third edition
Harry Lawrence
REVISED PRINTING

AVIATION
& THE ROLE OF GOVERNMENT

Kendall Hunt
publishing company

P9-CSC-174

Kendall Hunt
publishing company

www.kendallhunt.com
Send all inquiries to:
4050 Westmark Drive
Dubuque, IA 52004-1840

ISBN: 978-1-4652-7074-0

Printed in the United States of America

TO SUSAN

And to Colburn, Lachlan, Greyson, Sarah, Sadie, Connor (born on the 100th anniversary of the Wrights' epic flight), Reid, Alex, Ruby Jo, & Grace—memories of my first solo flight in a small, yellow airplane on July 16, 1956, cause me to paraphrase these thoughts to you:

“ As I run my hand over the wing and take in the poised majesty of this small machine, you should know that this plane can teach you more things and give you more gifts than I ever could. It won't get you a better job, a faster car, or a bigger house. But if you treat it with respect and keep your eyes open, it may remind you some things you used to know—that life is in the moment, joy matters more than money, the world can be a beautiful place, and that dreams really, truly are possible. And, because airplanes speak in a language beyond words, I will take you up in the evening summer sky and let the airplane show you what I mean. ”

From the "Eyes of a Child," *Flying Magazine,* February 2000

CONTENTS

STATUTES

1968 Civil Service Reform Act

1969 National Environmental Policy Act

1970 Airport and Airway Development Act of 1970

1970 The Clean Air Act, Amended

1972 Noise Control Act of 1972

1973 Airport Development Acceleration Act

1974 The Age Discrimination Act

1974 Independent Safety Board Act of 1974

1976 Airport and Airway Development Act Amendments

1976 The Railroad Revitalization and Regulatory Reform Act

1977 Air Cargo Deregulation Act

1978 Airline Deregulation Act

1979 Aviation Safety and Noise Abatement Act

1980 Motor Carrier Act of 1980

1982 Airport and Airway Development Act of 1982–FAA

1984 The Commercial Space Launch Act

1990 Airport Noise and Capacity Act (ANCA)

1994 FAA Authorization Act of 1994

1994 Independent Safety Board Act of 1994

1996 Airport Privatization Program

1998 The Commercial Space Act

1999 Wendell H. Ford Aviation Investment and Reform Act
      for the 21st Century (AIR-21)

2001 Air Transportation Safety and System Stabilization Act

2001 Aviation and Transportation Security Act

2002 Homeland Security Act

2003 Vision 100-Century of Aviation Reauthorization Act

2004 The Commercial Space Launch Amendments Act

2007 Implementing Recommendations of the 9/11 Commission Act

2010 Airline Safety and Aviation Administration Extension Act of 2010

2012 The FAA Reauthorization Act of 2012

Antitrust Legislation

1890 Sherman Antitrust Act

1914 Clayton Antitrust Act

The United States Bankruptcy Act

The bankruptcy laws of the United States have been consistently
amended since 1801.

CASES

FIGURES

PREFACE

For over 100 years, the evolution of commercial aviation has been a worldwide phenomenon. It has been the result of a combination of individual and corporate effort, and it has proceeded because of, and sometimes in spite of, the involvement of governments. In the United States, commercial aviation developed under principles of private enterprise in tension with government in its role of protecting the public interest. In contrast, throughout most of the rest of the world, governments had assumed the lead in innovation, development, and promotion of civil aviation, consistent with their more socialized economic systems and philosophies.

The cornerstone of the American experiment is government-protected individual freedom, in the words of the Declaration of Independence, the right to "life, liberty, and the pursuit of happiness." This freedom extends to business: the freedom to risk capital and ingenuity in return for financial gain. Failures resulting from these risks are borne individually or corporately, while the fruits of success often accrue to the benefit of the many.

The government of the United States traditionally has not been an intrusive government; rather, it was created in reaction to intrusive, oppressive foreign government. The powers of the federal government are derived from the people and are granted specifically in the Constitution of the United States. The government has no other source of power. Involvement of the federal government in the affairs of its citizens is authorized only as a result of duly enacted legislation (statutory law) by the Congress, and then only as to those matters over which it is given jurisdiction by the provisions of the Constitution.

When the American government was created, land transportation was primarily a private affair. The federal government took cognizance of its admiralty (maritime and shipping) responsibilities, but otherwise gave little heed to matters of travel. The obligation of government to attend to the "public welfare" extended to matters of interstate commerce, banking, defense, and the delivery of mail through the Post Office Department. The government experimented with trail improvement on its western margins (Ohio Territory, for instance) and road building (Post roads) incident to the delivery of the mails, but did little else. As the technological advances of the Industrial Revolution proceeded, so did the manufacturing and commercial enterprises that utilized them. Corporate forms of existence came into general use. Westward migration followed the steam locomotive and the telegraph across the country. The government was increasingly drawn into subsidy and regulation. These developments were followed by the reciprocating gasoline engine, the automobile, and the telephone. The transmission of electricity, wireless communication, commercial radio, and the airplane came after. The role of government continued to expand as the technological advances of the Industrial Revolution increasingly impacted the nation's commerce and its people.

The concepts of the federal maritime law were applied to the railroads when they appeared, and the law was modified as necessary to account for differences between these two modes of transport. Government experience with the railroads was applied to the new air transport industry when, in turn, it appeared. The result has been the development of a similar government methodology for the treatment of all forms of commercial transportation. Government in the United States remained mostly in the background even into the early part of the 20th century, but it remained ready to apply a steadying hand to prevent excesses of private or corporate self-interest.

The other primary interest of government in modern transportation involved issues of safety, which was legally appropriate under the Constitution in the interest of the public welfare. Government involvement in transportation safety issues first appeared in connection with railroad employees, who were suffering egregious personal injury due to the nature of railroading in the late 19th and early 20th centuries. Government's first involvement with aviation safety issues, in 1925, related to certification of pilots and aircraft, and airworthiness concerns. Safety would become the overriding governmental interest in commercial aviation as the 20th century progressed and as economic regulation by the government was phased out, beginning in 1978.

The early involvement of the government of the United States in transportation issues was mainly reactive, but also partly proactive. The railroad industry-government relationship was fairly well-established by the time the first practical airplane was developed. The railroads were privately owned, but the government actively regulated them. The United States experimented with government ownership of the railroads during World War I, but ended up returning them to corporate ownership after the war.

When the airplane appeared, there was no practical reason, nor any legal justification, for any government involvement. The audacious and romantic notion of flight was not put to practical use for over a decade after the Wrights' first flight, then in war in Europe in 1914. By war's end in 1918, in the United States the airplane was quickly returned to curiosity status, being used in barnstorming exhibitions, banner towing, and the occasional sightseeing flight. In the first part of the 20th century, America ran on wheels, steel ones and ever increasingly on rubber-tired wheels, and it did not have any immediate need for the airplane.[1]

In Europe, a limited commercial success had already been seen in Germany with the rise and deployment of dirigibles by 1909. European governments soon appreciated the potential commercial use of the airplane, particularly given the ruinous state of Europe's railroads after the devastation of World War I. The English Channel lay between London and Paris, separating two of the premier commercial and cultural metropolitan centers of the world, and it provided an obvious reason for commercial aviation to succeed. European governments owned the railroads. It was natural that the first commercial airlines created after World War I would also be owned by European governments.

But the United States was staunchly capitalistic. If aviation for any purpose was to succeed in this country, it was going to be up to a new breed of adventurer and entrepreneur to make it happen. Who they were and how they made it happen is the larger part of the account of the first century of flight. The story of airmail, the politics of the Great Depression, the creation of private airlines, the impact of World War II, the dawning of the jet age, the deregulation of the airlines, the advent of world competition, the space age, and the commercialization of space are all part of that adventure. The achievements of the first century of flight required the best from many worlds. The realms of business and finance, of engineering and science, and of government struggled together to overcome the uncertainties at the leading edge of a new technology. These struggles continue even today as the air transport industry, the flying public, and the government attempt to define the role that air transportation should play in the 21st century.

As a new millennium gets underway, government is being called upon to play perhaps its most decisive role ever in air transportation: the protection of the traveling public from international terrorism, and the pursuit of its ultimate defeat.

Endnote

1. In 1900, there were 8,000 automobiles registered in the United States. By 1920, there were 8 million automobiles registered. *Wall Street Journal* 5/17/03.

ABOUT THE AUTHOR

Harry W. Lawrence is a member of the faculty of Embry-Riddle Aeronautical University, Worldwide, and holds the rank of Adjunct Assistant Professor.

He received his Juris Doctor degree from the University of North Carolina at Chapel Hill, 1965, and was admitted to practice in Florida, Tennessee, and the District of Columbia. He was admitted to practice before the Supreme Court of the United States and Courts of the Fifth, Sixth, and Eleventh Circuits of the United States. He served as counsel for Seaboard Coast Line Railroad and Clinchfield Railroad Company (now CSX). He is Board Certified in Civil Trial Law by the Florida Bar. His practice of law had an emphasis on insurance, maritime, aviation, and railroad transportation issues.

He holds a Commercial Pilot Certificate with instrument, multiengine, glider, seaplane, and jet type ratings. He has been corporate owner and operator of fixed-base operations for general aviation, including turbojet commercial aircraft.

Foundation

©MO_SES

Part 1

Foundation

1 Beginnings

This is a story that begins with man's earliest reported technological accomplishment, the invention of the wheel, and continues with an ever-increasing intensity. A curve plotted on one axis as time and on the other as the rate of technological advance will depict a flat to gradually rising line, becoming at a point a rapidly rising line, disclosing a recent very high rate of technological accomplishment. (See Figure 1-1.) Between 1790 and 1870, for example, there were just over 40,000 patents granted in the United States for that entire 80-year period. During the 30 years between 1870 and 1900, the Patent Office granted over 400,000 patents, a 10-fold increase in slightly more than one third of the time. In 1870, there was nothing in America that could be called a steel industry; but by 1900, over 10 million tons of steel were being produced annually, more than the rest of the world combined. As men struggled to fly, the rate of technological innovation was beginning to move up, but it had been a long time coming.

All modern-day accomplishments are based, to one degree or another, on the efforts and accomplishments of those who went before. The ancient Phoenicians sailed the confines of the Mediterranean Sea by reference to land, and also by reference to the sun and stars. The length of the Mediterranean, its east and west limits, were known to them as Asu (east) and Ereb (west), the word roots that form the names of Asia and Europe in use today. Ocean travel was coastwise. Improvements were made to the shapes of sails and hulls used in early maritime commerce. Insurance and accounting came into vogue in the maritime trading centers around the Mediterranean, in the city-states such as Venice. Gunpowder arrived by the 9th century and, by the late 12th century, the magnetic compass was coming into common use on land and sea.

But the rising curve of progress really only begins with the rise of Western Civilization and the Rule of Law. Circumstances conducive to invention and innovation depend on many factors, including incentive to innovate—like the profit motive—and protection for the results of invention, like patent law. These and other relevant factors depend on a stable, progressive, and lawful society, and a strong government. Magna Carta (The Great Charter), in 1215, establishing for the first time limitations on the arbitrary powers of the King of England, is widely regarded as the cornerstone of personal liberty. Its principles have evolved into broad constitutional concepts embraced today. In 1420 began a period of progress and enlightenment known as the Renaissance

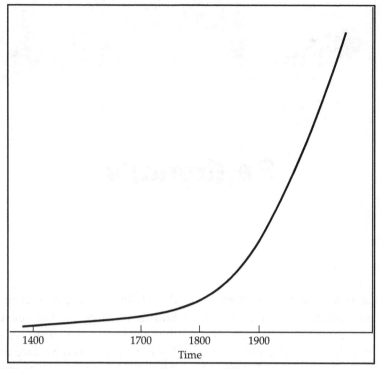

FIGURE 1-1 The rate of technological advance.

(rebirth), a time of advances in astronomy, anatomy, engineering, physics, and art. Great leaps of mind made by the luminaries of that day included the idea that man might actually fly—or so believed Leonardo da Vinci (1452–1519). His sketches depicting wings to support manned flight disclose that he understood the same basic airfoil concept used today. His ideas on the subject were lost for a period of 300 years before rediscovery.

❝ When once you have tasted flight, you will forever walk the earth with your eyes turned skyward, for there you have been, and there you will always long to return. ❞

Leonardo da Vinci

That enlightened period was followed by the era of European exploration and discovery,

of long distance open water navigation, and the opening of extended trade routes still in use today, along with a commercial appreciation of the meaning of time and distance. Latitudinal position, or north–south location, had for some time been capable of being established by reference to the celestial bodies, using instruments from early times like the gnomon or the Arabian kamal, and later the astrolabe, the cross-staff and, in 1731, the sextant. While a laborious methodology using the sextant could approximate longitude after 1731, the lack of a definitive longitudinal reference had prevented from time immemorial the accurate determining of positions of longitude, which resulted in costly navigation errors, loss of life and property, and commercial uncertainty.

In 1714, British Parliament offered a prize of 20 thousand pounds sterling for a reliable method of determining longitude on a ship at sea.

The best minds in Europe, including astronomers and physicists, worked on the project for 50 years without success. John Harrison, a carpenter and clockmaker with little formal education, reasoned that if a ship's local time at sea could be compared to the time at the port of origin, the calculation could readily be made to find the ship's longitudinal location. Local time could be accurately calculated at any point on earth by reference to astronomical observation and, although accurate pendulum clocks existed at the time, there were no portable clocks. Due to the water's motion, pendulum clocks would not work at sea.

Harrison produced a series of timepieces beginning in the early 1730s that produced increasingly accurate results, ultimately settling on a design that resembled a very large pocket watch. By 1762, a sea trial of his clock on a voyage from London to Jamica showed it to be only 5.1 seconds slow. A second trial at sea in 1764 proved the clock's error to be three times better than required to win the prize. Yet, the prize was not awarded.

The body set up by the royal government to judge the longitude prize, known as the Board of Longitude, consisted of astronomers, mathematicians, admirals, and a variety of other leading lights, who collectively could not bring themselves to believe that a mere carpenter could possibly have solved the longitude problem that had stumped civilization all for all time. The dispute was finally presented to Parliament and to King George III, the latter of whom said, ". . . these people have been cruelly wronged . . . , and By God, Harrison, I will see you righted!" But it was not until 1773 that an Act of Parliament finally awarded the full prize and the recognition for having solved the longitude problem to John Harrison.

The missing universal frame of reference, the Prime Meridian, was officially established in 1884 at Greenwich, England, at which Universal time is now found.

In transportation, while marginal improvements were seen in matters nautical, no significant advance had been otherwise made since the dawn of time. Motive power for land transport was provided either by animals or by men themselves. George Washington, for instance, in 1776, was unable to travel from Philadelphia to New York City any faster than Julius Caesar could cover the equivalent distance from Rome to Pompeii. In the middle of the 18th century, the problem was the lack of motive power.

We will begin the study of aviation, and the role of government, with the advent of the Industrial Revolution. The fruits of this period in world history would, for the first time, drastically alter essentially every aspect of human existence, and would, within the space of 54 years in the 20th century, accomplish a journey from the bicycle age to the space age.

2   The Industrial Revolution

The City of London, although of ancient Roman origin (Londinium), had little to distinguish it from the other potential candidates of Europe and the Middle East (Paris, Venice, Athens, Alexandria) for the honor of becoming the jumping-off place for the economic and military conquest of the world. One might have thought, for example, that such a place might more logically be somewhere in the Cradle of Civilization—the Middle East—or at least the Mediterranean, where for centuries commerce had steadily proceeded as invaders and traders crisscrossed the area bartering food, raw materials, and spices. Those people developed new and better sailing ships and means of propulsion (such as the triangular sail as an improvement on the square rigger), and they had a leg up when it came to understanding and practicing the art of politics, the use of centralized power, the formulation of ideas, and the development of institutions through centuries of inheritance. The earliest cities, governments, law codes, and alphabets were of Middle Eastern origin, as were the earliest forms of religion—Judaism, Christianity, and Islam.

The roots of the Industrial Revolution, however, can be found in English inventiveness. In 1750, most people in the world lived in relative self-sufficiency, filling their needs from the sea and through the husbandry of their own or others' land. People produced not only their food, but also their clothes, fuel, candles, and even furniture. Items that could not be produced locally, such as spices, tea, and precious stones, could be purchased in limited quantity from entrepreneurial efforts. The issue of labor was rather simple: one essentially did for oneself.

But there was a difference between England and the rest of Europe. England had developed a type of middle class, a mercantile base that dealt in the leather and wool trades, shipping, and banking. Most of Europe was still stuck in the vestiges of the feudal system of the Middle Ages where one's future was defined by one's status at birth. In England, trade had become a leveler of class distinction to some degree, where the opportunity to engage in free market exchange brought the opportunity for financial gain. Financial success meant escape from dependency on the upper classes and service to those with wealth and property. A lack of dependency brought with it not only self-sufficiency, but also freedom from the servile bondage of a class-bound society. It brought hope to the common man, and it invigorated him.

Production of woolen goods was revolutionized by inventions, like the flying shuttle in 1733 by John Kay, and the spinning jenny in 1764 by

James Hargreaves. These and other inventions led to machinery that provided a mechanized means of production whose places of operation came to be known as factories. Factories required people to operate the machines, men and women who could offer their labor in return for wages. In a society that was primarily agrarian, employment opportunities were not widespread. But among the descendents of feudal peasantry, the opportunity to work for a wage, and thus gain a measure of independence, was a step up.

The implementation of the factory system brought with it a significant change in the organization of work. While the production of goods had always been an individual endeavor, requiring the application of some skill in the craft, the factory system introduced a repetitive, routine, and boring set of hand–eye coordination that required, at the most, minimal skill. Over time, workers became more restive, dissatisfied, and unconnected.

Perhaps the most seminal of all developments during this time was the 1769 appearance of the reliable steam engine by Scottish inventor, James Watt. This invention would institutionalize the factory system, both in terms of the development of the labor movement and in terms of the efficient production of goods. It would change the course of the maritime trade, beginning with the installation of a steam engine on a barge to provide motive power, the forerunner of the steamship. Not long after, the steam engine would inaugurate an entirely new mode of transportation on land when installed on a carriage, the precursor of the locomotive.

The Industrial Revolution set the stage for the modern age to come. Figure 2-1 lists important events in the Industrial and Technological Revolution. It provided the impetus for the creation of the modern corporation as a legal entity, which developed as the vehicle by which to raise the large sums of money that were required to engage in the business opportunities that were generated by the Industrial Revolution. It provided the means necessary to commence the first land mass transportation system, the railroads. As the relationship was being established between the

railroads and labor, and between both of them with government, the paradigm for the airlines in these same areas was being set. Procedures among the various maritime countries of the world, defining the relative rights and obligations of nations engaged in international shipping, would similarly be made applicable to the airlines.

The Industrial Revolution caused a new involvement by government in the affairs of business, and spawned an era of regulation and legislation. It gave rise to the labor movement and cast the die for early labor-management strife. It created a new demand for manufactured goods, ranging from steel for use in the construction of railroad tracks, locomotives, and cars to cloth for denims for their workers, a consumerism that continues unabated today. It fueled an explosion of new industries, and new companies within each industry to compete under primitive free enterprise, or laissez-faire principles. And it produced a dependent worker class whose members, because of industrialization, urbanization, immigration, and specialization, were no longer self-sufficient.

An understanding of the history and experience of the railroads is important to our purpose for at least four reasons:

1. As the first modern form of national transportation, the railroads set the model in many ways for the succeeding modes of transport, particularly air transportation.
2. The experience of the railroads defined the relationship between carriers and the government, particularly in respect to the concept of the public interest.
3. The experience of the railroads defined the relationship between carriers and the public, the shippers, and passengers.
4. The railroad experience saw the beginning of a cohesive labor movement that was inherited by the airlines and that has been central to the airlines' experience in the 20th century.

We will review each of these developments in more detail in the next two chapters.

1452	(April 15) Leonardo da Vinci born.
1492	Columbus discovers the New World.
1502	The first watch is made.
1512	Copernicus concludes that the earth circles the sun.
1519	(May 2) Leonardo dies in Amboise; Magellan launches first round-the-world voyage.
1733	John Kay invents flying shuttle.
1765	James Hargreaves invents the spinning jenny, automating weaving the warp (in the weaving of cloth).
1775	Watt's first efficient steam engine.
1779	First steam-powered mills.
1793	Eli Whitney develops a device to clean raw cotton, called a cotton gin.
1801	Robert Trevithick demonstrates a steam locomotive.
1807	Robert Fulton's *Clermont* is the first successful steamboat.
1811–15	Luddite riots: laborers attack factories and break up the machines they fear will replace them.
1821	Michael Faraday demonstrates electro-magnetic rotation, the principle of the electric motor.
1837	Samuel Morse develops the telegraph and Morse Code.
1844	First long-distance telegraph message (Washington to Baltimore).
1858	First transatlantic cable completed. Cathode rays discovered.
1859	Edwin Drake strikes oil in Pennsylvania. Etienne Lenoir demonstrates the first successful gasoline engine.
1860	Science degrees awarded at University of London.
1863	Steel begins to replace iron in building: steel framing and reinforced concrete make possible "curtain-wall" architecture—i.e., the skyscraper.
1867	Alfred Nobel produces dynamite, the first high explosive which can be safely handled.
1873	Christopher Sholes invents the Remington typewriter.
1876	Alexander Graham Bell invents the telephone.
1877	Thomas Edison invents the phonograph.
1878	Microphone invented.
1879	Edison invents the incandescent lamp.
1883	First skyscraper (10 stories) in Chicago. The Brooklyn Bridge opens. This large suspension bridge, built by the Roeblings (father and son), is a triumph of engineering.
1885	Karl Benz develops first automobile to run on an internal-combustion engine.
1888	Heinrich Hertz produces radio waves.
1892	Rudolf Diesel invents the diesel engine.
1895	Wilhelm Roentgen discovers X-rays.
1896	Guglielmo Marconi patents the wireless telegraph.
1897	Joseph Thomson discovers particles smaller than atoms.
1900	First Zeppelin built.
1901	Marconi transmits first transatlantic radio message (from Cape Cod).
1903	Wright brothers make first powered flight.
1908	Henry Ford mass-produces the Model T.

FIGURE 2-1 Important events in industrial and technological development.

3

The Railroads

The steam engine, first fitted to a wagon in 1804, evolved into a primitive railroad locomotive to pull the first railroad carriages in 1830. (See Figure 3-1.) The first chartered railroad, the Baltimore & Ohio Railroad, operated from Baltimore to Ellicott's Mills, a distance of just 13 miles. Short-haul railroads like this began springing up all over the East Coast of the United States about this time. The noisy, dirty, and generally terrifying apparition of an early steam locomotive, spitting steam and hot coal cinders in its wake and upon the few discomfited passengers who may have been loaded in the open cars behind it, rudely intruded on the sedate horse and buggy countryside. Yet few questioned its future. It was, after all, the most significant transportation advance in the history of the world, even at its maximum speed of 16 miles per hour, and even though it had the worrisome tendency of setting fire to the countryside through which it passed.

Like most inventions, the locomotive was gradually improved through the contributions of many people until it worked smoothly and readily achieved its designed purpose. This was advanced technology. The various small lines began meeting up, forming interchange points and exchanging the relatively small amount of freight traffic available. Passenger service was tentative, and the destinations sparse. These early rail lines were constructed to meet local needs, and there was no overall plan for lines to serve the nation or any particular geographic region.

Railroads were considered, legally and practically, to be monopolistic enterprises. The large capital investment required to begin operations virtually guaranteed little competition. Land had to be purchased, then the land had to be made level—requiring fills or bridges to connect over low places, valleys, and rivers, and causing cuts or tunnels to be dug to eliminate hills and mountains. Once that was done, the roadbed, consisting of ballast, ties, and finally the rails themselves, had to be laid. This process was required in one form or another for every linear foot of road. Even as the road was laid, and large sums of money spent, the question was unanswered: How should and would the government consider this new industry?

This was a time of forging new relationships all around, relationships that, once defined, would extend into the as-yet-unimagined air age of the future.

- What was the responsibility of a railroad to passengers and shippers?
- Was there any responsibility to communities served?
- Where was the higher allegiance—to stockholders or to the public?

Source: U.S. National Atlas, 1970.

FIGURE 3-1 An early steam engine.

Prior to the construction of the great transcontinental road that linked the West Coast of the United States with the Midwest, government had generally refrained from intervening in the affairs of the infant railroad industry. There was no federal governmental interest in railroad regulation since, in the early 19th century, federal issues like the "public interest" or "interstate commerce" had yet to be framed. Local governments treated the small railroads as any other business. When it would later come, federal government intervention would be characterized as either "positive" or "negative." Positive intervention could be described as government action that is designed to support or benefit the railroad, such as favorable tax treatment, subsidies, land grants, and the like. Negative intervention takes the form of restrictive legislation, the curbing of pre-existing rights enjoyed by the railroads, and the forcing of certain behavior deemed to be in the public interest, such as prohibiting arbitrary or unequal treatment of shippers.

The sheer magnitude of the proposed transcontinental railroad construction dictated that the government's participation would be required.

No corporation, group of corporations, bank, or group of banks was big enough to make it happen. Only the government was big enough, and only the government had the money and other resources necessary (including the land), and the sovereignty necessary to assuage the conflicts, partisanship, separate interests, and legal questions guaranteed to arise in the vast undertaking.

The western land over which most of the transcontinental railroad would run was composed of acquisitions by the government beginning in 1803. Known as the "Louisiana Purchase" (see Figure 3-2), this vast tract consisted of over 800,000 square miles that extended from the Gulf of Mexico to the Canadian border and from the Mississippi River to the Rocky Mountains. The land area of the United States was doubled. Fifteen new states, in whole or in part, would come from this tract.

In three years between 1845 and 1848, the land area of the United States would be enlarged again by a third, as the State of Texas was annexed in 1845, the Oregon Territory was negotiated with England in 1846, and the great southwestern territory was ceded by Mexico to

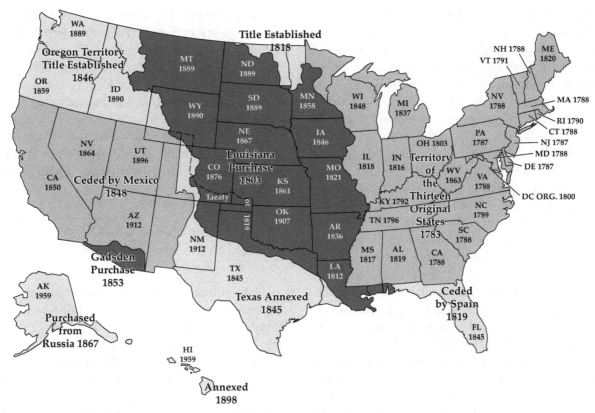

FIGURE 3-2 Map showing the accretion of land to the United States along with their individual dates.

the United States in 1848. The United States now extended all the way across the continent, from sea to shining sea.

> In 1860, there were 30,000 miles of railroad in the United States.

The passage by the Congress in 1862 of the Pacific Railroad Act became the first of government's involvements in the world of modern transportation. The law provided for the creation of two private corporations, the Union Pacific (building from the East) and the Central Pacific (building from the West), whose charters were to build a railroad and a telegraph line[1] between the Missouri River and Sacramento, California. The government would issue its bonds, bearing interest at the rate of 6 percent, to the railroads

for sale to the public. The improvements and the land on which they were placed would stand as security for the government's obligation to pay the interest on the bonds and to pay the face amount of the bonds when due. The government was not subsidizing the construction; rather, it was loaning its credit in order to raise the construction funds.

The government would, however, grant to the railroads the right of way (200 feet on each side) for the roadbed, and it would also deed land adjacent to the right of way in square miles amounting to 6,400 acres per mile. This was land expected to be used to entice settlers from the East who would create and work farms and ranches. The land would be used to build towns and to provide for industry, all of which in turn would provide passenger and freight traffic for the railroads and insure westward expansion and population of the Great Plains and points west. This was truly a win–win situation, even for the government, since the value of the remainder of the land that the government owned would be greatly enhanced by the efforts of the railroad companies and those who would follow them. The interests of the government would also be served by facilitating a viable railroad system to serve the nation and to advance the national economy and the public welfare.

The line began in the East on the Missouri River, at Omaha, Nebraska, and made its way west to Promontory Summit, Utah, where in 1869, the line of road that began in Sacramento, California, was joined. Along the way it laid down settlements which were to become the cities of the future, with names like Cheyenne, Laramie, North Platte, and Elko, names which 50 years later would also figure prominently in the annals of early flight as the first cross-country air mail service struggled to create yet another, but altogether different, fledgling transportation system. This transcontinental railroad is shown in Figure 3-3. With air transport, the government, once again, would take the lead and then step out of the way, leaving the captains of industry to their own devices in making the system run.

But turmoil lay ahead. It has been said that the years between 1860 and 1868 laid the foundation for the uprooting of the society of America. The Civil War, beginning in 1861, tore the country apart for four years, and the so-called Reconstruction era that followed effectively rendered the South a land occupied by a foreign power for many years. Centuries-old traditions in both the North and the South were eradicated or radically altered. Politics and social life changed.

> In 1870, there were 53,000 miles of railroad in the United States.

The impact of available and relatively fast railroad transportation on the stability of the population compounded the problem. People began to move and to follow the railroads as they connected sections of the country and both coasts, and as the heartland was settled. People could more readily live and work anywhere in the country, leaving behind their pasts, their established social networks, and sometimes their principles and mores. Political power was for sale in the legislatures of the states and in Congress as graft and corruption became prevalent.

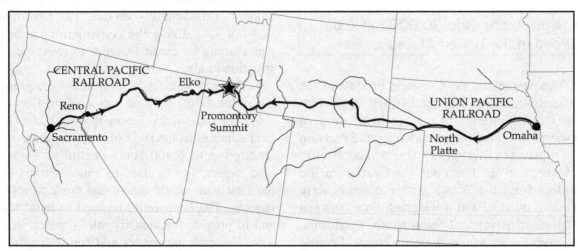

FIGURE 3-3 The transcontinental railroad.

The new opportunities afforded to corporations led to a time of unbridled capitalism at the hands of rapacious men of industry like the Vanderbilts, the Goulds, and the Carnegies. The power of corporations, like the Pullman Company, Standard Oil, and United States Steel, joined with the new political structure to create a vast gulf between owners, known as the "robber barons," and workers. Labor was set against management in an epic struggle that would poison labor relations in the railroad industry for generations to come and that would be carried over to the airlines. The government's initial assistance, as positive legislation, would soon turn to regulation of the restrictive kind with the passage of the first comprehensive national legislation regulating transportation.

▣ The Railroads, Laissez-Faire Economics, and the Basis of Regulation

As the railroads spread out from the East, they connected with other lines, north and south, and created interchange points between them. For the first time, goods began to be moved from origins far distant from their destinations. Markets that at one time had been local now became regional and even national. Manufacturing, meatpacking, farming, and the cattle business were becoming interdependent, and America was beginning to depend on transportation—the railroads—as the lifeblood of its commerce.

The railroads wielded vast economic power. Like government, they possessed the power of eminent domain. They set passenger fares as they wished. Freight rates varied according to the whim of the railroads, and were often discriminatory and unevenly applied.

Farmers, in particular, were at the mercy of the railroads in marketing their produce. Grain elevators were necessary as storage facilities for farmers, and these often were owned by the railroads.

Various states, in response to petitions from its citizens, enacted laws designed to curb the excesses of the railroads. But the railroads ran from state to state, and generally considered themselves immune from attempts at local regulation. These laws, therefore, were uniformly ineffective and were ignored or legally challenged by the railroads. It was not until shippers as a group began to assert influence on a national level that the Congress did eventually begin to address the problem.

In the United States, governmental authority to regulate lawful enterprises must be based on constitutional principles. In 1887, although these principles were not well defined, it was clear that the national government in Washington had express Constitutional authority to regulate commerce between the states. So it was that Congress that year debated the first regulation of transportation.

Historically, governmental regulation has been grounded on two primary concepts:

1. Economic necessity
2. Legal authority

The concept of economic necessity presumes (1) that there are certain businesses that are necessary in the public interest (e.g., transportation companies, gas companies, electric companies, etc.); (2) that these types of companies should be required to serve all of the public without discrimination; and (3) that these companies should be stable and be able to make a reasonable, but not too large, profit. To assure that these conditions exist, the government has undertaken to regulate them. This regulation controls entry into the business (which controls competition, expertise, and financial stability), the rates that are charged the public, and to some extent the manner in which the business is operated.

In the United States, most businesses are run under the principles of private enterprise. While businesses that are considered necessary in the public interest are mostly privately owned, they are considered to be "quasi-public," that is, operated in the public interest. From 1887, when the regulation of transportation began, the federal government considered interstate transportation to be a quasi-public undertaking, thus a legitimate object of regulation.

The second basis of regulation is legal. The legal basis of regulation is founded in the U.S. Constitution and the laws that are enacted by Congress. With regard to transportation, the commerce clause of the Constitution is most often invoked to authorize regulation of companies conducting business among the states (interstate commerce). The commerce clause is based, in part, on the realization that the people of the various states must be guaranteed equal access to a necessary service. It is also recognized that, in matters between the states, the presumed impartiality of the federal government should make it, and not the states, the arbiter of the law.

Once enacted pursuant these constitutional principles, regulation is *implemented through* either the common law or statutory law.

- *Common law* is the law that has resulted from judicial decisions derived from litigated cases between individual parties. This law is contained in written opinions of judges and is referred to as "judge-made" law. The common law that existed in England before the American Revolution was applied in the American colonies, and after independence was won and the United States Constitution was adopted, English common law continued to serve as legal precedent in the new United States.
- *Statutory law* is the law that Congress or the state legislatures have enacted by vote of elected representatives in those bodies. On the federal level, this law is codified in the United States Code, a sequentially numbered series of volumes that contain all current federal statutory law. The United States Code is kept updated by means of supplements published on a regular basis. Some statutes provide for the creation of federal agencies, like the Federal Aviation Administration or the Interstate Commerce Commission, to administer the

mandates set down in the statute. Such agencies are given rulemaking authority, which means they may conduct public hearings and make rules having the force of law to govern the manner in which the affected business or activity is conducted, like the Federal Aviation Regulations, for example.

■ The Interstate Commerce Act of 1887

The first legislation in the United States regulating transportation was the Interstate Commerce Act, in 1887. This statute heralded the era of "negative" legislation, or legislation that had the effect of curbing or restricting railroads in their conduct of business.

The thrust of the Act was to prohibit the railroads from paying rebates (kickbacks), from giving unreasonable preferences to shippers, and from discrimination against any shipper. Railroads were required to publish tariffs, which disclosed rates and schedules, and they were required to charge according to those tariffs. The Act brought uniformity to the relationship between the railroads and the public.

The Interstate Commerce Act and its amendments also created the Interstate Commerce Commission, the agency assigned the role of administering the terms and provisions of the statute. It was empowered to monitor railroads to ensure compliance with the terms of the statute, to hear complaints from the affected public, and to make rules and enter orders in furtherance of the statutory mandate.

Subsequent federal enactments continued the era of negative legislation toward the transportation industry, including:

- The **Elkins Act of 1903** (focused on person discrimination and established a system of fines and criminal penalties)
- The **Hepburn Act of 1906** (set maximum rates)
- The **Mann-Elkins Act of 1910** (focused on place discrimination)

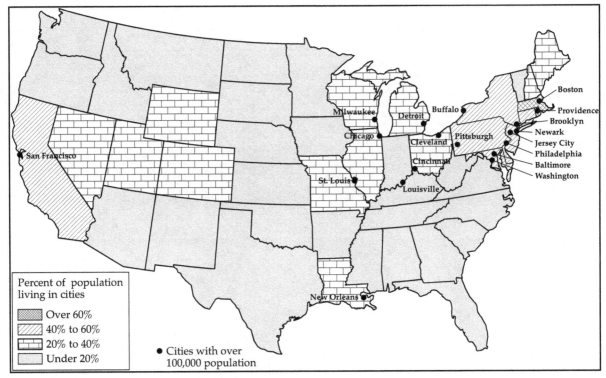

FIGURE 3-4 The emergence of cities, 1880.

The pendulum had swung too far in the early and energetic days of railroading, and the government was now catching up to balance things out in the public interest. The days of unbridled capitalism in the railroad business were over. In the early years of the 20th century, the railroads were nearing what was to be their maximum trackage (miles of laid tracks), and they were just about to experience the effects of continuing industrial and technological development (Figure 3-4 displays the emergence of U.S. cities in 1880) that would lead to alternative forms of transportation that would overpower them. The days of the internal combustion engine, the open road, and the machines of the air lay just over the horizon.

In 1890, there were 164,000 miles of railroad in the United States. Railroad mileage would peak at 254,000 miles in 1916, and then begin a gradual decline.

Endnote

1. The government issued a patent for the telegraph in 1837 to Samuel Morse. The first intercity telegraph message was transmitted in 1844.

4 The Industrial Age and the Rise of Unionism

Before proceeding further into the 20th century, we need to visit the labor movement in the United States. This phenomenon became a force and an institution in American industry that, beginning in the middle to late 19th century, has had a significant impact on national modes of transportation.

The development of trade unionism is highly correlated to the progression of industrialization. Although trade guilds existed from medieval times in Europe, they were composed of artisans who banded together to promote their craft, and to improve their products and methods. As such, guilds had an exclusionary aspect not seen in modern trade unions, which welcome wage earners of all kinds and strive to increase their membership numbers and power base.

Trade unions were formed as associations of workers as a natural counter-balance to owners. Historically, the formation of such groups was illegal under the laws of most countries. These groups were seen as hostile to the order of the day, revolutionary even, and their objectives were often sought through disorderly and violent means.

Prior to the Civil War, most of what could be called "industry" was controlled by small individual owners, often families, or sometimes small partnerships. These industries included the cotton and woolen mills of New England, iron and steel factories of Pennsylvania and New York, the various short-line railroads that served their local areas all over the eastern United States, oil drillers in Pennsylvania, and coal mining operations in the Appalachian Mountain chain. Most of the wealth of the country lay in land ownership. The United States was primarily a nation of farmers.

The Civil War spurred development in most areas of industry. The woolen mills were called upon to clothe a million men with uniforms. Boots and saddles were needed from the leather industry. Union Army contracts for pork and cattle created the Chicago railroad stockyards and packing plants. The manufacture of iron and steel products boomed. The railroads proved their efficiency during the war through the movement of troops and matériel. And the railroads demanded more coal, iron, and oil.

After the end of the Civil War, railroad construction exploded. Some 35,000 miles of track were laid from 1866 to 1873. Building railroads was an expensive undertaking, and the use of the corporation found favor as a means of raising money. Corporations also became the preferred form of business ownership and operation in most other industries. The shares of public corporations were traded on the stock exchanges of New York and Chicago, although large blocks of stock were owned by very wealthy individuals and families. In the days before any social regulation, corporations determined all the rules and working conditions of employment, including the hours to be worked and the rates of pay.

As industrialization grew, so did the organization of workers. Some of these organizations were more like fraternal organizations than unions, although they ultimately progressed into trade unionism and condoned work actions and strikes. Some of these groups were politically oriented, being populated by anarchists, socialists, and communists. The writings of Karl Marx, a German philosopher and bohemian, formed the basis of a philosophy of class strife (e.g., the haves against the have-nots, or class warfare), which was adopted by many groups. His Communist Manifesto, published in 1849, detailed the decline and fall of the capitalist economy and the ultimate triumph of the worker over the owner-class. Union leaders were usually the most aggressive of the workers.

The first railroad unions appeared in the 1860s. Their original purpose was to provide life insurance for their members, since life insurance companies refused to insure railroad workers due the high risk of injury and death. Railroads provided union organizers with the opportunity to organize workers on a national level instead of the local level usually associated with factories. Railroad unions were formed according to the class or craft of service that the employer rendered, whether engineer, fireman, conductor, or other.

After the Civil War, the railroads were the largest industrial employer in the United States. Money was flowing from the private sector into the railroads as they rapidly expanded and, as might be expected, the expansion rate proved to be too great. The overbuilding of the railroads,

along with the great investment in money made by speculators, led to widespread economic failures. First profits dried up and then credit. The first industrially induced recession, known as the Panic of 1873, resulted in bank closures and depositor losses. The crisis caused the failure of more than 18,000 businesses, and 89 of the nation's 364 railroads went bankrupt.

The relationship between the unions and the owners of the railroads was exceedingly antagonistic, with good cause on both sides. Although not illegal,[1] unions were not recognized by business or by the government as quite legitimate. Union members often resorted to violence and civil disturbance; the railroads reciprocated with hired police forces and strike-breakers.

The economic conditions surrounding the Panic of 1873 resulted in the railroads cutting wages and terminating workers. In 1877, the first serious railroad strike of the new industrial age began on July 14 in Martinsburg, West Virginia, and spread along the lines of railroad into Pittsburgh and Philadelphia, then on to the Midwest, St. Louis, and Chicago, becoming more violent as it went. Railroads across the country were brought to a standstill by rioting and bloodshed. In Chicago and St. Louis, a political group known as The Workingmen's Party, which was the first Marxist-influenced political party in the United States, organized mobs of up to 20,000 demonstrators who battled police and federal troops in the streets.

Gradually, the troops suppressed both strikers and rioters city-by-city and, 45 days after it began, the Strike of 1877 was over. But the unions came out of the fray empowered by the knowledge of what their combined action could produce. The unions became better organized, and their numbers and membership grew. Their leaders espoused the general belief that they were justified in resorting to any means to overcome the power of the corporations. The Strike of 1877 was to mark the beginning of a particularly violent period in labor relations in the United States.

During the next decade there would be thousands of strikes, lockouts, and work interruptions in American industry as management–labor relations deteriorated further. But railroad strikes gained the most notoriety because of the widespread effect they had on the transportation system of the country. The biggest of all, called the Pullman Strike, occurred in 1894.

The Pullman Palace Car Company manufactured luxurious railway sleeper cars that were used by most railroad companies in their passenger trains. Due to another cyclical economic downturn (known as the Panic of 1893), production at the Pullman plant located in south Chicago was severely curtailed. As a result, the work force was reduced from 5,500 to 3,300, and the wages of the remaining workers were reduced by 25 percent. The workers at the Pullman plant were required to live in Pullman City, where the plant was located, in houses built by the company and leased to the workers. Everything in the town was owned by the company, and the company provided everything for the people, except saloons. When wages were reduced, the workers petitioned for a reduction of lease payments, but the company refused. This led to a strike by the Pullman workers in May 1894.

The American Railway Union (ARU) had been established just the year before, in 1893, by Eugene V. Debs, a former railroad worker and union officer in the Brotherhood of Locomotive Firemen. The ARU was unlike railroad trade unions in that it included railroad workers of all classes and crafts. It shortly became the largest union in the United States with over 140,000 members by 1894. In August 1893, it had called a strike of the Great Northern Railroad in response to a series of wage cuts. The shutdown of the railroad caused the company to reverse its wage decision. So when the Pullman Company cut wages, the ARU voted to join the Pullman strikers in order to bring all of the union's clout down on Pullman.

The largest strike in the history of the United States ensued, involving hundreds of thousands of participants and 27 U.S. states and territories. One hundred twenty-five thousand railroad workers refused to handle Pullman sleeping cars or any trains in which they were placed. Thirteen railroads were forced to abandon all service in Chicago and 10 others were able to operate only passenger trains. *The New York Times* announced that the strike had become the greatest battle between labor and capital that had ever been inaugurated in the United States. Public sentiment shifted against the strikers as the disruption dragged on and as national transportation remained interrupted. Still, there was no federal intervention.

In July, the railroads began attaching the Pullman cars to U.S. mail cars, which then caused a disruption of interstate mail. Debs and other union officials were arrested for interfering with the delivery of U.S. mail. On July 2, a federal court injunction was issued against the ARU and its leaders. On July 3, President Cleveland ordered in federal troops to end the strike and to operate the railroads. On July 4, mobs of rioters began roaming the streets and destroying railroad property. Fires set by the mobs on July 6 and 7 destroyed 700 rail cars and seven buildings. Twelve people were killed by gunfire.

Debs was arrested on July 7 for violating the court order, and the violence began to subside. Trains began to move again and the strike whimpered to an end. Debs spent six months in prison.

These violent conflicts between organized labor and business during the latter part of the 19th century would lead to a federal legislation in the years to come designed to address the legitimate concerns of both labor and management. Eugene Debs would later be a candidate for President of the United States for the Socialist Party of America, standing for election four times between 1904 and 1920. His best showing, 6 percent of the vote, occurred in the election of

1912, and is the highest voter result for a Socialist Party candidate.

The disruption and violence of strikes were unpopular, and the courts routinely issued injunctions against unions on the basis of the *Sherman* Antitrust Act of 1890. This statute, while enacted primarily to eliminate corporate monopolies, contained language that prohibited "every contract, combination in the form of trust or otherwise, or conspiracy, in restraint of trade or commerce." The courts interpreted this language as prohibiting strikes, which did, of course, restrain trade and commerce. In 1914, Congress passed the *Clayton Antitrust Act*, a further enactment against corporate trusts, but which contained provisions expressly exempting labor unions from the operation of the "restraint of trade" prohibitions found in the Sherman Antitrust Act.

The early part of the 20th century saw many changes in the American way of life.

- Horses and buggies were giving way to the automobile.
- Factories were going full blast, turning out production goods as never before.
- The assembly line, perfected by Henry Ford in the production of automobiles, was further aggravating the relations between workers and owners.
- The entry of the United States into World War I caused many young servicemen to be exposed to foreign culture for the first time, and to the bohemian ways of European life.

Still, America was very conservative during this time. The Bolshevik Revolution in Russia in 1917 and its aftermath raised further concerns in this country as aggressive union activity seemed to bring the United States a step closer to socialist and communist ideology. Workers in heavy industry, such as mine workers, steel workers, and railroad workers, were highly organized and pursued a militant relationship with management.

The coming of the Great Depression during the 1930s and the Roosevelt New Deal, however, reflected a change in the way government looked at workers and their place in society. The New Deal brought a great wave of legislation directed toward fixing what was coming to be regarded as a broken economy and assisting those at the lower levels who functioned within it.

- Working conditions, hours, and rates of pay were the subjects of contention, and as the 20th century progressed, these conditions gradually improved due to the American system of self-determination through legislation.
- Child labor laws and a minimum wage were enacted.
- Laws addressing the safety of workers were put on the books for the first time.
- Broad legislation protecting the right of workers to organize and to strike was passed.
- National work programs, like the Works Progress Administration (WPA), a relief program established by Presidential executive order, were instituted to alleviate the high unemployment numbers experienced due to the adverse economic conditions of the 1930s.

The postulations that Karl Marx had made with respect to the class warfare that, in his view, were inevitable were proved incorrect by the flexibility of the American governmental system. As substantial problems induced by the Industrial Revolution that affected the working population of the United States were perceived, Congress reacted with remedial legislation. These laws had the effect of acting like a relief valve in a pressure cooker, as workers perceived that their legitimate concerns were being addressed. Although union membership rose steadily from the latter part of the 19th century through the 1930s, it reached its peak in the 1950s. As economic conditions improved in the United States and worldwide, and as the workforce shifted from heavy industry to technology, union membership dropped off, and is still in the process of falling. Negative perceptions of thug-like union activity increased among the American population. Connections between some large unions, like the Teamsters, and the underworld or Mafia, were shown to exist. Unions have been accused of misappropriating members' pension funds, and union officials have frequently been indicted and successfully prosecuted. The good that some unions accomplished was often overshadowed by these events.

The most important observation that can be made concerning the course of labor and management relations over the last century and a half is undoubtedly the success of the American system of government in coping with the often diametrically opposed positions of these participants in business. That system, based on the structure of the Constitution of the United States, has proven stronger than the differences that divide its population, and it has enabled a cooperative endeavor between labor and management that has benefited the world.

We will later consider specific developments in the country's labor laws and their impact on the airline industry.

Endnote

1. Trade unions were adjudicated to be legal organizations in the 1842 case of *Massachusetts Commonwealth v. Hunt*.

PART II

Dreamers

©kropic1

5   The Beginnings of Flight

" Many wonderful inventions have surprised us during the course of the last century and the beginning of this one. But most were completely unexpected and were not part of the old baggage of dreams that humanity carries with it. Who had ever dreamed of steamships, railroads, or electric light? We welcomed all these improvements with astonished pleasure; but they did not correspond to an expectation of our spirit or a hope as old as we are: to overcome gravity, to tear ourselves away from the earth, to become lighter, to fly away, to take possession of the immense aerial kingdom; to enter the universe of the Gods, to become Gods ourselves. "

Jerome Tharaud, 'Dans le ciel des dieux,' in *Les Grandes Conferences de l'aviation: Recits et souvenirs,* 1934

It is generally acknowledged that the success of the Wright brothers' Kitty Hawk flight on December 17, 1903, was due to their success, for the first time, in combining into a single machine the three essential elements needed for heavier than air powered flight:

1. A source of lift (the wings properly shaped),
2. Propulsion (an engine of appropriate power versus weight, and efficient propellers), and
3. A means of control (a "warping" or bending of the wings for banking, vertical rudders for turning, and an elevator for pitch).

To the date of their first successful flight, no one else had been able to assemble all three of these essential elements into one machine under conditions conducive to flight. It is generally acknowledged that the Wrights' machine was not so much an "invention" as it was a "development," one that relied upon the efforts, trials, failures, and successes of many who went before. In spite of that fact, the U.S. Patent Office issued a patent to the Wrights in 1906.

The flight experience of mankind prior to the Wright brothers' success was limited to balloons, dirigibles, and gliders. Balloons and dirigibles are classified as "lighter than air" craft. The Federal Aviation Administration (FAA) classifies gliders as a category of aircraft separate from airplanes, but the essential and only significant difference is propulsion, or the lack thereof. The wing of the glider produces lift, just as with the airplane, and the control surfaces of the glider (the ailerons, elevator, and rudder) are the same as the airplane. Early work and experimentation with gliders proved much more valuable to the long-term effort of sustained, controllable flight than did lighter than air experimentation. Since no history of flight would be complete without treatment of the history of all successful flight forms, we begin with the first flights of man.

Balloons

To fly has been a dream, although an elusive dream, of humankind from time immemorial. Through the ages, mockingly the birds of the air swirled and swooped with graceful ease over earthbound man. Man continued to look to the sky, and to dream on. The first flights of man were not to be patterned after the winged creatures; that had proven over the millennia to be too complex. Man's first exploration aloft was the result of the observations of two wealthy French brothers, Jacques-Étienne and Joseph-Michel Montgolfier, who happened to be papermakers in Annonay, France. They observed that fire seemed to have the quality of supporting certain light solid objects, like paper, and that they were borne aloft on what they theorized was a lighter than air gas. Experimentation led to the first hot air balloon ascent in 1783. This was followed that same year by a successful two-hour flight of a balloon filled with hydrogen gas, the brainchild of a French chemist, Jacques-Alexandre-César Charles. Hydrogen gas had been first isolated in 1766 by the British chemist Henry Cavendish. The first ascent by humans in a balloon was also recorded in 1783 near Paris, piloted by Jean-François de Rozier.

Within two years, there were people who called themselves "aeronauts," and who devoted significant effort to getting off the ground and going somewhere. In 1785, aeronaut Jean-Pierre Blanchard, accompanied by an American, John Jeffries, made the first successful crossing of the English Channel from Dover to Calais.

Balloons immediately found a use as observation platforms during the French Revolution and, later, during the American Civil War. (See Figure 5-1.) War again provided function to the balloons in the Franco-Prussian War (1870–1871) as observation vehicles, and even as an escape vehicle when French minister Leon Gambetta floated out of the besieged city of Paris to the very great consternation of the opposing forces. Progressing from war to war, it seems, once again balloons were used for observation in World War I, but now they were joined by, and opposed by, fighter aircraft.

Until the modern age, the record for distance traveled in piloted balloons stood from 1914, when the balloon *Berliner* covered a distance of 1,896 miles from Bitterfeld, Germany to

FIGURE 5-1 An observation balloon during the Civil War.

Source: Library of Congress.

Perm, Russia. Toward the middle and latter 20th century, extraordinary feats have accompanied balloon flight. In 1960, Capt. Joe Kittinger of the U.S. Air Force ascended in a polyethylene balloon to an altitude of 102,800 feet, setting an altitude record. He then bailed out of the gondola to set a free-fall parachute descent record for the time. The balloon altitude record was broken the next year during an ascent to 113,700 feet. In 1984, Kittinger piloted a 3,000 cubic meter balloon from Caribou, Maine to Cairo Montenotte, Italy, covering 3,543 miles. He thus became the first, and only, person to solo a balloon across the Atlantic Ocean. Kittenger's free-fall parachute jump record stood for over 50 years until broken by the Austrian, Felix Baumgartner, on October 12, 2012. Although the Kittinger ascent and jump was a government project (United States Air Force), the Baumgarnter adventure was funded by the Austrian company Red Bull GmbH, which produces the eponymous energy drink, Red Bull; Kissinger served as technical advisor on the project. Baumgartner also became the first man to break the sound barrier without an airplane, reaching an unofficial speed of mach 1.24 in freefall.

◼ Dirigibles

The second entry into the lighter than air category was the craft known as the dirigible. The marked distinctions between a balloon and a dirigible are the elongated shape of the dirigible; the control planes to allow pilots of the dirigible to turn, descend, and climb; and the presence of engines to provide thrust.

Both balloons and dirigibles used hydrogen gas to provide a lifting substance until the gas helium was extracted from natural gas in 1917. Since the United States had a monopoly on helium, no other country was privileged to use it in their airships. Instead, they were required to continue to rely on the very flammable hydrogen gas.

The first dirigibles (the term used here interchangeably with the term "airship") flew in France between 1851 and 1884. The word dirigible is derived from the French *diriger*, meaning to steer. Airship, on the other hand, is a literal translation of the German, *Luftschiff* (airship).

Airships are of two main types, rigid and non-rigid. (See Figure 5-2.) The rigid airship was highly developed after the turn of the 20th century by Ferdinand Adolf von Zeppelin, a former German cavalry officer, who became acquainted with balloons during a visit to the United States. His *LZ-1* became the first rigid airship to fly in a 17-minute sojourn over Lake Constance in 1900. This craft was 420 feet in length, supported by hydrogen gas, and cruised at 20 miles per hour with two 16 horsepower engines. Count von Zeppelin became a national hero because of his development of the very imposing and exciting "Zeppelins," which could be seen overhead proceeding majestically through the German countryside. In 1909, Count Zeppelin formed the first passenger line for the carriage of passengers by air, Deutsche Luftshiffahrts A.G. (DELAG). DELAG, the airship company, carried passengers all over the country of Germany after its inauguration, and by 1913 had conducted over 1,600 flights, carrying 35,000 passengers without mishap.

With the advent of World War I, Germany and England geared up to produce airships by the hundreds. The British navy produced 200 airships between 1915 and 1918, more than Germany, and almost all of them were used for antisubmarine patrol. Germany produced 125 Zeppelins between 1914 and 1918, and employed them in offensive engagements over the English countryside, dropping bombs and otherwise wreaking havoc among the terrified population. The Zeppelins proved quite vulnerable to antiaircraft battery fire and to fighter aircraft. Of the 125 Zeppelins manufactured and placed in service during the war, only 6 survived.

Non-rigid airship (blimp)

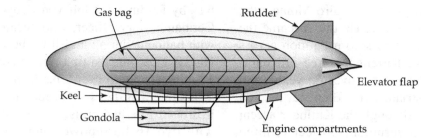

Semirigid airship

Rigid airship (Zeppelin)

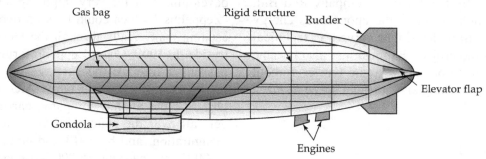

FIGURE 5-2 Types of airships.

Several countries produced airships after the war. Both England and France built dirigibles, but accidents and mysterious disappearances caused the French to cancel their program in 1923. England continued operating dirigibles until 1930. Aerodynamic improvements were made as the technology advanced. The English *R-34*, completed in December 1918, had a total air resistance of only 7 percent of a hypothetical flat disc of the same diameter. The United States built its own dirigibles and even received a Zeppelin as a war prize from Germany after the cessation of hostilities in 1918. The 660-foot *ZR-III* was the 126th Zeppelin constructed by Germany

and was later renamed *Los Angeles* and placed in service by the U.S. Navy.

After the war, the Zeppelin continued to be used in passenger service between America and Germany, as well as between Germany and South America. Zeppelin flights continued until the occurrence of the *Hindenburg* disaster in Lakehurst, New Jersey, in 1937. The *Hindenburg* was undoubtedly the greatest airship ever constructed, boasting restaurants, staterooms, lounges, and other amenities for the enjoyment of its transatlantic passengers.

The Goodyear Company built airships for the United States, including the *Akron* in 1931, commissioned for service in the U.S. Navy, and the *Macon* in 1933, also a navy craft. Both the *Akron* and the *Macon* were lost to weather, the last of a long line of airships that had come to similar grief. It was believed that the rigid airframe employed in the dirigibles was not sufficiently flexible, given its rather large dimensions, to withstand the vicissitudes of rough air and storms. The days of the rigid airship thus came to an ignominious close with their last production in the 1930s.

The non-rigid airship, or blimp, was placed in service by the United States Navy in World War II in convoy operations, and proved effective as an anti-submarine weapon. The only service to employ blimps in World War II, the United States Navy, worked 170 of the non-rigid airships over the Atlantic during the war, escorting 89,000 ships and logging some 500,000 hours flying time.

Today, blimps are used almost exclusively as promotional devices, employing television cameras for golf event coverage or other sporting events, or displaying brand names of commercial products on their ample sides. The advent of international terrorism after September 11, 2001, however, has caused renewed interest in the subject of blimps as a potential countermeasure against terrorist attacks in the United States.

Gliders

From the early to mid 19th century, to the Wright brothers' success in 1903, controllable flight of "heavier than air" craft was a preoccupation throughout the civilized world among dreamers, engineers, and assorted tinkerers. The sketches and writings of **Leonardo da Vinci** in 1505 were the only known serious, theoretical treatment of the subject of flight until the publication in 1810 of a series of articles by the Englishman **Sir George Cayley**.

Today, Cayley is considered to be the founder of the science of aerodynamics because of his pioneering experiments with wing design and the effects of lift and drag, and his formulations concerning control surfaces and propellers. He concluded, by observing birds, that a curved surface (a wing) would support weight and, under the proper configuration of fuselage and other accoutrements, would permit flight. As a scientist, he kept meticulous records of his observations and the results of his experiments. In years to come, this documentation would greatly assist those who followed him in the quest for flight.

In 1804, Cayley built and flew a model of a glider that incorporated the principles of the cambered wing, and in 1808 he flew a full-scale version of this glider as a kite, thereby proving his basic wing theory. Cayley worked on his theories all his life. Between 1849 and 1853, he designed and built the first human-carrying gliders in history. His research probed the engineering essentials of aircraft design today, including the ratio of lift to wing area, the determination of the center of wing pressure, the importance of streamlining, the concept of structural strength, and the concepts of stability and control. Cayley's work became the foundation of most of the future experimentation in flight.

Throughout the course of the 19th century, many pioneers contributed to the persistent quest of manned flight. Some got the cart before the horse, like the Englishmen **John Stringfellow** and his cohort **William S. Henson**. In their zeal they attempted to form a company called the "Aerial Steam Transit Company" in 1843, for the purpose of operating an international airline. The first problem the company had was the absence of any form of aerial conveyance, such as an airplane. There also was no form of propulsion to make the aerial conveyance go anywhere, although Stringfellow apparently worked at high pitch to develop a lightweight steam engine to be placed on the yet undesigned airplane. The attempt came to naught when the English House of Commons rejected the motion to form the company, with great laughter.

In apparent recognition of the unlikely commercial success of their venture, Henson married and moved to the United States, where no record has been located to support evidence of any further aeronautical involvements. But Stringfellow persisted and, in 1848, he was successful in developing a three-winged model aircraft on which he placed a lightweight steam engine that actually flew a distance of 120 feet. He is thus credited with producing the first engine-driven aircraft capable of free flight and, under the auspices of the Aeronautical Society, exhibited his machine at the world's first exhibition of flying machines held in the Crystal Palace in London in 1868.

Others, such as the French sea captain **Jean-Marie Le Bris**, are noted more for their efforts than their successes. His legacy was a series of glider crashes occurring after short, unmanned flight. **Francis Wenham** was an Englishman who pursued the elusive reality of flight without success, but who did design and build the first wind tunnel. Wenham was a marine engineer, as was the Frenchman **Alphonse Penaud**, who brought to their interest in flight an engineering discipline that would enhance the ultimate success of achieving manned flight.

Penaud's work was important to the Wright brothers' success, by their own admission. Penaud is known for his experimentation with model aircraft, with results long studied by aeronautical engineers and historians. Penaud had shown that models are effective for purposes of experimentation. He demonstrated the usefulness of the twisted rubber band as a means of propulsion for model airplanes. These models were among the first powered, heavier than air objects ever to fly and went far to encourage experimenters that manned, powered flight was possible. Penaud's "planaphore," a model monoplane with tapered dihedral wings, an adjustable tail assembly, and a pusher-type propeller mounted on the tail of the airplane, flew as a demonstration in 1871 in Paris. The planaphore covered a distance of 131 feet and is acknowledged to be the first recorded flight of an inherently stable aircraft.

Efforts to find a workable means of propulsion, or thrust, for aircraft were the primary interests of two other engineers. **Clement Ader**, a French electrical engineer, and **Hiram Maxim**, chief engineer for an early electric utility, experimented with steam engines, at the time the only known reliable form of moveable power.

During the 1880s Ader built flying machines to which he attached 40-horsepower and 20-horsepower steam engines. The engines were effective in producing sufficient power to propel his clumsy and unwieldy machines, all of which were completely without any effective means of control, and by turns they all suffered the ignominy of the crash and burn.

In 1893, Hiram Maxim built an enormous biplane. It was 200 feet in length with a wingspan of 107 feet, and he mounted on it not one but two 180-horsepower steam engines. The platform for the engines, the boiler, and the three-man crew was 40 feet long and 8 feet wide. The machine was effectively affixed to the ground by attachments to a track over which it ran. It was made to move along the track at speeds of up to 42 miles per hour in a fashion described at the time by a journalist at the scene:

> When full steam was up and the propellers spinning so fast that they seemed to become whirling disks, Maxim shouted, "Let go!" A rope was pulled and the machine shot forward like a railway train with the big propellers whirling, the steam hissing and the waste pipes puffing and gurgling, it flew over the 1800 feet of track in much less time that it takes to tell it.

Otto Lilienthal (see Figures 5-3 and 5-4), a German engineer who believed that glider flight was a necessary prerequisite to powered flight, constructed and tested a series of monoplanes in the nature of what we today would call hang gliders. He made the most accurate and detailed observations about the properties of curved

FIGURE 5-3 Otto Lilienthal and his glider.

Source: Library of Congress.

surfaces, presenting for the first time observations concerning aspect ratio, wing shape, and profile, and conducted various experiments in his workshop that were built on the already proven idea of the cambered wing. In 1889 he published *Birdflight as the Basis of Aviation*, which contained the findings and conclusions from his experiments and which were presented in tabulated format. Beginning in 1894, he proved, through repeated successful glides of distances of over 1,000 feet, that manned flight was possible.

Between 1891 and 1896, Lilienthal made over 2,000 gliding flights, many over distances in excess of 1,000 feet, and for this period there are 137 known photographs of him in flight. He wrestled with the concept of control, using dexterous movements of his body to keep the glider in proper attitude, but was unable to develop an otherwise effective means of control. On August 9, 1896, the lack of control took its toll when his glider stalled at an altitude of 50 feet and plummeted to the ground, fatally injuring him. As he lay dying in the open field where he crashed, he was heard to have said, "*Opfer müssen gemacht werden.*" Thus was started the tradition that has transcended the epoch of aviation, in the translation of his last words, "Sacrifices must be made."

Lilienthal's exploits were publicly acknowledged, and photographs, interviews, and publication of his experiments and calculations were widely circulated. **Percy Pilcher**, a Scotsman and marine engineer and lecturer in naval architecture at Glasgow University, was intrigued by Lilienthal. He fashioned his own form of glider, but did not fly it until after he was permitted a visit to Lilienthal with the opportunity to practice in his proven machines. Pilcher died in his own gliding crash in 1899. He was later cited by Wilbur

Wright as having influenced the brothers' experiments, who credited both Pilcher and Lilienthal in the success of the Wrights' experiments.

Octave Chanute was arguably the most important single influence on Orville and Wilbur Wright as they relentlessly pursued their goal of manned, powered flight. Chanute was an accomplished and successful civil engineer, president of the American Society of Civil Engineers, and

FIGURE 5-5 Octave Chanute.

Source: Library of Congress.

designer of the first railroad bridge over the Missouri River. (See Figure 5-5.) His interest in flight can be best understood as a hobby until he was in his sixties, when he published a book called *Progress in Flying Machines*, which compiled his extensive investigation of flight experimentation and research up to that time. (See Figures 5-6 and 5-7.) In 1896, Chanute began a series of experiments using gliders of his own design and construction. A short train ride from Chicago to the south lies the Indiana state line, along the shore of Lake Michigan. In June of that year, Chanute, his associate Augustus Herring, and two others established a campsite outside of Miller Junction, Indiana, among the famous dunes along Lake Michigan. Winds from the lake and the elevation of the dunes provided a very suitable venue for glider experimentation, and the isolation of the region provided some degree of privacy. (See Figure 5-8.) These physical characteristics of the topography were later noted by the Wrights in the selection of the Outer Banks of North Carolina for similar, although even more favorable, characteristics.

During this encampment, the Chanute party experimented with Lilienthal glider designs, making modifications that to them seemed appropriate. Progress was made, particularly in the six-winged version known as the "Katydid." The party returned to the area in August 1896, and continued experiments with gliders, this time

FIGURE 5-6 Lilienthal-type glider tested by Octave Chanute.

Source: Library of Congress.

FIGURE 5-7 Box-type glider (double-decker) design later used by the Wright brothers.

concentrating on the double-deck kite version that would become the model for the Wright's successful efforts a few years later. Chanute was encouraged by the results of the double-decker tests, and upon his return to Chicago he published the results in an article entitled "Recent Experiments in Gliding Flight." The next year he followed this up with an article in the *Journal of the Western Society of Engineers*, wherein he recounted not only the 1896 experiments but also additional flights conducted by Augustus Herring in 1897. This free distribution of information was typical of the generous Chanute, who was genuinely committed to the advancement of manned flight regardless of any issue of credit for it.

The Wright brothers became seriously interested in the subject of manned flight in 1899. They wrote to Secretary Langley at the Smithsonian Institution, who was also in the process of experimenting with the idea of manned flight, and in that way became aware of the efforts of Chanute. Wilbur Wright first corresponded with Octave Chanute in 1900, and expressed particular interest in the structural engineering concept of strut and wire bracing that Chanute first introduced to aircraft design with the double decker. From this developed a lengthy and prolific correspondence and association between Chanute and the Wright brothers that extended for a decade, until his death in 1910. Chanute became a friend and confidant to the Wrights, and even accompanied them to the Outer Banks on several occasions. As a man of some stature as compared to the unknown Wright brothers, he defended them and vouched for their accomplishments during the secretive five-year period following their first successful controlled and powered flight in 1903, when, as we shall see, no one else would.

" All agreed that the sensation of coasting on the air was delightful. "

Octave Chanute, regarding first glider flights, 1894

FIGURE 5-8 Box-type glider showing dunes near Lake Michigan where Chanute held experiments.

6 Prelude to Powered Flight

In the fall of 1903, aerodynamic research had proved the practicality of gliding flight, capable of carrying a man on wings of various designs. Rudimentary control had been shown in gliding flight, but with inconsistent results, and lack of control had caused the recent deaths of at least two gliding aeronauts. Sustained powered flight had been shown using models with steam engines. Reaching the goal of sustained, manned, and controlled flight was tantalizingly close, and was seemingly within the grasp of several different experimenters, yet it remained completely out of reach—as far away as the moon. The combined knowledge and experience of all of the preceding pioneers of flight hung in suspension just above their heads, awaiting some catalyst—some insight or development—that would crystallize all of it into successful, sustained flight. Of all such contenders, the most promising in the fall of 1903 seemed to be Samuel P. Langley (see Figure 6-1), an astronomer, mathematician, physicist, and third Secretary of the Smithsonian Institution in Washington, D.C.

Langley's formal education ended on his graduation from the Boston Latin School, but he was self-taught in mathematics, physics, and astronomy. When he was nine years old, he was heavily into reading books on astronomy, and

FIGURE 6-1 Samuel Langley.

Source: U.S. Air Force.

he built telescopes of various types, using them to observe the moon and the planets. He secured placement as an assistant astronomer at Harvard College Observatory during the middle 1860s, and then took a position at the U.S. Naval Academy as a professor of mathematics. His work in

37

Annapolis mostly related to the restoration of the observatory at the Academy.

After a year, Langley went to the Allegheny Observatory of the Western University of Pennsylvania (now the University of Pittsburgh), where he began to engage in pioneering work in solar observation and discovery, and where he developed astronomical instruments and conducted research that brought him a degree of recognition and fame. His work naturally led to publications in scientific journals and periodicals, and in turn he met and became familiar with inventors and scientists in many cognate fields of exploration, including the pursuit of heavier than air flight.

From his university life he moved to Washington, D.C., in order to take the appointment to the Smithsonian Institution as its third Secretary in 1887. The Smithsonian Institution was founded in 1846 by Congressional act to establish a charitable trust to create a museum, a library, and a program of research, publication, and collection in the sciences, arts, and history. The Secretary of the Smithsonian is the chief executive officer of the Institution.

After arriving in Washington, D.C. in 1887, Langley continued the research that he had earlier begun in studying aerodynamic lift. He constructed a whirling table (in order to generate wind) on which he affixed various bird wings, by which means he was able to observe the lifting characteristics of the particular designs. Langley worked briefly with gliders, consulting the work of Sir George Cayley of some 75 years earlier, who had also studied bird wings in shaping wings he constructed. The Smithsonian was a refuge and bulwark of naturalists, and it was easy for Langley to conduct research in that environment. He mused at the time, "I watched a hawk soaring far up in the blue, and sailing for a long time without any motion of its wings . . . How wonderfully easy, too, was its flight! I was brought to think of these things again, and to ask myself whether the problem of artificial flight was really as hopeless and as absurd as it was then thought to be."

This was also the time of other true believers, like Lilienthal and Chanute, whose work concentrated on lift experiments with gliders. But Langley moved away from gliders, favoring the development of a complete, self-sustaining aerial machine that would, by its own power, show that manned flight was ultimately possible.

He did this by building a series of models, which he called "Aerodromes" sequentially numbered, the first of which was completed in 1892, but not flown. By 1894, he had settled on a design that used two sets of equal-sized wings in tandem (one set of wings located behind a first set forward), on which he placed small contrivances of motive power, using compressed gas or steam. He converted a 38-foot houseboat, with a workshop, into a launch platform and towed it down the Potomac River to a point near Quantico, Virginia.

From here he tested Aerodrome 4 (all attempts were failures, resulting in each of the models falling into the water), and Aerodrome 5, which sustained a flight in October, 1894, for 35 feet and three seconds. A year and a half later, on May 6, 1896, Aerodrome No. 6 was launched from the houseboat's catapult but its left wing collapsed and the model landed in the water. At 3:05 p.m. that same day, Aerodrome No. 5, 13 feet long and weighing about 24 pounds, is launched and flies for a minute and a half, covering about one-half mile and reaching 100 feet altitude. This is the first successful sustained flight of a heavier-than-air machine ever recorded. At 5:10 p.m., Langley does it again as the machine climbs to 60 feet and flies in circles for 1 minute and 31 seconds. Dr. Alexander Graham Bell, the only witness to the flight who was not a staff member, photographed the accomplishment. Joy abounded.

The see-saw battle against gravity proceeded in fits and starts. In June, Chanute conducts his acclaimed glider experiments at the Lake

Michigan dunes using his box glider design, which will be later borrowed by the Wright brothers to good effect. In August, after over 2,000 gliding flights, the intrepid Lilienthal dies when his glider stalls and crashes from an altitude of about 50 feet. On November 28, Langley repeats his success as Aerodrome No. 6 flies 4,800 feet in 1 minute and 45 seconds.

On February 15, 1898, the USS *Maine* sank in Havana harbor, with the death of 266 sailors, due to a massive explosion. The *Maine* was in Cuba to protect American citizens during revolutionary unrest caused by Cuban freedom-fighters against Spanish colonial rule. A Navy Board of Inquiry concluded that the *Maine* had been sunk by a mine placed on her hull. Although the government did not affix blame for the mine's placement, an outraged public blamed Spain. This was one of the precipitating factors to the American entry into war with Spain (the Spanish-American War), which began on April 21, 1898.

Between the sinking of the *Maine* and the declaration of war, on March 25, 1898, the Assistant Secretary of the Navy, Theodore Roosevelt, suggested the development of Langley's Aerodrome as a possible weapon of war to Navy Secretary John D. Long. This shortly resulted in a grant from the War Department of $50,000 to Langley for the construction of a full-sized version of the Aerodrome model capable of carrying a man in controlled flight.

The Smithsonian is intricately connected to the federal government, and has always been largely funded by federal dollars and administered by officials from the three branches of the federal government. It was natural, then, that the federal government would fund advanced research that had already been started under the auspices of the Smithsonian Institution. It is not clear that this was a welcome development to Langley, as many have supposed that he intended to complete his aeronautical experiments and contributions with the successful flights of the models he had already produced.

Still, Langley accepted the assignment and was immediately confronted with several significant challenges. First, his plan was simply to scale up the models that he had successfully flown into a full-sized flying machine capable of carrying a person. Based on later analysis by the Smithsonian National Air and Space Museum,[1] this was an error of failure-producing proportion since the aerodynamics, structural design, and control system of the smaller craft were not adaptable to the full-sized version. However, Langley's primary focus was not on the integrity of the craft's structure, but on its propulsion.

In 1898 there existed no available engine that could produce sufficient horsepower for mounting on a full-sized flying machine, primarily due to considerations of weight. The best ones available produced only about one horsepower for each 20 pounds of engine weight. In spite of his accomplishments, Langley was not an engineer, nor was he an expert in either propulsion or structure. He had concluded, however, that steam engines were not suitable for large flying machines. This left as the only alternative the gasoline internal combustion engine, which had been invented by Gottlieb Daimler in 1885. Meaningful advances in the internal combustion engine were, at that time, awaiting the arrival of the automobile industry. Langley also concluded that he could use some engineering assistance.

Charles Manly, who was set to graduate from Cornell University as a mechanical engineer in 1898, was recommended to Langley by a professor friend of his at that school. Langley hired Manly in June 1898, and by October the two of them had begun major work on the Great Aerodrome, as it was called (see Figure 6-2). Manly had calculated that the machine would require at least two 12 horsepower motors, each weighing no more than 100 pounds. Finding none available, Langley contracted with automobile engine manufacturer Stephen Marius Balzer of New York to build it. After two years of effort, Balzer's engine, which was a 5-cylinder radial type, was not functional

Source: National Air and Space Museum.

FIGURE 6-2 Samuel Langley and Charles Manly. Note magnetic compass attached to the left leg of Charles Manly.

and Balzer was near bankruptcy. Manly prevailed upon Langley to assign the project of building the engine to him, and by September of 1900, Manly had produced an experimental engine weighing 108 pounds and producing 18½ horsepower. Manly had, in effect, produced a motor that would perform to almost twice the specifications of the original. As he later said, "At the time very little was known about the 'proper way of constructing' an engine and what work had been done was jealously guarded against patent theft by the automobile industry."

By January 1902, the 5-cylinder radial engine had been successfully developed and tested, and it produced 51 horsepower while weighing only 207 pounds, including water for cooling (see Figure 6-3). His weight to power ratio was an unbelievable 4 to 1. The unsuccessful Balzer engine's design specification had been 8 to 1.

The remaining news about the finished aircraft known as the Aerodrome A, on the other hand, was not so good. The fuselage was constructed of steel tubing. The wings and tail were of wood covered by Percaline (lightweight cotton). The frame of the craft, and both the design and construction of the tandem wing setup, was produced without the benefit of manned glider testing. Given its large size (it was 52 feet long with a wing span of 48 feet), it was flimsy. It did not help that the structure had to sit 11 feet above the ground to provide propeller clearance. Strangely, the Aerodrome had no landing gear or flotation devices. There were no specific provisions for lateral control except for a rudder mounted aft and beneath the fuselage of the craft. The press assigned it the moniker "the Dragonfly."

Refinements and finishing touches were made during 1903, and on October 7, things were all in order for the launch. Although Langley had planned to use ballast or dummy passengers, Manly insisted that he be permitted to pilot the craft. The launching mechanism had been enlarged, inspected, and tested. The Aerodrome had been affixed atop the launching mechanism and stood ready. The engine was cranked and was running smoothly. Wearing a cork-lined coat for flotation, and with a compass affixed to his left trouser leg to assist in navigating a lengthy flight, Manly mounted the Aerodrome atop the houseboat and signaled that he was ready. Two sky rockets were launched and the tugs holding the houseboat into the wind tooted to signal the launch.

With the press in full attendance, what happened next is described by Dr. A. G. Bell in a speech ten years later:

. . . but when the catapult was released the aerodrome sped along the track on the top of the houseboat attaining sufficient headway for normal flight; but at the end of the rails it was jerked violently down at the front, and plunged headlong into the river.

Source: National Air and Space Museum, Smithsonian Institution (SI 2003-35050).

FIGURE 6-3   The Aerodrome atop Langley's barge.

Langley was lampooned in the press, his aircraft maligned as a "buzzard," and his launch platform and houseboat ridiculed as the "Ark." *The Washington Post* said the Aerodrome plunged into the Potomac "like a handful of mortar." Despite the very public failure, the commitment to flight remained steadfast. Manly was chagrined but unhurt, the engine was undamaged, and the Aerodrome was repairable. On December 8, 1903, with the Wright brothers hard at work on their craft at Kitty Hawk, all was again in readiness for history to be made. According to Dr. Bell:

> This time the rear guy post was injured, crippling the rear wings, so that the aerodrome pitched up in front and plunged over backwards into the water . . .

The Washington Star headlined on December 9, 1903, "AIRSHIP FAILS TO FLY," accompanied by a distressing photograph of the Aerodrome just after launch, captioned "Collapse of the Airship." (See Figure 6-4.) Within three years Langley was dead, the object of ridicule. In 1913 Dr. Bell believed that the catapult was the only problem:

> It will thus be seen that Langley's aerodrome was never successfully launched, so that it had no opportunity of showing what it could do in the air. The defect lay in the launching mechanism employed and not in the machine itself, which is recognized by all experts as a perfectly good flying machine, excellently constructed and made long before the appearance of other machines.

The remains of Aerodrome A were carefully packed up in crates and stored at the Smithsonian Institution. But the end of the story of the Aerodrome was not yet at hand. In fact, the Aerodrome failure just two weeks before the Wright brothers' first successful manned flight in Kitty Hawk,

Source: National Air and Space Museum, Smithsonian Institution (SI 2002-16637).

FIGURE 6-4 The crash of the Aerodrome.

N.C. was to fuel a controversy that would fester for decades to come. It would cause the Smithsonian Institution to question the Wright brothers' claims to be the true "inventors" of the airplane, which, in turn, would cause the original Wright Flyer to be sent to the London Science Museum for exhibition rather than to the Washington Smithsonian. It would play a part in the rupture of the close and fraternal early aeronautical community and become a foil in the patent wars to come between the Wright brothers and the rest of the world over the issue of who owned the right to fly. The failure of the Aerodrome was to be just one poignant vignette among many as man strived to produce the world's first practical airplane in the early years of the 20th century.

Endnote

1. http://www.nasm.si.edu/collections/artifact.cfm?id=A19180001000

7 The Wright Brothers

❝ More than anything else the sensation is one of perfect peace mingled with an excitement that strains every nerve to the utmost, if you can conceive of such a combination. **❞**

Wilbur Wright

In 1908, Wilbur Wright responded to an inquiry concerning the circumstances of his and Orville's interest in flight. He said:

Late in the autumn of 1878, our father came into the house one evening with some object partly concealed in his hands, and before we could see what it was, he tossed it into the air. Instead of falling to the floor as we expected, it flew across the room till it struck the ceiling, where it fluttered awhile, and finally sank to the floor. It was a little toy, known to scientists as a "helicoptere," but which we, with sublime disregard for science, at once dubbed a "bat." It was a light frame of cork and bamboo, covered with paper, which formed two screws, driven in opposite directions by rubber bands under torsion. A toy so delicate lasted only a short time in the hands of small boys, but its memory was abiding.

Later, the boys became experts in kite building and in flying them until their age made this activity unseemingly childish. They also built model "helicopteres," making them larger and larger. The larger they become, they discovered, the less they flew. In this way they began to learn the rudimentary physics of aerodynamics, that a machine having only twice the linear dimensions of another would require eight times the power to achieve lift. Thus, were they introduced to coefficents of aerodynamic lift.

In the late 19th century, the bicycle was advanced technology, and its popularity made its commercial appeal very great. The Wrights opened a bicycle shop in Dayton, Ohio, and became adept at machinery and mechanics. In the middle of the decade of the 1890s, the brothers had some limited knowledge of the small group of engineers and scientists who had conducted experiments with gliders and flying machines. But it was not until the death of Otto Lilienthal, in 1896, that they seriously took up the study of aeronautics. They began reading works by Chanute, Lilienthal, Langley, and articles published by the Smithsonian Institution. They saw at once that the field of aviation was neatly divided between the advocates advancing theories and experimentation related to propulsion, or powered flight, like Langley and Maxim, and those advocates of soaring flight, like Lilienthal, Mouillard, and Chanute. The sympathies of the Wright brothers lay with the latter group, based on the sound logic that until the problem of control of an aerial vehicle could be solved, the question of power would not be relevant. They, therefore, zeroed in on the problem of control.

As they educated themselves with the available literature, they also noted that the years between 1895 and 1900 represented a brief time of heightened activity in aeronautics, and a time of great public expectation that a solution to the problem of flight would be found. But successful flight did not materialize. Maxim, after spending $100,000 in the effort, abandoned his work. The Ader machine, built at the expense of the French government, was a failure. Lilienthal and Pilcher were killed in experiments, and Chanute and most others seemed to be having little success. The Wrights concluded that the public, distressed and disappointed by the failures and tragedies, had given up on the idea of manned, powered flight. As they said, the whole process seemed to have been shuffled off to that purgatory of science and engineering that was concerned with such things as the perpetual motion machine.

So it was that they harked back to their days of kite flying. They began their active experimentation in October 1900 at Kitty Hawk. (See Figure 7-1.) They chose that venue for its constant, substantial breezes, and because of the elevation of the sand dunes and unobstructed terrain that joined the sea. Their machine was designed in large part from the work of Chanute with its struts and wire bracing, and from the Lilienthal tables from which the coefficient of lift could be calculated. It was to be flown tethered to the ground, as a kite with a man aboard, and also as a glider. The 1900 experiments failed to confirm published data on wind pressures and lift, although they did confirm the basic effectiveness of lateral and vertical control, innovations that were original to the Wrights. The main problems

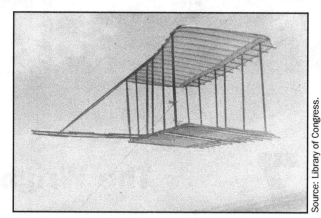

FIGURE 7-1 The Wright brothers' kite—1900.

Source: Library of Congress.

of lift and drag were daunting, but as the brothers left Kitty Hawk as winter approached, they were encouraged enough to plan improvements to be tested the next summer.

On their return to North Carolina on July 11, 1901, the design of the glider was essentially the same (see Figure 7-2), except that it was made larger and the camber of the wings was increased in order to attempt to provide for greater lift.

FIGURE 7-2 The Wright brothers' kite, also flown as a glider.

Source: Library of Congress.

Still, the amount of lift achieved was disappointing. The brothers reluctantly concluded that the published data of flight, particularly as concerned lift, could not be trusted. The center of pressure calculated from the tables was too far forward, resulting in a nose-heavy trim. Even attempts to manipulate the "warping mechanism" of the wings while attempting on-board gliding did not result in the satisfactory trials experienced the year before. Wilbur and Orville were so dispirited that they broke camp a month earlier than they had planned, and returned to Dayton. As recollected by Orville:

> . . . we doubted that we would ever resume our experiments. Although we had broken the record for distance in gliding, and although Mr. Chanute, who was present at that time, assured us that our results were better than had ever before been attained, yet when we looked at the time and money which we had expended, and considered the progress made and the distance yet to go, we considered our experiments a failure. At that time I made the prediction that men would sometime fly, but that it would not be within our lifetime.[1]

When they returned to Dayton, Wilbur and Orville began to believe that the information that had previously been developed, particularly the Smeaton coefficient and data compiled by Otto Lilienthal regarding pressures, were in error. They determined to verify all of the necessary data, such as coefficient of lift and wind pressures, from their own experimentation. Rather than secure this information from building and crashing more gliders, they set about to make these determinations more scientifically. They constructed a state-of-the-art wind tunnel and developed instruments to quantify lift and drag. They tested over 80 different wing configurations in their wind tunnel and, in the process, confirmed that prevailing data on coefficient of lift were wrong. They also were able to identify an optimum shape of wing, one much longer and narrower, for their new machine. Tests

also provided insight into the need of a vertical "vane" as they called it; what today is known as a rudder. (See Figure 7-3.)

The design of the 1902 glider (see Figure 7-4), incorporating the results of their testing in the wind tunnel, was the first aircraft that solved the fundamental problems of soaring flight, lift and control, and it constituted a major departure from their first two gliders. They returned to Kill Devil Hills in the late summer of 1902 and by the middle of September, they had begun kiting experiments. In a letter to Milton Wright on October 2, 1902, Wilbur wrote:

> Our new machine is a very great improvement over anything we had built before and over anything any one has built. We have far beaten all record for flatness of glides as we in some cases have descended only $5\frac{1}{3}$ degrees from the horizontal while other machines descended from 7.5 to 11 degrees. . . . This means that in soaring we can descend much slower, and in a power machine can fly with much less power. The new machine is also much more controllable than any heretofore built so the danger is correspondingly reduced. We are being

FIGURE 7-3 Glider—1901.

Source: Library of Congress.

FIGURE 7-4 Glider turning—1902.

careful and will avoid accident of serious nature if possible. Yesterday I tried three glides from the top of the hill and made 506 ft, 504.4 ft, and 550 ft, respectively in distance passed over. Everything is so much more satisfactory that we now believe that the flying problem is really nearing its solution.

Upon completion of the 1902 tests, the Wrights returned to Dayton, and they were now ready to confront the only remaining problem: propulsion.

Motive power, thrust, or propulsion, all words of similar meaning, was shown to have been effective using the steam engine. The weight and complexity of the steam engine, with its water, boiler, and piping, argued forcefully for a gasoline engine. But, to their knowledge, a lightweight gasoline engine did not exist.[2]

With the Wright brothers' travels to the Outer Banks becoming a regular thing, their bicycle shop was left unattended for extended periods of time. They hired a machinist in 1901 by the name of Charlie Taylor to mind the store in their absence and to take on bicycle repair work that they would have to miss due to their absence. It was Taylor who built the one-cylinder engine that the Wrights used to drive their wind tunnel for the 1902 Dayton experiments. When the Wrights finally got to the matter of propulsion for the *Flyer*, they turned to Charlie Taylor.

They calculated that the engine could weigh no more than 180 pounds and that it would take at least 8 horsepower to sustain the *Flyer* in flight. Taylor came up with a 4-cylinder in-line water cooled engine that weighed 178 pounds and produced 16 horsepower, that is until the valves heated up, and then it put out only 12 horsepower. It had no carburetor, and with a weight to power ratio of 14 to 1, this was not nearly the engine that Charles Manly had built for Langley, whose ratio was 4 to 1, but it was enough for the Wrights' purposes in 1903.

The second part of the propulsion problem was the propeller. There were no available data on aircraft propellers, and their research into marine propellers turned out to be a dead end. They approached the problem in the same way as they had approached the wing lift. They just rotated the wing 90 degrees, put a twist in it and they had created a propeller. The efficiency of the propeller designs was tested in the wind tunnel until the best was found.

There was no guesswork in the 1903 experiments. The Wright brothers had brought the scientific method to their task, and the total design had been proven on paper. They also possessed the skills of mechanics and craftsmen to put it all together in the final product and in a workmanlike manner. Free, controlled, and sustained powered flight was at last achieved on December 17, 1903 in their design known as the *Flyer I*. (See Figures 7-5 and 7-6.) This

craft was damaged after its fourth flight (852 feet in 59 seconds), although it was salvaged and returned to Dayton, Ohio. In 1928, Orville sent it for display to the London Science Museum. Since 1949, it has been on display at the Smithsonian Institution.

The Wrights continued their research and development at Huffman Prairie, Ohio, beginning in 1904. They built a second powered model, the *Flyer II* (see Figure 7-7), that was virtually identical to the *Flyer I*, but 320 pounds lighter. They attempted short hops in the *Flyer II*, but they were having difficulty with the underpowered engine and the lack of the favorable winds enjoyed at Kitty Hawk. In September 1904, they developed a catapult launching system to get the airplane quickly up to flying speed. This system allowed them to again concentrate on flying and on extending the range of their flights. On May 23, 1904, the Wrights invited newspaper reporters to view their experiments on condition that no photographs be taken. Lack of

Source: Library of Congress.

FIGURE 7-5   The first powered flight—December 17, 1903.

Source: Library of Congress.

FIGURE 7-6 The third powered flight—December 17, 1903.

Source: Library of Congress.

FIGURE 7-7 *Flyer II* at Huffman Prairie—1904.

wind, a cranky engine, and control problems left the reporters less than impressed, all of which contributed to the belief that the Wrights' claims were overblown. This failure also reinforced their penchant for conducting their work in secret. Yet they persevered, and by the end of 1904 they had made 105 successful flights and logged a total of 45 minutes flying time.

In 1905 the *Flyer III* was launched (see Figure 7-8). After a series of serious mishaps, the Wrights made several significant changes to the *Flyer* based on their conclusion that longitudinal stability was the problem. They increased the area of the elevator to almost two times its former dimension. Believing that the elevator was too close to the wings, they extended it to a point almost twice as far from the leading edge of the wing as previously. When testing resumed, it was immediately apparent that these changes had made the *Flyer* truly airworthy. This was regarded by the Wrights as their final design, having with it solved all major control problems, and it became generally acknowledged to be the world's first practical airplane. (See Figure 7-9.) On October 5, 1905, the Wrights completed a flight of 24 miles in 38 minutes, landing only when the gas tank on the airplane ran dry. Being highly satisfied with their design, but wondering what practical use

the airplane could be, they lobbied the U.S. government, suggesting that the airplane might be used for military scouting and reconnaissance. The War Department was not interested, advising the Wrights that the United States had "no requirements" for their invention.

The Wrights had applied for, but still had not secured, a patent in 1905 and they were not willing to make the details of their product public. After the negative press received in 1904, reporters were not invited to view the machine or its performance and the few articles published about it during this time were generally inaccurate. Their sole support came from Octave Chanute, who had seen the aircraft, had seen it fly, and who knew the details of its construction. His correspondence with his contacts throughout the world was about the only sustaining force that kept the Wrights' accomplishments above rank rumor. When visitors began to come to Dayton to view their machine and to interview them, the

Source: Library of Congress.

FIGURE 7-8 *Flyer III* at Huffman Prairie—1905.

FIGURE 7-9 *Flyer III*—the world's first practical airplane—1905.

Source: Library of Congress.

Wrights shunned all publicity and even disassembled the *Flyer* and stowed away the parts from view for almost three years. The *Flyer* did not fly again until 1908 when it was adapted to carry two people.

Rejected at home, the Wrights turned to Europe, where aviation was taking hold. The asking price for the aircraft was $200,000, a very large sum in those days. Although they guaranteed its performance, they refused to demonstrate it to a prospective purchaser until a price had been negotiated and paid. Not surprisingly, no sales were recorded. At the same time, experimenters were proceeding with their own individual designs and making progress, although none had come close to accomplishing what the Wrights had. This fact, in addition to the secrecy that surrounded the Wrights' 1905 experiments, produced widespread skepticism in the aviation community. Skepticism even took the form of

sarcasm and taunting. Consider the tone of the following article from the very prominent *Scientific American* magazine, entitled "The Wright Aeroplane and Its Fabled Performance."[3]

A Parisian automobile paper recently published a letter from the Wright brothers to Capt. Ferber of the French army, in which statements are made that certainly need some public substantiation from the Wright brothers. In the letter in question it is alleged that on September 26, the Wright motor-driven aeroplane covered a distance of 17.961 kilometers in 18 minutes and 9 seconds, and that its further progress was stopped by lack of gasoline. On September 29 a distance of 19.57 kilometers was covered in 19 minutes and 55 seconds, the gasoline supply again having been exhausted. On September 30 the machine traveled 16 kilometers in 17 minutes and 15 seconds;

this time a hot bearing prevented further remarkable progress. Then came some eye-opening records. Here they are:

- October 3: 25.535 kilometers in 25 minutes and 5 seconds. (Cause of Stoppage, hot bearing.)
- October 4: 33.456 kilometers in 33 minutes and 17 seconds. (Cause of Stoppage, hot bearing.)
- October 5: 38.956 kilometers in 33 minutes and 3 seconds. (Cause of Stoppage, exhaustion of gasoline supply.)

It seems that these alleged experiments were made at Dayton, Ohio, a fairly large town, and that the newspapers of the United States, alert as they are, allowed these sensational performances to escape their notice. When it is considered that Langley never even successfully launched his man-carrying machine, that Langley's experimental model never flew more than a mile, and that Wright's mysterious aeroplane covered a reputed distance of 38 kilometers at the rate of one kilometer a minute, we have the right to exact further information before we place reliance on these French reports. Unfortunately, the Wright brothers are hardly disposed to publish any substantiation or to make public experiment, for reasons best known to themselves. If such sensational and tremendously important experiments are being conducted in a not very remote part of the country, on a subject in which almost everybody feels the most profound interest, is it possible to believe that the enterprising American reporter, who, it is well known, comes down the chimney when the door is locked in his face—even if he has to scale a 15-story sky-scraper to do so—would not have ascertained all about them and published them for broadcast long ago? Why, particularly, as it is further alleged, should the Wrights desire to sell their invention to the French government for a "million" francs. Surely their own is the first to which they would be likely to apply.

We certainly want more light on the subject.[4]

On May 22, 1906, the U.S. Patent Office granted Patent No. 821,393 to the Wrights for their design. The patent was broad enough to cover the entire craft, although the main claim in the patent was to the means of control. Diagrams, accompanied by step-by-step explanations of the workings of their three-dimensional means of control, clearly show the originality of their design.

Ultimately, the infant aviation community did not accept that the work of the Wright brothers was worthy enough as to command royalties. In Europe, the patent was to be ignored and the Wrights' lateral control innovations were to be shamefully duplicated, as in the Bleriot monoplanes, for example. In the United States, Glenn Curtiss would begin developing designs of airplanes with a form of aileron control without payment of royalties. But he strenuously maintained that the incorporation of the "aileron" into the wing was outside of the Wrights' patent. It was subsequently demonstrated, in fact, that the "warping" of the wing had the long-term physical effect of weakening the structure of the wing. The aileron, of course, has no such effect.

In 1907, though, things began to improve for the secretive Wrights. The War Department that year announced a competition for an airplane for government use. The specifications tracked those that the Wrights had earlier advertised to the government. The Wrights returned to Kitty Hawk, a more isolated venue than Huffman Prairie, re-established their camp, and began testing their modified *Flyer*, which now had two side-by-side seats mounted in the upright position. This version was known as the *Model A*.

By 1908, the Wrights were satisfied with their modified design and were ready, not only for the Army competition, but to begin the European marketing of the *Flyer*. The Wrights decided to divide their efforts. Orville returned to Dayton and prepared a machine for demonstration. Wilbur journeyed to France to fulfill the terms of a contract that had finally been successfully negotiated for the sale of the *Flyer*. The terms of the French contract varied significantly from the bid submitted by Orville to the U.S. War Department.

The bid to the United States government was for one aircraft, for $25,000, deliverable in 200 days with an additional 30 days allowed for flight demonstration. The French contract agreed to deliver four aircraft, for $4,000 each, and to receive a lump sum payment of $100,000 and a 50% interest in the French purchasing company. The French contract also required that the aircraft successfully complete flights of 31 miles each, while carrying a passenger, and that the Wrights teach three students to fly and solo.

Wilbur was to be the subject of extensive ridicule on his arrival in France, where the terms of the contract had been widely publicized, and where it was generally believed that no aircraft was capable of accomplishing the requirements of the contract. As far as the French knew, the successful short flight of M. Santos-Dumont in 1906 outside of Paris not only established him as the first to fly, but also created the "operations envelope" for the "aeroplane" in general (that original flight covered a distance of 200 feet). Wilbur set up operations outside of Paris and resolutely went about preparing to meet his part of the bargain. After flawless demonstrations in August 1908, not only of the capabilities of the Model A but also of his piloting skills, the combination of which greatly surpassed anything the French had ever seen, he almost overnight became a national hero. Wilbur then began a series of record-setting accomplishments:

1. September 21, 1908—A record for distance and duration that brought a $1,000 prize from the Aero Club de France.
2. October 7, 1908—The first flight with a female passenger, Mrs. Hart O. Berg.
3. October 10, 1908—A record for distance and duration with a passenger.
4. November 18, 1908—An altitude record of 90 meters, earning a prize of 1,000 French francs from the Aero Club de Saitte.
5. November 23, 1908—A new altitude record bringing with it a prize of 2,500 French francs.
6. December 31, 1908—A new duration and distance record (2 hours, 18 minutes) for the Coupe de Michelin Trophy and a prize of 20,000 French francs.

Wilbur became the toast of France, the recipient of medals, commendations, and the honoree of testimonial dinners. He was even given a standing ovation by the French Senate. Flights were conducted throughout Europe for the remainder of 1908 and into 1909 with increasing acclaim from the Europeans. (See Figure 7-10.) Audiences were had with King Alfonso of Spain, King Victor Emmanuel of Italy, and King Edward VII of England. During the demonstrations in Italy, the American industrialist J. P. Morgan chanced to see one of the flights and was later instrumental in helping the Wrights secure financial backing from wealthy investors in New York. In England, the Wrights met Charles Rolls of Rolls-Royce renown, who purchased a Wright *Flyer* for his personal use, the first private airplane purchase in history.

Meanwhile, in September 1908, Orville began the demonstrations for the U.S. government in Ft. Myer, Virginia. (See Figure 7-11.) The demonstrations were attended by Lt. Thomas Selfridge, as a government representative, and he was authorized to accompany Orville as a passenger on one of the flights being evaluated by the government. (See Figure 7-12.) As we will see in the next chapter, Selfridge was a member of the Aerial Experiment Association (AEA), which had designed and, for the first time in America, publicly flown an airplane. The Wrights, in fact, regarded the activities of the AEA as an infringement on their patent.

Orville was not pleased that Lt. Selfridge was to be given an up-close look at the *Flyer*, but the flight proceeded aloft with the two antagonists aboard. As the aircraft flew at 80 feet, one of the propellers somehow struck a bracing wire,

Courtesy of Special Collections & Archives, Wright State University.

FIGURE 7-10 Wilbur Wright flying in France—1909.

Source: Library of Congress.

FIGURE 7-11 Orville Wright at Fort Myer, Virginia—1908.

Source: Library of Congress.

FIGURE 7-12 Lt. Thomas Selfridge and Orville Wright prior to a take off at Ft. Myer, Virginia—1908.

causing it to snap in two. Orville was unable to control the *Flyer*, and it dove almost vertically into the ground in front of the horrified spectators. Lt. Selfridge was killed, becoming the first fatality due to an airplane accident, and Orville was very seriously injured. The demonstrations were cancelled.

❝ If you are looking for perfect safety, you will do well to sit on a fence and watch the birds; but if you really wish to learn, you must mount a machine and become acquainted with its tricks by actual trial. ❞

Wilbur Wright, from an address to the Western Society of Engineers in Chicago, 18 September 1901

After his release from the hospital, Orville traveled to France as a part of his recuperation and participated along with Wilbur and their sister Katherine in the victorious tour of Europe. When the Wrights returned to the United States in May 1909, they were welcomed as national heroes. President Taft feted them at the White House and awarded them a Congressional medal.

The War Department had extended the time for completion of flight tests that had begun in 1908 until Orville could recover from his injuries. The tests were resumed on June 29, 1909 with a new model of the former *Model A Flyer*. This version was called the *Military Flyer*, weighing 740 pounds and with a Wright 4-cylinder 34 horsepower engine, which offered more speed. On July 12, Orville completed the duration portion of the Army requirements by staying aloft for 1 hour and 12 minutes with Army Lt. Frank Lahm aboard the aircraft, exceeding the test parameters. Orville next began the flight to meet the Army speed requirement of 40 miles per hour. He climbed the *Flyer* to 400 feet and, assuming a slight nose-down attitude, streaked past his launching derrick at 42.583 miles per hour. He flew a victory lap around Arlington National Cemetery and landed. The first military aircraft

had just been purchased at a cost of $30,000 ($25,000 contract price plus bonus of $5,000 for the extra two miles per hour attained in the test). Wheels were installed on this version in 1910.

The Wright Company was formed in November 1909 as an aircraft production company with the backing of New York financiers, and the brothers continued to improve on the *Model A* design. The *Model B* was the first production airplane with a 75-horsepower Rausenberger engine, and was the first Wright aircraft to fly without a canard in front. It was also the first to have a single elevator located aft, although it continued to use wing warping for banking control. The military version of the Model B adopted ailerons for the first time for lateral control.

The Wright Company produced a number of different models through 1916, the last year of production, with various design modifications, although Orville Wright sold his interest in the company to a group of financiers in 1915. The *Model F* was the first Wright airplane to adopt a fuselage, on which the elevator was placed atop the rudder located on the tail of the aircraft. The *Model K* was the first tractor (forward-facing propellers) airplane produced by the Wright Company, and on the K model wing warping was finally abandoned completely in favor of aileron control.

Wilbur Wright died of typhoid fever in 1912, and although Orville remained in the aviation arena for years, he was never to take another principal role.

❝ It may be that the invention of the aeroplane flying-machine will be deemed to have been of less material value to the world than the discovery of Bessemer and open-hearth steel, or the perfection of the telegraph, or the introduction of new and more scientific methods in the management of our great industrial works.

To us, however, the conquest of the air, to use a hackneyed phrase, is a technical triumph so dramatic and so amazing that it overshadows in importance every feat that the inventor has accomplished. If we are apt to lose our sense of proportion, it is not only because it was but yesterday that we learned the secret of the bird, but also because we have dreamed of flying long before we succeeded in ploughing the water in a dugout canoe. From Icarus to the Wright Brothers is a far cry. "

Waldemar Kaempffert, *The New Art of Flying*, 1910

Endnotes

1. Kelly, Fred. *The Wright Brothers: A Biography authorized by Orville Wright* (New York, Ballantine Books, 1956).

2. Charles Manly had been working on the Balzer engine since 1900 and, by the first part of 1902, had successfully upgraded the Balzer motor from a heavy 12 horsepower engine to a marvel of 51 horsepower weighing only 207 pounds. It had a weight to power ratio of 4 to 1.

3. January 13, 1905, Vol. XCIV, No. 2, page 40.

4. See Appendix 2, an address by A. G. Bell on the presentation of the Langley Medal to Gustave Eiffel in 1913. In this speech Dr. Bell provides a then contemporary explanation of the confusion and general lack of awareness that the public and the scientific community labored under regarding innovations of flight.

PART III

Pioneers

©Sergey Nivens.

8   Glenn Curtiss

Glenn Curtiss' efforts were to overlap the Wrights' and, as has been said, he was to take off where they left off. He began as a young man excelling in bicycle racing in 1896, becoming champion for western New York State. In 1900 he started his own bicycle shop in Hammondsport, N.Y., where he built a version he called the *Hercules*. He took to installing on these bikes a 1-cylinder gasoline engine kit, which he bought and assembled. Due to its poor construction, he began to modify this engine and before long he had designed and produced a motorbike with his own 2-cylinder air-cooled engine design that was handily defeating all competing models. In 1902 he formed the G. H. Curtiss Manufacturing Company, where he produced the *Hercules* motorcycle, a favorite all over the United States due to the excellence of its engine. He set an unofficial speed record of 64 miles per hour in 1903 at Yonkers, N.Y. with the *Hercules* and a world official speed record of 136.27 miles per hour at Ormond Beach, FL four years later atop his V8, 268-cubic inch, 40-horsepower model.

◼ Introduction to Aeronautics

His introduction to aeronautics occurred as a result of his engines. Thomas Scott Baldwin, a former circus trapeze acrobat, had for some years been performing in balloons at country fairs across the country. Baldwin was thus in the perfect place to begin experimentations with motorized balloons when lightweight gasoline engines began to appear shortly after the turn of the century. After Alberto Santos-Dumont circled the Eiffel Tower in Paris in 1901 in one of the world's first practical dirigibles, Baldwin visited him in France and returned resolved to build America's first controllable airship.

While building his *California Arrow* at a ranch in California, a visitor showed up on one of Curtiss' *Hercules* motorcycles. Baldwin knew at once that this was the engine needed for his dirigible. Although skeptical of the proposed use of his engine, Curtiss filled the order sent in by Baldwin, finally deciding that people could use his engines however they liked. Baldwin entered his dirigible in the competitions at the 1904 World's Fair in St. Louis, where in October and November that year he was credited with the "first controlled dirigible flight" in the United States, and where his flights won first prize at the exposition. Baldwin was a world-wide sensation almost overnight.

Baldwin credited the Curtiss engine freely for his dirigible's success in St. Louis. He then

Source: Library of Congress.

FIGURE 8-1 The Baldwin dirigible equipped with Curtiss motors was delivered to the Aeronautical Division of the U.S. Army Single Corps in Washington in the summer of 1908. Baldwin operated the controls of the craft from the rear, while Glenn Curtiss took care of the engine forward. The airship succeeded in meeting government specifications during its two-hour trials.

and there determined to meet the developer of the magnificent engine, and without further ado, he hopped a train for Hammondsport and arrived there before Curtiss even knew of Baldwin's feat using his engine. Baldwin's visit to Hammondsport, where he was a houseguest of Curtiss, changed completely Curtiss' attitude toward the use of his engines for aviation purposes. This marked the beginning of an aeronautical business association and friendship that would last for many years, and which brought Curtiss to a more intimate relationship with the flying community. Baldwin ultimately moved his operations to Hammondsport, where he continued building airships using Curtiss engines. In 1908, he sold to the Army Signal Corps the very first aircraft of any type ever purchased by the U.S. government—an improved dirigible with a 20-horsepower Curtiss engine (see Figure 8-1) that passed Army trials (proving an endurance of two hours flight time and being steerable in any direction). Beginning with its first powered aircraft, designated the *SC-1*, the military operated an airship program for the next 34 years.

At the beginning of 1906, there was an air of expectation in the small but growing aeronautical community. Although the Wright brothers had allegedly flown, few people really believed it. The Wrights had certainly done nothing publicly to convince anyone of it and their patent for the "airplane" would not be granted until May 22, 1906. This was a time when "dirigible balloons" were the only motorized aerial contrivances known to be capable of carrying a person aloft. Curtiss, therefore, continued to concentrate on the improvement of his gasoline engine and to develop its sales potential. This was the reason that he attended the New York City Auto Show in January that year, where the latest developments in the automotive and engine community were exhibited.

■ The Aerial Experiment Association

For the first time, the Aero Club of New York had been invited to attend, and in response to invitations from the exhibits committee, the leading lights of the aeronautical world, including Chanute, Langley, and Baldwin provided displays. Alexander Graham Bell, the inventor

Source: Library of Congress.

FIGURE 8-2 Members of the Aerial Experiment Association (from left to right) Glenn Curtiss, J. A. D. McCurdy, Alexander Graham Bell, Frederick W. Baldwin, Thomas E. Selfridge.

of the telephone, was also there exhibiting his "tetrahedral kite," a strange-looking contraption that he believed provided a means of lift. Although invited, the Wright brothers declined to attend, saying "It would interfere with our plans if we should make public at once a description of our machine and methods."[1]

Bell visited the Curtiss exhibit (see Figure 8-2), and came away convinced that Curtiss was the greatest motor expert in the country. Curtiss was a practical, down-to-earth kind of man. Although intrigued by his experiences with Baldwin and others whom he had met in the aeronautical groups, he was not altogether convinced that winged flight was to be a practical reality. But Dr. Bell was practical, and he was a proven commodity—his reputation was fully established. Bell's enthusiasm rubbed off on Curtiss, so a correspondence relationship between the two was established based on the idea that manned, controlled flight of an airplane was possible.

Curtiss wrote to the Wright brothers in May 1906, inquiring of their interest in his engines. The Wrights were not interested, but in September that year Curtiss was in Dayton at the behest of Baldwin in order to make repairs to a Curtiss engine being used on a

Baldwin dirigible. Baldwin, as a well-known aeronaut, knew the Wrights and introduced Curtiss to them. Curtiss was able to discuss with them their flying machine progress in some detail, and they showed him photographs of their machine in flight taken during the previous two years at Huffman Prairie. Although Curtiss remarked that it was the first time he had been able to believe that manned flight was possible, no one of any recognized credibility had ever actually seen the Wrights in the air. Although Baldwin would later say that Curtiss never had any thought at this time of taking up flying, it is reasonable to think that this visit with the Wrights might have combined with the Bell relationship to ignite that very interest.[2]

In October that year, Alberto Santos-Dumont made the first public airplane flight in the world in Paris. His *14-bis* flew a distance of 200 feet at a height of 10 feet at 25 miles per hour. Spurred on by these developments and his own long-standing belief and commitment to flight, Bell bought one of the Curtiss engines and asked Curtiss to deliver it, in person, to Bell's Nova Scotia home. He said he would pay Curtiss a consulting fee of $25 per day, plus expenses. He also invited Curtiss to join a small group of men dedicated to finding a practical solution to the problems of flight. They agreed to meet at the Bell estate on Cape Breton Island in July 1907.

Bell had arranged to have the other members of his proposed investigative group at his house at the same time; there were Douglas McCurdy and Casey Baldwin, both recent graduates of the University of Toronto with master's degrees in engineering, and Lt. Thomas Selfridge, whom we discovered in Chapter 7. Selfridge was a military expert in gliders and aeronautics and, like Curtiss, had some prior acquaintance with the Wright brothers. The group spent the next week at the Bell estate, becoming acquainted and discussing a wide range of issues relating to the scientific and engineering aspects of the problem of flight. General concepts of the operation and funding of the proposed undertaking were laid out by Dr. Bell. When he left at the end of the week, Curtiss came away favorably impressed with the great enthusiasm exhibited by the 60-year-old Bell, and with the way in which each man's talent and experience complemented that of the others.

Details of the undertaking were worked out on a subsequent visit to the Bell house in September 1907. The group, known as the Aerial Experiment Association (AEA), was formally established on the next visit in October 1907, and although no profit was expected from their activities, it was agreed that all benefits and discoveries would be shared equally among the members. They began with gliding experiments using Bell's strange tetrahedral design and then working with the proven Chanute designs of the biplane glider. They experimented with lift and control before moving on to any motorized attempt at flight.

The group moved operations from Nova Scotia to Hammondsport, where fabrication and machine working expertise was available at Curtiss' shop. They were learning fast, and they had a lot to learn; yet they were making excellent progress. At the end of that year Curtiss wrote to the Wrights telling them of the work of the AEA and offering a gift to the Wrights of his latest 50-horsepower engine. He also alluded to the publication

of the government's recent request for proposals and specifications for the purchase of a flying machine, adding: "You, of course, are the only persons who could come anywhere near doing what is required."[3]

On January 15, 1907, Thomas Selfridge wrote to the Wrights asking if they would share details of their glider construction and the results of their experiments with reference to the center of pressure "both on aerocurves and aeroplanes." The Wrights responded three days later and referenced the requested information as being available in public addresses by Wilbur Wright and Chanute, both from 1903. They also referenced the information available in their patent. Everything that was disclosed by the Wrights to Selfridge was apparently already in the public domain.

By March of 1908 the AEA had its first powered machine. Called the *Red Wing*, it was a biplane with the Curtiss V8 40-horsepower engine, with a rudder mounted aft and an elevator forward, like the Wrights' *Flyer*. Although Selfridge had been in charge of its design (each of the members took responsibility for one aircraft design), on the day of the inaugural flight he had been recalled by the Army to Washington, so it fell to Casey Baldwin to pilot the craft. Mounted on ice runners on the frozen surface of Lake Keuka near Hammondsport, the *Red Wing* lifted off and actually flew almost 100 feet before settling back on the ice. Its second flight five days later was its last, but it covered 318 feet, 11 inches, before crashing back onto frozen Lake Keuka due to lateral control problems. Contemporary reports described the flight as the first public heavier than air trip in America.

Casey Baldwin oversaw the next design, the *White Wing* (see Figure 8-3). It incorporated the salvaged engine from *Red Wing* and sported motorcycle wheels and tires, the first known aircraft to do so. An innovative steerable nose wheel was fashioned allowing a more controllable take off. After their learning experience with *Red Wing*, the group brain-stormed the problem

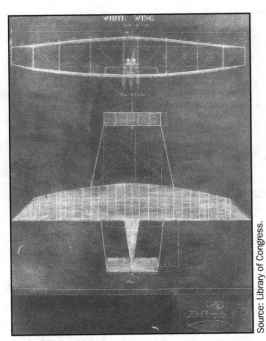

FIGURE 8-3 *White Wing.*

Source: Library of Congress.

of lateral control. They did not plan to incorporate "wing warping" since they were aware that this was the Wrights' patented method of lateral stability and that, by law, a royalty would have to be paid for its use. Because of Professor Bell's reputation and wide experience as an inventor, and because all of the flights of the AEA were open to the public, they took pains not to use any devices that might infringe the Wright patent. Bell came up with the idea of moveable panels located on the extreme ends of the wings which could be tilted up or down to either reduce or increase lift for that wing. He called these devices "ailerons," or little wings.

Although unknown to the members of the AEA, the idea for ailerons had been first proposed some 40 years earlier by an English inventor, M.P.W. Boulton, who secured an English patent in 1868. Ailerons had also been experimented with in 1904 by the Frenchman, Robert Esnault-Pelterie, and again in 1906 by Santos-Dumont. Bell said that his idea for ailerons came from studying birds.

Beginning on May 18, 1908, *White Wing* made a series of seven flights before being destroyed in another crash. Baldwin, Selfridge, and Curtiss all flew the machine, with Curtiss setting a distance record of almost 1,000 feet on his first attempt. The AEA was making steady progress. Every flight was a new and important learning experience. Curtiss was next in line to design and supervise construction of a successor to *White Wing*.

About this time the weekly magazine *Scientific American*, in conjunction with the Aero Club of America, offered a beautiful silver trophy and a monetary prize to any aeronaut who could achieve certain prescribed flying goals in each of three successive years. The goal for the first year was that the airplane must fly in a straight course for a distance of one kilometer (3,281 feet). This was a feat already easily accomplished by the Wright *Flyer* (although few believed it), but the additional requirements set by the contest were that the flight be made in public and that the aircraft take off and land on wheels. The Wright *Flyer* did not have wheels. Besides, Wilbur had arrived in Paris on May 29, 1908 to begin a series of public flying displays planned for the European scientific community and the crowned heads of Europe. At the same time, Orville was putting the final touches on his plans for the public trials with the U.S. Army at Ft. Myer, scheduled for September. The Wrights were not interested in mere contests, and although they were especially invited by the Aero Club to make the first attempt, Orville declined.

But Curtiss was interested, and he began modifying the *White Wing* design in order to produce an entrant for the *Scientific American* Cup. The new craft, dubbed by Dr. Bell the *June Bug*, incorporated the same 40-horsepower engine as the previous biplanes as well as the ailerons used in *White Wing* (see Figures 8-4 and 8-5). Its wings were painted yellow. Curtiss flew the *June Bug* successfully three times on June 21, 1908 and again on June 25, achieving sustained flight of 3,240 feet. The AEA was the first entrant to

Source: National Air and Space Museum, Smithsonian Institution (SI 2003-35048).

FIGURE 8-4 *June Bug* with Glenn Curtiss at the Controls—1908.

Source: Library of Congress.

FIGURE 8-6 Glenn Curtiss winning the *Scientific American* trophy with the *June Bug*—July 4, 1908.

Source: Library of Congress.

FIGURE 8-5 Glenn Curtiss seated in the *June Bug*.

contact the Aero Club and to request a trial for the *Scientific American* trophy (see Figure 8-6). A demonstration was scheduled for July 4, 1908 at Hammondsport.

The event was well attended by the July 4th crowd, most of whom had never seen an airplane, but thunderstorms prevented any flying until late in the afternoon. The assemblage lolled about for most of the day, sprouting umbrellas against the periodic thunderstorms. When the weather permitted, about 5 p.m., the *June Bug* was rolled out from under its tented enclosure and was made ready for flight. When the *June Bug* rose into the air, the astonishment of the crowd was evident, but the result was less than

satisfactory: a flight of only 2,200 feet. The problem was due to an incorrect attachment of the tail section to the fuselage. Once corrected, the *June Bug* again became airborne at 7 p.m. and flew over one mile in 1 minute and 42 seconds, successfully winning the trophy for the first time (of three required wins).

Everyone in the aviation community had glowing praise for Curtiss and the AEA for their magnificent achievement, with one exception. On July 20, 1908, Orville Wright sent a letter to Curtiss warning that use of the Wright's control system was a violation of their patent and was not to be used for a commercial purpose or for exhibitions. Although the members of the AEA did not agree that their use of ailerons on the *June Bug* infringed the Wright patent, they all realized that the days of the AEA were numbered (see Figure 8-7).

Two months later, on September 17th, Thomas Selfridge, one of the original four, was killed in the crash of the Wright *Flyer* (see pages 53–55) at Ft. Myer. On September 26, the day after Selfridges' funeral, Dr. Bell convened the remaining members of the Aerial Experiment Association and in an address to the group summed up their extraordinary association together:

❝We breathed an atmosphere of aviation from morning till night and almost from night to morning. Each felt the

stimulation of the discussion with the others, and each developed ideas of his own upon the subject of aviation, which were discussed by all. I may say for myself that this Association with these young men proved to be one of the happiest times of my life. "

It was agreed that the AEA would continue but for six months more. As the last project of the AEA, McCurdy oversaw the design and construction of the *Silver Dart*, an improved version of the *June Bug*, with a larger, liquid-cooled engine and a more efficient propeller. This craft was first flown in December, and on February 23, 1909, became the first flight of a controlled airplane in Canada at Baddeck Lake. In March,

FIGURE 8-7 Lt. Thomas E. Selfridge and Dr. Alexander Graham Bell at Baldwin trials, August 18, 1908.

Source: Library of Congress.

after the *Silver Dart* flew a circular course for over 22 miles, the AEA held its last meeting and closed its activities.

McCurdy and Baldwin would go on to form the Canadian Aerodrome Company with the goal of making airplanes for sale to the Canadian Army. Although they continued to fly the *Silver Dart*, and to construct several more airplanes of similar design, their efforts ultimately come to naught.

Curtiss, on the other hand, was just getting started. In March 1909, he produced a variant of the *June Bug*, called the *Golden Flyer* (also known as the *Gold Bug*), which he sold to the Aeronautic Society of New York for $5,000. This was the first commercial private sale in the United States. The Aeronautic Society, which began flying the craft at commercial exhibitions, agreed to pay the Wrights a royalty, but Curtiss refused.

Instead, he entered the *Scientific American* competition and, on July 17, 1909, was awarded the *Scientific American* trophy for the second time, flying a distance of 25 miles. On August 29, 1909, Curtiss won the speed competition (Gordon Bennett Cup) over a closed course at Rheims, France against stiff competition that included Louis Bleriot, who had made the first international flight on July 25, 1909 by flying the English Channel between Calais and Dover. Bleriot's airplane, incidentally, also utilized ailerons for lateral control. Flying a stripped down version of the *Golden Flyer*, Curtiss set a world speed record of 43 mph at Rheims, barely edging out Bleriot.

The Patent Litigation Begins

Along with his refusal to pay royalties, the publicity and success that Curtiss was obviously attaining was too much for the Wrights to bear, so they filed their first patent infringement lawsuit against Curtiss and the Herring-Curtiss Company in August 1909. Curtiss had formed the Herring-Curtiss Company with Augustus M. Herring in March 1909, primarily on the strength of Herring's representations of having a patent for the airplane that preceded that of the Wrights, and further of having been extensively associated with Octave Chanute and Samuel J. Langley in their aeronautical experiments. It soon turned out that Herring possessed no patent, but Curtiss still refused to pay royalties to the Wrights. So did many other aviators. Few people could believe that the two brothers owned, to the exclusion of everyone else in the world, the right to fly.

The Curtiss litigation was only one of many lawsuits the Wrights had filed against purported patent infringers. The Wrights sued the Aeronautic Society of New York. They sued this one and then that one, in the United States and in the courts of Europe, including England, France, and Germany. Judgment was ultimately entered in over 30 lawsuits brought by the Wrights. The Wrights' attention had turned completely away from the excitement of flying that now gripped the European and American aviation community. Their concentration was on litigation. They set up a corporation to own and manage their patent and to prevent any competition through litigation. They were consumed with the commercial exploitation of their airplane, but they were being left behind as the aeronautical world flew on.

Most of those who had been active in the small fraternity of aeronauts were appalled by the Wrights' actions. Octave Chanute, who had so openly shared the results of his experimentation in gliding and airfoils (which had been adopted by the Wrights in large measure), was highly critical of the Wrights and publicly rebuked their patent litigation. Perhaps the best illustration of the public feeling at the time was expressed in the *Evansville* (Illinois) *Courier* of December 2, 1909:

" For the purpose of controlling absolutely in this country and Canada all aviation by means of heavier-than-air machines, the Wright Company, backed by financiers controlling probably nearly a billion dollars, was formed several days ago. The men behind the latest, The Flying Machine Trust, are nearly all prominent in financial and trust affairs. The capital of the company is modestly placed at $1,000,000, and it is announced that there is no stock for sale. The company, which has been formed to take over all of the Wrights' patents and to prosecute infringements, claims as an asset even the principle of the plane and the control of the equilibrium of the machine.[4] **"**

The Wrights' suit against Curtiss resulted in the first court decision on the patent issue in January 1910. The federal court in the Western District of New York found that Curtiss had, indeed, violated the Wright patent. Although the Wright machines used wing "warping," and Curtiss used "ailerons" to accomplish lateral control, the court ruled that the Wrights' discovery of a workable means for achieving lateral equilibrium or balance was what was protected under the patent, not the method for achieving it. Thus, the dissimilarities between wing warping control and aileron control to produce lift differential of the wings "had no bearing upon the means adopted to preserve equilibrium."[5] Curtiss immediately appealed the decision, posted a bond to supersede the judgment, and then went back to work.

He moved forward energetically in many areas, innovating, testing, and improving his machines. He agreed to participate in an air meet in Los Angeles at the beginning of 1910, the first such major event in the United States. Although the Wrights did not compete in the event, they were there to try to shut it down. Louis Paulhan, the French aeronaut and early aviation record holder, was greeted upon his arrival by Wright lawyers serving a patent infringement suit and complaint for an injunction to prevent anyone from flying. The event ran, nevertheless, from January 10 to January 20 and was attended by 254,000 spectators. The *Los Angeles Times* said it was one of the greatest public events in the history of the west. Even the federal courts must have thought so, as no injunctions were issued.

Curtiss won $6,600 in prize money in the categories of fastest speed, endurance, and quick starting and set a new air speed record of 55 mph. From Los Angeles he traveled east and accepted the challenge issued by *New York World* publisher, Joseph Pulitzer, to compete for the first successful flight between New York City and Albany, New York. The challenge carried with its successful conclusion a $10,000 prize for completion of the 152-mile distance, which allowed two landings en route and completion within a period of 24 hours. Curtiss chose to fly down the Hudson River from Albany, successfully completing the competition requirements on May 29, 1910. It was the first official cross-country airplane flight in the United States.

In July 1910, six months after the trial court ruling in the Curtiss case, the Court of Appeals of New York reversed the trial court and sent the case back for further evidentiary hearings at the trial level, effectively putting the parties to the litigation back where they had started.

◼ The Beginning of Naval Aviation

Curtiss remained busy. His sojourns in California during 1910 convinced him of the benefits of the winter climate there compared to the snow of Hammondsport and frozen Lake Keuka in New York. Late that year he leased North Island in San Diego Bay and offered free pilot training to both the Army and the Navy, receiving his first military students early the next year. In November 1910, a pilot employed by Curtiss, Eugene Ely, was the first to take off an airplane from a Navy vessel, the USS *Birmingham*, anchored at Hampton Roads, Virginia. (See Figure 8-8.) Two months later in January 1911, Ely became the first to land an airplane back aboard a vessel, the USS *Pennsylvania* anchored in San Francisco Bay, utilizing in both cases specially constructed wooden platforms on the ships, and in both cases without the benefit of any wind over the decks of the anchored ships. (See Figure 8-9.)

He set up shop facilities for conducting experimentation with floats in order to develop a successful seaplane, at that time called a

Source: Florida State Archives.

FIGURE 8-8 Eugene Ely performing the first take off from a Naval vessel—November 1910.

Source: Florida State Archives.

FIGURE 8-9 Eugene Ely making the first landing aboard a Naval vessel, January 1911.

hydroplane. Although he had experimented with floats on the *June Bug* in 1908, and again in May and June 1910 with a canoe fitted centrally beneath one of his D2 machines, he had not been successful in getting an airplane off the water. At North Island, tests showed that significantly greater engine power was required to permit a takeoff from water as compared to land, so various hull designs were tested.

A breakthrough known as a "stepped" configuration essentially solved the problem of the water takeoff. The "stepped" hull design incorporated a recessed aft section, so that the bottom of the aft section of the hull was higher than the forward portion of the hull. As speed increased, the aft section of the hull came out of the water first, which greatly reduced drag and produced a planing effect of the hull on water that later came to be known as "being on the step." These original designs were modified and improved, spray patterns were controlled, and the improved hulls ultimately allowed take off from the water with close to the same horsepower as that required from land. By 1912, the Curtiss-designed aircraft hull had become state-of-the-art for the world. Further improvements were made as engines were mounted on the upper frame of the airplane, and as airframes were redesigned to account for pitch changes caused by these changes in the center of thrust. The Curtiss flying boats proved highly popular and sales were made to many foreign countries all over the world.[6] (See Figure 8-10.)

In February 1911, he built his first tractor seaplane, with the engine and propeller at the front of the airplane (to avoid damaging water spray to the propeller) and the elevators at the rear. At the request of the Navy, he personally flew this craft out to the USS *Pennsylvania* anchored in San Diego harbor, where the airplane was winched aboard and then redeployed to the

Source: U.S. Navy.

FIGURE 8-10 Curtiss Flying Boat—Model E.

water, completing the demonstration for what would become a common practice for the use of airplanes for scouting missions from warships. On May 8, 1911, the Navy ordered two Curtiss hydroplanes.

■ The Wright Patent Is Upheld a Second Time

Meanwhile, the Wright-Curtiss litigation dragged on. In February 1913, the same judge who had rendered the first judgment in favor of the Wright brothers in 1910 now issued a second opinion in which he specifically found that the Wrights' discovery of the use of a combination of rudder and wing deflection to maintain lateral control was the breakthrough that was patentable. The court then held that the use of ailerons was the functional equivalent of wing warping, thus the use of ailerons fell within the orb of the Wright patent.[7] But it was too late for Wilbur Wright. He died on May 30, 1912 at the age of 45 because, many said, of the stresses of the patent litigation.

Curtiss, however, was not retreating; he was regrouping. To his side came none other than the automobile magnate Henry Ford. Ford had recently won a protracted patent battle with one George Seldon, who had claimed a prior patent right to Ford's lightweight "road engine," which was central to Ford's ideas for mass production of automobiles. Ford's patent attorney was W. Benton Crisp, and Ford volunteered Crisp's services to Glenn Curtiss. Under attorney Crisp's guidance, a new strategy for defeating the Wright patent was initiated. The appellate decision that enjoined Curtiss' use of ailerons as being in violation of the Wright patent had cited only the simultaneous use of ailerons in opposite directions, which provided the lift differential for the two wings, causing the banking effect used in a coordinated turn. Crisp suggested that the Curtiss aircraft be rigged so that the ailerons would be used singly,

not simultaneously. This use of ailerons had not been enjoined by the court since it had not been adjudicated. It was, therefore, necessary for Orville to bring another lawsuit against Curtiss. Thus, the patent litigation rolled on in a seemingly endless procession of trials and appeals as the wheels of justice ground slowly on, and exceedingly fine.

In the next chapter we will see why and how this enduring legal contest was to be surprisingly resolved for the good of the country and for aviation itself.

■ The Langley Aerodrome Controversy[8]

Not content to leave the issue to be exclusively determined by the lawyers, at the invitation of the Smithsonian Institution in 1914, Curtiss entered into a contract with the Smithsonian to rebuild and fly the Langley Aerodrome for the consideration of $2,000. The Smithsonian was seeking to rehabilitate the reputation of Langley by demonstrating that the Aerodrome was, indeed, flyable and that the problem with the December 8, 1903 flight attempt was the defective launch mechanism, not the airplane. Curtiss was only too happy to accommodate the Smithsonian, since he too wanted to prove that the Aerodrome could have flown before the Wrights' machine.

The disassembled Aerodrome arrived in Hammondsport at the Curtiss facilities in crates loaded into a railroad boxcar. On arrival, it was clear that modifications would have to be made to the Langley machine. The 1903 Manly engine had been in storage for 10 years and would develop only two-thirds of its original power. The carburetor had to be changed. Curtiss provided it with magneto ignition instead of the original dry cell batteries. The airplane had no wheels, no skids, and no floats. Curtiss added pontoons to the Aerodrome, which required additional support and bracing. The floats added about 340 pounds of weight and added drag. The central stiffening keel was removed. The original propellers were used but one wing had to be rebuilt, as well as replacing several broken ribs in other wings. The wings had to be recovered with cloth and varnished. The Aerodrome did not have ailerons or wing warping; control was limited to the dihedral of the wings, the vertical tail rudder, and the shifting of the pilot's weight in order to maintain lateral balance. No changes were made to the system of balance. Curtiss stated that not a single change had been made to the Aerodrome that could have improved its flying qualities.

The reassembled machine was taken down to Lake Keuka where it was successfully made airborne for several short hops in the late spring of 1914. This proved to the satisfaction of Curtiss and the Smithsonian that the Aerodrome was, and always had been, flyable, and but for the defective launch mechanism on the Langley barge, it would have been the first powered, controlled flight in history. The Aerodrome was then fitted with a larger and more powerful engine and, during September and October 1914, it was able to lift off the water for flights of up to 3,000 feet.

◼ The Jenny

While aircraft development had been seriously stagnated in the United States by the Wright patent litigation, somehow Curtiss kept driving forward. He visited the factory of Thomas Sopwith in England in 1913, and was impressed by the progress shown in the development of the tractor designs Sopwith was producing. The Model J, a 90-horsepower tractor, was launched on May 10, 1914, followed by the Model N, also with a 90-horsepower tractor engine. These were supplied to the British and American armies and navies as trainer aircraft during 1914. In 1915, Curtiss produced the aircraft that was to be

known as the "Jenny," and which combined the best aspects of the "J" and "N" models.

World War I had begun in the summer of 1914, and the demand for aircraft and engines spiraled upward. Although the Jenny was too slow, too underpowered, and lacked the performance capabilities required of fighter aircraft in World War I, it fit well as a trainer both in England and the United States. Rapid improvements in design and increased horsepower in the Jenny made it the trainer of choice for the war. The Jenny first used the Curtiss OX 90-horsepower engines, but later in the war the 150-horsepower Hispano-Suiza engine, built by the Wright Company, was installed.

Thousands of Jennys were produced during the war, and afterward were used by both the Post Office in the airmail service (before being replaced by the De Havilland DH-4) and by the Army for training. The private sector was flooded with Jennys, which made for bargain prices for barn-stormers, banner-towers, and flight schools and made the Jenny a household word in an era when hardly anyone flew. A newly designed Jenny was placed on the market in 1920 as the "Oriole," and flew in the competitive market for almost twenty years.

◼ Transatlantic Flight

In 1919, the largest flying boats constructed by Curtiss, the NC-1 through the NC-4 (see Figure 8-11) were launched. In May, three of these, the NC-1, NC-3, and the NC-4, set out to make the first-ever transatlantic flight from Long Island to Lisbon, Portugal. The NC-1 and the NC-3 were forced down prior to reaching the Azores, but the NC-4, after 23 days en route, finally arrived in Lisbon—the first aircraft to cross the Atlantic Ocean.

Although Curtiss did not produce more of the flying boats, the design advances he made were replicated or became the starting point for

Courtesy of the National Museum of Naval Aviation.

FIGURE 8-11 The NC-4, the first plane to cross the Atlantic.

all future improvements on aircraft hull design. Boeing became the leading flying boat exponent in the United States, along with Martin and Sikorsky, and produced the beautiful Clipper Ships of Pan American Airways fame. See Chapter 15.

America's First Black Aviator and the Curtiss Connection

As a notable and related fact from newly discovered evidence,[9] it appears that the first licensed African-American pilot, Emory Malick,[10] received flight instruction from Curtiss at North Island in San Diego. Malick grew up in central Pennsylvania, where he built and flew his own gliders over the Susquehanna River. At some point (the evidence is still sketchy) he began flying powered aircraft and wound up at the Curtiss School, receiving his pilot's license on March 12, 1912 from the Federation Aeronautique Internationale, number 105. Very little is currently known about his later life in aviation. It is likely that research in the near future may alter the course of history concerning black aviators in the United States.

Postlude to the Wrights and Curtiss

The innovations, designs, and experimentation of Glenn Curtiss and the Aerial Experiment Association provide a study in contrast with those of the Wright brothers. The legacies of both groups continue to be studied and debated, but it is true that both were necessary to the development of aviation in the United States and in the world. It is ironic that the methods of the Wright brothers actually tended to inhibit flight when it was

Courtesy of The Malick Family Collection.

FIGURE 8-12 Emory Malick America's First Black Aviator- 1912 Solo Flight.

they who had initiated successful, controlled, and powered flight, while the methods of Curtiss tended to expand the concept and application of flight even though he was not first to succeed. In spite of the combination of brilliance and dedication, on the one hand, and striving and enmity, on the other, that existed in the early world of aeronautics, the resolution of the differences between the two camps and their allies would be forthcoming, as we shall see in Chapter 9.

Endnotes

1. Shulman, *Unlocking the Sky: Glenn Hammond Curtiss and the Race to Invent the Airplane*, Harper and Collins, 1903.

2. Dayton History Books Online http://www.daytonhistory books.com/the_wright_brothers_18html.

3. Dayton History Books, ibid.

4. The Wrights' commercial venture, like many to come, could only be deemed a failure. Orville Wright sold his interest in the company on August 26, 1915 for $250,000, one-fourth of its initial capitalization.

5. *Wright Co. v. Herring-Curtiss Co. et al.*, 177 F. 257 (W.D.N.Y. 1910).

6. See remarks in Appendix 2 by Dr. A. G. Bell on February 13, 1913, to the Board of Regents of the Smithsonian Institution regarding Curtiss' contributions to flight safety using floatplanes.

7. *Wright Co. v. Herring-Curtiss Co. et al.*, 204 F 597 (W.D.N.Y. 1913).

8. Please see Appendix 3 for a discussion of the specific details of the Curtiss revisions to the Langley Aerodrome in 1914 and the flights made at Hammondsport that year. Note that this is a Smithsonian report from the year 1942 that had the approval of Orville Wright, and it is likely part of the reconciliation made between Orville Wright and the Smithsonian in order to allow the Wright machine to be taken to the Smithsonian for exhibition.

9. This reported information was first discovered by a white family member in 2004 in a family album. It was reported in *Air & Space Magazine* in the March 2011 issue.

10. 1881–1958.

9 World War I, NACA, and the End of the Wright Patent Litigation

In 1913, the state of aeronautical advance in the United States was primarily represented by the accomplishments of Glenn Curtiss. Conversely, leaders in Europe had invested heavily in aircraft technology. Competitions were regularly sponsored to encourage advances in aircraft speed, range, and altitude. Europeans had also incorporated aircraft units in their armed forces prior to the first world war. In 1913, the United States had only six pilots in the entire U.S. Army.

In July 1914, the conflict that was to become known as "The Great War" or World War I opened with the Austro-Hungarian invasion of Serbia, which was soon followed by a German invasion of the low countries of Western Europe, Belgium, and Luxembourg, as well as France. Russia attacked Germany. The combatants aligned into the Allied Powers, consisting mainly of Great Britain, France, Italy, Russia, Japan, and the United States, and the Central Powers, mainly Germany, Austro-Hungary, Turkey, and Bulgaria. The conflict ended on November 11, 1918.

As in most wars, technological advances in weapons and support were greatly accelerated between 1914 and 1918. The United States was late entering the conflict (1917) and did not participate in the major aircraft innovations that occurred

during the war. European manufacturers and designers had jumped ahead in aircraft and engine design, partly out of necessity. On the Allied side, the French Nieuport, followed by the SPAD, manufactured by the French company Société des Productions Armand Deperdussin (hence the acronym), and the English S. E. 5, Sopwith Pup, and Sopwith Camel, provided the fighter aircraft. In 1918, close to the end of World War I, Glenn Martin was responsible for contributing the only American design for combatant aircraft in the war with his MB-1 bomber. On the Central Powers side, the German manufacturers Junkers and Albatros Werke GmbH produced formidable fighter aircraft, but the Fokker designs proved to be the best, particularly the D.VII, which is widely regarded as the best fighter of the war. This aircraft was flown by Hermann Goering, who was to become the second-in-command to Adolf Hitler in the 1920s and the leader of the German Luftwaffe in the 1930s and during World War II.

Although the Curtiss Aeroplane and Motor Company was the largest aircraft manufacturer in the world during the war, producing 10,000 planes by 1918, the JN-4 did not come close to matching European models in speed, power, ceiling, and reliability. First produced in 1916, the

Jenny mounted the OX-5 engine, 90 horsepower and water-cooled. When Curtiss improved his O model engine in 1913, he wanted to publicize its advances by designating it the "O Plus." But neither the "O Plus" nor the "O+" designation looked particularly good when printed, and the "+" could even be confused with the letter "T." Someone suggested rotating the Plus sign by 45 degrees, depicted as "OX," and the new series of engines became known as the OX-2.

The Curtiss models, although behind the Europeans, were higher performance machines than those built by the Wrights. The Wright Company had fallen by the wayside in aircraft design by World War I, its designs being almost entirely based on the outmoded *Flyer* models.

Manufacturing in the United States upon its entry into the war was made subject to the oversight and control of the Aircraft Production Board, the creation of which was a recommendation of the National Advisory Committee for Aeronautics (see below) which decreed that the United States should gear up to produce 22,000 aircraft for delivery to France within a year. Isolated between two great oceans, America was far removed from the vast destruction war had brought to Europe just since 1914, and the world was about to appreciate how valuable the heavy manufacturing reserve of the United States could be. But America was too far behind the design performance standards of aircraft already in use in Europe, so much of the American production effort was limited to manufacturing aircraft under license from European designers.

The De Havilland DH-4, a single-engine bomber/observation plane, was the primary military airplane built in the United States during the war. The Dayton-Wright Company (see Chapter 11 for the interesting story of the creating of the Dayton-Wright Company) built the most, 3,106 planes, followed by Fisher Body at 1,600, and Boeing, which produced 150.

The Wright Company concentrated on the production of engines under license, notably the 150-horsepower Hispano-Suiza aircraft engine,

much in demand by the French. Hispano-Suiza was a Spanish engine and automobile company that, in 1915, refined its V8 liquid-cooled automobile engine for aeronautical use. This engine represented a quantum advance over the rotary engine, which at the time was the primary aircraft engine in use. The French government in 1915 placed orders in the United States for 800 engines, which were required to be built in the United States due to the lack of capacity in Europe during the war. The Wright Company contracted to supply 450 of these. To facilitate filling the order, the Wright Company arranged a merger with Glenn L. Martin in 1916 to form the Wright-Martin Aircraft Company. By the end of the war, the company had produced over 10,000 of the engines, known as the Wright-Hispano. Along the way, the Wright-Hispano replaced the 90-horsepower Curtiss OX-5 in the Curtiss Jenny, which was limited to training use. After the war, in 1919, the Wright-Martin combination was dissolved and the company became the Wright Aeronautical Corporation. Much was to be heard from this company for its contributions to aircraft engine development during the 1920s.

With the entry of the United States into the war, the Aircraft Production Board ordered the production of 44,000 American-built aircraft engines to be used in conjunction with the ambitious goal of manufacturing over 22,000 aircraft. The immediate problem was, however, that the United States did not possess an aircraft engine capable of providing sufficient horsepower or speed for military airplanes. Packard Motors happened to have in its design inventory an experimental, but tested, 8-cylinder liquid-cooled automobile engine that was to prove the basis for America's greatest contribution to the war effort. On May 29, 1917, automobile engineers at Packard began a redesign of the engine with the purpose of supplying the ordered military aircraft engine, and five days later, a revised design was presented for aircraft use. But it was still an automobile engine, having battery ignition instead of magnetos, for example. It was redesigned again, this time expanding its power to 12 cylinders like the British Rolls engine, and with magneto ignition. The new design, the water-cooled Liberty, weighed only 710 pounds and, producing 410 horsepower, it surpassed the performance of all other aircraft engines in the world. By war's end, some 17,935 Libertys had been produced, of which 5,827 had been delivered to Europe for use in aircraft there. The Liberty was installed in the DH-4, and by November 1918 deliveries to the Army numbered 3,431 airplanes. Of these, 1,213 arrived in Europe, but only 248 ever flew at the front.

When the Armistice was signed, so many airplanes and engines had been produced for war use that engine and airplane manufacturing literally stopped cold. Surplus equipment was everywhere, and it was cheap. Curtiss Jennys were so numerous that, for $500, a student pilot could receive his instruction and upon solo be awarded a Jenny in the bargain.

As peace settled once again over the world, as the railroads were returned to their owners by the government, as the automobile began hitting the open roads being built by the government, and as all of the planes appeared to be sitting on the ground, many wondered what would become of aviation in America.

The National Advisory Committee for Aeronautics (NACA)

As early as 1912, forward-looking leaders in the United States, including people from the scientific, industrial, and government sectors, had attempted to create a center for the study and advancement of aviation. President Howard Taft appointed a group labeled the National Aerodynamical Laboratory Commission that year, but Congress voted down its funding. Most of the energy in aviation in America seemed to be spent on patent litigation between the Wright brothers and Glenn Curtiss.

By contrast, the countries of Europe were well ahead of the United States in aircraft research and development primarily due to their government-sponsored approach. The countries of France, Germany, Russia, and England all had government-funded agencies dedicated to the coordination of industry, scientific, and government efforts to advance aviation.

On the death of Samuel Langley, the Smithsonian Institution appointed Charles D. Walcott its Secretary in 1907. Although Walcott was a paleontologist, whose interest and previous scientific efforts were far removed from aviation, he nevertheless took up the call to end aviation's plight as an orphan of government. In collaboration with Congressional sponsors, he outlined a bill that was introduced into both houses of Congress in January 1915 to create an advisory committee patterned along the lines of the British Advisory Committee for Aeronautics.

Assistant Secretary of the Navy Franklin D. Roosevelt endorsed the idea and the legislation was attached to the Naval Appropriations Bill. It provided funding in the grand amount of $5,000. The enabling legislation for the National Advisory Committee for Aeronautics slipped through practically unnoticed by opponents on March 3, 1915, and became law on the same day when signed by President Woodrow Wilson. The mission statement of the NACA reads: "It shall be the duty of the advisory committee for aeronautics to supervise and direct the scientific study of the problems of flight with a view to their practical solution . . ."

The original committee was composed of 12 unpaid members selected from the military (Army and Navy), government (National Bureau of Standards, U.S. Weather Bureau, and Assistant Secretary of the Treasury), and academia (professors from Stanford, Columbia, Northwestern, and Johns Hopkins Universities). Walcott of the Smithsonian Institution became the committee's chairman.

The members soon began promoting the idea of a research laboratory and proposed a budget of $85,000 to fund their research. Against opposition, this amount was approved in August 1916 and led to the establishment of the Langley Memorial Aeronautical Laboratory in Virginia. It soon became clear just how little was known in the United States about the science of aeronautics, and there was a lot of wasted motion as the committee sought to find its way in uncharted waters. The first technical employee was an engineer selected from the Curtiss Aeroplane & Motor Corporation. Its first efforts centered on experimentation with propellers.

But there were as yet no representatives from business or industry involved in the proceedings. It soon became clear that, if the work of the NACA was to advance, it would be necessary to have industry at the table as well as the government and its scientific advisors from the halls of ivy. And it was not long before everyone realized that horsepower was driving the quest for superiority in the skies over Europe in 1916, and horsepower was beginning to be seen as the main requirement of any advance in aircraft evolution.

The automobile industry had been for some years the main authority in reciprocating engines in the United States, and automobile manufacturers had naturally become the principal builders of aircraft engines as well. Since the United States was not a belligerent in the European war in 1916, American manufacturers had not been presented with any particular stimulus to drive innovation or improvements as their counterparts in Europe had been. America continued to fall behind.

Thus it was that all the major engine manufacturers were invited to meet under the auspices of the NACA with military procurement officials from the government in June 1916. The main question presented was, what was holding back competitive engine production in the United States?

Howard E. Coffin emerged as the chief industry spokesman during the NACA meetings in 1916. Coffin had built a steam-powered automobile and designed his first internal combustion engine while studying engineering at the University of Michigan in 1899. By 1905, he was the chief engineer for the Olds Motor Works and later a vice president of the Hudson Motor Car Company. He was chiefly responsible for the standardization of parts in the automotive industry and became president of the Society of Automobile Engineers. He had been appointed to the Naval Consulting Board in 1915, so he had seen the interaction between industry and the government from both sides.

Coffin showed that the relationship between industry and government was tied up in bureaucracy and red tape to the point that hardly anything beneficial or constructive could be accomplished. He said that the solution was to rely on engineering instead of bureaucracy, as had been demonstrated by the record of cooperation between the automobile industry and the Society of Automobile Engineers. His words did not fall on deaf ears. The NACA had early on developed a system of appointing committees to address specific problems that fell within its authority. The NACA established a Committee on Motive Power that began to provide a venue where industry people and government representatives could meet, discuss, and work out specifications for what the government needed and wanted in aircraft engines. The automotive industry would then provide those engines.

Thus, the men at the NACA had been instrumental in solving, or at least understanding and diminishing, the conflict that was preventing the cooperation necessary for the advancement of aeronautical science and industrial production in the United States. There was optimism all around and, in fact, this spirit of cooperation did ignite the creation of the Liberty engine, which would begin production within the year.

But interdisciplinary cooperation was only part of the problem. The question remained, "What was to be done about the stifling patent litigation?"

The Cross-Licensing Agreement

Patent law is akin to medieval French to the modern mind. It operates in mysterious ways to the uninitiated. Since the first airplane patent was issued to the Wright brothers in 1906, which covered the entire airplane, the Patent Office had granted numerous patents in the field of aeronautics by the time World War I began. In spite of the issuance of the patent to the Wrights in 1906, and the ensuing litigation brought by the Wright brothers in 1909 against Glenn Curtiss for infringing their wing warping idea, the Patent Office on December 5, 1911 granted Curtiss and the other members of the AEA a patent for the idea of the aileron.

The Patent Office, as it were, has tunnel vision; it does not adjudicate rights that flow from patents, nor does it decide issues of infringement, the existence of prior art, or other defenses to lawsuits claiming patent infringement. These issues are decided by the federal courts. The function of the Patent Office is to grant or refuse to grant patents.

One of the results of this confusing progression of patent practice is that one patent may have the effect of "blocking" another patent, so that the holder of neither patent is able to move forward with the implementation of his ideas and incorporate them into practical products for public use without encountering claims of infringement. It was this "blocking" of patents, along with the pervasive litigation that had sprung up because of it, that had been instrumental in hamstringing innovative aircraft technology in the United States. This was a primary reason that there were no competitive American airplane designs and no engines powerful enough to participate in the war that was now raging in Europe.

By the spring of 1917, it looked increasingly likely that the United States was going to be drawn into the European war, yet its aircraft and engine production was paralyzed by patent litigation. Many in the United States feared for its defense in the new era of aviation warfare.

Wilbur Wright had died in 1912, and Orville Wright had assumed the presidency of the Wright Company and all its activities, including the engineering and manufacturing responsibilities of the company. He also continued to pursue the myriad lawsuits that he and his brother had initiated, almost as in memoriam to his deceased brother. But in 1915 Orville decided to move on. He bought up most of the outstanding shares of the Wright Company and then sold them to investors in New York. In 1916, the Wright Company merged with the Glenn L. Martin Company and became known as Wright-Martin (see above).

Thus, the main problem confronting the NACA men in 1917 was the Wright-Martin Company, which had paid in excess of $1,000,000 for the 1906 Wright patent. At the end of 1916, Wright-Martin issued a notice that all aircraft manufacturers would be required to pay a royalty of 5 percent on every aircraft they sold, with a minimum annual royalty of $10,000 per manufacturer. This royalty structure was to be imposed on all aircraft manufacturers irrespective of the means of control used, wing warping or aileron control. By that time, of course, all aircraft manufacturers used ailerons for lateral control.

Further compounding the issue, Curtiss was now also demanding royalties for his several patents as they may apply to new aircraft. Many believed that Curtiss was forced into this practice as a self defensive move due to his significant attorneys' fees and costs of litigation, but the result was that aircraft prices in the United States were becoming prohibitively costly. Lawsuits and threats of lawsuits were the most prominent feature of aeronautics in the USA. It was obvious that something had to be done, and it was going to have to be done by government.

Alternatives were discussed, including nationalization of the aircraft industry and the taking of the patents through the power of eminent domain. There was also another possibility: years earlier in a similar case in the automotive industry a cooperative arrangement had been agreed to between auto makers to resolve conflicting patent claims. This agreement had been made possible when Henry Ford broke the "Selden" patent. In that case a man named Selden claimed a patent on the entire automobile, not unlike the Wright brothers with the airplane, but the celebrated patent attorney, W. Benton Crisp, had prevailed in the infringement case brought by Selden against Henry Ford.

W. Benton Crisp had later represented Howard E. Coffin (who was now head of the NACA) in the Hudson crankshaft case. Through the influence of Henry Ford, Crisp now represented Glenn Curtiss against the Wright patent. Reluctantly, Wright-Martin was beginning to see the logic in compromise.

Under the proposal, all aircraft and parts manufacturers would join an association to be known as the Aircraft Manufacturers Association. For each aircraft produced, the manufacturer would pay a modest sum into the Association, which amount would be shared by Wright-Martin, the Curtiss organization, and the Association. The effect of the cross-licensing agreement was that the aviation manufacturing industry would produce aircraft without regard to patents, subject to the modest stipends mentioned, and all ideas, practices, techniques, and procedures would be shared between the members. Aircraft engines were excepted from the Agreement.

Although the Agreement soon came under criticism from some aircraft manufacturers on grounds of favoritism (of Wright-Martin and Curtiss) and on antitrust principles, the cross-licensing agreement is considered one of the outstanding contributions of the NACA during World War I. Even though the Agreement had a proposed limited lifespan, no patent litigation relating to the original aircraft patents was ever revived.

The National Advisory Committee for Aeronautics (NACA) in 1958 became the National Aeronautics and Space Administration (NASA).

10   Airmail Story

It was not long after the Wright brothers were first successful in marketing their airplane to the French and to the U.S. Army, in 1908 and 1909, that the idea occurred to someone in the Post Office Department that the airplane could be useful in delivering the mail—and faster than the railroads. Federal funding for airmail delivery was not forthcoming in spite of a bill introduced in Congress in 1910 by Congressman Morris Sheppard for that purpose. Beginning in 1911 without specific government funding, limited experimentation with airplanes hauling mail (15 pounds a load) was initiated. Congress was not convinced that the entire process of flying mail to a point over a United States Post Office, and dropping it from various heights to the ground, was not too hare-brained to be dignified by appropriations. Only in 1916 did Congress finally approve limited funding ($50,000 from the "Steamship Fund") for the establishment of a trial airmail route, in large part because of the rapid improvement in the reliability of aircraft. In 1918, specific funding was finally approved (the Sheppard bill had been hung up in Congressional debate for eight years) with a $100,000 appropriation for the purchase, operation, and maintenance of airplanes for use by the Post Office Department.

◼ A Rough Beginning

Operations began by using airplanes and pilots furnished by the Army Signal Corps. It soon was clear that the airmail experiment was, in reality, a training device and exercise for the Army, and that delivery of the mail often amounted to an afterthought. It also became clear that the lack of training and experience of Army pilots, particularly in cross-country flying and navigation, was going to be a problem. Otto Praeger was Second Assistant Postmaster General of the United States from 1915 to 1921. He believed that the carriage of mail by air would be a logical next step in mail service to the country, and he also believed that the carrying of mail would have the secondary benefit of proving the use of the airplane for commercial purposes. After World War I, it seemed that business interests in the United States could not figure out how to put the airplane to any beneficial or productive purpose. This was the age of barnstormers, daredevils, adventurers, and a sideshow mentality that overshadowed most other thinking on the subject of airplanes. Banner towing, the selling of rides, and the occasional charter hop from one municipality to another was about the extent of commercial benefit associated with aviation. Besides, flying was fraught with danger.

The aircraft available after World War I were numerous, but they were mostly JN-4s, the latest version of which was the H model. This airplane had an average speed of 50 miles per hour, 60 tops, and could carry some 150 pounds of mail. The route fixed as the first experimental airmail route was between New York and Washington, D.C., a distance of 218 miles, with an intermediate stop at Philadelphia, and the date set for its inauguration was May 15, 1918. Airplanes would depart both New York and Washington at the same time. In Washington, President Woodrow Wilson was in attendance, attesting to the magnitude and portent of the event, as was Otto Praeger and other Post Office dignitaries. (See Figure 10-1.)

The pilot selected for the Washington departure, Lt. George Boyle, was chosen more for his family contacts than for either his experience or his skill. (See Figure 10-2.) As the president watched, Lt. Boyle called "contact" and the propeller was pulled through for start, but nothing happened. After several attempts, amid an embarrassing silence from the august assembly, someone thought to check the airplane's gas tank. It was empty. Upon being filled, the engine coughed to life and presently brand-new airmail pilot Boyle was finally airborne, and the airmail service had been launched, much to the relief of the Post Office and Army officials gathered there. (See Figure 10-3.) But there was yet another problem.

A pilot wishing to fly from Washington to Philadelphia is required to follow a generally northerly course, owing to the fact that Philadelphia is north of Washington. Lt. Boyle, however, turned to the south shortly after take off and landed in a pasture farther away from Philadelphia than where he started. The day was saved by the southbound mail, which arrived in Washington 3 hours and 20 minutes after it left New York. The second leg of the northbound route, from Philadelphia to New York, was salvaged when Boyle's difficulties became known, whereupon the second-leg pilot loaded his airplane with Philadelphia mail and took off for New York.

FIGURE 10-1 President Woodrow Wilson at the inauguration of airmail—May 15, 1918.

FIGURE 10-2 Major Reuben Fleet (on the left) briefs airmail pilot Lt. George Boyle before he begins his flight on May 15, 1918.

Courtesy of the National Postal Museum, Smithsonian Institution.

FIGURE 10-3 Lt. George Boyle takes off for Philadelphia.

Courtesy of the National Postal Museum, Smithsonian Institution.

▇ Scheduled Airmail Service

The experimental airmail service continued for about three months, until August 10, 1918, with an impressive record of 88% completion of flights attempted. The experiment using Army personnel had come to an end, and since it was the intention of the Post Office to use civilian pilots to operate the new, permanent airmail system, six new pilots were hired and new planes were put in service. (See Figure 10-4.) On August 12, 1918, the world's first regularly scheduled airmail service was begun between New York

and Washington. On May 15, 1919, service was commenced between Cleveland and Chicago, the first segment of what was to ultimately become the transcontinental airmail route of the United States Post Office. Service on the segment from New York to Cleveland was deferred due to the adverse terrain, the Allegheny Mountains, which lay between those two cities.[1] Attempts to inaugurate that service in December 1918 had failed due to the fact that every airplane sent aloft had been forced down by weather. But by July 1, 1919, that service had been begun as well. The

FIGURE 10-4 The first civilian airmail pilots (from left to right): Edward Gardner, Captain Benjamin Lipsner, Maurice Newton, Max Miller, and Robert Shank.

FIGURE 10-5 De Havilland—DH-4 with a Liberty engine.

FIGURE 10-6 DH-4.

New York–Chicago route segment would come to be known as the "graveyard run," and it would claim the lives of 18 airmail pilots.

The mail was mostly flown in Curtiss Jennys from the beginning of experimental service, but it was clear that more powerful and larger airplanes were needed. The Army had developed an appreciation for Glenn Martin's airplanes during World War I, and was about to order the improved MB-2 bomber when the Post Office took over airmail delivery from the Army. In 1919, the Post Office applied some of the Congressional airmail appropriation to order six Martin MPs (mail planes), specially designed with nose cargo compartments capable of holding up to 1,500 pounds of mail, which were put into service in 1919 and 1920. Pilots crashed four of the new Post Office MPs on the New York to Chicago route, and the Post Office finally transferred the other two to the Army Signal Corps.

The Jennys gave way to the De Havilland DH-4 with Liberty engines, also leftovers from the war, that had earned the name "flying coffins" because of their propensity to catch fire on crashing, a not uncommon occurrence. (See Figures 10-5 and 10-6.) These planes generally had as instrumentation an airspeed indicator, an altimeter of sorts, and an oil compass. The planes had to be flown visually, by reference to horizon, sky, and land outside of the cockpit. Navigation was also by outside reference, referred to as "pilotage," "contact flying," or "ded reckoning."[2] Landmarks on the ground were the prime navigational reference for these early cross-country pilots, and when clouds or fog obscured these, finding one's way became problematical, indeed. The airmail service did not operate at night; the mailbags were delivered to the trains for continuation of the journey until the next day, when once again the mail flew.

Courtesy of the National Postal Museum, Smithsonian Institution.

FIGURE 10-7 Wild Bill Hopson, airmail pilot.

These two incapacities severely hampered the fledgling airmail service from fulfilling its promise.

- First, the lack of instrumentation to fly "blind," or by instruments alone, was a problem that had to be addressed by the aircraft manufacturers, their vendors, and by the pilots themselves.
- Second, the lack of any land-based navigational infrastructure by which airplanes might find their way at night or in adverse weather conditions was a problem too big for individuals or the fledgling aircraft community.

A navigational infrastructure was an undertaking for government.

The first airmail pilots (see Figures 10-4 and 10-7), like Max Miller and Wesley Smith, began pushing the limits of "blind" flying, usually in order to extricate themselves from situations inadvertently encountered, like flying into clouds

or fog. Smith is said to have taken a half empty bottle of whiskey aloft, which he placed on top of his instrument panel, to practice flying wings level with the whiskey level. Soon, he found that a curved tube filled with liquid and containing a ball, like a carpenter's level, was available, and this he fastened to his instrument panel. And so it went. It was found that turns made at a constant, steady rate could be timed and the airplane could be rather accurately rolled out on predetermined headings. Sperry introduced a two-axis gyroscopic instrument that allowed a pilot to determine whether his airplane had inadvertently entered a turn. This was followed up with a three-axis instrument that showed changes in pitch attitude.

William Charles Ocker, the Father of Blind Flight

It was one thing to have these new tools available; it was yet another thing altogether to be able to use them in actual flight. U.S. Army pilot William C. Ocker nearly crashed one day in 1918 testing the Sperry turn indicator. He could not convince himself to trust these new instruments instead of his senses, as he and every other military pilot had been taught: "Ignore them"; "Fly by the seat of your pants," they were told. Pilots who relied on anything other than a magnetic compass and the altimeter were considered lightweight and weak.

During a routine Army physical exam in 1926, Ocker was subjected to a Jones-Barany chair, which is a spinning, swiveling seat designed to measure balance and equilibrium. When deprived of his visual cues, he naturally became completely disoriented and confused. He could not tell if he was stationary or spinning, or which way. With the doctor's help, he practiced using the turn indicator and a pen light rigged up in a shoe box as he was spun around. Watching only inside the box, he could tell the doctor which way he was going, and how fast. This

Source: U.S. Air Force.

FIGURE 10-8 Charles Ocker.

device, the "Ocker Box," became the first blind flying trainer. (See Figure 10-8.)

In spite of the Army's refusal to teach instrument flying, Ocker became something of an advocate, and convinced many pilots of the worth of his designs. The Army forced Ocker to undergo psychological exams for his penchant for sitting in spinning chairs. He invented the idea of the covered cockpit, used by Jimmy Doolittle for a flight around the pattern in 1929, but Ocker made the first cross-country flight in a completely covered cockpit on June 24, 1930, flying 900 miles from Brooks Field, Texas to Scott Field, Illinois.

Pan American pilots soon began using Ocker's techniques and instruments. In 1932, in cooperation with Col. Carl Crane, he published the world's first instrument flight manual, *Blind Flight in Theory and Practice*. The Soviet Air Force adopted the book before the U.S. Army did. Orville Wright called him a "missionary" and he considered among his friends Eddie Rickenbacker, Billy Mitchell, and Jimmy Doolittle. A year after his death in 1942, the Army made his training procedures standard for all military pilots.[3]

At the same time, experimentation was proceeding on various fronts, including with radio, not only as a means of voice communication from air to ground, but also as a means of navigation. By May 15, 1920, airmail service had been extended westward from Chicago to Omaha, Nebraska, establishing a through route all the way from New York. On August 16, 1920, a route was added southward from Chicago to St. Louis. On September 8, 1920, the transcontinental route was completed to San Francisco. Although the airmail service operated only during daylight hours, the railroad coast-to-coast mail time was bettered by 22 hours.

The promise of airmail was yet unfulfilled. Moreover, Otto Praeger was concerned that the entire airmail program might be cancelled if better results were not soon achieved. Night flying was the only way to free the airmail service from its earthbound dependence on the railroads. Flying at night had been experimented with, and successfully under certain conditions, like clear, moonlit nights, for short distances. But what about transcontinental distances on a regular schedule? Could it be done?

■ Transcontinental Airmail

On February 22, 1921, the first attempt at a through, continuous transcontinental airmail service was made. The plan called for a westbound plane to leave New York to fly the initial segment of the route to San Francisco, and an eastbound plane to leave San Francisco initiating the first segment to New York. (See Figure 10-9.) The trip each way would be sequentially flown by fresh airplanes and pilots, like the Pony Express, handing off the mail at predetermined points along the route. Two aircraft were assigned to begin at each end of the route.

The first airplane to leave New York discontinued shortly after take off. The second plane flew to Chicago but was grounded due to weather. The first plane out of San Francisco crashed in Nevada, but the second plane made

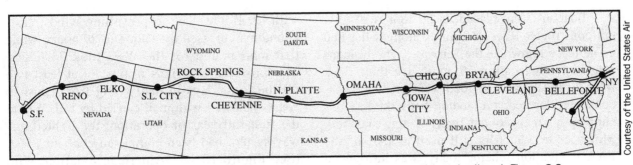

FIGURE 10-9 Original transcontinental airmail route—compare to the transcontinental railroad, Figure 3-3.

it to Reno, and 12 hours after leaving San Francisco, the mail arrived in Cheyenne. Another plane took the mail on to North Platte, Nebraska, and there it was turned over to the next segment airmail pilot, Jack Knight.

A combination of ground personnel and volunteers built bonfires along Jack's route, which was to be traversed at night, and he made it to Omaha, his segment complete, by 1:00 a.m. There he learned that the plane scheduled to meet him in Omaha had not left Chicago due to weather. He volunteered to continue, armed only with an automobile road map to guide him over unknown terrain, a landscape he had never flown. This part of the country is chilly in February, and this night was accompanied by cold, ice, and snow, along with the low clouds that produce snow. He was unable to land at Des Moines, Iowa, as planned. He continued to Iowa City, and arriving, searched for the airport that was unlighted because the ground crew had left for the evening, believing that no sane person would fly in the prevailing conditions. A lone employee at the airfield heard his engine, lit a flare and watched as Jack Knight glided in with an empty gas tank. After refueling and accepting a quick cup of coffee, Knight gamely flew on to Chicago, finally landing at Checkerboard Field at 8:40 a.m. From there, the mail relay was continued to New York and, when the results were announced, the mail had been successfully carried coast to coast in slightly more than 24 hours.

The best that the Post Office had been able to do up to that time using the railroads was a transcontinental transit of three days. The experimental policy of flying the mail during daylight hours and handing the mail off to the railroads at night had only marginally improved savings in time, and was generally considered to be not cost effective. But with the grand experiment of February 21, 1921, it was now clear that flying the mails for the entire route could be done.

The success of this first attempt caused Congress to favorably consider appropriations sought by the Post Office, granting a splendid sum for that time, $1,250,000, for airmail extensions. Paul Henderson, who became Second Assistant Postmaster General in 1922, was committed to the Otto Praeger principle that the mail could be flown. But it was clear that the mail had to be flown both night and day, and that bonfires as a means of nighttime navigation probably had only the most limited of possibilities.

The Lighted Airway

In 1923, Congress granted an appropriation to fund the construction of a system of sequential lighting on the transcontinental airmail route. The first segment completed was between Chicago and Cheyenne, a stretch of flat country most conducive to this original effort, and centrally located along the route. Airplanes launched at first light on either coast could reach the lighted segment by nightfall under most circumstances.

Beacons were placed on 50 foot steel towers constructed every 10 miles along what had come to be known as the "airway." The beacons rotated so as to allow pilots to see their flash from 40 miles away in good weather. If the beacons were located at a landing field, the beacons showed a green course light, if not, then red. Morse code, which is still used as part of the FAA navigation scheme today, was introduced into the airway system at the time of this first construction. Each beacon flashed an identifier in Morse code that corresponded to the number of the beacon within the airway segment.

Regularly scheduled airmail service was begun on July 1, 1924, just over six years from the inauspicious kick-off in Washington, D.C.

with Lt. Boyle. Due to prevailing winds, eastbound mail crossed the nation in 29 hours, while that mail bound for the West took 34 hours. This provided a savings in time of at least two full business days in mail going from coast to coast compared with mail carried by rail. Within the first full year of operation, the lighted airway system had been completed coast to coast. (See Figure 10-10.) American aviation, with the leadership of an enlightened government, had made a quantum leap into a technologically advanced civilian navigation system. Nothing like it existed in the world.

The American scene was almost set for the beginnings of a viable commercial aviation transportation system, but not quite. Still to come

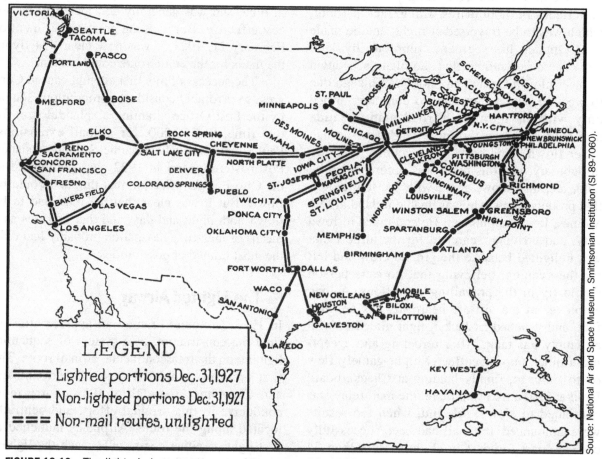

Source: National Air and Space Museum, Smithsonian Institution (SI 89-7060).

FIGURE 10-10 The lighted airway system as of December 31, 1927.

were more reliable engines, sturdier airplane designs, acceptance of flight by reference only to aircraft instruments, involvement of the banking and financial community, acceptance by the public of aviation as legitimate transportation and, lastly, those visionaries and adventurers, both physically and financially, who would make it all happen.

Endnotes

1. See Appendix 3 for Max Miller's narration of his survey flight to Chicago across the Allegheny Mountains.
2. Or "dead reckoning." There does not appear to be agreement concerning the use of the term "ded reckoning" or "dead reckoning." "Ded reckoning" is based on a contraction of "deductive reckoning."
3. Credit for some of this information goes to Mark Wolverton.

11 Horsepower

Fate had set apart a place for Fred Rentschler in the Age of Aviation that was just beginning. Today, his is not a name that springs to mind as central to the development of commercial aviation in the United States, but it should be. He changed the aviation world. Almost single-handedly, and certainly single-mindedly, his vision and dedication made the military air forces of the United States the strongest in the world, for the longest time, and at the time they were most needed for survival of western civilization because of the advent of World War II. The giant airliners of the pre-jet world were mainly powered by his designs.

Fred Rentschler (see Figure 11-1) came from solid German stock. His father, George Adam Rentschler, an immigrant from Württemberg, established a foundry in Hamilton, Ohio, where pig iron and machine castings were the mother's milk of his upbringing. The Rentschler family also owned the Republic Motor Car Company, which built automobiles until 1916. Hamilton is but a stone's throw from Dayton, not only the home of the Wright brothers, but also in the early years of the 20th century the locale of the National Cash Register Company, its biggest business. The Rentschler foundry supplied the company with castings for its cash registers, and

FIGURE 11-1 Frederich B. Rentschler.

Source: Vought Aircraft Industries, Inc.

George A. Rentschler became a friend of Edward Deeds, NCR's vice president.

Fred Rentschler grew up in Hamilton around the foundry and automobile business, graduated from Princeton University in 1909, and returned to Hamilton to work in the family businesses. In addition to NCR, Hamilton was a center of manufacturing of different types, including machine tools, steel products, railroad rail and steam engines, reapers, threshers, gun lathes, and many other heavy industry products. It was the home of Niles-Bement-Pond Company, one of the world's largest machine tool companies, which would later acquire the Pratt & Whitney Tool Company of East Hartford, Connecticut, and it was home to many powerful executives, bankers, and engineers. The social network of Fred Rentschler and his family was extensive.

Edward Deeds had the idea to fit NCR cash registers with electric motors in order to replace the mechanical finger-force needed to ring up the register. He brought into NCR Charles Kettering, an inventor and engineer (he would have 186 patents in due course) to create the electric motor application. Soon afterwards, Deeds and Kettering started a little company by the name of Dayton Engineering Laboratories to manufacture an innovation thought up by Kettering, an electric self-starter that could be applied to automobiles. DELCO, as the company was to be known, was to be credited with taming the horseless carriage, eliminating the need for the manly and strenuous art of hand cranking required at the time. The first starter was one of 5,000 installed in the 1912 Cadillac, and the idea rapidly spread throughout the automobile industry. DELCO forged close ties with the automobile industry. In 1916, Kettering and Deeds sold DELCO to United Motors Corporation for the whopping sum of nine million dollars.

With the profits from the DELCO sale, Deeds and Kettering formed the Dayton Airplane Company and then brought in Orville Wright as consultant. The name was changed to the Dayton-Wright Company with the idea of producing airplanes for private use. When the United States entered the war in 1917, Deeds volunteered for work on the Aircraft Production Board in Washington. He was placed in charge of all aircraft procurement for the United States and given the rank of colonel in the Army. The Dayton-Wright Company thereby received contracts from the government to produce 5,000 De Havilland warplanes under license.

The state of the art of American airplane and aircraft engine design was represented by the out-classed Curtiss Jenny and the OX-2. As discussed in Chapter 9, the redesigned Packard automobile engine became the Liberty engine that would be installed into the De Havillands, and it was Deeds who engaged his automobile industry contacts to effect that redesign. The Liberty engine became America's greatest contribution to the war matériel effort. The Dayton-Wright Company also produced a pilotless "flying bomb," another of Kettering's innovations, but too late for use in the war. The device was kept a military secret after the war, but the Nazi German government employed the same technology in the V-1 rocket, used with some success against England in World War II. These were smart and dedicated men.

When the United States entered the war in 1917, Fred Rentschler came to Edward Deeds. Deeds found a place for him at the Wright-Martin plant in Brunswick, New Jersey, where the French Hispano-Suiza aircraft engine was being produced under license for shipment to Europe. When Rentschler arrived at Wright-Martin, production and inspection of engines was the job of a French Commission, and it was Rentschler's job to replace the Commission. The Hispano 180, followed by the 300, were the dominant power plants of the final years of the war and gave the Allies superiority in the air. At the end of the war, Wright-Martin was turning out 1,000 engines a month under Rentschler's direction.

After the war most of the assets of Wright-Martin were sold to the Mack Truck Company. Fred Rentschler accepted an offer to manage the remnants of the company, under the name of Wright Aeronautical, for the production of postwar aviation engines. Starting from scratch, he located another plant site in Paterson, New Jersey, to refine and improve on the Hispanos, and to design an American product based on both liquid and air-cooled experimentation. During the postwar days of plentiful engines and planes, these engines were not for personal or private use, but for the military and the government market. The trouble was, no one knew if there would be such a market. Many of the Wright-Martin engineers and technicians returned to the automotive industry, but a few stalwarts remained with Rentschler at Wright Aeronautical. As it turned out, these were the most dedicated and gifted of the group, and soon the company was profitable and had established a credible reputation against the other two aircraft engine producers, Curtiss and Packard.

In the early 1920s, the aircraft engines of choice, for both the Army and the Navy, were the 500 horsepower liquid-cooled engine, the D-12 and the Liberty. These were produced by all three companies (Wright Aeronautical, Curtiss, and Packard), but it was the air-cooled engine that had caught the attention of Rentschler and, as it turned out, the United States Navy.

■ The Evolution of the Air-Cooled Engine

It was generally believed that no air-cooled type of engine could ever supplant the exceedingly efficient water-cooled engines that had been developed both in the automotive and aircraft industries. The ability to operate large displacement engines at high crankshaft speeds was central to this efficiency, and air-cooled engines could not match those crankshaft speeds. Cooling was a big problem. It was also believed that the excessive "head resistance" of radial engines would not compete with in-line water-cooled engines, generating excessive drag. Yet, if they could be made to work, air-cooled engines offered many advantages over liquid-cooled

engines, with their associated requirements of plumbing, radiators, and attendant weight. Hardly anyone believed that the radial would work, except Fred Rentschler, and perhaps Charles Lawrance. The Curtiss Aeronautical and Packard factories were firmly committed to liquid-cooled engines.

Lawrance Aero Engine Company was experimenting with a small, 3-cylinder French radial in Lawrance's New York City loft, but it was underfunded and disorganized and it was not making much headway. Lawrance and his backers approached Wright Aeronautical for talks, and Rentschler was assigned to confer with them. The Lawrance group said that the Navy was interested in the air-cooled engine and would contract for a properly developed radial that could be produced in sufficient numbers. This was soon confirmed by the head of the Bureau of Aeronautics, Admiral Moffet, who asked Rentschler to come down to Washington to talk about the Lawrance situation. As a result of this discussion, Wright Aeronautical took over the Lawrance operation and moved it to New Jersey in 1923.

The engine at the time was known as the J-1 radial, but the Lawrance group lacked the funds and technical expertise to bring its power up to military standards. Within several months, the Wright engineers had redesigned the engine into a workable product, and they continued to improve the design, reliability, cooling, and fuel consumption. The engine design would ultimately be known as the "Whirlwind," a 200-horsepower, 790-inch displacement radial designated the J-5 or R-790, and it was introduced in 1925. The Navy bought it and used it, mostly in trainers. It made an unheard-of endurance flight of over 50 hours in April 1927 and it was selected by Charles Lindbergh for his transatlantic flight from New York to Paris in May 1927.

But Rentschler would not be there at the end. In the summer of 1924 it became apparent that the board of directors of Wright

Aeronautical, which was composed of investment bankers who had no appreciation for what Rentschler was trying to accomplish, was going to make the arduous effort of creating a competitive radial engine very difficult, if not impossible.

The Whirlwind was a fine machine, but Rentschler was convinced that the radial engine concept could be much more powerful and much more efficient, and that it could compete with the 400- and 500-horsepower liquid-cooled engines on which the military relied. But development would take more time and much more money, and the Wright board of directors was not interested in such costly projects.

Rentschler had decided to leave the company. He was discouraged and he had taken ill. He resigned and was determined to give it all up. But on recovering his health at the beginning of 1925, he set out to find a way to continue his quest in radial aviation engines. Although he had little money, he did have hometown contacts, and his brother, Gordon, was a vice-president of National City Bank of New York. Gordon had also been recently elected to the board of directors of Niles-Bement-Pond, a Hamilton company well known to both Gordon and Fred. Colonel Deeds was also on the Niles Board, and Niles owned Pratt & Whitney Tool Company. Pratt & Whitney was sitting on piles of cash from World War I operations.

Rentschler went down to Washington for a confidential talk with Admiral Moffet, and to seek some insight as to how the Navy might view his move from Wright Aeronautical. The discussions went extremely well; the admiral told him that the Navy would be "overwhelmingly" interested if such a powerful radial could be produced.[1]

Rentschler's next stop was an all-day appointment with the president of Niles-Bement-Pond in New York City, James K. Cullen, who was a close friend of Rentschler's father in Hamilton. Rentschler told Cullen that he estimated he would need $500,000 through the design, construction, preliminary tests, and proof of the new

FIGURE 11-2 Rentschler and William.

engine. If the engine proved reliable, he would need up to another one million dollars before any return could be expected. Cullen didn't blink; instead he said he would provide the money from "surplus funds." It got better. Cullen said there was empty space at the Pratt & Whitney plant in East Hartford and that Rentschler could have it for his use—he could also use the P&W name!

Contract arrangements were completed on July 14, 1925, with Rentschler taking 50 percent of the stock of the new company, which was to be called Pratt & Whitney Aircraft Company, and Pratt & Whitney Tool Company taking the other 50 percent. The core engineering group from Wright Aeronautical, George Mead, Don Brown, and Andrew Willagoos, committed to joining him. They roughed out the general characteristics of the proposed new engine, including displacement, power range, and a weight limitation. They included innovations never before used, either in the United States or in Europe.

Wasting no time, the group set up shop and went to work in the Willagoos garage in Montclair, New Jersey, while the move to Hartford was arranged. The goal was understood by all: an air-cooled radial in the 400-horsepower class. By August the plant was operating in Hartford, and by Christmas Day 1925, the new engine had been completely designed, machined, and assembled. Within a few hours on the test stand, power readings showed well above 400 horsepower. It weighed 650 pounds. It was proving to be a thoroughbred.

Navy personnel were swept off their feet. By October 1926, the Navy sent a contract for 200 of the engines and Pratt and Whitney Aircraft was on its way. Due to the sound it made, the group decided on "Bees" as a general designation for the P&W engine types. Rentschler's wife suggested that the first engine type be called the "Wasp." And so it was.

There was still the question of "head resistance"; Packard and Curtiss maintained that the radial could never match their engines in speed, even though their engines were heavier. Rentschler believed that, if properly cowled, the radial could be cooled at high speed. Nine out of ten "experts" disagreed. In side-by-side tests, however, the Wasp held a slight edge in speed over the Curtiss D-12, and the Wasp out climbed and turned inside its competitor. The installed weight differential between the Wasp and the Liberty was 1,000 pounds, and between the Wasp and the D-12, 650 to 700 pounds. These figures translated into useful load for a Wasp-driven airplane.

The P&W engineers continued to design and test, and soon they had developed the 500-horsepower "Hornet," which the Navy liked as well. By 1927, when the first large aircraft carriers, the *Lexington* and the *Saratoga*, were launched, all 160 airplanes on deck had either Wasp or Hornet engines. It took the Army two years to come around to the Wasp and Hornet for their fighters. For the rest of the decade, P&W engines set the standard. By 1929, 2,500 Wasps had been delivered, and the engine was to remain in production until 1960. When the last Wasp was turned out, the production run numbered 34,966.

But the company was soon in for some competition. After the departure of Rentschler and his engineers from Wright Aeronautical, the company regrouped. By 1929, Wright Aeronautical had perfected the 575-horsepower air-cooled Cyclone that was to see extensive use in the coming years in both civilian and military aircraft, installed in the DC-3 and B-17. Wright Aeronautical, ironically because of the long-standing enmity between the Wright brothers and Glenn Curtiss, merged with Curtiss Aircraft on July 5, 1929 and operates under the name Curtiss-Wright to this day.

The development of the heavy radial engine in 1925 and 1926 transformed the aviation industry, leading to the privatization of airmail, the building of larger aircraft, the creation of the first safe passenger airlines, and creating a reliable, lighter-weight engine. It would lead to the first transcontinental airline, composed of Boeing and P&W, and to the merging of P&W with Chance Vought Aircraft, Hamilton Standard, and Sikorsky. We will get more into those details in the next chapters.

Because of these developments, the role of government was just beginning to define itself in the new world of commercial aviation.

Endnote

1. *An account of Pratt & Whitney Aircraft Company, 1925–1950*, Frederick B. Rentschler, 1950, Pratt & Whitney Archives, East Hartford, CT.

Regulation

©Digital Media Pro

Chapter 12 The Privatization of Airmail

Chapter 13 The Founding of the Airlines

Chapter 14 New Deal—The Roosevelt Administration

Chapter 15 State of the Airlines before the Civil Aeronautics Act

Chapter 16 The Civil Aeronautics Act of 1938 (McCarran-Lea Act)

Chapter 17 World War II

Chapter 18 A New Beginning

Chapter 19 On the Way to the Jet Age

Chapter 20 The Federal Aviation Act

Chapter 21 The Next Jets

Chapter 22 The Department of Transportation

Chapter 23 Airports

12 The Privatization of Airmail

Delivery of mail was a feature of colonial America, although a haphazard and irregular practice, and was mainly a function of private enterprise. Mail was often left and picked up at taverns and inns. Benjamin Franklin served as Philadelphia's postmaster beginning in 1737, and was appointed the deputy postmaster general for the American colonies in 1753. He brought order to the system by mapping routes between stations, establishing post roads and mileposts, and inaugurated the use of stagecoaches to deliver mail under contract. He was appointed postmaster general by the Continental Congress in 1775 and the practices he had put in place continued.

The Constitution of the United States specifically authorizes Congress to establish post offices and post roads. When California was admitted to the Union in 1850 and the discovery of gold (a main source of wealth for the United States at the time) made rapid communication essential between the seat of government and commercial centers in the east and the new, developing west coast, the government contracted with the privately owned "Pony Express" to deliver the mail. The Pony Express shortened mail delivery over the 2,000-mile route to about 10 days. Expedited communication has, from time immemorial, been a highly valued quality of civilization and a legitimate, necessary governmental function.

Congressional legislation in the 19th century made railroads officially "post roads." The Post Office Department contracted with the railroads to deliver intercity and transcontinental mail, which was the mainstay of national mail delivery until well into the 20th century. In the late 19th century, passenger trains included "postal cars," where mail was sorted en route by postal employees.

The government "airmail" experiment that was begun in 1918 was a government operation because there was no reliable private sector to perform that mission. Contrary to the practice in other countries, passenger and cargo transportation has not been a government function in the United States. Even when the railroads were nationalized between 1917 and 1920 due to the requirements of transportation control in World War I, they were returned to private operation as soon as practicable. Although the government dalliance with airmail delivery was a successful experiment to advance a legitimate government function, it also hastened the building of an aviation infrastructure of lighted airways and landing fields that could inure to the benefit of a private aviation transportation system. As late as 1925,

Source: Florida State Archives.

FIGURE 12-1 Benoist flying boat—1914.

Source: Florida State Archives.

FIGURE 12-2 Benoist flying boat—1914. Inauguration of the St. Petersburg–Tampa airboat line.

however, it was hard to find much evidence of an emerging privately operated transportation system.

From the Wright's first flight in 1903 to the middle of the 1920s, there had been only two known attempts to start a scheduled passenger flying service, or airline, in the United States. The first was the St. Petersburg–Tampa Airboat Line inaugurated on January 1, 1914 to serve the 18-mile over water route between the two Florida cities with a 26-foot Benoist XIV flying boat. (See Figures 12-1 and 12-2.) Although the little air service carried 1,200 passengers over the twenty-three minute route during the next several months, at a fare of $5.00 each, business sagged with the departure of the northern tourists and their money in the spring, and the company folded.

The other one was a short-lived idea of a Manhattan Cadillac dealer by the name of Inglis M. Uppercu. Uppercu ran an aerial sightseeing service in New York that he had started as an offshoot of having manufactured seaplanes (see Figure 12-3, Aeromarine Corp) for the Navy during World War I. In 1920, he bought out a small Key West to Havana mail line and began to supplement the cargo with passengers. Prohibition (which outlawed the manufacture and sale of alcoholic beverages) went into effect in the United States beginning in 1920 as a result of the 18th Amendment, and Uppercu correctly figured that Cuba and the Bahamas, with their plentiful rum and sunshine, would make a fetching destination for thirsty and cold Americans.

He formed Aeromarine West Indies Airways and during his first year carried 6,814 passengers in seven flying boats, flying 95,000 miles. He noted that people who seemed to be terrified of flying at altitude over land appeared to have no fear of flying a few feet above water in a flying boat. The airline published schedules and met them. During its second year, the fleet was expanded to 15 aircraft, which carried 9,107 passengers on 2,000 flights. After two widely publicized accidents, resulting in the deaths of several passengers, and receiving exceedingly bad press that emphasized the complete absence of any kind of government mandated safeguards for the flying public, the bloom was off the rose. Uppercu shut down his airline in 1923.

Henry Ford, who by the middle of the 1920s was quite successful as the manufacturer of automobiles, saw that he had a legitimate business use for airplanes in the middle 1920s. Ford Motor Company had automobile plants in various locales, including Detroit, Cleveland,

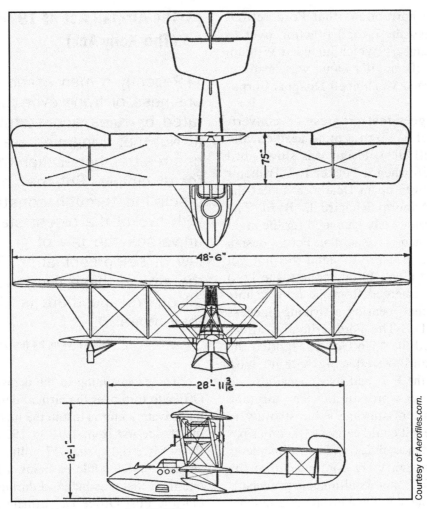

75"

48'-6"

28'-11 3/16"

12'-1"

Courtesy of Aerofiles.com.

FIGURE 12-3 Aeromarine 50-U8D.

Chicago, and Dearborn, and it was necessary to carry parts and machinery between them on a regular basis. Ford became acquainted with William E. Stout, an idea-man and former airplane designer, who had a passion to build an all-metal airplane. The craft would be built of duralumin, not quite as light as aluminum but twice as strong. Ford decided to back Stout who did, in fact, produce a single engine high wing monoplane constructed almost completely of metal, all as advertised. Its corrugated metal sides and thick wings looked remarkably like those produced in Germany by the Junkers Company,

but no one said anything. It was powered by the Liberty water-cooled engine, carried eight passengers and was dubbed *Maiden Detroit*.

Ford not only bought the plane, he bought the plant as well. He started Ford Air Transport and began a regular service between his plants. He then set Stout on a course to develop a bigger all metal airplane, one that would go down in history as the Ford Trimotor.

In 1924, Stout's efforts resulted in the trimotor Ford 3-AT, a bulbous-nosed monstrosity configured with the pilot seated in an open cockpit above the high-winged fuselage. The design was so horrendous that Ford retired Stout and turned the design function over to his team of engineers, which included William McDonnell. McDonnell's name was destined to lead the merged McDonnell Douglas Corporation in 1967.

The story goes that progress on converting the mongrel 3-AT to a more aesthetically pleasing and efficient design was slow, until one day in 1926 when a Fokker F-7 Trimotor monoplane showed up in Dearborn, under the command of Admiral Richard E. Byrd. The airplane was gratuitously hangared for the night at Ford's field, and it is said that Ford's design team with tape measure in hand did not get much sleep that night. In due course, the Ford 4-AT Trimotor emerged from the Ford team's plans and sketches, bearing a striking likeness to the Fokker F-7. The Ford Trimotor, affectionately dubbed the "Tin Goose," sported the same heavy cantilevered wing without wire bracing as did the F-7, and its dimensions and engine mountings were similar. The airplane conveyed a sense of sturdiness and stability to the 14 passengers it could carry at 100 miles per hour over a distance of 250 miles. Refinements in this basic design were continued into the 1930s, with 199 Trimotors ultimately produced.

In spite of the individual efforts of a number of adventurers and various businessmen, in 1925 there was no momentum to be found in the world of commercial aviation. Progress was measured in fits and starts, like the two defunct airlines mentioned above, and popular confidence was justifiably lacking due to the unreliability of the engines and aircraft of the time. Passenger air traffic was basically unknown. We saw in Chapter 11 how things were about to change for the better in the quality and reliability of aircraft engines, and progress was also being made in airframe design and construction, yet aviation wandered aimlessly over the countryside. That is, except for the airmail. What the private sector needed was a reason to fly.

The Airmail Act of 1925 (The Kelly Act)

" Recently a man asked whether the business of flying ever could be regulated by rules and statutes. I doubt it. Not that flying men are lawless. No one realizes better than they the need for discipline. But they have learned discipline through constant contact with two of the oldest statutes in the universe—the law of gravity and the law of self-preservation. Ten feet off the ground these two laws supersede all others and there is little hope of their repeal. **"**

Walter Hinson, 24 July 1926, *Liberty Magazine*

The exact timing of the decision by the Post Office to turn over the airmail delivery service to the private sector is lost in the mists of time. During the period from 1918 to 1925, however, the Post Office did spend $17 million to operate the airmail service while realizing a return of about one-third that amount. And during the nine years that the Post Office Department carried airmail (1918–1927), 32 pilots—about one out of every six—were killed in the service.

The railroads also made it clear that they were opposed to any long-term government intrusion on their longstanding mail contract subsidies. In 1925, Postmaster Harry S. New, a former Congressman himself, worked with Congressman Clyde Kelly (who represented railroad interests) to formulate a legislative bill designed to put the airmail delivery service up for competitive bid.

Congress passed the Kelly Act (so-called after the name of the bill's sponsor) on February 2, 1925. The act was appropriately titled "An Act to Encourage Commercial Aviation and to

Authorize the Postmaster General to Contract for the Mail Service." The statute called for the Postmaster General to seek competitive bids to operate the airmail feeder routes to the transcontinental main airmail trunk line between New York and San Francisco. The operation of the transcontinental trunk was to be initially retained by the Post Office service; it made its last flight on that route on September 9, 1927.

Advertisement for bids was published in the middle of 1925, and bids were received from 10 companies. Although eight routes were to be awarded, financial responsibility concerns caused the Post Office to delay assigning some of them until later.

Seven contract airmail (CAM) routes were awarded at the beginning of 1926:

1. CAM 1: *Boston–New York,* awarded to a group including Juan Trippe, later to found and operate Pan American Airways. Colonial Air Transport operated the airmail service.

2. CAM 2: *Chicago–St. Louis,* awarded to Robertson Aircraft Corp., a forerunner to American Airlines. Robertson hired Charles Lindbergh as chief pilot. (See Figure 12-4.)

3. CAM 3: *Chicago–Dallas,* awarded to National Air Transport, a forerunner of United Airlines.

4. CAM 4: *Salt Lake City–Los Angeles,* awarded to Western Air Express, a forerunner of TWA.

5. CAM 5: *Elko, Nevada–Pasco, Washington,* awarded to Varney Air Lines, a forerunner of United Airlines.

6. CAM 6: *Detroit–Cleveland,* awarded to Ford Air Transport.

7. CAM 7: *Detroit–Chicago,* awarded to Ford Air Transport.

Ford was the first to begin service, on February 15, 1926, with the others following

FIGURE 12-4 Charles Lindbergh on CAM 2, flown between Chicago and St. Louis.

Courtesy of the Minnesota Historical Society.

within four months. The last to begin service was Colonial Airways on CAM 1. Subsequent awards that year were:

8. CAM 8: *Los Angeles–Seattle,* awarded to Pacific Air Transport, a forerunner of United Airlines.

9. CAM 9: *Chicago–Minneapolis,* awarded to Charles Dickenson. Northwest Airlines began operating the route in 1926.

10. CAM 10: *Atlanta–Jacksonville,* awarded to Florida Airways Corp, a forerunner of Eastern Air Lines.

11. CAM 11: *Cleveland–Pittsburgh,* awarded to Clifford Ball, later absorbed by United Airlines.

12. CAM 12: *Pueblo, Colorado–Cheyenne, Wyoming,* awarded to Western Air Express.

The aircraft available to serve the new airmail companies were limited and unreliable. The Post Office had largely relied on the World War I British-designed DH-4, but its Liberty engines were pretty much used up. Varney had to begin airmail service with the underpowered Swallow biplane, and Western Air Express bought the Douglas M-2, all six of them. Ford had the

Courtesy of the Minnesota Historical Society.

FIGURE 12-5 Ford Trimotor.

Courtesy of the National Postal Museum, Smithsonian Institution.

FIGURE 12-6 Ford Trimotor loading mail.

first of the Ford Trimotors (see Figures 12-5 and 12-6), producing 14 in 1926. Juan Trippe of Colonial Air Transport, impressed by Fokker's monoplane design and its absence of wires and struts, ordered the first three Fokker Trimotors produced, but they would not be available until 1927. In 1928, Western Air added Fokkers for its Los Angeles–San Francisco passenger service.

One of the most advanced airplanes in 1926 was the Boeing 40, which had been designed around the Liberty engine. A joint study done by Boeing and Pratt & Whitney showed that a Wasp mounted on the Boeing 40 airframe would be able to carry a payload of 1,200 pounds as compared to 300–400 pounds using the Liberty engine. This was interesting information to have when the Post Office announced in the fall of 1926 that the Chicago–San Francisco airmail route was going up for bid (the eastern leg of the transcontinental route from New York to Chicago was awarded to National Air Transport).

The western route was challenging when viewed from any angle: the Rockies, the weather, the distance, and the fact that night flying was a requirement. Boeing had been flying the international airmail route between Seattle and Vancouver with seaplanes under contract with Canada and the United States since 1919, but that route

was basically flat and over tidal water. Another problem was that the U.S. Navy had dibs on the first 200 Wasps that P&W could produce.

Rentschler's contacts once again proved fruitful. An agreement was made for Boeing to step ahead of the Navy for delivery of these engines, at the rate of five per month for a total of 25 Wasps. Thus, the Boeing 40 A, with a single Wasp mounted upfront, was born and the fuselage revised to accommodate two passengers behind the firewall. Based on the results of the joint study, Boeing submitted a bid that was about one-third of that of any of its competitors.

Over protests of bad faith and "low-ball" bidding, Boeing began flying the Chicago–San Francisco route on July 1, 1927, and it made money in the process. This was only possible because of the Wasp, and it put private airmail carriage off to an excellent start.

❝ I've tried to make the men around me feel, as I do, that we embarked as pioneers upon a new science and industry in which our problems are so new and unusual that it behooves no one to dismiss any novel idea with the statement that "it can't be done!" Our job is to keep everlasting at research and experimentation, to adapt our laboratories to production as soon as possible, and to let no new improvement in flying and flying equipment pass us by. **"**

William E. Boeing, founder, The Boeing Company, 1929

Orders for the Wasp began to flood in from the commercial side as well as the military. Varney Airlines was the first to order the Boeing 40 A with the Wasp engine. The Wasp quickly began to replace the smaller Wright engines in the Trimotor Ford and Fokkers and practically every other large aircraft type. The Wasp was destined to reign supreme over its competition for several years before larger P&W and Wright engines became available. Soon the Boeing 40 B was designed with an enclosed four-place passenger compartment, with glass windows on each side, located between the Wasp/Hornet engine and the pilot in his open cockpit behind.

The 40 Bs set a completely new standard of reliability in the air. Proven reliability was an absolute necessity before transporting passengers on any broad scale could be seriously considered. With the Liberty engine, making the long-distance run without an engine failure or forced landing was practically unknown. The Wasps began running 250 hours and more without adjustment of any kind or requiring overhaul.

These engines actually ended the long-standing superiority of European engine manufacture that began before World War I and led to the establishment of American air supremacy for decades to come, well through World War II. They also laid the groundwork for the successful beginning of the commercial air transport business.

13   **The Founding of the Airlines**

The process of creating an air transportation system had begun as an incidental consequence of privatizing the United States airmail delivery system. While a partial and rudimentary navigation infrastructure was in place, there was very little else on which to base a civil air transportation network. In 1925, it was difficult to imagine air travel ever overtaking the familiar modes of travel by sea or rail. Flying was not only still the province of adventurers, it was prohibitively expensive. About the only thing that would recommend travel by air was the element of speed, but this was more than offset by the discomfort of the associated noise, heat, cold, or turbulence, as well as the likelihood that mechanical failures would result in unscheduled landings, causing delays or, heaven forbid, even worse.

But aside from the optimistic efforts of the undaunted enthusiasts of aviation, there were national interests to be considered. In Europe subsidized national flag carriers were being formed, Imperial Airways in Britain in 1924, for instance, and there were rumors of Lufthansa in Germany (which did form in 1926). Other European countries were forming airlines. There was criticism heard in the United States and recollections of how far behind Europe America had been before and during the First World War.

The United States had no civil aviation policy. President Calvin Coolidge, like most everybody else, had never been inside an airplane. But Coolidge was in a position to do something about it—he formed a commission to study what should be done. It was called the Morrow Board.

Coolidge and Dwight Morrow had been classmates at Amherst. Morrow had gone to Yale Law School and was in law practice in New York in 1925 when Coolidge asked him to head up a "blue-ribbon" committee to make a general inquiry into U.S. aviation. Coolidge biographer Robert Sobel characterized Coolidge's style this way: "Find the right man, tell him what has to be done, then step aside."[1]

Having such a man was particularly important since two related committees had preceded this one: (1) the Secretary of War had convened the Lassiter Board in 1923 to try to resolve competing interests of the Army and Navy regarding airpower and how it should be controlled, and (2) the House of Representatives had appointed the Lampert Committee in 1924 to look into allegations of malfeasance by the Chief of Air Service, General Mason Patrick, regarding budget cuts for military aviation and the policy of the Army that placed air units under control of ground commanders. It was in the Lampert Commission hearing that General Billy Mitchell got in such hot water with his insubordinate statements about military aviation that President Coolidge ordered his court-martial. In short, the state of American aviation was in turmoil.

Now the Morrow Board was formed in September 1925 to look into the future of aviation in both the military and civilian aviation sectors. It was composed of a federal judge, an engineer on the National Advisory Committee for Aeronautics (NACA), several former military officers, and the World War I head of the Board of Aircraft Production. Morrow himself knew little about aviation, although he was a member of the Guggenheim Fund Board of Trustees (see below).

The Morrow Board

The Board heard from 99 witnesses, including the Secretary of War, the Secretary of the Navy, the Postmaster General, and even Wilbur Wright, whom the Chairman jokingly chided as "being responsible for it all."

The board heard the testimony of Herbert Hoover, then Secretary of Commerce in the Coolidge administration, which said that the government was obliged to lend its support to commercial aviation, as it had always done in the maritime industry. Hoover pointed out that the government had for a century maintained aids to navigation in the coastal waters of the country, provided education and competency standards for ships' officers, required federal inspections of ships, and funded improvements in and about the navigable waters, including ports. He noted that the 25 years since the flight of the Wright brothers in 1903 had brought little advance in commercial aviation, and that America was lagging the Europeans in engaging the subject of transport by air.

The Morrow Board heard from another strong voice in support of governmental action. By the early 1920s, the National Advisory Committee for Aeronautics (NACA)[2] had become a loosely organized group of scientists and engineers who were developing into leaders in aeronautical research and experimentation. NACA conducted pure research in its Langley Laboratory unconstrained by bureaucratic influences. Independence from political pressures contributed greatly to NACA becoming the premier aeronautical research facility in the world beginning in the 1920s. By the time the Morrow Board was convened, NACA had even then gained a great level of respect. The NACA testimony laid the foundation for initiating the examination and licensing of pilots and the imposition of airworthiness standards for aircraft, as well as for the creation of an Aeronautics Branch within the Department of Commerce to administer these activities.

Based on all of the testimony produced before his board, Morrow prepared a report that was to become the blueprint for the development of commercial aviation for years to come. Among other things, the report concluded:

1. Aviation is vital to the national defense. The means of aircraft design and production must be supported in the national interest, and a military procurement program should be initiated.

2. Non-military aviation, comprising the largest potential for commercial development, serves a national purpose, and deserves the support of the government.

3. The government should enhance the safety and reliability of flying by establishing standards for pilots and aircraft. It should establish and maintain airways for navigation and enlarge its support for airmail contract carriers under contract with the Post Office. All this would have the collateral effect of bolstering both public and banking confidence in aviation.

The Morrow Board was central to the second major federal statute affecting commercial aviation, the Air Commerce Act of 1926.

The Air Commerce Act of 1926

The next hurdle was actually getting a bill passed through both Houses of Congress. Some of the original recommendations did not make it into law. Debate was vigorous: construction of airfields, they said, should be left to local governments, like docks and port facilities; some Congressmen did not like the government taking control of the air over their real property (thus violating the long-standing law of real property ownership *ad coelum* or "to the sky"); some tried to exempt intra-state aviation under the doctrine of "states' rights." Finally, the statute was enacted and on October 20, 1926, President Coolidge signed it into law.

Prior to this enactment, there had been no official government statement identifying what role, if any, the federal government would play in the field of aviation. There had been no structure, no plan, no strictures, and no standards. In one fell swoop all of this uncertainty vanished, and in its place was laid a solid foundation for the building of a national commercial aviation industry.

The purpose of the act was to promote air commerce. It specifically charged the federal government with the obligation of creating and maintaining a national system of navigational aids and of adopting rules and regulations to promote safety of flight.

The Department of Commerce, in turn, was charged with the responsibility of promulgating and enforcing safety regulations, including the registration and licensing of aircraft, producing aeronautical charts, providing meteorological advice and reports, investigating accidents, and certification and medical examination of pilots. The Aeronautics Branch of the Department of Commerce was created to administer and carry out the requirements placed on the department. This agency was renamed the Bureau of Air Commerce in 1934 and assumed all safety responsibilities. The Interstate Commerce Commission assumed all rate and fare authority.

The black letter law was on the books, the Commerce Department had its marching orders, the banking community had taken note, the manufacturing sector was in place, and the entrepreneurs were emerging. Still, the hearts and minds of the public were with the railroads. Those in government and in aviation wondered how the public imagination could be captured.

Lindbergh

Charles Lindbergh had been hired by Robertson Aircraft, one of the original airmail contractors, following a short career in which he fully qualified as an all-around daredevil. He parachuted from a plane in 1922, even before he had soloed an airplane for the first time. He adopted an itinerate life first as a wing-walker and stunt man and then as a barnstormer pilot. With Robertson, he flew the mail between St. Louis and Chicago, a route known for its range of temperatures and volatile weather.

An offer of $25,000 prize money had been made in 1919 by a New York businessman, Raymond Orteig, to anyone who successfully completed a nonstop flight between New York and Paris. Although the Atlantic had been successfully crossed in 1919 in three separate efforts, including one nonstop flight from St. Johns, Newfoundland to Clifden, Ireland, no one had succeeded in claiming the Ortieg prize by 1927. Several attempts had been made during the intervening years, including French World War I ace, René Fonck, in 1926. In early 1927, Fonck was rumored to be readying another attempt, and Admiral Richard E. Byrd was also said to be preparing to make the crossing in his Fokker Trimotor. Advances in technology by 1927 made the chances of success increasingly likely, and the race was heating up with great publicity.

Lindbergh was backed by a group of St. Louis businessmen, but his budget was limited to $15,000. No airplane existed for that sum of money that had any chance of making the

3,600-mile flight successfully. He decided to fly solo, a controversial decision in an otherwise foolhardy endeavor, but a decision that lent itself to a smaller airplane, one that could possibly be built for a cost within his budget. The Ryan Airplane Company, a small aircraft manufacturer located in San Diego, California, agreed to build the airplane to his specifications for $6,000, plus the cost of the engine. He decided on the Wright Whirlwind engine, whose endurance had been proven earlier in 1927 when two pilots kept their Bellanca aloft with it for a period of 57 hours.

Lindbergh decamped to San Diego where he supervised the construction. Although the airplane type had never before been built (it was a custom job), it was completed in 77 days, and with the Wright Whirlwind installed, the total price was $10,580. To save weight, the *Spirit of St. Louis*, named in honor of his backers, had no brakes and no radio. Gasoline tanks occupied the forward portion of the cockpit where a windshield would normally be placed. To see forward he was required to use a small periscope. The airplane's range was 4,200 miles, just 600 miles over the flight-planned distance necessary to reach Paris.

Lindbergh had accumulated just over 2,000 hours of flying time, but his airmail experience had given him exposure to practically all types of weather conditions. He felt that he was ready. He flew the *Spirit of St. Louis* from San Diego to New York on what was really a "shake down" flight, stopping in St. Louis to refuel, and in the process he set a coast-to-coast record of slightly less than 22 hours. The press coverage of the transcontinental flight only served to heighten the public attention that had been building.

The *Spirit of St. Louis* left Roosevelt Field on Long Island at 7:52 a.m. on May 20, 1927, with 450 gallons of gasoline, half the total weight of the airplane. Thirty-three hours and 30 minutes later, Parisians flooded the field at Le Bourget to welcome Lindbergh, and the entire world was consumed by aviation fervor.[3]

"Science, freedom, beauty, adventure: what more could you ask of life? Aviation combined all the elements I loved. There was science in each curve of an airfoil, in each angle between strut and wire, in the gap of a spark plug or the color of the exhaust flame. There was freedom in the unlimited horizon, on the open fields where one landed. A pilot was surrounded by beauty of earth and sky. He brushed treetops with the birds, leapt valleys and rivers, explored the cloud canyons he had gazed at as a child. Adventure lay in each puff of wind.

I began to feel that I lived on a higher plane than the skeptics of the ground; one that was richer because of its very association with the element of danger they dreaded, because it was freer of the earth to which they were bound. In flying, I tasted a wine of the gods of which they could know nothing. Who valued life more highly, the aviators who spent it on the art they loved, or these misers who doled it out like pennies through their antlike days? I decided that if I could fly for 10 years before I was killed in a crash, it would be a worthwhile trade for an ordinary life time."

Charles A. Lindbergh, *The Spirit of St. Louis*

If the flying feat itself were not enough to sufficiently impress the mind, then the proceedings that followed, conducted on the world scene, would certainly do the trick. He went on a triumphant tour of European capitals, and

FIGURE 13-1 Charles Lindbergh pays a visit to Orville Wright at Wright Field, Dayton, OH, June 22, 1927.

FIGURE 13-2 Juan Trippe and Charles Lindbergh.

was given audiences with the kings of Belgium and England. President Coolidge sent a United States warship to fetch the young Lindbergh home, where he was met by the dirigible USS *Los Angeles* and a ticker tape parade. He was awarded the Congressional Medal of Honor and commissioned a colonel in the Army Reserve. He was also introduced to Dwight Morrow.

He went on a three-month tour, sponsored by the Guggenheim Fund, of all 48 states, parading in 82 cities, and flying over 22,000 miles in the process. He was a fine hero, conducting himself at all times in his trademark modest and dignified manner. (See Figure 13-1.) He was invited to Mexico by Dwight Morrow, who was then ambassador there, for a Mexican tour and then for a sojourn through Latin America. Ambassador Morrow's daughter, Anne Spencer, met Lindy on one of his visits to the ambassador's residence in Mexico and, mutually taken with each other, in due course they were married.

It would be difficult to overstate the effect that Lindbergh had on the nascent airline industry in the late 1920s. Dormant aviation stocks across the board ignited as money poured in from all quarters. In 1926, total passenger enplanements in the United States had numbered less than 6,000. By 1930, the flourishing airline industry carried over 400,000 adventurous souls. Production of aircraft soared.

Back in New York, what might have been the first of all celebrity endorsements occurred when Lindbergh joined the new airline, Transcontinental Air Transport (TAT), lending his name to a commercial product in return for cash and stock. Juan Trippe, (see Figure 13-2) having been deposed from Colonial Air Transport, also signed him up as a technical adviser to his new airline venture, Pan American Airways. This was the beginning of a long-standing relationship between Lindbergh and Trippe[4] that would play a key role in the expansion of air commerce around the world and, with it, American influence.

The Daniel Guggenheim Fund for the Promotion of Aeronautics

In the middle of the 1920s, aviation in America was emerging from its long period of confusion and stagnation. But aviation in Europe had captured the imagination of the people and of industry almost immediately after the Wright brothers' tour of Europe in 1908–9, and it still led the way. The United States government had been significantly involved in promoting aviation at least since 1918 with subsidy and direct investment in infrastructure, and in 1926 it would begin to legally promote safety and standards in aviation in order to boost the public confidence. But the job was big. The list of individual citizens with ardent interests in aviation in the 1920s was long, and the record of their contributions was even-then impressive. Corporate America, as well, had shared in the promotion and advancement of aviation. But the going was still slow.

One of the more beneficial byproducts of the American system of private enterprise is the philanthropic activity of its successful practitioners. The giving of one's time, interest, and assets to causes of one's choosing is a time-honored tradition in America. The Guggenheim family of New York made its money in the mining industry. In 1924, Daniel Guggenheim and his wife, Florence, established a foundation to promote a variety of charitable causes. One of their sons, Harry Guggenheim, was a pilot during World War I and became committed to the advancement of aviation. Father and son established, in 1926, a separate fund called the Daniel Guggenheim Fund for the Promotion of Aeronautics, and by 1930 the family had given almost $3 million to aviation-related projects.

The Guggenheims believed, like the government, that the public would embrace air travel if confidence could be established in its safety. A significant part of the safety of air travel depended on reliably designed and constructed aircraft, yet there was no such thing as what we now know as an aeronautical engineer in 1925. The Guggenheims began to fund the establishment of schools at universities across the country, and by 1929 aeronautical engineering programs or research centers had been set up at the California Institute of Technology, Stanford, the Massachusetts Institute of Technology, Harvard, Syracuse, Northwestern, the University of Michigan, and others.

In 1927, the Guggenheims offered a prize of $100,000 for the construction of safe aircraft in a contest called the "Safe Aircraft Competition." The prize went to the Curtiss Tanager, which had incorporated into its design the first short takeoff

and landing (STOL) characteristics, including reduced stall speeds, ever demonstrated.

The Fund subsidized an operation in California by Western Air Express (WAE) in 1928 known as the "Model Airway," between Los Angeles and San Francisco. Airmail was not carried on this route since no award had been made by the Post Office to WAE. Instead, the airline carried only passengers along the corridor in an effort to show that commercial passenger service was feasible without airmail subsidies, as well as safe and reliable. The Fund provided a Fokker F-10 Super Trimotor to WAE for this scheduled service and had implemented a weather-reporting regimen along the route that utilized two-way radio. This was the first PIREPS (pilot weather reporting system) in history. The passenger operations ended in 1929, and although the experiment was not profitable, it did demonstrate that passenger-only (non-airmail) service could be feasible and popular with the public, at least between certain population centers. At a time when one of the most frequent causes of airplane crashes was allocated to adverse weather conditions, not one weather-related incident was recorded. Upon the termination of the experiment in June 1929, the weather bureau assumed the reporting of aviation weather locally, and the practice ultimately spread all across the country.

When Charles Lindbergh, in 1928, suggested that it would be helpful to navigation if the names of cities and towns could be painted on the roofs of large buildings, the Guggenheims funded the cost. The Postmasters of some 8,000 communities arranged for the painting on rooftops of their towns' names in large letters, with arrows pointing to the north and, if available, to the nearest landing field.

The Guggenheims made a very significant contribution to advances in instrument flying by funding research involving gyroscopic instrumentation invented by Elmer Sperry (directional gyrocompass and artificial horizon) and Paul Kollsman (precision altimeter). Guggenheim-funded engineers worked with the Aeronautics Branch of the Commerce Department and the Bureau of Standards to advance radio navigation, and with Jimmy Doolittle to test and implement instrument procedures in 1929 that made safe instrument flight routine within a decade.

■ Airways—From Lighted Beacons to Radio Navigation

By the end of 1927, the government had extended the lighted portion of the airway system from New York to Salt Lake City on the transcontinental route, and on portions of feeder and parallel segments, such as Los Angeles to Las Vegas, New York to Atlanta, Chicago to Dallas, and between Los Angeles and San Francisco. That year there were 4,121 miles of lighted airways operated by the Aeronautics Branch of the Department of Commerce. By 1933, there were 1,500 beacons in place, extending the lighted airway systems for a length of 18,000 miles. While the lighted airway was of significant aid in navigation, it had serious limitations in the context of an all-weather air carrier system. It was still a visual navigation system, dependent on reasonably good weather in order to operate effectively.

The Bureau of Standards in the Department of Commerce began, in 1926, to work with radio as a means of communication and navigation. As government involvement in aviation began to kick in as a result of the Air Commerce Act, money and effort were applied to solve problems and to attempt to eliminate limitations on the commercial development of air commerce. In 1926, for instance, there was no two-way voice communication possible with aircraft in flight. This amounted to a serious limitation in safety, including a lack of pilot awareness of developing weather. By 1927, the first radio transmitter was established at Bellefonte, Pennsylvania, allowing communication with aircraft in a 150-mile radius.

In 1928, the Bureau of Standards developed a new radio beacon system of navigation, the first non-visual navigation system in the world. The Aeronautics Branch, which had authority over the lighted airway system, took over the installation and control of the new radio navigation system in 1929. The system was known as the "four-course radio range," and it would provide the first step in allowing a true all-weather air carrier system to begin to develop. It would remain the standard navigation system in use until World War II.

The four-course radio range utilized low frequency radio waves (190 to 535 kHz radio band) transmitted from powerful 1,500-watt beacons spaced 200 miles apart on the airway. The beacons transmitted two Morse code signals, the letter "A" and the letter "N." In Morse code, these signals are opposite, "dot-dash" for A, and "dash-dot" for N. When the aircraft was centered "on the beam," these signals merged into a steady, monotonous tone. If the aircraft ventured to one side of the airway, the signal heard was either the Morse A or N, depending on the aircraft's position from the beacon. (See Figure 13-3.)

Each beacon defined four airways, thus the name "four-course radio range," and the beacon's identification was broadcast in Morse code twice each minute. The so-called beam width was 3 degrees, so that at the halfway point of 100 miles between beacons, the on-course deviation was about +/–2.6 miles. Station passage was

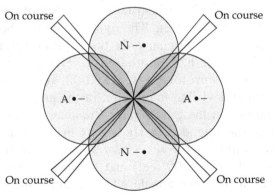

FIGURE 13-3 Schematic of the four-course radio range.

marked by a "cone of silence," at which point the aural tone would disappear as the aircraft passed overhead. Distance from the station was later provided by marker beacons placed along the airway at intervals of 20 miles or so.

By today's standards, the four-course radio range was primitive. Low frequency radio was subject to electrical static and other weather aberrations and distortions, but it constituted a quantum leap forward over the visual, lighted beacon system in use at the time. Pilots became very adept at flying the four-course system, and as the airlines began establishing schedules on their new routes. All-weather navigation allowed adherence to schedules that theretofore would have been impossible.

Amelia Earhart

Lindbergh was not to be the only aviation celebrity of the late 1920s. Building on the women pioneers before her,[5] Amelia Earhart was to emerge shortly after the Lindbergh flight as the foremost female aviator up to that time and, arguably, even to the present day. (See Figure 13-4.) She certainly captured the public imagination in much the same way that Lindbergh had, and thereby contributed to the enthusiasm that helped to create the airlines.

When Earhart soloed in 1922 at a small field in south Los Angeles, California, there were fewer than 100 female pilots in the United States. Her flight instructor, Neta Snook, was one of those women. The right to vote had been achieved by women only three years before, in 1919. Earhart purchased a yellow Kinner "Airster" prototype for $2,000 and began making a visible impression in the area, being featured in the *Los Angeles Examiner* declaring that she intended to fly across the continent. She immediately set a new women's altitude record (of 14,000 feet) and was advertised as one of only two female pilots in an air meet at the Glendale airport. She was awarded a flying certification in May 1923 from the Fédération

FIGURE 13-4 Amelia Earhart.

Source: Library of Congress.

Aéronautique Internationale, although flying licenses were not required, nor even issued, by the U.S. government. The certification was necessary in order to have official recognition for any record-breaking or record-setting achievements.

In 1924, Earhart moved with her mother to Boston, Massachusetts, arriving there by a "motorcar" which she drove all the way from California by way of Banff, Canada. This was a daring adventure at the time, as the U.S. Army had only performed the first sustained cross-country convoy in 1919. In Boston, her flying activities once again prompted curiosity from local interests, including *The Boston Globe,* in which she was featured in an interview in June 1927, shortly after the Lindbergh flight. She was billed as "one of the best women pilots in the United States" and began to be mentioned increasingly in the local press. Earhart bore a remarkable resemblance to Charles Lindbergh, and some say that was the main reason for the event that set her career skyward. She was to be the first woman to fly the Atlantic Ocean.

"You haven't seen a tree until you've seen its shadow from the sky."

Amelia Earhart

We have already seen what excitement Lindbergh's spectacular solo transatlantic flight had caused in 1927. By 1928, women in both Europe and America were making plans to be the first woman to make the crossing, but with a difference—they planned to have the flying actually performed by male pilots. (See Box 13-1.)

Amelia Earhart had no such plans. The flight that was to make her initially famous was entirely planned and paid for by others. She had nothing to do with the selection of pilots, the selection of aircraft, or with flight planning. She was, in effect, chosen as a passenger. At the time, she was making a living as a social worker with immigrants in Boston.

The adventure began in early 1928 when another female patron, the wife of a wealthy Londoner, Frederick E. Guest (she was formerly Amy Phipps of Pittsburgh), purchased a Fokker Trimotor from Commander Richard E. Byrd with plans to hire a pilot to fly her to England. Mrs. Guest was soon dissuaded from this venture by her family, but she stuck with the plan for the trip to be made by "an American girl with the right image,"[6] and a committee was formed to find her replacement.

On the committee was George Palmer Putnam, a New York publisher and writer. He had, in fact, published Lindbergh's *We,* the firsthand account of the first solo transatlantic crossing, and was in the process of publishing Richard E. Byrd's chronicle of his flying and exploring adventures in the book, *Skyward.* He heard of Amelia Earhart, then residing in Boston, and invited her to New York for an interview. It went well, and the agreement was sealed in April 1928.

Box 13-1 Who Would Be the First Woman Across the Atlantic?

The first attempt was by Princess Anne Lowenstein-Wertheim, a German aristocrat who for some years had exhibited an affinity for aviation and who held several aviation records in her own right. She departed England on August 31, 1927, bound for Ottawa, Canada with two experienced Royal Air Force pilots, Leslie Hamilton and Fred Minchin, at the controls. Although the aircraft was spotted once en route, it disappeared.

Another, Ruth Elder, was only a student pilot when she announced in August 1927 plans to fly the Atlantic. Her flight instructor was George Haldeman, and she acknowledged that he would do the flight planning and most of the flying. The route he chose was the longer southern route via the Azores. The aircraft chosen for the flight was a Stinson Detroiter, a single engine monoplane that Elder had named *American Girl.* The project was a promotion for the manufacturer, Stinson, and was likened to a publicity stunt. The pair left Roosevelt Field, Long Island, New York, on October 11, 1927, for Paris and completed most of the planned flight route (over 2,600 miles) but the craft was forced down just 300 miles short of their destination by an overheating engine caused by a leaking oil line. A passing ship off the Azores rescued them. Their return to New York was celebrated almost as if the flight had succeeded, which, admittedly, it nearly did. Ruth Elder continued to fly and, in 1929, placed fifth in the first Women's Air Derby.

Frances Grayson was another female patron with money. She hired an all-male crew for her attempt in a Sikorsky amphibian, which was readied for the flight at Curtiss Field on Long Island. Ruth Elder and George Haldeman were preparing for their departure at the same time from the same airfield. Frances Grayson's flight planned the shorter northern route to Europe. This aircraft took off from Newfoundland on December 23, 1927, and was never seen again.

Earhart would be a passenger on the *Friendship*, a Fokker F-7 Trimotor fitted with floats that had been already scheduled for a transatlantic attempt in June. The crew consisted of a mechanic, Bill Gordon, and the pilot, Lou Stultz, the latter of whom was proficient in multiengine aircraft, float plane flying, and instrument flying. Amelia Earhart had none of these qualifications nor, for that matter, did many male aviators. Nevertheless, she was billed as the "Commander" of the flight, which left Newfoundland on June 17, 1928 and arrived in New South Wales, England the next day after a flight of 20 hours and 49 minutes.

Gordon and Stultz were soon forgotten, but the public embraced Amelia much as they had Lindbergh. This was a matter of some embarrassment to Earhart, who felt that she had done nothing to deserve such adulation and that the credit should go to the crew, and she had the courage to say so. But the public clamor continued. She received congratulations from many government quarters, including President Coolidge, and under the tutelage of George Putnam, she embarked on a lecture circuit during 1928 and 1929 that gave her worldwide recognition. She thereby became acquainted with aviation luminaries of the time like Admiral Byrd and Colonel Lindbergh. Because of the physical resemblance to Lindbergh and the Atlantic transit similarity, she soon garnered the moniker "Lady Lindy."

After her return from Europe in 1928, Earhart began to earn the celebrity that had been handed to her by fate. She crossed the continent solo from New York to Los Angeles in September 1928. She was swamped with offers to endorse products in advertising media. She began writing articles for national magazines, including *Cosmopolitan* and *McCall's,* and she was hired by Transcontinental Air Transport (the Lindbergh Line) as Assistant to the General Traffic Manager. She acquired a Lockheed Vega and began entering air races around the country and set several speed records.

In 1929, she was largely responsible for inaugurating the Women's Air Derby, a grueling nine-day race from Santa Monica, California to Cleveland, Ohio, dubbed by Will Rogers as "the Powder Puff Derby," a name that has remained with the event. The race was limited to women who had been licensed and who had logged at least 100 hours of solo time. It was estimated at the time that only 30 women could qualify for the event. Twenty fliers started the race, 15 finished, and there was one fatality. Earhart finished third.

Earhart improved her flying proficiency, particularly in instrument qualification. With her publicist (and now husband) George Putnam, she planned and advertised her intention of becoming the first woman to solo the Atlantic. On May 19, 1932, AE (as she had begun to sign her name) left Harbor Grace, Newfoundland for Paris. Mechanical difficulties en route, including a leaking reserve fuel line, an inoperative altimeter, and a broken weld on an engine manifold, caused her to alter course for Ireland. Fifteen hours and eighteen minutes after leaving Harbor Grace, AE landed the Vega in a sloping field outside of Londonderry. Her acclaim rose higher and higher, and she had earned it.

Amelia Earhart was destined for even bigger accomplishments, and for tragedy, as the decade of the 1930s unfolded. We will jump ahead in our chronology of the development of aviation to briefly consider the rest of her story. So far, Earhart had only tried to duplicate what men had done. She had set no significant records for the first time in aviation on a genderless basis. But on January 11, 1935, she left Wheeler Field in Hawaii and successfully soloed her new Vega across 2,400 miles of Pacific Ocean to Oakland, California. No person, man or woman, had ever done that before. The Vega performed flawlessly and required only eighteen hours and fifteen minutes en route. She followed this up with other aviation firsts, a nonstop flight from Burbank, California to Mexico City on April 20, 1935, and from there she flew nonstop across the Gulf of

Mexico and on to Newark, N.J., in 14 hours and 19 minutes on May 8 that year.

In June 1935, AE took on a new role as visiting aeronautics advisor at Purdue University, which had begun an ambitious plan to develop one of the nation's first academic aviation curricula. As it turned out, this assignment would provide Earhart with the airplane with which she would make her final mark—her unsuccessful attempts to circumnavigate the globe. The Lockheed Electra 10E was purchased by Purdue to be used for research purposes in connection with AE's duties, but soon after taking possession of the Electra in July 1936, she flew it in the 1936 Bendix air race from New York to Los Angeles. Shortly thereafter, the airplane was fitted for long-distance flight and the latest radio navigation equipment.

Earhart made two attempts to fly around the world in the Electra, both on a flight-planned route close to the equator of over 29,000 miles.[7] In both attempts she carried navigator Fred Noonan, who had flown the Pacific extensively with Pan American. The first attempt was planned from east to west, beginning in Oakland with the initial stop in Hawaii, and then on to tiny Howland Island. This effort was abandoned when Earhart ground looped the Electra on take off from Hawaii on March 19, 1937, with serious damage to the airplane. The plane was shipped back to the Lockheed plant in California where it was repaired.

For her next attempt, AE decided to reverse course and fly the route from Oakland to Miami, thence to South America, and on to Africa and points east. The Pacific itinerary was to be the last part of the flight, but it still included Howland Island, which is truly a relative speck of land in the vast Pacific Ocean. By late June 1937, the route had been successfully flown all the way to Lae, New Guinea, a distance of 22,000 miles. On July 2, Earhart and Noonan departed New Guinea for the long over-water flight to Howland Island. In spite of all precautions, including the Coast Guard vessel *Itasca* standing off Howland to broadcast

homing signals and to plot her position, the Electra never made landfall at Howland. Although she was heard on several occasions attempting to make contact with *Itasca*, her location was never established, and no provable trace of her, Noonan, or the Electra has ever been found.[8]

While Amelia Earhart had little direct effect on the establishment of commercial aviation in the United States, her efforts to overcome and transcend the boundaries encountered by the aviation pioneers of the 1920s and 1930s engendered public admiration and a greater acceptance of the new industry of flight. She became a model for both male and female aviators and, like many of them, her time was too short.

From Mail Carriers to Airlines—1925 to 1930

Before 1930, the airplane industry was a very scrambled lot. The main aircraft manufacturers were Curtiss, Martin, Consolidated, Douglas, Boeing, and Vought. These comprised the list of military contractors, but these companies were also being drawn into the commercial field due to the sudden expansion of participants in the fledgling air transport business. The main engine producers were Pratt & Whitney and Wright Aeronautical, the latter of which merged with Curtiss Aeronautical to become Curtiss-Wright in 1929. The air transport companies, according to Fred Rentschler, numbered as many as one hundred.[9] Most of these operators did not have CAM routes and flew one or two airplanes from any place to practically anywhere else hauling what passengers or cargo there was. These companies, operated mainly by aviation enthusiasts, had little realistic hope of ever developing a successful business. Yet they were eager to bid on any government-offered route or proposal, irrespective of their chances of operating success.

To qualify for government airmail contracts, bidders had to establish some reasonable degree of soundness in financial and operating responsibility, which by itself quickly had the effect of separating out the contestants. Among the relatively sound new business entities were Colonial Air Transport, Boeing Air Transport, Transcontinental Air Transport, Western Air Express, National Air Transport, and Pacific Air Transport. But under its competitive bidding requirements, the Post Office had made CAM awards to marginal companies who were operating at a loss and engaging in marginal operational practices, using obsolete, cheaper airplanes and engines. Clear cases of fraudulent billing practices to the government were commonplace.

The larger companies were better capitalized, could afford newer and more modern equipment, and generally observed better operating practices. These attributes translated into greater reliability and safer air transport. In the late 1920s the broad aircraft industry came under the control of a few large companies that combined the primary air industry sectors: airmail carriers, airplane manufacturers, and engine manufacturers. Three groups, in particular, formed the core of the vertical holding companies that were to figure prominently in the future of the airline industry. These groups were:

1. United Aircraft & Transport Corporation
2. North American Aviation (NAA)
3. Aviation Corporation of America (AVCO)

■ United Aircraft & Transport Corporation

Fred Rentschler had early on formed a working relationship with Chance Vought in negotiating with U.S. Navy personnel. They had cooperated in marrying the Wasp engine with the Vought-built original Corsair for use on early Navy carriers. William Boeing and Rentschler had combined to create the most effective aircraft of the time, the

Boeing 40 B with the Wasp engine for Boeing Air Transport. These three men represented the three sectors mentioned, namely engine manufacture, aircraft manufacture, and airmail carrier. Led by Rentschler and Boeing, these three formed United Aircraft & Transport Corporation. Soon they added Hamilton Propeller to the group.

The company was set up with Pratt & Whitney owning 50 percent of the stock and the rest being divided among Boeing Aircraft, Boeing Air Transport, the Vought Corporation, and Hamilton Propeller. United then added Standard Propeller, Sikorsky, and Stearman Aircraft Company.

United next embarked on acquiring air transport companies, including Pacific Air Transport, which operated from Seattle to San Francisco and Los Angeles, Varney Air Lines, operating from Salt Lake City to Seattle, and National Air Transport (through a proxy fight), which held the eastern leg of the transcontinental route from New York to Chicago, as well as the line from Chicago to Dallas/Ft. Worth. Upon the acquisition of NAT, United operated the entire transcontinental airmail route, and soon decided to break it out into a wholly owned carrier subsidiary called United Air Lines.

■ North American Aviation

North American Aviation (NAA) was the brainchild of Clement Keys, a vice president of the Curtiss Aeroplane and Motor Company during World War I. He gained control of that company during the early 1920s and began acquiring an assortment of additional companies, including National Air Transport, which was later to be absorbed by United. Next, he lined up and bought out several airmail routes operating between the Northeast and Florida (which would ultimately form the basis for Eastern Air Lines), while continuing to fly the mails on the midwestern routes. Before the great Wall Street crash of 1929, he merged the Curtiss holdings with Wright Aeronautical Corporation, creating Curtiss-Wright, completing the triad acquisition of companies capable of airplane building, engine manufacture, and air carriage. General Motors would gain controlling interest in NAA for a time in the early 1930s. At this time, NAA's holdings included Eastern Air Transport, Transcontinental Air Transport, and a substantial interest in Douglas Aircraft.

Aviation Corporation

Aviation Corporation was the work of Averell Harriman and Robert Lehman, New York financiers. Robert Lehman was of the Wall Street banking house of Lehman Brothers. Harriman was to later serve in key government posts, including lend-lease administrator, ambassador to the Soviet Union, Secretary of Commerce, and was to be a confidant of presidents. Together they salvaged the Fairchild Aircraft Company in 1929 through a stock sale before the financial crash in October of that year. The new company proceeded to acquire 5 airmail carriers, themselves holders of 11 airmail routes; they bought all sorts of aviation properties, including aircraft and engine plants, and even some airports. The air carriers were combined to form American Airways.

Harriman and Lehman did not remain in the aviation business very long, losing out in a proxy fight to E. L. Cord in the early 1930s. Harriman then began his government service, while Lehman returned to Wall Street. But Lehman would be heard from again, this time at TWA with Yellow Cab magnate John Hertz.

More on Transcontinental Air Transport—A Novel but Unworkable Idea

Flying was not yet very appealing to travelers in the late 1920s. Forced landings, cancellations due to weather, and airsickness from the heat, noise,

and sometimes-violent motion of the primitive aircraft combined to make the experience more of an adventure than a reliable mode of transport. The passenger service that was available was mostly short-haul, and there were parts of the country where there was no service at all, like between New York and Chicago, which was the heavily traveled train route through the Allegheny Mountains. The experience of the early airmail pilots over that route, as well as the subsequent trials of the contract airmail carriers, had convinced National Air Transport (Clement Keys), which flew the mails over the route, not to attempt passenger service. Still, Keys believed that airline service was destined to be a marketable and timesaving device for transcontinental passengers.

In 1928, Keys seized upon the idea of providing air transportation by day, then turning the passengers over to the trains for the standard luxurious Pullman service by night. He established a joint venture with the Pennsylvania Railroad in the East and the Santa Fe in the West to round out the full passage. The air carriage portion of the deal was carried out by the newly formed Transcontinental Air Transport (TAT), which had no airmail routes or subsidies, and it had to rely solely on passenger fares for its income. The westbound trip began in New York at Penn Station, where passengers boarded the Pennsylvania Railroad for the overnight run to Columbus, Ohio. Once beyond the Alleghenies, TAT took over at Columbus, flying passengers all day on the next leg to Waynoka, Oklahoma, where they again boarded a Santa Fe overnight train to Clovis, New Mexico. From there, they continued in Ford Trimotor discomfort to Los Angeles. The complete itinerary could be completed, at least on paper, in 48 hours, saving a full day over the fastest through train schedule then being operated. (See Figure 13-5.)

The operation, although highly touted by the railroads and accompanied with big-name fanfare (Charles Lindbergh himself was at the controls of the inaugural flight), was really only

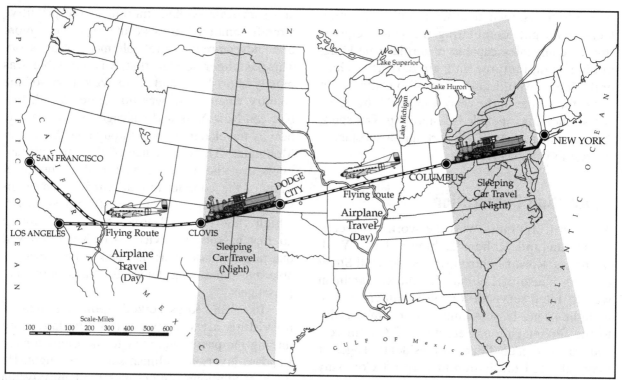

FIGURE 13-5   Route of Transcontinental Air Transport—depicting night and day portions of the route.

a novelty. The Ford Trimotors held 10 to 14 seats, but the passenger load was usually only six or seven passengers, and sometimes just three. With no airmail subsidy, the airline lost money, $2.7 million in 18 months. The Wall Street crash of 1929 impoverished many of the potential passengers, and by 1930, TAT was barely hanging on.

The Hoover Administration and Walter Folger Brown

Former Secretary of Commerce Herbert Hoover was elected President of the United States in November 1928, and took office in 1929. As we saw at the beginning of this chapter, in his testimony before the Morrow Commission Hoover strongly supported a robust aviation system for the country. As we also saw above, the state of commercial aviation after the passage of the

Airmail Act of 1925 was far from optimal, being perhaps better described as chaotic. It was clear, however, that the health of the emerging aviation industry at the time depended on airmail government contracts.

Hoover appointed Walter Folger Brown as his new Postmaster General in 1929. Brown, a lawyer, had served as Assistant Secretary of Commerce beginning in 1927 under Hoover. Brown had no particular affiliation with aviation prior to his appointment, but he took seriously the mandate that came with his job to "encourage commercial aviation." The Postmaster General, since 1925, had the responsibility of making awards of airmail contracts, which under the Airmail Act of 1925 were required to be made on a competitive bid basis.

Under the terms of the original Act, airmail carriers were paid 80 percent of the revenues derived from the postage charged. This had provided too little income for the CAM route operators to survive, so the law was changed in 1926 to provide for CAM operators to be paid according to the weight of mail carried plus a factor for distance carried. As he immersed himself in his new duties, Brown noticed that sometimes smaller companies submitted unrealistically low bids in order to get the business, and then played games with the weights of mail carried in order to increase their income. Postage rates were not set to cover the actual cost of airmail delivery, but to encourage the use of airmail and to promote commercial aviation. The difference in revenue received by the Post Office and the amount paid to the CAM operators based on weight/distance of airmail carried was a subsidy. Unscrupulous operators were known to have mailed telephone books and machine parts to themselves, paying the upfront postage and then charging the Post Office the much higher contract rate based on weight.

Brown saw that the system in place encouraged fraud, was costly to the government, and did little to promote commercial aviation. He realized that the government subsidy for airmail was open-ended, subject to little government control. It was like an oil gusher that could not be capped.

Although the government controlled the award of CAM routes, it had little control over the operators after the award was made. Control of stock companies was subject to change and was beyond the control of the Post Office under the system in place. In fact, in 1929 a proxy fight for control of National Air Transport, which held the New York to Chicago portion of the transcontinental airmail route, had resulted in United Aircraft & Transport Corporation taking control of that company from the North American Aviation group. This gave the United group monopolistic control of airmail carriage all the way across the nation, without Post Office approval, although the government was footing the bill.

Within a relatively short time after taking office, Brown had formed well-researched and thought-out conclusions about what was wrong with the airmail service. Brown believed that the Post Office was paying too much for the carriage of mail, partly because the airline passenger business had not been developed. He believed that by developing passenger traffic, a new, untapped source of income would become available to the carriers. This new income would then be available to help offset the cost of airmail operations.

Brown thought that tying the mail contracts to the size of aircraft (bigger) and requiring on-board state-of-the-art communication equipment (radios) and instrumentation would have the effect of making airline flying safer and more acceptable to the potential flying public.

He noted that a system of illogical short routes had been created through the process of competitive bidding, and that competitive bidding had resulted in a nonsensical pay schedule to the airmail contractors with rates of pay varying from 62 1/2 cents to the maximum of $3.00 per pound. He believed that competitive bidding on airmail contracts was counterproductive and that a system of appointing qualified, well-financed, and experienced operators would render a more stable and efficient system. He felt that those operators who had "pioneered" airmail routes in certain parts of the country, and who had expended effort and money in promoting the airmail system, developing good will and encouraging aviation should be given preferred consideration in the award of airmail contracts. (See Figure 13-6.)

The Airmail Act of 1930 (McNary-Watres Act)

On December 9, 1929, Brown appeared before the Appropriations Committee of Congress and related his concerns and suggestions about the airmail system in place, and the lack of an efficient passenger service. Members of the committee were receptive to Brown's ideas and

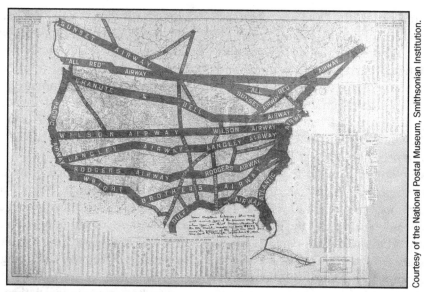

FIGURE 13-6 Airmail airways.

requested that he draft a bill and send it to them as soon as possible.

On February 4, 1930, Brown sent to Congress a proposed bill that contained the majority of his ideas about how to fix the system. The bill expressly allowed the Postmaster General to award contracts based on negotiated rates rather than competitive bidding. Although the bill was reported favorably out of committee, a minority report was filed containing objections by two members of the committee to the proviso allowing awarding contracts on other than a competitive bid. One of those was Representative Kelly, the sponsor of the Airmail Act of 1925 (Kelly Act).

The form of bill that was passed by Congress was substantially the same as the draft submitted by Brown, with the exception of the removal of the proviso allowing award of contracts based on negotiation, and the removal of provisions allowing consideration of "equities" or "pioneering rights" to carriers based on prior contributions. The bill became law when signed by President Hoover on April 29, 1930.

Accordingly, the main provisions of the act required that the carriers would no longer be paid on the basis of weight, but by the volume of the available space in the aircraft for the carriage of mail. This encouraged the carriers to invest in larger aircraft to earn more money. It further provided that bonuses would be paid if the aircraft were multiengined and had certain navigational devices installed.

Although the Act did not permit the award of contracts based on negotiation, as Brown had requested, it did amend the prior requirement of straight competitive bidding to a modified version of competitive bidding. The Postmaster was authorized to circumvent the actual low bidder in favor of the "lowest responsible bidder." Precedent for awarding contracts on this basis can be found in the Foreign Airmail Act of 1928.[10] A "responsible bidder" was defined in the Act as one that had flown daily scheduled service over a 250-mile route for a period of at least six months. In actual practice, Brown redefined the definition of "responsible bidder" to require that the applicant not only show that it had flown a daily scheduled route for six months, but that it had been flown in both daylight hours and at night. This requirement favored the larger, more experienced airmail carriers.

The law also granted the Postmaster General the discretion to "extend or consolidate" routes then in effect and to grant carriers who had flown existing routes for at least 2 years extensions on their contracts for an additional 10 years. The law gave near dictatorial powers to the Postmaster General.

◼ The Big Four

Immediately after passage of the legislation, Brown summoned to Washington representatives from the major lines around the country, who assembled in the Postmaster General's office on May 19, 1930. It was his belief, he said, that the mail should be carried by substantial, established air carriers, the vast majority of which fell within the ownership of the three largest holding companies, United Aircraft & Transport Corporation, North American Aviation, and Aviation Corporation. He explained his master plan to them in conjunction with the expressed and unexpressed terms of the new law. He decreed that there could be no monopoly of transcontinental service, but that competition along that route would be required, to the dismay of United. Brown explained, in effect, that the country would be carved up among a few lines, with United flying the transcontinental route to San Francisco, another line flying the New York–Los Angeles route by way of Pittsburgh and St. Louis, and still another line proceeding from New York via Washington, Atlanta, and Dallas, thence on to Los Angeles. He also outlined a north–south route along the east coast. He told the representatives in attendance that they should decide among themselves who would take which routes.

Brown brought in William P. MacCracken, aviation's first regulator as head of the Bureau of Aeronautics in the Commerce Department in 1926, to monitor the ensuing meetings among the carrier representatives in attendance. Not surprisingly, the strong-willed leaders of the industrial and financial interests that controlled these carriers were unable to agree among themselves, as directed by the Postmaster General, as to how the country should be split up. Representatives of the carriers remained in Washington, attending meetings with each other, until June 4, 1930. On that date, the carriers reported to the Postmaster General that they were unable to agree on allocating the five major routes in the country, including the transcontinental routes, and submitted the issues back to Brown. The carriers advised the Postmaster General that they would agree to be bound by his decision as to the route awards.

During June and July 1930, negotiations and correspondence continued between the parties with a view toward an agreement that would be fair to all concerned and that would take care of smaller lines having some "equity" due to their "pioneering" efforts. Brown suggested that the central transcontinental route should go to the beleaguered TAT, the plane and train airline, which had been flying without airmail subsidy. TAT had no night flying experience, however, and was ineligible for consideration for the transcontinental route because Brown had added this experience requirement under his "discretionary" authority. Western Air Express, however, did have the requisite night flying experience. Brown, in effect, ordered the merger of TAT with Western Air Express. This merged airline was to be TWA, or Transcontinental and Western Air. As consolation for sacrificing its independence, Western Air Express was allowed to survive as an independent entity and retain its passenger service between San Diego and Los Angeles, and between Los Angeles and Salt Lake City.

United kept its New York–San Francisco route through Chicago, and was allowed to expand northwest. Eastern was assigned New York–Miami, along with Atlanta, New Orleans, and Houston. TWA got New York–Los Angeles through St. Louis and Kansas City. American would fly New York–Los Angeles via Nashville, Dallas, and points in the Southwest. Thus were the "Big Four" (United, Eastern, TWA, and American) born.

Although the smaller lines were not invited to the meetings in May, the Post Office–carrier conferences were no secret. The Post Office had even put out a press release about the whole affair. Representatives of several small operators showed up, including Southwest Air Fast Express (SAFE), owned by oilman Erie Halliburton, Pittsburgh Aviation Industries, U.S. Air Transport, Curtiss Flying Service, Delta Air Service, and Thompson Aeronautical Corporation. During the summer of 1930, prior to the request for bids being sent out by the Post Office, discussions and negotiations continued. The financial interests of some of the smaller lines were taken into consideration, like SAFE and Delta, and mergers and buyouts were agreed to between them and the larger carriers who would be serving the routes on which the smaller lines had "pioneered." The parties even agreed that Walter Folger Brown would be the arbiter of the value of the stock transactions made to complete the arrangements. Some of the smaller operators received "extensions" of the major routes as additional consideration for the overall agreement.

The airlines paid lip service to the requirements of the Watres Act by going through the motions of competitive bidding with all of the carriers duly submitting bids. The only thing was, none of the Big Four submitted competing bids on the routes that had been assigned by Brown to others. Lower bids on the assigned routes submitted by small carriers were rejected as "not responsible." In this way, modern commercial aviation was born.

Hindsight will not compel a uniform judgment of Brown's actions. It cannot be doubted that the struggling world of commercial aviation was given a mighty boost by the arrangements put in place, and that it evolved at a much accelerated pace over what would otherwise have been the case. At the end of Brown's tenure in 1933, passenger traffic was rising, and the airlines were competing on their transcontinental routes. The cost to the government was less than it had been 4 years before, down from an average of $1.10 per mile in 1929 to half that in 1933, $.54 per mile. The airlines were in good shape financially. It is clear, therefore, that the public interest was served. As we shall see in the next chapter, the 1932 election of Franklin D. Roosevelt as President of the United States (he assumed office in 1933) would have a profound effect on the new commercial aviation community. The allocation of airmail routes and the award of airmail contracts would be the subject of a political Congressional investigation, and Walter Folger Brown, himself, would be the subject of intense scrutiny and criticism.

No evidence would be adduced that would even suggest any financial or material gain by Brown. His actions appear to have been the result of a sincere desire to promote aviation, and he did so with success. It is, however, beyond dispute that the procedures employed by Brown were outside of the requirements of the Watres Act. The Congress did not remove the requirement of competitive bidding in 1930, yet that requirement was not observed. The bill that was passed by Congress had removed consideration being given to "pioneering" efforts of some of the operators, yet such consideration was given. But, with the aid of hindsight, it can be seriously argued that his vision for the future of aviation was far superior to any of his peers'.

Although the results of Brown's actions would be undone at the beginning of the next administration, the reality is that the Big Four put in place by the Brown policy were still the Big Four for the ensuing 48 years, until deregulation in 1978, in fact. It was then, in 1978, that the country would finally have the chance to glimpse what might have happened during the 1930s had it not been for Walter Brown.

Endnotes

1. Sobel, *Coolidge, An American Enigma*, Regnery Publishing, Inc. 1998.

2. For a more detailed discussion of NACA, see Chapter 15.

3. See Appendix 4 for details of Lindbergh's flight, including hourly log entries.

4. Lindbergh served as technical advisor to Pan American for 45 years.

5. See Appendix 5.

6. Moolman, Valerie, *Women Aloft,* Time-Life Books, 1981.

7. By contrast, the around the world flight in 1938 by Howard Hughes was 14,456 miles in length, incorporating the itinerary New York-Paris-Moscow-Omsk-Yakutsk-Fairbanks-Minneapolis-New York. Except for New York, Paris, and Minneapolis, all stops were above 55 degrees north latitude. Hughes' flight set a new around the world speed record of 3 days, 19 hours, and 8 minutes, beating both of Wiley Post's world records of 8 days and 16 hours in 1931 and 7 days 19 hours in 1933 along a route similar to that flown by Howard Hughes in 1938.

8. In 2012, the International Group for Historic Aircraft Recovery (TIGHAR) began its 11th expedition to Nikumaroro (formerly Gardner Island) in search of evidence of Earhart's aircraft. An underwater search of the waters off the western end of the island was conducted using unmanned submersibles. This coral atoll is about 400 miles southeast of Howland Island, which was Earhart's intended destination. Although TIGHAR departed the area with no known positive results from their underwater search, in August 2012 TIGHAR announced that a review of high-definition video footage taken during the expedition revealed aircraft parts similar to Earhart's Lockheed Electra. Further analysis will be required to correlate this find definitively to Earhart.

9. *An Account of Pratt & Whitney Aircraft Company 1925–1950*, Frederick B. Rentschler, 1950, Pratt & Whitney Archives, East Hartford, CT.

10. See discussion of Pan American in Chapter 15.

14 New Deal—The Roosevelt Administration

A New Broom Sweeps Clean

The Great Depression was getting seriously underway in 1933, at the time that the Republican Hoover Administration was vacating office and the Democratic Franklin Roosevelt Administration was sweeping in with reform on its mind. Big business had ruled during the Roaring Twenties. The stock market increasingly through that decade had reflected in price the explosion in commerce and development, much money had been made and people were happy. But in 1933, the bread lines were long and were filled with disillusioned and angry men. The majority of voters had voted, in effect, to "throw the bums out." And so it was that the Democrats arrived in town with an agenda, a mandate even, to begin to set things straight. In the process, a rare opportunity was seen to make a little political hay and find out who and what was to blame for the mess the country found itself in.

Hugo Black came to the U.S. Senate in 1926 as a Democrat from Alabama, where he had enhanced his political career by winning local judicial elections and with membership in the Ku Klux Klan. While a lawyer there, he mostly sued corporations representing personal injury claimants. He considered himself a populist, and was re-elected to the Senate in 1932. He was a supporter of Franklin Roosevelt's bid for the presidency, and after Roosevelt's election, he was an ardent supporter of New Deal (anti-corporate) initiatives.

In fact, the 1932 election gave the Democrats the control of the Senate, the House of Representatives, and the White House. Control of the entire government was theirs. In February 1933, Black proposed a resolution to establish a special investigatory committee to inquire into the government's system of awarding ocean mail and airmail contracts, claiming that during the Hoover Administration they had become government giveaways to Hoover's friends and associates. The tension between the Democrats and Republicans was only heightened during the last days of the Hoover Administration when the Democrats requested the Postmaster General to defer awarding any further mail contracts. Black had been tipped off by a reporter that the Post Office Department was planning to sign an ocean mail contract with Philadelphia Steamship Company before the Democrats had a chance to replace the Postmaster General. Walter F. Brown awarded four new contracts anyway.

The Committee began its investigation on March 4, 1933, and for four months plowed through documents and testimony without uncovering much in the way of skullduggery. In fact, it was shown that all contract awards had been approved by the guardian of the national purse, Comptroller General McCarl. When Black started digging into the airmail awards, he thought he had finally struck pay dirt when he learned of the 1930 meetings in Brown's office with the Big Four. The press, who *Time Magazine* reported was feeding the questions to Black,[1] quickly labeled those meetings "the spoils conferences." The label stuck.

Small airline operators told of being excluded from the bidding process, or having their lower bids thrown out in favor of higher bids from larger carriers. Black cast his net wide. He sent out Interstate Commerce Commission agents with synchronized watches, armed with subpoenas to swoop down on the aviation companies without warning. When it was learned that Republican William P. MacCracken (the former head of the Bureau of Aeronautics) was present at the 1930 meetings, he was subpoenaed to produce his personal files for examination. On MacCracken's refusal, he was held in contempt of the Senate and ultimately jailed for 10 days by the Committee. But the main object of scorn was Walter F. Brown, whom Black saw as the author and architect of the whole scheme.

To Black, what the hearings produced was confirmation that the air carriers had exploited the public through inflated contract rates charged to the government, that the airlines' manufacturing arms had made huge profits from military procurement contracts, and that speculation in airline stocks had profited them all. It was not fully explained how these conclusions compared with the undisputed fact that the cost to the government of airmail delivery under Brown's administration had been cut in half, from $1.10 per mile to $.54 per mile, in four years. But such are the hazards of credibility in politically

motivated pursuits. Nor was it appreciated that the air carriers were stable, growing, and though still formative, rendering an air transportation service. Of what interest were airlines to a populace that did not have enough to eat? This was a relevant, if short-sighted, question.

James Farley was appointed Postmaster General in the new Roosevelt Administration. To him fell the duty of carrying out the verdict of Black, sanctioned by the president by way of presidential order, that all of the existing airmail contracts held by the airlines then operating were to be cancelled forthwith on the basis that they were fraudulently procured. The airmail, decreed Farley, would be carried by the Army Air Corps. All this was made official on February 9, 1934 by Executive Order 6591, signed by President Roosevelt. On February 11, 1934, Charles Lindbergh sent a letter to the president that stated, in part:

"Your action of yesterday affects fundamentally the industry to which I have devoted the last 12 years of my life. Therefore, I respectfully present to you the following considerations. The personal and business lives of American citizens have been built up around the right to a just trial before conviction. Your order of cancellation of all air mail contracts condemns the largest portion of our commercial aviation without just trial. The officers of a number of the organizations affected have not been given the opportunity of a hearing and improper acts by many companies affected have not been established. . . . Your present actions do not discriminate between innocence and guilt and place no premium on honest business. . . . The United States today is far in the lead in almost every branch of commercial aviation. In America we have commercial aircraft, engines, equipment, and airlines superior to those of any other country. The greatest part of this progress has been brought about through the airmail. Certainly . . . this development has been carried on in cooperation with the existing government and according to law. If this is not the case it seems the right of the industry and in keeping with

American tradition that facts to the contrary be definitely established. Unless these facts leave no alternative the condemnation of commercial aviation by cancellation of all mail contracts and the use of army pilots on commercial airlines will unnecessarily and greatly damage all American aviation."

Army pilots were basically untrained in cross-country flying and had neither knowledge of nor experience in flying the routes that the mails took across the country. Their airplanes were all open cockpits and contained few of the instruments that had become standard in just a few short years due to Brown's enticements to the airlines. By the end of the first week of flying, five pilots had been killed in accidents and six were critically injured. The Army pilots began flying only in daylight hours, thus delaying mail delivery. Within five weeks, 12 Army pilots had died. It became clear that a major mistake had been made. New bids to reinstate private carriage of the airmail were called for, but under a revised set of rules.

A temporary arrangement had to be put in place immediately, pending adoption of legislation. Postmaster General Farley called a meeting of airline representatives, like Walter Folger Brown had done. But this time, none of the airlines involved in the "spoils conferences," nor any of the executives who attended them, could participate in the new round of bidding. Neither could a bidding airline be involved in the manufacture of aircraft designed to be used in the airline business, like the Boeing-Rentschler combination at United. Vertical holding companies that exercised control over the actual airlines were disallowed. Rectitude reigned supreme in public, but in private, practicality ruled the day. Cosmetic name changes by the Big Four were accepted as serious compliance with the new rules, changes like American Airways becoming American Airlines and Eastern Air Transport becoming Eastern Air Lines. In fact, after the bids were opened on April 20, 1934, the commercial

airline industry looked very much the same as it did before Black started his quest for justice the year before.

Two significant changes did occur. An upstart airline named Braniff Airways beat out United on the Dallas–Chicago route, and the crop dusting C. E. Woolman, operating as Delta Airlines, had secured the Dallas to Charleston, S.C. route. Each of these new airlines would ultimately make the most of their opportunity.

Walter Brown would continue unrepentant and dignified amidst the righteous alarms of Black and other politicians who sought to capitalize at the expense of his reputation. The airlines whose contracts had been terminated, although back in the airmail business within a short time, had lost a significant amount of money by continuing operations in the interim, but only United Air Lines resorted to litigation against the government because of the contract cancellations. That litigation would drag out for another 10 years. And, when finally concluded, it would uphold the government's right to terminate the airmail contracts.[2] The court did, however, award money damages to the United group for contract payments earned prior to the cancellations. The opinion, which is 104 pages in length, is a detailed chronology of the events that transpired after passage of the Watres Act.

The Airmail Act of 1934 (The Black-McKellar Act)

The Black-McKellar Act, passed by Congress in June 1934, codified the arrangements for the award of airmail contracts made in April 1934 (see Figure 14-1), and repealed the powers and prerogative of the Postmaster General as established in the Watres Act. Competitive bidding was reinstated. The newly named airlines bid on the routes. Airline executives involved in the Brown meetings were prohibited from occupying positions of authority in the new airlines. The vertical structure of the airlines

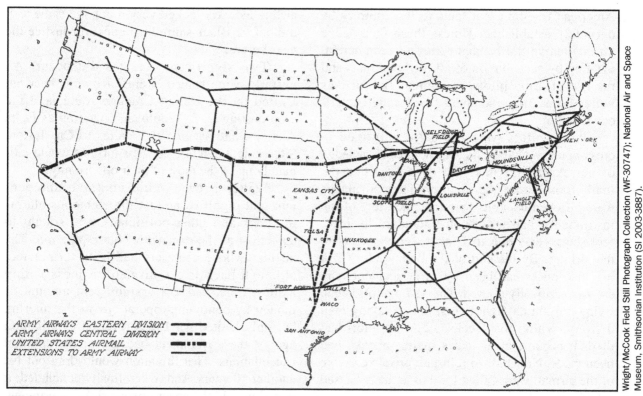

FIGURE 14-1 1934 airmail routes.

and manufacturing companies was prohibited. United Aircraft and Transport, for example, was dismantled and its operations split three ways:

- Boeing took over all operating properties in the West;
- All eastern United States' functions were assumed by United Aircraft Corporation (today known as United Technologies), run by Rentschler;
- Finally the airline itself, United Air Lines, became a separate and independent entity.

The air carrier industry was reorganized under the Act by separating oversight and regulatory authority among:

1. The Post Office, which would continue to award contracts, designate routes, and establish schedules;

2. The Interstate Commerce Commission, which would establish reasonable rates through competitive bidding oversight;

3. The Department of Commerce, which through the Bureau of Air Commerce would attend to safety.

Ultimately, the effect of the Act would be to divest the other large airline operations from their holding companies. Aviation Corporation (AVCO) divested itself of American Airlines, now to be run by C. R. Smith as an independent corporation. North American Aviation (NAA), a complex and diverse entity, was the parent of both TWA and Eastern Air Transport, and had substantial manufacturing interests. NAA first sold off TWA, which was then run by Jack Frye, a pilot's pilot. In due course, Eddie Rickenbacker cobbled together Wall Street financing to the tune of some 3.5 million dollars and bought out the Eastern Air Lines interest. Thus, all of the Big Four were positioned independently for the advent of commercial air transportation and the first comprehensive federal regulation of it.

Pan American, meanwhile, had been unaffected by the so-called Brown scandal and still had its airmail contracts awarded under the Foreign Airmail Act of 1928 by the Postmaster General. The Brown philosophy that the international airmail business should not compete with the domestic airmail business, and vice versa, was intact. The international trade routes that had emerged from the Brown era were not in the least affected by the new law, nor by anything that Black had done, and Pan American was set to become the premier airline of all.

The Railway Labor Act

Transportation during the 1920s was the domain of the railroads, which carried nearly all of the intercity passengers in the nation. The railroads delivered essentially all of the freight of the nation, and employed by far the most workers of any industry in the country.

The hazards of being a railroad employee, particularly those working as members of train crews, like brakemen, conductors, and engineers, or those working on the bridges, tunnels, and rights of way of the railroad, had resulted in a level of deaths and maiming previously unknown. Congress, taking note of the plight of railroad workers, passed a spate of remedial legislation aimed at improving their working conditions and safety. Examples are the Boiler Inspection Act to lessen the risk of locomotive boiler explosions; the Safety Appliance Act to establish safety standards regarding ladders, handholds, and coupling devices on freight cars; and the Air Brake law, which required the installation of air brakes on each railroad car.

Congress also addressed the concerns of workers who had little or no control over their wages or working conditions, and the concerns

of railroad management and the public regarding disruptions of the nation's primary transportation system through labor strife, work stoppages, and violence carried out by railroad workers. The result was the Railway Labor Act of 1926.

The Railway Labor Act, for the first time, provided a legislative scheme to insure workers the right to organize themselves into legally recognized bargaining units, or unions. This required railroad management to accord the workers a voice in their conditions of safety, wages, and working conditions. At the same time, the law restricted the unions' right to disrupt the nation's transportation system through work stoppages and strikes except under the most controlled conditions, and only after federally mandated mediation between workers and management proved fruitless. Even then, the law provided that the president of the United States could require, under certain conditions, that employees continue to work under their existing labor agreements so as not to paralyze the nation's commerce.

Except for the enactment of the Railway Labor Act in 1926, there had been no meaningful federal legislation affecting the larger world of workers and management since the Clayton Antitrust Act of 1914. That statute had exempted labor unions from the constraints of the Sherman Antitrust Act, legislation that had been used by the courts to great effect in enjoining union strike activity. In 1932, Congress passed the Norris-LaGuardia Anti-Injunction Act,[3] which further severely limited the power of courts to issue injunctions in labor disputes.

When the Roosevelt Administration took office in 1933 amidst the distress of working people during the Great Depression, it turned its attention to the general condition of workers outside of the railroad industry. In 1935, Congress passed the Social Security Act to provide protection to workers to cover the risks of old age, death, and the dependency of children, and to provide for the payment of unemployment benefits. Congress also, in 1935, passed the National Labor Relations Act (the Wagner Act),[4] which extended to workers in the nation generally the right to organize, bargain collectively, and to "engage in concerted activities for the purpose of collective bargaining or other mutual aid and protection."

At this point, recognizing that the fledgling air carrier industry, similar to the railroad industry before it, appeared to be on the threshold of assuming some of the transportation needs of the country, Congress exempted airlines and their workers from the broader labor relations law of the Wagner Act and placed the air carrier industry under the Railway Labor Act (RLA), where it has remained. The pilots' union, the Air Line Pilots Association (ALPA), maintains that this result came about, at least in part, because of lobbying efforts by their organization in the early 1930s.

The first airline employee's union, ALPA, was formed in 1931, but it had no legal standing. The airlines required pilots to fly 120 hours a month, but during the depression in 1933, they announced that flight hours would be increased to 140 per month, and at a lower pay scale. A strike was called by the pilots and, in the absence of any law governing the situation, the parties agreed to refer the issue to mediation. Judge Bernard Shintag of the New York Supreme Court took evidence and ruled, among other things, that pilot monthly flight time should be limited to 85 hours per month. Although without the legal standing of enforcement, the ruling, known as Decision 83, was ultimately incorporated into the Civil Aeronautics Act of 1938.

Under the provisions of RLA, airline workers were given the same rights of organizing and collective bargaining as were railroad workers, and airline employees were similarly constrained from conducting work stoppages except under the very specific provisions of the statute.

The main purposes of the Act are:

- The statute intends to establish a system that resolves labor disputes without disrupting interstate and foreign commerce. The statute imposes on both labor and management the obligation to use every reasonable effort to settle disputes. This is the "heart of the Act," as stated by the Supreme Court.
- The statute requires that no change in working conditions or wages be made during negotiations between labor and management. This is called "maintaining the status quo" and generally prohibits management from changing working conditions or wages and prohibits unions from striking or conducting any other type of "work action," like slowdowns or sick outs, during this time.
- The statute prohibits management from interfering with any attempt by workers to organize themselves into collective bargaining units.

There are only two types of "issues" recognized under the Act. Every type of actual or potential disagreement or dispute between the parties is classified as:

- A "major dispute" is one that concerns wages and benefits, working conditions, or rules. These types of disputes are also called "Section 6" disputes and may, after exhaustion of all remedies under the statute, and while the "status quo" is being maintained during negotiations between the parties, result in strike action.
- A "minor dispute" describes all other disputes, and mainly concerns individual employee issues such a disciplinary action. Strikes are prohibited in minor disputes; instead binding arbitration is required in the event that the parties are unable to resolve the issue.

Procedures to be followed are:

1. The party desiring to change the provisions of the labor agreement must give a Section 6

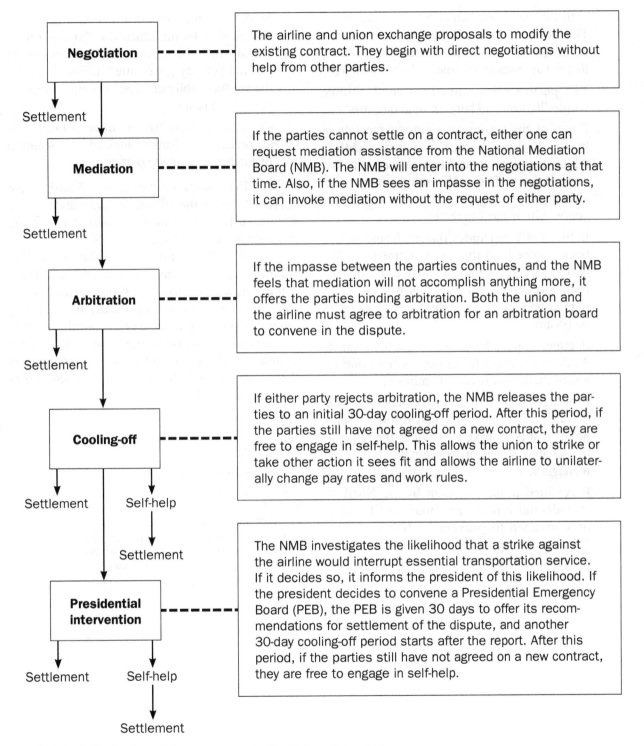

TABLE 14-1 Collective bargaining process under the Railway Labor Act.
Source: GAO analysis of NMB data.

notice of the desired change to the other side. This notice includes the initiation of negotiations after the "amendable date," or the date that the agreement becomes subject to change.

2. The parties must enter into negotiations within 30 days and bargain in good faith.

3. Either of the parties may request mediation by the National Mediation Board (NMB), which appoints a mediator to assist in the negotiations. The NMB may not require either party to agree or to take any other action with respect to the issue.

4. If the NMB concludes that an impasse has been reached, so that no settlement of the issue is likely, it may offer to arbitrate the issue and issue a decision that will be binding on the parties. Both parties must agree to be bound.

5. If either party refuses binding arbitration, a 30-day "cooling off" period begins, during which mediation usually continues.

6. If no agreement is reached by the end of the 30-day period, either side may resort to "self-help," that is, a strike by labor or the imposition of new wages or working conditions by management.

7. If certified to the president by the NMB, a Presidential Emergency Board (PEB) may be convened to prevent "self-help." The PEB has 30 days to investigate and report to the president, after which time an additional 30 days (a total of 60 days) is imposed on the parties to maintain the "status quo." During this time, considerable pressure is exerted both by government officials and by the media (public opinion) to cause a resolution of the issue.

8. Congress is empowered upon a failure of all preceding efforts to legislate a resolution that is binding on the parties.

No Presidential Emergency Boards were convened during the 1930s, nor until after World War II. In fact, the first labor agreement in the airlines was not negotiated until 1939.[5]

It should be noted that the RLA was extended only to airlines, or "carriers" as defined in the Act, and not to other forms of transportation. The trucking industry, buses, and shipping under the Merchant Marine fall under the NLRB.

Significant developments in airline labor relations, both before and after the deregulation of the airlines in 1978, will be discussed beginning in Chapter 29.

Endnotes

1. *Time Magazine*, August 26, 1935.
2. Pacific Air Transport v. U.S., et al.
3. 27 USC §101–115.
4. 29 USC §151–166.
5. Presidential Emergency Boards under the Railway Labor Act <http://www.ilr.cornell.edu/library/e_archive/miscellaneous/airlines/emergency.pdf>.

15　State of the Airlines before the Civil Aeronautics Act

The Big Four, having been established largely through the efforts of Walter Brown, and having survived the Black investigation and the resulting remedial legislation (Black-McKellar), were well positioned for the beginnings of the modern era of commercial air transportation. The airlines were hurting financially, however, due to the losses experienced during the stand down period when the Army had flown the mail after the cancellation of all CAM routes in February 1934, and because the new rates mandated by Black-McKellar were set to a maximum of 33.5 cents per mile, less than a third of the going rate in 1929.

But progress had been made. In 1929, the contract mail carriers (who were to become the country's major airlines) were still flying wood and wire airplanes, although a few had acquired the very latest technology in the Fokker or Ford trimotors. By the late 1930s, when the Civil Aeronautics Act was passed, great innovations in aircraft manufacture had occurred, largely due to a combination of commitments and risks undertaken by the airlines, by the aircraft manufacturers and engine manufacturers, and to government innovations achieved at the National Advisory Committee on Aeronautics.

■ The National Advisory Committee on Aeronautics (NACA)

We first learned about NACA in Chapter 9 in connection with the ending of the patent litigation between Glenn Curtiss and the Wright brothers. This one accomplishment freed up the development of aerodynamics for the country, which had been paralyzed by the patent litigation. NACA's importance cannot be understated (in 1958 it would become NASA) as a progressive force in American aeronautics. Because of its importance, it will appear from time to time in this book.

As we saw, it was created in 1915 as an aeronautical research laboratory, at a time when the national government had fallen well behind European countries in developments in aviation. World War I (1914–1918) had the effect of pointing out that aviation was rapidly becoming an issue of national defense. The year 1915 was a transformational one for the United States and the world, even aside from the effects of World War I. The Panama Canal, which had opened just the year before, was treated as a national asset and essential in the defense of the United States. Robert Goddard had started experimenting with rockets and Albert Einstein had announced his general theory of relativity. Alexander Graham Bell made the first transcontinental telephone call and a new automobile speed record had been established of 102.6 miles per hour (still slower than Curtiss' motorcycle speed record of 136 miles per hour set in 1907).

In the United States, aerodynamic research was a far-flung undertaking. Experiments were conducted at the Navy Yard, the Bureau of Standards tested engines, experiments in aeronautics were sometimes undertaken at Catholic University in Washington, a curriculum in aeronautics was being developed at the Massachusetts Institute of Technology, and Stanford University ran propeller tests. Although the NACA charter provided for the possibility of an independent laboratory, by 1917 none existed. NACA was set up as a loose organization, consisting of a main committee of 12 members, who met semiannually in Washington, and an Executive Committee of 7 members who did the actual work of supervising NACA activities and proposed activities. They decided their best bet was to tag along to the Army's new proposed airfield construction across the river from Norfolk, Virginia, to be called Langley Field after Samuel Pierpont Langley, formerly of the Smithsonian. NACA named its new laboratory the "Langley Memorial Aeronautical Laboratory," or just "Langley."

When completed in 1920, the small Langley NACA component consisted of a staff of just 11 people, mostly civil or mechanical engineers, who did their work without the normal formalities of government institutions. By 1925 the staff had grown to 100. At that time the engineers had 19 airplanes dedicated to test operations with two wind tunnels, as well as a new engine research lab for high altitude flight and increased climb capabilities.

NACA's variable density wind tunnel, recognized in the 1920s to be the world's best, allowed the engineers to develop and test various airfoil shapes, resulting in 78 different airfoil cross-sections with designated camber lines, thicknesses, and nose features. Independent aircraft designers by 1933 could select an airfoil from the catalogue for any desired performance they wished in any airplane they were in the process of designing.

A new propeller wind tunnel was completed at Langley in 1927. For the first time, this 20-foot diameter tunnel allowed the testing of full-sized aircraft models, and it was put to work on attempts to solve the problem of drag associated with radial engines.

As we saw in Chapter 11, conventional wisdom in the 1920s held that inline liquid-cooled engines were superior to radial engines because of several factors, including "head resistance," cooling, and horsepower. In 1926, the Navy asked NACA to conduct cowling research for radial engines at the same time that Pratt & Whitney was developing the Wasp. The Navy had found that carrier landings by aircraft using liquid cooled engines resulted in cracks in the cooling system and attachments, which mandated a different engine solution than the Army had found acceptable.

By 1927, after hundreds of tests, a technical breakthrough was achieved, and subsequent practical tests showed that the military test aircraft increased its speed from 118 to 137 miles per hour solely by use of the NACA-conceived cowling. When applied commercially, NACA estimated savings to the airmail/airline industry of over $5 million, which was more than all the money that had been appropriated for NACA from its inception to 1928.[1]

The results of cowling research alone justified NACA's creation. The cowling-drag breakthrough boosted the preeminence of American engine and aircraft design, and allowed the creation of the modern reciprocating-engine airliners of the 1930s, like the Boeing 247 and the DC-3 with their all-metal construction, retractable landing gear, and powerful radial engines.

Now let us take a look at the commercial side of aviation as we progress through the 1930s.

■ The Big Four
American Airlines

American Airlines emerged as the surviving corporate entity after Black-McKellar. Aviation Corporation (AVCO) had been formed in early 1929 as a holding company by a group of New York financiers, and it rapidly proceeded to acquire aviation-related companies left and right. Its holdings included airports, instrument manufacturers, and engine makers, and finally totaled more than 80 separate companies, some having absolutely nothing in common with the others. In early 1930, AVCO consolidated its aviation holdings into American Airways, the name under which the airmail contracts would be serviced in the early 1930s.

American Airways had been formed from eleven smaller lines. Some had their beginnings as early as 1925, notably Embry-Riddle Company (first to be acquired), and 1926, such as Colonial Air Transport, Southern Air Transport, Robertson Aircraft Corp, and Southern Air Fast Express (SAFE).

E. L. Cord, who had bested Harriman and Lehman for control of Aviation Corporation, made C. R. Smith, who had come from Southern Air Transport, president of the new American Airlines in 1934. Smith had a penchant for detail worthy of his training and experience as a bookkeeper and part-time bank examiner, and he ran the company with a hands-on approach that, by 1939, would make American Airlines the nation's foremost air carrier in passenger miles flown. Upon his election as president, and while American was flying a conglomeration of airplanes ranging from the trimotor monoplanes to the bi-wing Curtiss Condors, he immediately placed orders with Douglas Aircraft for the new DC-2. Then, in 1935, he ordered the DC-3, the airplane that was to revolutionize commercial air travel. The DC-3, in fact, was a direct result of collaboration between Smith and Douglas to make modifications to the DC-2 that American wanted. The main change desired by Smith was a wider cabin, but in the process of this change, other significant changes in the DC-2 were made, including a new wing, a hydraulic system, insulation, and a much better landing gear and suspension system.

In 1937, American Airlines' route structure included New York to Los Angeles, the southern route, via Washington, D.C., Nashville, and Dallas. It also had New York to Boston, New York to Montreal, and New York to Buffalo and thence to Chicago, St. Louis, and Oklahoma City.

Eastern Air Lines

Eastern Air Lines emerged in 1934 as the surviving entity following Black-McKellar. The predecessor company, Eastern Air Transport, was owned by the holding company, North American Aviation, which in turn was controlled by General Motors as of 1933. Eddie Rickenbacker (see Figure 15-1), World War I hero and fighter ace, was hired by General Motors as a consultant and then was made general manager of Eastern Air

FIGURE 15-1 Eddie Rickenbacker.

Source: Library of Congress.

Transport in 1934. Eastern Air Transport was successor to the original line, Pitcairn Aviation, and it later absorbed the Luddington Line and New York Airways before becoming Eastern Air Lines. When General Motors tired of the airline business in 1938, Rickenbacker purchased the company and steadily increased its business and its mileage.

In 1937, Eastern Air Lines had routes from New York to Miami and to Atlanta and points south and west, New Orleans, Houston, and San Antonio, all through Washington, D.C. It also flew the Chicago to Miami route through Indianapolis, Nashville, and Atlanta.

TWA

TWA was the designation taken by the airline combined at the behest of Walter Folger Brown. A combination of the former Transcontinental Air Transport (TAT) and Western Air Express, it flew the middle transcontinental route from New York to Los Angeles under the name Transcontinental and Western Air. After Black-McKellar, the airline simply added "Inc." after its name in order to comply with the prohibition of Postmaster General Farley that precluded those airlines which had participated in the Brown meetings from bidding on the new airmail contracts in 1934.

TWA had been a part of North American Aviation in the early 1930s, and General Motors controlled the holding company. After Brown-McKellar, General Motors sold its interests to John D. Hertz and Lehman Brothers, who then had effective control of TWA.

Jack Frye, at the age of 26, was TWA's operational vice president in 1930. He had founded Standard Air Lines in the 1920s, after stints at flight instructing and stunt flying, and went with the company when it was purchased by Western Air Express. With the merger of Western and TAT, he suddenly found himself in charge of operations of a transcontinental airline. TWA, and most other airlines, relied heavily on the trimotors in the early 1930s. With the 1931 crash of the Fokker Trimotor in which Notre Dame football coach Knute Rockne was killed, government-mandated inspections of that plane's wooden wing structure became cost-prohibitive, not to mention the fact that the flying public thereafter was not keen on stepping aboard that airplane. Frye needed new equipment.

In 1932, Frye had heard the buzz in the aviation community of a new prototype in the works at Boeing, the model 247. (See Figure 15-2.) This airplane was to be a giant leap forward with its low mono-wing, and two engines instead of three that were mounted into the wings in nacelles (taking

Source: National Air and Space Museum.

FIGURE 15-2 The Boeing 247 was to be a great leap forward with its low mono-wing and two engines instead of three that were mounted into wings in nacelles that greatly reduced drag.

advantage of NACA research) that greatly reduced drag. The 247 used stressed all-metal skin, retractable landing gear (a first), insulated cabin walls, hot water heating, and double ventilation systems. This airplane would fly from one coast to the other in only 19$\frac{1}{2}$ hours, 12 hours less than with the trimotors. Fueling stops were reduced from 14 to 6. Frye decided that TWA had to have these airplanes.

When he inquired, he was advised that United Airlines (the sister company to the Boeing manufacturing arm) had already placed an order for 60 of the new planes, an order that it would take all of two years to fill, thus precluding any deliveries to other airlines. The 247 became operational in June 1933.

In the fall of 1932, Frye wrote to a number of aircraft manufacturers setting out airplane performance specifications for new equipment that TWA would be interested in purchasing. Although the specifications included that the airplane have three engines, the engineers at a small company located in California, known as Douglas Aircraft, believed that the performance specifications could be met with a twin engine design, including the requirement for a 10,000 foot minimum service ceiling on one engine (necessary to clear the Rockies).

A prototype was fielded in July 1933, the DC-1 (see Figure 15-3), the designation for the Douglas Commercial Number 1. If this had been poker, the DC-1 would have called the B-247 and raised it. The DC-1 engine mountings and cowling were similar to the 247, incorporating the design developed by NACA, but the landing gear of the DC-1 folded up into the engine nacelles. The engines, Wright Cyclones, had been engineered to produce 710 horsepower due to 87-octane gasoline having become commercially available during the period of the plane's construction. Although the constant speed propeller was still a few years off, the DC-1 did have a 2-speed propeller that could be set either for takeoff or for cruise (a first). Additional firsts included an automatic pilot and efficient wing flaps. Flight tests showed that Frye's performance specifications had been met. Only one DC-1 was built and that one was purchased by TWA. It was placed in limited service in 1933.

When Postmaster General Farley sent his notice dated February 9, 1934, canceling all airmail contracts effective February 19, 1934, Frye decided to make his own statement. With Eddie Rickenbacker of Eastern Air Transport as co-pilot, on February 18, 1934, Frye took off from Los

FIGURE 15-3 DC-1, designation for the Douglas Commercial Number 1. This was the only one ever built.

Angeles in the DC-1 loaded with airmail and flew it to Newark, with fueling stops in Kansas City and Columbus, in 13 hours and 4 minutes, setting the transcontinental speed record at the time.

The DC-2, with 14 seats, was brought to production in 1934, and 193 were built. The next year, in 1935, Douglas came out with the DC-3 (see Figure 15-4) (21 seats) with 900-horsepower

FIGURE 15-4 DC-3—The plane that changed the world.

Source: Florida State Archives.

Wright Cyclones (DC-3A with 1,200-horsepower P&W engines), and Douglas would, before it was all over, build 455 of them for commercial use and 10,174 for the military. By 1936, the DC-3 had reduced the transcontinental flying time to about 17 hours. The airplane was awarded the Collier Trophy in 1936 and became known as "the plane that changed the world." And, indeed, it was used all over the world—in World War II in Burma, this airplane, which at normal configuration seated 21 passengers, set a load record of 72 refugees safely delivered, and 6 more stowaways were discovered on landing.

By late 1938, pressurized airplanes were on the drawing boards. Boeing designed a commercial transport, the 307 (see Figure 15-5), scheduled for delivery in 1939. It was based on the basic B-17 design with four 900-horsepower Wright R-1820 Cyclone engines. This airplane had a service ceiling of 26,200 feet and was the first commercial liner pressurized for high-altitude flight. The airplane came to be known as the "Stratoliner." Jack Frye decided that TWA had to have them too, so he placed an order

FIGURE 15-5 Boeing 307.

Source: Florida State Archives.

with Boeing for five of the new planes. But his board of directors, chaired by John D. Hertz of Lehman Brothers, did not agree. In December 1938, TWA's board voted to cancel Frye's order to Boeing for the B-307.

Jack Frye knew that this dispute represented an essential disagreement concerning his and the board's vision for the future of TWA. He also knew that this disagreement would likely mean his being removed if control of the company remained in the hands of the present directors. Jack Frye was acquainted with Howard Hughes (see Figure 15-6), the eccentric multimillionaire and aviation pioneer in his own right, who was then living in Los Angeles and involved in the movie-making business. Hughes had an abiding interest in aviation and had even worked for American Airlines, under an assumed name, as a co-pilot in 1932, flying between Los Angeles and Chicago. He listened to Frye, sided with his logic in the B-307 dispute with the board of directors, and agreed to buy the company. He began secretly buying up TWA stock. By April, it was public knowledge that Hughes was becoming a substantial stockholder in the airline, so much so that the significant interests represented by Lehman and Hertz decided to pull out of the company, the second time Lehman had

FIGURE 15-6 Howard Hughes, the eccentric multimillionaire and aviation pioneer.

departed the field. Control was effectively passed to Howard Hughes, the Boeing order for the 307 was reinstated, and the future of TWA remained firmly in the grip of Jack Frye, now with Howard Hughes. On July 8, 1940, the 307 was placed into service on the New York to Los Angeles route, reducing the transcontinental flying time to 14½ hours.

Hughes was a singular individual and unique in all known respects. He was born wealthy, son of the founder of the Hughes Tool Company of Houston, Texas. As soon as he could, he left Houston, began traveling the world, and wound up in Hollywood. He entered the film business and, in the process of directing his first film, *Hell's Angels,* a story of British pilots in World War I, he became fascinated with aviation and learned to fly.

Even as a young man, Hughes was obsessive, wanting to be the best, to know the most, and never to fail. With absolutely no concerns about money, he began the design and building of an airplane racer, the H-1, with which he would set a world's speed record of 352 miles per hour in 1935. He set a transcontinental speed record of 7 hours and 27 minutes with the H-1 in January 1936. He flew practically every commercial airplane in production over the next several years, gaining experience in long-distance navigation and planning, as well as execution at the controls, until he launched his most ambitious attempt yet: a round the world flight in the Lockheed Electra.

The record in 1938 stood from Wiley Post's solo circumnavigation in 1933 at 7 days and 18 hours. Hughes' route took him from New York to Paris in less than half the time it took Lindbergh, then across Europe into Russia and Siberia to Alaska. From Fairbanks he refueled in Minneapolis and returned to Floyd Bennett Field in New York triumphant in three and a half days, halving Post's record.

Hughes had some prior acquaintance with TWA; in fact, one of its vice presidents had been a stunt pilot for Hughes' movie, *Hell's*

Source: Library of Congress.

Angels. Hughes was also more pilot than businessman. As Jack Frye would later remark, "One thing about Hughes, he did have an understanding about the airplane." He fully understood the advantage of having an airplane that could top most of the weather, so he agreed with Frye's position on the Boeing 307.

United Airlines

United Airlines' name came through the Black and Brown affair unscathed. This was because each of the airmail carrying lines operated in their own names, for example, Boeing Air Transport, Pacific Air Transport, and United Air Lines Transport Corporation. The chief operating officers of the companies caught up in the Brown affair were banished. Thus, United's Phil Johnson left the stage and the presidency of United Airlines was assumed by Pat Patterson, a 34-year-old former banker who came up through the ranks from Pacific Air Transport.

Patterson is credited with initiating the in-flight passenger service staffed by young women, initially nurses, in 1930. The United group was the strongest of the airlines of the 1930s. It was United's lead that counted with the other airlines when Patterson decided to continue passenger and freight service in spite of the cancellation of the airmail contracts in 1934, as he said, "no matter what the losses." United maintained its schedules but at tremendous cost. Even with the return of airmail contracts, given the reduced rate then paid and the losses suffered during the cancellation period, United lost more than two million dollars in 1934, and continued to struggle financially over the last years of the 1930s, falling behind American Airlines with revenues less than half of American by 1938.

The United group, in their individual operating names (Pacific Air Transport, Boeing Air Transport, etc.) had been the lone airline group to sue the government over the airmail cancellation decision in 1934. That litigation would drag

on and not be finally resolved until 1942, when the decision of the U.S. Court of Claims was handed down.[2] The court upheld the right of the government to cancel the contracts, but awarded damages to United for those sums representing United's airmail carriage up to the date of cancellation. The language of the opinion is generally considered to be favorable to United and not in keeping with the tone of the Black investigation and the negative airline press it generated.

It can be argued that United's difficulties beginning in 1934 were due to an unfriendly relationship between the Roosevelt Administration (which would remain in office until 1945) and United due to the litigation, and exacerbated by a general anti-corporate attitude in certain government quarters. For example, the Interstate Commerce Commission (ICC) had assumed responsibility for rates and mergers as a result of Black-McKellar. In 1936, the ICC refused to approve a merger between United and a money-making line serving New York–Washington. When the Civil Aeronautics Authority took over the ICC function in 1938, it denied purchase authority for United's bid for Western Air Express (the split-off branch that did not merge with TAT to form TWA). United, with its 10-passenger Boeing Model 247s, was struggling to compete against the larger and faster DC-2s and DC-3s of the other lines.

In 1937, United still had its transcontinental route, but that was in heavy competition with the other routes awarded by Brown. It did not have the strength of the eastern lines that resulted from their consolidation of the shorter route structure between cities of the more populous eastern United States. Not until the 1960s would United be once again the airline industry leader.

The Lesser Lines

In 1938 it was the Big Four and then everybody else. Some of the smaller lines would fade away; others would prosper under the new law. When the Civil Aeronautics Act passed Congress, notables among the small lines were Delta, Northwest, Western Air Express, Braniff, National, and Continental. Much would be heard from them in the future. And then there was Pan American.

Pan American Airways

Pan American Airways was to occupy a singular place in the annals of American aviation and in the relationship of an airline company with the U.S. government. What Pan Am came to be was mostly a product of the efforts of Juan Trippe, a true visionary, an indefatigable worker and thinker, a man of exceptional personal and professional contacts in both the world of business and government, and a man who stayed at the helm of his company longer than any of his contemporaries.

Trippe was instrumental in the formation and early operation of Colonial Airlines, one of the original airmail contract flyers in 1926 that ultimately became part of American Airways. His vision for that airline was much too aggressive for its conservative directors and stockholders, and Trippe was soon out. He had actually formed a small airline in 1924, before the financial benefits of airmail carriage became available, but it had been unable to survive. After Colonial Airlines, he was soon underway with his concept of an international airline, lining up financing from his wealthy friends and his father's Wall Street contacts.

By 1927, Pan American was in the firm control of Juan Trippe and his friends. That year, wheeling, dealing, merging, and negotiating their way, the young men of Pan American had an airmail contract for the Key West, Florida to Havana, Cuba route. The contract stipulated that service must commence at the latest by October 19, 1927, and since other companies were waiting in the wings hoping Pan American would default, it became a matter of some importance to meet the deadline.

The Fokker Trimotors that Trippe had ordered to service the route had not shown up by that date, so the inaugural flight of Pan American Airways was hastily arranged on the dock at Key West on the drop-dead date. A transient floatplane pilot, bound for a job in Haiti, made a fortuitous fuel stop that day and unwittingly became a part of the grand history of Pan American, for a cash fee of $175.00. In fact, this unknown itinerate pilot was an essential catalyst to the creation of the Pan American Airlines that came to be.

Trippe's vision was fueled not only by his expansive imagination and unbridled determination, but also by the circumstances in which America found itself in the late 1920s. The 1920s had been a decade of progress, experimentation, expansion, and success. World War I had caused Americans to look outward, mainly toward Europe, but now toward the untapped vast South American continent and the Latin American connection. The region was ideally suited to air transportation because of its island-hopping availability. South America was also largely undeveloped, ruled by mountains, smothered by jungles, and it had largely skipped the era of railroad expansion. Transportation was about to go from pack mule and water skiff directly to air travel.

Europeans, mainly Germans seeking respite from the turmoil and inflation of their defeated nation, had opened up aerial trading routes to South America in 1919. They were expanding their influence along its eastern coast and up into the Caribbean. The expatriates formed a company called Sociedad Colombo-Aleman de Transposes Aereos (SCADTA) under the laws of Colombia that had become, as one of the world's first airlines, an example of what aviation could do under extremely challenging conditions. In the process, SCADTA had become the pride of the people of Colombia.

The United States looked with some alarm at this development. The long-standing policy of the United States, as articulated in the "Monroe

Doctrine,"[3] after all, essentially decreed the Americas for Americans, not Europeans, and certainly not the Germans. The governmental policy toward commercial aviation that was forming during the 1920s held that, while competition among business interests within the United States was good for the public, competition between American businesses outside its borders could be harmful. To properly compete with foreign airlines that were strongly supported by their governments, American international aviation would have to have some form of American government support and should follow some kind of governmental policy.

Pan American was ideally positioned to take advantage of this political and economic situation, and Juan Trippe commanded the confidence of the right people in government and business to enhance Pan American's opportunities. The first Trippe ploy was to take advantage of a practice common in the domestic aviation market to "extend" route authority by fiat of the Postmaster General. This he did by securing an extension authority from the Key West to Havana route to Miami from Key West. After Lindbergh's epic transatlantic flight and the ensuing public clamor and appeal that it engendered, Trippe signed Lindy up as a consultant, and Lindbergh became an integral part of the Pan Am strategy to extend its routes across the Caribbean and into Central America and then down into South America. In time, he would also figure prominently in Pan American's westward Pacific expansion.

The second significant development was the passage by Congress in 1928 of the "Foreign Airmail Act." This statute allowed the Postmaster General the discretion to grant routes to bidders that, in his opinion, were the "lowest responsible bidders that can perform the service satisfactorily." The Act provided, in so many words, that only airlines capable of operating on a scale and in a manner that would project the dignity of the United States in Latin America would be granted the right to carry international mail. The only airline that fit this description was Pan American.

The first three airplanes purchased by Pan American were land-based Fokker Trimotors. (See Figure 15-9.) With these, the first passenger service between Key West and Havana was begun in January 1928. Given the lack of airports over the region and the fact that most of the flying was over water, Pan American made two significant decisions about its near-term future:

1. The line would employ flying boats to the exclusion of other types of aircraft.
2. The line would fly only multiengine planes.

These decisions weighed favorably with the public and with the government.

It was also required that a form of navigation be developed that would allow flight over the trackless ocean. There were obviously no railroads to follow, no landmarks to navigate by, and no open fields to land in. Celestial navigation, long used in maritime transportation, was available, but it had serious limitations as the sole method of navigation for relatively fast moving airplanes. Voice radio was being experimented with on domestic air routes, but the equipment necessary to be placed on board approximated the size and weight of a small piano. Pan American had decided that radio was a near necessity from a safety standpoint, and it was searching for alternatives. An employee of RCA well versed in radio, Hugo Leuteritz, began experimenting with radiotelegraphy with devices that were installed on some of the airplanes. The equipment on board was very light, and the signals were clear and not beset by the static that made voice communication at these latitudes almost impossible. The procedure developed by Leuteritz utilized two land-based listening stations equipped with loop antennae that could pick up and then directionally locate the dots and dashes emitting from the en route aircraft. When the two stations drew lines from their separate positions to that of the aircraft, and the two lines crossed, the latitude and longitude thus determined were transmitted by the shore station to the radio operator aboard the

Source: ATA Annual Report 1937.

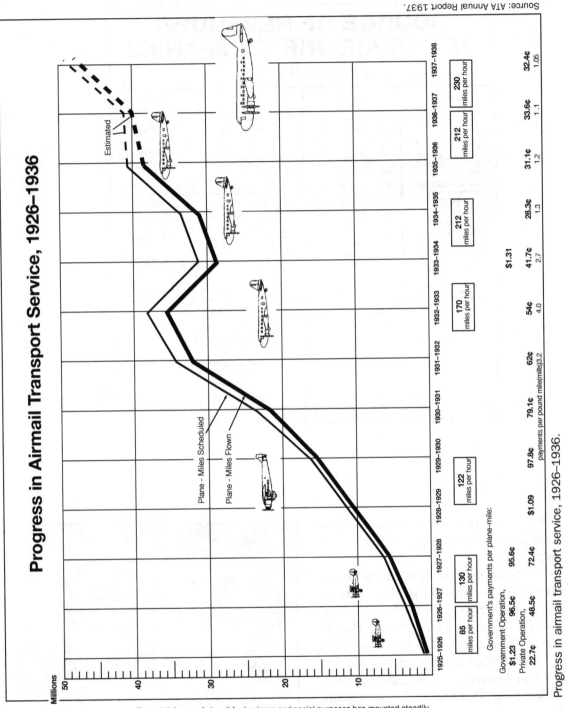

Progress in Airmail Transport Service, 1926–1936

	1925–1926	1926–1927	1927–1928	1928–1929	1929–1930	1930–1931	1931–1932	1932–1933	1933–1934	1934–1935	1935–1936	1936–1937	1937–1938
miles per hour	85 miles per hour	130 miles per hour		122 miles per hour				170 miles per hour		212 miles per hour	212 miles per hour	230 miles per hour	

Government's payments per plane-mile:

	1925–1926	1926–1927	1927–1928		1929–1930	1930–1931	1931–1932	1932–1933	1933–1934	1934–1935	1935–1936	1936–1937	1937–1938
Government Operation,	$1.23	96.5¢	95.6¢						$1.31				
Private Operation,	22.7¢	48.5¢	72.4¢	$1.09	97.8¢	79.1¢	62¢	54¢	41.7¢	28.3¢	31.1¢	33.6¢	32.4¢
payments per pound mile (mills)						3.2		4.0	2.7	1.3	1.2	1.1	1.05

Plane - Miles Scheduled

Plane - Miles Flown

Estimated

Millions
50
40
30
20
10

The public's use of airmail for business and social purposes has mounted steadily.

(The decline during the fiscal year 1934, and in the subsequent interval required for repairing the decline, was caused by the cancellation of the airmail contracts.)

As volume has mounted, the unit cost to the government has steadily decreased. (Note figures at extreme bottom of chart.)

FIGURE 15-7 Progress in airmail transport service, 1926–1936.

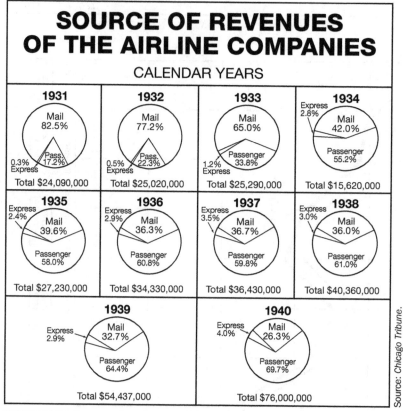

FIGURE 15-8 Source of revenues of the airline companies.

aircraft and its fix would be established. This method allowed pinpoint accuracy in making the desired landfall.

When the Sikorsky S-38 twin-engine flying boats arrived (see Figure 15-10), Pan American's chief pilot, Captain Eddie Musick (see Figure 15-11), began to make survey flights beyond Havana to anticipated destinations even before the Post Office advertised for bids. It seemed that Pan American had an uncanny knack for already knowing where the routes were going to be offered, and for sewing up the local political and logistical support, including landing rights, necessary to make the routes immediately feasible and successful.

FIGURE 15-9 Fokker F-7 to Havana, Pan American 1928.

FIGURE 15-10 S-38.

FIGURE 15-12 Charles Lindbergh and an S-38 in Miami.

FIGURE 15-11 Igor Sikorsky and Eddie Musick.

FIGURE 15-13 Charles Lindbergh and an S-38.

The next two routes awarded to Pan American were (1) from Havana to the Mexican island of Cozumel, then down Central America to Panama, and (2) from Havana to San Juan, Puerto Rico which suddenly increased Pan American's annual airmail revenues from $160,000 to $2 million. Passenger service was then initiated on February 4, 1929, with Lindbergh at the controls flying the 100-mile per hour S-38. With the first flying boats,

service was commenced directly between Miami and Panama. (See Figures 15-12 and 15-13.) These two lucrative routes were soon followed by a third, from Miami to Mexico City, where linkups were made to the west coast of the United States. Airmail revenues soon topped $3 million a year.

Airmail routes in the Caribbean, Central America, and South America were consistently awarded only to Pan American in what was becoming the obvious policy of the United States government of allowing Pan American to be the "Chosen Instrument" of U.S. foreign influence.

This was despite the emergence of another American-formed airline, the New York, Rio, and Buenos Aires Airways (NYRBA), which began a head-on competition with Pan American in the region utilizing flying boats.

While Pan American went with the S-38, NYRBA ordered 14 of the Consolidated Commodore (see Figure 15-14), an amphibian designed as a patrol boat for the United States Navy, but which was converted to commercial use by September 1929. The Commodore mounted two 575-horsepower Hornet engines beneath its high wing. It was put into service on the Miami to Santiago, Chile route down the west coast of South America, a 9,000-mile route requiring seven days en route. It was also used on the east coast route to Buenos Aires.

Big names associated with NYRBA, like James Rand (of Remington Rand), former Assistant Secretary of Commerce for Aeronautics William McCracken, and William J. Donovan (credited with forming the Central Intelligence Agency), were unable by the middle of 1930 to secure even one foreign U.S. airmail contract. The airline was losing money on a then-gargantuan scale ($50,000 a month) and, without help from the government, its backers saw no alternative to a sellout. On August 19, 1930, Pan American, with unofficial Post Office approval, bought out the NYRBA line. The next day, the Post Office Department advertised the east coast of South America airmail route. Pan American, of course, was the only bidder and it bid the maximum allowable rate.

By 1930, Pan Am was flying 20,000 route miles to 20 different countries, and it was still within the Western Hemisphere. (See Figure 15-15.) Trippe was obviously the American government's "fair-haired child," but his efforts at establishing transatlantic service were continuously thwarted by the British. Although the British agreed in principle with the proposition of bilateral rights between America and England, the standing position was that they were not physically or financially ready to compete with the United States, and until they were, no American rights would be granted. Because of the long distances, Europe was not considered a feasible destination without landing rights in Bermuda, and

FIGURE 15-14 The Consolidated Commodore was originally designed as a patrol boat for the United States Navy, but was converted to commercial use by September 1929.

Source: Florida State Archives.

Adapted from Orion Books.

FIGURE 15-15 Pan American airways route map 1933.

since that island was strictly English, no European schedules of any sort were considered possible. Trippe turned his attention to the Pacific.

The range, in miles, of available aircraft was the most severely limiting factor in attempting a traverse of the vast Pacific Ocean. Sikorsky was the first to complete an aircraft design that attempted to address this problem, the S-40 flying boat. (See Figures 15-16 through 15-18.) This model boasted four engines, had a capacity of 44 passengers, and a range of 1,000 miles. The first S-40 was delivered to Pan American on October 10, 1931, and was christened by Mrs. Herbert Hoover at the Annapolis Naval Air Station. She broke a bottle of Caribbean seawater across the prow of the S-40, after which Juan Trippe dubbed the airplane a Pan American "Flagship." Thus was the appellation "Clipper" born.

Shortly thereafter, the S-42 (see Figures 15-19 and 15-20), with a range of 2,520 miles, came off the line. This was still a bit short for the 2,410 mile San Francisco-to-Honolulu run, if any reserve of fuel for weather or other contingencies were to be made. Trippe turned to Glenn Martin for help, while at the same time flying the S-42 configured with extra fuel tanks to assure another 500 miles.

With Lindbergh's help, it was Trippe's plan that the Pacific would be conquered by way of Alaska, Japan, China, and points south, the kind of Great Circle route Lindbergh had used in 1927 to Paris. No airmail contract had been awarded to Pan Am, but Trippe was proceeding anyway. He bagged a majority interest in an airline with operating rights in China called the China National Aviation Corporation, but then, in 1934, Japan was becoming militarily aggressive, and the U.S. State Department advised against the

FIGURE 15-16   The S-40 was the first aircraft to address the problem of range over the vast Pacific Ocean.

Source: Florida State Archives.

FIGURE 15-17   S-40. Approaching Pan Am's Dinner Key Terminal, FL.

Source: Florida State Archives.

FIGURE 15-18 S-40. Taking off from Biscayne Bay, FL.

Source: Florida State Archives.

FIGURE 15-19 The S-42 had a range of 2,520 miles.

Source: Florida State Archives.

proposed route. To go straight across the Pacific would require a route including Honolulu, Midway, Wake Island, and Guam before reaching Manila, Philippines. Aside from the fact that the Sikorsky aircraft was limited in range, there were absolutely no facilities on Midway, Wake, or Guam.

In typical fashion, Trippe had a freighter loaded with the necessary equipment, supplies, workmen, and supervisors and dispatched it to each of the proposed landing sites to construct the necessary passenger and aircraft support facilities, including terminals and hotels. With this service archipelago in place, and with

FIGURE 15-20   An S-42.

Source: Florida State Archives.

FIGURE 15-21   S-43—on glassy water.

Source: Florida State Archives.

landing rights in Hong Kong, Pan American was poised to be the first transpacific airline with service from the American to the Chinese coasts.

In October 1935, the first M-130 Martin flying boat was delivered (the first of three). (See Figures 15-22 through 15-24.) This craft was larger than any other flying at the time. It had a range of 4,000 miles configured for mail and 3,200 miles with 12 passengers, a cruising speed of 163 miles per hour and redundant hydraulic and electrical systems. With the airmail contract secured, service was inaugurated for mail and cargo delivery on November 22, 1935, in a ceremony at the dock in San Francisco attended by Postmaster General Farley. In October 1936, with the support facilities now in place, passenger service across the Pacific Ocean began to Manila. A New Zealand route followed after Australia was blocked by the British, and then a second, southern transpacific route was initiated

FIGURE 15-22 In October 1935 the first M-130 Martin Flying Boat was delivered.

Source: Florida State Archives.

FIGURE 15-23 M-130 and Commodore at Dinner Key Terminal.

Source: Florida State Archives.

via Kingman Reef and Pago Pago. On April 21, 1937, the transpacific route was extended to Hong Kong, with connecting flights to destinations in China serviced by the Pan Am subsidiary, China National Aviation Corporation. Then, within a six-month period, December 1937 to the summer of 1938, Pan American suffered two highly publicized clipper accidents that brought unaccustomed criticism, both from the press and from government quarters. Chief Pilot Eddie Musick, who had surveyed the original Latin American routes 10 years before, was at the controls of an S-40 off of Somoa when it exploded in

midair. In July 1938, one of the three Martin 130 Clippers disappeared between the Philippines and Guam. The intense expansion of routes over the Pacific was taking a heavy toll and, while Pan Am banked over $1 million in profits from Latin American operations in 1938, it was losing large sums of money in the Pacific. Trippe turned his energies back to the Atlantic.

On February 22, 1937, the British Air Ministry issued Pan Am a permit to operate a regular air service between the United Kingdom and the United States via intermediate points in Canada, Bermuda, Ireland, and Portugal. The agreement by Pan Am to pool passengers and cargo with the British airline, Imperial Airways, had a lot to do with this breakthrough. Technological advances, however, followed shortly on the heels of diplomacy. On order from Pan American since 1936, Boeing in 1938 produced its B-314 clipper (see Figure 15-25), the largest aircraft to be used in scheduled service then or thereafter until the arrival of the jumbo jets of the late 1960s. This airplane was configured in two decks, had a speed of 193 miles per hour and a range of 3,500 miles, enough range to allow Pan American to fly right over Bermuda en route to Europe. It carried 74 passengers seated or 40 passengers in the sleeping berth configuration. The Clipper went into the Pacific route service on February 22, 1939. (See Figures 15-26 and 15-27.)

In the Atlantic, Pan American launched its passenger service between New York and Marseille, France, on June 28, 1939 with the Dixie Clipper, a Boeing 314A, followed on July 8, 1939, by Yankee Clipper service from New York to Southampton.

■ Summary of Airlines' Condition

The effects of the Great Depression were lessening by 1938. The economy was recovering, jobs were being restored, and manufacturing was picking up, including in the aircraft industry.

FIGURE 15-24 M-130 at Dinner Key.

FIGURE 15-25 The B-314 was the largest aircraft to be used in scheduled service until the arrival of jumbo jets in the late 1960s.

Although the airlines' income from airmail carriage was down from what it had been before 1934, passenger revenues were up and exceeded airmail revenue for the first time. Airlines began to expand their passenger facilities and corporate infrastructure, and their traffic and sales departments. The airline industry was beginning to have an impact on the public and on the economy. As the government lost more control over the airlines because of the lessening effects of airmail revenue, and as the airlines began to develop passenger traffic and revenue, it was time for the government to put into effect some kind of comprehensive control of the industry.

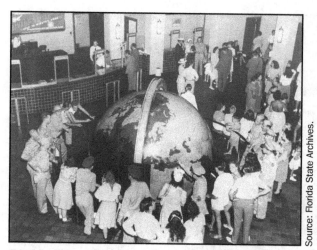

Source: Florida State Archives.

FIGURE 15-26 Inside Pan Am's Dinner Key Terminal.

Source: Florida State Archives.

FIGURE 15-27 Passengers boarding a Pan Am flight for an adventure.

The situation was not unlike that of the railroad industry with the Interstate Commerce Act of 1887, or the trucking and bus industry in the Motor Carrier Act of 1935, except for one thing: The airlines wanted regulation.

Endnotes

1. *History. NASA.gov/SP—4406/chap1.html—from which much of this section was taken.*

2. *Pacific Air Transport v. U.S.; Boeing Air Transport v. U.S.; United Airline Transport Corporation v. U.S.*, 98 Ct. Cl. 649 (1942).

3. The Monroe Doctrine was first expressed by President James Monroe in the State of the Union address to Congress on December 2, 1823. According to this policy, the American continents (North and South America, and including Central America) were to be henceforth free of any further colonization attempts by any European power. This statement of American national interest implied the use of American military and economic power in its enforcement. International adventures by Spain and Portugal triggered this policy.

16 The Civil Aeronautics Act of 1938 (McCarran-Lea Act)

Since 1926, what little regulation the government had imposed on the aviation community had been administered by the Department of Commerce, specifically the Aeronautics Branch first and then the Bureau of Air Commerce beginning in 1934. Even with these rules, regulation was decentralized. Jurisdictional disputes existed among the Post Office Department, the Interstate Commerce Commission, and the Bureau of Air Commerce.

In the meantime, flying had progressed from mail planes constructed of wood and wire with open cockpits to all-metal stress-skinned monoplanes flying in instrument conditions at speeds over three times that of early aircraft. In the middle 1930s, flying was still something of an adventure, for navigation facilities were primitive, instruments rudimentary, and weather prognostication an immature art form.

The TWA crash of the Fokker Trimotor in 1931 that killed Knute Rockne was the most notorious domestic airline crash until the death of Senator Bronson Cutting on May 6, 1935, aboard another TWA airplane, a DC-2, on a transcontinental flight from Los Angeles to Newark. Cutting boarded the aircraft at Albuquerque, N.M., where it was reported that the plane's radio transmitter was faulty. The

weather at Kansas City, which had been predicted to be good, had deteriorated to a ceiling of 600 feet, 100 feet below minimums, by the time of the flight's arrival in the area. Unable to communicate or to make the appropriate instrument approach, and with fuel low, the DC-2 crashed while attempting to fly visually at treetop level.

Cutting was much beloved in the Senate. The congressional investigation of the crash centered on the Department of Commerce and its administration of aviation safety. It was determined that the Department had been lax in enforcing what few rules were in place. Then a controversy arose between the Department and TWA as to whether the 45-minute fuel reserve rule had even been properly published, or whether TWA was otherwise notified of the rule. There were questions of conflict of interest over the Department of Commerce investigating itself concerning the adequacy of existing rules and their enforcement. The Department was shown to have a propensity for laying blame on the pilot in command, a tendency, some may argue, that continues to this day. The press stirred the pot well, and the public reaction ranged from a loss of confidence in the system to outrage. The sense of the Congress was that the Department of Commerce had failed to keep pace with the ongoing progress of commercial aviation.

Then, on October 7, 1935, a United Airlines crash near Denver killed 12 passengers and crew. On April 7, 1936, another TWA DC-2 crashed in Pennsylvania with 12 more fatalities. On August 6, 1936, a Chicago & Southern Lockheed went down in St. Louis with fatalities of all 8 aboard, and on February 10, 1937, a DC-3 flown by United Airlines crashed in San Francisco and all 11 on board were lost. The winter of 1937, in fact, recorded 5 airline crashes with fatalities.

The airlines took it upon themselves to develop operating rules and regulations for the governance of their pilots, still a rather undisciplined lot, who looked upon flying as another form of freedom, not restriction. The management of the airlines understood that, in order to win the confidence of the public and take their place as a legitimate form of public transportation that could compete with the railroads, order must be brought to the rather free-form society of aviation, up to that time primarily known for its airmail deliveries and stunt pilots.

In 1935, the airlines knew that someone had to control the growing number of airplanes plying the skies, particularly where they converged for landing, like in Newark, New Jersey. Newark Airport had a departure or an arrival every 10 minutes. It was American Airlines that took the lead in designating a "boss," someone in charge who could direct planes to maintain separation from each other. This was primarily accomplished by assigning to each aircraft an altitude as they approached for landing. An agreement among six airlines created a company known as Air Traffic Control, Inc., and it was manned by employees of those companies.

The first facility was set up at Newark (see Figure 16-1) on December 1, 1935, followed by one in Chicago in April 1936, and another in Cleveland in June 1936. At first, the controllers sought to track flights within 50 miles of the controlled airport, using blackboards, a large

Source: FAA.

FIGURE 16-1 The beginnings of air traffic control—Earl Ward (left) organized the Newark, New Jersey air traffic facility in the mid-1930s. Here he tracks a flight with the aid of a caliper as R. A. Eccles watches. The pointed markers representing aircraft were moved across the map as flights progressed.

table map, a telephone, and a Teletype. Flight plans were filed by departing pilots who would then keep in contact with their company's radio operator, relaying their position at designated waypoints with their speed and altitude. This information would then be telephoned to the center guarding the destination airport, and the airplane's position would be marked using brass weights that were moved along the table map to represent the airplane's progress. When an aircraft approached one of the staffed centers, directions to the incoming airplane would be issued by the controller to the airline's radio operator by telephone, who would then radio the pilot of the incoming airplane to descend to a certain altitude, to hold at the beacon, or that he was cleared for the approach.

The authority of the controllers was debatable, particularly among the more independent pilots who were used to doing things their own way and in their own time. It was at first considered by the pilots that the controllers' directions to them were advisory only, not mandatory, so that a direction to hold while another aircraft landed might or might not be honored. With air traffic control being taken over by the Commerce Department's Bureau of Lighthouses in 1936, procedures at last began to change. Discipline and self-control were becoming as much a requirement of good piloting technique as airspeed and altitude.

The regulations governing aircraft control adopted by the Commerce Department were actually not known to all airlines and pilots, since they were not required to be published in the Federal Register, a publication whose purpose it was to advise of the adoption of agency regulations. The Supreme Court case of *Panama Refining Co. v. Ryan*[1] established the proposition that, in order to be binding, a regulation must be published in the Federal Register as notice to all concerned. The next year, 1937, saw the first codification of air traffic regulations promulgated by the federal government. They came to be known as the Civil Air Regulations. Not only did these first regulations establish rules governing the movement of airplanes within the designated airspace, they required, for the first time, that the airlines themselves draw up a detailed operations manual, approved by the government, containing procedures for that airline regarding weather, minimum altitudes, approach, departure, and en route procedures. These Department of Commerce regulations did not apply to airport control towers, however, which remained under local city control until just before the United States entered World War II, just as the airports did themselves.

"Before take-off, a professional pilot is keen, anxious, but lest someone read his true feelings he is elaborately casual. The reason for this is that he is about to enter a new though familiar world. The process of entrance begins a short time before he leaves the ground and is completed the instant he is in the air. From that moment on, not only his body but his spirit and personality exist in a separate world known only to himself and his comrades. "

Ernest K. Gann, foreword to *Island in the Sky*

Standardization of aircraft procedures was only one aspect of the emerging airline industry that the airlines felt needed the steady hand of government control. Passenger traffic and airmail carriage had tripled since Black-McKellar, but the airlines were still suffering financially and had, in fact, all lost money each and every year since 1934. The airlines formed their own group, the Air Transport Association, and one of its first acts was to drum up support for and draft a bill creating federal rate and route regulation designed to stabilize the airline industry. The airline industry was demanding to be regulated.

Government involvement in the airline business since 1925 had been inconsistent. It had been both proactive and reactive, and both tentative and heavy-handed. The growth of aviation in all respects caused the airline industry in 1938 to bear little resemblance to what it was in 1925.

As the reliance on airmail subsidy gradually diminished because of the growth of freight traffic and passenger counts, heightened concerns about safety naturally edged forward. Insuring safety was seen as a government obligation. Like the railroads before them, the airlines were also beginning to be viewed as a national domestic resource, if not a necessity. World political and military turmoil, particularly in the Far East and in Europe, caused the government increasingly to include the aviation sector in its plans for national defense.

As a result of the Airmail Act of 1934 (Black-McKellar), government regulation was broken down into three basic jurisdictional divisions: the Post Office Department controlled the bidding and award of postal contracts; the Interstate Commerce Commission controlled the rates that were paid for the carriage of mail, passengers, and freight by the airline carriers; and the Bureau of Air Commerce within the Department of Commerce controlled the issuance and enforcement of safety regulations. This arrangement was cumbersome, divisive, and increasingly ineffective.

Never a supporter of the New Deal or Franklin D. Roosevelt, although he was a Democratic senator from Nevada, Pat McCarran felt that the regulation of aviation should be centralized. In 1935 he wrote a bill to place full control of the airline industry with the Interstate Commerce Committee, in part to rectify what the Roosevelt Administration and the Black committee had done by the 1934 Airmail Act. The 1934 Act was regarded as punitive to the airlines, and concentrated on limiting rates and eliminating excess profits. In the House, Clarence Lea, from California, introduced a bill to create an independent Bureau for Aviation within the Executive Branch. These moves were opposed by the Post Office Department and the Department of Commerce, both of which would lose important control, influence, and funding under centralization.

Vigorous debate roiled the Senate and House as members sought to ensure that the airlines and routes that served their states and districts would not be adversely affected and that any advantages to their constituents would not be lost. Neither bill received necessary support for passage because of these turf battles until 1938, when both bills were passed and then sent to joint committee conferences for the resolution of differences, from which emerged the Civil Aeronautics Act of 1938, the McCarran-Lea Act. The statute passed by Congress on June 23, 1938 provided a uniform basis of regulation for aviation in the United States and created three independent agencies to discharge the statute's mandate: the Civil Aeronautics Authority, the Administrator of Aviation, and the Air Safety Board.

"Civilian aviation," wrote President Roosevelt on January 24, 1939, "is clearly recognized as the back log of national defense in the Civil Aeronautics Act which set up the effective machinery for a comprehensive national policy with respect to the air."

"Underlying the statute is the principle that the country's welfare in time of peace and its safety in time of war rest upon the existence of a stabilized aircraft production—an economically and technically sound air transportation system, both domestic and overseas—an adequate supply of well trained civilian pilots and ground personnel."

"This new national policy set up by the Congress views American aviation as a special problem requiring special treatment. . . . One fact which stands out is that hardly another civil activity of our people bears such a direct and intimate relation to the national security as does civil aviation."

Problems quickly arose with the new statutory setup. The jurisdiction and authority of the three agencies created by the Act (the Civil Aeronautics Authority, the Administrator of Aviation, and the Air Safety Board) overlapped, causing friction and inefficiencies in meeting the mandates of the Act. The president shortly ordered an investigation into these problems. Within a period of two years from its passage, Congress enacted the 1940 Amendment to the Civil Aeronautics Act, which dissolved the three agencies originally created by the Act and redistributed their functions between two new agencies that would administer the Act for the next 20 years.

■ The Civil Aeronautics Board (CAB)

The CAB was established as an independent board of five individuals who reported directly to the president and whose function was primarily to exercise control over air carrier economic regulation, such as rates, routes, and mergers. The CAB was also given the responsibility to investigate aircraft accidents and for safety rulemaking. It was specifically charged with "the promotion, encouragement, and development of civil aeronautics."

The Civil Aeronautics Administration (CAA)

The CAA was created as an agency, headed by an administrator, which was placed back within the Department of Commerce. Responsibility for all non-military air traffic control, safety programs, and airway development was now assumed by the CAA. Compliance with Civil Air Regulations became mandatory. Training centers were established to educate and standardize training for air traffic controllers and others affected by safety regulations. Coordination of all controllers followed, with towers and en route centers falling under the CAA umbrella.

The Major Economic Effects of the Civil Aeronautics Act of 1938, as Amended in 1940

The major economic effects of the Act came in three areas: routes, mergers, and rates. The airlines were exempted from the operation of the antitrust legislation of the United States (Sherman and Clayton Acts) and the CAB took over this function, which included mergers.

The CAB decided which carriers would serve which routes, and they did this by granting certificates of "public convenience and necessity" to the existing 16 trunk carriers then operating, which thereafter became known as the "grandfather clause," and those 16 airlines continued to serve the same routes that they had served before the Act was passed. No additional certificates of "public convenience and necessity" would be granted for any trunk line operations for the next 40 years, although "feeder" routes would be established by the CAB later and authority granted for some 21 feeder service providers to operate over those routes. These supplementary carriers would supply the trunk lines with passengers, but could not compete with them. The CAB thus controlled entry into the market.

The CAB assumed one of its functions was to preserve the market that existed when the Act was passed. It assured, therefore, that no carrier could leave the system or abandon any route without its approval. In the few cases where airlines would face financial difficulties that prevented their continuing to operate in the system, the CAB simply ordered the failing carrier to be merged with a healthy one. It thus controlled exit from the market.

The CAB set rates that the airlines could charge for all services, including passenger fares. Since the CAB determined which routes would be flown by which carriers, and also determined how much the airlines could charge for that carriage, there was no competition, as that word is normally understood, between carriers. There was a philosophical departure from the punitive aspects of the 1934 Act to one of insuring that rates were sufficiently adequate to insure survivability. Rates were set to provide sufficient income so as to prevent the failure of a reasonably well-run operation, but not high enough to render any excess profits. It was basically a cost-plus fare. The government assumption and intent was that airlines were henceforth public utilities.

By the time the 1940 Amendment to the Civil Aeronautics Act was passed, it was becoming clear that developing stability and strength in the American air carrier system was a prudent course. World War II had already begun in Europe, and Japan was on a rampage in the Far East. The world was on edge, and the role that the American airline system would have thrust upon it very shortly could not, at this point, even be imagined.

Endnote

1. 298 U.S. 388, 55 S.Ct. 241, 79 L.Ed 446 (1935).

17 World War II

As the world approached the end of the third decade of the 20th century, the United States had overcome its disadvantaged position of being the last in the world of aviation to gradually becoming the first. The advances made in engine development during the 1920s by Pratt & Whitney with the Wasp and Hornet radials and by Curtiss-Wright (formerly Wright Aeronautical) with the Cyclone radial established those companies as the industry leaders. Airframe manufacturers during the 1930s had also gone through a "monoplane revolution," which had completely transformed the design and manufacture of commercial aircraft from the biplanes of earlier years.

The 1930s had proved to be a turbulent period, dominated by the economic "Great Depression." The promise of airline development springing from government-subsidized airmail had been sacrificed on the altar of politics when the Roosevelt Administration took office, and the airlines were having an exceedingly hard time making ends meet under the rate cuts mandated by the Black-McKellar Airmail Act of 1934.

The state of the art in airplane design and manufacture had evolved in the United States during this time, and it was represented first by the Boeing 247 and then by the Douglas aircraft

(DC-1 and DC-2) that evolved into the DC-3 design. Yet, in 1938 there was not much market for airline transports. That year only 42 civilian aircraft were built of any type designed to carry five or more passengers.

The military forces were a little better off in airplane numbers, but many were obsolete, and several hundred of the Navy's aircraft were biplanes. Japan had been building militarily both in its air arm and its navy since the 1920s. Beginning in the middle of the decade, Germany began designing and then producing superior military aircraft. America was in a lethargic phase, separated from Asia and Europe by two great oceans and not vulnerable to air attack, but trouble was brewing.

About the time the Civil Aeronautics Act was passed, with war clouds on the horizon, Congress authorized funds for upgrading the Navy, but mostly for ships, not carrier planes. The Army received little funding, and none for bomber aircraft.

◼ War Beyond the Great Oceans

Japan was on the march in Asia in the late 1930s. It had militarily occupied Korea, Manchuria, and parts of China and appeared to have designs on Southeast Asia and the Philippines for their rubber resources. In Europe, after concluding a non-aggression pact with the Soviet Union, Hitler invaded Poland to start World War II in September 1939. Japan, Germany, and Italy aligned to form the "Axis Powers." Britain and France declared war on Germany. In 1940, Germany overran most of Europe north of the Alps, including France, the Low Countries, and Norway. The Soviet Union invaded Finland. Italy controlled Sicily, several other Mediterranean Islands and, along with Germany, several countries in North Africa. Italy attacked Greece, but had to be backed up by Germany in 1941, which also took Yugoslavia and then Albania. Germany invaded Russia in 1941 for oil resources in the Southern Russia and Caucasus region and for "Lebensraum" in the Ukraine.

Great Britain stood alone as the last democracy against Fascist aggression in Europe. Many people believed an accommodation with Hitler was unavoidable, including some senior British Ministers in government. Appeasement and avoidance of war characterized the policies of Prime Minister Neville Chamberlain and Foreign Secretary Lord Halifax. When the Chamberlain government fell in May 1940, Sir Winston Churchill, whose mother was an American, became Prime Minister and he set an entirely different tone.

Three days after taking office, with expectations of an imminent German invasion of England, he expressed his resolve against Hitler in a speech to the House of Commons, saying "I have nothing to offer but blood, toil, tears, and sweat." On June 4, 1940 he gave his famous "We shall fight them on the beaches" speech in the House of Commons, adding "we shall fight on the landing grounds, we shall fight in the fields and in the streets, we shall fight in the hills; we shall never surrender." As the aerial war over England progressed between the Royal Air Force and the Luftwaffe during the summer of 1940, which was a prelude to Hitler's plan to invade the island

nation (Operation Sea Lion), he gave his third stirring speech, a tribute to the RAF and its brave pilots, saying: "Never in the field of human conflict was so much owed by so many to so few."

In spite of all this, sentiment in the United States was mostly isolationist. After all, the peoples of Europe had been engaged in mutual combat from time immemorial, and the carnage of World War I was still fresh in the minds of most adult citizens. Neutrality Acts were passed by Congress to prevent the United States from "taking sides" in the growing hostilities worldwide. These Acts prohibited American vessels from transporting passengers or articles to the belligerents. There were even those who held up the recent industrial advances and full employment of the German nation as something to be admired. Charles Lindbergh was a prominent and active isolationist, frequently taking the stump to caution against "foreign entanglements." In the 1940 election, Roosevelt had promised America's mothers that he "would not send American boys to fight in any foreign wars."

Yet, England and the United States were historically closely bound together—by language, by culture, and by common law. A secret correspondence had begun in September 1939 between Roosevelt and Churchill, even though Chamberlain was then still Prime Minister, centering on details of the coming war that had been precipitated by the German invasion of Poland only days earlier. There was a kind of kindred spirit between Roosevelt and Churchill—both had in their earlier years been identified with their countries' navies, Roosevelt as Assistant Secretary of the Navy in the Wilson Administration and Churchill as First Lord of the Admiralty before and during the First World War, a position he again held in the run up to World War II. This personal correspondence provided a "back door" channel between the two countries that served to allow the United States an inside look at the dire situation England would find itself in after the fall of France the next year. And it gave

Churchill a direct line to the United States to plead for help.

The Royal Navy was fighting for its life against German U-boats, which were sinking prodigious amounts of tonnage, and the new battleships *Bismarck* and *Tirpitz* were prowling the North Atlantic sea lanes. In the summer of 1940 the aerial "Battle of Britain" was a touch and go affair with daily bombing raids on London and other English cities and on Royal Air Force airbases. Although the Office of Home Defense had developed a primitive form of radar that enabled the RAF to anticipate the approach of Luftwaffe planes, the resulting daily aerial dogfights were depleting the fighter capability of the RAF, and new aircraft production in England could not keep up with the losses being sustained. The same situation existed with naval transport vessels and warships. The HMS *Hood*, pride of the Royal Navy, was sunk in May 1941 by the *Bismarck*.

There was little doubt that Roosevelt believed that the future of Western Civilization depended on preserving the British nation and defeating Nazi and Japanese aggression. Roosevelt's public persona reflected the isolationist sentiment of the country, and he was legally bound by the law of the land, which required strict neutrality. But the 1937 Neutrality Act contained a loophole that allowed the president to authorize the sale of matériel to belligerents in Europe as long as they paid for the goods in cash and arranged for their transport, which provided a little daylight to the Roosevelt Administration to quietly begin to help England.

The Destroyers for Bases Agreement

On September 2, 1940, the United States and Great Britain sealed an agreement that transferred 50 U.S. destroyer-type warships to England in return for land rights on several British

possessions, including Newfoundland, the Bahamas, Jamaica, and other Caribbean islands. This was the first move toward extending the defenses of the United States and at the same time laying the groundwork for a ferry system for the future transport of war matériel to Europe and Africa. On April 9, 1941 the Danish Ambassador (who had relocated to Washington after the Nazi takeover of Denmark in 1940) signed an agreement allowing the United States to build airfields and associated facilities, as well as placing personnel on the island of Greenland (Greenland had been a colony of Denmark since the early 18th century).

The Lend Lease Act

American public opinion was gradually changing from predominately isolationist to one of limited involvement, "as long as we don't have to go to war." On March 11, 1941 Congress passed the Lend Lease Act, which empowered the president "on behalf of any country whose defense the president deems vital to the defense of the United States, to sell, transfer title to, exchange, lease, lend, or otherwise dispose of, to any such government any defense article . . . not expressly prohibited." This Act allowed the United States to legally provide war matériel to England, China, Russia, and to 35 other nations. Roosevelt had earlier announced that the United States, although not involved in the war, was to become the "arsenal of democracy." The industrial capacity of the United States was about to be tapped, and a mighty force it would prove to be.

The Secret Meeting and the Atlantic Charter

In the summer of 1941, Roosevelt and Churchill agreed to a secret meeting to discuss the deteriorating military and economic situation confronting Britain. Using cover stories, Roosevelt boarded the heavy cruiser USS *Augusta* from the

Presidential yacht, *Potomac*, off New London, Connecticut, and Churchill departed Scapa Flow in Scotland aboard the battleship *Prince of Wales* for a rendezvous in Placentia Bay, Newfoundland, which occurred on August 9, 1941. Although the meeting produced what was to be called the "Atlantic Charter," no specific progress was made for either getting the United States into the war or providing additional war matériel to Britain, but the "Atlantic Charter" contained eight separate points on which the two agreed, including that "Nazi tyranny" must be destroyed, a statement that was well outside the parameters of the neutrality position of the United States. It also cemented the coalition between the United States and Great Britain for the difficulties that lay ahead. Based on the totality of the agreement, it is commonly concluded that this document also formed the basis of what was to become the United Nations.

In the months that followed, Churchill continued his ardent dialogue with Roosevelt for ever increasing participation by the United States in the European war theater, but it was not until December 7, 1941, that the United States became fully committed to World War II. For on that day the Empire of Japan, using aircraft launched from six aircraft carriers located to the northwest of Hawaii, carried out air strikes against the naval and air facilities at Pearl Harbor, resulting in over 2,000 servicemen deaths and the near destruction of the American battleship fleet at anchor there. Fortuitously, all American aircraft carriers, with their full complement of aircraft, officers, and men, were at sea.

The World at War

The United States declared war on Japan the next day. Although taken by surprise by the Japanese attack at Pearl Harbor, Germany declared war against the United States on December 11, justifying this action on American provocations against German ships and submarines

since September 1941. In fact, three American destroyers, the *Greer*, the *Kearney* and the *Reuben James* had fired on German submarines. These developments brought the United States fully into the European conflict. The world now was truly in total war.

In 1941, the most reliable way for the delivery of goods to Europe was by cargo ship, but the German U-boat threat to the mercantile transport fleet was very real. Several innovations were instituted, including the convoy system across the North Atlantic. At the same time, the United States military, in conjunction with the domestic civilian air transport fleet, created a series of Atlantic Ocean air routes for the purpose of delivering war matériel from the United States to the war zones in Europe and Africa. These routes were generally operational beginning in 1942.

The primary air routes were the North Atlantic Air Route, the Mid-Atlantic Air Route, and the South Atlantic Air Route. Because no aircraft existed that had sufficient range to bridge the entire Atlantic Ocean from the United States, aircraft were required to "hop" from one landing field to the next over large expanses of ocean. The DC-3, whose military designation was the C-47, was the mainstay of transport aircraft at the time. Pilots were advised to place their trust in God and Pratt & Whitney.[1]

The South Atlantic Route began at one of four bases in Brazil, to which aircraft arrived from Florida, and then proceeded to Ascension Island, which is located in the South Atlantic some 1,400 miles from Natal or Recife, Brazil. From there aircraft landed on the African continent, usually in French Morocco or Liberia.

The Mid-Atlantic Route ran from Morrison Field in Florida to Bermuda and thence to the Azores, from where landings were made in Marrakech or Casablanca, French Morocco or RAF St. Mawgan in Cornwall, England.

The North Atlantic Route commenced in either New Hampshire (Grenier Army Air Base) or in Maine (Presque Isle Army Airfield) and progressed thence usually along the route to Newfoundland (Gander), Labrador (Goose Bay), Greenland (Bluie-West-One), Iceland (Meeks Field, Patterson Field, or Reykjavik Airport) to Prestwick, Scotland. Due to North Atlantic weather patterns, the North Atlantic Route was by far the most perilous, particularly in winter.

Bluie-West-One in Greenland, for instance, was a steel mesh runway located over 30 miles up a rocky fjord with vertical walls, which increased in height farther inland. The chart designation of the terrain north of the field was marked "Unexplored." There were three separate but nearly identical fjords with entrances from the ocean in the vicinity of Bluie-West-One, but only the middle one led to the runway. In low ceiling conditions pilots had to enter the fjord at near sea level altitude, and visibility was usually minimal. Once in the fjord, turns of 180 degrees were out of the question, as was climbing through the overcast without colliding with terrain. There were no distinguishing features that would identify one fjord from another, so selecting the correct one was of paramount importance. Once entered, this was a one-way route.

The visual approach to the fjord entrance was on a bearing from Semitak Island, which was a rock outcropping located offshore. Ernest K. Gann explains the procedure in his book, *Fate is the Hunter*,[2] as he made his first approach at 50 feet over the rolling ocean surface under a low cloud ceiling:

"A jumble of rocks proved to be Semitak Island. It swept past our right wing and became lost almost instantly in the mist. Now for the fiord. The *correct* fiord. We held on straight for the coast line. We would soon be committed. The distance between the island and the mouths of the three fiords was only two miles. How could we be sure we had entered the fiord in the middle unless it was possible to see the other two? Eenie-meenie-miney-mo. . ."

Although the DC-3 was the mainstay of American transport aircraft in 1941, the Douglas DC-4 and the Lockheed Constellation, both four-engine designs, were in development. While these two aircraft appeared at about the same time, they were very different from each other and the reasons for their appearance were based on very different circumstances.

The DC-4 was created under specifications requested in the late 1930s by United Airlines to provide that carrier with a longer range passenger airliner. It first flew on February 14, 1942 and because the United States had recently entered World War II, the production line was requisitioned by the military. It was designated the C-54 for military cargo transport. The DC-4 carried twice the number of passengers as the DC-3, had a much longer range, and was the first transport aircraft to have tricycle landing gear. It had a relatively simple fuselage design and could be produced in large numbers easily.

The Lockheed Constellation, on the other hand, was the brain child of Howard Hughes, who in 1939 had taken over control of TWA. His support for the creation of the Boeing 307 had so far caused five of the pressurized Stratoliners to be delivered to service, but he had bigger plans—plans that would create one of the most impressive shapes in the history of the commercial airlines.

The shark-like Constellation was to be pressurized, unlike the DC-4 that would be limited to lower altitudes. Hughes favored pressurized aircraft partly due to his prior experience with the H-1 Racer that he had designed and flown in 1935. Pressurized aircraft had the advantage of flying above most of the weather, without the requirement of oxygen masks, and could seek the further advantage of favorable winds. Hughes provided Lockheed with the essential specifications and told them that he would buy it if Lockheed would build it.

There was at Lockheed a young aeronautical engineer by the name of Kelly Johnson, who headed up a small team of engineers in the Advanced Development Programs division. His team developed the P-38 Lightning in 1939, the world's first 400 mile-per-hour aircraft, and much of his design was beyond government specifications and without a written contract. That was his style. He set up his team in a separate, walled-off section of the Lockheed building that was off-limits to all but a few. His mode of operation led to his group garnering the label "Skunk Works," from which astounding aircraft developments would later appear, including the super-secret U-2 (1955), A-12 (1962) and SR-71 (1964) spy planes, and stealth aircraft like the F-117 (1977). His was a reputation for speed, innovation, informality, and on-time, under-budget aircraft productions.

In 1939 Kelly Johnson was put in charge of the design, development, and production of the Constellation. Lockheed agreed to Howard Hughes' terms, including that TWA would get the first 40 planes off the line and that the project be held in the strictest secrecy (Hughes was developing his reputation for paranoia even then). The deal was made with Hughes Tool Company, not TWA, both to ensure secrecy and because of the fact that Hughes Tool had the money. The project was begun, drawings were prepared, reviewed, revised, and by 1941 about half of the original prototype was done.

World events in 1939 and 1940 caused the War Department to conduct a survey of United States airplane manufacturing plants with a view to ascertaining production levels in the event of the United States being brought into the hostilities. The secret Constellation design was thus disclosed. The war atmosphere had also caused the United States to create the War Production Board, whose job was to allocate the industrial and manufacturing resources of the country in a way to best ensure its defense and guarantee the production of essential goods. This higher cause was understood by all concerned, including Howard Hughes, and by agreement it was determined that Pan American would participate in the Constellation project along with TWA. Pan Am was the only international air carrier for the United States, and it was not a competitor of TWA at that time. Further, Pan Am had the international experience, the routes, the landing rights, and the foreign contacts that could make the best and highest use of the Connie's range and speed. Thus amended, the project went ahead under the auspices of the War Production Board.

General "Hap" Arnold was Chief of the Army Air Corps in 1941. He was one of the first military pilots in the Army and he had even received flight instruction in 1911 at the Wright brothers' aviation school in Ohio. He was to play a central role in wartime aviation. His duties before and during World War II included the monitoring and evaluation of aircraft production at plants around the country. The design shape and relative complexity of the Constellation (military designation C-121) caused him to halt production work on the airplane several times in favor of the simpler and less expensive DC-4. Because of this, the Constellation would not actually fly until December 1943, almost two years after the first flight of the DC-4. After the first Connie was rolled out of the Burbank, California plant, and as a part of its test flight regimen, Howard Hughes and Jack Frye would fly it to Washington, D.C. in a new record time of under seven hours, nonstop.

The Connie would not contribute in any significant way to the war effort. The DC-4, on the other hand, would take center stage as the transport workhorse for the military for the duration of the war. With the exception of the five Boeing 307 Stratoliners in service, the DC-4 was the first serious transoceanic aircraft to become available. The first of these aircraft did not go to United Airlines, which had provided its specifications and had submitted the first orders for it, but ironically to its competitor, TWA, which was flying the southern transatlantic route to Africa for the military. During the war, these planes would log over a million miles a month over the Atlantic, some 20 ocean sorties every day.

The Chosen Instrument

As the sole American airline with prewar operations overseas, Pan American became an important asset of the United States during World War II. Pan American operated flying boats, in part, because of the lack of airfields. But Pan Am also had experience in building airfields in remote areas. Roosevelt had secured rights to bases on many of the islands of the Caribbean from the British under the "Destroyers for Bases Agreement." He now called upon Pan American to build airfields on these islands as a part of a larger plan to supply the war effort against Germany. Airports would be built down through the Caribbean to South America and along its east coast, for ferrying equipment and supplies across the Atlantic narrows to Africa. The British were engaging the Germans in North Africa, and North Africa would be the location of America's first military engagements in World War II. Although the United States paid for all of the airport construction (over $90 million), Pan American held title to these facilities initially for appearance purposes since the United States was diplomatically neutral prior to its entry into the war. After the war, negotiations caused these improvements to revert to the United States, but with limitations on their use by airlines other than Pan Am.

The Airlines at War

At the beginning of the war, there were only some 365 commercial transport aircraft in the United States. The airplane manufacturing community would shortly begin to produce 50,000 aircraft a year, the largest manufacturing activity in the United States during the war, and at war's end over 300,000 airplanes would have been produced. America's main contribution was in production,

not development, for the existing fighter and transport aircraft designs were considered sufficient, at least in the short run, to win the war if only there were enough of them. The P-51 Mustang was the only new development in airplane technology supplied by the United States after the onset of war.

The main production effort was, of course, directed toward fighter and bomber aircraft, although over 10,000 DC-3s, designated for the military as C-47s, were built, along with over 1,000 DC-4s (as C-54s). America needed every bit of transport potential it could muster during the years 1941–1945, including railroads as well as air carriers, and while the railroads enjoyed a resurgence of their former glory during these years, the air carriers came into their own for the first time. Aircrews flew everywhere, either as military or civilian to military or civilian airports, on domestic and overseas routes. Flying transoceanic routes became routine.

TWA, the only airline with land-based four-engine aircraft at the beginning of the war, set up a training center at government direction in New Mexico for instructing American and British pilots how to fly the four engine bombers, the B-24 and the B-17. (TWA had purchased the new Boeing Stratoliner, the 307, in 1940.) Pan American also contributed to four engine training, sharing its pilots' experience in long-range ocean and celestial navigation. (See Figure 17-1.)

Domestically, the airlines discovered after the onset of hostilities that they had only 165 airplanes to service their routes. The armed forces had commandeered the rest for military purposes. Travel space on the relatively few air carrier aircraft was allocated according to a government imposed "priority system":

- Priority One was for persons traveling under the authority of the president.
- Priority Two got military pilots a seat.
- Priority Three was other military personnel or civilians on essential wartime business.
- Priority Four was military cargo.

Source: Florida State Archives.

FIGURE 17-1 Military airmen in training with Pan Am.

The remaining seats, of which there were precious few, went to everyone else. The lexicon of future airline travel was being established too. "Standbys" were those who hoped a priority above them would become a "no-show" so that a seat would become available. To be "bumped" was to have a higher priority passenger show up to take your seat.

American air carriers began to make money for the first time since 1934, and although the high load factor of domestic commercial operations contributed to profitability, the main effort of the airlines during the war was as contract carriers for the military.

The government allocated the airlines' responsibility during the war in logical fashion. Northeast Airlines was given the North Atlantic route as far as Greenland and then Reykjavik, Iceland. Northwest was assigned to the Alaska route, Eastern to the Caribbean and Brazil. American flew to South America and, in the process, caused a radio range to be built along its route from the United States. TWA had its five Boeing 307s, the only four-engine land-based transoceanic aircraft available at the time, commandeered by the military and was given the transatlantic route to Egypt, the most significant long distance route of any airline except Pan

American. TWA set up its transcontinental division immediately at the beginning of the war, no doubt with an eye on the postwar period. At first, TWA flew to Africa via the South American route, and later, after Portugal granted landing rights, via the much shorter North Atlantic route by way of Prestwick, Scotland. TWA flew military supplies and equipment, like the other airlines, but it was the preferred carrier for VIPs and, in fact, TWA carried President Roosevelt to the three wartime conferences with Churchill in Casablanca, Tehran, and Yalta.

It is not surprising that Pan American, as the only overseas carrier in existence before the war, was counted on as the major civilian arm of the military during the war. Yet, it is noteworthy that Pan American's five divisions, the Alaskan, Pacific, North Atlantic, Caribbean, and Africa-Orient, flew half of all contract miles flown by all airlines for the U.S. military. In the process, Pan American began flying landplanes instead of the flying boats that had been its trademark during its early years, thus marking the end of the romantic and adventurous era of the Pan American Clipper. The range and speed of the DC-4 and the airplanes to follow, the availability of the airports that Pan American and others had built around the world, and the relative high maintenance costs and requirements of amphibious planes over landplanes sounded the death knell of the flying boat airliner, and Pan American never ordered another one.

Most of the flying done during World War II was not by the personnel of the commercial airlines but by the military forces created and trained by the government. The exigencies of war, shown once again to be a mighty motivating force, had caused a great technological leap forward in aircraft, engines, and systems. The feats of the non-combat pilots of the military lift branches, some 25,000 of them, during the four-year duration of the war testify to the great advance in air transportation over that short span of time. Feats only imagined a mere four years before were now commonplace. Distances had been covered and heights had been overcome for the first time in the airborne delivery of personnel and goods that would henceforth be considered routine. There was a confidence born not only of victory, but also of studied accomplishment.

Contrasted to the unspeakable devastation visited on the landscapes and structures of Europe that had been created by the world's most advanced civilization for the better part of two millennia, the homeland of the United States emerged from the war unscathed, and with the robust industrial complex that had supplied the weapons and material of war intact. America had:

- The pilots
- The planes
- The know-how
- The international presence on the ground
- The financial structure and stability to lead the world into the postwar realms of commercial aviation.

And the United States was ready to use all of it.

Endnotes

1. Gann, Ernest K., *Fate is the Hunter,* Simon and Shuster, New York, NY, 1961.
2. Simon and Shuster, 1961.

18 A New Beginning

Before the war, air travel had begun to catch on, and in 1941 domestic airlines carried four million passengers. With the war over in 1945, air travel quickly picked up again, and by the end of 1945 the airlines had enplaned some 7.5 million passengers. In 1946, the number almost doubled to 12.5 million passengers. The commercial airline fleet before the war provided about 6,200 seats. By 1946, the airlines had tripled capacity to 19,000 available seats. The cost of airline travel had fallen enough to be competitive with first class railroad fares, and the four-hour plane ride between Chicago and New York offered a real choice for any time-sensitive traveler over the sixteen-hour railroad Pullman. It was a new day in commercial aviation.

The development of transport aircraft had progressed rapidly during the war. The expectation was that the prewar traffic would be promptly reclaimed and then exponentially developed using the new era of airliners. Some of the aircraft were suited to expanding the first class travel begun in the 1930s, particularly on the transcontinental and transoceanic runs. Modern airlines of the postwar era were on the verge of entering the first class travel market long held by the steamship lines and the transcontinental Pullman trains. While it was true that some

airlines using DC-3s had offered berths for sleeping on overnight flights, now airliners could fly much higher and faster, and in pressurized and air-conditioned comfort.

TWA launched transatlantic service on December 5, 1945, with a VIP flight to Paris that was completed in the record time of 12 hours and 57 minutes. Pressurized, and with a cruise speed of 280 miles per hour, the Connie was ready to contribute to the anticipated revolution in transatlantic and transcontinental air travel.

The number of airports used by the airlines more than doubled between 1941 and 1947, from 2,484 to 5,343. Outside the terminals, new sleek aircraft for the first time took on the look of flying in place with their new tricycle landing gear. Interspersed among the ubiquitous DC-3s that appeared to be sitting back on their haunches, these new planes stood tall over them and gave an impression of progress, comfort, and safety. The airplanes were getting larger than the terminals in some places. Mass transit, facilitated by the big airliners, was about to begin.

The DC-4, which had been commandeered by the military upon its appearance in 1942, became available to the domestic fleet in 1946. (See Figure 18-1.) Unpressurized, seating 44 passengers and barely able to muster 200 miles per hour at

Source: Florida State Archives.

FIGURE 18-1 The DC-4 became available to the domestic fleet in 1946.

cruise, the DC-4 was out-classed by the Connie, yet it became in the late 1940s the four-engine airplane of choice. Its service during the war had proved it to be safe and reliable, something yet to be proved in the Constellation and other advanced aircraft emerging from the war. The tapered lines of the Constellation, its more complex systems, its three vertical stabilizers, and the number of parts required to be stored and available also caused it to be significantly more expensive to maintain than the DC-4. (See Figure 18-2.) The straight lines of the DC-4 proved to be much cheaper to repair, maintain, and to fly.

The availability of these new aircraft increased the airlines' capacity and brought with them options for airline management that had never before been possible. This may be the point in history when the concept of the passenger seat as a "grapefruit," as in a perishable commodity, was articulated as a marketing truism. Every unfilled seat at takeoff was like spoiled grapefruit for that flight; it was forever lost to use. Competitive management thinking recognized that high-density seating brought with it pure profit after boarding enough passengers to cover costs.

The scheduled airlines were, and had always been, of one class, and that was first class. When comparisons were made between the airlines and the railroads as to cost, an airline seat was compared to a Pullman berth (these accommodations were seats during day travel and were converted to beds for night travel). The high cost of air travel could be favorably compared to first class rail fares because of the time–distance advantage between comparable points enjoyed by the airlines.

After the war, the CAB began loosening the regulations that bound the air-traveling public to the scheduled airlines (first class service). This allowed aircraft charter, or as some called it, the nonscheduled lines, or "nonskeds." Using DC-3s and then DC-4s, these charter operators flew at off hours, at night, and most importantly, with full airplanes. Not bound to a schedule, these operators were not required to leave the terminal at any particular time. Their schedule was simply dictated by the passenger count. And passengers flocked to them. Soon the nonskeds were going coast to coast and at prices that were 30 percent less than the scheduled airlines. They did the same thing on some international routes, notably to Puerto Rico.

Pan Am's official name had been changed in 1945 from Pan American Airways to Pan American World Airways. Juan Trippe was again ahead of the game and ready for the postwar contest. He saw that by seating five abreast in the DC-4, the passenger count could increase from 44 to 63. But the question remained in what market such a configuration could be put to use. And fares would certainly have to be reduced in order to induce anyone to put up with such crowding. Here, Juan Trippe was about 30 years ahead of his time, ahead of the days of deregulation that would come in 1978.

In 1948, Pan American began flying DC-4s from New York to San Juan, Puerto Rico. Puerto Rico was a relatively impoverished island, and most of its inhabitants could not afford expensive travel of either kind, ship or plane. The low standard of living in Puerto Rico and its mortality rate combined to provide motivation to some people to leave the country. Pan Am tapped this large market for mass air transit in the newly configured DC-4,

Source: Library of Congress.

FIGURE 18-2   The Constellation was much more expensive to maintain than other comparable aircraft.

which had no galley and only one flight attendant. Any Puerto Rican with $75 was given the opportunity to begin a new life in New York, which had a Puerto Rican population of 70,000 at that time. By 1950, there would be 250 thousand Puerto Rican residents in New York City. By 1975, five million of the island's former residents had migrated to the United States.

Domestically, the airlines were losing money to the nonskeds, so they petitioned the CAB for authority to operate a second class of service. "Air coach," as it was called, was introduced by the scheduled airlines in 1948. Some of the crews began to refer to the new passengers as "cattle class." The airlines saw that they could compete with the railroads, not just for first class passengers, but also for coach passengers. Capital Airlines became the first established carrier to offer "coach-class" service, inaugurated on the New York–Chicago route. At a fare of two-thirds

the standard, there were few complaints of overcrowding, late night departures, or the lack of a meal service. TWA and American followed suit with their transcontinental service. By the end of 1951, nine domestic carriers offered coach or tourist class service to 34 cities. In 1952, fares were $99 coast-to-coast; $32 between Chicago and New York. Airline passenger traffic doubled in the five years between 1948 and 1952. By 1955, the airlines had passed the railroads for the first time in the number of passengers carried.

For a while the "coach" or "tourist" class flights operated as separate airplanes both domestically and internationally. The smaller international carriers complained to the International Air Transport Association (IATA) that they could not compete with larger airlines since they did not possess the necessary number of aircraft to operate both first class and tourist class airplanes. When IATA authorized them to operate their equipment carrying both first class and tourist in the same airplane, the modern form of aircraft configuration was born. TWA was the first to begin domestic operations with both fare classes on the same airplane after CAB approval.

A new group of air carrier, known collectively as local service lines or feeder lines, completed their first full year of service in 1946. While the CAB would not expand the total number of trunk airlines beyond the sixteen that were grandfathered under the Civil Aeronautics Act of 1938, these smaller carriers received authority to operate on short routes to some 350 small cities. The average distance flown between stops was about 60 miles, and some of the communities served had populations of as few as 3,000 people. By the end of 1951, there were 18 local service airlines operating 130 airplanes.

(Selected Years)

	No. of Engines	1940		1945		1948 1/		*1949 1/	
		No. Planes	Av. Mi. Per Day	No. Planes	Av. Mi. Per Day	No. Planes	Av. Mi. Per Day	No. Planes	Av. Mi. Per Day
Beechcraft	2	—	—	0.8	66	6.5	219	—	—
Boeing									
247-D	2	34.9	468	—	—	0.8	800	—	—
SA-307B	4	3.1	1,354	3.6	2,094	5.0	1,326	5.0	1,306
377	4	—	—	—	—	—	—	7.0	306
Consolidated-Vultee									
Convair	2	—	—	—	—	9.3	907	92.0	834
Douglas									
DC-2	2	42.2	715	—	—	—	—	—	—
DC-3	2	145.2	1,198	314.4	1,756	429.2	1,194	404.0	898
DST	2	38.6	1,569	—	—	—	—	—	—
DC-4	4	—	—	—	—	155.0	1,317	158.0	947
DC-6	4	—	—	—	—	46.3	1,825	104.0	1,626
Lockheed									
Electra	2	33.8	58.3	1.3	727	—	—	—	—
Lodestar	2	4.4	661	17.7	1,545	12.0	258	11.0	909
Constelation	4	—	—	—	—	30.9	1,828	51.0	1,688
Sikorsky	2	6.0	203	2.0	184	—	—	—	—
Stinson									
Single Motor	1	—	—	10.9	404	7.0	439	—	—
Tri-motored	3	2.0	109	4.0	61	—	—	—	—
Martin 202	2	—	—	—	—	15.4	843	24.0	1,107
Curtiss 46	2	—	—	—	—	2.0	73	2.0	129

*1/includes local service and territorial lines. 1949 data for 10 months only.

FIGURE 18-3 General aircraft utilization, domestic airlines.

LESS TIME TO CROSS THE CONTINENT

1858
Mail Coach
and Rail

1861
Pony Express
and Rail

1869
First
Transcontinental
Train

1921
First
All–Air Mail

1929
First Air-Rail
Passenger Service

1944
Regular
Air-Passenger
Service

= 24 hrs.

The Continent Grows Smaller

Coast-to-Coast

1840	The ox-drawn covered wagon	6 to 8 months
1846	Sailing vessels around the Horn	6 1/2 months
1849	Steam vessels around the Horn	4 1/2 months
1858	Overland mail coaches and rail	24–30 days
1861	Pony Express and rail	11–13 days
1869	First transcontinental train	7 days
1903	First transcontinental automobile trip	61 days
1911	First transcontinental airplane trip Calbraith P. Rodgers: Sheepshead Bay, L. I. to Pasadena, California	49 days
1919	First transcontinental round trip by air: Lt. Belvin W. Maynard	9 days 4 hours 25 min.
1920	First air-rail mail: New York-San Francisco	72 hours
1921	First all-air mail: San Francisco-New York	33 hours 20 min.
1923	First non-stop coast-to-coast flight: Lts. John A. Macready and Oakley Kelly New York-San Diego, May 2-3	26 hours 50 min.
1924	Fastest transcontinental railroad trip	69 hours 7 min.
	Standard transcontinental railroad trip	87 hours
	Regular air mail, day and night schedule	32 hours
	First dawn-to-dusk coast-to-coast flight: Col. Russell L. Maughan, New York-San Francisco, June 23	21 hours 44 min.
1927	First coast-to-coast commercial air passengers: New York-San Francisco	31 hours 45 min.

1929	Round-trip record by Frank Hawks: New York-Los Angeles	19 hours 10 min.
	Los Angeles-New York	17 hours 38 min.
	First air-rail passenger service	48 hours
1930	New round-trip record by Frank Hawks: Los Angeles-New York, August 12	14 hours 50 min.
	New York-Los Angeles, August 15	12 hours 25 min.
1931	Record by Jimmy Doolittle: Burbank-Newark, September 4	11 hours 15 min.
1933	Regular coast-to-coast air passenger, mail, and express schedule	19 hours 35 min.
1934	Jack Frye and E. V. Rickenbacker in regular commercial transport plane: Los Angeles-Newark, February 18-19	13 hours 4 min.
	Jack Frye with mail: Los Angeles-New York, May 8	11 hours 30 min.
1935	Record by Leland S. Andrews and H. B. Snead: Los Angeles-Washington, February 20	10 hours 22 min.
1937	Record by Howard Hughes: Los Angeles-New York, January 19	7 hours 28 min. 25 sec.
1938	Westbound record by A. P. DeSeversky: Brooklyn-Burbank, August 29	10 hours 2 min. 55 sec.
1943	Regular schedule for passengers, mail, express	16 hours
1944	New record by Howard Hughes and 17 passengers in transport plane: Burbank-Washington, April 17	6 hours 57 min. 51 sec.
1945	Regular extra fare service: New York-Los Angeles	14 hours 35 min.
	Record in transport plane: Seattle-Washington, January 10	6 hours 3 min. 50 sec.

FIGURE 18-4 Less time to cross the continent.

19 On the Way to the Jet Age

" To put your life in danger from time to time . . . breeds a saneness in dealing with day-to-day trivialities. "

Nevil Shute, *Slide Rule: The Autobiography of an Engineer*

The last of the big airliners mounting reciprocating engines on their wings were stretched versions of the airliners that had gone before. The DC-6 and the DC-7 were from the DC-4 model with various refinements to go along with the increase in length, breadth, and power. The Super Constellation was 19 feet longer than the original. With increased length came additional seating and with more seating came more revenue. Range was extended so that nonstop service was possible— not only coast-to-coast but transatlantic.

The DC-6 was launched in coast-to-coast service on April 27, 1947, with one stop en route for fuel. United advertised its service as ten hours total. (See Figure 19-1.) TWA's Constellations could do about the same, advertised as ten hours, ten minutes.

Boeing, a late entry to the new postwar aircraft building party, in 1948 introduced the double-decked B-377 Stratocruiser, a four-engine landplane larger than either the DC-6 or

Constellation and designed with an emphasis on luxury reminiscent of the Pan Am Clippers. The airplane featured two decks with a cocktail lounge with leather seating located below, accessible by a curved stairway, and with a honeymoon suite in the aft section. Take off performance in the Stratocruiser was marginal, with the DC-6 routinely outperforming it, but it was bigger and faster at 340 miles per hour than any other airliner. It was also expensive, costing over $1.5 million, and its high operation costs did not help matters. It had engine problems (the P&W Wasp Major had 112 spark plugs in 28 cylinders and delivered 3,500 horsepower) and the propellers had a tendency to go flying off on their own. Still, these airplanes were the ultimate in passenger comfort. New York to London was a pleasant affair of 12 hours duration, including cocktails, a five-course dinner, a good night's sleep, and plenty of attention. But the Stratocruiser had the worst safety record of the postwar big planes; six were involved in fatal crashes with the loss of 108 passengers and 28 crew. United unloaded their Stratocruisers early; Northwest kept theirs for years. In the end, the airlines seemed glad to see them go. Figure 19-2 pictures the Boeing 377, the Constellation 049, and the DC-4.

Source: Florida State Archives.

FIGURE 19-1 The DC-6 was launched in coast-to-coast service on April 27, 1947 with one stop en route for fuel.

Source: Florida State Archives.

FIGURE 19-2 Boeing 377, Constellation 049, and DC-4.

The DC-7 proved to be the first true transatlantic airplane, flying either west or east with a full load. With it, Pan American regained its leadership position over TWA, which was flying the Super Constellation. The DC-7 had engines that were reaching the limits of reciprocating-engine power possibilities. With four Wright turbo-compound engines providing 3,250 horsepower, each weighing over 3,500 pounds, engine maintenance was a problem; American Airlines reported 10 engine failures a day on average. Westbound DC-7 service to the Pacific coast was advertised as nonstop, but with headwinds the advertised flying time of seven and one-half hours was often missed. Eastbound, American was able to adhere to its scheduled arrivals. The DC-7 made the first nonstop transatlantic crossing in 1957.

But the strain was showing; the limits of the reciprocating engine had been reached. It was time for the jet age.

Jets

It has been said that World War II advanced the airplane by 50 years. Yet it can also be accurately stated that there were really only two revolutionary technological advances to come out of the war—radar and the jet engine—and America had nothing to do with the discovery of either. Not only were the Americans a bit slow at the beginning, they were even slower at appreciating how great a leap the jet engine represented in the potential for air commerce. This was demonstrated by the reluctance of American aircraft manufacturers and air carriers to pursue jet engine potential after the war.

The idea of turbine engines first manifested itself in England in 1884, when Charles Parsons, who was called the greatest engineer since James Watt, developed a stationary steam turbine that he applied to the generation of electric energy. Within his lifetime his patent was applied to all major world power stations, including in the United States by George Westinghouse. Although his original patent claimed the use of the steam turbine for ships, it was not until 1894 that he built a 100-foot vessel, the *Turbinia*, which he powered by means of a steam turbine to a speed of 34 knots. The British Admiralty adopted the steam turbine in 1905 as the exclusive propulsion system in all classes of its warships. The steam turbine was soon also applied to new construction for the mercantile fleet and by Cunard for luxury passenger liners.

In the early 20th century, attempts to apply the turbine technology to internal combustion engines, or gas turbines, met with disappointment. The design of the gas turbine called for the induction of air (as in a reciprocating engine) that would be compressed prior to ignition (as in a reciprocating engine). In the reciprocating engine, the compression is accomplished by means of the piston, but in the turbine engine, the compression is delivered by means of a series of rotating vanes (the compressor) located in front of the combustion chamber. Although the

idea of the gas turbine proved workable, its fuel consumption was four times that of the internal combustion engine, and the economics of the invention simply prevented its adoption into commercial use.

The use of compressors in aircraft engines, however, did find continued use as the combined technology associated with aircraft engines and aircraft designs matured during the early years of aviation. As early as World War I, a turbocharger was fitted to a French aircraft to enable increased engine performance at higher altitudes. Turbochargers use the engine's exhaust gases to propel the turbocharger's compressor, thus making use of the free fuel source of the exhaust to compress air for induction into the engine's cylinders as the aircraft climbs into the thinner air at altitude. This technology was used to good effect in the design of the American fighters and bombers used in World War II. The B-17, for instance, could carry its bomb load to 34,000 feet.

The idea of utilizing the smooth, vibration-free rotation of a turbine, instead of the oscillating pistons of the much more cumbersome internal combustion engine, continued to occupy the minds of engineers and inventors. The first serious work on developing the jet engine, or turbojet, was commenced almost simultaneously in the 1930s in both England and Germany.

In England, Frank Whittle, an officer in the Royal Air Force (RAF), conceived that the application of the principles of the gas turbine might be applied, not to drive a shaft or propeller, but to produce a source of thrust for propulsion. In 1930, he was awarded a patent for his design, which was replete with compressor, combustion chamber, and turbine. Although his ideas and designs appeared to be workable, no assistance was forthcoming directly from the British government. The RAF did allow him to continue his work while on duty, and even approved his securing engineering and advanced degrees at government expense, culminating in a master's degree from Cambridge. By 1935, Whittle had almost given up on his dream of producing a prototype jet engine when he was approached by two RAF officers willing to capitalize a company for this work. A company was formed, Power Jets, Ltd., and a workable prototype was achieved. At last, government interest was piqued, and direct funding of refinements of his engine was provided. Shortly, in 1939 and in conjunction with the Gloster Aircraft Company, Whittle was given a contract to produce England's first fighter jet airplane, the Meteor. It first flew in 1941.

In Germany, Hans von Ohain, a doctorial student in physics at the University of Göttingen, was similarly motivated to develop an efficient compressor for the gas turbine. His efforts led to early disappointments, but tests revealed enough success that his university mentors used their influence to introduce Ohain to Ernst Heinkel, the noted aircraft builder. Ohain found kindred spirits at Heinkel's company, and with that support a workable jet engine, of much simpler design than Whittle's, was incorporated into a newly designed airplane, the He 178, for its test flight in August 1939. The test was completely successful and ultimately produced the Jumo-004 (see Figure 19-3), later incorporated into the Messerschmidt 262 and Heinkel 280. These airplanes made limited but impressive appearances over the skies of Europe during World War II.

Although the United States did not have a jet research program, in 1938 General Hap Arnold (see Chapter 17), having taken command of the Army Air Corps was a member of the NACA Main Committee. One of the R&D projects underway at that time was called jet assisted takeoff (JATO), the purpose of which was to accelerate aircraft for takeoff using rockets. As a result of letters received from Charles Lindbergh while on a tour of Nazi facilities and equipment that same year at the invitation of Hermann Goering, in which Lindbergh related the speeds of German pursuit aircraft exceeding 400 mph, Arnold stepped-up propulsion research by bringing in scientists and engineers from Caltech and the Massachusetts Institute of Technology (MIT). But it was not until April 1941 that Whittle's jet engine research was made known to General Arnold by the British.

Upon receipt of those plans and specifications, in September of that year Arnold created a super secret production team composed of Bell Aircraft engineers and General Electric personnel. General Electric was chosen as the most experienced turbine producer in the country, and it was given the assignment of developing an American model along the lines of Whittle's design. Only 15 people composed the Bell/GE project, known as "Super-charger Type #1." It was assigned an old project number to avoid suspicion and the work teams were divided up in a manner that prevented any one person from realizing exactly what they were building. The resulting jet aircraft, the Bell XP-59A "Airacomet" first flew officially on October 2, 1942. But this airplane

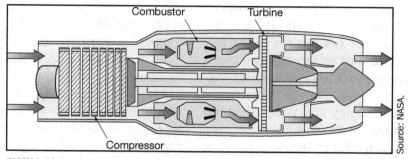

FIGURE 19-3 Germany's Jumo-004 engine.

was experimental, not a production model, and its limited range and further development precluded its application to the American effort in World War II. This initial American jet R&D, however, expanded to jet bomber adaptation that resulted in the North American B-45 Tornado and the vastly superior Boeing B-47 Stratojet, and to the first operational American fighter, the Lockheed P-80 Shooting Star.

Boeing had engineered and put in service in 1944 a very large wind tunnel capable of design testing shapes at speeds close to the speed of sound. Engineers had been dealing with drag at lower speeds for decades, but compressibility was a phenomenon that had only manifested itself as aircraft gained speeds approaching the speed of sound. Drag also appeared to increase exponentially as the speed of sound was approached. The Boeing tests concentrated on these phenomena and, unlike the B-45, were to result in a sweepback wing design never before incorporated in production aircraft. This design had the effect of delaying the onset of compressibility and of raising the speed at which the exponential increase in drag occurred. In short, it facilitated faster flight. Interest in production jet aircraft in the United States was in military aircraft, as evidenced by the B-47 medium bomber program, followed by the B-52 heavy bomber program. The first fully operational jet fighter, the Lockheed P-80, appeared in production in 1945 with its straight wings. The swept-wing North American P-86 (designation changed to F-86) appeared in production in 1948 and set the world speed record that year at 671 miles per hour. These and the other jet aircraft of the time incorporated the conventional turbojet engine with all of its drawbacks and shortcomings. Chief among these drawbacks was fuel consumption, followed by high initial cost, and frequent maintenance requirements. Airline chieftains were wary of the new, noisy technology. While there was little long-term operational data on jet engines available at the time, what was known

was daunting. The consensus among American airline executives was that the jet was too risky, too unproven, and too expensive to be seriously considered as an addition to the fleet.

In the late 1940s, a secret design concept for an improved jet engine, known as a "twin-spool turbojet" was in the works in military circles. The prototype of this engine would be known as the "J-57," and it was first tested aloft in 1951. After successful tests, it would be incorporated in a new generation of military airplanes, and it ultimately would make the difference the airline industry needed to consider turbojet propulsion in American commercial aviation. But in the early 1950s, the J-57 was still a military secret.

■ The British Comet

After World War II, commercial aviation interests in England conceded that the state of British aircraft technology and production was woefully behind that of the United States. The British, by necessity, had concentrated their efforts on fighter aircraft during the war, while the United States had been able to pursue transport development as well. The British concluded that they could never catch up with the Americans in existing technology, but they saw a chance at leveling the competitive playing field with the United States by using the conventional turbojet in a new series of passenger transports.

In 1949, the De Havilland Comet began flight-testing with a design expectation of speeds of 480 miles per hour at flight levels of 35,000 feet. (See Figure 19-4.) While pressurized aircraft had been flying since the late 1930s, no airliner had faced the stresses that would be imposed at this projected altitude. The De Havilland Comet completed testing and entered into service on British Overseas Airways Corporation (BOAC) in May 1952, to the thrill and applause of the world. The first turbojet airliner halved flight times over BOAC's world routes. To the surprise of many, the Comet made money even though

FIGURE 19-4 The Comet entered into service on British Overseas Airways Corporation in May 1952.

Source: © Hutton-Deutsch Collection/CORBIS.

its operating costs were three times that of the DC-6, even charging regular fares. The difference was that the Comet flew virtually full on all flights, proving that high-density seating was commercially feasible, at least on the vibration-free Comet. Next, Air France inaugurated jet service on some of its routes with the Comet. In the United States, it was still DC-7 and Superconstellation piston engine service.

The Comet had three serious accidents in 1953. The third one involved the airplane coming apart in the air, possibly due to a design flaw, but it had occurred in connection with suspected thunderstorm penetration and was written off to the expected result of thunderstorm force. A fourth accident on January 10, 1954 grounded all seven of the Comets. This fourth Comet was lost over the Mediterranean Sea as it climbed above 26,000 feet. Its wreckage fell into the sea and was not immediately available for study. A commission formed in England to study the accidents came up with some 50 fixes to be incorporated into the Comet fleet. These adjustments were made and the Comets resumed service.

The wreckage of the Mediterranean crash was recovered and taken to the Civil Aviation Investigation Branch in England for analysis. As the investigation was proceeding, another Comet disappeared on April 8, 1954 on a flight from Rome to Cairo as it climbed to 35,000 feet. The fleet was again grounded and an all-out investigation was ordered to resolve the cause. It was fully appreciated that the future and reputation of the English aircraft production industry was now at risk, as was the entire future of commercial jet transportation.

The Royal Aircraft Establishment at Farnborough, headquarters for British aeronautical research, was given the task of solving the mystery of the Comets' crashes. A test procedure was contrived to expose the fuselage to a lifetime of pressurization and depressurization cycles, but at a rate 40 times faster than would normally occur. On June 24, 1954, the Comet's fuselage failed, developing a structural crack at the corner of one of the square windows, and expanding away down the fuselage. This indicated that the Comets likely had exploded, not unlike a bomb, due to the interior pressure of the aircraft. In August 1954, the last section of the doomed Rome to Cairo Comet was recovered. The investigators' conclusion of the cause of the crash was confirmed as the Comet's fuselage disclosed an almost exact duplication of the test results. The Comet 1 never flew again. Two later iterations of the Comet never flew commercially. The official findings of the British government's inquiry included that "more study both in design and by experiment" was needed to secure an economically safe life of the pressure cabin. These requirements were not met until 1958, at which time the Comet 4 made the first transatlantic jet commercial flight, on October 4, 1958. By then, the British advantage had been lost, and the United States aircraft production community was just getting started.

America Catches Up

The U.S. aircraft industry took its cue from its potential customers. The industry was obviously not interested in designing and building airplanes unless and until a market existed for them. The concept of the turboprop (the turbine jet engine used to drive a propeller) was considered the likely next commercially successful form of propulsion, and research and development efforts were stepped up both in military and commercial circles, particularly at Lockheed.

There was one other possibility. Boeing's reputation as a builder of military aircraft, mainly bombers and tankers, was unequalled. But Douglas and Lockheed were far ahead of Boeing in the commercial transport field. Boeing had taken a back seat to Douglas and Lockheed in every commercial airliner contest thus far—the B-247 ran second to the DC-3, the B-307 lost out to the Connie and to WWII, and the B-377 could not compete with the DC-7 and the Super Constellation. Boeing had built the C-97 piston engine tanker for the Air Force, but it was not adequate for fueling the new jet bombers, the B-47 and the B-52. The Air Force, Boeing reckoned, would be in the market for a new jet tanker.

Boeing decided to take the gamble. On April 22, 1952, Boeing's board of directors authorized the expenditure of one-fourth of the company's total net worth, $15 million, to develop a prototype. Neither the airlines nor the military had actually expressed an interest in purchasing such an airplane, nor had any appropriation been secured in Congress for replacing the C-97. Boeing officially designated the project the model 367-80, and it was known internally at Boeing as the "dash 80" thereafter. But the designation that the world would come to know was the "707."

Boeing had the largest and the only state-of-the-art wind tunnel for testing aircraft shapes. The development of this wind tunnel, in fact, had been responsible for the adoption of the swept-wing design first incorporated in the B-47. (See Figure 19-5.) The 707 design was adapted through wind tunnel testing for over 4,000 hours. Redundant systems, overlapping structural components, multiple strength round windows, plug

FIGURE 19-5 A KC-97 refueling a B-47.

type doors for better pressurization seals, and spot welds set the standard for the jet aircraft production industry to come. The exterior shell of the 707 was engineered before the Comet disasters. Boeing decided that the skin of the aircraft would be aluminum, of a thickness that turned out to be $4\frac{1}{2}$ times as thick as the Comet's (the Comet's exterior shell was so designed in order to save weight). Boeing also incorporated a new alloy, known as titanium, that was as light as aluminum but stronger than steel, to bolster the strength and fatigue resistance of the 707's skin. Then the engineers put the design through 50,000 pressurization cycles with no evidence of metal fatigue.

Tests revealed that the positioning of the aircraft's engines on pylons slung underneath the wings provided the best lift efficiency and had the added benefit of allowing easy access to the engines for maintenance. The wings were also designed to carry 17,000 gallons of fuel, thus allowing for nonstop transcontinental range.

In 1952, Douglas was investigating the feasibility of jet-powered airliners but only went so far as to construct a full-scale wooden mockup of what was to become the DC-8. The problem in the industry, with both manufacturers and carriers, was one of confidence. None of the industry leaders could seem to project a solution to the financial impact of the cost of construction of the high-flying jet airliner and its cost of operation, particularly from the fuel standpoint. The J-57 was still not available. Projections of cost per aircraft approximated $4 million, contrasted to the $1.5 million price tag of the DC-7. Aviation industry leaders were not convinced that jets were commercially viable. C. R. Smith of American Airlines was of the opinion that in order to justify going to jetliners, the cost of operating them should be no higher than the cost of operating the DC-6. Of course, no one knew what the costs of operation of a jet fleet would be. Fuel consumption could be projected, but some costs, such as parts, maintenance, and engine life (time between overhaul, or TBO) would have to await experience. Among the Americans, only Juan Trippe dissented.

Trippe had been interested in the De Havilland Comet when it first came out, and had placed orders for three of the airplanes subject to their specifications meeting the United States Civil Aeronautics Administration requirements. There was, in fact, some concern that the CAA would not grant the Comet an airworthiness type certificate based on CAA reservations (prophetic, as it turned out) about the square corners of the windows in the aircraft. The CAA had recommended oval windows but De Havilland appeared to be satisfied with its design, citing design safety tolerances much in excess of expected stresses. Subsequent events would tragically vindicate the CAA's position but, without U.S. approval, Trippe was left in the age of piston aircraft. By the time the problems with the Comet had been rectified in the redesign of the Comet 4, in 1958, the 707 was light years ahead of the old Comet design. The Comet, for instance, had seating for 67 while the 707's capacity was 130.

Boeing's gamble paid off when, in March 1955, it received its first order for the 707, not as the anticipated passenger airliner, but as the

first jet tanker ordered by the Air Force. The first 707 was rolled out of its hangar at Renton, Washington, in May 1955, and completed its maiden flight on July 15, 1955. The 707 prototype would undergo flight testing for the next three years before being placed in commercial airline service. The largest aircraft then in commercial service was the Boeing Stratocruiser and the 707 was 15 times more powerful, twice as fast, and almost twice as big. Douglas, now convinced of the feasibility of building civilian jet aircraft, announced that it would complete its design and begin production of the DC-8.

Pan American, alone among the American carriers, seemed interested in jets, despite their projected economic indicators. Trippe had seen how the public had abandoned piston-powered airplanes in droves for the Comet, and it was his purpose to be the first to supply the high-flying, vibration-free, 500-mile-per-hour airplane of the future to America. Just as he had been among the first to abandon the wood and wire airplane and put the Fokker Trimotor all-metal cantilevered monoplane in service in 1928 (Key West to Havana), the first to inaugurate extended over-water service in the great Clipper amphibians, the first to offer his airline passengers hotel accommodations in his own hotels at their destinations, and among the first to switch to pressurized aircraft, he was now the first to order the first U.S.-produced commercial jet airliner. He did so against the prevailing industry tide in October 1955 with the announcement that he had ordered 20 Boeing 707s and, to the great delight of Douglas who did not actually have a real airplane in existence, twenty-five Douglas DC-8s. At a total capital outlay of $269 million, Pan American had committed to the largest airplane acquisition in the history of the industry.

The 707 and the DC-8 were so similar in appearance that it was hard to distinguish between them. But there were real differences to the potential customers, the airlines. First was cabin width, then length, then seating capacity, then the engines. The airlines seemed to prefer the DC-8 design. Before very long, Douglas had twice the orders for DC-8s than Boeing did for 707s. Boeing began making modifications, first to widen the fuselage to a dimension one inch wider than the DC-8, then to increase its length, wingspan, and range. Soon, it had another version of the original 707, and this time the airlines liked it. In 1955, Douglas outsold Boeing, only to be put in second place at the end of 1956. The airlines were now getting caught up in the idea of the jet age, and orders began to pour in. United States airlines bought, but so did foreign airlines. Eastern, Delta, KLM, SAS, Japan Air Lines, and Swissair all bought Douglas. American, Continental, Western, TWA, Air France, Sabena, and Lufthansa went with Boeing. Boeing had finally broken the old jinx of second best. All told, Boeing would win the numbers competition against Douglas by almost 2 to 1. The most satisfying event, though, might have been the selection by the president of the United States of the Boeing 707 as the first jet Air Force One, in 1959.

Lockheed declined to enter the competition, concentrating on the turboprop as its best guess of where the future of commercial aviation lay. Lockheed's contribution was to be the Electra, which in 1957 became the first propjet put in service by U.S. airlines. Only 169 planes were produced, some for the Navy, designated as the P-3. Convair submitted its 880 in 1959 but was unable to compete with the Boeing and Douglas jetliners, losing some $270 million for its efforts.

On October 26, 1958, Pan American became the first American air carrier to inaugurate scheduled jet service with the 707 on its New York to Paris flight. National Airlines was next on December 10, 1958, with a 707 leased from Pan Am that was put on the New York–Miami run to mark the first domestic jet service. Eastern was

flying the same route with Lockheed Electras, and immediately began losing out to National. American followed domestically by putting the 707 to work on the transcontinental route, then TWA. United was out of action awaiting the delivery of the first DC-8s, still in the production phase. Eastern could not seem to accept that the jet age had really arrived, and was woefully late in acquiring its first jets, much to its economic disadvantage against its competitors.

On any competitive route in the late 1950s, jets trounced the piston airplanes. The flying public loved jets, and this translated into filled passenger seats. The load factor went up dramatically on jet routes, and their capacity was almost twice that of the DC-7. The airlines were surprised to find that the reliability of the new jet engines greatly reduced failure concerns which had become commonplace with the great turbo-compound piston engines, and that replacement parts and maintenance costs were much lower than expected. Time Between Overhaul (TBO) was a federally mandated life expectancy of the piston engine used in commercial service in the late 1950s, and it was about 800 hours. The FAA found that jet engines could greatly exceed this limit, and gradually raised the TBO for jets to 4,000 hours. This artificial limit was ultimately discarded entirely in favor of a progressive maintenance schedule designed around the few critical components of the jet engine.

Passenger-mile costs proved to be about the same as on the DC-7. Although fuel consumption in the 707 was much higher than the DC-7, the actual passenger miles per gallon for the 707 was 42 compared to the 59 passenger miles per gallon for the DC-7. The lower cost for jet fuel (kerosene) compared to high-octane gasoline off-set this slight difference. The economics of commercial jet travel were working out after all, and the flying public embraced the jet age.

20   The Federal Aviation Act

Responsibility for aviation safety had been lodged in the Civil Aeronautics Authority (CAA) by virtue of the Civil Aeronautics Act of 1938, as amended in 1940. Over the course of the ensuing 20 years, aviation safety had dramatically improved, largely due to the reliability of aircraft and engines and the development of instruments and navigation aids. The skies were much more crowded in 1958 than they had been in 1938, no doubt; but progress had been made in refining the airway (navigation) structure since the days of the lighted (beacon) airways. Beginning in 1947, VHF Omni-directional Radio transmitters (VOR) were installed across the country. An aircraft with a VOR receiver could track inbound from any point, directly to the station, by means of visual reference to the display shown in the onboard aircraft receiver. The direct routes between the VOR transmitters were established in 1950, designated as Victor airways, and were given numbers to distinguish one from another. Instead of flying from city to city as previously, or from one low-frequency radio transmitter to another (the radio range navigation system), aircraft that were equipped with these high-frequency radio receivers flew these new routes as aerial highways.

For years the CAA had been authorized to fashion rules and regulations to promote aviation safety and to thus establish standards for aircraft, engines, propellers, and mechanics, as well as for flight schools and the training of airmen. It was also charged with developing and administering the Air Traffic Control system (ATC), the system operated by the federal government that regulated the movement of aircraft throughout the United States. Control of aircraft by ATC could range all the way from taxi to takeoff, departure and en route clearance, to arrival and landing clearance at destination. Most aircraft in the 1950s flew under Visual Flight Rules (VFR), which required little or no ATC control. Airline passenger operations, however, flew largely under Instrument Flight Rules (IFR), the procedure that was designed to ensure that an aircraft had airspace reserved specifically for it, so that no other airplane flying under IFR would occupy that same airspace. But it was not uncommon for airline traffic to also fly under visual flight rules, at least for part of the planned route of flight.

These regulations were known as Civil Aeronautic Regulations (CARS) and were published in the Code of Federal Regulations. The CAA appears to have dutifully performed its administrative function regarding such matters. It can be argued with the aid of hindsight, however, that there was a lack of long-range vision within the CAA during its first 20 years of existence, between 1938 and 1958.

For one thing, the CAA was buried within the Department of Commerce along with the agencies that dealt with highways, maritime issues, textiles, the census, and myriad other matters. To make things worse, its appropriations had been slashed following World War II. Voice communication between pilots and ground controllers using high frequency radio had only been completely implemented in 1955. CAA air traffic control centers, which exercised control over all IFR traffic within large geographical areas throughout the country, now had direct voice contact with most aircraft within their sectors, although in some remote areas of the country it was still necessary for aircraft to relay and receive communications with ATC through airline company channels, particularly in uncontrolled airspace. CAA controllers kept track of the location of each aircraft in the sector by means of position reports given by the pilots themselves. These position reports included time, altitude, last radio fix or location, next radio fix, and the estimated time of arrival at that fix. Position reporting was cumbersome and that system required extremely large blocks of airspace to be reserved for a single aircraft.

Radar, only recently invented (WWII), was slower to be adopted. Radar was first implemented by ATC only as an aid to making instrument approaches to airports during instrument or bad weather conditions. Gradually, as the number of large planes increased and began competing for the available airspace, it became more and more difficult for the air traffic control center personnel to keep track of aircraft. Distance Measuring Equipment (DME), the system that allowed an airplane to determine its distance from an equipped navigation facility, was incorporated into the VOR (Victor) airways system beginning in 1951. Now an aircraft could not only determine its azimuth location (bearing) from the station, it also could determine its distance. DME was a big help in tracking aircraft in the "voice only" system but, even so, the control problem was becoming unmanageable.

In 1955 there were surveillance radars in place at 32 locations to service traffic arrival and departure at airports, but there were no long-range radars to control en route traffic except in the mid-Atlantic

region at Baltimore. Concerns were raised that ATC traffic congestion increased the likelihood of mid-air collision. Extension of long-range radars to provide positive radar control for en route traffic was discussed, but not implemented. Then, on June 30, 1956, a United Airlines DC-7 collided with a TWA Super Constellation over the Grand Canyon, in Arizona, killing 128 people. (See Figure 20-1.)

In order to take a closer look at this tragedy, some background regarding how ATC did things at the time is helpful. Commercial airline flights at the time were conducted under both IFR and VFR rules, at different times during the same flight. ATC provided aircraft separation only to aircraft flying under instrument flight rules, and then only to aircraft flying within "controlled" airspace. It is also important to note that the aircraft separation provided was only as to other IFR traffic, not aircraft flying under visual flight rules.

En route controlled airspace (as opposed to terminal airspace) was basically limited to Victor airways that crisscrossed the country. A disadvantage to the Victor airways system was that its zigzag courses often did not suit either favorable wind conditions or preferred airline routing. Airline operations were thus permitted on "direct" routes between points, but these operations were "off airways," or in uncontrolled airspace, in which ATC did not provide either control or aircraft separation, even on IFR flight plans. Operations in uncontrolled airspace were therefore conducted under visual flight rules where flight crews were obligated to "see and avoid" all other aircraft traffic.

TWA 2 and United 718 both departed Los Angeles on IFR flight plans within minutes of each other. TWA 2 was assigned an altitude of 19,000 feet and United 718 was cleared to 21,000 feet. While still in controlled airspace at 19,000 feet, TWA 2 requested and was granted clearance to "1,000 on top," which allowed it to climb to and maintain any altitude at least 1,000 feet above the general cloud layer. TWA 2 then climbed to 21,000 feet.

As the two flights neared the Grand Canyon, both aircraft were at 21,000 feet on converging courses. They were in uncontrolled airspace, in clear weather with only scattered buildups that could be circumnavigated. Both aircraft were

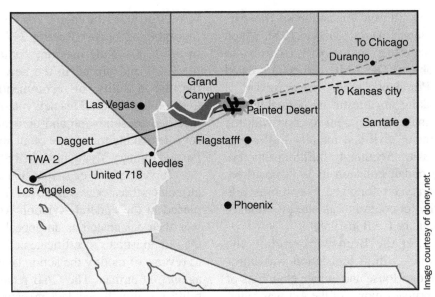

FIGURE 20-1 Collision of United Airlines DC-7 and TWA Super Constellation, June 30, 1956.

flying under visual flight rules that required each to "see and avoid" each other, but somehow they did neither. While no definitive causation could be established, the crash investigation panel suggested that the towering cumulous might have obscured the aircraft from each other.

This accident caused the largest loss of life since the beginning of commercial aviation. It focused public attention on the increasingly crowded skies developing over America as commercial aviation grew. The addition of jets to the aircraft fleet, flying at almost twice the speed of the fastest piston aircraft, would only increase the hazard. Another problem was the mix of military aircraft with civilian aircraft in common airspace. Bomber and fighter jet aircraft operated under one set of rules run by the military, and civilian aircraft operated under a different set of rules administered by the CAA.

The civilian-military dichotomy of aircraft control soon produced a second midair catastrophe. On January 31, 1957, a Douglas Aircraft owned DC-7 and an Air Force F-89 collided near Sunland, California at 25,000 feet. The DC-7 had a crew of four who were onboard in connection with a test flight of the aircraft, with no passengers. The F-89 Scorpion, with a crew of two, was conducting an unrelated test flight. Near head-on closure at high

speed was deemed the probable cause. A particularly regrettable and high profile aspect of this midair collision was the fact that aircraft debris fell onto the occupied school yard of Pacoima Junior High School, where hundreds of students happened to be engaged in athletic activities. Three boys were killed and some 71 children were injured.

The lack of uniformity and coordination in aircraft control between civilian and military authority was further highlighted by the midair collision of a United DC-7 with a U.S. Air Force F-100 on April 21, 1958 very near the Grand Canyon. The F-100 was based at Nellis AFB and the DC-7 was en route from Los Angeles to New York at 21,000 feet when the collision occurred. Neither aircraft was aware of the presence of the other, and neither were their respective controlling authorities. On May 2, 1958, yet another midair occurred when a military jet trainer and a civilian airliner collided over Brunswick, Maryland. This time the death toll was 12. It was clear that something had to be done.

Although it had been apparent to many people in authority since the early 1950s that technological advances in aviation and the growth of commercial aviation had compromised the government's function to properly promote safety in commercial air travel, no consensus for remedial action formed until this series of midair collisions occurred. The first action taken was the formation of the Airways Modernization Board (AMB) in 1957, which was really no more than a temporary fix to try to address the problem. The AMB had been created as a result of a Presidential report that warned of "a crisis in the making" as a result of the inability of the airspace management system to cope with the complex patterns of civil and military traffic plying America's skies. Seemingly fulfilling this dire prediction, the midair collision in 1958 occurred. Another temporary fix followed to combine rule making authority for control of all aircraft, military as well as civil, in the CAB in 1958.

The day after the Brunswick midair, the Federal Aviation Act draft legislation was introduced into both the House and Senate chambers of Congress. The primary mover of the Act was Senator Mike Monroney of Oklahoma, a frequent critic of existing aviation policy. President Eisenhower sent a special message to Congress soon after in which he referenced the "recent midair collision" and the "tragic losses of life," and through which he asked for the establishment of a federal agency to consolidate the functions required to administer the needs of both civil and military aviation in the country. Congress finally acted.

The Federal Aviation Act of 1958 was signed into law by President Eisenhower on August 23, 1958. While the Act incorporated virtually all of the provisions of the Civil Aeronautics Act of 1938 that related to economic regulation (entry, rates, routes, mergers, interlocking directorates, and agreements among air carriers), its great impact was on safety. The CAA was abolished and in its place was created the Federal Aviation Agency, which was organized as an independent agency answerable to Congress.

The Federal Aviation Agency was given authority to make long-range plans and to implement such plans without interference from competing government interests. All air safety research and development was consolidated and placed with the new agency; thus, the work of the Airways Modernization Board, the Air Coordinating Committee, and the National Advisory Committee for Aeronautics (NACA) was assumed by the Federal Aviation Agency. Recall that an example of the work of

NACA includes the engine cowl research originally incorporated on the Boeing 247 and DC-1 back in the 1930s. Rule making was taken away from the CAB and placed in the new agency, as was the responsibility for recommendation regarding aviation legislation. This new rule-making authority included consolidation and unification of authority for rule making for control of all aircraft, both civilian and military, flying in United States airspace.

Jurisdiction over suspension or revocation of airmen certificates was removed from the CAB and placed in the Federal Aviation Agency; the CAB was then designated as an appeal board to review the Administrator's certificate action with authority to reverse or modify the action taken by the agency against an airman. The CAB retained its responsibility for aircraft accident investigation as well as all aspects of economic regulation of the airlines.

In the fall of 1958, the first Federal Aviation Agency Administrator to be appointed was retired Air Force General Elwood R. "Pete" Quesada. (See Figure 20-2.) He stepped up enforcement procedures in the airlines, assessing fines and issuing suspensions for rules violations. He led the way for the adoption of military-style radar for control of civilian aircraft. His tenure with the Federal Aviation Agency was marked by stormy relations with the airlines and its pilots, as well as with general aviation, but it set the country on a course of placing safety first for the flying public, a priority constant to this day.

FIGURE 20-2 Pete Quesada being sworn in at the FAA in the fall of 1958.

21   **The Next Jets**

Boeing had upgraded the 707 in 1959 with the new J-75 engine. The DC-8 was flying. Big jets were flying long distances and setting records, and the public was fascinated. Governments the world over were buying these jets and setting up their own airlines. Flying in jets was a prestigious activity.

The government of France had been eclipsed in the jet design and production market. Its aviation representatives took note of something that was not in production and not even on the drawing boards—a medium-range jet that could carry 60 passengers up to 1,200 miles. This was the airplane for the European market and, presciently, was to become the airplane for the deregulated market of the future. This was the Regional Jet.

In response to a government-sponsored competition, Sud Aviation in Toulouse, France came up with a novel idea in aircraft construction. They placed the aircraft's engines on the side of the fuselage near the tail of the aircraft instead of under the wings. They called this prototype the Caravelle (see Figure 21-1), a name given small sailing ships during the age of exploration. Production began, and in 1956 Air France contracted for the first twelve airliners to come off the line.

Source: National Air and Space Museum, Smithsonian Institution (SI 82-14081).

FIGURE 21-1   The Caravelle was a prototype with the aircraft's engines on the side of the fuselage near the tail of the aircraft.

British European Airways, the government-owned airline, flew many of the same routes on the Continent using turboprops. Given the proven popularity of jets, already evident in the 1950s, Britain realized that it must build its own short-haul aircraft in order to compete. Its entry was the Hawker-Siddeley Trident, which incorporated the Caravelle aft-engine innovation but added a third engine housed within the vertical stabilizer and aft fuselage. The aircraft designers placed the horizontal stabilizer at the top of the vertical stabilizer, out of the way of the jet exhaust, an arrangement that provided more stability at low airspeeds.

Meanwhile, Boeing was testing the aft-engine concept with an aft-mounted engine attached to its 707 prototype, and it was pondering the viability of such an aircraft in the domestic market. Douglas had designed the DC-9, with its aft-mounted engines, in response to a request by United Airlines, but no other carrier expressed interest, and the design was put on hold. The airlines specified an aircraft with two or three engines, for cost effectiveness, that could operate from shorter runways like LaGuardia. Boeing's engineers were first to conclude that a three-engine airplane with a T-tail was the most likely airplane to succeed, borrowing from the Trident design, which had proven out in Boeing's tests. They designated the new airplane the Boeing 727 and incorporated the new Pratt & Whitney JT8D turbofan, with up to 17,500 pounds of thrust, as the power plant. Turbofans evolved from turbojets as early as 1960, mainly in response to complaints about the noise produced by straight jets, both while in taxi and airborne. The JT8D was not only quieter, but it was also more economical to operate than any other engine at the time.

The 727 was an aesthetically pleasing airplane. (See Figure 21-2.) It was said that building the 727 would have been warranted even if it could not fly. It utilized the same basic fuselage as the 707 and incorporated a new flap design that, at slow airspeeds, increased the wing area by 25 percent; thereby greatly reducing the aircraft stall speed. This reduction in speed enabled the 727 to operate from shorter runways, just as specified by the airlines.

The first production model of the 727 flew late in 1962 and immediately began to surpass its design criteria. It was faster, its fuel consumption was less, and its payload was greater. Short landing and takeoff was proven in operation, and its superb handling made it one of the most trusted and respected aircraft flying. Concerns arising from a series of four crashes occurring in 1965 were alleviated when it was determined that they were all caused by pilot error in allowing the airplane to descend at a rate from which recovery was difficult. These accidents established that the 727, in spite of its easy handling characteristics, had to be flown by the numbers, like most jets. The performance of the 727 would go on to earn it a reputation as the most successful commercial transport aircraft in the history of aviation. By the early 1980s, Boeing had delivered or contracted to deliver almost 2,000 of the very unique airplanes.

After Douglas had placed its DC-9 plans on hold in the late 1950s, the emergence of the short-to-medium range aircraft market caused Douglas to dust off its DC-9 blueprints. In April 1961, Douglas announced that it would begin production of the DC-9. Although Douglas had no orders placed at the time of its announcement, within a month Delta disclosed its contract to purchase 15 of the new jets. Boeing did not respond to the DC-9 until 1965, the same year the first DC-9 went into service. (See Figure 21-3.) Then Boeing unveiled its plans for the 737. The 737 was not a sleek airplane, having a width equal to the 727 and 707 but not the length—it was shorter even than the DC-9. Lufthansa Airlines was instrumental in the design of the 737 because they were first to order the airplane, insisting that it carry 100 passengers, ten more than the DC-9. The 737 entered service in 1968. (See Figure 21-4.)

Sales of the 737 were initially depressed primarily because the Air Line Pilots Association (ALPA) took the position that ALPA crews

Image courtesy of Corel.

FIGURE 21-2 Boeing 727.

Image courtesy of Corel.

FIGURE 21-3 Douglas DC-9.

Image courtesy of Corel.

FIGURE 21-4 Boeing 737.

would not fly the 737 with only two flight crew members; demanding that a flight engineer be included in the cockpit. ALPA was playing catch-up from its earlier failure to require three-man crews in the DC-9. This requirement made the 737's operating costs too high to be competitive, so the airlines largely rejected the airplane. ALPA abandoned its three-crew position in 1974, partly because of worldwide recession based on the fuel crisis that year, and partly because of the untenable and obvious featherbedding aspects of its three-crew position. Airlines then started buying the 737.

For the first time, feeder airlines began to buy the short-to-medium range jets and to bring jet service to the hinterlands of America. Piedmont, North Central Airlines, and Allegheny Airlines were able to expand their service, and in the later years of regulation, beginning in the early 1970s, these airlines were able to secure routes to destinations previously unavailable to them. These jets made routes between small airports—like Tri-Cities, Tennessee to Chicago, or to Washington, D.C., or to New York—convenient and profitable. The feeder lines preferred one class service and gave the world a glimpse of the age of deregulation to come. But first, the jumbo jets had to fly.

The Really Big Jets

In 1962, Lockheed won an Air Force contract to build the largest cargo plane ever conceived. The aircraft specified by the government included power plants of four 21,000-pound thrust turbofans, a range of 4,000 miles, and a useful load of 71,000 pounds plus fuel. When complete, the aircraft would be known as the C-141 Starlifter, and it would have shortcomings. Chief among these was the fact that the C-141 did not have the design volume required to house the cargo load specified. Already recognized by the Air Force was the need for a larger airplane. The Air Force had put out for competition the design of what was to be known as the C-5A, a truly mammoth creation. Lockheed won this competition too, even though Boeing's entry was a serious contender in the competition and, on reflection, perhaps the best of the three entries.

Second-place Boeing decided to convert its design and engineering effort to commercial passenger use. Juan Trippe, ever on the cutting edge, had indicated an interest in such an aircraft. Boeing showed that its cargo plane could be modified to accommodate 450 passengers, at 19 feet, 5 inches in width, and 231 feet in length. The JT9D turbofan, a high-bypass-ratio jet engine with 41,000 pounds of thrust, was chosen to power the aircraft. This airplane would also fly faster than previous models, at 625 miles per hour, and would be known as the 747. (See Figure 21-5.) Juan Trippe had long ago concluded that the key to making

FIGURE 21-5 The Boeing 747.

Source: Florida State Archives.

money in the airline business was to fill the airplanes with paying customers, like he did with the DC-4 in the late 1940s in the San Juan to New York migration. Now, this was a dream come true. He signed a letter of intent to purchase 25 of the "wide bodies," as they were to be known.

Boeing, just as it had during the design phase of the first American jet transport, the 707, took its safety responsibilities seriously. The "carnage factor" of a crash of such a large aircraft was daunting, and only increased Boeing's commitment to safety in the design stage. A "safety committee" was formed to review every aspect of the new aircraft. Concerns of the committee ran the gamut of engineering and construction, from hydraulics, to wing loads, and even to coffee pots. The airplane was so huge that Boeing did not even have a facility large enough to build it, so a new plant had to be constructed at Everett, Washington. It was the largest factory in the world.

The 747 first flew on February 9, 1969. Once again, Pan American was the first to place yet another new prototype airliner in service, this time the 747 Clipper Young America out of JFK for Europe. The 747 had initial problems, mostly because of its size. For instance, baggage

facilities were overloaded at destination, causing delays; cabin attendants were overwhelmed by the number of drinks, meals, and related requirements caused by the passenger count; the lavatories seemed inadequate for the needs of passengers; and so on. Each of the concerns was addressed, resolved, and the 747 gradually became a favorite of the flying public. The upper deck of the 747, complete with its cocktail lounge atmosphere for first-class passengers, which was sometimes converted to a restaurant, and its piano manned by a professional pianist, was reminiscent of the lower deck of the Stratocruiser of the 1940s.

In 1967, Lockheed completed its design for its wide-bodied entrant into the field, known as the L-1011 Tristar. (See Figures 21-6 and 21-7.) Lockheed utilized the fuselage tail-mounted

FIGURE 21-6 Comparison of the interiors of the L-1011 (top) and the F-7 (bottom).

Source: Florida State Archives.

FIGURE 21-7   Lockheed L-1011.

Image courtesy of Corel.

engine of the original Trident, together with two wing-mounted engines, for its combined power plant, and it could accommodate 300 passengers.

Circumstances, primarily financial, had required Douglas to merge with McDonnell Aircraft of St. Louis in 1967. The new company was known as McDonnell-Douglas. Its submission to the wide-body contest was the DC-10, which bore a marked similarity to the L-1011. Both aircraft had three turbofans, one mounted under each wing and one tail mounted. The L-1011's rear engine's intake was built into the vertical stabilizer above the top of the fuselage, with the engine mounted at the rear of the cabin. In the DC-10, the third engine was mounted through the vertical stabilizer, with the intake and exhaust in a direct line fore to aft. (See Figure 21-8.)

FIGURE 21-8   DC-10.

Image courtesy of Corel.

In 1970, European aircraft builders, funded by their national governments and comprising a loose consortium of French and British interests that were later joined by the Germans, established their own aircraft production company, Airbus Industrie. The purpose, as they said, was "to reduce dependence on foreign equipment, facilitate survival of a struggling European aircraft industry and address a market opportunity not being met by the Americans." This consortium designed the Airbus 300, a 300-passenger entry actually built by Sud Aviation in Toulouse, France. The A300 had only two turbofan engines, either Rolls-Royce or General Electric, but for various reasons the A300 was slow to materialize. The A300 did not fly until 1972, over three years after the 747, and over one year after the DC-10.

Problems related to structural integrity were encountered by the DC-10 shortly after its inauguration. First, in June 1972, an American Airlines DC-10 out of Detroit suffered a decompression incident when a baggage door, located on the lower deck, blew off and collapsed the supporting deck of the passenger section above. Hydraulic lines had been designed and built to run the length of the aircraft through the floor or deck between the upper and lower compartments, and when the floor collapsed, some of these lines were severed, causing serious control problems for the flight crew. Only the ingenuity and skill of the crew allowed the stricken craft to be brought in for a safe landing.

The baggage doors were not the plug-type doors designed into many jet aircraft, but were dependent on latch mechanisms that, upon investigation, were found to be defective. An aircraft directive mandating corrective action was issued and the modifications were performed with the exception of two airplanes.

One of these was found and fixed; the other was not. On March 3, 1974, the airliner that had been overlooked, a Turkish Airline DC-10, which was flying from Paris to London, suffered a similar baggage door failure with a similar floor collapse. This time the crew was unable to fly the aircraft, which crashed, taking all 346 lives aboard.

In the DC-10, no further baggage door incidents occurred, nor were any other serious failures experienced for six years. Then on May 25, 1979, as an American Airlines DC-10 climbed out from Chicago O'Hare after takeoff, the left engine separated from the wing pylon, causing the aircraft to roll inverted and nose down, a condition that the crew was unable to correct at such a low altitude. All 271 people on board were killed, along with two more on the ground. The NTSB determined the probable cause of the accident was "the asymmetrical stall and the ensuing roll of the aircraft because of the uncommanded retraction of the left wing leading edge slats." The separation resulted "from improper maintenance procedures which led to the failure of the pylon structure."

The wide-bodied experience of the American producers could be said to have been only marginally successful. Ultimately, McDonnell-Douglas sold 300 DC-10s while Lockheed sold only 244 L-1011s. By 1982 when production of the L-1011 was halted, Lockheed is said to have lost some $2.5 billion on the project.

Airbus, on the other hand, had managed to design a product that would crack the American airline market from Europe for the first time. The A300 had only two engines. This was of some concern initially for transoceanic flight, but it translated directly into reduced operating costs.

Secondly, the A300 had incorporated composite, lightweight materials in its structure, adding to its cost effectiveness. As Air France began in 1974 to operate the A300 around the world, the airplane soon began to sell in the European and Asian airline market. Korean Air Lines, Lufthansa, Indian Air Lines, and South African Airways bought the A300. Frank Borman of Eastern arranged a six-month trial of the A300 for its New York to Miami route, without any commitment to buy the airplane. This was an unprecedented deal, amounting to a manufacturer loss-leader arrangement whereby Airbus, in effect, loaned its airplane to Eastern on a trial basis. It turned out to be a brilliant stroke by Airbus that resulted in Eastern placing an order for 23 of the aircraft at the price of $25 million a copy, in April 1978.

With the Airbus 300, a trend began in airliner construction of wide-bodied, twin-engined, and lighter weight airplanes that still endures. Boeing contributed the 767 in 1983, using weight-saving composite materials and an advanced wing structure. Since the Boeing and Douglas face-off in the 1930s, beginning with the introduction of the 247 and the DC-1, the history of commercial airliner production competition had been an altogether American affair. Now, with the emergence of Airbus Industrie, combined with the shrinking number of American aircraft manufacturers, the contest was becoming not only international, but also specifically European versus American.

22 The Department of Transportation

Prior to the creation of the Department of Transportation, the broad function of the administration of transportation fell to the Undersecretary of Commerce for Transportation. The Department of Commerce, a cabinet-level executive department under the direction of a secretary and also a member of the president's cabinet, had been the catch-all repository for the various forms of transportation. The nation's regulation of transportation was administered by agencies, like the Interstate Commerce Commission and the Civil Aeronautics Administration, within the department created to deal with specific modes of transportation. Aviation matters had been removed from the Commerce Department by the Federal Aviation Act of 1958 so that, in 1966, both the CAB and the Federal Aviation Agency (formerly the CAA) were independent agencies. Others remained within the Commerce Department. Administration of the nation's transportation system was fragmented. Some transportation modes were over-funded and over-regulated, while others were under-funded and operated under a system of benign neglect.

The needs of the country from the earliest times were seen as including an efficient and accessible transportation infrastructure. But no overall plan had ever emerged to develop or administer transportation.

In 1965, the then-administrator of the Federal Aviation Agency, Najeeb Halaby, recommended to planners in the Johnson Administration that a cabinet-level Department of Transportation be created based, in part, on his experience as head of that agency. For one thing, Halaby believed that the Federal Aviation Agency had been frozen out of the deliberations surrounding the administration's consideration of a supersonic aircraft transport program. To Halaby, this aviation endeavor was something that the FAA should be consulted on. He wrote to President Johnson that there existed ". . . no point of responsibility below the president capable of taking an even-handed, comprehensive, authoritarian approach to the development of transportation policies . . ." and that no means existed ". . . to ensure reasonable coordination and balance among the various transportation programs of the government."

Others in the Johnson Administration also saw the need for unification of transportation activities, legislation, and oversight. At the urgings of Joseph A. Califano, Jr., Special Assistant to the President, and Charles Schultze, Director of the Bureau of the Budget, a special Task Force was created to explore the wisdom and feasibility of creating such a cabinet-level department. In October 1965, Alan S. Boyd, then Undersecretary of

Commerce for Transportation, and who had been appointed to head the Task Force, forwarded to the president recommendations that included the creation of a Department of Transportation. The Task Force report further recommended that all separate sub-agencies that dealt with transportation matters be included in the proposed department. Representative of these were the Federal Aviation Agency, the Bureau of Public Roads, the Saint Lawrence Seaway Development Corporation, the Interstate Commerce Commission, the Civil Aeronautics Board, and the Panama Canal Administration.

Legislation was forwarded to Congress on March 6, 1966, with a letter from Johnson in which he stated: "America today lacks a coordinated transportation system that permits travelers and goods to move conveniently and efficiently from one means of transportation to another, using the best characteristics of each." The thrust of the proposed legislation sought to create one venue for the coordination and management of government-funded transportation programs, and to provide a center for the development of a national transportation policy and its administration.

Debate on the bill was lively, given that many bureaucrats, with their supporters in Congress, had long staked out their turf with respect to their own agencies and authority. The maritime industry opposed the bill, and some in the Federal Aviation Agency voiced fears that its newly won independent status (by the Federal Aviation Act of 1958) would be lost. Nevertheless, by October 1966, a compromise had been reached, and President Johnson signed the bill into law. It was known as the Department of Transportation Act of 1967.

The Department of Transportation (DOT) began operations on April 1, 1967, becoming the fourth-largest cabinet-level department within the United States government. It combined over thirty transportation agencies and functions, and their employees, who numbered some 95,000. During the organizational phase of setting up the DOT were born the Federal Aviation Administration, the Federal Highway Administration, and the Federal Railroad Administration. DOT absorbed functions that previously belonged to departments other than Commerce. Urban mass transit, for example, was removed from the Department of Housing and Urban Development, which in turn caused the creation of additional agencies (the Urban Mass Transportation Administration, later renamed the Federal Transit Administration). The National Transportation Safety Board (NTSB) was created, which assumed the investigative responsibilities formerly carried out by the CAB's Bureau of Aviation Safety. The administration of aviation was placed in the new department and named the Federal Aviation Administration.

The Federal Aviation Administration

When the Department of Transportation Act created the Federal Aviation Administration (FAA), the function of the government in promoting, regulating, and enforcing aviation safety standards finally found a permanent home. A quick review of the history of the administration of aviation safety shows the torturous path that it had taken.

The Air Commerce Act of 1926 first authorized safety regulation, the administration of which was placed within the Department of Commerce. The Aeronautics Branch was created as an agency in the Department of Commerce and became the first government agency to concern itself with aviation safety. This agency was renamed the Bureau of Air Commerce in 1934. Under the Civil Aeronautics Act of 1938 (as amended in 1940), these functions were transferred to the Civil Aeronautics Administration (CAA) and remained within the Department of Commerce.

The Federal Aviation Act of 1958 significantly reallocated existing authority in aviation regulatory matters. The CAA was renamed the Federal Aviation Agency, removed from the Department of Commerce, and organized as an independent agency that reported only to Congress and to the president. The Federal Aviation Agency was given the responsibility previously exercised by the CAB for proposing air safety legislation (statutory) and for rule making, designated under the CAB as Civil Aeronautic Rules (CARs), and now known as the Federal Aviation Regulations (FARs). All air safety research and development authority was consolidated within the Agency, including that previously carried out by the National Advisory Committee for Aeronautics, the Airways Modernization Board, and the Air Coordinating Committee. The procedural responsibility in airman certificate actions was also transferred from the CAB to the Federal Aviation Agency. Under the Federal Aviation Act of 1958, the CAB retained its responsibility for the investigation of aircraft accidents as well as its economic regulation of the airlines, and it became an appeals review board for certificate action taken by the Federal Aviation Agency.

Under the provisions of the Department of Transportation Act, responsibility for aviation safety, and virtually all logical ramifications of safety issues, were placed within the authority of the Federal Aviation Administration. Its basic mission is defined by its legislative mandate, particularly the Federal Aviation Act of 1958. In 1984, Congress authorized commercial space launches by the private (nongovernmental) sector for the first time under the Commercial Space Launch Act. Regulatory authority was initially placed within the Department of Transportation in the Office of Commercial Space Transportation (AST), but in 1995 this function was moved over to the FAA under the same name, Office of Space Transportation (AST). This office conducts the only space-related function within the FAA. FAA/AST regulates the commercial space transportation industry to ensure compliance with international obligations of the United States and to enhance safety and national security. It also licenses commercial space launches of both

orbital and suborbital rockets and nonfederal launch sites, or spaceports.

The scope of the functions assigned to the FAA are pervasive. While safety has always been the mainstay of the FAA mandate, ongoing developments in aviation have caused new emphasis to be placed on related but separate concerns, such as security,[1] the environment, airport funding, international relations, and commercial space activities.

The functions of the FAA could logically be examined from several different perspectives, but for our purposes the following breakout of FAA responsibility should be the most instructive.

Regulation

The FAA, as a government agency with rule-making authority, is required to follow certain procedures when originating or altering regulations that it issues. All federal agencies are required to issue Notices of Proposed Rule Making, published in the Federal Register, which are designed to allow those who may be affected by the proposed rule to be put on notice that a new regulation may be coming, and to allow input to the FAA on the impact of the proposed rule. Input from the aviation industry, or others who may be affected by the rule, often causes modification or abandonment of the proposed rule, and is an important and practical aspect of the regulatory function of the FAA. Industry groups, such as the Airline Transport Association, Aircraft Owners and Pilots Association, National Business Aviation Association, and National Business Aircraft Association, closely monitor the FAA for these Notices of Proposed Rule Making.

See Chapter 41 for a full discussion of FAA responsibilities for commercial space launch activity.

Regulations adopted by the FAA are published in the Code of Federal Regulations,

Title 14, and referred to in the aviation community as Federal Aviation Regulations (FARs). These regulations have the force of law and are primarily concerned with safety, although environmental (noise) and funding issues are also addressed. The FAA is required by the provisions of the Aircraft Noise Abatement Act of 1968 to consult with the Environmental Protection Agency (EPA) to establish noise standards and to enforce those standards by regulation. In addition to the FARs, the FAA issues mandatory orders that have the force of law in the form of Airworthiness Directives (ADs). These directives generally require inspections or modifications to aircraft that are already certified and in use in the aviation community, and may be prompted by accidents, operating experience, or observations of pilots and mechanics.

Certification

The FAA enhances the safe operation of aviation by controlling, through certification, who may legally function in civil aviation, and by certification of certain equipment used in domestic civil aviation. Certification by the FAA applies to eight major categories:

1. Airmen
2. Aircraft
3. Air Carriers
4. Air Navigation Facilities
5. Air Agencies
6. Airports
7. Designees (representatives of the Administrator)
8. Unmanned Aircraft Systems

Airmen

Certification is required of pilots, flight engineers, navigators, air traffic controllers, aircraft dispatchers, mechanics, repairmen, and parachute riggers. Certification of airmen includes procedures not only for the written and oral testing of applicants, but also the requirement of practical demonstrations of required levels of proficiency.

Minimum physical and mental health standards are applied through periodic medical examinations of airmen. The FAA issues separate medical certificates to airmen through its network of Aviation Medical Examiners. The amorphous standard that airmen possess "good moral character" has been consistently required of all certificate holders since passage of the Air Commerce Act of 1926.

Aircraft

The FAA issues three types of certificates applicable to aircraft and their components—Type, Production, and Airworthiness. The aircraft components that must be certified include aircraft engines, propellers, and appliances. Every civil aircraft manufactured in the United States is subject to this inspection and certification regimen beginning with the design of the aircraft. A Type Certificate is issued to the aircraft manufacturer after flight and static testing confirms that the design conforms to the standards adopted by the FAA and published in the FARs. The issuance of a Production Type Certificate follows on the manufacturer meeting all FAA standards designed to assure that all aircraft produced pursuant to the Type Certificate will faithfully conform to the approved design of the aircraft. This certificate is a sort of quality assurance requirement based on the manufacturer's production and inspection methods at its plant. The final requirement imposed by the FAA is the Airworthiness Certificate, which is awarded to each and every aircraft that comes off the assembly line and is required before the aircraft can be delivered to a purchaser. This certificate is valid only for a period of twelve months.

Air Carriers

There are two types of certificates issued by the federal government to air carriers in the United States. Air Carrier Operating Certificates are issued by the FAA under Part 121 of the FARs to carriers operating aircraft for hire with 10 or more seats. The compliance requirements of Part 121 are numerous, but the two major areas addressed are the training of flight crews and aircraft maintenance programs. Air Carrier Fitness Certificates, also referred to as Certificates of Public Convenience and Necessity, are issued by DOT, not the FAA, and establish that the carrier has shown that it has the financial capacity and management expertise to carry on a scheduled airline operation. These are required only of carriers operating aircraft with 61 or more seats. While some Fitness Certificates authorize only cargo operations, the majority of such certificates apply to both passenger and cargo operations.

Air Navigation Facilities

Air navigation facilities include radio directional equipment and landing aids and are inspected and rated by the FAA to ensure compliance with safety operational standards. A certificate issued by the FAA to such a facility establishes such compliance.

Air Agencies

FAA regulations applying to aircraft repair stations and to maintenance technician facilities, pilot schools, and training centers include the requirement of meeting certification standards relating to procedures, instructors, equipment, tools, and personnel.

Airports

Since 1982, the FAA has been charged with certificating operators of airports serving certificated air carriers (Airport and Airway Development Act). FAA regulations containing the requirements applicable to such airport operators are found in Part 139 and relate primarily to maintenance of minimum safety standards in airport operations.

Designees

The FAA designates individuals possessing certain skills, training, or education to assist it in carrying out its examination and inspection duties and through whom FAA certificates are issued. These individuals must first be certified, themselves, as representatives of the administrator and must hold that certificate issued by the FAA. These individuals include Aviation Medical Examiners who are issued a Certificate of Designation, and Pilot Examiners (Flight Standards Designated Examiner) who are issued a Certificate of Authority. In addition, Certificates of Authority are issued to Technical Personnel Examiners, Designated Aircraft Maintenance Inspectors, Designated Engineering Representatives, Designated Manufacturing Inspection Representatives, and Designated Airworthiness Representatives.

Unmanned Aircraft Systems

There are three categories of Unmanned Aircraft Systems (UAS) now operating under FAA authorization in the National Air Space (NAS) in the United States: Model aircraft, Experimental UAS, and Public UAS.

Model Aircraft

FAA Advisory Circular (AC) 91-57, entitled "Model Aircraft Operating Standards" applies to the recreational use of the NAS by model airplane operators. Issued in 1981, these standards limit the operation of model aircraft to less than 400 feet above the surface, away from populated areas, and when operated within three miles of an airport, notice must be given to the airport operator or control tower.

Experimental UAS

The FAA issues Special Airworthiness Certificates in the Experimental Category (SAC-EC) to civil operators of UAS and optionally piloted aircraft (OPA) for research and development, market survey, and crew training operations. This certificate does not extend to the carrying of persons or property for compensation or hire. The FAA has issued these certificates since 2005 to a limited number of applicants who work with the FAA to collect technical and operational data to improve the UAS certification process.

Public UAS

The FAA issues Certificates of Waiver or Authorization (COA) to public entities, including military, law enforcement, and other government agencies. These certificates are issued on a case-by-case basis for a limited period of time, usually one year, and with restrictions for their use, such as the requirement for being transponder equipped.

Future FAA Role in UAS

Under the provisions of the FAA Reauthorization Act of 2012, the FAA has been directed to develop regulations to facilitate the widespread use of UAS within the United States and to present its plan to do so to Congress by the end of 2012. The FAA has announced that it will authorize at least six UAS test sites in the United States, and has created the Unmanned Aircraft Program Office (UAPO) to oversee the development of procedures, standards, and policies that will govern this activity. These sites will be operational sometime in 2013. The FAA says that it plans to fully integrate flights of UAVs into the NAS by September 30, 2015. But this conclusion presumes that issues of privacy and possible encroachments on 4th Amendment rights will have been settled by then. As of this writing, it appears that a battle may be looming over the general deployment of drones over the United States.

Investigation

The FAA conducts investigations of aircraft accidents subordinate to and in cooperation with the National Transportation Safety Board pursuant to an arrangement known as the Accident Investigation Selectivity Program. This program is formalized in an agreement between the NTSB and the FAA and is designed to delineate responsibility in accident investigations and to avoid conflicts.[2] Previously, separate investigations conducted by the NTSB and the FAA sometimes resulted in contrary findings and conclusions, and were the occasion for embarrassment to one or both agencies.

The types of accidents investigated by the FAA are normally limited to general aviation accidents or those that, by comparison to airline accidents, are relatively limited in scope or impact in the aviation community. It should be noted that the objectives of an FAA investigation are different from those of the NTSB. In particular, the FAA is looking for violations of the FARs, and it scrutinizes whether the accident was a result of deviations from standards adopted by the FAA. FAA investigations seek to determine whether FAA facilities were a factor and whether the FARs were adequate. The FAA also investigates aircraft incidents that do not result in accidents, such as "near misses" by passing aircraft or other instances when aviation safety may have been jeopardized. The FAA is also mandated by Congress to investigate all reports of violations of the FARs.

Enforcement

Since passage of the Federal Aviation Act of 1958, responsibility for carrying out enforcement procedures for violations of the FARs has resided with the FAA. Enforcement options open to the FAA in

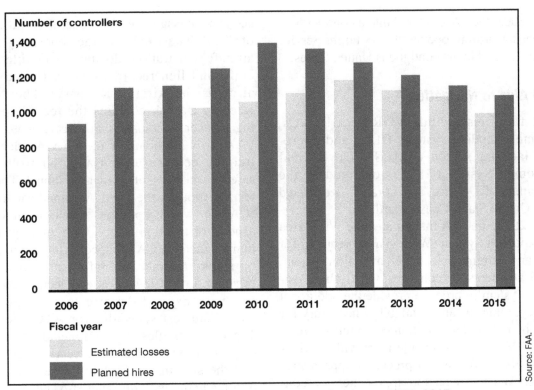

FIGURE 22-1 Estimated controller losses and planned hires, fiscal years 2006–2015.

any given case are normally dictated by considerations already well-established within the agency, and are generally handled either as administrative dispositions (warning notices and letters of correction) or by certificate action (suspension or revocation). Occasionally, civil penalties are assessed in lieu of certificate action (historically against corporations or against working pilots where certificate suspension is deemed too harsh).

Operations

The FAA is charged with the operation and maintenance of a vast array of facilities and equipment within the aviation system. We will briefly review the major categories of FAA responsibility.

Air Traffic Control

The ATC system includes airport control towers, air route traffic control centers (ARTCC), terminal radar approach control (TRACON), and flight service stations (FSS).

The FAA estimates that it will lose 10,291 controllers, or about 70 percent of the controller workforce, between 2006 and 2015 due to retirements. The large percentage loss is due to the unlawful PATCO strike in 1981, when President Reagan fired almost 11,000 controllers. From 1982 through 1991, the FAA hired an average of 2,655 controllers each year. These controllers will become eligible for retirement during the next decade.

In 1982, the FAA began a program of outsourcing operation at a limited number of VFR towers. As of 2006, 231 towers in 46 states participate in the FAA's Contract Tower Program.

In 2005, the FAA entered into a contract with Lockheed Martin to operate the 58 Flight Service Stations located in the contiguous United States.

Radio Aids to Navigation

These facilities include VORs, VORTACs, instrument landing systems (ILS), and micro-wave landing systems (MLS). The Global Positioning System (GPS) is operated by the Department of Defense, and Loran C is operated by the United States Coast Guard.

In 2003, the FAA inaugurated the Wide Area Augmentation System (WAAS) as a precursor for a new and extremely accurate navigation system. WAAS augments, or enhances, the Global Positioning System in order to provide the additional accuracy, integrity, and availability necessary for its use by the civilian aviation community. Previously, GPS data were unable to provide navigation capability for use in precision approaches. Through WAAS, precision approaches are conceivable for all 5,400 public use airports in the United States without local airport ground support facilities.

WAAS is an integral part of the FAA plan to replace ground-based Navaids entirely with satellite-based navigation capability, thus eliminating VORs, VORTACs, ILS, and MLS. (See Chapter 36 for the Next Generation Air Transportation System plan.)

National Airports

The FAA no longer is responsible for the two major airports located in and near Washington, D.C., Reagan National and Dulles, since their operation has been assigned to the Washington Metropolitan Airport Authority.

Monroney Aeronautical Center

The Center was named for Oklahoma Senator Mike Monroney, who was instrumental in securing passage of the Federal Aviation Act of 1958. The Center is the repository for all aircraft registration, documents of title to aircraft, and lien recordations on United States aircraft (the Aircraft Registry). The Airman Records Branch contains the records pertaining to every person issued a certificate by the FAA. It is the home of the FAA Academy, the training center for air traffic controllers, air safety inspectors, and other personnel. The Center also houses the Civil Aeromedical Institute (CAMI), which conducts research on various aspects of aviation safety, with an emphasis on human factors. CAMI specialists conduct tests on smoke toxicity, aircraft seats and restraint systems, air traffic controller selection and training methods, and the effects of fatigue, age, work, and rest schedules for ATC personnel. Teaching activities at CAMI include the training of pilots in water and arctic survival techniques and the sharing of the latest research in aviation medicine with designated Aviation Medical Examiners.

William J. Hughes Technical Center

Research and development programs are conducted at the Technical Center located just outside Atlantic City, N.J., on a former Navy airfield. Activities conducted at the Center include test and evaluation in air traffic control, communications, navigation, airports, and aircraft safety and security. The Center strives to develop innovative systems and concepts, new equipment and software, and modifications of existing systems.

Education

The FAA supports a large effort in the aviation community directed toward education of the flying public and the public at large. Periodic publications, such as the Advisory Circulars and Service Bulletins, and safety seminars for pilots, instructors, mechanics, and others reach out to all certificated airmen in an effort to facilitate improvements in all aspects of aviation safety.

Funding

Responsibility for distribution of federal grants under the Airport Improvement Program is assumed by the FAA under the Airport and Airway Development Act.

Registration and Recordation

A central registry for U.S. civil aircraft (N-numbered aircraft) is located at the Aeronautical Center in Oklahoma City. All aircraft operated within the United States are required to be registered, and it is the responsibility of the owner of every aircraft to secure the registration. The FAA issues its Certificate of Registration in the name of the owner upon satisfactory completion of the registration process. The Aircraft Registry also functions as the recordation site for establishing or determining legal title to aircraft, and is the one place that contains the entire chain of title of any aircraft. All legal encumbrances, or perfected security interests, in aircraft must be filed with the FAA at the Aircraft Registry.

Commercial Space Transportation

The responsibilities of the FAA discussed above grew and were assumed over time as civilian aviation sector activities developed. All of these responsibilities relate to civil aviation operations occurring on the surface of the earth and within the earth's atmosphere. When the United States began operations beyond the earth's atmosphere with the first U.S. space launch in 1958, and for many years thereafter, all U.S. space activities were the exclusive province of either NASA or the military.

With the passage by Congress of the Commercial Space Launch Act of 1985, the Office of Commercial Space Transportation (referred to as FAA/AST) was created within the FAA. Under this statute, AST has the responsibility to:

* Regulate the commercial space transportation industry, only to the extent necessary to ensure compliance with international obligations of the United States and to protect the public health and safety, safety of property, and national security and foreign policy interests of the United States;
* Encourage, facilitate, and promote commercial space launches by the private sector;
* Recommend appropriate changes in federal statutes, treaties, regulations, policies, plans, and procedures;
* Facilitate the strengthening and expansion of the United States space transportation infrastructure.

FAA/AST is organized into three divisions:

* Space Systems Development Division (AST-100)
* Licensing and Safety Division (AST-200)
* Systems Engineering and Training Division (AST-300)

Because the FAA has been assigned an entirely new role in aviation safety, staffing and expertise concerns have been expressed both within and outside the agency. This has been compounded by the fact that, while the original thrust of the FAA's oversight related to unmanned launches of expendable launch vehicles, commercial space activity is rapidly expanding into space tourism, so that the FAA's responsibility for licensing reusable launch vehicle missions will need to expand correspondingly. As of the end of 2009, FAA's Office of Commercial Space Transportation had a staff of 71 full-time employees, including 12 new aerospace engineers, and had established field offices at Edwards Air Force Base and NASA's Johnson Space Center.

For a more thorough discussion of commercial space launch activities in the United States and the role of FAA/AST, please refer to Chapter 41.

Dual Mandate

The historic mission of the FAA has been to not only administer the requirements of safety in the aviation community, but also to "promote" aviation in the overall national transportation scheme. The FAA has come under criticism from time to time that this dual role really amounts to a conflict of interest in promoting the airlines, on the one hand, and enforcing its regulations applicable to them, on the other hand. The issue resurfaced in the high visibility aftermath of the Valuejet crash in the Florida Everglades in 1996. The FAA had determined that the discount carrier was not in significant violation of the FARs, that FAA oversight and inspection of the airline had been standard, and reported its conclusion that the airline was "safe." Within six weeks, the FAA had shut down the company based on additional findings of serious violations of regulations relating to the transportation of hazardous materials, which led to the conclusion that such violations were the direct cause of the catastrophic crash, with the loss of all lives on board.

In 1996, Congress revised the FAA's mission in the Federal Aviation Reauthorization Act, removing the "dual mandate" by repealing the duty of the administrator to "promote civil aeronautics." Instead, Congress directed the FAA to consider as its highest priority the "maintaining and enhancing of safety and security of air commerce."

■ The National Transportation Safety Board

The National Transportation Safety Board (NTSB) was created by the Department of Transportation Act of 1966 as an agency within DOT. The general responsibilities given to NTSB were to investigate transportation accidents, to determine the "probable cause" of the accident, and to make recommendations based on its findings designed to assist in preventing similar accidents in the future (see page 205 for list of primary responsibilities). The range of transportation modes subject to the scrutiny of the NTSB was commensurate with the DOT itself, that is, railroad, highway, aviation, marine, and pipeline. It was assigned the additional role of acting as a review board for airman appeals from certificate actions or penalty assessments by the FAA.

In 1974, the NTSB was removed from the DOT and established as an independent agency answerable to Congress pursuant to the provisions of the Independent Safety Board Act. This action was taken by Congress because it was determined that, given its unique role in investigation and recommendation, the agency should be completely independent of other agencies and departments to ensure that it could be direct, impartial, and uninfluenced in making assessments of fault and recommendations for changes.

The agency is headquartered in Washington, D.C., and maintains 10 field offices nationwide and a training center in Ashburn, Virginia, in suburban Washington, D.C. In recent years, the agency has shrunk in size. In 2003, NTSB had 438 full-time employees compared with 386 in September 2006. During the same period, the number of full-time investigators and technical staff decreased from 234 to 203. (See Figure 22-2.) NTSB's modal offices vary in size in relation to the number of investigators; as of September 2006, the aviation office had 102 investigators and technical staff; the rail, pipeline, and hazardous materials office had 31; the highway office had 22; and the marine office had 12 employees. An additional 36 technical staff worked in the Office of Research and Engineering, which provides technical, laboratory, analytical, and engineering support for the modal investigation offices. For example, it is responsible for interpreting data recorders, creating accident computer simulations, and publishing general safety studies.

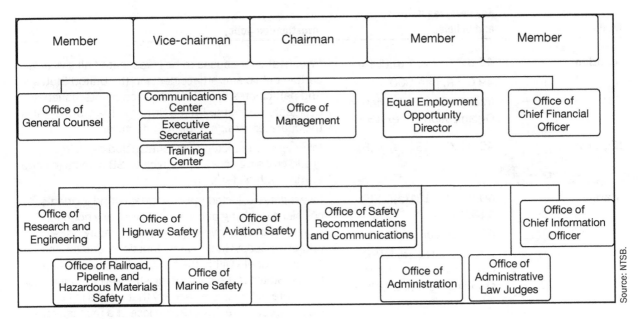

FIGURE 22-2 NTSB's organization.

The investigative role now performed by the NTSB dates back to the Air Commerce Act of 1926 when Congress gave the Department of Commerce responsibility for investigation of air crashes. An Aeronautics Branch of the Commerce Department was created to carry out this responsibility and it did so until renamed the Bureau of Air Commerce in 1934. In 1938, the CAB took over the investigative role and performed this duty until the creation of the NTSB in 1966.

To facilitate its investigative and reporting responsibility, Part 830 of the FARs requires aircraft operators to provide notification to the NTSB of certain accidents and incidents, and in certain cases to follow up such notice by required reports. This notification and reporting regimen is important to the role of the NTSB in staying current with problem areas in aviation safety.

Mode	2002	2003	2004	2005
Aviation[a]	1,949	1,997	1,870	1,937
Highway	52	45	45	33
Rail	11	9	12	8
Pipeline	1	2	2	1
Hazardous materials	2	1	2	1
Marine	6	6	7	4

[a]Aviation accidents include limited investigations in which NTSB delegates the gathering of on-scene information to FAA inspectors.

FIGURE 22-3 Number of accident investigations completed by NTSB by mode, fiscal years 2002–2005. Source: GAO analysis of NTSB data.

The role of the NTSB was extended to the investigation of nonmilitary public aircraft accidents under the provisions of the Independent Safety Board Act of 1994. Public aircraft, generally those aircraft owned or operated by various

Mode	Key laws, regulations, and policies	Investigation policy
Aviation	49 U.S.C. 1131 (a)(1)(A) 49 C.F.R. part 800 International Civil Aviation Organization annex 13	Investigates or causes to be investigated all civil and certain public aircraft accidents in the United States and participates in the investigation of international accidents where the United States is the state of registry, operator, designer, or manufacturer.
Highway	49 U.S.C. 1131 (a)(1)(B)	Investigates selected accidents including railroad grade crossing accidents, which NTSB selects in cooperation with a state.
Marine	49 U.S.C. 1131(a)(1)(E); 1131(b) 49 C.F.R. part 850 U.S. Coast Guard/NTSB memorandum of understanding from 9/12/2002	Investigates selected major accidents and incidents, collisions involving public vessels with any nonpublic vessel, accidents involving significant safety issues related to Coast Guard safety functions, and international accidents within the territorial seas and where the United States is the state of registry. Major marine accidents are defined as a casualty that results in (1) the loss of six or more lives; (2) the loss of a mechanically propelled vessel of 100 or more gross tons; (3) property damage initially estimated as $500,000 or more; or (4) serious threat, as determined by the Commandant of the Coast Guard and concurred with by the Chairman of NTSB, to life, property, or the environment by hazardous materials.
Railroad	49 U.S.C. 1131(a)(1)(C); 1116(b)(5) 49 C.F.R. part 840	Investigates railroad accidents involving a fatality, substantial property damage, or a passenger train.
Pipeline	49 U.S.C. 1131(a)(1)(D)	Investigates pipeline accidents in which there is a fatality, substantial property damage, or significant injury to the environment.
Hazardous materials	49 U.S.C. 1116(b)(5)	Investigates releases of hazardous materials in any mode that involves a fatality, substantial property damage, or significant injury to the environment. For all modes, NTSB also evaluates the adequacy of safeguards and procedures for the transportation of hazardous materials and the performance of other departments, agencies, and instrumentalities of the government responsible for the safe transportation of that material.
All modes		Investigates selected accidents that are catastrophic or of a recurring nature.

FIGURE 22-4   Key laws, regulations, and NTSB policies for investigations by mode.
Source: GAO summary of law, regulations, and policies.

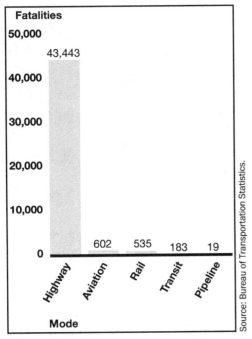

Source: Bureau of Transportation Statistics.

FIGURE 22-5 Fatalities by transportation mode, 2005.

federal government agencies, were excluded from compliance with the airworthiness and maintenance requirements of the FARs by the Federal Aviation Act of 1958. In 1993, the Governor of South Dakota, George S. Mickelson, was killed in the crash of a government aircraft in which he was a passenger. In the wake of the investigation into that accident, Congress rewrote the law to bring most nonmilitary government-owned or operated aircraft within the authority of the FAA and the NTSB.

In 1996, Congress further charged the NTSB, pursuant to the provisions of the Aviation Disaster Family Assistance Act, with the task of coordinating all federal assistance to survivors and families of victims of catastrophic transportation accidents. The NTSB strategic plan developed as a result of this mandate ensures that such people receive timely assistance from the carrier involved, and from all government agencies and community service organizations included in the program.

The Primary Functions of the NTSB

1. Aircraft accident investigation
2. Probable cause determinations
3. Accident report preparation
4. Safety recommendations
5. Receipt of Part 830 notifications and reports
6. Appellate review of FAA certificate actions and penalty assessments
7. Disaster assistance

The primary functions of the NTSB are outlined in the box shown on this page.

It should be noted that the NTSB has no authority over any other federal agency or any industry group. It has no regulatory or enforcement powers. Its effectiveness is enhanced by its resultant impartiality. The NTSB operates with a very small staff, historically fewer than 400 employees. Since 1967, the NTSB has investigated over 114,000 aviation accidents and issued more than 11,600 safety recommendations in all transportation modes. More than 80 percent of its safety recommendations have been adopted by those empowered to effect changes in the transportation system and in government agencies. At a cost of less than $.24 annually per citizen, it is said to be one of the best bargains in government.

Endnotes

1. In 2001, responsibility for aviation security was transferred from the FAA to the Transportation Security Administration (TSA).
2. See FAA Order 8020.11c and preceding orders that provide direction and guidance to inspectors performing accident investigations.

23   Airports

Before Herbert Hoover was President, he was Secretary of Commerce in the Coolidge Administration. He was called on to testify before the Morrow Board in 1925. The Morrow Board had been created for the purpose of studying the state of aviation and recommending to the president an aviation policy for the nation. Aviation, as the newest form of commerce joining maritime and land-based transportation, naturally followed some of the paths previously established by the older forms. It was also recognized that the promotion of aviation was in the national interest, much the same as it had been acknowledged that the nation needed the Post Office, a merchant marine, and the railroads.

Secretary Hoover drew an almost complete parallel between the needs of the fledgling aviation industry and the government's policy toward maritime commerce in the United States. He pointed out that government had accepted the responsibility of providing aids to navigation in the nation's ports and waterways by establishing markers, buoys, and lighthouses, and by providing surveys and geodetic charting. The government had provided land grants to the railroads in order to open up the West, in the name of the national interest. Roadways, too, were within the realm of government responsibility in part

to facilitate motor commerce. The analogy was complete. Aviation needed and deserved federal assistance and direction if it was to develop in an organized manner. Otherwise, a fragmented and chaotic system of air transportation could be expected.

Included within the analogy was the need for airports to serve the various cities of the country. In the 1920s airmail service was being provided to some cities but not to others, often based on the fact that no landing fields were available to receive the planes. Airports then were truly landing "fields," sometimes referred to as "all-way airfields" since landings and takeoff could be made in any direction. Runways were the exception. Notwithstanding the favorable national policy toward aviation, there was no authorization for the direct participation of the federal government in the construction of airports. Municipalities, counties, and state governments recognized that their participation in air commerce was going to be dependent, in large part, on their own financial contributions. The Air Commerce Act of 1926 authorized the Commerce Department to survey and rate airports, and by 1929 some 181 airports had been catalogued. Only half of the airports had some kind of "prepared" runway, ranging from an oil-treated surface to cinders and concrete. Major cities, including Cleveland, Detroit, Buffalo, Milwaukee, Denver, and Boston, had fields acquired and improved with local money. Indeed, prior to World War II, most of the airports of the country were financed, developed, and operated by local or regional government, since no federal airport program had ever existed.

New York's LaGuardia airport was a local project. It started out in 1929 as North Beach Airport and, when Mayor Fiorello La Guardia began his expansive program of municipal works during the 1930s, including the city's famous bridges, tunnels, and highways, the airport was included. New York had been a central maritime port for over a century and had developed into a major transatlantic passenger seaport by the 1930s. Its piers, visibly surrounding the island of Manhattan, provided a gateway to the world. They also provided an aviation analogy for the advanced planners of New York.

LaGuardia airport was only eight miles from the center of Manhattan, and Pan American had built its Marine Terminal there. There was a concrete apron for the parking of the new DC-2s and DC-3s, and its runways were a mile long. La Guardia took advantage of a Depression era program known as the Works Progress Administration (WPA—the name was changed to the Works Projects Administration in 1939), which was begun to provide work for the millions of unemployed men during the 1930s. At a time when practically all construction of any kind was stopped by the rigors of the Great Depression, and with commercial aviation just beginning to emerge as a new and viable transportation medium, federal monies expended through the WPA program greatly enhanced the progress of commercial aviation in the 1930s.

The Civil Aeronautics Act of 1938 lifted the ban on direct federal contributions for airports. One of the first cities to benefit was Washington, D.C., whose airport, Washington-Hoover Airport, was described at the time by historian John R. M. Wilson:

" Bordered on the east by Highway One, with its accompanying high-tension electrical wires, and obstructed by a smokestack on one approach and a smoky dump nearby, the field was a masterpiece of inept siting. Incredibly, the airport was intersected by a busy thoroughfare, Military Road, which had guards posted to flag down traffic during takeoffs and landings. In spite of such hazards, Washington-Hoover had a perfect safety record—for the simple reason that whenever even a slight breeze was blowing, planes refused to land there.[1] "

By 1941, Washington National Airport had taken the place of Washington-Hoover, having been literally dredged up out of the swampy ground next to the Potomac. It immediately became the second busiest airport in the country.

Civil airport construction languished, however, largely because of World War II. During the war, the federal government had created many airfields for military use under a program known as Development of Landing Areas for National Defense, spending $3.25 billion. After the war, pursuant to the Surplus Property Act of 1944, about half of these bases were turned over to local and state governments. Still, airports of the size and quality for use by growing commercial aviation were few, and those few were abysmal. As reported in *Fortune* in 1946:[2]

The half-dozen largest city airports handle millions of people a year. LaGuardia airport with 2,100,000 people, Washington with 757,000, Chicago with 1,300,000, and Los Angeles' Lockheed Air Terminal with 760,000 give clear indication of the size of the new air traffic. By standards of the huge railroad terminals, such as New York's Grand

Central, which handles 65 million people a year, a million passengers is not so much. But a million passengers jamming through one small room, such as Chicago's filthy little air terminal, instantly creates a problem solvable only by a fresh start in new surroundings, by new design on functional lines.

Chicago is the worst; its airport is a slum. Chewing gum, orange peel, papers, and cigar butts strew the floor around the stacks of baggage. Porters can't keep the floor clean if people are standing on it day and night. At almost all hours every telephone booth is filled, with people lined up outside; the dingy airport cafe is filled with standees. To rest the thousands there are exactly 28 broken-down seats. One must line up even for the rest rooms. The weary travelers sit or even lie on the floor. The drooping grandmothers, the crying babies, the continuous, raucous, unintelligible squawk of the loudspeaker, the constant push and jostle of new arrivals and new baggage tangling inextricably with their predecessors, make bus terminals look like luxury.

To say that the airports at San Francisco or Los Angeles are less squalid than Chicago is faint praise, for the difference is so slight that anyone passing hastily through would notice no real improvement. Almost all U.S. airports are utterly barren of things to do. The dirty little lunch counters are always choked with permanent sitters staring at their indigestible food; even a good cup of coffee is a thing unknown. The traveler consigned to hours of tedious waiting can only clear a spot on the floor and sit on his baggage and, while oversmoking, drearily contemplate his sins.

Federal Airport Act of 1946

In 1946, Congress authorized the expenditure of federal funds for use by the political subdivisions of state, county, and city governments in building or improving the airport infrastructure. Under the provisions of the Federal Airport

Act of 1946, the government would contribute 50 percent of the cost of these improvements, and the local government would fund the rest. Small communities found it difficult to come up with even 50 percent of such large expenditures. The program worked better in large cities that could float bond issues to finance their portion of the cost. A series of amendments to the Act extended the duration and funding of the program and added provisions designed to guarantee proper standards of construction and operation, open and nondiscriminatory access by the public, and appropriate zoning of lands adjacent to the airport.

New York utilized the program to construct a third major airport, named Idlewild (now JFK), and then expanded the original construction with $60 million of terminal buildings and parking areas. Los Angeles raised a bond issue in the amount of $60 million for its international airport. St. Louis expanded its airport and built a new terminal. The busiest airport in the country was Midway, in Chicago, with an arrival or departure every 80 seconds. The activity at Midway led to the building of O'Hare, which opened in 1955. Dulles airport, conceived to serve Washington, D.C., finally found a home in Chantilly, Virginia, in 1958. Still, it was generally realized and noted at the time that United States airports were not ready for jets, and that they were not keeping up with the growth of commercial air travel. The number of passengers enplaning on domestic flights would almost double between 1954 and 1959, from 32 million to 55 million. And it was reckoned that less than 10 percent of the American population had ever set foot on a commercial airplane.

Airports faced new problems as a direct result of the larger piston airplanes, and these problems were compounded by the arrival of jets. Fuel storage facilities were inadequate, both in size and in type, since jets burned a form of kerosene, not the gasoline of piston engines. Taxiways had to be redesigned, relocated, and widened, due both to the size of the aircraft and to allow for the new, low positioning of jet engines on the pylons hanging below the wing. FOD, the new acronym for foreign object damage, was a major concern to the health and integrity of jet engines because they could not tolerate ingesting small rocks, gravel, and debris of any kind lying about the taxiway. Runways were too short for jet aircraft, particularly those needing a full load of fuel for transatlantic or transcontinental routes. These requirements were exceedingly costly to the airport owners, usually a governmental entity, whether city, county, or regional political subdivision.

Not only was it costly and time-consuming to enlarge and upgrade existing airports, new construction was becoming a contentious issue in the communities in which they were located. Noise associated with jet operations was becoming a serious environmental issue, an issue that had constitutional and legal ramifications that extended far beyond the boundaries of the airports. And if improvement of existing airport facilities was a problem, then the building of new airports was next to impossible to pull off. In 1952 when authorities began looking for a site near Washington, D.C., to relieve the already overcrowded National Airport, an exercised public in Fairfax County, Virginia, rose in protest. It would require six years of effort spent in negotiation, in cajoling, in conducting studies, and in spending lots of money before the eventual site for Dulles International Airport was selected and approved. It was worse in the metropolitan New York area. Attempts to locate an agreeable site anywhere in northern New Jersey were defeated; 22 other proposed sites in New York and New Jersey went down in flames. A group composed of the New York Port Authority, the FAA, and some airlines finally settled on a site 48 miles from the city, but opposition cancelled that one too. Plans to expand and upgrade the ancient White Plains Airport were defeated by local opposition. To this day, New York has the same three airports that it had in 1950.

The resistance was not limited to the Northeast. Attempts in Dade County, Florida, to build a new airport to serve Miami failed. Miami International Airport, like most metropolitan airports, has been situated in the same place since bi-wing, open cockpit airplanes first began using it. One exception is the DallasFort Worth Airport, in Texas, which only came about because of the cooperation of the citizens and local governments of the two cities that it serves. Located midway between Dallas and Fort Worth, DFW was completed in 1974. It became a symbol of pride and progress for the area, and it was appreciated by its business and leisure travel communities. One motivating factor for success was the appallingly inadequate Love Field in Dallas, which it replaced, as well as the fact that Fort Worth had no commercial airport at all. After completion of DFW, no new airport would be built in the United States for another 20 years.[3]

The launch of the Airbus 380, the world's largest airplane, in December 2000 created another challenge for U.S. airports, as well as airports all over the world. The size of the A380 requires that modifications be made at airports that will serve the new gigantic aircraft. Although the A380 can land on runways that will accept the Boeing 747, modifications to taxiways, terminal gates, and aprons will have to be made. Airports will also have to fund the purchase of new servicing vehicles for the A380.

By 2011, six airports in the United States had been equipped to handle the A380, including Los Angeles, San Francisco, Miami, JFK, Dulles, and Houston. The Houston Airport Authority reported that it spent $8 million to widen runways (with an additional $30 million to $40 million planned to upgrade runways to FAA requirements), $7.5 million for gate bridges to allow loading and unloading, and $15 million to $20 million for interior gate hold areas and improvements.

As of 2012, although not one United States airline had ordered the A380, it was being flown by seven world airlines, including Air France, Korean, China Southern, Lufthansa, Singapore, Qantas, and Emirates.

▪ Airport Security

Exploding passenger traffic after World War II and the advance in aircraft technology were only part of the problem confronting airports. Aircraft hijacking began as a means for oppressed citizens from communist regimes to escape to freedom in the West. As long as the hijackings were of communist-controlled airlines and the destination was freedom, the public generally applauded this audacity. But when the hijacking traffic started moving in the other direction, from the United States to Cuba, people began to view hijacking a bit differently. The first such United States to Cuba effrontery occurred in 1961 when a National Airlines airliner was commandeered to Havana, and was followed by more. It was unthinkable. No federal laws adequately covered the activity, so Congress hurriedly passed appropriate legislation making the hijacking of an aircraft a federal crime. Things then cooled off and it began to look as though the few hijackings from the United States had been an aberration. But in 1968, there were 17 hijacking attempts; in 1969, there were 33 more.

Hijacking commercial airliners soon became a worldwide phenomenon when two Arabs grabbed a TWA flight bound for Tel Aviv. Hijacking was gradually evolving into terrorism; that is, hijacking to accomplish a political purpose. Palestinians seized a Pan American 747 in September 1970 and forced it to Cairo, where it was blown up. This kind of terrorism was repeated on several occasions, resulting in destruction of the aircraft amid full-blown television coverage. Hostages were taken; ransoms and the release of imprisoned terrorists were demanded.

The United States initiated a program of air marshals, G-men who rode anonymously aboard selected airliners for the purpose of foiling would-be hijackers. Eastern Air Lines began using metal detectors for boarding passengers. Then the infamous D. B. Cooper, a thief with no particular social or religious philosophy, took over a Northwest Airlines 727. He directed the aircraft to a designated landing site where he released the passengers but demanded and got $200,000 and four parachutes. After the aircraft departed, and while airborne over the vast forests of the northwestern United States, he lowered the 727's unique rear stairwell and disappeared, with his cash, into the night.

But hijackings worldwide were taking on a deadly and tragic caste. In October 1972, an Eastern 727 was hijacked to Havana by wanted murderers, and in November, an escaped convict and two accomplices seized a Southern Airways DC-9 and proceeded to take the airplane and crew on an extended 29 hour odyssey, making eight landings. The airplane and crew finally wound up safely in Havana, even after agents in Miami shot out the tires during takeoff. The FAA responded by ordering the installation of metal detectors at all gates at airports serving certificated carriers.[4] In December 1972 the FAA changed the passenger airline business forever by ordering the airlines to carry out electronic screening of all boarding passengers, as well as the inspection of carry-on luggage.

In the years since the first electronic screening began, scrutiny of airline passengers has steadily intensified. The list of prohibited carry-on items has persistently lengthened. Surveillance methods and sources have increased. Many more security personnel have been employed. Since the terrorist attacks on September 11, 2001, security procedures have been greatly amplified, as well as modified to address the threat of international terrorism. Responsibility for airport security has been removed from the FAA and given to the new Transportation Security Administration (TSA). Please see Chapter 35 for a more thorough discussion of the TSA.

Evolution of a New National Airport Policy

The operation of airports changed in many other ways. The physical size of new airports serving modern jet airline traffic, the noise considerations inherent in airport operations, the large facilities necessary to accommodate the millions of passengers passing through the airports, and the newfound safety concerns resulting from the criminal and social developments of the 1960s called for a new and aggressive national airport policy.

Under the Federal Airport Act of 1946, the Federal-Aid Airport Program (FAAP) had been the first peacetime program of financial aid aimed exclusively at promoting development of the nation's civil airports. It endured for 24 years, but the growing demands of modern commercial aviation rendered that program obsolete.

In 1970, Congress passed the Airport and Airway Development Act in order to address the obvious shortcomings of the nation's airports and the airway system. The policy statement for this law recognized the inadequacy of the nation's airport and airway system, and committed the government to its substantial expansion and improvement in order to meet the demands of interstate commerce, the national defense, and the postal service. Congress thereby created the Airport and Airway Trust Fund, which receives revenues from excise taxes paid by users of the National Air Space. Excise taxes are placed on domestic airline passenger tickets, domestic airline flight segments, international arrivals and departures, air cargo waybills, and aviation fuels used by general aviation. See Table 23-1.

In 1982, after deregulation, Congress amended the existing statute with the Airport and Airway Development Act of 1982, reestablishing the FAA's airport grants program (which had been inactive since 1981) and renaming the Trust Fund program the Airport Improvement Program (AIP). The Trust Fund was originally administered by the CAA in 1946, and sequentially thereafter by the Federal Aviation Agency and then the Federal Aviation Administration.

This Act also amended the Federal Aviation Act of 1958 by requiring, for the first time, that operators of airports serving certificated air carriers secure "Airport Operating Certificates" by application to the FAA, demonstrating the ability to conduct safe and properly equipped airport operations. These requirements are set forth in Part 139 of the Federal Aviation Regulations.

Endnotes

1. Wilson, John R. M., *Turbulence Aloft*, 34–35.
2. *Fortune* magazine, August 1946, 78.
3. Denver International Airport opened in 1995.
4. FAR Part 107, effective March 18, 1972.

Aviation Taxes	Comment	Tax Rate
PASSENGERS		
Domestic Passenger Ticket Tax	Ad valorem tax	7.5% of ticket price (10/1/99 through 9/30/2007)
Domestic Flight Segment Tax	"Domestic Segment" = a flight leg consisting of one takeoff and one landing by a flight	Rate is indexed by the Consumer Price Index starting 1/1/02 $3.00 per passenger per segment during calendar year (CY) 2003 $3.10 per passenger per segment during CY2004. $3.20 per passenger per segment during CY2005. $3.30 per passenger per segment during CY2006. $3.40 per passenger per segment during CY2007.
Passenger Ticket Tax for Rural Airports	Assessed on tickets on flights that begin/end at a rural airport. Rural airport: <100K enplanements during 2nd preceding CY, and either: 1) not located within 75 miles of another airport with 100K+ enplanements, 2) is receiving essential air service subsidies, or 3) is not connected by paved roads to another airport.	7.5% of ticket price (same as passenger ticket tax) Flight segment fee does not apply.
International Arrival & Departure Tax	Head tax assessed on pax arriving or departing for foreign destinations (& U.S. territories) that are not subject to pax ticket tax.	Rate is indexed by the Consumer Price Index starting 1/1/99 Rate during CY2003 = $13.40 Rate during CY2004 = $13.70 Rate during CY2005 = $14.10 Rate during CY2006 = $14.50 Rate during CY2007 = $15.10
Flights between continental U.S. and Alaska or Hawaii		Rate is indexed by the Consumer Price Index starting 1/1/99 $6.70 international facilities tax + applicable domestic tax rate (during CY03) $6.90 international facilities tax + applicable domestic tax rate (during CY04) $7.00 international facilities tax + applicable domestic tax rate (during CY05) $7.30 international facilities tax + applicable domestic tax rate (during CY06) $7.50 international facilities tax + applicable domestic tax rate (during CY07)
Frequent Flyer Tax	Ad valorem tax assessed on mileage awards (e.g., credit cards).	7.5% of value of miles
FREIGHT/MAIL		
Domestic Cargo/Mail		6.25% of amount paid for the transportation of property by air
Aviation Fuel		
General Aviation Fuel Tax		Aviation gasoline: $0.193/gallon Jet fuel: $0.218/gallon
Commercial Fuel Tax		$0.043/gallon

TABLE 23-1 Aviation excise tax structure (Taxpayer Relief Act of 1997, Public Law 105-35).

Deregulation

American Spirit/Shutterstock.com

Deregulation

24 Prelude to Deregulation

In Chapter 3 we saw that government regulation of public utilities in the United States is grounded primarily on the concept of economic necessity, supported by legal authority. Since 1887, the railroads had been considered to be monopolistic, quasi-public corporations, although privately owned and operated. This meant that the public interest (the right of the public to equal access to travel opportunity and to non-discriminatory passenger fares and freight rates) and the governmental interest (in having a reliable interstate transportation system) had to be protected by federal law. The administration of this function was performed by the Interstate Commerce Commission, the agency whose rules and regulations largely controlled how the railroads operated, who could operate them, where they could operate, and how much they could charge. It also mandated safety regulations.

We also saw how the early airmail routes operated by the Post Office generally followed the railroad lines laid down across the country, with air fields in or near the settlements and towns created during the westward expansion of the emerging nation. The early airlines were largely controlled by the Post Office through airmail subsidies, and the airmail routes awarded by the Post Office gradually evolved into passenger and freight routes operated by established, independent airline companies. The government viewed the airlines in the same light as the railroads and, in turn, regulated them in a similar manner.

We know that the first federal regulation of aviation occurred with the passage of the Air Commerce Act of 1926, with a modest mandate from Congress to promote air commerce. Beginning with the licensing of airmen and aircraft and the creation of navigational aids and other mostly safety-oriented rules, government regulation expanded in lockstep with the expansion of the commercial aviation industry itself. The government assumed control of airline labor relations and air traffic control and, with the passage of the Civil Aeronautics Act of 1938, the government began deciding who could enter the airline business, as well as where they could fly and how much they could charge. Approval of mergers and rate and route regulation were performed mainly by the Civil Aeronautics Board, with safety regulation ultimately residing with the Federal Aviation Administration.

Historically, the government's interest in regulating transportation has also extended to insuring that the various modes of transport (water, overland, railroad, air) remain individually viable by limiting or forbidding interlocking relationships between them, thus insuring competition. When the United States took over the former French construction of the Panama Canal under the Panama Canal Act of 1912, for example, the railroads were precluded from having any ownership interest in competing water carrier companies that would operate through the canal. The fear was that the railroads would compromise the promise of the Panama Canal and doom its success by cutthroat competition amongst the coastwise trade carriers, thus preserving their transcontinental railroad monopolies. Likewise, when the airlines came along the railroads were forbidden from owning any interest in those fledging airline companies so as to insure that airline passenger and freight markets were unfettered and free to develop on their own and in their own way.

Before launching into the historical developments that precipitated the dismantling of federal economic regulation under the Airline Deregulation Act, let us take a look at the economic nature of transportation in general.

The Economic Nature of Transportation

Unlike most consumer services, transportation provides an intermediate product—only a means to an end. In air transportation specifically, hardly anyone flies in the airline system just to go for an airplane ride. The reason people fly is to accomplish another goal, whether it is for a business purpose or a personal one.

This characteristic of the transportation industry likens it to a commodity, for example, wheat or petroleum. Wheat is not purchased because anyone wants a bushel of wheat, but rather to create something else, perhaps a cake or a loaf of bread. Oil has no use except to facilitate a secondary purpose, like the lubrication of machines or as a means of propulsion.

There are no unique characteristics within a class of commodity; one bushel of wheat is like any other. One quart of oil is indistinguishable, and worth no more, than any other quart of oil. Economic theory teaches that the price of a commodity will seek the lowest possible level based on supply and demand. If the supply of a commodity is adequate to the demand, unit profit on any given quantity of a commodity will be very small and the price will be low.

If an airline seat is like a bushel of wheat, its price will be valued like any other airline seat absent some distinguishing characteristic, assuming an adequate supply of airline seats. Government economic regulation of the airline industry effectively thwarted this economic truth by controlling the supply and the price of airline seats. The cost of air transportation was, therefore, very high causing the system to be mainly used for business travel. By the 1960s, economists and others began to ask "Why?"

The Nature of Regulated Transportation

Since early in their history airlines had been considered by government to be, to some degree, instruments of national policy. Airlines were used:

- To carry the mail
- To facilitate commerce between the cities and states
- To establish a fast and efficient passenger transportation system
- To function in the national defense system in times of emergency
- To carry the flag internationally

To carry out these functions, the airlines had to be financially stable, they had to be dependable in the long run and reliable at all times. Government regulation of the airlines facilitated these ends well, and they were among the primary reasons that the federal government began controlling entry, rate, and route allocation in 1938 under the Civil Aeronautics Act. The nascent airline business was a fragile concept at the time and it was by no means certain that unlimited competition would not bring down the whole endeavor. Widespread public acceptance of air travel had not yet occurred. Deficiencies in equipment, weather forecasting, and air traffic control contributed to well-publicized airline crashes; flying was still an adventure. The airlines needed to be stabilized, protected against absolute competition, and developed into an acceptable and safe form of transportation in order to accomplish these government goals.

Thus, for nearly 40 years, entry into the airline business had been controlled by the Civil Aeronautics Board. Under this system no major new entrants had ever been permitted, although the CAB did authorize a limited number local service providers for a subsidized service on less dense routes and to provide feeder lines for the trunk carriers. The number of trunk lines had decreased from 16 in 1938 to 10 in 1978. That year the 5 largest airlines accounted for two-thirds of all domestic revenue and the exclusive 10 trunk carriers accounted for 90% of all air traffic. There were 8 regional service carriers and 10 supplemental carriers.

Under the CAB system routes were supposed to be awarded among the existing carriers based on the perceived needs of the communities and cities requiring service, and on the equitable allocation of routes to the existing airlines desiring and capable of delivering such service. In fact, the performance of the CAB fails to indicate that it fulfilled even this task, as confirmed by Senate hearings in 1974 and 1975, as the CAB enforced a de facto moratorium on new route awards after 1969, effectively stagnating the system.[1] Fares and rates were established mainly as a function of the airlines' cost of doing business, which cost was set using an assumption of a 55% load factor for all airlines. This produced a

system not particularly designed or administered to be cost efficient, but it was stable. Not one airline in 40 years had been allowed to go into bankruptcy.

Competition in the airline industry had been regulated, but competition had not been eliminated. The more efficient the airline, the better its operating ratio and the more money there was at the bottom-line. Northwest was the most efficient airline with a breakeven load factor of 43%. This compared with United, whose breakeven load factor was 59%. The average of all airlines' load factors at the time was between 50% and 55%.

The effect of airline economic regulation was to create both a financial ceiling and floor for the companies, guaranteeing that neither profits nor losses were excessive. While the support of the CAB limiting airline loss was comforting to management, the ceiling limiting innovation and profit was frustrating, particularly to the types of men who rose to run the airlines. The technological advance in aircraft and engine design kept airlines busy trying to stay ahead of one another in order to have the most appealing fleet available for the limited passenger market, most of which were business travelers.

Aesthetics and quality of service were high on the list of concerns, since these were two of the few discretionary operating decisions available to management. Marketing schemes were also highly competitive, the effort being limited to the best way to sell essentially the same product that every other airline sold. Each new innovation thought up by an airline, no matter how minor, was pushed as the reason to fly that airline. For instance, the introduction in 1965 of in-flight movies by TWA was highly advertised; it resulted in six to eight more passengers per flight. Delta had a piano in its upstairs bar on the domestic 747, accessible from below by a circular staircase. Southwest dressed its stewardesses in hot pants. National Airlines fielded a suggestive advertising program, with TV clips featuring stewardesses inviting passengers to "fly me" to

Miami. Their 727s featured a painted likeness of a beautiful stewardess on the side of the plane with "Fly Me" painted just to the side. Airline management continually strove to bring some quality of uniqueness to their commodity-like operations.

Until the 1960s and early 1970s, leadership of the major airlines had remained mostly in the hands of the young men who took over in 1934 after the Black investigation of the so-called "spoils conference" scandal. There was a sameness about those early airline leaders since they had all been tempered by the same conditions affecting airline growth and essentially all had been both pilots and CEOs. Newcomers like Robert Crandall at American and Richard Ferris at United were natural competitors and often went head to head on issues like market share, computer reservation system development, and travel agent loyalty. While these new leaders brought a new entrepreneurial spirit to the airline business, they did so in different ways. Crandall preferred to compete within the established regulatory framework, while Ferris, who came from the hotel industry, was open-minded about deregulation. For the most part, however, airline management was firmly opposed to airline deregulation.

Factors That Influenced the Deregulation of the Airlines

Charter Operations

As we saw in Chapter 18, the market for cheaper air travel had been recognized since shortly after World War II, when charter operators began to fly using war surplus DC-3s. Charter operators were definitely second class citizens in the airline world and in the view of the CAB. They not only got no respect from the scheduled airline world but they were hindered at every turn by regulations designed to insulate from competition the trunk air carriers who had been accepted into the system by the CAB in 1938.

Charterers could not sell individual tickets, nor could they fly published schedules. They were essentially relegated to selling the entire aircraft capacity to large, established groups by advance sales. The CAB monitored these operations carefully; ever watchful lest charter operations encroach on the CAB-controlled scheduled airlines' established routes. But the charter operators showed that a profit could be made with low fares, sometimes as much as 50 percent lower than CAB-mandated fares, so long as the aircraft flew filled with passengers.

The CAB then allowed the trunk lines for the first time to include a cheaper class of airfare in the same aircraft with standard fares; these were the first "coach fares" and this was the creation of separate seating and amenities for second class passengers on the same flight. Still, the CAB retained its stranglehold on the economics of commercial aviation.

Intrastate Air Carrier Operations and Scholarly Publications

One of the first economic studies to question the advisability of the airline system run by the CAB was published in 1962.[2] The conclusion of this study was that there was nothing inherently monopolistic about the airline business and there was no need for any government limitation or control over entry into it or exit from it. Shortly thereafter, in 1965, a Yale law student by the name of Michael Levine wrote a law review article about the largely unregulated intrastate airline business in California. In comparing the intrastate airline fares with those mandated by the CAB, he concluded that CAB policies "fostered unnecessarily high fares, encouraged uneconomic practices, and limited the variety of service available to the public." He found that intrastate fares were about half as high as interstate airline fares, yet the intrastate carriers were making a profit and they were flying more passengers.

In 1970, Alfred Kahn, a professor of economics at Cornell University, produced a two-volume work, *The Economics of Regulation*, which basically postulated that the heavy hand of government regulation was inimical to the public interest, and that competition would naturally produce the best product for the best price for the public.

By 1971, a new intrastate carrier, Southwest Airlines, answering not to the CAB but only to the Texas Public Service Commission, began service between the three largest cities in the very large state of Texas, setting its fares far below those mandated by the CAB. It, too, proved successful charging lower fares and flying with full airplanes.

The conclusion was becoming inescapable that government regulation of air carriers was largely preventing low-fare air travel and restricting travel.

The Failure of Railroad Regulation

By the 1970s, the railroad industry had been heavily regulated by the Interstate Commerce Commission for over 80 years, and the airline industry had been regulated by the Civil Aeronautics Board for almost 40 years. The railroads were in serious financial trouble under regulation. Mergers entered into to stave off financial collapse, like the Pennsylvania Railroad and the New York Central, only succeeded in delaying the inevitable as the Penn Central entered bankruptcy in the 1970s. Six Northeast railroads were in bankruptcy. In order to preserve passenger rail traffic in the Northeast corridor and environs, Conrail was created from the remains of the six railroads at a cost of billions of dollars of taxpayer money. Railroad passenger service could not be sustained anywhere in the private sector, as Amtrak, subsidized by the government, was required to take over that service nationally. It appeared that it was only a matter of time before the airlines were going to be in the same position.

Mistrust of Government

It also seemed that the government was not trusted, nor was it respected as before, perhaps due to public disgust and unease created by the divisive issues of the 1960s and 1970s. It hardly mattered from which end of the political spectrum one viewed the situation. On the left, the Vietnam War and Watergate, resulting in the unprecedented resignation of a sitting president of the United States, were examples of inept or corrupt leadership. On the right, the social experimentation of the Great Society programs of Lyndon Johnson, the rapid deterioration of inner cities, and civil disturbances seen nightly on the evening news were evidence of misguided governmental policy. Government seemed to be contributing to the problem, rather than offering rational solutions. Nixon had imposed wage and price controls, effectively putting the government, not the business owners or the workers, in charge of prices and wages. These efforts were ineffective, and added to the general frustration of people with government.

❝ I really don't know one plane from the other. To me they are just marginal costs with wings. ❞

Alfred Kahn, 1977

The Civil Aeronautics Board Procedures and Practices

The way that the CAB chose, over the years, to discharge its regulatory functions over the airlines heavily contributed to the ultimate decision to deregulate the airlines. It goes without saying that it was completely impossible to have the CAB grant new entry for any trunk carrier at any time during the 40-year period that it operated. Between 1950 and 1974, for instance, the CAB rejected all 79 applicants who applied for authority to create new certificated airlines. Moreover, any change to the status quo for existing carriers required the filing of an appropriate petition, the scheduling of hearings, and the presentation of evidence to support the petition, after which the CAB would proceed to mull over the issues presented in its own good time. The laborious routine by which "business" was done before the CAB effectively prevented practically any change in the status quo, or any expansion or improvement to the air transportation system.

The following examples are representative of CAB practices:

Example 1: When Continental Airlines sought permission to add a new route to its system from San Diego to Denver, the CAB studied the matter for eight years before finally granting the petition, but only after being ordered to do so by the United States Court of Appeals.

Example 2: When World Airways applied to fly a scheduled low-cost passenger service between New York and Los Angeles in 1967, the CAB considered the petition for six and a half years and then dismissed the case because the record was "stale."

Example 3: When Federal Express entered the freight market it had to do so as an "air taxi," whereby the size of its aircraft were limited to 12,500 pounds. When FedEx business increased, Fred Smith found that he had to fly two aircraft in trail from Memphis to the same destination in order to carry all of his cargo. He applied to the CAB for permission to fly a larger aircraft on these occasions on the reasonable principle that it was almost twice as expensive to fly two small aircraft as it was to fly one larger one. The CAB denied that request.

Example 4: The CAB occupied itself largely with trivialities, from fixing the exact price of drinks on airplanes to setting special fares for skiers.

Politics

Deregulation in general had become a common subject of conversation in the halls of Congress, applied to several areas of quasi-public activity. Railroads, trucks, public utilities,

telecommunications, gas pipelines, banking, and natural gas were among the infrastructures discussed. As such, deregulation became a political topic, and it was bipartisan.

The drive toward deregulation was led by President Gerald Ford almost immediately upon his taking office on the resignation of Richard Nixon in 1974. As an economic conservative, he felt that the consumer was best able to "signal his wants and needs through the marketplace" and that government "should not intrude in the free market" except to preserve "well-defined social objectives."

He found an unlikely ally in Senator Ted Kennedy, who convinced a young Harvard law professor named Stephen Breyer, who was to become an Associate Justice of the Supreme Court 20 years later on, to join his staff for a sabbatical in August 1974. In September Breyer attended a meeting of the major airlines with the Secretary of Transportation at which the Secretary openly urged the airlines to all "raise their prices" in order to help Pan Am. Breyer was shocked at this blatant price fixing and convinced Kennedy to hold hearings on the subject of airline deregulation. Committee hearings began in November 1974, and continued into 1975.

The hearings disclosed a history of impropriety at the CAB that extended nearly top to bottom. Breyer's report issued at the conclusion of the hearings amounted to an indictment of the CAB commissioners, finding that there was "a strong likelihood of highly improper and possibly criminal behavior on the part of the Board members themselves."[3] Among the specific findings of the report were that the CAB had covered up the existence of an airline slush fund for illegal contributions to the Board and that the Board had observed an "unofficial moratorium" on granting any new route awards since 1969.

De Facto Deregulation

As a result of the hearings, President Ford caused the resignation of the Chairman of the CAB, Robert Timm, and in early 1975 appointed John

Robson, an Undersecretary at the Department of Transportation and a career bureaucrat, in his place. Although Robson knew little about the airline industry, he set about to remedy the shortcomings and failures that had been disclosed in the Kennedy hearings, including the liberalization of charter rules and the approving of new routes, which continued during Robson's tenure at the CAB. A CAB staff report was issued in July 1975 recommending deregulation within five years. Incredibly, in April 1976, all of the CAB commissioners announced that they supported deregulation.

The changes kept coming under what was now known as "de facto deregulation." Liberalization of charter rules had these operations flying more routes, longer distances, and with fewer restrictions, thus creating immediate competition for the scheduled airlines. This, in turn, caused the scheduled airlines to make application to the CAB for permission to make a legitimate, long-range competitive response to the charterers. The CAB then began granting those applications, thereby setting up an incipient competition theretofore unknown under regulation. Airlines were then allowed to unilaterally raise or lower prices "within zones of reasonableness," and on specified routes, they could enter or exit without prior authority.

The CAB had no jurisdiction over intrastate carriers like Southwest Airlines, and although Southwest could charge what it pleased subject only to the rules of the Texas Public Utilities Commission, its fares were substantially less than those mandated under the CAB regimen. Southwest was stiff competition for any airline flying within the borders of Texas and that competition included interstate carriers Texas International and American Airlines. When Texas International sought CAB authority for its "peanut fares," (its regular CAB-mandated fare discounted 50 percent) in order to compete with Southwest, the CAB obliged. Again, when American Airlines wanted to institute its "Supersaver" fare in March 1977, a charter-like

discount theretofore prohibited by CAB philosophy, the CAB approved. Significantly, the "Supersaver" fares applied to seats on regularly scheduled flights on which standard fare passengers had purchased tickets. Thus began the confusing and seemingly inequitable pattern of full-fare passengers seated beside someone who had paid a fraction of full fare. These low fares also invited into the cabin leisure passengers, bringing with them their small children and babies, to occupy the center seat previously left unfilled. American Airline's coast-to-coast traffic soon increased by 61 percent.

Word spread and the trend continued as Allegheny Airlines instituted "Simple Saver" fares and TWA started "Super-Jackpot" fares to Las Vegas. By 1978, discount fares were widely available, prices had fallen by 8 percent, and air traffic had increased by 17 percent. Whether noticed or not, deregulation had already begun.

Deregulation of Air Cargo

Under CAB regulations, air cargo was allowed to be carried by certificated carriers in the belly of any type of aircraft and over any route for which the carrier had passenger authority. As of 1978, more than half of all cargo still moved in the bellies of passenger aircraft. No "all-cargo" commercial carriers appeared on the scene at all until after World War II. In the 1970s, there were only a few all-cargo certificated carriers, including Flying Tiger and Seaboard World Airlines, and only one air taxi cargo operator. The air taxi was Federal Express, and it had been allowed entry into the cargo field by using the CAB exemption for small airplanes—under 12,500 pounds. Once a cargo plane landed, it was limited to a delivery radius of 25 miles by ICC regulation. The CAB set cargo prices and did not allow higher prices for faster transport.

In June 1976, John Robson proposed to Congress that cargo be treated separately from passenger operations and, going beyond what either Kennedy or Ford had authorized, suggested that air cargo be completely freed of regulatory control. At the time, the pending airline deregulation bill applied to both passenger and cargo carriage, but the main problem with advancing the legislation lay with the passenger side of the legislation. This was due to powerful interest groups on the passenger side who were opposing airline deregulation vociferously. On the cargo side, there were no such interest groups working against the bill; in fact, most all of the interested parties supported complete deregulation of air cargo. This was the opening that John Robson saw and was the reason for his proposal to split the legislation and seek full deregulation for air cargo.

Federal Express and Flying Tiger representatives worked closely with Congressional committees to separate the passenger legislation from the cargo legislation, and on October 20, 1977, the cargo bill was signed into law by President Jimmy Carter. By this statute, the cargo carriers were free to use aircraft of any size, to fly them wherever they chose, and to set rates that were justified by market conditions.

The share price for Federal Express on the day of the passage of this law in October was $9.16. By December, it had catapulted to $34.75. Share prices for Flying Tiger also rose. Federal Express began acquiring large jet aircraft, up to seven times larger than those permitted during regulation. Total shipments increased by 38 percent in 1978. Overnight shipping was born, with pricing based in part on speed. In the world of air cargo and on the New York Stock Exchange, the name "FedEx" took on new meaning.

The deregulation of cargo also created opportunities for companies engaged solely in surface transportation. In 1981, United Parcel Service (also known as UPS) entered the overnight air delivery business and is today one of the largest cargo airlines in the country. It is an interesting fact that labor relations between UPS management and its employees are governed by the National Labor Relations Act, while FedEx is subject to the Railway Labor Act. This seeming contradiction is, of course, due to the fact that UPS was subject to the NLRA from its inception as the American Messenger Company in 1907.

The success of the air cargo carriers due to deregulation was a positive sign for air passenger deregulation. Arguments that chaos would follow deregulation of the air carrier industry were to some degree muted by the success of the air cargo carrier experience, but not everybody agreed.

Endnotes

1. Barnum, John, *What Prompted Airline Deregulation 20 Years Ago*, http://library.findlaw.com/1988/Sep/1/129304.html.

2. Caves, Richard E., *Air transport and its regulators: an industry study*, Harvard University Press, 1962.

3. Martha Derthick & Paul J. Quirk, *The Politics of Deregulation* 241 (1985).

25 The Airline Deregulation Act of 1978

Bills to deregulate airline service were submitted to Congress by both the Ford Administration and Senator Kennedy. In April 1975, hearings began on these bills before the Senate Aviation Subcommittee chaired by Nevada Democrat Howard Cannon. Support for the airline deregulation bill came from many quarters and from both sides of the aisle. Republican President Ford supported it, as did Senator Orrin Hatch (R-UT) and Senator Strom Thurmond (R-SC). Democrats from Kennedy (D-MA) to presidential candidate Jimmy Carter supported it.

But the airline industry as a group was strongly against it. The most vehement opponents of deregulation were the weaker and less financially strong airlines, like Eastern, American, and TWA. Under regulation they had protection of their most profitable routes, and they feared deregulation would unleash competitive vultures to take away their only lifeline to sustainability. Most local service providers opposed deregulation because they feared that the trunk lines would take over their most dense and profitable routes.

Democratic Congressman Elliott Levitas (D-GA), using procedural tricks and Congressional rules, stalled the bill in Congress specifically for Delta Airlines, whose principal office was in

Atlanta, for a period of time. He added to the bill the provision for terminating the authority of the CAB, thereby ending its existence, which many believed would kill the legislation. It didn't.

The airline industry remained solidly opposed to deregulation until the hearings in the spring of 1977, when for the first time United Airlines split from the carrier group. United CEO Richard Ferris came from the hotel industry, not the airlines, and some said that his conversion to the need for deregulation was the result of a failure to understand the workings of air transportation. But there were other supporters, including the intrastate carriers, particularly Southwest, which with deregulation could break forth from the confines of Texas to challenge the airline industry country-wide. Hughes Airwest and Frontier Airlines were two local service providers who favored deregulation. Then there were the commuters, who wanted to be free of the CAB-imposed limitation of 30-seat aircraft; they supported the bill.

Labor groups were opposed to the proposed law, fearing new airlines would hire nonunion labor, thereby reducing wages and threatening job security and favorable work rules. Commercial banks and insurance companies, which provided capital and loans to the air carrier industry and aircraft manufacturers, opposed the law. These companies lived according to well-established amortization and annuity tables that predicted future performance based on past experience. Nobody could say with any reasonable certainty exactly what would happen under a deregulated airline industry.

Missing in all of the debate was any articulation of a national public policy for air transportation in the United States. Most industrialized countries had integrated public transportation systems that included rail, highway, and air. These foreign transportation systems were primarily owned and operated by their governments at taxpayer expense as a function of national pride and necessity.

In the United States, there was no coherent national transportation policy. With the exception of the air transportation and maritime infrastructure and the national highway system, the United States relied on private enterprise and local municipalities to furnish its transportation services needs.

The closest thing to a national air transportation policy that existed in the United States was the Civil Aeronautics Act of 1938, as administered by the CAB. But this statute was enacted primarily to protect the airlines from destructive competition and to promote safety and popular acceptance of air travel. As national policy, it was probably time for a change, but very little was heard in the Kennedy hearings about national policy; rather, the subject focused on anecdotal evidence of overpricing, inefficiencies, lack of capacity, and governmental mismanagement.

Carter had been elected president in 1976, and by early 1977 he began appointing people to head various affected agencies who shared his views on deregulation. To the ICC he appointed deregulator George Stafford as Chairman. To the CAB he appointed Alfred Kahn, the author of *Economics of Regulation*, to replace Robson. Carter went at deregulation across the board,

pushing bills to deregulate the railroads, motor carriers, moving companies, and the gas industry.

Even before passage of the Airline Deregulation Act, Kahn attacked regulation of the airlines in order to create, in his words, "something as close to total deregulation as the (existing) law will permit, to be achieved as quickly as possible."[1] He told his staff that they "were going to get the airline eggs so scrambled that no one was ever going to be able to unscramble them."[2]

Carter continued to push the airline deregulation bill. In April 1978, the Senate passed the bill 83 to 9. In the House of Representatives, Carter enlisted the powerful Speaker of the House, Tip O'Neill, to corral votes from undecided Representatives. By 1978, the relaxed administration of the CAB initiated by Robson and Kahn showed (1) a decline in fares for the first time since 1966, (2) an expansion of air traffic at a rate faster than in the preceding 10 years, and (3) the highest carrier profitability in 10 years. All this had been achieved even while the rate of inflation steadily rose.

Based on these results observed during the spring and summer of 1978, and on the growing support of leaders of both political parties, opposition to the deregulation of the airlines virtually vanished. The deregulation bills passed both Houses.

On October 28, 1978, Carter signed the Act into law. The Airline Deregulation Act (ADA) amends the Federal Aviation Act of 1958, stating as its purpose "to encourage, develop, and attain an air transportation system which relies on competitive market forces to determine the quality, variety, and price of air services." The Act completely changed the economic foundation for the domestic airline industry and provided for its full implementation over the course of a four-year period. It provided, among other things:

1. For the phase-out of the CAB and its authority over domestic routes and fares,

2. For the phase-out of existing economic regulations formerly constituting barriers to competition,

3. Safeguards for the protection of air carrier service to small communities,

4. For the facilitation of entry of air carriers into new markets, and

5. For certain protection of airline employees who may be adversely affected by the results of the Act.

CAB route authority was scheduled to end on December 31, 1981, and rate authority was set to terminate on December 31, 1983. The CAB itself was mandated to cease to exist as of the close of business on December 31, 1984.

This policy of fixing specific termination dates, laddered out into the near future, was to allow the airlines time to develop responses to the changes caused by the Act. The specific provisions for airline guidance during the CAB phase-out period included the following changes:

1. Immediate automatic market entry in certain cases.

2. Shifted the burden of proof in route authority cases from the requirement to show that public necessity and convenience (PNC) was required (in order to secure the route) to one requiring opponents to show that the new award/entry would be inconsistent with PNC.

3. Allowed carriers to obtain authority to fly unused routes of other carriers.

4. Established a range of fares within which carriers could immediately select fares on their own without CAB approval.

5. Established notice procedures to facilitate abandonment of unprofitable routes.

6. Provided a 10-year Essential Air Service Program to ensure air service to small communities.

7. Provided employee protective measures for workers dislocated by changes in the airlines' procedures.

Because of the speed that the Board began to confer new authority, within a year of the passage of the Act certificated lines were able to serve virtually any route they wished. New entries were also granted during this time, although not as quickly as route authority.

The Board arranged a series of meetings throughout the country to address the needs of small communities to facilitate the transition of service mandated by the local service subsidy program and the new essential air service program mandated by the ADA.

Although the Act was designed to offer temporary federal payments to airline employees adversely affected by the Act (see 7 above), this provision of the Act was never implemented. This was due to the inability of the government to make any objective determination as to the cause of job losses or dislocations among airline employees, given the simultaneous onset of the Act, fast-rising fuel prices, and the resulting recession that began in the early 1980s.

Transition from a regulated to an unregulated economic airline environment proved difficult in two particular areas: fares and mergers. Prior law of the Supreme Court had exempted the airlines from compliance with the antitrust laws (the Sherman Antitrust Act and the Clayton Act) that governed other commercial enterprises in the United States. Instead, antitrust oversight and enforcement of the airlines had been conferred on the CAB. This authority had been consistently exercised for over 40 years in the airline industry.

The liberalization of CAB practices that began in the 1970s continued during the phase-out of CAB authority in the early 1980s. There were charges of price-fixing among the airlines as they raised fares and rates almost in lockstep due to the doubling of jet fuel prices between 1979 and 1980. Mergers were approved during this time that most certainly would not have been approved under prior CAB practice.

Upon the demise of CAB authority, airlines became subject to the same antitrust laws as all other commercial business with enforcement jurisdiction initially residing in the Department of Transportation.[3]

With deregulation in place, there was no longer any requirement to secure from the CAB certificates of convenience and necessity before commencing service on a route. No longer were there artificial barriers to entry into the previously exclusive airline carrier club, nor was there any requirement to secure approval from the CAB for rate increases.

When deregulation became law, all of the pent-up competitive instincts of airline bosses were suddenly unleashed. Like adolescents let loose on a first unsupervised journey away from home, excesses might have been expected. The choices of how to proceed were practically unlimited. Unbridled optimism coupled with a fear of being left behind in the race to gain position on their competitors spurred frenzied activity of all sorts, and not a few miscalculations.

■ Braniff International Airways—A Case History Under Deregulation

Braniff's conclusion that deregulation would be only temporary, and that re-regulation was inevitable, was probably the biggest mistake of all. That conclusion prompted Braniff to believe that new routes should be established as quickly as possible, before the window of opportunity slammed shut, and that the equipment to serve these new routes should be immediately acquired before the aircraft manufacturers became backlogged with orders from all of the other airlines that were sure to come.

In 1978 Braniff International Airways was a successful, established carrier with a reliable business clientele responsible for about 70 percent of its traffic. When Postmaster General Farley ordered the re-bidding in 1934 for airmail routes after the so-called "Spoils Conference" affair of 1930, Braniff Airways, Inc, as it was

known then, had acquired the coveted Dallas–Chicago route. As it grew, its route system centered on the Midwest, primarily on a north–south axis. Braniff was profitable and had been for much of its proud history as one of the 16 trunk carriers grandfathered under the Civil Aeronautics Act of 1938.

After World War II, Braniff became the first international competitor to Pan American certificated by the United States government when it began service to South America along its east coast. In 1950, Braniff was granted landing rights in Buenos Aires by the Peron government in Argentina.

By the late 1950s, Braniff had expanded to airports across the country using the DC-7, the last of the large piston engine airplanes, and would soon convert its entire fleet to turbine powered aircraft, including Lockheed turbo "Electras" and Boeing 707s. At this time Braniff was still a conservatively run organization with a solid balance sheet, excellent routes both domestically and internationally, and new aircraft. The future looked bright, indeed.

In 1965, Braniff was bought by GreatAmerica Corporation, an insurance holding company whose expansion into transportation included the purchase of National Car Rental. With its history as a solid Midwestern company serving conservative business and corporate clients, its livery, as well as its management style, was considered rather staid. Under new management Braniff began to take on a different image, one that defines how it is usually viewed today.

Harding Lawrence, as Braniff's new CEO, inaugurated a "makeover" that became the talk of the airline industry. Madison Avenue advertising agencies, folk artists, Italian fashion designers, and architects were called in to recreate the "Braniff look." The airplanes were painted in solid colors, a different color for each airplane, and the colors ranged across the pastel spectrum. During the 1960s, Braniff airplanes sported a total of 15 different colors, including ochre, turquoise, and lemon yellow.

Harding Lawrence loved the abstract, multicolored paintings of the modern artist Alexander Calder and hung some 50 of his original creations around Braniff's executive offices in 1972. Soon, Calder was engaged to design a paint scheme for an entire jet airplane, the first of several, in original, swirling, multicolor designs unique to each aircraft. Calder oversaw the painting as an original work of art and insisted on personally painting one engine nacelle on each airplane with a special design. He was paid a fee of $100,000 for each aircraft design. This fee did not include the paint.

In December 1965, Braniff expanded its international reach by buying the 50 percent interest of W. R. Grace in "Panagra," an airline operated as a joint venture with Pan American World Airways to serve the Andean countries of South America from the United States. Four months later, Braniff bought out Pan Am and continued to fly these South American routes as far south as Santiago, Chile. Pan American continued to fly the east coast of South America.

Between 1975 and 1980, Braniff doubled in size. By this time 95 percent of the Braniff fleet consisted of jets.

Within a few days after the Airline Deregulation Act was passed in October 1978, Braniff had applied for 626 new routes. By early November the CAB had granted Braniff 67 of these new routes, and by the middle of December, the airline had begun service to 16 new cities. During the three months following the signing of the ADA, Braniff hired over 338 new pilots. It bracketed the American continent by establishing new hubs in Boston and Los Angeles. It expanded its fleet by buying and leasing all manner of new aircraft, including the expensive-to-operate 747, which served to compound the error as its cavernous interior flew practically empty on Braniff's new routes.

But possibly the most astonishing development after deregulation was in 1979 when Braniff began service with the new supersonic Concorde between Dallas/Fort Worth and Washington, D.C. as the first leg of international routes to London and Paris with British Airways and Air France. The Concorde was the product of a joint enterprise of the British and French governments to develop the first supersonic transport (SST), and it had been introduced to the aviation world at the Paris Air Show in 1973. The advantage of the Concorde was its ability to fly at Mach 2; its disadvantage was that it could fly at Mach 2 only over the open ocean due to the shock wave produced by supersonic flight. Where Braniff flew the Concorde, which was over the continental United States, there was no advantage—it was limited to an airspeed of .95 Mach, barely over the normal operating speed of a Boeing 727. Worse, even with a nominal surcharge of only $100 added to the DFW-Dulles fare, the cramped 100 seat-configured Concorde usually flew at 15 percent capacity. Some wag observed that all of Braniff's airplanes should have been painted yellow since the airline had gone completely "bananas."

Beginning in 1980 and extending into the early years of the decade, fuel prices spiraled upward due to the OPEC oil crisis, interest rates shot up to 20 percent, and the attendant recession had a stifling effect on passenger traffic. When deregulation did not end, and upstart airlines continued to enter the field and pose significant competitive pressures on Braniff's expanded routes, Braniff began suffering catastrophic losses. In order to maintain cash flow, Braniff began to sell off its newly acquired fleet of aircraft at distressed prices to its competitors, further weakening its position. It then turned to selling off its biggest prizes, its European routes and then its Asian routes, as well as some of its domestic service. This was a pattern that had never been seen before in American aviation, but it was only the beginning.

By 1982, Braniff could no longer keep its doors open against the clamor of creditors, and it filed for Chapter 11 protection under the Bankruptcy Act. It was the first United States airline to do so since airline regulation was begun in

1938. Due to the crushing debt that had accumulated under Braniff's bizarre management style since deregulation, the company could not secure an agreement from its creditors to continue operations under Chapter 11. On May 12, 1982, Braniff grounded all of its beautifully designed and painted aircraft and shut down its operations. It had been 52 years since Paul Braniff first coined the slogan, "The World's Fastest Airline."

▨ The United States Bankruptcy Act[4]

The Constitution of the United States (Article 1, Section 8) specifically provides that Congress be empowered to establish "uniform laws on the subject of bankruptcies throughout the United States." Congress has done so on repeated occasions since 1801. Bankruptcy in the United States, therefore, is mainly a federal exercise, administered in the federal bankruptcy courts, which are an adjunct of the United States District Courts located in each state across the land.

The concept of bankruptcy first implies that one's debts exceed one's assets. This is called "insolvency." Under U.S. law, a petition in bankruptcy can be initiated either by creditors of the insolvent debtor, called "involuntary bankruptcy," or by the debtor himself, called "voluntary bankruptcy." As we saw in Part I of this book, the industrial revolution, and particularly the advent of the railroads, caused the rise of the corporate form of business entity. Under U.S. law, corporations are entitled to the same basic privileges as individuals, including the protection of the bankruptcy laws.

The bankruptcy code is sub-divided into "Chapters," each one dealing with a separate kind of bankruptcy. The most common form of bankruptcy, known as "straight bankruptcy" is found in Chapter 7 of the Code and results in the shutting down of the business. This procedure provides for the appointment of a trustee to liquidate all of the debtor's assets and to distribute the proceeds to the creditors. Chapter 11 is a more complex procedure that allows the debtor to remain in business under the supervision of the bankruptcy court while it goes through a "reorganization" of its debt structure and contractual obligations.

The intent of Chapter 11, in allowing a company to remain in business under reorganization, is to provide a way to pay most if not all of the creditors, to save jobs, to preserve the engine of profitability (which is the corporation's operations in place, good will, experience, and hope of the future), and to allow the business to earn a "fresh start." One trade-off to accomplish this result is the cancellation or renegotiation of previously incurred debts and contracts, including labor contracts. This is accomplished either by compromise between the debtor and the creditors, or by rulings of the bankruptcy judge.

During the reorganization process, which may take months to years depending on the complexities of the reorganization, the debtor is considered "under the protection" of the bankruptcy court. This means that the debtor is shielded from lawsuits that could otherwise be brought by creditors, and from general harassment associated with its unpaid debts. At the same time, the operations of the debtor are subject to the scrutiny of the bankruptcy court and the creditors.

In the following chapters of this book, we will see how Chapter 11 bankruptcy has become an integral part of the air transportation business in the deregulated world. Other sophisticated free market techniques, previously unheard of in commercial aviation, would be brought to bear as airlines attempted to cope with the new world of competition. Hostile corporate takeovers, leveraged buyouts, downsizing, outsourcing, and employee pay givebacks and salary cuts were only some of the new developments that loomed over the horizon. Chief practitioner of these ideas was a Harvard MBA by the name of Frank Lorenzo.

Endnotes

1. Derthick & Quirk, supra, 73.
2. Alfred E. Kahn, Deregulation: Looking Backward and Looking Forward, 7 *Yale J. on Reg.* 325, 331 (Summer 1990).
3. See Chapter 32—Antitrust Enforcement after Deregulation.
4. The bankruptcy law is codified at Title 11 of the United States Code. The U.S. Code is a series of books containing all of the laws of the United States arranged sequentially from Title 1 through Title 50A. Each Title is devoted to a particular subject matter. Title 49, for example, contains the federal statutes in the field of transportation.

26　The Age of Lorenzo

> **❝**I think it is a pity to lose the romantic side of flying and simply to accept it as a common means of transport, although that end is what we have all ostensibly been striving to attain.**❞**
>
> **Amy Johnson, *Sky Roads of the World*, 1939**

Francisco A. Lorenzo, the son of Spanish immigrants, grew up in Queens, New York. He worked his way through Columbia University, earning a degree in economics in 1961, and then graduated from the Harvard Business School with an MBA in 1963. He learned airline financial analysis from the inside as an employee with Eastern Air Lines and TWA in New York City before starting his own financial consulting company, Lorenzo & Carney, in 1966, concentrating on the airline industry. In 1969, the partners formed Jet Capital Corporation, issuing shares to themselves for pennies and then taking the company public by offering shares at $10. In this way the company was capitalized in an amount of $1.5 million. Lorenzo was the prime shareholder.

◼ Texas International

Another Harvard MBA by the name of Donald Burr, a friend of Lorenzo, was a mutual fund financial analyst in New York City specializing in airline stocks. An airline of interest to Burr was a small interstate airline in Texas which, despite its rather small size, had the grand name of Texas International Airlines. It was known in Texas as "Tree Top Airlines" after its original name of Trans Texas Airlines, and it was losing lots of money. Its routes were mostly in Texas and the southwest United States. It claimed its "international" status due to routes to Veracruz and Tampico, Mexico.

As a result of the Burr-Lorenzo friendship, Texas International became a client of Jet Capital Corporation. In the process of arranging a refinancing plan to save the company from bankruptcy, Lorenzo infused most of Jet Capital's money into Texas International Airlines in return for voting control of its stock, and then he secured an additional $5 million in new equity for the airline. By 1972, Lorenzo at 32 years of age had become the youngest airline CEO in the country.

235

FIGURE 26-1 Frank Lorenzo at a press conference, June 1984.

Lorenzo's aggressive management style, which included labor confrontation, wage cutting, equipment upgrades, and streamlining operations, had Texas International turned around by 1974. The airline had lost some $7 million annually for the three years before Lorenzo's arrival, but in 1974 the company was at break even. He had been joined in 1973 by Don Burr as a sort of second banana, and after reversing the airline's financial course, they began developing ways to confront their competition.

The main competition faced by Texas International came from a small intrastate carrier called Southwest Airlines. Unlike Texas International, Southwest was not governed by the Civil Aeronautics Board and, subject only to the rules of the Texas Utilities Commission, it could charge any fare it wanted. Southwest's fares were substantially lower over the same routes than those mandated by the CAB.

Burr and Lorenzo realized that to compete with Southwest, Texas International needed to fill its airplanes' seats, and to do that they had to lower fares. As luck would have it, the CAB was just then beginning to experiment with discounted fares under John Robson, as we saw in Chapter 24.

Texas International petitioned the CAB for authority to discount fares by 50 percent of the standard, CAB-mandated fare. When the CAB unexpectedly approved the lower fares, Lorenzo began a high-profile marketing blitz touting his "Peanut Fares." The consumer response was overwhelming. Between 1972 and 1978 Lorenzo went from a $7 million loss on $63 million in gross revenues to a $13.2 million profit on $158 million in revenues. This was all before the Airline Deregulation Act had passed, but Lorenzo was only warming up.

Texas International had grown to number 16 in the size hierarchy of United States airlines by 1979, a year after deregulation became law, but for Lorenzo that was not big enough. Growth is often accomplished by merger with another carrier, but that did not seem to be in the cards; none of the other airlines was interested in Texas International or Frank Lorenzo.

A hostile takeover, the process by which control of a corporation is taken through stock acquisition, followed by election of a new board of directors and a new slate of officers giving control of the company to the takeover group, had never been attempted in the airline industry. But there was really nothing about the airlines after deregulation that differentiated them from most any other kind of corporation. Times had changed since CAB Chairman James Landis, in 1947, had forced Howard Hughes out of the control of TWA with the words, "I don't believe one man should own a public utility."

Stock acquisition of an airline company, however, requires lots of money, and Lorenzo was not in the same league as Howard Hughes. Lorenzo did, however, have access to the assets of Jet Capital, which had increased along with the value of Texas International stock. These assets could be used for acquiring the stock of another airline, at least in the short run. National Airlines was the ninth largest carrier in the United States in 1979, and Lorenzo discovered that it had practically no debt. The assets of the ninth largest airline unencumbered by debt are valuable collateral at the bank if one wished to borrow on those assets, something the management of National obviously did not wish to do. Lorenzo, however, saw these assets as a way to finance a possible takeover of National with a relatively small investment outlay. This process was the paradigm of what would come to be known in financial circles as the "leveraged buyout."

Jet Capital began buying National stock in the open market until it had acquired almost 10 percent of stock outstanding. Lorenzo then conveyed his intentions to National's president, who immediately began to seek ways to fend off the hostile takeover. The simplest way to defeat a hostile takeover is to gain control of more shares of stock than the takeover group. That usually involves getting into a bidding war for the available stock, which, in turn, causes the stock to increase in value.

Pan American Airways, looking for domestic routes, of which it had absolutely none, joined in the bidding, and the stock of National went up and up. Lorenzo could not or would not compete with Pan American and decided to simply cash in his National stock—for $108 million, or about a $35 million profit. As we will see in Chapter 28, Pan American ultimately purchased 100 percent of National stock and National became a wholly owned subsidiary of Pan Am.

Lorenzo's war chest was now bigger than ever. He formed a new company called Texas Air Corporation in 1980 as a holding company. Texas Air now owned Texas International. Lorenzo began looking for new corporate opportunities to bring under its control. Using Texas Air, Lorenzo took the no frills concept to the east coast, to his home town of New York City, and

started a new subsidiary airline called New York Air to compete with the Eastern Shuttle between Washington, D.C., and Boston.

To Lorenzo, creating a new airline company was much preferred to an expansion of Texas International for the main reason that the new company would be nonunion, unlike Texas International. Like most of the scheduled carriers, Texas International was burdened by union labor contracts that governed wage rates, seniority, and work rules. The pilots of Texas International, on the other hand, were not happy to see their company's money being used to form a nonunion carrier instead of an extension of the Texas International network. An expansion of Texas International, as opposed to the creation of a new nonunion airline, would have brought with it new left seat opportunities for the Texas International pilots, openings for new co-pilots, and a larger union contingent. But this was contrary to Lorenzo's plan. Lorenzo was now beginning to build his reputation as the nemesis of organized airline labor, a union buster even, and there was nothing the unions could do about it. Somehow nobody had thought to mention this aspect of deregulation to the rank and file, to the public, or even to Congress. The sudden and bold elimination of economic regulation of the airlines did, indeed, have unintended consequences.

Lorenzo wanted New York Air to begin operations from LaGuardia Airport. The main problem there was that LaGuardia was slot-allocated, and New York Air had no slots. This conundrum was accommodated when Lorenzo hired a young man by the name of Phil Bakes, a politically well-connected Harvard law graduate. Bakes had worked on the staff of Attorney General Archibald Cox in the prosecutions related to the Watergate break-in affair, as had Harvard professor and future Supreme Court Justice Stephen Breyer.

It was Breyer who recruited Bakes to work on the deregulation effort in 1975 on the Kennedy staff, and it was Bakes who was largely responsible for engineering the deregulation legislation successfully through Congress for Kennedy. He then worked on the unsuccessful 1980 presidential campaign of Ted Kennedy. Lorenzo had hired Bakes just as the dismal Kennedy campaign came to its sad end. Now, Bakes used his knowledge and contacts to deliver the slots to New York Air. New York Air was launched to great fanfare in New York, and the fare wars with Eastern Shuttle commenced, to the delight of the traveling public. New York Air was the first in a long line of new airlines that would come to be known as the "Upstarts." And it was very successful.

People Express

In the meantime, Don Burr had concluded that he wanted to run his own airline, in his own way. Burr had basic philosophical differences with Lorenzo about how to treat employees and people in general. Labor strife at Texas International was increasing due to Lorenzo's business practices.

Burr left Texas Air Corporation, taking with him several other executives, and launched his own airline on April 30, 1981. He named it People Express. People Express made its headquarters in an old abandoned terminal at Newark, and began operations with hand-me-down 737-100s purchased from Lufthansa. The airplanes were reconfigured for high density, one-class seating. The first routes of the new airline were from Newark to Buffalo, Columbus, and Norfolk.

From the early days of commercial passenger service there had been a certain cache and attempt at elegance and elitism in the airlines' treatment of passengers. And although Texas International had dispensed with many of the historical amenities of airline travel, the extreme People Express approach was a shock. With the exception of wartime, nobody in the early 1980s had ever seen anything like it.

There were no meals, no free beverages (coffee was $.50), and no free checked baggage. Passenger baggage that had been checked, for a charge of $3.00 (a substantial amount in 1980s money), was not even transferred to connecting carriers. This required connecting passengers to pick up their bags upon deplaning and carry them to their next departure point. People Express distinguished itself in other ways. Fares were the lowest in the industry, perhaps ever. Greyhound Bus Lines lost business to People Express.

Equality was the order of the day—there were no vice-presidents and no secretaries. Non-technical employees were cross-trained in most jobs and were required to lend a hand where necessary, and there were no nine-to-five days. It was difficult to distinguish the pilots' uniforms from those worn by cabin stewards. In the 1980s, People Express had an air of the communistic People's Republic except for one noticeable difference—it was clearly profitable.

People Express began operations during one of the most turbulent economic times in memory. Interest rates, fuel prices, recession, and the air traffic controllers strike all combined to test the new theories of deregulation. In spite of the difficult economic situation, both New York Air and People Express began to thrive, and that was instructive. The no-frills concept took flying to the masses, where the main consideration was price. The effects of deregulation, good and bad, were beginning to be defined.

We will return to the People Express phenomenon later in this chapter.

> **People Express is clearly the archetypical deregulation success story and the most spectacular of my babies. It is the case that makes me the proudest.**
>
> **Alfred Kahn, Professor of Political Economy, Cornell University, *Time Magazine*, 13 Jan 1986**

Takeover at Continental Airlines

Frank Lorenzo next set his sights on Continental Airlines, which had a proud history going back to 1934 as Varney Speed Lines. The airline was renamed Continental Air Lines in 1937, even before the passage of the Civil Aeronautics Act, and before Frank Lorenzo was born. Lorenzo had earlier attempted to interest Robert Six, founder and chief executive of Continental, in a merger with Texas International, to no avail. Six was among the group of original oil-stained visionaries who had started it all in the airline business, along with Jack Frye, Eddie Rickenbacker, and Juan Trippe, and he wanted nothing to do with the financial whiz-kid from New York. By 1980, Continental's all-jet fleet flew routes coast to coast and over the Pacific to the Far East and Australia. But by 1980, the effects of deregulation and a long strike by flight attendants had produced a loss of $27 million for the year. An attempted merger with Western Airlines did not succeed, and Continental was at risk.

By 1981, Al Feldman had replaced Robert Six as CEO. Feldman was also of the old school and was no more interested in hooking up with Lorenzo than Six had been. Before joining Continental, Feldman had successfully turned around Frontier Airlines using traditional business methods. Unable to secure a voluntary merger agreement with Feldman, Lorenzo, using the assets of Texas Air, began buying Continental stock in another hostile takeover bid.

Feldman fought the takeover energetically, combining with Continental's labor forces to present a united front in opposition. Attempts were even made to get financing that would allow the employees to buy into the company through an employee stock ownership plan (ESOP). In spite of these frantic efforts, which included the employees giving up $180 million in projected pay raises, the ESOP failed. Lorenzo ultimately acquired enough company stock through the open market to get voting control. Al Feldman committed suicide in his office on August 9, 1981.

When Lorenzo took over, a new board of directors was selected, which included Alfred Kahn and John Robson, both former chairmen of the CAB. Because of their roles in bringing about economic deregulation, it could be said that they were both indirectly responsible for the emergence of the voracious Frank Lorenzo as a force in the airline industry. Lorenzo brought in Stephen Wolf from Pan Am as president of Continental. Lorenzo decided to merge Texas International operations and assets with those of Continental, to jettison the Texas International name for good, and to move forward as Continental.

As the consolidation proceeded and Lorenzo's accounting team probed deeper into Continental's finances, it soon became clear that the company was in much worse shape than Lorenzo had been led to believe. It began to look like Lorenzo might have finally made a fatal miscalculation. If Lorenzo's investment was to be salvaged, drastic measures were going to be called for.

Phil Bakes, still Lorenzo's right-hand man, determined that the airline's main expense challenge was the cost of labor. Pilots averaged around $90,000 per year, but flew only about a third of the month. Flight attendants drew $37,500 annually. Mechanics' wages were $40,000 a year. If Continental was going to survive, labor would have to yield to the competitive market consequences of deregulation. Attempts at conciliation between the two sides proved fruitless. The machinists' union, International Association of Machinists (IAM), went on strike at Continental in August 1983. On September 24, 1983, Continental became the second major airline to file for Chapter 11 protection under the Bankruptcy Act.

Lorenzo turned over operation of the airline in Chapter 11 to Phil Bakes. A recent decision of the U.S. Supreme Court, *National Labor Relations Board v. Bildisco*,[1] established that labor contracts, to the extent that their provisions impaired the claims of other creditors, were not enforceable against the debtor corporation (the airline). This decision opened the way for

Continental to unilaterally abrogate all wage scales and work rules, which it did immediately. In effect, Lorenzo was able to legally cancel all labor contracts that were in force at Continental. He then invited back its employees to work longer hours at half the rate of pay. Those who did not agree were simply out of a job. New hires were made in all areas of the company and, despite the fact that the company was in bankruptcy, the pilots' union called a strike. Through the efforts of Phil Bakes, schedules were largely maintained, additional pilots were brought into the company, fares were lowered to attract more passengers, and gradually the company took on a semblance of normalcy. Two years after Continental entered Chapter 11, it became the first airline to successfully emerge from bankruptcy and to pay its creditors close to 100 cents on the dollar. The restructured and reconfigured airline was now ready to cope with the deregulated world.

Computer Reservation Systems

Lorenzo was by no means through acquiring airlines. In 1985, just prior to Continental's coming out of reorganization, Lorenzo made a play for TWA. Some said this was because he needed its computer reservation system to manage the traffic in his growing conglomerate of airline companies. Nobody had yet heard of the Internet. Computer reservation systems were proprietary with each of the Big Four, and it was realized that these systems gave huge advantages to those airlines by increasing their passenger market share, to the detriment of the smaller lines.

Travel reservations, the process of matching an available seat with a named passenger to occupy it, had always been a complex undertaking. Even with the railroads, where it was largely a matter of recognizing where passengers on the line of road were getting on and getting off, keeping up with the availability of seats was a daunting task. In the early airlines, as with the railroads, reservations were tracked manually, usually at a central location. Entries representing reservations were made in pencil so that they could be erased if the reservation was cancelled.

When traffic picked up in the 1930s, ledgers became even more impractical, and the system was expanded to chalkboard displays in large rooms, also at a central location, on which entries and cancellations were noted. Clerks who took the reservation request from passengers handed off the information to runners who relayed the details to writers at the chalkboards. In time chalkboards were replaced by electric light displays, also in large rooms, and despite the advanced technology of electricity, the process was still manual, cumbersome, and inaccurate. Increased service to multiple cities in random directions, even on one airline, exponentially increased the difficulties of keeping track of reservations manually. Booking seats on multiple airlines made the job even harder.

By the 1940s, efforts were being made to automate the process. Makers of computational equipment, like adding machines, were the logical choice to assist in solving these mathematical complexities, but in turn these companies advised that they could not handle the number of variables presented in the problem.

C. R. Smith of American Airlines, himself an accountant and numbers man, was preoccupied with the reservations dilemma. Unable to secure assistance outside of the company, he authorized American's technical people to come up with a solution. The result was a massive mechanical monstrosity consisting of vertical cylinders, each one representing a different flight on a given day, which was filled with marbles representing available seats. When a seat was booked, an agent activated a switch that released one marble from the cylinder. A reciprocal arrangement at the top of the cylinder released a marble back into the cylinder for each reservation that was cancelled.

This arrangement was an improvement, but it was no match for the growing problem of reservations as traffic increased. With the beginning of the jet age in commercial air traffic, once again the problem was made exponentially more difficult. The process was not only marginally inaccurate, but also very costly for the company as personnel and terminals had to be added to the system.

IBM, through its primitive computer technology, during the 1950s was out front in developing solutions for the federal government related to the problems of monitoring the potential for incoming ballistic missiles. The acronym for the IBM program was SAGE, Semi-Automatic Ground Environment. SAGE was the first computer game in real time as strategic and tactical planners engaged each other in simulations of nuclear warfare.

Under contract with American, IBM began applying its SAGE technology to the reservations problem, and for almost 10 years its best minds labored away. The project was originally known as SABER, Semi-Automatic Business Environment Research, and later as SABRE, and the first commercial activation of the system did not occur until 1962. At that time computer technology was truly rudimentary, and almost all commercial computers were engaged in solving mathematical equations, or in streamlining the problems of accounting in corporate America, like payrolls. And these applications were applied to dealing with numbers in a historical context, not real-time. With SABRE, real-time computing in business applications was born.

With this development American Airlines had a real commercial advantage over its competitors. In the 1960s, the Civil Aeronautics Board was still in control of all meaningful decisions related to the running of an airline, so SABRE's function was expanded to not only solve American's reservations problems, and to assure consistent and accurate reservations for the very first time, but also to track every passenger's name, address, personal information, and most details of that passenger's travel preferences, such as hotel usage. Not only could SABRE track customer information, but the technology was soon

expanded to begin to solve the company's day-to-day operational problems. But management at American was slow to realize the full potential of the advantage given them by the computer system they had developed.

The other airlines began their own experimentations with computers, particularly as applied to the reservations system. The technology was still relatively primitive, and the cost was enormous. In 1966, TWA committed $75 million to solving the problem, hiring Burroughs Corporation to come up with a proprietary computer reservations system (CRS). By 1970, no workable system had been achieved, although in time TWA would perfect a system known as PARS. United began its own program, called APOLLO, and made reasonable progress. At the same time at American, SABRE was losing its advantage as management failed to upgrade equipment, and as uninstalled computers sat in storage, allowing its competitors to catch up. Still, all computer reservation systems at the time were considered works in progress.

In 1970, in spite of their individual efforts up to that time, the major airlines realized that, from a cost-effectiveness standpoint, it made a lot more sense to pool their resources to develop the ultimate computer reservations system than for each to go it alone, thereby duplicating effort and wasting untold sums of money. When presented with the airlines' plan, the Justice Department announced that it would consider such a combination between the major carriers to be a violation of the Sherman Antitrust Act, and would prosecute the airlines criminally if they proceeded. Many considered this an extreme example of government abuse of power, but there was little the airlines could do. The opportunity was thus lost to have a single, unbiased reservations program developed for the benefit of all of the airlines and the public at large. The only course left for the airlines was for each of them to develop their own, proprietary system. Few in 1970 realized the commercial potential of the computer, or the great benefits that would inure to the owners of these proprietary systems. The joint plan proposed by the airlines would have allowed the unbiased computer reservations system to be used by all travel agents in servicing the flying public. Now the public would have to wait, as would the travel agents.

Around 1975, the travel agents got together to announce that they were planning to develop their own CRS. United had its APOLLO up and running, and by 1974 it was generally considered to be the best in the industry, having surpassed SABRE. It was, however, still in development. No one at the major airlines believed that it was in their interest to lose control of CRS, and be faced with a giant travel agent computer network where all flights of all airlines would be available to all travel agents everywhere. It was feared that such a system would require the airlines to pay a transaction fee for every reservation, in addition to the commission that they paid.

Another effort was made by the airlines to convince the government of the desirability of the joint approach. The CAB this time gave the airlines antitrust immunity, but only to permit the airlines to explore the possibilities of such a system—to talk, but not to proceed, with building the program. It was at this stage, in July 1975, that United unilaterally declared that it would no longer participate in seeking government approval for the joint effort, and that it would go it alone. United, as the biggest bear in the woods, believed that it had a competitive advantage over the other airlines in its CRS, and it began to appreciate what favorable nuances could be incorporated into the program to heighten that advantage. United's plan was to gain control of the travel agent business by supplying travel agents with its APOLLO program which would, of course, have built into it biases in favor of United.

The world of travel agents at the time was one of telephones and paper transactions. The Official Airline Guide (OAG) was a periodical publication containing all the world's airline departures and arrivals, displayed in a city pair format. The procedure was for the travel agent, upon receiving a request from a traveler for flight information preparatory to booking a reservation, to go to the OAG, discern the flight information and the airline that most closely matched the traveler's request, and then secure authority from the traveler to book the flight. The travel agent would then telephone the airline, confirm the reservation, secure the airline's authority, and then telephone the traveler back with the confirmation. The agent would then write the ticket and ultimately transmit it to the traveler, usually by mail. The travel agent was paid a commission by the airline.

The United plan would simplify this procedure greatly. The plan was to install computer terminals in the travel agents' offices for a fee, and then provide the agents with all of the flight information available in the OAG on an interactive, real-time basis so that the travel agent would be able to confirm the reservation while the traveler was still on the phone, then the computer would issue the ticket. Unstated, but appreciated by some of United's competitors like Bob Crandall at American, was the fact that APOLLO would contain preferences for United through outright biased presentations that would likely cause the travel agent to favor a United flight over any other.

Typical of the types of bias that the computer could generate was the positioning of the flight information on the computer screen. American had conducted research that showed that 50 percent of the time, travel agents selected the flight that appeared on the first line of the computer screen. Ninety percent of the time, the travel agent picked a flight that appeared on the first page of a multi-page computer display. If the proprietary CRS program were configured to offer its own flights on the first line, or at least in a favorable position on the first page, there was an advantage to that airline. Various algorithms were developed to accomplish these ends.

Dick Ferris of United and Bob Crandall of American, with their companies in a nip and tuck race to lead the industry in the middle 1970s, were head-to-head competitors. Crandall resolved to bring SABRE back up to a competitive level, and to pitch SABRE to the travel agents as the best system for them. Crandall did his homework, made presentations at national travel agent conventions, conducted mail-out campaigns, and before long, American was out in front again.

The agents who signed up with American were provided with terminals, computers, monitors, and the essentials for using the system in their business, and they were charged a fee. Only the largest "commercial" agencies could afford to participate, but the hardware was getting cheaper by the month. Then United struck back by providing some of the agencies with the equipment without a fee, and allegedly gave rebates (kickbacks) to the agencies for using United's CRS.

By 1983, the proprietary computer reservation systems included American's SABRE, United's APOLLO, TWA's PARS, Delta's DATAS II, and Eastern's SODA. All of these systems began as in-house reservation systems, but their databases were expanded and their access systems were configured to allow distribution to travel agents under either lease or outright sale. The airlines' mainframe computers were operated by the airlines, telecommunications equipment connected the airlines' computers with the travel agents, and the travel agents equipped their offices with computer terminals and printers.

SABRE (American)		Apollo (United)		PARS (TWA)	
Anchorage	92%	Denver	72%	Kansas City	71%
Dallas–Ft. Worth	88	Portland	66	St. Louis	57
Cincinnati	84	Cleveland	64	Columbus	51
Phoenix	69	Milwaukee	57	Pittsburgh	41
Boston	69	Sacramento	52		
Rochester	69	Salt Lake City	52		
Houston	68	Seattle	48		
San Diego	54	Honolulu	47		
Detroit	53	Buffalo	44		
Wash., D.C.	51	Chicago	42		
New York	50				
Miami	49				
Minn.–St. Paul	49				
Hartford	44				
Los Angeles	43				
Salt Lake City	42				
Chicago	41				

TABLE 26-1 CRS shares of travel agencies in $100 million urban markets (CMSAs) (18 Months Ended June 1983)
Source: U.S. Department of Justice Comments, November 17, 1983 (Appendix).

The game was now on. It became a contest to program the airline's CRS to give the greatest advantage (bias) to that airline, preferably without disclosing the bias to the travel agent or anyone else. CRS owners were known for being slow to adjust changes made by their competitors in their schedules, particularly if those changes operated to the detriment of that CRS owner. Preferences were introduced, like providing advance boarding passes only to travel agents who were subscribers to SABRE. "Bonuses" were paid to travel agents. Various dirty tricks were not uncommon. When Lorenzo's New York Air refused to pay the $3.00 transaction fee imposed first by American, and then by all other CRS owners, all New York Air flights were dropped to the bottom of the last page. United dropped People Express completely from its APOLLO system. And the CRS owners began selectively charging booking fees to the smaller airlines. This caused the CAB to order in 1984 that CRS owners desist from discriminating against the smaller airlines in booking fee charges.[2] So the CRS owners simply raised fees for everyone, and it was a huge burden. Midway Airlines is reported to have paid nearly $150 million in booking fees over a 12-year period. Only Southwest and People Express, of all United States carriers, chose not to participate in CRS bookings offered by the large proprietary systems.

Travel agents in hub cities overwhelmingly used the CRS system owned and provided by the dominant hub carrier. The airlines candidly admitted that their computer screen displays favored their own airline, justifying the practice on the airlines' vast expenditure of funds in development of the CRS. After a Justice Department investigation, the CAB in 1984, as one of its last official acts, ordered the airlines to cease all bias in their programs' displays.[3]

It was becoming increasingly clear as business and the public became more dependent on computers that the airlines were increasingly dependent on computer reservations systems.

By 1984, travel agencies were responsible for almost three-fourths of all airline tickets sold, and 57 percent of their revenues were produced through the use of computer reservation systems.

CRS was important before deregulation when all airlines charged the same fare as set for them by the CAB. With deregulation in 1978 and the freedom to set fares as the airlines wished, CRS became the prime conduit for the flow of information in the travel industry; CRS was becoming indispensable, and Lorenzo did not have one.

Acquiring a computer reservations system is only one justification for waging a hostile takeover war. As Lorenzo was making his play for TWA, another wealthy financier, Carl Icahn, became enamored of owning an airline since in all his life he had never owned one. Deregulation, it appeared, allowed moneyed individuals the opportunity to buy and sell airlines like railroads in a large Monopoly game. The vaunted concept of the "public interest," one of the main bases invoked for governmental regulation of public utilities, including the airlines, appeared to have been lost forever. When TWA got wind of Lorenzo's interest in them, they literally jumped into Icahn's arms, believing that anything would be better than a Lorenzo takeover. After engaging in a series of thrusts and parries, Lorenzo once again acquiesced and backed off, content with his multimillion dollar stock appreciation. Carl Icahn took control of TWA, to be discussed in Chapter 27.

■ Takeover at Eastern Air Lines

Eastern Air Lines, one of the venerable Big Four, had a proprietary computer reservations system. Eastern had largely grown and developed under the reign of Eddie Rickenbacker, World War I ace and champion racecar driver. Eastern's reputation in labor relations was not what one would call "progressive"; rather, it was contentious to the extreme, particularly with the machinists union under the leadership of Charlie Bryan. One might say that labor relations at Eastern were more like the railroads than the airlines.

Eastern was losing money in 1983, so much so that insolvency appeared to Frank Borman, the first American astronaut to orbit the earth and Eastern's CEO, to be a distinct possibility. The rigors of deregulation, along with the serious economic situation that existed in the early 1980s, were taking a toll. Borman, like others in the industry, went to the rank and file with pleas for help in the form of "givebacks," or voluntary wage cuts, in order to meet the emergency. Reluctantly, the pilots and the flight attendants cooperated, but the machinists did not. In fact, they demanded and got a 32 percent wage increase on threats of a strike, which created a rather incongruous situation among the respective crafts. The pilots were not happy, nor were the flight attendants, and morale plummeted. And Eastern continued to lose money.

In 1985, Eastern's debt approached $2.5 billion and income was dwindling. But Eastern had a computer reservations system. Texas Air was still flush with cash but Lorenzo still did not have his own CRS. Lorenzo offered to supply the needed cash to Eastern through a straight buyout. Because of Lorenzo's reputation, neither management nor the employees favored this idea. Borman desperately sought ways to right the ship, appealing to the working crafts for even more concessions, but it was clear that without the support of Charlie Bryan and the machinists, there was little hope. With all options exhausted, Borman and the Eastern board of directors, at a midnight meeting, reluctantly agreed to the sale to Texas Air. While awaiting government approval for the Eastern purchase, Lorenzo turned his attention to People Express.

■ Takeover at People Express

❝ Be Luke Skywalker, not Darth Vader. Ultimately love is stronger than evil. ❞

Donald Burr, founder of People Express

People Express had done exceedingly well at the beginning, expanding its route structure and

purchasing more and more aircraft. Revenues grew at an astonishing rate, from $38 million in 1981 to $1 billion in 1985. People Express even bought Frontier Airlines, headquartered at Denver, to give it a western hub and to rapidly increase its rate of growth. This purchase also gave People Express an elementary CRS system, the lack of which Burr concluded was severely undermining his airline's ability to compete in 1985. But Frontier was a union airline, and its culture did not mesh well with People Express, not that any conventional carrier could.

It was said that working at People Express was akin to being in a cult, with its emphasis from the top down on philosophical intangibles like love, equality, peace, and brotherhood. All this was the direct influence of Don Burr, who had been caught up in the message of a popular inspirational and self-help book called *The Greatest Salesman in the World*. The tenets of this book became the basis for his personal philosophy. Attempts to put these teachings into practice at Texas International inevitably brought him into conflict with Frank Lorenzo, who had a very different approach to running a corporation for profit. Now at People Express Burr was free to apply these teachings liberally, and he did, in upbeat posters, presidential messages, manuals, and meetings. Morale was high, and most employees joined in the upbeat new-age philosophy that infused the company, attending pep rallies in the company auditorium by chief cheerleader Burr. The employee stock purchase plan swelled, as workers paid out substantial portions of their salaries to the company in stock purchases, stock that went up and seemingly never could go down.

Burr had pulled off the Frontier acquisition right out from under his mentor, Lorenzo, who was also vying for the property. But it had been costly. Lorenzo had offered $22 per share in October 1985, but Burr had successfully lined up employee support at Frontier because of Lorenzo's anti-union reputation, and secured significant employee concessions. These, coupled with Burr's countering bid of $24 per share, were enough to convince Frontier's board of directors to vote in favor of the People Express acquisition.

People Express's cash stores were immediately and firmly tapped in order to pay Frontier's expenses. It was much worse than anyone had expected. Burr learned from his financial people right after the deal was closed that People Express could expect to lose $100 million in just the next few months covering Frontier's hemorrhaging. By June 1986, less than a year after acquiring it, Burr realized he had to dump Frontier if People Express was to survive. Within a period of nine months after the Frontier acquisition, People Express was essentially out of cash.

There were not a lot of suitors interested in Frontier. United offered to take Frontier off Burr's hands for less than one-half of what Burr had paid just a few months earlier. But United's pilots soon put an end to the takeover discussions with People Express, and United pulled out of the discussions. With no more cash to infuse into Frontier, Frontier filed for Chapter 11 protection on August 28, 1986.

When all other possible deals had fallen through for People Express, Lorenzo became the only option. Burr had come full circle. On September 15, 1986, it was announced that Texas Air had purchased People Express.

■ The DOT Approves the Eastern Takeover

The Department of Transportation gave its approval to the Eastern takeover by Texas Air later that year. That Eastern was a basket case was known, but, like Frontier, it had not been appreciated just how bad the situation was. Phil Bakes had performed well for Lorenzo after the Continental takeover. Under Bakes, Continental had been turned around and was profitable again. Like Continental, the most pressing problem

facing Eastern was labor costs. But the labor problems at Eastern could not be handled like they were at Continental four years before by simply filing under Chapter 11, then unilaterally abrogating the labor contracts in place with the unions. Congress had passed legislation in 1984 that restricted the effect of the holding in *Bildisco,* so that the debtor in possession (the bankrupt airline) could no longer unilaterally cancel labor agreements.[4]

Bakes relocated to Miami and took over the helm at Eastern. The magnitude of Eastern's problems dwarfed those encountered at Continental. The culture was different, the personnel were hostile, and the history of labor relations was dismal. Eastern's record of labor relations over the years was largely a chronicle of the intransigence of the International Association of Machinists, whose leader was the powerful Charlie Bryan. Without a solution to the labor problem, for starters, there did not appear to be any way to salvage the airline.

Judging by subsequent developments, it appears that Lorenzo also came to that conclusion early; there likely was no way to salvage Eastern. Even as Bakes worked to solve the company's seemingly insurmountable problems, Lorenzo began the systematic dismantling of Eastern for the benefit of Texas Air and its viable holdings. Eastern's computer reservation system had been appraised for an amount between $250 million and $450 million, an astonishing fact when it is realized that the entire purchase price for the company was $615 million. Lorenzo had financed the purchase in such a way that less than half of the purchase money came from Texas Air, the rest of the money came from Eastern itself, validating once again the old leveraged buyout strategy that had worked so well. The computer reservation system was sold to Texas Air for the insider bargain price of $100 million, but the terms were even better: Texas Air put up no money, but gave Eastern a promissory note for the purchase price, payable at the end of a period of 25 years at a severely discounted rate of interest. Texas Air then leased back the system to Eastern for a fee of $10 million a month.

> **" As a businessman, Frank Lorenzo gives capitalism a bad name. "**
>
> **William F. Buckley**

Lorenzo next transferred Eastern's newest airplanes to Continental, paying Eastern again by promissory note for part of the payment. Continental then sold the airplanes for cash, and at a profit. Continental bought 11 Eastern Air Lines gates at Newark Airport for half price, again paid for by promissory note. The purchasing of fuel was outsourced to a subsidiary of Texas Air at a cost to Eastern of $1 million per month. Eastern paid Continental another $2 million per month for the training of non-employee pilots who, ironically, would be used to replace Eastern's pilots in case of a labor disruption.

Eastern's service was also being curtailed for lack of cash flow, and was stopped completely at New Orleans, Seattle, and San Diego. Then came the sell-off of the routes, beginning with Eastern's shuttle, which was sold to Donald Trump. The expected machinist strike came in March 1989, which marked the absolute beginning of the end. Although Eastern immediately went into Chapter 11, the reorganization amounted to little more than the gradual selling off of all remaining assets in order to raise operating cash. The bankruptcy court took control of the reorganization from Eastern in April 1990, appointing as Trustee Martin Shugrue, former Continental president. The court used the opportunity to judicially note that Lorenzo's stewardship of Eastern had been a catastrophe. The reorganization was turned into a liquidation of Eastern's assets and, in 1991, the charade finally ended. Eastern Air Lines was no more. Creditors were left holding the bag to the tune of almost $3 billion, and even the lawyers were shorted their fees, a most uncommon occurrence.

> **" Pilots are a rare kind of human. They leave the ordinary surface of the world, to purify their soul in the sky, and they come down to earth, only after receiving the communion of the infinite. "**
>
> **José Maria Velasco Ibarra, President of Ecuador**

◼ Lorenzo Departs

Frank Lorenzo was obviously not cut from the same airline cloth as were the early aviation chieftains like Jack Frye, Eddie Rickenbacker, and Juan Trippe, people who loved to build things and loved to fly. Lorenzo was first and foremost a financial guy, the quintessential MBA focused on finance, with little thought or care for tradition, history, or national concept. Whereas the airlines had been built by men who expected to make money from their efforts, not every decision they made was a financial one; not every action taken was with a view toward the bottom line. Empire building in the early days was done one step at a time, not in one fell swoop like the hostile takeovers, leveraged buyouts, and unrestrained mergers that became the *modus operandi* of the deregulated 1980s. Lorenzo had turned the venerable airline industry on its head: Continental had absorbed People Express (and Frontier) and New York Air. Texas Air, in turn, owned Continental, and had then acquired Eastern Air Lines. By 1987, Texas Air controlled 20 percent of the domestic airline market, and it had only 20 employees.

By the late 1980s, Lorenzo and his business methods were wearing thin in most quarters, including labor, the banks, other airlines, and the agencies of the federal government. His reputation was preceding him. It was said that the Berlin wall, before it began to come down in 1989, bore Lorenzo's name in red with a slash through it, signifying the negative. The ultimate industry rejection came from the bankruptcy order of Judge Burton Lifland, in his termination of Lorenzo's status as debtor in possession of Eastern. Judge Lifland noted that Lorenzo was "not competent to reorganize" the company. Lorenzo himself seems to have tired of the game. Pickets from Eastern regularly appeared outside of his home and there was some concern for his safety and that of his family.

Jan Carlzon had built SAS (Scandinavian Airlines System) into a niche airline operation within the continent of Europe, competing with the large state-owned airlines. His vision was to beat his European competition to the markets of America now opening due to deregulation. Thus, he began overtures in the middle 1980s to establish a relationship with a United States carrier. After negotiating unsuccessfully first with Eastern, then TWA, he approached Lorenzo with a proposition for a partnership arrangement with Continental, based out of Newark. This led to an agreement in October 1988 for SAS to purchase a minority interest in Texas Air for $50 million, to be followed the next year with another payment of $40 million. Texas Air, in the late 1980s, was suffering hefty losses, and the experience with Eastern after its purchase by Texas Air was draining.

Lorenzo's reputation had made its way to Europe, where labor interests looked askance at the prospect of the Texas Air–SAS alliance. One European tabloid ran a cartoon depicting Carlzon and Lorenzo in bed together with the caption "It's fine if you go to bed just don't go to sleep." Even Lorenzo had to acknowledge that his reputation detracted from the ongoing success and potential of Texas Air holdings. In 1990, Texas Air was reorganized into Continental Air Holdings, and in the summer of that year Lorenzo struck a deal with SAS for the sale of his entire personal stake in the company for $50 million.

Seemingly always at the top of his game, and a master of timing, Lorenzo sold out just before Iraq invaded Kuwait in August 1990. The invasion and resulting worldwide reaction spurred fuel costs and depressed airline travel. Continental was unable to meet the financial strain imposed, and filed for Chapter 11 protection again in December 1990, prompting some wags to suggest that Continental was now in "Chapter 22."

Lorenzo made one last appearance on the airline scene in 1993. His idea was to inaugurate a new carrier called "Friendship Airlines." He made application to the DOT, as required by law, for a Certificate of Public Convenience and Necessity. Since deregulation, this procedure has been used to determine the "fitness" of an applicant to conduct an interstate air carrier operation. The DOT denied the application. Lorenzo was finally gone.

Endnotes

1. 459 U.S. 1145, 103 S.Ct. 784, 74 L.Ed. 992 (1983).

2. 14 C.F.R. 255; Regulation ER-1385, 49 Fed. Reg. 32540 (Aug. 14, 1984), aff'd *United Airlines v. CAB*, 766 F. 2d 1107 (7th Cir. 1985).

3. The Department of Transportation allowed this CAB regulation to expire in 2004 due to the effect of the Internet.

4. See Bankruptcy Code, 11 U.S.C § 1113, et. seq. Under this amendment to the Bankruptcy Code, the debtor in bankruptcy may petition the Bankruptcy Court to void or modify union contracts and impose lower pay scales or more reasonable work rules. The Court must find (after presentation of evidence) that wage and benefit cuts or changes to work rules are necessary for the debtor (airline) to successfully emerge from bankruptcy and that these changes are equitable and not arbitrary. This was not the case when Lorenzo unilaterally canceled the Continental labor agreements.

27   Carl Icahn and TWA

"You learn in this business: If you want a friend, get a dog."

Carl Icahn

TWA was one of the original "Big Four," created out of the so-called "Spoils Conference" in 1930 by the edict of Walter Folger Brown, which forced the combination of Western Airlines and Transcontinental Air Transport (TAT). TWA had participated in the major developments of American airline history under the leadership of Jack Frye, and later under the secretive and unpredictable Howard Hughes. It had pioneered both the early transcontinental routes and the early airliners used on those routes, like the DC-3 and later the Constellation. TWA had contributed significantly to the war effort between 1941 and 1945, flying the only land-based four-engine aircraft in existence at that time (the Boeing 307) on transatlantic routes to Africa from South America and to Europe. By war's end, TWA had gained transatlantic experience that only Pan American could rival. Howard Hughes, then firmly in control of TWA, changed the name of the company. Since 1930, the initials TWA had stood for Transcontinental and Western Airlines, but after the war the company name became Trans World Airlines, still using the TWA brand.

Perhaps owing largely to its war effort, TWA was rewarded after World War II with the first transatlantic routes that went to any established American airline other than Pan American. On February 5, 1946, TWA made its first scheduled international flight, from New York to Paris. TWA was also granted access to London's Heathrow Airport, known as the "Gateway to the World," and it continued its international route expansion for years to come, including the polar route in 1957 from Los Angeles to London.

In 1961, TWA severed its relationship with Howard Hughes, who by that time had become a recluse, and by 1965 the company had redeemed all of his shares of stock. New management, led by Charles Tillinghast, made changes within the company that caused it to prosper. TWA's profits in 1965 were the largest of any airline.

TWA thrived under the regulatory scheme in place during the 1960s and 1970s, but with deregulation, things began to come undone. The very nature of TWA's routes, including many long distance ones, had mandated that its fleet be composed of large airplanes. The use of large aircraft when smaller ones would have sufficed, with the resulting substantial expense differential, increased the financial burden. TWA was also slow to appreciate the hub concept, and its

249

labor costs were way out of line. Its unions were not willing to grant the wage and working condition concessions that looked necessary. By the 1980s, TWA was losing money, some $100 million by the middle of the decade. TWA began to look appealing as a corporate takeover target. All of the symptoms were there, including low stock valuation, troubled management, and relatively high asset value. It had also accumulated $200 million in depreciation, which could be used as a tax deduction directly against income. This scenario drew the Wall Street raider types like sharks to blood in the water.

Carl Icahn (see Figure 27-1), like Frank Lorenzo, grew up in Queens, New York. He received his A. B. degree from Princeton in 1957, and then attended New York University School of Medicine, without graduating. As a young man, he had some talent at chess and, it was rumored, at poker as well. When he left medical school he joined the Army, where he gained a reputation for his gambling skills. By 1961, he was employed on Wall Street in New York in the stock brokerage business and drifted into the super-specialty of arbitrage, the trading of both the long and the short side of stocks and options that allows the taking advantage of slight differentials in price. This led to trading in

FIGURE 27-1 Carl Icahn began buying up shares of TWA in 1985, and by April he had acquired enough stock in the company to trigger the mandatory public filings with the Securities and Exchange Commission.

issues of companies rumored to be the object of takeover strategies, companies that usually experienced large and volatile price fluctuations.

Icahn went from simply trading the stocks of these companies to practicing strategies to gain actual management control of them. Control of a company can be gained either by outright stock purchase or through proxy fights. Proxy fights involve persuading other stockholders, usually through intensive mailing campaigns, to allow their shares to be voted by someone who is leading the proxy fight. The rationale is usually to effect a change in management through gaining seats on the board of directors.

Icahn's aggressive corporate acquisition strategies were originally bona fide efforts to win stock proxy fights in order to gain control of undervalued corporations so that their management and value could be improved. In 1979, Icahn won his first proxy fight for a seat on the board of directors of the stove manufacturer, Tappan, by which he subsequently forced the sale of the company, rendering him a profit of $3 million for his stock.

He soon learned that he did not always have to be successful in his takeover bids in order to make money. This tactic usually involved isolating a target company, starting to buy up its stock or gaining control through a proxy fight, running up the stock's price, and then retiring from the field with a nice profit when the target's management successfully fought him off with counter offers for control. This practice came to be known as "greenmail," a play on the better understood word "blackmail." Icahn gained the reputation as a "corporate raider"[1] when the business community realized that he had adopted this practice as a vocation and business lifestyle.

Icahn followed the Tappan bid with raids of Marshall Field's, Anchor Hocking, American Can, and Owens-Illinois. His image was blackened forever when he attempted to take over the textile company Dan River in 1982. Dan River was a 100-year-old Danville, Virginia company and mostly locally owned when Icahn began buying up stock. The employees and the people of Danville got together to fight the takeover, using their retirement money to successfully buy up the stock. When it was all over, Icahn was roundly seen as a villain.

Along the way Icahn developed deep pockets for financing his deals, including the investment banking house of Drexel Burnham and junk bond king Michael Milken. Icahn next successfully acquired the rail car manufacturing and leasing company, ACF Industries, which was followed by the unsuccessful, but profitable, takeover effort of Phillips Petroleum. Icahn's targets appeared to be getting bigger and bigger.

Icahn began buying up shares of TWA in 1985, and by April he had acquired enough stock in the company to trigger the mandatory public filings with the Securities and Exchange Commission. TWA management sprang into action. By this time one thing was known for sure: Icahn could not be a good steward for any company. Icahn's corporate raider reputation was seen as having developed from "greenmail" to "acquisition and dismemberment," and TWA pulled out the stops in mobilizing against him.

At first there was a combined effort by both management and labor against the takeover attempt. Suits for injunctions were filed on various grounds, the unions conducted campaigns against Icahn, and both groups lobbied Congress for help. An Employee Stock Option Plan (ESOP) was considered. TWA sought merger partners, but only Eastern made any attempt to investigate the possiblities. A TWA–Eastern merger would probably not have survived the anticompetitive test by the government anyway, but the unions at Eastern defeated that effort.

By the beginning of the summer of 1985, Icahn had invested over $100 million in TWA. With all defensive stratagems failing to prevent a hostile takeover, management began to consider alternatives to Icahn, including Frank Lorenzo (Texas Air). This is where management and labor parted company. Lorenzo's use of the bankruptcy court to void labor contracts and cut wages at

Continental, as well as his starting his new shuttle airline in New York as a nonunion airline, were to have a long legacy. The unions were convinced that if Lorenzo won control, TWA would be folded into the Texas Air–Continental operation and would cease to exist. Yet Lorenzo was not about to go away. Management brought in Drexel Burnham to broker a deal between Icahn and Lorenzo that would have paid Icahn $95 million and given control of TWA to Lorenzo. Management believed that they could work better with Lorenzo than Icahn.

During the negotiations, Lorenzo and Icahn were about $7 million apart on the money when the unions, led by the Airline Pilots Association, began negotiations directly with Icahn. The pilots and the machinists offered concessions to Icahn that they would not offer to Lorenzo and had not offered even to TWA management— they agreed to wage cuts (26 percent) and to work rules changes in exchange for a profit-sharing arrangement and stock ownership. This allowed Icahn to raise his stock offer price to match Lorenzo's rather than sell out his stock investment in TWA under the Drexel Burnham deal. Lorenzo actually offered slightly more than Icahn for stock control, but by this time Icahn had acquired over 50 percent of the stock, and because of the bitter resentment of the unions against Lorenzo, the board acceded to the decision to go with Icahn.

In the end, it was labor that handed TWA to Icahn.[2] Lorenzo, once again, pocketed a nice gain in the value of his stock acquired while pursuing control of the company—in this case $50 million. Icahn meanwhile set out to maximize his investment with further acquisitions by TWA.

TWA's main competition in St. Louis in 1986 was Ozark Airlines. In the middle 1980s the Department of Transportation under Elizabeth Dole was in charge of reviewing proposed mergers, and the stance at DOT at that time was rather relaxed on airline mergers. This was, after all, the era of deregulation. Still, many people, like Alfred Kahn, the so-called father of deregulation, were concerned that the industry was rapidly becoming too centralized, too anti-competitive, and that the benefits of deregulation as they saw it would suffer from such lack of competition. Their views were largely dismissed as the DOT routinely signaled its approval of anticipated combinations in the industry, particularly with relatively minor players like Ozark.

Icahn closed the deal for the acquisition of Ozark for $239 million. The Justice Department decried the merger and came out against it. But it was the DOT's call (the DOJ would not be given authority over mergers until 1988), and the merger was approved as expected. With this deal, Icahn had essentially eliminated competition out of St. Louis. It came as no surprise that St. Louis fares were quickly raised, now that the CAB no longer existed, but it was also clear that this was not what deregulation was supposed to be about. It became obvious that the anticompetitive safeguards formerly monitored by the CAB, and now by the DOT, were being ignored—another unintended consequence.

As TWA proceeded under the new arrangement and Icahn's management practices took hold, the unions at TWA would learn what bitter fruit their deal with Icahn was about to produce. The flight attendants had not been part of the deal with Icahn, and their labor working agreement expired in 1986. When no progress was seen in their attempted negotiations with Icahn, they walked out. Icahn hired replacements, at a significant savings to the company, and when the flight attendants called off the strike a few months later and wanted to return to work, Icahn refused to rehire them. Lawsuits abounded.

The wage concessions that the pilots and machinists had earlier agreed to in their deal with Icahn provided for "snap back" wage increases when their labor agreements were to be renewed. To their dismay, Icahn insisted that they extend their contracts at present wage rates. When the unions resisted, Icahn threatened to dismantle the airline—and he meant what he said. The unions folded.

In what might be considered to be less than good faith follow through, Icahn sold all of the Ozark fleet of airplanes and then leased them back to TWA. As majority shareholder, this was like cash in Icahn's pocket. The airplanes then had to be paid for out of operating expense.

TWA's assets also included its computer reservation system (PARS). Icahn sold a 50 percent interest in the CRS to Northwest Airlines for $140 million, thus raising even more cash. Icahn denied that his management style included "dismemberment," but it did bear some resemblance to what Lorenzo was doing to Eastern Air Lines at the same time.

In fairness to Icahn, the steps he took to streamline TWA's operations, including converting hard assets to cash, laying off nonunion workers, and fighting union wage and rules demands began to show up at the bottom line. From a stock price of around $14 per share when he took over, TWA stock was trading at $34 two years later.

This was when he decided to take the company private by merging TWA into a newly formed private company, where he would own 90 percent of the stock (he held 73 percent in the public company), and which would free him from many regulatory requirements and much government oversight necessary in a public corporation. The company's cash would go to partially pay for shares not controlled by Icahn. The 10 percent of stock not owned by Icahn would be owned by the employees. Since this deal was a leveraged buyout, Icahn was able to recover $469 million personally. TWA assumed over $539 million in debt.

This heavy debt load gave TWA a negative net worth, and it required a lot of money to pay interest on the debt. Profitability was short lived as its domestic and foreign market shares fell to new lows. TWA had failed to appreciate the necessity of the hub concept after deregulation and it did not develop adequate feeder lines to supply its long-range routes, resulting in lower passenger counts.

TWA's fortunes did not improve over the following years, as competition increased with new entrant airlines amid rising fuel prices. The first Iraq war in 1990 coupled with an economic downturn that resulted in reduced travel demand. Airline losses as a group in 1990 were $1.9 billion, in 1991 $1.8 billion, and in 1992 they were $2.4 billion. Icahn continued the dismemberment of the airline by selling TWA's most valuable routes. In 1991, he sold the prized Heathrow London routes to New York, Los Angeles, Boston, and Chicago to American Airlines for $445 million.

On January 31, 1992, TWA entered into Chapter 11 reorganization. As debtor in possession, Icahn still had control over TWA's assets, and he sold its London routes to Philadelphia and Baltimore to USAir for $50 million. All that was left of the proud world-wide network of TWA was the London–St. Louis route.

During reorganization, Icahn agreed to step down and sell his shares to the employees and the creditors. The deal was solidified with TWA's three primary unions taking a 45 percent equity stake in the company in return for concessions. TWA's creditors would forgive some $1 billion in debt in return for 55 percent of company stock. Icahn would loan the airline $200 million for operating cash, secured by TWA's remaining assets, until the company emerged from bankruptcy. Everyone, it seemed, was tired of Icahn, and Icahn was tired of the airline business.

TWA came out of bankruptcy in November 1993 and a succession of senior executives went through the head office until Jeffrey Erickson, from Reno Air, took over as CEO. Over the next two years, management and the labor groups, the latter of which owned 45 percent of the company, together made extraordinary efforts to see TWA succeed, but it was not enough as share prices continued down, reflecting the lack of profit. TWA entered Chapter 11 for the second time in 1995 under a prearranged deal with its creditors to shed some $500 million in debt, so the company was able to reemerge quickly from reorganization in August 1995.

In 1996 things looked up for TWA, with plans to purchase new aircraft and to make new hires of around 10 percent. But on July 17, 1996, flight 800, a Boeing 747 bound from JFK to Paris, exploded over Long Island killing all 230 people on board. Theories abounded as to the cause of the explosion of flight 800, including a rocket attack by terrorists, conspiracy theories of various kinds, as well as a fuel tank detonation. The cause was ultimately determined by the NTSB to be due to a short-circuit spark in the center wing fuel tank, but that did not really matter to the profit and loss question that controlled the fate of TWA. At the end of 1996, all TWA had to show for its efforts was a $259 million loss. Erickson resigned and was replaced by Gerald L. Gitner, who ironically had previously been with Lorenzo at Texas Air.

The late 1990s were good times for United States airlines, yet TWA was unable to post a profit for 1997, the only airline, in fact, that lost money for the year. It lost money the next year too, the 10th straight year in the red. The board of directors appointed one of their own pilots, William Compton, as president in 1998 to bring a hands-on approach to operations, with Gitner remaining as chairman of the board.

Compton ventured out on an airplane buying spree, concentrating on smaller aircraft like the Boeing 717-200s, to replace TWA's large aircraft and aging fleet. He ordered 125 planes and took options on 125 more. Still, TWA had not turned a profit since 1988. TWA lost $353 million in 1999 and over $115 million during the first nine months of 2000.

TWA finally threw in the towel and reached an agreement with AMR Corporation, American Airlines parent company, to acquire the airline. TWA entered Chapter 11 for the third time in 2001 in order to be able to finalize the AMR takeover. The Justice Department approved the acquisition and the proud and historic Trans

World Airline, the "Lindbergh Line," became just TWA Airlines, LLC. AMR Corporation now controlled 22.6 percent of the entire airline market, another unintended consequence of deregulation.

In September 2001, operations of TWA were consolidated with those of American Airlines, 138,000 TWA employees were let go, and the TWA terminal at JFK was closed. The brand TWA ceased to exist.

Endnotes

1. A corporate raider has been defined as an investor who buys large amounts of stock in corporations whose assets appear to be undervalued for the purpose of effecting a hostile takeover of the company or merely running up the value of the stock for subsequent sale and profit, called "greenmail."

2. *Barthelemy et al. v. Air Line Pilots Association*, 897 F.2d 999 (9 Cir 1990). Not all union members agreed. Suit was brought against Alpa by its own members to set aside the Alpa—Icahn agreement that cut wages and allowed Icahn to gain control of TWA—the members lost.

28 Pan American and Deregulation

Among the trunk carriers of the United States, Pan American had enjoyed a monopoly on America's international traffic from 1927 until after World War II, with two exceptions. First, American Airlines was awarded a route between Dallas and Mexico City in 1942. Next, and the only other exception, was a small startup called American Export Airlines, originally a subsidiary of one of the largest shipping companies in the country, American Export Lines. Pan American successfully challenged the shipping line's ownership in court, and forced a divestiture of the airline operation. The airline became American Overseas Airlines and struggled along during the war flying mail and cargo mostly between New York and Ireland, using Vought-Sikorsky flying boats. After the war, Pan American's fortunes began a gradual decline in direct proportion to its loss of its monopoly. On July 5, 1945, the CAB approved the acquisition of American Export Lines by American Airlines, and granted routes across the North Atlantic to the United Kingdom and other European countries. Pan American had proposed to the government a continuation of the prewar relationship that granted Pan Am "Chosen Instrument" status. But Congress rejected the idea of a continuing monopoly. Times had changed since prewar days. The

United States had nothing to fear from foreign power competition, nor any need for a "Chosen Instrument" to represent the country in aviation internationally. In fact, the government decided that the more United States airlines spreading out over the world the better.

TWA was granted access across the Atlantic, Northwest Airlines began operations over the north Pacific, Braniff went into South America. But these airlines had domestic routes too. Pan Am had none. Everyone wanted to fly Pan Am's routes; almost 20 domestic airlines had applied for its Pacific routes alone. The applicants included passenger, cargo, scheduled, and charter airlines. Through the administrations of Truman, Eisenhower, and Kennedy (1944–1963), the previous monopoly enjoyed by Pan Am disappeared, but Pan Am was still in a competitive position. During the Johnson Administration (1963–1968), however, everything went up for grabs. The chairmanship of the CAB, the body that would make the route awards, was a recent Johnson appointee friendly to Texas-based American Airlines and to Braniff. Juan Trippe retired in 1968, but earlier in the 1960s he had hired the second administrator of the Federal Aviation Agency (created by the Federal Aviation Act of 1958), Najeeb Halaby, who succeeded him as

CEO. Since Pan American was exclusively an international carrier with no domestic service, it had no boosters in the Congress, unlike the major domestic carriers. Delta in Georgia, Eastern in Florida, and Northwest in Minnesota, for example, had their loyal delegations to lobby for them.

Pan American had pioneered all of the international routes and had represented the United States as the "Chosen Instrument" of American influence. Pan Am had served America's interests during the war and had even been largely responsible for the development and original use of the 707 and DC-8 jet fleet. But now it seemed like it was all politics. Routes to Hawaii went to Continental, Braniff, American, and Northwest. TWA got round-the-world rights and even Flying Tiger got the Pacific cargo routes. Although incoming President Nixon (1969) reviewed and amended some of the awards, the result was the same to Pan Am. And still, Pan Am could not get a domestic route from the CAB.

Merger talks were carried on between Pan Am and several carriers, including Braniff and American. But it was with TWA that the deal was struck to combine operations. Not only would the joining of the two international carriers render savings of $200 million a year, but merging the TWA-owned Hilton International hotel chain with Pan American's Intercontinental Hotel assets would mean that the new airline would own the most elite hotel system in the world.

The Antitrust Division of the Justice Department would have to approve the combination of TWA and Pan Am as posing no undue competitive threat to international commercial aviation. In spite of the plethora of carriers now plying the international routes since the end of the war, approval was not forthcoming. So Pan Am struggled on, knowing that it had to have domestic routes to survive. With losses mounting and market share dwindling, Pan Am's board of directors appointed a new president, a former Air Force general by the name of William T. Seawell. A

West Point graduate, a B-17 Group commander during World War II, as well as a Harvard law graduate, Seawell had been a senior vice-president at American Airlines and president of Rolls-Royce Aero, Inc. Seawell came on board in 1971 as Pan Am was losing another $45 million, and by 1972, as Pan Am concluded a three-year losing period of $120 million, Seawell was made CEO and Halaby was out.

Seawell had not only been a general in the Air Force, he had been a general in the Strategic Air Command (SAC), with its iron-fisted rule by General Curtis E. Lemay. Many SAC pilots found the assignment to be sort of a purgatory. Pan Am's pilots wondered what the strict organizational procedures of SAC might mean to Pan American.

Seawell set about cutting and paring staff, offices, and expenses. The number of employees was cut to 27,000 from 42,000. Levels of management, like staff vice-president, were eliminated altogether. Service was curtailed and bases were closed. These measures were dictated not only by the bloat that Pan Am had acquired, but also by the first OPEC-generated fuel crisis that occurred in the early 1970s. Pan Am's fuel bill doubled. Although Pan Am was still *persona non grata* at the CAB and at the White House, the CAB did, in 1975, grant both TWA and Pan American some relief in approving some route swaps, thus lessening the competition between them. Still, Pan Am had no domestic routes.

Pan American lost $364 million in the early years of the 1970s. But by 1976, under the direction of Seawell, Pan Am started making a comeback. In 1976 it realized a net profit of $100 million. In 1977 it made $45 million, and in 1978 it was over $120 million. Still, all was not well. As shabbily as Pan Am felt it had been treated by the postwar administrations, particularly the Johnson and Nixon administrations, it was not prepared for the largesse bestowed on Pan Am's competitors by the Carter White House. There were more international routes for almost everyone: Delta to London, Braniff to London, and National to Paris and Amsterdam. Northwest was assigned Copenhagen and Stockholm. Pan American, incredibly, was losing even more market share.

With the passage of deregulation in 1978, Pan Am no longer needed the long-sought-after approval of the CAB. Under deregulation, Pan Am could fly wherever and whenever it wanted and charge any fare it pleased. The only problem was, so could everybody else. Pan Am did not have time to build a domestic route structure under these circumstances; it would have to find an airline to merge with or to buy.

The circumstances of the attempt by Frank Lorenzo to take over National Airlines in 1978 have already been considered above. We know that Lorenzo was not successful in that effort and that he lost out to Pan American after Pan Am trumped his best stock offer. Now we need to look at the results of the National takeover by Pan American.

National Airlines in 1978 was a tempting takeover target: undervalued stock price, low debt, and high assets. National was the first all-jet U.S. carrier. It had been flying the Atlantic since 1970 between Miami and London, and after that it went into Amsterdam, Paris, and Frankfurt. National, headquartered in Miami like Eastern, was also very similar to Eastern in its labor experience. Almost every contract renewal ended up in a strike. No trust existed between labor and management. The culture at National was much different from that at Pan American. National, in spite of its international routes, was really a southern airline dedicated to small destinations, while Pan American was the international sophisticate. The attitudes of its pilots said it all. From the early days of the Clippers, there had been a certain swagger to the Pan American pilots: their uniforms were patterned after the maritime officers of the deck, like the Queen Mary. They wore white hats. They were chosen, and superior, just like their airline. What's more,

National's pilot roster was considerably younger than was Pan Am's.

It was an accepted fact that Pan American, in its zeal to get domestic routes, was caused to grossly overpay for National. All told, it cost Pan Am $374 million to acquire National, and the financial drain was just beginning. All 8,350 National employees were now working for Pan Am. Seawell had to raise National's pilots' wages to match those of Pan Am's pilots, and he had to increase their benefits packages to match those at Pan Am. The cost of acquisition was over half a billion dollars, and the year of acquisition was not even over.

The fleets of the two companies did not jibe. Although both carriers had 727s, the wide bodies were different: National had DC-10s and Pan Am had L-1011s. Each type of aircraft had a different power plant, whether Pratt & Whitney, Rolls Royce, or General Electric, and each had to be maintained and serviced by a mechanic specially trained and qualified on that engine. Each type of engine and each type of aircraft had to have parts and spares available and storage space to put them.

Prior to the acquisition of National, Pan Am appeared to be on the road back to profitability, and it was, in fact, sitting on significant cash. But that was the only good news; all the rest of the news was bad.

Matters were getting worse as the work forces of each company regarded each other warily. Pilot seniority has always been a fact of life in the airline industry. It is the measure by which a pilot knows what he is: a captain, a first officer, a journeyman, hired out, unemployed, furloughed, riding high, or down and out. It was, therefore, central to the pilots' interest in the merger to have their position in the seniority roster protected. A new seniority list was being prepared, one that would have to merge the two companies' seniority rosters into one new roster. The numbers, that's what the pilots called it, defined the pilots' past, present, and future.

Most of the Pan Am pilots were senior to the National pilots, so that if the respective rosters were to be merged on a chronological date basis, most of the National pilots would be at the bottom of the combined new roster. Captains would be first officers or even out of a job. A merger of the two rosters on the basis of relative position between the two, on the other hand, would mean that a National pilot with a seniority number of 100th from the top on the National roster might very well be many years junior to a pilot ranked 100th on the Pan Am roster, the effect being that a Pan Am pilot hired in 1965 might find himself serving under a National pilot hired in 1975. Each group of pilots was adamant about its view of the roster.

The issue was finally referred to binding arbitration. A complicated formula was decreed in March 1981 and the new Pan Am seniority list was posted. The result was not pleasing to either side, but it had to be accepted. On the National side, at least, the National 727 pilots retained their captains' positions. The rest had to sort out their numbers, most with a sense of disbelief.

When the two companies were combined, Pan Am had its domestic routes so long denied. But in 1980 it was losing a million dollars a day. The assets of Pan American included its landmark building astride Park Avenue in midtown Manhattan, with the Pan Am name emblazoned in 12-foot-high letters for all to admire. Other assets included its hotel system and its coveted routes to almost every corner of the world. The options were considered by management, by the Seawell team, and it was obvious that some assets had to be converted to cash to satisfy the insatiable demands of the creditors. The Pan Am building was sold to Metropolitan Life Insurance Company for $400 million, but insolvency still loomed. Next came the Intercontinental Hotel chain, sold for $500 million. Deliveries of new airplanes were deferred, and unfilled orders were cancelled. General Seawell, no longer regarded as the savior of Pan American by the stockholders, retired early, in 1981.

Ed Acker took over Pan Am in 1981. Acker had been president of Braniff International in the 1970s and was acknowledged to have done a good job, leaving the company in good shape and with a better future before it. At length he wound up at Air Florida, a startup intrastate airline with revenues of less than $10 million a year as of 1977. In just three years, by 1980, Air Florida under his direction netted over $160 million.

Acker perceived his main job, like most of the new CEOs after deregulation, to secure givebacks from the union rank and file. After all, that was about the only place to look for relief. Everyone knew that the unions had had it too good during the old CAB days, and now it was time to get real. Typical of the time, wage and working condition concessions were agreed to by the unions, which represented 24,000 of the company's 33,000 employees, in return for a stock position in the company and, for the first time in the industry, a seat on the board of directors.

Yet, after Acker's first year as CEO, Pan Am lost $485 million. And the losses continued. The expected labor "snap backs," the increased pay to make up for the concessions given earlier by the unions, could not be made as scheduled because of the ongoing monthly losses. Negotiations did not produce any movement, and on February 28, 1985, the unions went out on strike. This was a new and unpleasant development for the old Pan Am pilots, who had always considered themselves as professionals, in service to their passengers and in league and in parity with the company.

Pan Am fired all the strikers, as was the custom, but in short order the sides came together, each claiming victory, and the strike was over. Everybody went back to work. But a strike is a serious financial blow to an airline, even a healthy one, and can be devastating to a crippled one like Pan Am in 1985.

In an ironic turn of events, the international routes were breaking even, but the long-sought domestic routes of the former National Airlines were losing $250 million a year. Acker looked around for something else to sell; he came up with the Pacific routes so laboriously and bravely secured almost a half-century earlier. These were the routes of the Clippers: Hawaii and on to the romantic Orient, Singapore, Hong Kong, and Bora Bora. United wanted the Pacific routes, and shortly a deal was announced that United would buy the routes for $750 million. In the "first of a kind" deal, United agreed to take the sixteen 747 SPs (see Figure 28-1) (the outdated short-range model), the six L-1011s, and a DC-10 that serviced the routes, as well as the personnel at Pan American who were dedicated to those routes. All told, the personnel transfer to United was about 2,700 employees, including managers, 1,200 flight attendants, and 410 pilots. These cost savings, and the influx of three-quarters of a billion dollars, allowed the airline to continue its existence, at least for the time being.

By 1988, the United money was gone and Pan Am was still losing money. Terrorism had taken its toll on Pan Am: a takeover of a 747 in Karachi had ended badly in a highly publicized shootout. In 1988, Acker was out as CEO, and Tom Plaskett, fired by Lorenzo from Continental, was in. More wage and work rules concessions for the unions were negotiated. Later, in 1988, Plaskett announced that Pan Am would have an operating profit for the first time in years. It was a great day. And then came December 21, 1988, the day Pan American would be ever identified with the small village of Lockerbie, Scotland. On the evening of that day the Clipper *Maid of the Seas* disintegrated at altitude, spreading itself, its passengers and crew, and all of their baggage over the Scottish countryside.

For days afterward, the forward section of the 747, painted in the white with blue trim colors of Pan American, was displayed on the evening news to the entire world as it lay on its side in an open field, a metaphor for the formerly

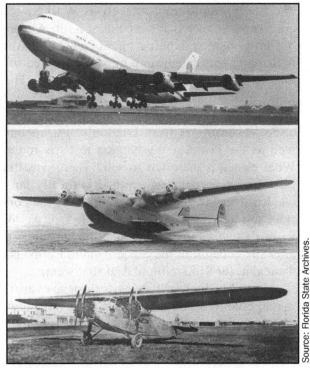

Source: Florida State Archives.

FIGURE 28-1 Boeing 747 (top), Boeing 314 (middle), Fokker F-7 (bottom).

great Pan American World Airways. Investigation revealed that the flight was brought down by a terrorist bomb, but it did not seem to matter. Passengers did not fly Pan American in 1989, and Pan Am was losing $2 million a day.

In 1990, traffic picked up as the summer vacation crowd to Europe seemed to be coming back. Then, in August, Saddam Hussein invaded Kuwait. Passenger counts went down, and fuel prices went up. Plaskett could see the end coming. He had to sell something else. This was not like selling your blood; this was like selling your body parts. United wanted the crown jewels, the London routes. Pan American had been the first to fly to London from the States, in the Boeing 314 flying boat, over a half-century earlier. Now 50 years of Pan American tradition in the Atlantic service was suddenly bestowed on United, and another Pan Am era was to be closed out for mere filthy lucre, some $400 million.

Many employees, as well as Wall Street observers, wondered at the point of it all. A morbid humorism was being circulated: "Pan Am is like a coyote caught in a trap. It's chewed off three of its legs and it's still in the trap."[1] The London deal included service from New York, Washington, Los Angeles, Seattle, and San Francisco, seven routes from London to Europe, as well as the Pan Am Washington to Paris route. What else was there left to sell? There was the Berlin service that Pan Am had faithfully husbanded over the years of the Cold War, the corridor through the Iron Curtain to the free world. Even though Germany was just being reunified after the collapse of the Soviet Union, Lufthansa wanted it, for $150 million. And so it went.

Pan Am was in its death throes, even if management would not admit it. It was now getting quite unseemly, with Airbus Industries taking back 20 Airbuses, and with Pan Am stock selling for 75 cents instead of $75. Pan American did not have enough money to pay its creditors. In January 1991, Pan Am went into Chapter 11. But even with the protection that Chapter 11 gave the airline from having to keep its creditors current, it was losing up to $3 million a day. The vultures gathered around, seeking to know whether the remains of the airline might be picked up cheap, or merged. The creditors' committee was interested, after all, since that was likely the only way unsecured creditors were going to get anything at all.

The biggest surprise was the interest of Delta Airlines, probably the most conservative airline of all, which in the summer of 1991 offered $310 million for Pan American World Airways. Finally, following hurried and intense negotiating sessions, a deal was closed between the creditors' committee and Delta. Delta would pay $416 million in cash and assume $389 million in pre-existing liabilities, making an immediate cash infusion of $80 million to prevent immediate shutdown. Pan American was to be salvaged as a corporation, 45 percent of its stock would be owned by Delta and creditors would hold the remaining 55 percent. Pan Am II, the new name of the restructured company that was to continue operation mainly down in the Caribbean, was set to emerge from Chapter 11 in December.

Pan Am ran through the $80 million deposited by Delta, and then another $35 million deposited by Delta. It seemed that Pan Am had no way to stop the bleeding, not even long enough

Source: Florida State Archives.

FIGURE 28-2 Pan American Field at Miami before the sale by Pan American to the city of Miami.

to be saved. Nobody apparently wanted to fly Pan American under bankruptcy circumstances. On December 3, 1991, Delta's lawyers advised the bankruptcy court that the deal was off. Delta would infuse no more money into Pan Am.

The Clipper *Goodwill*, a Boeing 727, was the last Pan American airplane in the air after the company shut down. Pan Am operations directed the Clipper to Miami, to the airport that was first known as Pan American Field because Pan American had built it; to the airport that Pan Am had sold to the city of Miami in 1930 even when the city could not afford to finance the purchase—Pan Am had graciously bought the city's bonds. Pan American operations at Miami requested a last fly-by over the airport and the control tower approved. Down runway 12 to the southeast it flew, out over the first Pan Am hangars and the old marine terminal at Dinner Key in Biscayne Bay, where the clippers used to load up for South America. Reluctantly, it seemed,

© Courtesy of panamair.org.

FIGURE 28-3   Pan American Dinner Key Terminal.

the Clipper *Goodwill* turned back to the airport; it came around, landed, and slowly taxied to the gate under saluting streams of water from airport fire trucks, sadly marking the end of an era.

Endnote

1. Gandt, Robert, *Skygods*, p. 289.

29 Airline Labor Relations

It would be easy to excuse a person's confusion today when told that airline labor matters are governed by the Railway Labor Act (RLA).[1] But in 1936, when the RLA was made applicable to the neophyte airline industry, the differences between the two transportation systems were not at all clear. Both systems carried passenger and freight traffic in interstate commerce, across state lines, and from coast to coast. Both were considered quasi-public utilities obligated to conduct their operations in a manner consistent with the "public interest." And both were capable of causing severe disruption to the nation's commerce by labor-management disagreements and work stoppages.

We have already considered the temper of the times. The United States was deep into the Great Depression, distrust of the corporate world and capitalism was in vogue, unemployment was widespread, labor protective legislation was being cranked out of Congress, and membership in unions was high and on the rise. The airline industry seemed poised to take over from the railroads, which were on the wane, and it was assumed that the confrontational model of labor relations fashioned out of the experience of the railroads would serve the interests of labor and the nation in aviation as well.

But experience has shown that the airlines were not very much like the railroads after all; they were, in fact, very different. Aside from the fact that railroad labor relations arose out of the violent confrontations of the late 19th century, airlines were much more technologically oriented, the product of inventions and developments that had largely first come into being after the labor pattern of the railroads had already been established.

The job classifications (the "crafts" in the words of the RLA) were very different. The railroads had their train crews composed of engineers, firemen, brakemen, and conductors, which ranged from semi-skilled to laboring work, and owing to coal used for fuel, they were mostly soot-covered jobs. Job names like hostlers, boilermakers, car repair workers, maintenance of way laborers (gandy dancers), and blacksmiths filled the railroad roster. The airlines' occupational groups were pilots, powerplant mechanics, and clerical employees. Only baggage handlers, ground crew, and cleaners came close to matching the personnel types common on the railroads. The knowledge and skill requirements of the pilots and mechanics were federally mandated and tested. As time went on, many pilots came from the ranks of the college educated, and because of the federal limitations on hours flown, many of those would have second careers, some even professional careers based on advanced university degrees.

Railroad style unionism was promoted by the policies of the National Mediation Board (NMB), the federal body established under the RLA to mediate the relative positions of the two sides, which assumes a power-based equality of collective bargaining and promotes a "digging in" of the heels, rather than a cooperative effort based on a "mutuality of interests" approach. This has produced a history of labor strife marked by work stoppages and severe disruptions in the national transportation system over much of the life of the airline industry. Contributing to the encouragement of militant union activity has been a competition between the different unions' leadership to produce the best "package" in the industry, to set the standard for union gains. Resistance from management to such union activity was, during regulation, lessened due to the practice of the CAB of increasing rates and fares to cover the increase in employee wages and benefits. Management also appeared to be willing to trade off increased income from productivity gains due to technological advances, such as increased efficiencies

associated with jet aircraft, to achieve peace with the labor unions.

Major Airline Unions

The major certified bargaining units (unions) in the airline industry are:

- The Air Line Pilots Association (ALPA), representing the majority of pilots
- The Allied Pilots Association (representing American Airlines pilots since 1960)
- The Southwest Airlines Pilots Association (Southwest pilots)
- Frontier Pilots Association (Frontier pilots)
- The International Association of Machinists and Aerospace Workers (IAM)
- The Association of Professional Flight Attendants (APFA)
- The Association of Flight Attendants (AFA)
- The Transport Workers Union (TWU), representing a range of employees from maintenance employees to flight attendants and dispatchers
- The Brotherhood of Railway, Airline, and Steamship Clerks (BRAC), representing mostly clerical and passenger service employees
- The Aircraft Mechanics Fraternal Association

Airline	Pilots	Flight attendants	Mechanics and related	Dispatchers	Fleet service/ramp
Alaska	ALPA	AFA	AMFA	TWU	IAM
America West	ALPA	AFA	IBT	TWU	TWU
American	APA	APFA	TWU	TWU	TWU
Continental	ALPA	IAM	IBT	TWU	(none)
Delta	ALPA	(none)	(none)	PAFCA	(none)
Northwest	ALPA	IBT	AMFA	TWU	IAM
Southwest	SWAPA	TWU	AMFA	SAEA	TWU
United	ALPA	AFA	IAM	PAFCA	IAM
US Airways	ALPA	AFA	IAM	TWU	IAM

TABLE 29-1 Unions representing selected crafts or classes at major passenger airlines as of February 1, 2003.

- The Communications Workers of America
- The International Brotherhood of Teamsters
- The Professional Airline Flight Control Association

Most of the crafts of the largest 19 airlines in the country, accounting for 95 percent of industry revenues, were unionized in 1977. Only Delta, which had a nonunion work force with the exception of its pilots (who are represented by ALPA), and Southern Airways deviated from the norm. As of 2012, Airlines for America stated that about half of all airline workers belong to professional unions and are governed by collective bargaining agreements.

■ Strife and Presidential Interventions

From the time that the RLA was applied to the airline industry in 1936, there were no strikes until 1946, when the first Presidential Emergency Board (PEB) was established in a dispute between TWA and its pilots. Six more PEBs followed during the late 1940s, and then 19 occurred during

	Carrier	Union	Craft	Duration of negotiations	Dates of strike	Duration of strike
1	Alaska	IAM	Mechanics	2/17/84–6/3/85	3/4/85–5/4/85	2
2	American	APA	Pilots	6/30/94–5/5/97	2/15/97	24
3	American	APFA	Flight attendants	11/18/92–10/10/95	11/18/93–11/22/93	5 days
4	American	TWU	Flight instructors	Not available	11/4/79	1 day
5	Comair	ALPA	Pilots	Not available	3/26/01–6/22/01	88 days
6	Continental	ALPA	Pilots	Not available	10/1/83–10/31/85	2 years
7	Continental	IAM	Mechanics	1981–1985	8/13/83–4/16/85	1 1/2
8	Continental	IBT	Flight engineers	Not Available	9/23/79–10/6/79	13 days
9	Continental	UFA	Flight attendants	Not available	12/5/80–12/21/80	16 days
10	Continental	UFA	Flight attendants	Not available	10/1/83–4/17/85	1 1/2
11	Continental	IAM	Flight attendants	1985–1989	3/15/89–12/15/89	9
12	Northwest	ALPA	Pilots	8/27/96–9/12/98	8/29/98–9/12/98	15 days
13	Northwest	AMFA	Mechanics	Not available	8/20/05–10/9/05	416 days
14	Northwest	IAM	Mechanics Flight kitchen	9/29/81–6/16/82	5/22/82–6/25/82	1 month
15	Southwest	IAM	Mechanics	Not available	1/13/80–2/1/80	19 days
16	Spirit	ALPA	Pilots	Not available	6/12/10–6/16/10	5 days
17	United	ALPA	Pilots	1/30/84–6/17/85	5/17/85–6/14/85	29 days
18	United	IAM	Mechanics Ramp and stores Food services Dispatchers Security officers	10/1/78–5/24/79	3/31/79–5/27/79	2
19	USAir	IAM	Mechanics	2/14/90–10/13/92	10/5/92–10/8/92	3 days

TABLE 29-2 Airline strikes that have occurred since deregulation through 2005.
Sources: NMB and, airlines.

	Carrier	Union	Craft	Amendable date	Presidential intervention date	Actions taken
1	American	APA	Pilots	8/31/94	2/15/97	Presidential Emergency Board
2	American	APFA	Flight attendants	11/1/98	2001	Presidential Emergency Board warning
3	American	APFA	Flight attendants	12/31/92	1993	Presidential recommends binding interest arbitration
4	Northwest	ALPA	Pilots	11/2/96	September 1998	Presidential Emergency Board warning
5	Northwest	AMFA	Mechanics	9/30/96	3/12/01	Presidential Emergency Board
6	United	IAM	Mechanics	7/12/00	1/19/02	Presidential Emergency Board

TABLE 29-3 *Number of presidential interventions since deregulation.*

the 1950s—11 during 1957 alone. These 1957 strikes involved Eastern, National, Capital, Northeast, Northwest, United, TWA, and American. Most of these involved the mechanics, although two were pilot initiated. Through 1978, domestic airlines had experienced a total of 191 strikes.

The number of strikes decreased significantly after deregulation. Only 19 strikes of domestic passenger airlines have been called since 1978, 12 of them before 1990. The duration of these strikes ranged from 2 years to 24 minutes. See Table 29-2 for a summary of strike incidences, presidential interventions, and nonstrike work actions between 1978 and 2002.

Presidential interventions may include the convening of a Presidential Emergency Board (PEB), or they may be limited to pressuring or "jawboning" with the parties. The president has also intervened in labor-management disputes to recommend binding arbitration. PEBs are normally not instituted except in circumstances where significant interstate commerce disruption is expected to result. See Table 29-3.

Work actions, which is the term for union organized slowdowns, sickouts, or other nonstrike activity, have increased since deregulation. Many of these disruptions go unheralded, but there have been 10 instances of such activity that have been recognized by various courts as being in violation of the RLA. Some of these nonstrike work actions

are presented by labor in a context of safety concerns. One tactic used by Alaska flight attendants was a technique called "CHAOS" (Creating Havoc Around Our System) that involved intermittent but unpredictable walkouts. These tactics do not shut down the airline but attempt to make their point by harassment. See Table 29-4.

■ The Mutual Aid Pact

In 1958, the airlines entered into the Mutual Aid Agreement (MAA), also called the Mutual Aid Pact (MAP), which amounted to a self-insured strike fund. This airline cooperative agreement was to be in place for the next 20 years, until deregulation. Under this arrangement, the largest nine trunk carriers in the United States contributed to a fund from which amounts were paid to struck airlines to defray losses directly attributable to strike action. During the initial stage of MAP, the period 1958 to 1962, struck carriers received only "windfall benefits"—relatively small amounts equal to nonstruck carriers' increased revenues realized due to the strikes. In the second stage of MAP, from 1962 to 1969, the plan assured that a struck carrier would recover at least an amount equal to 25 percent of the struck carrier's normal operating expenses. In the third stage, between 1969 and 1978, the fund paid a struck carrier between 35 and 50 percent

	Carrier	Union	Craft	Work action	Plaintiff request	Date of court decision
1	American	APA	Pilots	Sickout	TRO* sought	2/10/1999
2	American	TWU	Mechanics	Slowdown	TRO sought	2001
3	American	TWU	Mechanics	Slowdown	TRO sought	1998
4	American	TWU	Mechanics	Slowdown	Injunction sought	1999
5	Delta	ALPA	Pilots	Refuse overtime	Injunction sought	2001
6	Northwest	AMFA	Mechanics	Refuse overtime	Injunction sought	5/11/2001
7	Northwest	IAM	Clerical Flight kitchen stock	Slowdown	Injunction sought	2/25/1999
8	Northwest	IBT	Flight attendants	Sickout	Injunction sought	1/5/2000
9	TWA	IAM	Mechanics	Sickout and work stoppage	TRO sought	1998
10	United	IAM	Mechanics	Slowdown	Injunction sought	7/1/2002
11	US Airways	ALPA	Pilots	Slowdown	Injunction sought	January 2012

TABLE 29-4 Court-recognized, nonstrike work actions since deregulation through 2012.
Sources: NMB, airlines, and courts.
*A "TRO" is a temporary restraining order, which requires the union to cease the offending activity.

of such expenses. At the beginning of the third stage, in 1970, local service carriers (feeder airlines) came into the program, along with the trunk carrier Western Airlines.

The major beneficiary of the strike insurance was Northwest, which received over $187 million, followed by National ($120.1 million), and TWA ($37.1 million). The three major contributors to the fund were United, American, and Eastern, none of which had actually benefited from the fund.

The unions fought the MAP from its inception in 1958, first before the CAB, which had to approve the plan, next by lobbying Congress, then by litigation brought in the courts, and finally in the collective bargaining arena. The unions lost on all fronts, and the MAP remained in force until the Airline Deregulation Act (ADA) passed Congress in 1978. The ADA provided that the MAP as approved by the CAB would terminate, and that any subsequent plan entered into by the airlines would be constrained by very specific rules

and requirements. Thus far, the provisions of the ADA have effectively terminated the strike insurance fund of the airlines.

It should be noted that the MAP was used to great advantage by Texas International beginning with Frank Lorenzo's takeover of that airline and during his battles with that airline's unions in the early 1970s. During the period 1970 to 1974, Texas International received over $11 million from the fund, while paying in only $732,000. Rumblings of discontent over Lorenzo's activities were heard even from the other airlines.

■ Airline Labor Relations after Deregulation

The Airline Deregulation Act initiated two primary changes in the *status quo ante* in the airline industry that were to have profound effects in labor relations. First, the practical effects of competition from new entrant, nonunion carriers were largely beyond the negotiating parameters practiced by the incumbent carriers and their unions; that is, concessions in wages and rules to match the start-ups would have been rejected out of hand by the unions as being too severe. This provided the start-ups with the advantage of being able to provide essentially the same service as the major airlines at greatly reduced rates and fares, and still make a profit. Second, the effects of economic pressures from outside the airline industry, such as recession, fuel prices, and interest rates, could no longer be assuaged or compensated for by the CAB. The airlines and their unions, in other words, were going to have to learn to deal with each other in the real world where profit margins, or the lack thereof, were going to drive the relationship.

The overall economic climate that prevailed after the passage of ADA was first seen as a limited decline that turned into a recession by 1980, followed by a deeper sustained recession into the early years of the 1980s. Interest rates soared to 20 percent and inflation went into double digits. The OPEC fuel embargo caused fuel prices to rise from $.40 in 1978 to $1.15 in 1980. The airlines' bottom line was hit hard. There was no safety net to prevent bankruptcy, as Braniff faltered and then fell. Management practices, at Braniff for instance, which completely misapprehended the effects of deregulation, compounded the problem. Between 1979 and 1984, the airlines as an industry lost $4 billion. Other airlines followed Braniff into insolvency, including Air Florida, Air New England, and Laker.

Between 1979 and the end of 1984, 47 airlines filed under the Bankruptcy Act.

The takeover tactics of Lorenzo, and the creation of subsidiary airlines of incumbent carriers, like New York Air as a nonunion carrier owned by unionized Texas International, constituted wake-up calls to union leadership. Incursions by startups caused a general reassessment by both management of incumbent carriers and their unions. The apparent willingness, even eagerness, of pilots to work for these new carriers

without the benefits of union representation was proven by the large number of applicants for the relatively few available positions.

As we saw in Chapter 24, deregulation also created apparent inconsistencies in the application of the Railway Labor Act, with UPS being subject to the National Labor Relations Act and FedEx being governed by the Railway Labor Act, even though they now perform the same functions.

ALPA and the Crew Size Issue

When technological advances in the railroad industry introduced the diesel locomotive to render obsolete the steam locomotive, and with it the firemen who had been necessary to stoke the steam locomotive's fireboxes, the unions successfully fought the railroads' attempts to eliminate the firemen's position. The firemen thenceforth sat in the engine with little or nothing to do and were paid their regular wage. The name given to this development was "feather-bedding," and it effectively reduced the productivity gains that diesel technology had produced.

When the DC-9 and the Boeing 737 were introduced into the airline fleet in the 1960s, the FAA certified these new types for operation with two-pilot crews. ALPA adopted a hard stance against the FAA certification on the 737, and refused to fly the aircraft with a two-pilot crew. United was originally the largest purchaser of the 737, and to avoid a pilot strike during the regulated 1960s, United agreed to binding arbitration to resolve the issue notwithstanding the FAA certification. In spite of the FAA certification and the proven experience of other airlines, like Lufthansa and Piedmont, that were flying the 737 with two-pilot crews with spotless safety records, the arbitration panel surprisingly ruled that safety concerns mandated that the United 737s be operated with three-pilot crews.

ALPA's stance was now further hardened and extended to the upcoming new Boeing types, the 757 and 767. At ALPA's National Convention in 1980, the delegates voted for a nationwide strike by March 1, 1981, if the crew-size issue on the new aircraft types was not resolved in favor of a three-pilot crew by that date. Such a strike would be a blatant violation of the provisions of the RLA, as ALPA well knew, and as the strike date approached, ALPA pressed for the appointment of a Presidential Task Force to review the FAA's prior certifications. In July 1981, the Task Force reported its findings that safety concerns did not justify the use of three-pilot crews on the new types of aircraft under consideration.

Prior to the publication of the Task Force report, United had concluded that its short-haul routes serviced by the three-man crewed 737 would have to be discontinued or severely cut back as too costly, with significant pilot furloughs. Although United had reported a profit in 1978 of $296 million, the subsequent years of 1979 and 1980 resulted in losses of $235 million and $65 million, respectively. In a first-of-its-kind turnabout, ALPA under these circumstances reversed its position on the crew size issue and announced that it would accede to the findings of the Task Force. Reminiscent of the days of old, however, ALPA did extract a concession from United, namely, that the airline would agree never to form a startup, nonunion subsidiary like New York Air.

The PATCO Strike

The Professional Air Traffic Controllers Organization (PATCO) walked off their jobs on August 3, 1981, in violation of the Civil Service Reform Act of 1978 (CSRA), which forbids strikes among civil service workers. That same day, President Reagan went on radio and television to announce that any striker who did not return to the job within 48 hours would be fired, and would also be permanently prohibited from being reemployed at any federal agency in the future.

Of those controllers who went on strike (some 4,199 did not), 875 returned to work before the expiration of the deadline set by the president. The remainder of the strikers, over 11,000 controllers, were fired.

The FAA had made preparations to meet the strike. Controller positions were staffed by those who had refused to strike, supplemented by supervisors, military personnel, and retirees who were called back. Within 10 days the ATC system was operating at about 70 percent effectiveness. The FAA recruited new trainees and ran them through its Air Traffic Service Academy to fill the remaining vacancies. When the air traffic system regained full operational capacity less than two years later, a head count showed that there were 20 percent fewer controllers required to run the system safely and efficiently, implicit proof that ATC was over-staffed when the strike began.

PATCO was decertified as the bargaining agent for FAA controllers. The FAA and the Airline Transport Association filed civil lawsuits seeking damages and injunctive relief, and the PATCO strike fund, which in August 1981 held over $3 million, was impounded to pay damages and fines. Criminal proceedings were commenced and federal court contempt orders were entered.

The controllers hired after the PATCO strike subsequently formed their own union, the National Air Traffic Controllers Union (NATCO), which represents controllers today.

Response from other union groups in support of the strike was muted. ALPA, in fact, publicly countered PATCO assertions that the ATC system was unsafe. Any tepid support voiced for the strike was seen as merely symbolic. Still, union leadership countrywide was apprehensive over the effect of such a devastating defeat suffered by any labor organization. They could not help but notice the overwhelming support that the administration's response to the strike had engendered.

The strike caused large airline losses at a time when the airlines were having a difficult time due to deregulation and the economic downturn then ongoing. It inconvenienced millions of air travelers, and reinforced the wisdom of the anti-strike provisions applicable to federal employees. Unions also took note of the public resentment generated by the strike and by the disruptions that it caused. It might even be concluded that the PATCO strike and its aftermath had a chilling effect on militant union activity—during the ensuing three-year period there were only two strikes in the airline industry, an IAM strike against Northwest in May 1982 and another IAM strike in August 1983, this time against Lorenzo's Continental. Each of the IAM strikes deserves further comment.

The strike against Northwest was called by the mechanics after negotiations had produced agreements with all of the other crafts. It was also generally conceded that the company's offer to IAM was substantial. Union solidarity, most visibly expressed by a refusal by one union's members to cross picket lines set up by different unions, has been a traditional and effective tool in job actions. When IAM struck Northwest, the pilots crossed the picket lines and continued to fly, as did the flight attendants represented by the Teamsters, thereby greatly reducing the effectiveness of the strike.

The Continental strike is technically still in progress given that Continental's entry into Chapter 11, and the subsequent firing of its employees under the *Bildisco* decision, caused the loss of all of those employees' jobs.

▪ Concession Bargaining

Wage concessions first appeared as a result of the financial setbacks experienced by Eastern in the middle of the 1970s, before deregulation. Eastern's unions agreed to a one-year wage freeze in 1975, and in 1976 signed on to a new employee participation plan, known as the Variable Earnings Program (VEP), under which employees would return 3.5 percent of their wages to the company beginning in 1978 in return for profit sharing.

In 1981, the unions at Braniff agreed to a 10 percent wage reduction, but Braniff went into liquidation shortly thereafter anyway. Pan American unions agreed in October 1981 to a 10 percent wage cut, in return for an employee stock ownership plan and a seat on the board of directors. This was the first time that labor had negotiated a seat on any airline's board, and of the 13 largest carriers in the United States, it was the only board seat. At United, the pilots gave work rule concessions, agreeing to more flying time and to the crew-size issue. They also gave up some bonus pay provisions.

Concession bargaining appeared to be limited to situations where the financial condition of the airline had been directly impacted by either claimed economic conditions or the effects of deregulation, or both. It also is clear that concession bargaining most often resulted in a *quid pro quo* back to the unions, as well as a "snap back" provision designed to reinstate the wage concession when the carrier was again financially stable.

Concession bargaining included wage reductions, work rule changes, delay or elimination of future wage increases, current wage freezes, and reductions in vacation allowances and fringe benefit reductions. Concession bargaining also appears to have been most effective with pilots and flight attendants, but less so with the mechanics. In fact, for many years IAM refused further wage concessions after the Braniff agreement in 1981. The practice of concession bargaining continued over the ensuing years.

In April 2003, American employees agreed to $1.8 billion in wage, benefit, and work rules concessions to help the airline avoid bankruptcy. That same month, United employees represented by ALPA, Association of Flight Attendants

(AFA), the International Association of Machinists and Aerospace Workers (IAM), the Transport Workers Union (TWU), and the Professional Airline Flight Control Association (PAFCA) agreed to $2.2 billion in average yearly savings to avoid liquidation. Through January 2003, US Airways employees agreed to over $1 billion in cuts to avoid liquidation. Of the three airlines, only American was able to remain out of bankruptcy.

■ Two-Tiered Wage Agreements

Two-tiered wage agreements, or b-scale wages, are a form of concession bargaining that first arose at American Airlines in 1983. The b-scale refers to a wage rate applied to workers solely on the basis of their having been hired after a specified date. The plan is, therefore, prospective in benefit rather than immediate. Once in place at American, the two-tier system rapidly proceeded through the ranks of most carriers, and was readily adopted. By 1986, with the exception of Braniff and Continental, all major carriers had the system in place for at least one craft of employees, and 70 percent of all union contracts carried b-scales.

The agreement typically involves a gradual "payoff," or a limited period during which the new employee will be paid under the reduced pay scale. The plan typically will be merged with the higher wage scale, usually within five years. The wage reduction historically has ranged from 20 percent to 45 percent.

■ Airline Union Characteristics

From a historical point of view, the machinists' union, IAM, can be considered to remain the most intransigent in labor negotiations. IAM is a centralized union with bargaining units outside of the airline industry. As a union with strong, central leadership that generally controls ultimate decision making in negotiations and concessions, there is a more consistent negotiating position throughout the union, and much less fragmentation due to local union authority. Mechanics are also less affected by either work stoppages or the fear of long-term unemployment due to bankruptcies of their employers since they are readily employable at other carriers or outside of the airline industry. One drawback to IAM is the fact that it represents significant numbers of much less skilled, or even unskilled, workers both within and outside of the industry. Aircraft cleaners and other ground employees, in some locations, are able to control the union. It is apparent that the interests of these disparate groups are not identical.

Pilots, 90 percent of whom are represented by ALPA, are all employed with the airline industry, and their mobility within the industry is seriously constrained by the seniority system employed on all airlines. They are also much more impacted by work stoppages or by carrier bankruptcies since they have no comparable opportunities outside of the industry, or even within the industry due to the seniority rosters. Finally, local ALPA chapters have had much more autonomy than IAM and have been more amenable to concession bargaining on an individual carrier basis.

Flight attendants traditionally have had less bargaining power than pilots and mechanics. They were organized much later than the other two crafts, and they have been less unified. In the early 1980s, there were 11 bargaining units representing flight attendants. Their training is much less extensive than pilots or mechanics and, before 2004, there was no FAA certification requirement for flight attendants. In the fall of 2003, Congress established a flight attendant certification requirement under the Vision 100— Century of Aviation Reauthorization Act. The Act requires that after December 11, 2004, no person may serve as a flight attendant aboard an aircraft of an air carrier unless that person holds a Certificate of Demonstrated Proficiency (certificate) issued by the FAA.

How Did Stewardesses Become Flight Attendants?

There were no unions for cabin attendants working for the airlines prior to the early 1940s. Their roles had been defined early on by passenger ship service, and these attendants were usually males who were termed "stewards" or "pursers." During the 1920s, Pan American World Airways first employed male stewards on their Key West and Miami service to Havana, using 10-passenger Fokker aircraft (see Figure 15-9, p. 144).

Domestically, women came into the airline work force in 1930 when Boeing Air Transport, later United Airlines, hired Ellen Church, a registered nurse. Church was enamored of aviation and had applied unsuccessfully for a pilot's position with Boeing Air Transport. Having been rejected as a pilot, she suggested that having a registered nurse on board would help alleviate passengers' fear of flying in those early days and that she could professionally attend to air sickness as well.

Church became the world's first stewardess on May 15, 1930, in a three-month experiment that ultimately used eight registered nurses on the west coast to Chicago routes. The addition of these nurses was an unqualified success and, within a short time, most airlines in the country also began adding nurses to their flight crews. They were called "stewardesses."

Stewardesses in the 1930s were required to be unmarried, younger than 25 years old, weigh less than 115 pounds, and be under 5'4" tall. At the time, there was some correlation between these physical requirements and the size of the interior of most passenger planes. In addition to attending to passengers, their duties included fueling the airplanes, hauling baggage, and light cabin maintenance.

In 1953, American Airlines imposed an upper age restriction for continued employment for stewardesses that called for their retirement upon reaching 32 years of age. Their union was able to limit this rule to new hires, exempting current employees. By this time, many airliners had pressurization systems that allowed flights to be conducted at higher altitudes in quite comfortable conditions, out of most of the weather and turbulence inducing air sickness and fear of earlier times. These aspects of commercial flight were significantly enhanced with the introduction of passenger jets late in the 1950s.

By 1960, the stewardesses were represented by a division of the Air Line Pilots Association known as the Air Line Stewards and Stewardess Association (ALSSA), now an independent union known as the Association of Flight Attendants.[2]

The Civil Rights Act of 1964—Title VII

Title VII of the Civil Rights Act barred employers from discriminating against both employees and job applicants on the basis of sex, race, national origin, or religion.[3] The statute contained an exception known as the "bona fide occupation qualification" (BFOQ), which recognized that there are "certain instances where religion, sex, or national origin is a bona fide occupational qualification reasonably necessary to the normal operation of that particular business or enterprise." This exception provided a "gray area" that allowed an argument for the airlines to continue current employment policies, but it also provided a "wedge" issue to the unions to seek the complete elimination of discrimination against stewardesses in employment.

The agency charged with administering Title VII of the Civil Rights Act is the Equal Employment Opportunity Commission (EEOC). Stewardesses wasted no time in filing charges of sex discrimination against the airlines, citing age ceilings and marriage bans. The "no-marriage" rule was the first to fall when a grievance filed against Braniff, alleging discrimination under its work rules, resulted in September 1965 in a ruling favorable to the union, citing Title VII. This was followed later the same month by the EEOC issuing its general guidelines on sex discrimination, finding that the firing of female employees for marriage was discriminatory when the policy was not also applied to male employees.

Agency rulings are often only way stations to the ultimate resolution of the issue(s) under consideration. And so it was with the major issues being contested by stewardesses, which included limitations on marriage, age, weight, height, and appearance. The contest between the airlines and female cabin employees or their unions gyrated around the filing of grievance procedures under the Railway Labor Act, filing civil actions in the federal courts based on federal statutes and the BFOQ exception, providing testimony in hearings before Congressional committees, and appearances in hearings before various state agencies.

These efforts continued with mixed results as to the particular limitation at issue, until the case of *Diaz v. Pan Am*[4] was brought in the federal court in Florida in 1971. The sole issue in this case was whether or not sex was a bona fide occupational qualification for the flight attendant occupation. Efforts by men to enter this class of airline employment had been resisted by the airlines ever since the advent of Title VII, and in the *Diaz* case the plaintiff was a man.

The federal trial judge ruled with the airline, basically saying that the BFOQ exception requiring females as cabin attendants was valid in the airlines for cabin service. You will recall that, in these pre-deregulation days, most air travel was by businessmen, and as long as the airline could show that having females in the cabin for service was better for business than having men, then the BFOQ exception was deemed valid. The trial court specifically found that the performance of female attendants was better in that they were superior to men in "providing reassurance to anxious passengers, giving courteous personalized service and, in general, making flights as pleasurable as possible within the limitations imposed by aircraft operations."

This case was reversed on appeal[5] by the Fifth Circuit Court of Appeals in 1971. The court noted that the *preference* of passengers was not sufficient to justify the exclusion of males in cabin service, given the statutory language requiring "necessity" in order to support exclusion. The court also noted that Pan Am, at the time this case was brought against it, already had 283 male stewards employed on some of its foreign flights.

Stewardesses would become flight attendants as a result of this case.

Still to come were the battles over weight and appearance limitations of female cabin attendants, and on the further polarizing limitation regarding pregnancy. In 1978, Congress passed the Pregnancy Discrimination Act as an amendment to Title VII. Henceforth, pregnancy had to be treated on the same basis as other temporary worker disabilities.

■ The Progression of Labor Impacts Due to Deregulation

While almost every aspect of commercial air transportation has in some way been changed by deregulation, perhaps the most consistent impact of the effects of deregulation has been to the airline employee. Due to the relatively liberal wage and benefits package that airline employees as a group enjoyed during the period of CAB fare and rate control, it is understandable that employee wages and benefits would be a primary target for correction when passenger fares and airline revenues began to fall due to competitive pressures after deregulation. In addition, deregulation caused increased activity in mergers and downsizing by the legacy carriers, as well as bankruptcies, which had never before been experienced in the airline industry. This resulted not only in downward pressure on wages and benefits, but in the reduction of the number of airline employees overall.

Because no one in government, in academia, or in the private sector had actually analyzed the vast ramifications of deregulation before Congress passed the Airline Deregulation Act, the industry was thrown into a state of turmoil and confusion as it attempted to deal with the realities of unchecked competition. As these realities played out over the first decade or so of deregulated air transportation, both the legacy carriers and the new entrant airlines tried to find a workable business model. The fluctuation of oil prices and the onset of economic recessions complicated this process immensely.

In the legacy airlines, over the course of deregulation there has ensued a cycle of wage and benefit concessions during recurring times of financial distress, followed by intermittent periods of airline profitability when some rebound in wages has occurred. But one thing has been constant: the trend line for historical airline employee wages, along with the total number of airline employees, has continued down. With the early new entrant airlines, wages and benefits were significantly lower that the legacy airlines, and during the early days of deregulation, the further bad news was that most new entrant airlines were mostly unsuccessful and left the field.

Although the Southwest Airlines business model has proved consistently profitable since deregulation, the legacy airlines and the new entrants have had to continuously make adjustments to their way of doing business. Beginning with JetBlue in 2000, a new kind of entrant airline, designated "low cost carrier," has emerged that appears to be successful and growing. The legacy airlines, on the other hand, continue to enter bankruptcy, shrink and cut services. As of November 2011, there had been 173 bankruptcy filings by domestic carriers since 1978.

The total number of airline employees as of March 2010 was the lowest since 1990, according to the Department of Transportation. But that is not the whole story. While legacy airlines continue to downsize, the new breed of low cost carriers, including Southwest, are growing, adding routes and hiring more employees.

There appears, in fact, to be developing a convergence of business models and methods among all airlines.

Finally, domestic airlines have all dramatically increased their use of outsourced maintenance facilities. From 1996 to 2006, outsourced maintenance dollars increased from 37 percent to 64 percent, and the number of foreign facilities servicing U.S. carriers increased by 344 to 698. The Inspector General of the Department of Transportation, in testimony before Congressional hearings on aviation, has stated "We have identified challenges in FAA's ability to effectively monitor the increase in outsourcing."[6] Most troubling, there do appear to be critical regulatory differences between repair shops run by the airlines and those by outside vendors, and the concern remains about how effectively the FAA is able to conduct timely inspections over such a wide-spread repair community.[7]

Endnotes

1. To review the provisions of the RLA and its mandated procedures for the resolution of labor disputes, refer to Chapter 14.

2. The Airline Stewardess Association was founded in 1945 and merged into the Air Line Stewards and Stewardesses Association in 1949. In 1973, ALSSA left ALPA and formed an independent union under the name Association of Flight Attendants (AFA). AFA was chartered by the AFL-CIO in 1984, and merged with the Communications Workers of America in 2004.

3. The Age Discrimination Act in Employment was not passed until 1967, which banned discrimination regarding certain employees 40 years of age or older. The Age Discrimination Act of 1975 bars discrimination on the basis of age in programs and activities receiving federal financial assistance, and applies to all ages.

4. *Diaz v. Pan American World Airways, Inc*, 311 F.Supp. 599, (S.D. Fl 1971).

5. *Diaz v. Pan American World Airways*, 442 F. 2d 385 (5 Cir. 1972).

6. www.oig.dot.gov/item.jsp?id=2068.

7. McGee, USA Today, October 2007.

30

The Progression of Deregulation

When Congress passed the Airline Deregulation Act in 1978, there existed no empirical data, nor any experience, to reliably predict what would happen to the U.S. air carrier industry under economic deregulation. During the three years that Congress held hearings on the matter before the Act was actually passed, scores of proponents and opponents testified. The arguments made for deregulation were largely just that, arguments, and they were premised on anecdotal data. Economic theory was given much credence, but it was still just theory. The effect that economic deregulation would have on the airline industry and on the nation was simply unknown.

In the following chapters we will examine some of the specific, unexpected developments that deregulation produced and their impact on the promise of deregulation. But here, let us take an overall look at how the progression of deregulation has unfolded since the passage of the Act.

■ Airline Fares

A study conducted by the Government Accounting Office (GAO) in the early 1970s concluded that airline fares under the CAB regulated system were anywhere from 22 percent to 50 percent higher than they would be under a deregulated system. By 2010, domestic fares had actually declined more than 40 percent in inflation-adjusted dollars since 1978. Fares have declined the most in long-distance and heavily trafficked markets, and the least in shorter-distance and less-traveled markets. Figure 30-1 provides a comparison of the cost of air travel versus the cost of other goods and services as of 2013.[1]

Historically, airline fares have been the standard used in the airline industry and by government to track travel costs and to set taxes on travel services, in order to determine how much it costs a passenger to go from Point A to Point B. Since 2008, a new development has arisen in the legacy airlines that calls into question this time-worn standard for evaluating passenger travel cost. This new development, the addition of add-on fees by all carriers, requires airline fares to now be compared with the more realistic totality of "cost of travel," which includes not only basic airfares but also all the other costs charged to the passenger by the airline while getting from Point A to Point B. This will be discussed below.

For many years after deregulation, most of the price benefit in reduced fares went to

Product (Unit)	1978*	2000	2010	2013	2013 vs. 1978	2013 vs. 2000
Walt Disney World (One Day Pass, Adult)[0]	$6.50	$46	$82	$95	1362%	107%
College Education: Public, Undergraduate (Year)[1]	$688	$3,508	$7,605	$8,893	1193%	154%
College Education: Private, Undergraduate (Year)[1]	$2,958	$16,072	$27,293	$30,094	917%	87%
National Football League Game (Ticket)[9]	$9.67	$48.97	$76.47	$81.54	743%	67%
Prescription Drugs (BLS Index)[2]	61.6	285.4	412.79	442.58	618%	55%
Major League Baseball Game (Ticket)[10]	$3.98	$16.22	$26.74	$27.48	590%	69%
Gasoline (Gallon, Unleaded)[4]	$0.67	$1.51	$2.90	$3.53	426%	134%
Vehicle (New)[12]	$6,470	$24,923	$29,793	$31,762	391%	27%
Single-Family Home (New)[5]	$55,700	$169,000	$221,800	$265,900	377%	57%
Consumer Price Index (CPI-U)[2]	65.2	172.2	218.1	232.957	257%	35%
Movie Ticket[6]	$2.34	$5.39	$7.89	$8.13	247%	51%
Food & Beverage (BLS Index)	72.183	168.35	220.0	237.0	228%	41%
Postage Stamp (First-Class)[7]	$0.15	$0.33	$0.44	$0.46	207%	39%
Whole Milk (Index)[2]	81	156.9	194.45	214.68	165%	37%
Air Travel (R/T Domestic Fare + Ancillary)[8]	**$187**	**$316.96**	**$338.10**	**$385.32**	**106%**	**22%**
Air Travel (R/T Domestic Fare Only)[8]	**$186**	**$314.46**	**$316.27**	**$362.85**	**95%**	**15%**
Apparel: Clothing/Footwear/Jewelry (BLS Index)[2]	81.3	129.6	119.50	127.41	57%	-2%
Television (BLS Index)[2]	101.8	49.9	7.99	4.58	-96%	-91%
Cable TV (Monthly)[11]	N/A	$31.22	$54.44	$65.07	N/A	N/A

* Domestic fare data commences in 1979; international fare data commences in 1990.

FIGURE 30-1   Price of air travel versus other goods and services.

A change in the price of any good or service over time has little value in isolation. Therefore, it is common practice to adjust the values in a time series for inflation. The adjusted (restated) values are then presented in "real" (rather than "nominal") terms.

leisure travelers, who were not required to fly on short notice, like the business traveler. Due to computer reservation systems and the yield management programs available to the incumbent airlines, ticket prices were discounted most heavily for those who could purchase early, stay longer, and travel at non-peak times. The airlines were able to charge much higher fares for those who could not plan very far ahead and were otherwise constrained in their travel options.

In the early years of deregulation, the computer generated systems of yield management and other competitive pricing schemes resulted in an almost indecipherable pricing regimen, where the passenger in 20A, for example, may find that his fare is twice that of his seatmate in 20B, for no discernible reason. Business fares actually increased after deregulation, at one time by as much as 70 percent over similar fares charged during the CAB era.[2]

Recent evidence, however, discloses that businesses that were punished by the economic downturn beginning in 2000 began to resist such disparate pricing. Corporate travel offices were set up for the express purpose of economizing on costs of air travel. By 2002, airlines began to reduce fares across the board, and an increased corporate use of the Internet caused some tempering of fare disparity. Fares still remain higher at "fortress hubs," where one or two airlines have disproportionate market share, and at some small airports where there is little or no competition.

Passenger Travel

Passenger enplanements since 1978 have increased dramatically. In 1978, 275 million people flew on domestic airlines. By 1995, that figure had doubled, to 548 million. In 2000, the number had increased to 693 million. Because of 9-11, passenger travel dropped significantly, to a low of 641 million in 2002, but by the end of 2005, passenger enplanements were almost

780 million. Between 2006 and 2010, cycling once again primarily due to economic factors, the average annual passenger count declined to 736 million. It is beyond argument that deregulation opened up air travel to the vast general population of the United States primarily because of a falling fare structure.

Number of Carriers

The number of carriers operating in any given year since deregulation has fluctuated greatly, although there has been an increase overall. This variation has been referred to as the "ebb and flow" of entrants by former CAB chairman John E. Robson. The "flow" of entrants has been marked by high expectations, and the "ebb" of failures in the industry by excuses. A variety of reasons has been given for new entrant failures: inexperienced management, unrealistic business plans, lack of solid financial backing, public doubts about airlines' reliability, and poorly conceived pricing structures. Recently, new entrant airlines have stabilized their performance record, with far fewer failures than were seen in the period just after the airlines were deregulated.

In 1938 when the CAB took over economic regulation of the airlines, there were 16 trunk carriers; by 1978, that number had shrunk to 10 airlines, although local service airlines and commuters had brought the total number of airlines to 43. While airlines have been classified in a number of different ways, the Department of Transportation defines airlines based on annual revenues as major airlines, national airlines, and regional airlines. In 2000, there were a total of 90 airlines operating in the United States, of which 10 were classified as "major" airlines, a rough equivalent to the trunk airlines of regulation days. By reason of volume and inflation costs, by 2010 the number of "major" airlines had grown to 18. As of 2012, through mergers and acquisitions, the number of incumbent "major" airlines had declined to five. The number of surviving legacy airlines remains a moving target as carriers continue to adjust to the factors that seem to control their individual destinies.

Market Share

After deregulation, and for many years thereafter, the incumbent (legacy) airlines increased market share over that which existed during CAB regulation. In 1978, for instance, the five largest (incumbent) airlines took in 66 percent of domestic revenues. This excessive control of market share was recited by proponents of deregulation during the Congressional hearings to demonstrate the anti-competitive impact of CAB regulation. The implication was that under a deregulated market, the share of the largest carriers in the overall market would decrease. In 2001, the five-carrier share had actually increased to 72 percent, revealing a central failure of deregulation theory. By 2010, largely because of mergers and acquisitions (American took over TWA, US Airways merged with America West, Delta merged with Northwest, and United merged with Continental), the largest legacy carriers still owned 72 percent of market share.

Figure 30-2 is an interesting and informative graphic. Represented here is the period of time between 1975 and 2009, depicting six surviving airlines (four legacy carriers and two low-cost carriers) as of 2009, along with their merger histories with numerous other airlines over that period. Shown also on a continuum is the market share, based on passengers flown (not revenues), of each surviving airline over the applicable period of time.

Mergers have also altered the rankings of airlines based on measures most traditionally used. As of 2012, the largest airlines ranked by passengers carried were 1. Delta Airlines, 2. United Airlines, 3. Southwest Airlines, 4. American Airlines, 5. US Airways, 6. Air Canada, 7. Republic Airways, 8. JetBlue Airways, 9. Alaska Airlines, 10. WestJet, 11. Frontier Airlines, 12. AeroMexico, 13. Spirit Airlines, 14. Hawaiian Airlines, and 15. Allegiant Air.

Safety

The airline accident rate has been steadily declining since the 1940s. With the introduction of jet aircraft into the civilian airline fleet, the rate of decline increased even faster, so that by the late 1980s, the total annual number of airline accidents had become historically miniscule. Commuter carriers, flying more turboprop equipment than their larger brethren, have had a proportionately higher accident rate, but over the last two decades even that rate has declined by 90 percent. Since deregulation, the overall fatal accident rate per million miles flown has averaged 0.0009, compared to 0.0135 during the 40 years of regulation. It can be logically surmised that the difference in the accident rate before and after deregulation probably has more to do with the technological advance of aircraft and equipment than with regulation. It should be remembered that economic deregulation did not extend to safety issues. The United States airline industry remains today one of the most heavily regulated endeavors in the world. See Table 30-1 for accident statistics for U.S. airlines.

Worldwide, the year 2012 marked the lowest rate of fatal accidents since the dawn of the jet age. Including both passenger and cargo flights, in 2012 there were 22 fatal crashes, down from 28 in 2011. The 10-year average is 34. None occurred in the United States. Of those 22 crashes, just 10 involved passenger aircraft and only 3 of those were jets. The remaining 7 involved Western-built or Russian turboprops.

Turboprop operations have significantly higher crash rates, particularly world-wide. Turboprops serve smaller airfields and use less advanced air traffic control equipment than major Western airports.

Russian-built planes historically have accounted for much higher crash rates than American or European-built planes. Crash rates in underdeveloped areas of the world, like Africa, Latin America, and the Caribbean are over four times that of the rest of the world. These regions account for only 7 percent of all global passenger traffic but have recorded nearly half of all accidents in 2012.[3]

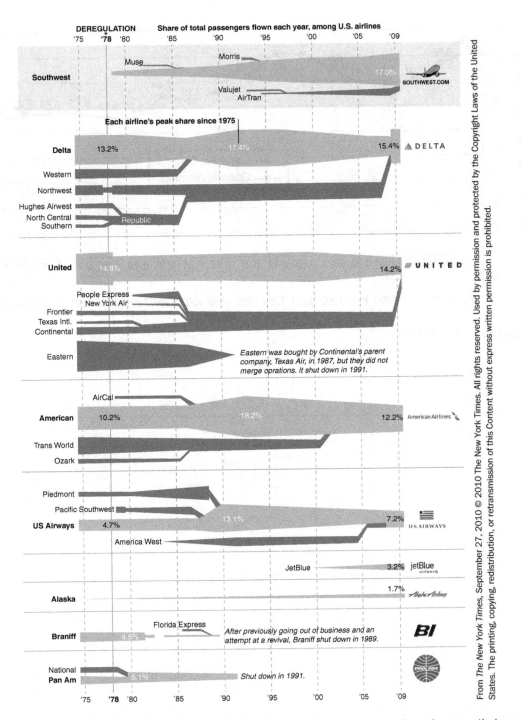

FIGURE 30-2   Converging flight paths. (Note: Some airlines that merged with others are not shown because their passenger data was not available.)

The deregulation of the airline industry in 1978 led to a wave of mergers that continues to this day. But even as the legacy carriers have been consolidating and growing, they have been losing market share to low-cost carriers. Two of them, SouthWest and AirTran, have just agreed to merge and carried the most passengers in 2009 combined.

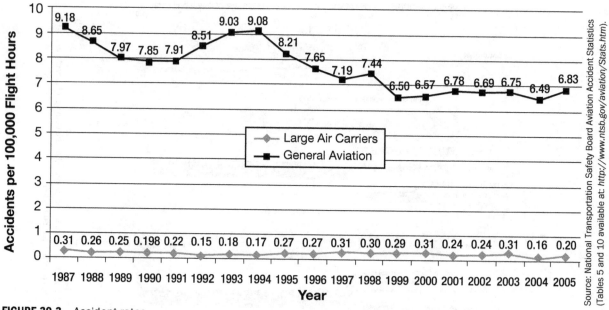

Source: National Transportation Safety Board Aviation Accident Statistics (Tables 5 and 10 available at: http://www.ntsb.gov/aviation/Stats.htm).

FIGURE 30-3 Accident rates.

US Air Carriers Operating Under 14 **CFR 121**, Scheduled Service (Airlines)

Year	Accidents		Fatalities		Flight Hours	Miles Flown	Departures	Accidents Per 100,000 Flight Hours		Accidents per 1,000,000 Miles Flown		Accidents per 100,000 Departures	
	All	Fatal	Total	Aboard				All	Fatal	All	Fatal	All	Fatal
1994*	18	4	239	237	12,292,356	5,112,633,000	7,824,802	0.138	0.033	0.0033	0.0008	0.217	0.051
1995	30	1	160	160	12,776,679	5,328,969,000	8,105,570	0.235	0.008	0.0056	0.0002	0.370	0.012
1996	31	3	342	342	12,971,676	5,449,997,000	7,851,298	0.239	0.023	0.0057	0.0006	0.395	0.038
1997	43	3	3	2	15,061,662	6,339,432,000	9,925,058	0.285	0.020	0.0068	0.0005	0.433	0.030
1998	41	1	1	0	15,921,447	6,343,690,000	10,535,196	0.258	0.006	0.0065	0.0002	0.389	0.009
1999	40	2	12	11	16,693,365	6,689,327,000	10,860,692	0.240	0.012	0.0060	0.0003	0.368	0.018
2000	49	2	89	89	17,478,519	7,152,260,000	11,053,826	0.280	0.011	0.0069	0.0003	0.443	0.018
2001*	41	6	531	525	17,157,858	6,994,939,000	10,632,880	0.216	0.012	0.0053	0.0003	0.348	0.019
2002	34	0	0	0	16,718,781	6,927,954,000	10,276,107	0.203	-	0.0049	-	0.331	-
2003	51	2	22	21	16,887,756	7,015,935,000	10,227,924	0.302	0.012	0.0073	0.0003	0.499	0.020
2004	23	1	13	13	18,184,016	7,604,248,000	10,782,989	0.126	0.005	0.0030	0.0001	0.213	0.009
2005	34	3	22	20	18,712,191	7,843,717,000	10,910,460	0.182	0.016	0.0043	0.0004	0.312	0.027
2006	26	2	50	49	18,647,896	7,851,864,000	10,627,481	0.139	0.011	0.0033	0.0003	0.245	0.019
2007	26	0	0	0	19,014,677	8,024,313,000	10,734,170	0.137	-	0.0032	-	0.242	-
2008	20	0	0	0	18,580,166	7,813,371,000	10,282,575	0.108	-	0.0026	-	0.195	-
2009	26	1	50	49	17,182,970	7,248,702,000	9,564,891	0.151	0.006	0.0036	0.0001	0.272	0.010
2010	27	0	0	0	17,235,121	7,352,374,000	9,467,282	0.157	-	0.0037	-	0.285	-
2011	28	0	0	0	17,464,623	7,473,520,000	9,419,064	0.160	-	0.0037	-	0.297	-
2012	27	0	0	0	17,271,783	7,443,366,000	9,241,935	0.156	-	0.0036	-	0.292	-
2013	20	1	2	2	17,150,000	7,334,170,000	8,927,000	0.117	0.006	0.0027	0.0001	0.224	0.011

Notes:
- 2013 data are preliminary.
- Flight hours, miles, and departures are compiled by the Federal Aviation Administration.
- Since March 20, 1997, aircraft with 10 or more seats used in scheduled passenger service have been operated under 14 CFR 121.

- Years followed by the symbol * are those in which an illegal act was responsible for an occurrence in this category. These acts, such as suicide and sabotage are included in the totals for accidents and fatalities but are excluded for the purpose of accident rate computation. Other than the persons aboard aircraft who were killed, fatalities resulting from the September 11, 2001 terrorist acts are excluded from this table.

Source: NTSB

TABLE 30-1 Accidents, fatalities, and rates, 1994 through 2013.

Employment

From the passage of the Airline Deregulation Act through the first year of the 21st century, the number of airline employees had increased by 50 percent, to 536,400 as measured in full-time equivalents (FTEs).[4] Due to the effects of September 11, 2001 and other economic factors during the first decade of the new century, airline employment fell to a low of 376,200 FTEs in April 2010, at which point a slow recovery began.

The Evolution of Operating Practices

The air carrier industry has passed through a series of changes or "waves" since deregulation in 1978.[5] The initial wave was the creation of the hub and spoke system. The second wave was the inauguration of low-fare, point-to-point service, pioneered by Southwest Airlines. The third wave was the entry into the airline fleet of the regional jet. The fourth wave, now in process, is the abandonment of the financial and operational model of the legacy carriers from the period of CAB regulation, and a process of convergence of practices of legacy carriers and low-cost carriers (LCCs). This process of convergence has been driven by the reality of all five of the largest legacy carriers having entered Chapter 11 bankruptcy as of the end of 2011. The relative success of the low-cost carriers during the same period underscores the bottom-line effects of the differences in the business practices of the two groups. Also underscoring the success of the LCC group is their increase of domestic passenger market share—from 13 percent in 1997 to 28 percent in 2009.

Hub and Spoke

Before deregulation, it was said that if you traveled in the southeastern part of the United States and you wanted to get to heaven, you would have to go through Atlanta and change planes. Delta Airlines is credited with creation of the hub and spoke concept that it centered in Atlanta, and, as discussed earlier, Delta began this service during the 1940s at the behest of the CAB in order to bring service to small outlying communities in the Southeast. The other trunk airlines that operated during regulation, however, were all point-to-point carriers.

After deregulation, the opportunities to serve when and where the airlines wanted, coupled with the economic necessity to fill their airplanes with as many passengers as possible, caused the adoption of the hub and spoke system nationwide. This system had two main advantages to the traveler:

- The passenger who lived in the hub city gained access to a greatly increased number of destinations directly from the hub airport.
- The passenger who lived in one of the smaller communities at the end of a spoke, who may not have had any service under regulation, was offered access to the same greatly increased number of destinations after one stop at the hub airport.

Hub and spoke brought to the airlines a much more efficient use of aircraft by allowing many more destinations to be served using far fewer airplanes. By way of example, if a carrier had 20 airplanes engaged in point-to-point service between city pairs, as was the case before deregulation, the number of origin and destination operations (O&D) would be limited to 20. In the hub and spoke system, the O&D number would suddenly jump to 400 (20 × 20). The truth is that there will never be nonstop service between most cities. Recognizing this fact, the hub and spoke system should be recognized as a major, positive development of deregulation.

The hub and spoke system has also drawn complaints.

- First, passengers were said to be traveling "around their elbow," being required to stop at hub airports that were considerably distant from a direct line of travel, and losing the main advantage of jet aircraft, which is speed and the efficient use of time. According to this view, these passengers were traveling at the convenience of the airline, not themselves.

- Second, the system produced the natural result that the dominant airline gained tremendous market share at the hub city, a potential anticompetitive development. Dominated hubs include Atlanta (Delta), Denver (United), Detroit (Northwest), and Chicago (American and United).

- Third, the system required that all aircraft returning to the hub do so at or about the same time in order to make connections with aircraft departing from the hub to new destinations. This confluence of activity placed a huge strain on air traffic control and airport operations.

The introduction of these relatively short-haul operations altered the airlines' needs as to types of aircraft. Boeing, it is said, was in the process in the late 1970s of phasing out production of the 737. This decision was reversed after deregulation due to the adoption of the hub and spoke system, and production of 737 aircraft soared. The hub and spoke system also gave rise to an entirely new line of short-range aircraft, like the MD-80, shorter Airbus planes, and regional jets (RJs). Suddenly there was less need for the larger, fuel-hungry 747s, and a general downsizing of aircraft began.

Low Fare, Point-to-Point Service

Southwest Airlines was a wholly intrastate carrier before deregulation, having been founded in 1971. It had developed a no-frills approach to air carrier service that it brought to the interstate market after deregulation, gradually expanding in a deliberate and cautious way. It used just one type of aircraft, the Boeing 737, thereby greatly reducing its parts inventory requirements and the training of its airframe and powerplant people, as well as its pilots. Southwest chose secondary airports, like Love Field in Dallas and Midway Airport in Chicago, where

the turn-around time for its aircraft would be minimized. This practice avoided the congestion, the ATC delays, and the airport confusion that were becoming symptomatic of the hubs. Southwest's success moved it into the top 10 airlines in the United States during the 1990s, and it continued to expand its service into the eastern United States market, opening up service to underserved or unserved airports. By 2012, Southwest had grown to be the third largest air carrier in the country as measured by passengers carried.[6]

As Southwest has grown, it has developed a "rolling hub" system instead of strictly point-to-point service. In practice, an appreciable number of Southwest passengers are being flown by way of connections (via LAS, LUV, and BWI, for example).

The success of Southwest caused new entrant airlines (increasingly known as "low cost carriers," or LCCs) to imitate its model of low cost and no frills, thereby creating even more service to even more destinations. The legacy airlines also began, in self-defense, to imitate the model of Southwest by creating subsidiaries that provided the same kind of no-frills service and that used lower-paid crews operating a single type of airplane, just like Southwest. These subsidiaries have not met with any substantial success.

The Regional Jet

The concept of the "regional aircraft" was born after World War II to describe the kind of airplanes used by feeder airlines or local service airlines authorized by the CAB to supplement the mainstay air carrier fleet. These airplanes were thus described to differentiate them from the long-haul aircraft flown by trunk carriers. At first these aircraft were older aircraft previously flown by the trunk lines, like the DC-3; Convair 240, 340, and 440; and the first commercial turboprop, the Vickers Viscount.

During the late 1950s and early 1960s, a new kind of turboprop was conceived to service the short-haul and feeder market. These were airplanes like the high-winged, 28-seat Fokker F27, delivered in 1958, and larger iterations of the same basic design. The F27 and its successor types would go on to become the most successful turboprop of all time. In 1963, the low-winged Avro 748 turboprop took to the skies, carrying over 20 passengers.

Turboprops worked well in this market, as their operating characteristics allowed them to service smaller airports, and their fuel economy was much better than turbojets. After deregulation, and during the 1980s, other manufacturers entered the 30- to 40-seat commuter market, like De Havilland with the Dash 8, also a high-wing turboprop. While these turboprops were well liked by passengers because of their relative roominess, they were slow compared to jets.

The regional jet (RJ) was introduced into the aviation community in 1992 by the Canadian aircraft manufacturer, Bombardier, with its 50-seat CRJ100 (Canadair Regional Jet), in part fashioned on its business jet, the Challenger 604. In 1998, the company announced a stretched version holding 64 to 70 seats, designated the CRJ700, Series 701, and the 75-seat CRJ700, Series 705. A 90-seat version, CRJ900, joined the fleet in 2001. Canadair had some 55 percent of the regional jet market in 2002.

The Brazilian aircraft manufacturer, Embraer (Empresa Brasileira de Aeronautica, South America) entered the field in 1996 with the ERJ145, with 50 seats. The 35-seat ERJ135 was introduced into service in June 1999 to begin replacing the Brasilia, Embraer's turboprop workhorse. In 1999, Embraer launched a new family of twin-engine passenger aircraft consisting of the EMB170, 175, 190, and 195 jets with seating in the 70 to 110 range. The first of this new family, the 170, flew on February 19, 2002. Embraer claimed about 40 percent of the regional jet market in 2002.

The Embraer 190 received FAA certification in September 2005. JetBlue Airways took the first delivery of this 106-seat RJ and ordered 100 more. The EMB190 is a state-of-the-art airplane, which relies on digital modeling and virtual reality concepts in its design. This airplane has an all-digital cockpit and is equipped with fly-by-wire flight controls except for ailerons. Winglets at the wing tips are standard. The fuselage design features the "double bubble" idea, instead of the traditional circular cross section, which provides the look and feel of a larger cabin. There are no "middle" seats in its 2 by 2 seating configuration. See Figure 30-4 for a partial list of aircraft in the regional jet fleet.

The Sukhoi Superjet 100 is a 75- to 95-seat RJ, developed by the Russian aerospace firm Sukhoi in collaboration with Ilyushin and Boeing and with subsidy from the Russian government. Its first flight occurred in May 2008 and on February 3, 2012 the European Aviation Safety Agency (EASA) issued a type certificate for the airplane. The first aircraft was delivered to Amavia, an Armenian airline, and eight others have been delivered to the Russian company Aeroflot. Although orders and options are pending with other airlines and leasing companies, no other deliveries have been made. On May 9, 2012, a Superjet 100 on a demonstration flight out of Jakarta, Indonesia crashed into the side of a mountain, killing all 45 passengers aboard.

The Chinese are in the developmental stage of an RJ called the ARJ 21, with 80 seats for the first phase production and 100 seats for its next phase. Deployment of this aircraft was originally announced for 2008, but delays of various kinds have now pushed delivery to at least 2013.

There have been few other entrants into the RJ production market. Fairchild Dornier, a subsidiary of the U.S.–German partnership, Fairchild Aerospace Corporation, marketed the 329Jet. Production stopped with Fairchild's financial reverses in the 1990s. The only other

Scheduled Passenger Carriers for Select Aircraft (as of July 2014)

Manufacturer	Aircraft Type		Number of Aircraft	% of Total Aircraft	Average Seats	Total Seats
Bombardier	CRJ100/200		461	19.6%	50	23,050
Embraer	ERJ 145		456	19.4%	50	22,800
Bombardier	CRJ 700/705		289	12.3%	70	20,230
Embraer	EMB 170/175		217	9.2%	70	15,190
Bombardier	CRJ 900		185	7.9%	86	15,910
Embraer	ERJ 135/140		63	2.7%	37	2,331
Embraer	EMB 190		31	1.3%	114	3,534
Total			**1,702**	**72.3%**		**103,045**
Bombardier	DHC-8Q-400		128	5.4%	74	9,472
Bombardier	DHC-8-100/200		97	4.1%	37	3,589
Cessna 402	402		74	3.1%	9	666
Cessna	208-Caravan		73	3.1%	10	730
Raytheon	Beech 1900		52	2.2%	19	988
Embraer	EMB 120		51	2.2%	30	1,530
Saab	340		50	2.1%	35	1,750
Bombardier	DHC-8-300		44	1.9%	50	2,200
Bombardier	DHC-6 Twin Otter/Vistaliner		18	0.8%	19	342
ATR	ATR 42		14	0.6%	48	672
ATR	ATR 72		14	0.6%	60	840
Raytheon	Beech 90/99		12	0.5%	8	96
Britten-Norman	Britten-Norman BN-2 Islander		7	0.3%	9	63
Bombardier	DHC-3T Turbo Otter		4	0.2%	9	36
CASA	C-212		4	0.2%	26	104
Piper	Navajo Chieftain		4	0.2%	10	40
Bombardier	DHC-2T Turbo Beaver		2	0.1%	6	12
Cessna	180		2	0.1%	5	10
Quest	Kodiak 100		1	0.0%	9	9
	TOTAL		**651**	**27.7%**		**23,149**
	Grand Total		**2,353**			**126,194**

Source: Fleet database and Innovata schedules, via Diio online portal. RAA internal data.

FIGURE 30-4 Regional airline fleet.

Scheduled Passenger Carriers for Select Aircraft (as of July 2014)

Carrier	ATR		Beech		Bombardier/De Havilland										Britten-Norman	CASA	Cessna			Embraer					Piper	Quest	Saab	Grand Total
	ATR 42	ATR 72	1900	90/99	-2T	-3T	-6	-8 100/200	-8 300	-8Q 400	CRJ 100/200	CRJ 700/705	CRJ 900	BN2	212	180	208	402	120	145	190	135/140	170/175	Navajo Chieftain	Kodiak 100	340	
AeroLitoral																				28	26		7				61
Air Wisconsin											71																71
AirNet Systems																	6										6
Alaska Central Express			6																								6
Alpine Aviation			12	12																							24
Bering Air			2														6										8
Cape Air	1													4				74									79
Chautauqua Airlines																				43							43
CommutAir								16	5																		21
Compass Airlines																							42				42
Empire Airlines	13	9															36										58
Endeavor Air											82		65														147
Envoy												47								118		54					219
ERA Aviation			4					8																			12
ExpressJet Airlines											88	47	28							238		9					410
GoJet Airlines												47															47
Grand Canyon Airlines							16										6								1		23
Great Lakes Aviation			28																6								34
Horizon Air										51																	51
Island Air Hawaii		5								2																	7
Jazz Aviation								34	28	21	26	16															125
Kenmore Air					2	4										2	3										11
LC Peru								7																			7
Mesa Airlines												20	47										3				70
Mokulele Airlines																	12										12
New England Airlines														3										4			7
Penair																	2									15	17
Piedmont Airlines								32	11																		43
Porter Airlines										26																	26
PSA Airlines											35	14	9														58
Republic Airlines										28											5		91				124
Ryan Air															4												4
Seaborne Airlines							2																			8	10
Shuttle America																							68				68
Silver Airways																										27	27
SkyWest Airlines											159	98	36						45				6				344
Trans States Airlines																				29							29
Vieques Air Link																	2										2
Grand Total	14	14	52	12	2	4	18	97	44	128	461	289	185	7	4	2	73	74	51	456	31	63	217	4	1	50	2,353

RAA Member Airlines shown in shaded box.

Source: Fleet database, via Diio online portal. RAA internal data.

FIGURE 30-5 Regional aircraft distribution by carrier and manufacturer.

manufacturer of regional jets was Aero International, a consortium composed of Aerospatiale, Alenia, and British Aerospace. The BAE 146 series became the Avro RJ series (RJ 70/85/100) and 160 of these were produced before BAE Systems announced their discontinuation in the last quarter of 2001.

The history of the regional jet is not quite ready to be written in full, but there are signs that this concept has just about run its course. During the 1990s, RJs began to replace the turboprops used by commuter airlines. As airlines reconfigured and modified their hub and spoke concepts to utilize RJs, these small jets became commonplace and relatively popular in that service. The regional jets are faster, the engines are more reliable, and engine maintenance costs are lower. But compared to turboprops, the original small RJs were much more expensive to operate on a per seat basis. They were also more cramped than the larger turboprops, had less carry-on storage space, had lavatory issues, and minimal flight attendant service. See Figure 30-5 for a list of the airlines using RJ's, as well as the types of RJ's used.

As seen above, the trend in RJ size has consistently been toward larger and larger aircraft. As the new RJ designs have increased their seating capacity, the line between a medium-sized jet and a so-called RJ has been blurred. The Airbus 319, for instance, is normally configured for 124 seats, not much larger than the latest RJs. In 2005, a JetBlue spokesman refused to categorize the EMB190 as an RJ, saying that the aircraft was designed to fill the gap left by the DC-9. Many of these airplanes are being used by JetBlue to overfly hubs on point-to-point service (Orlando-MCO to Buffalo-BUF, for example).

The original RJ concept that emerged during the 1990s of producing jets to replace similar-sized turboprops is being phased out. Bombardier, for example, stopped production of its 50-seater in January 2006 and there is only limited production of the ERJ145 under license in China.

Because experience has shown that operating costs of RJs can make sense only on longer routes (400 miles seems to be the minimum), and as per seat operating costs, particularly fuel, have caused so-called "regional jets" to become larger, a market is appearing for a new era of turboprop aircraft to fill that niche. Most short-haul routes are less than 350 miles. Rising fuel prices have only reinforced this idea. Turboprops use about 30 percent less fuel than RJs.

The United States jet fleet is composed of four classes of aircraft: large, twin-aisle, single-aisle, and regional jet. In 1990, RJs accounted for 13 percent of this total, and by 2010 the RJ percentage had risen to only 15 percent. By reference to the chart in Figure 30-6, you will see that Boeing's prediction is that RJs in 2030 will have shrunk to only 5 percent of the jet fleet while the total number of jet aircraft will have doubled.

There were only two companies producing turboprops in the 40-seat-plus capacity range as of 2007: Bombardier and ATR. The economic factors discussed above have caused increased orders for these companies' turboprop aircraft. ATR as of July 2012 planned to boost production by 60 percent, to a rate of more than seven aircraft per month by 2014.

The old De Havilland Dash 8 production unit, which delivered the first Dash 8 in 1984, was sold first to Boeing and then to Bombardier in 1992. Bombardier turboprops are the Q100, first delivered in 1984 (33–37 seats); the Q200, first delivered in 1989 (33–37 seats); the Q300, a stretched version of the 100 (48–50 seats); and the Q400, first delivered in 2000 (68–78 seats). These airplanes have been fitted with a computer controlled noise and vibration suppression system since 1996 (the "Q" denotes "Quiet"), and produce a cabin decibel level equivalent to the CRJ regional jet. The Q400 has an impressive maximum cruise speed of 360 knots.

Total fleet

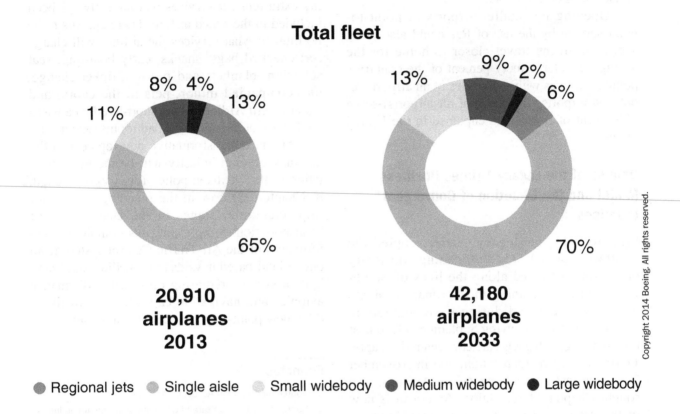

8% 4% 13%

11%

65%

20,910 airplanes 2013

13% 9% 2% 6%

70%

42,180 airplanes 2033

● Regional jets ● Single aisle ● Small widebody ● Medium widebody ● Large widebody

FIGURE 30-6 Composition of aircraft fleet—comparison between 2013 and 2033.

The European consortium ATR is a joint venture between EADS and Alenia Aeronautica. It produces the ATR 42-500 (48–50 seats) with a maximum cruise speed of 300 knots, and the ATR 72-500 (68–74 seats) with a maximum cruise speed of 276 knots.

Opening up smaller airports in point-to-point service by the use of RJs could also bring access to airline travel closer to home for the average traveler. Ninety percent of the country's population lives within 30 miles of an airport, yet only 64 airports (1 percent of all airports) serve 80 percent of passengers enplaned in the United States.[7]

Demise of the Legacy Airlines Business Model and the Evolution of Convergent Practices

Prior to 9-11, the legacy carriers copied the Southwest model only by creating subsidiary operations patterned along the lines of Southwest, while maintaining their primary business models that evolved during CAB regulation. During the years following September 11, four of the five largest legacy carriers[8] entered Chapter 11 bankruptcy reorganization, and in November 2011, the last holdout, American Airlines, also sought Chapter 11 protection. American is now in the process of attempting to slim down its cost structure and secure the benefits that earlier came to its competitors as a result of bankruptcy. Under Chapter 11, these airlines secured approval to make substantive changes to their basic structure, including eliminating employee pension plans, securing reductions in wages, amending work rules, cutting capacity, and downsizing generally. These changes are discussed in more detail in Chapter 35.

A comparison of relevant indicators, including cost per available seat mile (CASM), between these carrier groups will disclose that the margin between the two groups is narrowing. As the

first full decade of the 21st century closed, the legacy airlines had adopted many of the "no frills" standards of the LCCs, sometimes even exceeding the austere approach of the LCCs. In some instances, legacy airlines are now charging extra fees for services that have always been included in the stated airfare. There appears to be no limit to what services the airlines will charge for: checked bags, snacks, early boarding, seat selection, blankets and pillows, ticket change, unaccompanied minor, pets in the cabin, and water (Spirit Airlines). One short-lived idea was a fee for use of the on-board bathrooms (Ryanair).

The next transformative development in the air transportation industry will be the implementation of the NextGen policy (discussed at length in Chapter 35) now in the planning and earlier implementation stages in the Department of Transportation. Simply put, this complete transformation of the Air Traffic Control system from one of land-based navaids to a satellite-based navigation system, requiring on-board performance avionics and navigation capabilities, will likely drive new point-to-point operational models.

Endnotes

1. Source Air Transport Association—2014.
2. Kahn, Alfred E., The State of Competition in the Airline Industry, Statement before the U.S. House of Representatives Commission on the Judiciary, June 14, 2000.
3. Wall Street Journal, December 29–30, 2012.
4. A full-time equivalent is equal to two part-time employees.
5. The first three waves are suggested by Robert W. Poole, Jr. and Viggo Butler, "Airline Deregulation: The Unfinished Revolution," Reason Public Policy Institute.
6. Earlier in the decade, before the mergers of Delta and Northwest and United and Continental, Southwest was number two in size, measured by the number of passengers carried.
7. Miles, Richard B., Testimony before the Aviation Subcommittee, Committee on Transportation and Infrastructure, U.S. House of Representatives, Competition in the U.S. Aircraft Manufacturing Industry, June 26, 2001.
8. United Airlines, Northwest Airlines, Delta Airlines, and US Airways.

31 Deregulation and the Significance of Competition

If you were a traveler in the year 2000, 22 years after the airlines were deregulated, you would have been unable to fly nonstop between Springfield, Illinois and Washington, D.C. No airline in the country offered this service. Instead, you would be required to go through either Chicago or St. Louis. Your airfare would be about the same, $470 in that year, whether you went through O'Hare using United Airlines or through St. Louis using American. But say that for personal reasons you wanted to drive to your first stop of Chicago or St. Louis, and then take the same flight from that airport on to Washington. Your airfare from either Chicago or St. Louis to Washington would then be about $1,200, between two to three times as much, even though the distance to Washington is shorter by 178 miles through Chicago and by 86 miles through St. Louis. The reason is summed up in three words: Lack of Competition.

United competes with American for the Springfield traffic to Washington. Springfield passengers had a choice of almost equal proportions, in distance, convenience, and service. And the price is about the same for our Springfield traveler whether he goes through Chicago or St. Louis. At Chicago, however, United has little competition for the Chicago to Washington traffic. United has what is known as a "fortress hub" in Chicago. The same situation exists in St. Louis with American. The fares are, therefore, much higher, even though the distance traveled is less.

A Look Back at the Arguments for Deregulation

It is clear that many of the arguments made in support of deregulation were theoretical only; there was no practical or empirical basis in the airline industry for them. Airline markets since deregulation have not performed as expected. What happened?

First, predictions made before deregulation did not foresee the evolution of the hub and spoke system, a system that was adopted by every incumbent carrier. Point-to-point service as a primary marketing or operations strategy was maintained by only one major carrier, Southwest Airlines. The hub and spoke system has created major barriers to entry for the startup airlines.

Second, expectations that a simplified fare structure would be adopted, based on the assumption that startups with low operating costs would prevent the development or proliferation of complex fare structures, were not borne out. The computer reservation systems of the incumbent airlines, coupled with the captured market produced by the hub and spoke system, allowed the proliferation of yield management principles first introduced by American Airlines in the 1970s. The application of these principles had a significant impact on rate structures. The widening of the gap between the price of unrestricted full-fare tickets (purchased by the time-constrained or business passenger) and the price of the restricted low fares (purchased by the price-constrained, leisure class of passenger) has been due in large part to the workings of computerized yield management.

Third, it was predicted that there would be no "economies of scale" in a deregulated airline market. This expectation assumed that incumbent carriers would be unable to bring their size, their experience, their computer reservations systems, their borrowing power, their ownership of slots and gates, or the benefits of the unanticipated hub and spoke systems to create an advantage over smaller, startup airlines. The contrary, in fact, had been assumed, that the incumbent airlines would have difficulty in competing with the more efficient low-cost carriers that would emerge after deregulation. The lack of economies of scale argument had focused on the cost side of the equation, not on the revenue side. Experience has shown that there truly are few economies of scale on the cost side (e.g., costs of operation are not reduced because of economies of scale), but there are substantial economies of scale on the revenue side (e.g., the enhancement of revenues) due to the factors enumerated above. As a result, most of the startups that came into the market immediately after deregulation, not possessing these attributes, have vanished. With the exception of Southwest, most of the major airlines in operation after deregulation were the very same large airlines that existed before deregulation. More recently, certain low-cost carriers like JetBlue and AirTran have shown staying power utilizing the business model pioneered by Southwest Airlines.

The fact that the incumbent airlines were able to survive, and to expand, in spite of the lower costs of the smaller and more efficient startups, leads to the conclusion that there are economies of scale. Further, competitive responses of the incumbents to the entry of the startups in competing markets suggest the existence of anticompetitive practices by the incumbent lines, again possible because of the size and presence of the incumbent carriers. This leads to the next argument made for deregulation.

Fourth, it was said that airline markets were "contestable," that is, in a market where there are only relatively few participants to vie for and share the available market, low-cost carriers with low fares would necessarily cause the competing carriers to lower their fares. In actual practice, the market contestability theory has not proven out in the airline industry. Free entry into the market has been depressed by slot and gate scarcity. There has been an inequality of management acumen and operating experience. Costs associated with the beginning of operations are substantial, and they normally are not recovered in the short run. Predatory practices by the incumbent airlines are routine, resulting in fares being lowered on the incumbent airlines to match those charged by startups. These practices include increasing capacity on the routes flown by the new entrant and by the inauguration of new routes to compete with the new entrant. Marketing strategies, such as frequent flyer programs that grant advantages to the large, incumbent airlines, have also proven to be effective.

Deregulation was supposed to foster competition. Competition is what gives to the consumer the best possible deal in price and quality. Until recently, competition has been primarily the result of new airlines entering the market, as well as established airlines entering new markets. Freedom to compete since the industry was deregulated, however, has not been uniform, and competition has been stifled in many ways. We will now take a further look at how the promise of deregulation has been compromised.

Barriers to Entry— Limiting Competition

One of the biggest reasons for the failure of deregulation to meet its promise of widespread competition has been the existence of barriers to entry of new airlines. Some of the barriers to entry were identified by opponents to deregulation, but some were not anticipated. After some 20 years of actual experience in the deregulated environment, the Government Accounting Office and the Transportation Research Board released the results of studies on anticompetitive developments in the air carrier industry. These reports classified barriers to entry for new airlines as "operational barriers" and "marketing barriers."

Operational barriers include takeoff and landing slots at high-density airports, access to boarding gates, access to ticket counters, the availability of ground handling and airport apron facilities, baggage handling and storage facilities, and perimeter rules. Marketing barriers include strategies designed to bind travelers to a particular airline through frequent flyer programs and loyalty incentives, computer reservation systems, and code-sharing alliances.

Slots

Historically, arrivals and landings at U.S. airports have been on a "first-come, first-served" basis. In 1968, the increase in commercial air traffic at the nation's busiest airports caused the FAA to institute limitations on arrivals and departures under a regimen known as "High Density Rules"(HDR). This procedure capped the number of hourly arrivals and departures at five airports, Washington National (now Ronald Reagan National—DCA), O'Hare (ORD), and the three New York City area airports, Kennedy (JFK), LaGuardia (LGA), and Newark (EWR). This system of required reservations was implemented at that time by scheduling committees set up by the airlines themselves to allocate "slots" for arrival and departure operations. A "slot" is a reservation for an instrument flight takeoff or landing by an air carrier. A small number of slots were set aside for general aviation use.

During regulation, the slot system worked well since the number of air carriers, routes, and access to these airports were controlled by the CAB. With deregulation, however, new startup airlines appeared and established airlines sought out new markets for themselves, greatly increasing the demand for access to these airports. In 1985, DOT revised its rules and procedures to allow slots to be bought and sold by airlines.[1] Slots became a limited commodity, subject to being traded like a commodity. Under the buy/sell rule, DOT explicitly stated that slots were not carrier property and that DOT retains ownership of the slots, so that they can theoretically be withdrawn at any time, but DOT grandfathered all slot allocations to airlines holding them as of December 16, 1985. Under the buy/sell rule, slots have taken on the look of property rights and ownership that resides with the airlines. DOT retained about 5 percent of outstanding slots and, in early 1986, distributed these in a random lottery to airlines having few or no slots.

After 10 years, by the end of 1996, the General Accounting Office (GAO)[2] found that established (grandfathered) airlines had increased their total number of slots, while airlines that went into business after deregulation had lost slots. Slots held by startup airlines that went out of business were often acquired by lenders (banks and other financial institutions) since these slots had been pledged as collateral to the lenders. The lenders were then free to transfer ownership rights in the slots to the highest bidders, which were often the established airlines, although Southwest was able to gain access to LaGuardia by purchase of ATA slots out of bankruptcy court. Established airlines also acquired slots by absorbing startup airlines by merger or buyout.

By 1999, slots had become concentrated among incumbent carriers. The four largest carriers controlled 87 percent of all slots, and the largest six airlines controlled 98 percent of all slots.[3] Because the number of slots is limited, slots have become very expensive, even if they can be bought at all. This unforeseen development is a disincentive to competition.

As an alternative to sale, established airlines have leased slots to startup airlines. This procedure is anticompetitive, as well, since the established airlines often lease slots in order to avoid the "use or lose" rule, also known as the 80/20 rule, imposed by the FAA. This rule requires the airline to use the slot at least 80 percent of the time or the slot will revert to the FAA. When the established airlines do lease slots, they typically do so only on a short-term basis, from 30 to 90 days. Entrant airlines find it difficult to justify startup costs of new service at an airport with no guarantees of the right to continue to use slots, which are its only means of access to the airport and its market.

In 1994, by the FAA Authorization Act,[4] Congress authorized DOT to grant slot exemptions to new entrants where DOT found it to be in the public interest and based on "exceptional circumstances." Slot exemptions, unlike regular slots, could not be transferred. DOT interpreted this authorization narrowly and granted very few exemptions until GAO issued its 1996 report to Congress on the anticompetitive effect of the DOT's failure to grant slot exemptions. By 2000, DOT had amended its criteria such that, for example, slot exemptions at LaGuardia had been awarded to startup airlines Frontier, Spirit, Pro Air, AirTran, and American Trans Air. DOT also awarded 75 slot exemptions to startup JetBlue. Although major airlines continued to oppose it, the revised DOT practice of awarding slot exemptions stimulated competition at these airports.

In April 2000, Congress passed the Wendell H. Ford Aviation Investment and Reform Act for the 21st Century (AIR-21). AIR-21 mandated the phasing out of the slot rules at LaGuardia, JFK, and O'Hare. The effective date for the elimination of all slot restrictions at O'Hare was July 1, 2002, and at the New York airports, January 1, 2007.

Upon expiration of slot controls at O'Hare in 2002, resulting congestion during peak hours caused serious delays at that airport. In consultation with affected airlines, the FAA issued an order limiting scheduled operations at ORD. This order is under periodic review, and the arrangement in place is not viewed as a long-range solution to congestion nor a substitute for slots. The construction of a new runway (9L/27R) in 2008, however, provided significant relief to the problem of congestion since there are now seven primary runways. Pre-construction projections were that delays would be reduced by as much as 66 percent by this new runway.

This kind of renovation and reconfiguration is not an option at LGA (and possibly other HDR airports) due to physical land constraints. LGA is located eight miles from downtown Manhattan and bordered on three sides by water and by a multilane highway on the fourth side. It is, however, central to flight operations in the United States. One study showed that on one particular day, "some 376 flights traveling to 73 airports experienced flight delays because their aircraft had passed through LaGuardia at least once that day."[5] It is clear that delays at LGA are propagated throughout the National Airspace System on a daily basis.

In October 2004, DOT and FAA contracted with NEXTOR[6] a cooperative group of university departments named the "National Center of Excellence for Aviation Operations Research," to carry out research on the question of congestion management alternatives, centered on operations at LGA. The NEXTOR results were reported back to the FAA in 2005.

As the date approached for expiration of slot allocations for the New York airports, mandated by AIR-21 to take effect on January 1, 2007, it was clear to the FAA from prior experience that chaos would result if those expirations were allowed to go into effect as scheduled. On August 29, 2006 the FAA proposed new slot rules for the New York airports. Relying partly on NEXTOR study results, the proposed rules for LGA not only continued HDR caps, but also sought to impose minimum aircraft size requirements for much of the fleet, to limit the duration of slots (OAs),[7] and to employ market principles (probably auctions) for the reallocation of slots/OAs. Under this proposal the stage was set for the airlines to not only lose their implied property rights in the slots/OAs (and their value) but also to be told how large their aircraft must be if they were to service LGA.

The storm of protest was universal, and it came from every quarter, including the Port Authority of New York and New Jersey, the airlines, Congress, community groups concerned about losing service, and even the Canadian Embassy. Needless to say, this proposal would not fly. High Density Rules, therefore, remained in effect either partially or completely for the HDR airports in spite of the provisions for lifting those allocations as required by AIR-21. This was done under the escape clause in the Act that implementation of its provisions was subject to FAA discretion that placed safety in the National Air Space as a primary consideration under the Act.

In 2008, during the last year of the Bush administration, the FAA tried again to revise slot rules for the New York airports.[8] As to LaGuardia, the FAA proposed to initiate a detailed non-monetary "leasing" arrangement for a majority of slots with "historic" operators for 10 years, coupled with an annual auction of additional slots. While too detailed for discussion here, the plan was a first step, to be reviewed over the 10-year period and discussed by all stakeholders over that term. The proposal made two uncontestable points: (1) LGA required a cap on operations and (2) the allocation of available slots needed to be more

efficiently and fairly applied. But it also contained changes that the airlines were not ready to concede, including (1) that the FAA has authority to allocate slots in connection with its authority to determine the best use of the national airspace and (2) that the reallocation of slots by the FAA do not constitute a "taking" of property from the airlines in violation of the 5th Amendment.

This effort was met not only by objections, but also by lawsuits. In December 2008, a United States Court of Appeals entered a temporary stay order to the proposed rule pending further hearings on the effects of the rule. After the Obama Administration took over in 2009, Secretary of Transportation Ray LaHood unilaterally rescinded the entire congestion management plan incorporated in the proposed rule. At LGA, slot authorizations established in 2006 remain in effect. Temporary slot extensions continue to be made at JFK and EWR.

It is clear that the airlines are asserting ownership rights to slots in spite of the expressed reservation by the FAA at the time of their issuance that the FAA retained full authority over the allocation of all slots. This slot "property right" carries not only inherent value, but the right to make operating decisions incident to its use, like the size of aircraft the carrier wishes to use when filling the slot, where the airplane comes from when landing, and where it goes after takeoff. While the FAA has obviously not acquiesced in the airlines' position, it does appear that the FAA is not, at this point, willing to completely contest the issue—witness the withdrawal of the proposed rule to modify the HDR regimen on at least the two occasions in 2006 and 2009.

As this contest plays out new developments continue, and in the process maybe some insight is being offered on the question of ownership and control of slots. In 2011, Delta Airlines wanted to expand its presence and create a hub at LGA. At the same time, US Airways wanted to grow at DCA. The solution was a swap of slots between the two airlines; this was a deal that required DOT approval. Here is what happened: The DOT agreed to approve the Delta–US Airways proposal as long as the airlines agreed to give up and sell off, at auction, 8 daily slot pairs at DCA and 16 daily slot pairs at LGA, with the additional condition that bidders would be limited to airlines with less than 5 percent of the slots at either airport.

In November 2011, it was announced that JetBlue had submitted the winning bids for the eight LaGuardia slots (for $32 million) and for the eight Reagan National slots (for $40 million). The other eight LGA slots went to WestJet (for $17.6 million).

Several things are obvious here: Two new entrant airlines got bigger at two HDR airports; that is good for competition. The DOT forced two big airlines to divest slots to smaller airlines, asserting government control over slot allocation; that is good for competition. The two big airlines got a big payday for something (slots) that they did not pay for and the purchasing low-cost carriers had to pay that bill; assuming those costs are to be passed on to the traveling consumer, that is not good for competition.

While the FAA-supervised slot control issue affects only designated high-density airports,[9] congestion and delays are increasing throughout the National Airspace System. Because of this combination of issues, DOT and FAA have coined a new approach to the problem: congestion management.

"Congestion management" is a concept that encompasses a number of different policies designed to reduce congestion and delay. Among these policies are (1) the imposition of landing fees during peak hours; (2) the expansion of the airside (runway) environment of the airport; (3) reconfiguring runways and taxiways, especially to eliminate or minimize runway crossings; (4) incentives to airlines to use larger aircraft; and (5) the use of secondary and reliever airports.

The implementation of such a system will necessarily have to be the result of a cooperative effort among the DOT, the airlines, and the airports. Each of these entities has its own priorities and its own primary responsibilities. Revamping of the air traffic control system through NextGen, airport privatization or modification, and a workable revision of the slot allocation program will all be necessary.

■ Gates

When economic deregulation of the airlines was suddenly decreed by the federal government in 1978, America's commercial airports were poorly equipped or organized to service the new air transportation system. The relationship between the airlines and the airports they served was basically oriented toward airline control; airports were mostly junior partners that more or less accepted whatever the airlines dictated.

The decision to serve any particular airport, as well as the identity of the airline(s) to serve the airport, was in the first instance dictated by the CAB. When a community and its airport found itself fortunate enough to be designated by the CAB, it usually went out of its way to accommodate the airlines designated to serve it. This included the nature of contractual relationships between airports and airlines that governed gates, baggage areas, ticket counters, and ground support facilities. Both the airlines and the owners of the airports preferred reliable, long-term arrangements.

Exclusive, long-term gate leases restrict entry by new airlines at airports. A GAO survey in 1990,[10] 12 years after deregulation, revealed that at the 66 largest airports in the United States, 85 percent of their gates were leased to established airlines under long-term and exclusive-use arrangements. Most seriously affected were Charlotte–USAir, Cincinnati–Delta, Detroit–Northwest, Minneapolis–Northwest, Newark–Continental, and Pittsburgh–USAir. This greatly contributed to the creation of fortress hubs, one characteristic of which is the limiting or exclusion of competition from the market. In 1995, at all of these airports, with the exception of Newark, one carrier accounted for over 75 percent of all passenger enplanements.

New startups were often denied access to these airports, although incumbent airlines would sometimes sublease gates to entrant airlines. These arrangements often carried with them inequities to the new airline, such as being required to utilize the ground personnel of the lessor airline, usually at increased cost and diminished efficiency to the leasing airline. Occasionally, such subleases require that the entrant airline's aircraft be maintained by the lessor airline. Oftentimes, the duration of the sublease was also quite short.

Congress, in the year 2000, set about to correct some of these inequities in the Wendell H. Ford Aviation Investment and Reform Act for the 21st Century (AIR-21), to be further discussed in Chapter 33.

■ Perimeter Rules—LGA and DCA

In addition to the anticompetitive constraints of slot and gate access, at LaGuardia and at Ronald Reagan National, there is the additional constraint of perimeter rules. These restrictions prohibit nonstop flights of more than 1,500 miles into and out of LaGuardia[11] and nonstop flights of more than 1,250 miles into and out of Reagan National. The purpose of these rules was to promote the use of the new JFK and Dulles (IAD) airports as the long-haul airports for the area when they were built in the 1950s.

The effect of these rules is to restrict entry, particularly in the case of startup airlines with hubs outside of the established perimeter. Under these rules for instance, America West, the second-largest airline started after deregulation, was precluded from serving these two airports from its Phoenix, Arizona, base of operations.

At the same time, all seven of the largest, established airlines in the United States could easily serve these airports from one or more of their hubs.

By virtue of two federal statutes,[12] DOT was allowed to award 44 new slots to airlines at DCA, 24 of which could be used for flights to cities more than 1,250 miles away. These slots were awarded to airlines serving six cities (Denver, Las Vegas, Los Angeles, Phoenix, Salt Lake City, and Seattle). See Figure 31-1.

LaGuardia has one exemption to its perimeter rule—to and from Denver International.

The continuation of perimeter rule constraints, especially for LGA, has been roundly criticized as no longer necessary. Under these arguments, the protected airports (JFK and IAD) no longer need development, and the introduction of Stage 3 and Stage 4 aircraft into the fleet has reduced the airports' noise footprint for all types of jet aircraft such that the restriction on long-range jet aircraft is no longer necessary.

■ Marketing Strategies—Frequent Flyer Programs

Frequent flyer programs began in the early 1980s as a device to encourage customer loyalty and to entice frequent travelers to use a chosen airline to the exclusion of all other competing airlines. The customers who normally fly the most, and usually at the highest fares, are business travelers whose costs of travel are usually paid by their employers, or accounted for as a business expense. Frequent flyer awards are based on miles flown with the airline that go directly to the passenger, not the employer. So far these awards have not been considered taxable. Thus, the frequent flyer has a potential personal and financial incentive to continue to fly with the sponsoring airline, often paying its highest fares. A new entry into one of these markets, whether by a startup or by an established airline, is very difficult.

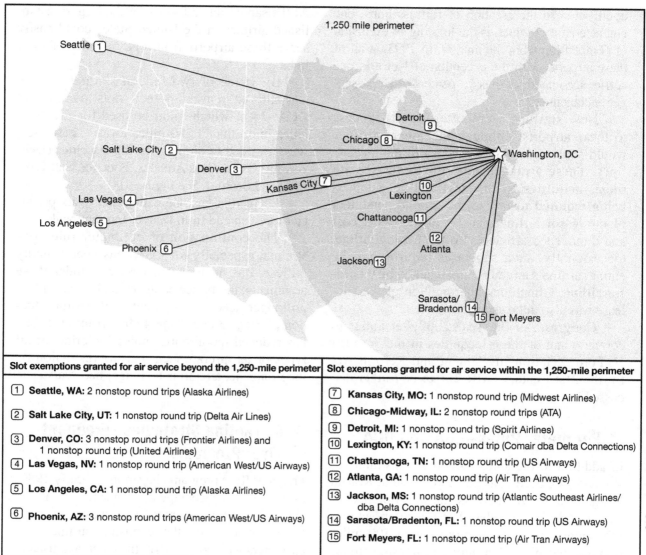

Slot exemptions granted for air service beyond the 1,250-mile perimeter

1 **Seattle, WA:** 2 nonstop round trips (Alaska Airlines)

2 **Salt Lake City, UT:** 1 nonstop round trip (Delta Air Lines)

3 **Denver, CO:** 3 nonstop round trips (Frontier Airlines) and 1 nonstop round trip (United Airlines)

4 **Las Vegas, NV:** 1 nonstop round trip (American West/US Airways)

5 **Los Angeles, CA:** 1 nonstop round trip (Alaska Airlines)

6 **Phoenix, AZ:** 3 nonstop round trips (American West/US Airways)

Slot exemptions granted for air service within the 1,250-mile perimeter

7 **Kansas City, MO:** 1 nonstop round trip (Midwest Airlines)

8 **Chicago-Midway, IL:** 2 nonstop round trips (ATA)

9 **Detroit, MI:** 1 nonstop round trip (Spirit Airlines)

10 **Lexington, KY:** 1 nonstop round trip (Comair dba Delta Connections)

11 **Chattanooga, TN:** 1 nonstop round trip (US Airways)

12 **Atlanta, GA:** 1 nonstop round trip (Air Tran Airways)

13 **Jackson, MS:** 1 nonstop round trip (Atlantic Southeast Airlines/ dba Delta Connections)

14 **Sarasota/Bradenton, FL:** 1 nonstop round trip (US Airways)

15 **Fort Meyers, FL:** 1 nonstop round trip (Air Tran Airways)

FIGURE 31-1 Summary of slot exemptions granted by DOT under AIR-21 and Vision 100 as of September 2006.

Marketing Strategies—Code Sharing

Code-sharing arrangements are devices used in advertising, sales, and reservations activities that allow originating airline designations to be carried through to connecting airlines' flight segments, including to the destination. These arrangements are often entered into between domestic and foreign airlines, or other end-to-end airlines, and between commuter carriers and major airlines. The first code-sharing arrangement was approved by the United States government in 1983, when antitrust immunity was given to Pan American to advertise origin and destination points on international routes that actually lay on domestic inland routes operated by northeastern U.S. regional carrier Empire Airlines, not Pan American. Empire Airlines became a feeder carrier to Pan Am, and was the first of many to come in the U.S. airline market.

Code sharing is also used to eliminate potential competitors from picking up an airline's customers at interchange points by reserving the customer's seat for his entire trip, and by issuing his through ticket, utilizing only the code-sharing partners' airlines. The code-sharing device is depicted in computer reservations systems in user-friendly ways that enhance the likelihood of selecting the code-sharing route from origin to destination. Often it is not readily apparent to the traveler that two or more separate airlines are involved in the itinerary.

“ British Airways believes that it is intrinsically deceptive for two carriers to share a designator code.”

—British Airways, comment on PDSR-85, Notice of Proposed Rulemaking, Docket 42199, 1984

▪ Marketing Strategies—Computer Reservation Systems

As we saw in Chapter 26, computer reservation systems were developed independently by United States airlines starting in the 1950s, beginning with American Airlines' SABRE, followed by United Airlines' APOLLO, TWA's PARS, Delta Airlines' DATAS II, and Eastern's System One. By 1988, these same five systems were in use in the United States and were also in common use by travel agents.

These proprietary systems had preferences built into them that favored the owning airline, created competitive disadvantages for airlines that did not possess these systems, and presented distorted options to travel agents. Travel agents typically used only one CRS, usually the one owned by the largest, closest airline to the travel agent's city, so that the travel agent naturally preferred that airline's offerings. The agent would also typically have an incentive contract with that airline. In 1984, the CAB adopted rules to insure fair competition among all airlines.

As computer reservation systems became diversified internationally, the CRS acronym yielded to the more accurate GDS, representing the "global distribution system." By the mid 1990s, U.S. airline owners had divested themselves of ownership in the domestic GDS systems, which by 2003 were dominated by SABRE (43 percent), Galileo (formerly APOLLO, 20 percent), and Worldspan (formerly PARS and DATAS II, 29 percent). These GDS companies accounted for 92 percent of all U.S. airline bookings.[13]

While U.S. airlines continue to use GDS booking services with accompanying fees, at the same time they began creating Internet applications, including their own websites, and the large airlines have also created their own travel technology companies, such as Orbitz. Southwest and some of the low-cost carriers do not participate in the global distribution system and rely instead on their own websites for information distribution, reservations, and ticket sales.

▪ The Internet

The appearance and growth of the Internet has generally contributed to a leveling of the competitive playing field in airline advertising and bookings, primarily because the consumer is the active, originating participant who searches out the desired information on the Internet. This access has been facilitated by the airlines revising their company access outlets to provide user-friendly websites available to travelers on a 24/7 basis right in their own home or office.

The aftermath of September 11, 2001 and the resulting economic downturn saw a significant increase in the use of the Internet by both business and leisure travellers for making travel arrangements directly with the airlines. This also had the effect of countering some of the incumbents' economies of scale and CRS/GDS advantages.

The Internet is also not a one-way street. It has provided consumers with a way to provide undesirable feedback, not only to the airlines, but also to the world of travelers out there. One example was the passenger who had his Taylor guitar trashed by some gorilla bag handlers at United in Chicago. When United apparently chose to ignore the problem, this guitar man wrote a very uncomplimentary description of the affair in a song entitled "United Breaks Guitars" and posted it on the Internet. At last count it had over 12 million hits.

Endnotes

1. FAR Amendment 93-49, 50 Fed. Reg. 52-180 (1985), 14 CFR pt 93.
2. General Accounting Office Report, *Airline Deregulation: Barriers to Entry Continue to Limit Competition in Several Key Domestic Markets* (Letter Report, GAO/RCED-97-4, October, 1996).
3. Dempsey, *Airport Monopolization: Barriers to Entry and Impediments to Competition*, Testimony before the United States House of Representatives, Committee on the Judiciary—Hearings on the State of Competition in the Airline Industry, June 14, 2000.
4. 49 USC sec. 41714.
5. Market-Based Alternatives for Managing Congestion at New York's LaGuardia Airport, Michael O. Ball, University of Maryland.
6. Nextor is a consortium of government, academic, and industry representatives dedicated to the advancement of aviation research and technology and is sponsored by the FAA. The eight universities associated with Nextor are George Mason University, Massachusetts Institute of Technology, University of California at Berkeley, University of Maryland at College Park, Virginia Polytechnic Institute and State University, Georgia Institute of Technology, Purdue University, and The Ohio State University
7. The FAA had determined that large carriers who control almost all slots at LGA are using the airport to serve their medium and large hubs, and that the average size aircraft operated into the airport has shrunk to 98 seats.
8. For a full discussion of the proposal applicable to LGA, see Congestion Management Rule for LaGuardia Airport, Docket No. FAA-2006-25709, RIN 2120-A170, April 16, 2008. The proposed rules were considered in two separate dockets, one for JFK and EWR, and one for LGA.
9. Long Beach, CA (LGB) and John Wayne Orange County (SNA) are slot-controlled under local airport authority.
10. General Accounting Office Report, *Airline Competition: Higher Fares and Reduced Competition at Concentrated Airports*, (GA)/RCED-90-102, July 1990.
11. The LGA perimeter rule was first established in the late 1950s under an informal arrangement between the Port Authority and the airlines. It was formalized in 1984 and unsuccessfully challenged in *Western Airlines v. Port Authority of New York and New Jersey*, 658 F. Supp. 952 (SDNY 1986), aff'd 817 F2d 222 (2nd Cir., 1987, cert. denied, 485 U.S. 1006 (1988).
12. AIR-21 in 2000 and Vision 100-Century of Aviation Reauthorization Act in 2003.
13. Europe-based GDS companies, like Amadeus, are not included in the discussion of domestic airline ownership.

32 Antitrust Enforcement after Deregulation

One of the recognized purposes of government is to protect the "public interest" under its constitutional authority to promote the general welfare. A full and complete definition of the term "public interest" has proven to be elusive. The concept of the public interest has, for example, been used to justify both the regulation of the airline industry and its later deregulation. It was invoked to justify the original restrictive regulation of the railroads in 1887 (The Interstate Commerce Act), and later used to justify financial assistance to the same railroads.

The nature of the activity deemed by society, or the government specifically, to be either in the public interest or against the public interest is often a function of the "times" or of the philosophy of the administration that happens to be currently in charge of running the government.

In this chapter we will look at how the government attempts to protect the "public interest," specifically in the air transportation industry. To do this we will have to review the history of Congressional legislation which makes it unlawful for the private sector or any business enterprise to prevent or limit competition. These laws are referred to generally as "antitrust" legislation, which is in the public interest because competition in the business sector is beneficial to the public, resulting in cheaper and more available products and services.

When this legislation was enacted by the Congress, the aviation industry did not exist. It was enacted primarily to curb abuses by the railroad industry during the late 19th and early 20th centuries. When the commercial airline industry came along, the courts had to decide whether or how the antitrust statutes would or should be applied to airline transportation.

Once Congress had enacted this type of legislation in the form of statutes, it fell to the executive branch of government to enforce the law. The executive branch does this through its departments and agencies. Jurisdiction over the airlines has bounced around in the executive branch of government, being first exercised by the Department of Commerce, then the agency known as the Civil Aeronautics Board. After deregulation of the airlines in 1978, jurisdiction swung between the newly formed Department of Transportation (DOT) and the Department of Justice (DOJ) and, finally, today, is shared by these two departments and their agencies.

The chronological sequence of statutory law and the agencies that have enforced that law are as follows:

1. The Sherman Antitrust Act
2. The Clayton Antitrust Act
3. The Department of Commerce and its agencies
4. The Civil Aeronautics Board
5. The Department of Transportation
6. The Department of Justice
7. A combination of DOT and DOJ

The Sherman Antitrust Act—Price Fixing and Trusts

Shortly after the appearance of large corporations in the late 19th century, particularly the railroads, it was deemed to be in the public interest to prevent concentrations of power that interfered with trade or reduced levels of economic competition. The Sherman Antitrust Act (1890) essentially prohibits any activity that:

1. Fixes prices
2. Limits industrial output
3. Allocates or shares markets
4. Excludes competition

This activity can be in the form of combinations of cartels, or agreements between corporations or individuals to accomplish any of these purposes. These combinations are often referred to as trusts. The second essential prohibition of the Act is to make illegal any attempt to monopolize any part of trade or commerce by any individual or corporation.

There is no "bright line" test as to what activity constitutes a violation of the Act, and it generally requires a court test and a judicial decision to settle the question of whether or not a specific activity is a violation of the Act. Perceived violations of the Act are enforceable by the Department of Justice through litigation in the federal courts.

The Clayton Antitrust Act—Mergers, Acquisitions, and Predation

In 1914, Congress supplemented the Sherman Act by passing the Clayton Antitrust Act, which prohibits:

1. Companies within the same field from having interlocking boards of directors (thus, essentially the same management)
2. Forms of price cutting (predatory pricing) or other pricing discrimination
3. Acquisition of stock or assets of one company by another if the acquisition tends to lessen competition or to create a monopoly

Enforcement is carried out jointly by the Department of Justice, Antitrust Division, and the Federal Trade Commission.

The Civil Aeronautics Act and the Department of Justice

When the airline companies first appeared during the 1920s and 1930s, it was rightly presumed that they were subject to the same antitrust laws as everybody else. The Department of Commerce had jurisdiction over the railroads and regulated that industry through its agency known as the Interstate Commerce Commission (ICC). When commercial aviation began, what little regulation there was of the airlines was also administered in the Department of Commerce, first by the Aeronautics Branch and then by the Bureau of Commerce and finally by the ICC.

In 1938, as commercial aviation expanded and became more important to the nation, the airlines came under the special legislation of the Civil Aeronautics Act, applicable only to the airlines, and that law was administered by the Civil Aeronautics Board (CAB). Although the Sherman and Clayton Acts did not specifically address the antitrust aspects of airline operation, the Federal Aviation Act of 1958 gave the CAB authority to approve all airline mergers and consolidations[1] and granted certain exceptions from the Sherman Act and other antitrust laws.[2] The broader question of whether, or to what extent, the airlines were subject to the Sherman and Clayton Acts was an open one until finally settled in 1963.

The Justice Department had long maintained that it had antitrust enforcement authority over the airlines, and the DOJ brought suit against Pan American and W. R. Grace & Co., as well as their jointly owned subsidiary, Pan American–Grace Airways (Panagra). In defense, the airlines contended that the Civil Aeronautics Board had exclusive authority over airlines, including antitrust matters, and that the Justice Department had no authority to bring the action. The lower federal court sided with the Justice Department, holding that Pan Am had violated the Sherman Act by combining with its subsidiary, Panagra, in agreeing not to parallel each other's South American routes, effectively agreeing not to compete. In *Pan American World Airways, Inc. v. United States*,[3] the Supreme Court reversed the lower court holding and established that the CAB had primary jurisdiction over the airlines in matters of "unfair practices" and "unfair methods of competition," as well as to consolidations, mergers, and acquisitions. This became established law and remained so until the CAB was legislated out of existence effective January 1, 1985, by the provisions of the Airline Deregulation Act of 1978.

Before deregulation, mergers of airlines were rare. The largest was United Airlines and Capital Airlines in 1961. The norm was represented by Delta's acquisition of Northeast in 1972 based on the "failing airlines" doctrine of the CAB. Simply stated, the "failing airlines" doctrine described the CAB practice that prevented any airline bankruptcies during regulation by "allowing, encouraging, and arranging" for stronger carriers to absorb weaker ones.

The Department of Justice and CAB—1978 to 1985

The Department of Transportation—1985 to 1988

During the first years after deregulation, and before 1985, antitrust jurisdiction was divided between the DOJ and the CAB. The DOJ prosecuted price-fixing violations of the Sherman Act and the CAB retained jurisdiction over mergers and acquisitions. When the sunset provisions of the ADA extinguished the authority of the CAB, jurisdiction over merger authority went to the Department of Transportation (in 1985). During this period, the DOJ function with respect to proposed mergers was limited to the submission of comments to the DOT. The DOJ agreed with many of the DOT positions on mergers and acquisitions. In 1986 alone, in fact, some 25 airlines were involved in 15 mergers.[4]

But the DOJ strongly opposed two mergers that the DOT approved, namely, the TWA acquisition of Ozark and the Northwest acquisition of Republic, both in 1986. The DOJ opposition was based on the fact that the merged carriers operated hubs at common airports, thus only they provided nonstop service to many city-pairs. With the mergers, all competition was lost.

The DOT approved the acquisitions rationalizing that the *threat* of entry into those markets by other carriers, who would be free to enter because of deregulation, would deter anticompetitive practices by the merged carriers. This thesis, known as the contestability theory, proved to be incorrect, and fare increases and service reductions followed the mergers.

The Department of Justice after 1988

The DOT's jurisdiction over mergers terminated effective December 31, 1988, and the DOJ then assumed sole responsibility for airline merger review. The DOJ now has primary authority in air carrier cases to enforce all antitrust laws. Although there were few merger proposals after 1988 (see Figure 32-1), it was clear that the days of merger accommodation were over. The Justice Department approach to antitrust activity was going to be very different from that of the Department of Transportation.

In 1998, when Northwest, then the fourth-largest carrier in the United States, proposed to acquire a controlling interest in Continental, then the fifth-largest air carrier, the DOJ opposed the action. The challenge of the DOJ was based on the fact that the two carriers are each other's most significant competitors (or only competitors) in nonstop service between cities where they maintain their hubs. In its complaint filed in federal court against the carriers, the DOJ asserted that the proposal would cause higher ticket prices and diminished service for millions of passengers. This proposed merger did not occur.

In 2000–2001, United proposed to acquire US Airways. The DOJ opened an investigation into the merger and concluded that it would be highly anticompetitive for a number of reasons. These carriers were the only competitors between the District of Columbia area and a number of cities; they were the most significant nonstop carriers in numerous hub-to-hub markets; only they connected several northeastern cities; and the merger would have lessened competition in several transatlantic markets. When the DOJ announced that it would sue to block the transaction, the airlines abandoned their merger plans.

Proposals that have been reviewed without adverse action by the DOJ include US Airways–America West (2005), Northwest–Delta (2008), and United–Continental (2010).

How Proposed Mergers and Acquisitions Are Reviewed

Carriers proposing to merge are required to provide notice to the DOJ and to the Federal Trade Commission (FTC). The DOJ reviews the

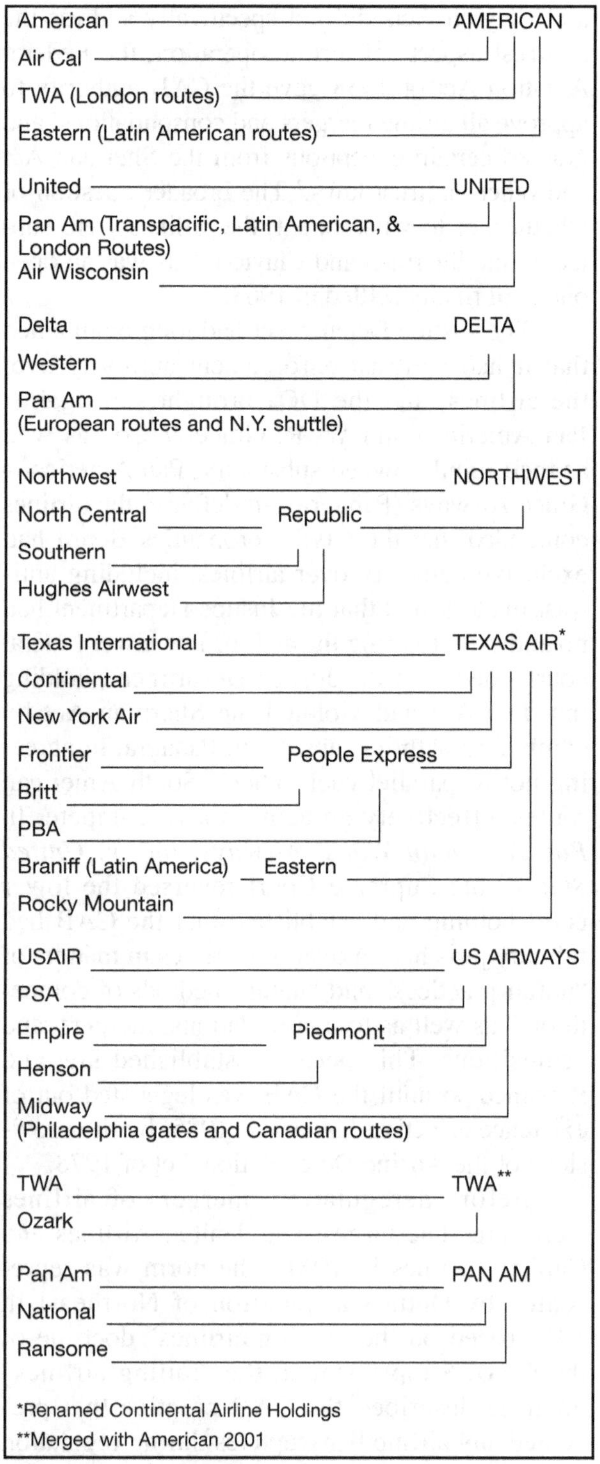

FIGURE 32-1 Historical major air carrier mergers, acquisitions, purchases, and consolidations through 2001. (Refer to Chapter 35 for an update of mergers and acquisitions.)

proposed merger plan, usually within a period of 30 days, and if no competitive issues are discerned by the DOJ, the parties are free to proceed. In some cases, the DOJ may issue its request for additional information, which prevents further action toward merger by the carriers for another 20 days. Often, concerns of the DOJ are addressed in this manner and any issues are resolved without formal action. Other times, litigation is required to resolve the issues.

The DOJ normally applies the provisions of Section 7 of the Clayton Antitrust Act, which prohibits the acquisition of stock or assets "where in any line of commerce or in any activity affecting commerce in any section of the country, the effect of such acquisition may be substantially to lessen competition, or to tend to create a monopoly." The statute provides the means for the proposed action to be prevented or delayed while the objections of the government are heard. The procedure reflects the fact that, once a merger process has begun or has been completed, it is very difficult to undo. Delay or prevention of the proposed merger activity is accomplished by the filing of a complaint in federal court and the seeking of a temporary restraining order or injunction to prohibit the airlines from proceeding with the proposed action.

The authority of the DOJ extends to instances involving the acquisition of relatively minor assets of one carrier by another, as in the case of gates or slots at airports. In 1989, for example, the DOJ moved to block Eastern's proposal to sell gates to USAir at Philadelphia International Airport, and again in 1991 when Eastern sought to sell slots and gates to United at Reagan Washington National Airport.

Finally, the DOJ has authority, jointly with the DOT, over airline acquisition of international route authority and mergers between domestic and foreign carriers. The DOT, in turn, works with the Department of State, which has final authority in dealing with foreign governments. The DOJ may challenge these proposals in the same manner as in domestic acquisitions.

The Department of Transportation after 1988

Even though the DOJ now has primary authority over domestic airline mergers and acquisitions, the DOT retains jurisdiction to regulate and investigate some aspects of domestic airline operations, including carrier fitness, ownership, and advertising. The DOT also has express authority to prohibit unfair and deceptive practices and unfair methods of competition. Section 411 of the Federal Aviation Act, recodified as 49 U.S.C. 41712, provides:

" [The] Secretary may investigate and decide whether an air carrier . . . has been or is engaged in an unfair or deceptive practice or an unfair method of competition in air transportation . . . If the Secretary, after notice and an opportunity for hearing, finds that an air carrier . . . is engaged in an unfair or deceptive practice or unfair method of competition, the Secretary shall order the air carrier . . . to stop the practice or method. "

DOT takes the position that it is authorized to prohibit conduct that does not amount to an actual violation of the antitrust laws, but is such that it could be considered anticompetitive under antitrust principles.[5] DOT also has authority to approve or immunize from U.S. antitrust laws cooperative agreements between domestic carriers and foreign carriers relating to international routes.[6]

Predatory Practices and Anticompetitive Responses of Airlines

A government study begun in 1990[7] found that the hub and spoke system, adopted by all major airlines after deregulation, resulted in airlines charging premium prices to local passengers originating from dominated hubs. But it also found that low-cost point-to-point service, such as that developed by Southwest Airlines, provided an effective counter to local hub and spoke market power. Further, DOT concluded that the rapid growth of Southwest and the entry into the market of other low-cost carriers appeared to be correcting the lack of price competition at hubs. Thus, governmental action was not warranted.

By 1995, nearly 40 percent of domestic passengers flew from hubs with low-fare competition, causing some major carriers to emulate the low-cost point-to-point carriers by forming their own low-cost divisions, like Delta Express, United Shuttle, and Metrojet. In 1998, the DOT concluded that the competitive stimulus supplied by new-entrant carriers had decreased, and that the number of new-entrant carriers had significantly declined. The reason, according to DOT, was because of anticompetitive activity on the part of some major airlines.[8]

Predatory activity by incumbent airlines historically has occurred when other airlines, usually smaller discount airlines, attempted to enter a market already served by the incumbent airline. The incumbent airlines may respond to this new competition by fare cuts, capacity increases by adding aircraft, or capacity increases by adding routes. The purpose of the response is to maintain market power and to diminish or eliminate competition. Since the cornerstone of a successful air transport system under deregulation depends on fair competition among the participating air carriers, predatory activity is harmful to the success of the system and to the ultimate interest of the consumer. Maintaining competition requires the assurance that carriers can enter new markets fairly.

It has been argued that the competitive responses of major hub carriers differ depending on which airline is supplying the competition. Major carriers' responses as to each other reflect a "live and let live" approach, that is, there is an implicit recognition that relatively equal financial strength and market power provide a control mechanism that allows a peaceful coexistence to be maintained in the competitive process.

The competitive response to new entrant airlines, however, is territorial and aggressive, including matching and even undercutting the smaller carrier's low-cost fares and adding capacity on the routes of the interloper. Historical examples may include United versus Frontier, American versus Vanguard, Delta versus (the former) ValuJet, Northwest versus Sprint and Reno, and Continental versus Kiwi.

In 1998, the DOT said:

❝ DOT believes that the responses of some large, established major carriers at their hub cities to service by small, new-entrant airlines have inhibited competition, resulting in higher prices for many passengers and preventing a large sector of air travel demand from being efficiently served. These responses, which protect major carriers' ability to charge higher prices in local hub markets, involve temporarily selling such large numbers of seats at low fares, comparable to new-entrant fares, that by sacrificing profits in the short term, they force the new-entrant carriers to exit from the local market❞ .[9]

Once the low-cost carrier had been forced out of the market, it was common practice for the incumbent airline to set its fares at least as high as they had been prior to the incursion by the new-entrant airline. It is believed that these anticompetitive practices against low-fare entrants caused new entries to virtually cease, beginning in the middle 1990s.

Having concluded that predatory activity by the incumbent airlines was, indeed, reducing competition, the DOT in 1998[10] announced its new enforcement policy directed at curbing predatory activities by the major air carriers. DOT policy regards an incumbent's competitive response to a new entry to be anticompetitive and predatory where it initiates fare cuts or capacity increases on the routes served by the new entrant, and where the incumbent's tactics appear to be economically rational only if they force the new entrant to exit the market or reduce service.

Since 2001, however, incumbent airlines have struggled financially. Bankruptcies and mergers of incumbent carriers have been the rule while, at the same time, a new breed of low-cost carrier has entered the market. Low-cost carriers have increased market share significantly, from 5 percent in the 1990s to around 30 percent currently. Incumbents have gone from trying to drive new carriers out of business to attempting to copy their way of doing business. As a result, anticompetitive practices have markedly declined.

Anticompetitive Practices at Airports

In Chapter 31, we discussed barriers to entry and how slot and gate ownership can have the effect of limiting competition. In Chapter 33, Airports and Deregulation, we will talk about how the operation of airports can also have anticompetitive results. The DOT has been concerned with all of these activities to the extent to which airlines participate in them. But the DOT is also concerned with anticompetitive practices by the airport owners and operators themselves.

As we will see in Chapter 33, DOT oversight of anticompetitive practices by airport owners was practically nonexistent until 2001. With the passage of the Wendell H. Ford Aviation Investment and Reform Act for the 21st Century (AIR-21), the DOT was given an important tool to use in monitoring and preventing these practices. In order to participate in federal monies, airport owners and operators must now submit for DOT approval "Competition Plans" designed to insure that gate availability is equitably provided. Under this program, the DOT can also monitor and, to some extent, control other anticompetitive and unfair practices associated with gate use, such as subleases, equipment leases, ground aircraft maintenance, and aircraft service agreements.

Endnotes

1. 49 USC sec. 1378.
2. 49 USC sec. 1384.
3. 371 U.S. 296 (1963).
4. Dempsey, Antitrust Law and Policy in Transportation: Monopoly Is the Name of the Game, 21 *Ga. L. Rev.* 505 (1987).
5. *See Pan American World Airways v. United States*, 371 U.S. 296, 306–308 (1963), and *United States v. CAB.* 766 F.2d 1107 (7th Cir. 1985).
6. See 49 U.S.C. sections 41308-41309.
7. GAO, Airline Competition: Higher Fares and Reduced Competition at Concentrated Airports, GAO/RECD-90-102; July 1990.
8. U.S. Department of Transportation, Statement of Enforcement Policy Regarding Unfair Exclusionary Conduct (Docket No. OST-98-3713, Notice 98-16) April 1998.
9. Ibid.
10. Ibid. This study was followed up by DOT in 2001, see: U.S. Department of Transportation, Enforcement Policy Regarding Unfair Exclusionary Conduct in the Air Transportation Industry (Docket ST-98-3713) January 17, 2001.

33   Airports and Deregulation

Throughout the period of Civil Aeronautics Board regulation of air carrier routes and rates, airports competed with each other for the limited amount of traffic that was available. Traffic was limited not only because CAB policy restricted the number of available routes, but also because it mandated high airfares. During the 1950s, 1960s, and most of the 1970s, airports maintained marketing departments whose functions included lobbying the airlines and the CAB for service.

After deregulation, the passenger counts flowing through the airports of the United States increased by a factor of three over those in 1978, with an all-time high of over 726 million in 2007.[1] The problem was no longer one of how to secure more service; rather it was one of how to service the existing, and increasing, traffic.

Commercial-service airports were suddenly faced with the need for more gates and runways (airside expansion) and for more groundside support facilities (parking, restaurants, rental car counters, ticket counters, and shops). Methods of funding for renovation and expansion had to be addressed anew. The developing operational practice of the airlines known as hub and spoke, with its concentration of passenger arrivals and departures all at the same time, put severe pressure on airport operations. Control of existing gates had to be reevaluated in view of the increasing number of airlines requiring access to the limited number of available gates. Environmental concerns, both from increased aircraft operations and from ground traffic to and from the airports, brought additional pressures on airport management practices.

The commercial air service industry consists of three essential components:

1. Air carriers
2. Air traffic control (ATC)
3. Airports

While all three of these components must combine to function in an orderly and cohesive manner, the provisions of the Airline Deregulation Act directly controlled only the air carriers. In other words, only the air carrier portion of this combination had been deregulated. The federal government is solely responsible for the operation of the ATC system, and it is significantly involved in the operation of airports. Airports operate under a matrix of federal regulations, and commercial-service airports are all owned by local, regional, or state governments or their political subdivisions. While deregulation had unleashed the power and innovative potential of

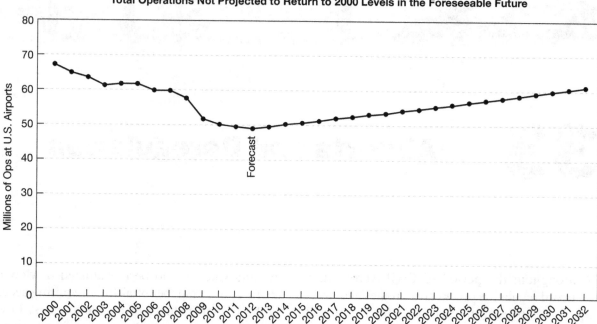

FIGURE 33-1   FAA forecasts suggest breathing room for airports.

Source: FAA Forecast Table 32 (http://www.faa.gov/about/office_org/headquarters_offices/apl/aviation_forecasts/aerospace_forecasts/
2012–2032/))

private enterprise in air carrier operations, the inherent limitations of government control in the ATC and airport sectors still overlay, and constrain, that potential. We will review how these factors have impacted modern airport operations.

■ Airport Ownership

The United States has the largest, most extensive airport system in the world. There are some 19,700 airports in the United States, ranging from world-class international airports to grass strips. Most of these airports are small, private fields, but 5,300 of these are for public use. Of these, 3,356 are designated as part of the National Airport System (NAS). NAS airports are entitled to federal aid, and they are categorized by the FAA as follows:

Commercial Service Airports (503 airports) are publicly owned airports that have at least 2,500 passenger boardings each calendar year and receive scheduled passenger service. Of these:

382 are **primary** airports designated as large, medium, small, or nonhub, with more than 10,000 passenger boardings per year; and

121 **nonprimary** airports with between 2,500 and 9,999 passenger boardings per year

Reliever Airports (269 airports) are designated by the FAA to relieve congestion at Commercial Service Airports and to provide improved general aviation access.

General Aviation Airports (2,560 airports) comprise the remaining airports including privately owned, public use airports that enplane more than 2,500 passengers annually and receive scheduled airline service.

All of these airports are included in the FAA's National Plan of Integrated Airport Systems.

	Thousands of passengers				
	Total enplanements	**Large hubs**	**Medium hubs**	**Small hubs**	**Nonhubs**
2004	668,648	467,082	126,898	52,787	21,881
2005	701,088	483,869	140,896	53,115	23,208
2006	703,517	487,176	140,614	53,047	22,680
2007	726,373	501,736	144,888	57,247	22,502
2008	697,100	478,700	142,096	54,303	22,001
2009	662,966	461,020	126,650	54,910	20,386
2010	328,239	229,309	60,375	28,330	10,225

NOTES: 2010 data are through September. Data are for all scheduled and nonscheduled (chartered) service by large certificated U.S. air carriers at all domestic airports served within the 50 states, the District of Columbia, and other U.S. areas designated by the Federal Aviation Administration (FAA). Not all scheduled service is actually performed.

Since 2007 air traffic hubs are designated as geographical areas based on the percentage of total passengers enplaned in the area. Under this designation, a hub may have more than one airport in it. (This definition of hub should not be confused with the definition used by the airlines in describing their "hub-and-spoke" route structures). Individual communities fall into four hub classifications as determined by each community's percentage of total enplaned revenue passengers in all services and all operations of U.S. certificated route carriers within the 50 states, the District of Columbia, and other U.S. areas. For 2004–2006, hub designation is based on passenger boardings at individual airports as designated by the FAA. Classifications are based on the percentage of total enplaned revenue passengers for each year according to the following: Large = 1 percent or more, Medium = 0.25 to 0.9999 percent, Small = 0.05 to 0.249 percent, Nonhub = less than 0.05.

SOURCE: U.S. Department of Transportation, Research and Innovative Technology Administration, Bureau of Transportation Statistics, Office of Airline Information, *Airport Activity Statistics Database (Form 41 Schedule T-3)*, special tabulation, October 2010.

TABLE 33-1 Domestic enplanements at U.S. airports: 2004–2010.

A limited number of these airports have contracted out some of their operations to private, commercial management, primarily at medium hub airports.[2] Airports are further classified by the FAA on the basis of percentages:

- Large hub airports (at least 1.0 percent of total national enplanements)
- Medium hub airports (less than 1.0 percent but more than .25 percent of total national enplanements)
- Small hub airports (less than .25 percent but more than .05 percent of total national enplanements)
- Non-hub airports

Even though commercial airports are mostly publicly owned, private enterprise plays a significant role in their operation. Private companies provide 90 percent of the employees who work at these airports, or work for the airlines themselves, or concessionaires and contractors.

Airport Funding for Operations and Capital Improvements

Each airport is operated under a master plan, the primary purpose of which is to provide safe and efficient air carrier service and to enhance airport capacity. Capital improvements include construction of new facilities or renovations of existing facilities. Sources of funding include:

- Airport Revenue Bonds
- The Airport Improvement Program (AIP)
- Airport user charges
- Passenger Facility Charges (PFCs)
- State and local funding programs

Airport Revenue Bonds

Bonds are the primary means of financing airport capital development projects. Bonds are debt instruments (like I.O.U.s) issued by the airport owner to raise the money necessary for new

Operations (Takeoffs + Landings)		(Thousands)	Passengers (Arriving + Departing)		(Thousands)	Cargo Metric Tons1 (Loaded + Unloaded)		(Thousands)
1	Atlanta (ATL)	980	1	Atlanta (ATL)	85,907	1	Memphis (MEM)	3,599
2	Chicago (ORD)	972	2	Chicago (ORD)	76,510	2	Anchorage (ANC)	2,554
3	Dallas/Fort Worth (DFW)	712	3	Los Angeles (LAX)	61,489	3	Los Angeles (LAX)	1,938
4	Los Angeles (LAX)	651	4	Dallas/Fort Worth (DFW)	59,176	4	Louisville (SDF)	1,815
5	Las Vegas (LAS)	605	5	Las Vegas (LAS)	43,990	5	Miami (MIA)	1,755
6	Houston (IAH)	563	6	Denver (DEN)	43,388	6	New York (JFK)	1,661
7	Denver (DEN)	561	7	New York (JFK)	41,885	7	Chicago (ORD)	1,546
8	Phoenix (PHX)	555	8	Phoenix (PHX)	41,214	8	Indianapolis(IND)	985
9	Philadelphia (PHL)	536	9	Houston (IAH)	39,685	9	Newark (EWR)	950
10	Minneapolis/St. Paul (MSP)	532	10	Minneapolis/St. Paul (MSP)	37,604	10	Atlanta (ATL)	768

TABLE 33-2   Top 10 U.S. airports—2005.

Source: Adapted from Airports Council International-North America (www.aci-na.org)

FIGURE 33-2 Airport activity statistics of certificated air carriers.

Source: U.S. Dept. of Transportation.

LEGEND

Large Hubs 29
Medium Hubs 31
Small Hubs 56

311

construction or renovations. These bonds are tax-exempt and are known as General Airport Revenue Bonds (GARBs). Some GARBs have maturity dates of 30 years or more and since 1982 they have comprised more than 95 percent of all airport debt.

A secondary source of revenue is derived from bonds known as Special Facility Bonds. These bonds are secured directly by the owner of the facility, such as a fixed base operation or aircraft maintenance facility, and the owner of the facility is usually responsible for paying off the principal amount of the bond and all interest charges.

Airport Improvement Program Funds (AIP)[3]

AIP funds are federal monies (derived from taxes and fees specifically collected for that purpose) administered by the FAA. These include a domestic ticket tax and flight segment fees on domestic flights, an international arrival and departure tax, a domestic tax on air freight, and a per gallon fuel tax on aviation fuels. The FAA distributes more than $3.8 billion annually out of AIP funds to airports. Airport owners and sponsors provide a minimum of 10 percent share in any project funded by AIP grants.

Airport User Charges

Airport user charges are either (1) aeronautical user charges or (2) nonaeronautical user charges.

1. Aeronautical user charges include landing fees, apron, gate-use or parking fees, fuel-flow fees, and terminal charges for rent or use of ticket counters, baggage claim areas, administrative support quarters, hangars, and cargo buildings.

2. Nonaeronautical user charges include rentals to terminal concessionaires, automobile parking, rental car fees, and rents and utilities for hotel, gas station, and related facilities.

Passenger Facility Charges (PFCs)

In 1990, Congress authorized airports to charge a per-passenger enplanement fee to be used for the financing of airport capital improvements and the expansion and repair of airport infrastructure. These are called Passenger Facility Charges (PFCs) and they are collected by the airlines as a part of the ticket price for the benefit of airports. As of 2012, the PFC program allows the collection of $4.50 for every boarded passenger at commercial service airports.[4] These funds may be used for three specific purposes: (1) to

All 74 S&P-Rated U.S. Airports have Investment-Grade Credit

Rating	Number of Airports	Name of Airport
AA	3	LAX, OKC, ORD
AA–	11	BOS, DCA/IAD, EWR/JFK/LGA, HOU/IAH, LAS, MSP, OMA, PDX, PHX, SEA, SNA
A+	18	ABQ, ATL, BUR, CLT, CMH, DEN, DFW, ELP, FLL, GEG, MCI, MCO, PHL, SAN, SAT, SDF, SFO, TPA
A	11	BDL, CHS, CLE, COS, CVG, DAY, DSM, GSO, LIT, MEM, MIA, MSY, MYR, ONT, RSW, SJC, STL, TYS
A–	18	AUS, BNA, BWI, DTW, HNL, IND, JAX, MDW, OAK, PBI, SMF
BBB+	8	ALB, GRR, MHT, PIT, PVD, PWM, TUL, VPS
BBB	4	FAT, GUM, MOB, PNS
BBB–	1	CRP

FIGURE 33-3 U.S. airports remain financially sound.

Source: "FAA Funding reductions could ground some U.S. Airport Projects," Standard & Poor's (April 5, 2012)

Allocation of Passenger Facility Charges (PFC) Funds Approved by FAA for Collection as of October 1, 2012

Airside	Landside	Noise Abatement	Access
runways	terminal	land acquisition	roads
taxiways	security	soundproofing	rail
aprons		monitoring	land
equipment		planning	planning
planning lighting			

Interest	Denver International Airport
payments on outstanding debt for eligible capital improvements	payoff of 1990s construction

FIGURE 33-4 Passenger Facility Charges (PFC).

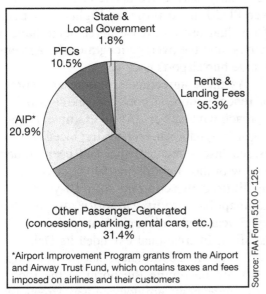

Source: FAA Form 510 0-125.

*Airport Improvement Program grants from the Airport and Airway Trust Fund, which contains taxes and fees imposed on airlines and their customers

FIGURE 33-5 98% of airport revenue comes from airport users. (U.S. Airport Sources of Revenue, 2001.)

of all airport capital investment in the United States. PFC funds are used for airside projects; terminal area projects; interest costs on airport bonds; access projects such as roadways, people movers, or transit projects; and noise mitigation projects. They have been used specifically for new runway construction and new gate construction, but they are not permitted to be used for parking garages, terminal concession areas, or areas leased by a specific airline for more than five years.

State and Local Government Programs

State and local funding is most often used as matching funds in order to receive federal support, although direct funding of maintenance projects is sometimes provided. During the 1990s, state and local funds accounted for 7 percent to 11 percent of airport capital development expenditures.

Funding of Annual Airport Operating Costs and Expenses

Most commercial service airports are self-sustaining[5] due to the receipt of rents, passenger and shipper expenditures, and business users. Entities doing business at airports as

preserve or enhance safety, security, or capacity; (2) to reduce noise or mitigate noise impacts; and (3) to enhance air carrier competition.

Over $84 billion in airport capital improvements have been made using PFC monies through September 2012. This amounts to over 30 percent concessionaires, such as car rental companies, restaurants, book stores, clothing outlets, and airlines pay rents for the space they occupy and also usually pay a gross receipts tax on the total income they receive from their business at the airport.

■ Airport Facilities Use Arrangements

Use of airport facilities, buildings, and land is normally arranged under use and lease agreements between the airport management and the user. Most of these agreements are between the airport owner and the airlines. These agreements generally fall into three separate categories: residual, compensatory, and hybrid agreements. In addition, the airlines normally pay landing fees based on the gross weight of the landing aircraft.

Residual Use and Lease Agreements

Under this type of agreement, which is more typically found in airport operating practices before deregulation, airlines agree to assume the financial risk of running the airport. Airlines guarantee that the airport will not lose money by agreeing to make up the difference between total cost of operations and the total of non-airline revenue received by the airport.

These types of agreements originated during the period of regulation when traffic volumes were low and the airlines were much more powerful than after deregulation. The trade-off an airport makes when entering into this kind of agreement is two-fold:

1. The airport gives up the opportunity to make any profit in its operations since any surpluses are credited to the airlines.

2. The airport gives up the right to make autonomous decisions over capital expenditure programs because of provisions in the agreements, called "majority-in-interest" (MII) clauses.

These MII clauses allow the airline to approve or disapprove, or at least delay, specific capital projects, the costs of which would be included in the future charges to the airline.

Some of these capital projects (like construction of new gates) could benefit new entrant airlines into the airport, which would be adverse to the interests of the signatory airline. The right to disapprove the project, of course, is anticompetitive, so that the airline has been placed in a position of unfair advantage over its would-be competitor. These clauses are also against the public interest in having better, bigger, and more efficient airport facilities for use by passengers. MII clauses, however, do not give the airline approval authority over projects funded by AIP, PFCs, or special facility bonds, and airlines are legally barred from exercising veto rights over PFC-funded projects. Eighty-four percent of residual use and lease agreements have MII clauses, and the average length of the agreement at large hub airports is 28 years.

As these agreements mature and come up for renegotiation, airports are taking a different approach with carriers. As an example, Dallas/Ft. Worth International recently replaced a 35-year residual use agreement that had been signed in 1974 with the "hybrid" model (discussed below) and limited the contract to a 10-year period. Indianapolis Airport Authority also reached a new 5-year deal with some of its airlines. Atlanta Hartsfield International extended its Delta leases for 7 years in 2010. These shorter-term agreements are becoming the norm in the industry. These agreements are not one-way streets favoring the airport, however, as negotiations include various concessions to the airlines in some areas, including reduced landing fees.

Compensatory Use and Lease Agreements

Under these types of agreements, which are progressively in use at more modern and successful airports, the airline pays only for the facilities and services actually used. The airport assumes the responsibility for meeting the costs of operation like any other owner. One survey reported that 20 percent of these types of agreements have MII clauses. Compensatory agreements, without MII clauses, allow the airport full latitude in the use of its funds and allow the incentive to add additional services in the interest of the public and the airport instead of the interests of the incumbent airlines at the airport.

Hybrid Use and Lease Agreements

These agreements typically exclude nonaeronautical uses (restaurants, rental car operations, etc.) from the residual pool, so that an airline's guarantee is limited to the cost of aeronautical operations only. The airport retains earned revenues from its nonaeronautical operations while being guaranteed a break-even on airfield activities. Seventy-four percent of these agreements contain MII clauses, the average length of which is 20 years. While these agreements are anticompetitive with respect to capital improvement and expansion projects, they do give the airport the incentive to expand its nonaeronautical sources of income.

▪ Gate Leasing Arrangements

Airport gates obviously are a finite commodity and an essential element of both airline service and competition in the airline industry. In combination with overriding use agreements, or as separate undertakings with airlines, airports have normally utilized three methods of allocating gate use to airlines serving that airport:

1. Exclusive-use contracts
2. Preferential-use contracts
3. Airport controlled gates

Exclusive-Use Arrangements

Exclusive-use arrangements typically assign to one airline the right to use and occupy gates and facilities for a specified duration, as well as the right to sublet or assign those gates and facilities conditioned on prior consent of the airport. These types of arrangements are recognized to constitute potential barriers to entry based on complaints by new entrant carriers that incumbent airlines hoard gates, require substantial sublease premiums, offer access at less preferable times, force the new entrant to use the incumbent's ground personnel, or refuse to sublease altogether. These arrangements also have the effect of hindering airport management from properly exercising its legislative mandate of providing equal, nondiscriminatory access to its federally funded facilities. Moreover, since gate leases are considered assets in law, secured creditors of bankrupt carriers, like banks, can wind up possessing the proprietary rights to airport gates, and preventing recovery and use of those gates by airport management.

The prevalence of exclusive use gates has been in consistent decline since 1968, and because of the effects of deregulation on airport traffic, that decline has accelerated. U.S. airports increasingly now prefer to maintain more control over gate access. This trend has been buttressed by the Wendell H. Ford Aviation Investment and Reform Act (AIR-21) that requires some airports to submit for approval "competition plans" to the FAA, more fully discussed below.

Preferential-Use Arrangements

Preferential-use arrangements normally give the tenant airline the primary right to use the facility only when it has operations scheduled. These arrangements constitute a shared control between the airport and the airline with an explicit contractual right remaining in the airport authority to allow use of the gate by other airlines. Importantly, this type of arrangement preserves the airports' ability to honor the legislative mandate of providing nondiscriminatory access to its facilities and to use the tenant's gates for new entrants.

Preferential-use agreements differ in their specifics, some containing "use-it-or-share-it" or "use-it-or-lose-it" requirements, as well as other types of recapture provisions. These types of gate arrangements have become more prevalent at large hub airports, increasing from 28 percent in 1992 to around 50 percent in 2004. For example, Reagan Washington National has reported a gate composition of all preferential-use gates, and Boston Logan has converted to all preferential-use gates or common-use gates. By 2005, Detroit Metropolitan Airport, with 16 carriers and 114 jet gates, had converted to all preferential-use gates, with the exception of 2 common-use gates.

Airport-Controlled or Common-Use Arrangements

Airport-controlled or common-use arrangements are completely under the control of the airport authority. The airport may assign gate and facility usage on a temporary, per-turn basis or for a short-term duration. These types of arrangements have been popular in Europe and other foreign regions for some time. The concept has gained popularity to the point that it has acquired the acronym C.U.T.E., or Common Use Terminal Equipment, to describe what is being increasingly seen as the best way for an airport to organize its gates and check-in counter facilities.

The International Air Transport Association (IATA) has even issued a recommendation (No. 1797) favoring common-use systems as a means of efficient and cooperative use of available terminal facilities worldwide.

Various proprietary contractors have developed expertise in assisting airports in setting up these common-use arrangements so that, rather than being blocked off, the available facilities can be distributed as needed to different airlines. These facilities include check-in counters, gates, holding rooms, and electronic equipment. The systems control and integrate all components necessary to the carrier, including computers, displays, and boarding pass printers and readers.

Two airports have all airport-controlled gates—Miami International with 121 gates and Phoenix Sky Harbor with 84.

DOT Interest in Airport Practices—Unfair Competition

Prior to 2001, the Department of Transportation's authority over the gate practices of commercial-service airports was severely limited.[6] While the DOT had jurisdiction over the gate practices of airlines, constitutional principles prevented interference in policies and practices of state-owned airports.

With the passage of the Wendell H. Ford Aviation Investment and Reform Act for 21st Century (AIR-21) in 2001, the DOT was given authority to require certain large and medium hub airports to submit competition plans as a condition of receiving federal grant monies and as a condition for authority to impose PFCs at their airports. These airports (including those at which competition among the airlines was threatened by airline domination, gate control, and other anti-competitive practices) were required to provide the DOT detailed information concerning their gate practices. The DOT has used its authority to approve or disapprove these competition plans as a means to insure that gate practices at those airports are fair. This includes insuring broader access to gates by new entrant airlines.

Airline gate practices continue to be monitored by the DOT to insure that airline control of gates does not unduly impede competition. This authority can compel an airline to surrender control of airport gates, or prevent tying arrangements involving subleases by one airline to another, where, for example, the lease requires the use of the lessor airlines' ground forces by the lessee airline. So too may the DOT apply its authority to situations where an airline, with market power, exercises its contractual rights under a MII clause to block the construction of facilities for competitors merely to maintain its own monopoly power.

Privatization of the Air Traffic Service Industry[7]

It would be fair to say that the promise of economic deregulation of the airlines has been compromised by continued government operation and control of the remaining two components of the air service industry: airports and air traffic control. Airports are virtually all owned by state and local governments or their subdivisions. Air traffic control is operated by the Federal Aviation Administration. Knowledgeable people are asking, "Would the system function at a higher service level if these other two branches of the air service system were also to be economically deregulated?"

■ Airports and Air Traffic Control— A Brief History

Airports

Federal subsidization of airports has a long history, as we have seen earlier in this book. Airports began in the early days of commercial aviation as local, municipal, state, and even private (Burbank Airport in California) operations. Federal financial participation began as part of the Works Projects Administration and other relief organizations in the 1930s (notably at LaGuardia Airport). After World War II, Congress dived into the airport business with the passage of the Federal Airport Act of 1946 and, while that was a relatively small effort, with it began the acceptance of the principle that airports were the primary responsibility of the federal taxpayer.

The federal government also has a long history of levying taxes on the air service industry, beginning with the placing of an excise tax on aviation fuels in 1932 and an excise tax on passenger airline tickets in 1941. These revenues were deposited in the General Fund, but in 1970, on the creation of the Airport and Airway Trust Fund (discussed above), revenues received from

various sources by the federal government were dedicated to be used for federal aid to airports and for air traffic control and other FAA purposes.

The Federal Aviation Administration is responsible today for the administration of these revenues, which currently amount to some $12 billion annually. Trust fund revenues paid for almost 80 percent of the FAA's $16.4 billion 2011 budget. The General Fund is still on the hook for the remaining 20 percent.

Airport authorities and their lobbying organizations have attempted to have Congress raise the PFC amount that airlines can charge each passenger, asserting that inflation has eroded the value of the PFC money received by them for airport upgrades, among other things. They have also offered to forego the AIP funds in return for being able to set their own PFC rates. The Congress passed the 2012 FAA Reauthorization Act, however, without raising the amount that airports may charge under the PFC program and without disturbing the distribution rationale of the AIP program. This may leave a shortfall in airport funding programs for airport improvement projects going forward. Environmental concerns have brought additional pressures on airport management practices and funding requirements.

The international community is well out in front of the United States on this issue. Over 32 of the largest 100 foreign airports are now fully or partly privatized, including Athens, Auckland, Brussels, Buenos Aires, Copenhagen, Dusseldorf, Frankfurt, Johannesburg, London, Melbourne, Naples, Rome, Sydney, and Vienna. Others are in the process of privatization, including Hong Kong and Tokyo. Most of these airports are operated under a lease of the entire airport facility to a private operator on a long-term basis, usually 30 years or more. The governmental owner of the airport normally retains ownership of the land and airport facilities. The privatization process was begun, of all places, in England with the 1987 privatization of the British Airports Authority, which owns Heathrow and other airports.

Government-owned and managed airports are characterized as risk-averse, passive, and non-innovative. Privatized airports are more willing to take new risks, like expansion of facilities and gates. The lack of gates is cited as one of the constraints on new entrant airlines, which is a competitive disincentive. As we have seen, long-term leases with incumbent airlines allow a large degree of control to be lodged with those airlines, another competitive disincentive. Oxford University has conducted recent research into airport management strategies and found that the management approach at privatized airports is significantly more "passenger-friendly" than at government-operated airports.

There are currently some 100 companies worldwide that own or operate airports, finance the privatization of airports, or participate in the design, financing, building, and operation of airports and terminals at airports.

The U.S. federal statutory regimen governing airports is a significant disincentive to privatizing airports. Under federal law, airport authorities that have received them must repay federal grants previously received if the airport is sold and, if it is sold, the FAA has said that all monies received in payment for the airport itself must in turn be used for "airport purposes," rather than placed into the local government's general fund to be used for other governmental purposes. The other possibility is to lease the airport grounds and facilities, retain title to the airport, and contract out the use of the airport to a qualified operator. These considerations led to the new statute discussed below.

There has been a quiet movement in the United States to convince Congress that privatization of the airports is in the ultimate interest of travelers and taxpayers. In 1996, Congress passed the 1996 Airport Privatization Pilot Program,[8] which created five "pilot program slots" that allow up to five airports (but only one large hub airport) to enter into a privatization test program. This program releases airport owners from the restrictions mentioned above and thus makes feasible the privatization of airports. The law, however, makes mandatory that the airport must secure at least 65 percent approval (by landing weight) from the airlines using the airport.

Progress under this statute has been slow. In fact, the only successful privatization under this program was concluded by Stewart International Airport, located north of New York City, by entering into a 99-year lease with a subsidiary of the British-owned National Express Group. This arrangement lasted only one year when the lease was terminated in 2007 by mutual consent and the operation of the airport was taken over by the New York and New Jersey Port Authority, which is not eligible under the privatization statute. This terminated the only successful privatization effort in the U.S. to date.

Applications were made by several other airports. Some of these applications have been withdrawn, while others are going forward, as indicated below. The following airports have made applications: Gwinnett County Briscoe Field in Georgia (application withdrawn June 2012), New Orleans International Airport (application withdrawn October 2012), Luis Muñoz Marin International Airport, San Juan, P.R. (application approved December 2009, Aerostar Airport Holdings selected as operator, July 2012, pending FAA approval, docket number FAA-2009-1144), Hendry County Airglades Airport in Clewiston, FL (application approved October 2012, negotiations ongoing with private operator, docket number FAA-2008-1168), and Niagara Falls International Airport (application withdrawn 2001).

By far the largest airport that has begun the privatization process is Midway Airport in Chicago. This effort has been ongoing for many years and at least one arrangement with a private operator collapsed because of the lack of funding by the City of Chicago. As of July 13, 2012, the City has awarded a new five-year $53.6 million contract for the airport's operation, but that is subject to FAA approval, so the process continues (docket number FAA-2006-25867).

Box 33-1 The Major Components of the Wendell H. Ford Aviation Investment and Reform Act

1. Safety
   a. Increases FAA facilities and equipment budget by almost 50 percent for ATC system modernization
   b. Increases funds for runways and airport equipment
   c. Provides funding for FAA hiring and retention of controllers and inspectors
   d. Makes runway incursion prevention devices eligible for AIP funding

2. Competition
   a. Funding for new terminals, gates, and taxiways
   b. Abolishes slots at O'Hare in 2002; modified by FAA in 2004
   c. Abolishes slots at LaGuardia and Kennedy in 2007
   d. Creates 24 new slots at Reagan National, 12 of which are to be used for flights within the 1,250-mile perimeter and 12 to be used outside of the perimeter
   e. Requires certain large and medium hub airports to submit a competition plan

3. Environment
   a. Increases funding for noise abatement
   b. Establishes guidelines for air tours over national parks

4. Small Communities
   a. Increases funding for non-hub airports
   b. Guarantees funding for general aviation airports
   c. Doubles the small airport fund
   d. Creates an incentive program to help airlines buy regional jets to be used to serve small airports
   e. Creates a new funding program to assist small airports in promoting their air services

5. Large Airports
   a. Doubles the amount of annual passenger funding for primary airports (those with 10,000 or more passengers per year)
   b. Raises the cap on annual funding for large airports from $22 million to $26 million
   c. Doubles the funding for cargo airports
   d. Raises the cap on Passenger Facility Charges (PFC) by $1.50 (to $4.50) to facilitate airport improvements that cannot be funded through the Airport Improvement Plan (AIP). PFCs can only be used to fund airport projects that increase safety and competition or are used for noise abatement

6. FAA Reforms
   a. Creates an oversight board (similar to IRS reform legislation)
   b. Makes changes in FAA management structure to ensure spending integrity
   c. Creates a management board to oversee the ATC modernization program (the DOT is to consult with Congress in board appointments)

Privatization of terminals, as opposed to the entire airport, is a likely continuing trend as Southwest plans its new terminal at Midway and Terminal 4 at JFK continues to be operated by the Dutch Schiphol Group, which also manages Amsterdam's Schiphol Airport, under contract with the New York and New Jersey Port Authority. Delta is expanding Terminal 4 to accommodate all of its international flights in a new $900 million undertaking.

As a part of the FAA Reauthorization Act of 2012, the Airport Privatization Pilot Act was expanded to allow up to 10 slots for the program, an increase from the original 5 slots. Under the privatization act, commercial service airports may only be leased out to operators, but general aviation airports may be sold. Privatization under this program has been nil to slow.

The only existing privately operated and privately owned commercial service airport in the United States was built in 2009 as Branson Airport by a group of investors known as Branson Airport LLC. The airport is located near Branson, Missouri, with the closest commercial service airport 50 miles away near Springfield, MO. Its largest carrier is Air Tran (Southwest is merging its operations with those of Air Tran and has announced that it will take over operations on March 9, 2013), with additional service being offered by Frontier and ExpressJet. One unusual aspect to the private ownership of the airport is that the airport is free to grant exclusive route authority to just one airline. The operators have said that they do not want "suicide fares," with two or three airlines bashing each other until one or more gives up and stops service. This should be interesting to watch.

Air Traffic Control

The commercialization of air traffic control is a much more difficult subject to broach than is the privatization of airports. The world leader in private aviation is the United States, and the United States remains the chief training venue in the world for both U.S. and foreign civilian pilots, with its training facilities, cheaper aviation fuel, good weather, and vast territory. The very large civilian private pilot population of the United States and its chief lobbying representative, the Aircraft Owners and Pilots Association, along with general aviation business aircraft operators and their organization, the National Business Aircraft Association, are dedicated to keeping the skies over America basically free from government-based user charges (other than aviation fuel taxes and landing fees at some airports). The airlines are on the other side of this issue, advocating the inclusion of general aviation aircraft in a regimen based on usage. A system of user charges has historically been utilized in any commercialization of ATC services. The question of commercialization of ATC services, therefore, becomes a very real political issue.

The fact remains that in the United States the FAA, like airports, is a governmental-funded undertaking. The FAA budget in the United States for the fiscal year 2011 was somewhere around $16.4 billion. Of that total, $9.7 million went to "operations," which includes $7.6 billion for air traffic control operations, $1.3 billion for safety regulation and certification, $3.3 billion for capital investments in ATC facilities, equipment, and research (which presumably includes NextGen expenditures) and the rest for grants to state and local governments for airport investments.

According to the Government Accounting Office consistently over the years, the FAA has also been criticized as not being set up to effectively manage the development of large projects, resulting in delays and cost overruns on major technology developments and their implementation. The Advanced Automation System project, for instance, was begun in the early 1980s at a projected cost of $2.5 million to be completed in 1996. By 1994, project costs were estimated to be $7.6 billion and the project was seven years behind schedule. A study by the DOT's Office of Inspector General in 2005 reviewed 16 other major ATC projects and found that the combined costs had gone from $8.9 billion to $14.5 billion.[9] Many of the same concerns are heard about FAA management acumen and procedures as the NextGen overhaul proceeds. The question occurs whether private enterprise could do the job better.

While there is no doubt that commercialization of ATC services is a global trend, the question remains whether it is the right answer for the United States. The commercialization of ATC services has been an expanding phenomenon elsewhere in the world since 1972. By 2005, at least 40 countries had fundamentally restructured their ATC systems. All of these countries have shifted from a tax-funded base to direct user fees. In a 2009 article based on a study comparing 10 commercialized ATC systems with the FAA ATC system,[10] the author concludes that the commercialized systems improved service quality, modernized workplace technologies, maintained or improved safety, and reduced costs. The study also concludes that other risks of commercialization, such as erosion of accountability to government, deterioration of labor relations, or worsened relationships between civil and military air traffic controllers, did not materialize.

The study includes analyses of air navigation systems of Australia, Canada, France, Germany, Ireland, the Netherlands, New Zealand, South Africa, Switzerland, and the United Kingdom, contrasting those with the FAA system in the United States. Among the advantages of reforming their air navigation systems as compared to the FAA system were the still lingering problems in the FAA of failing to take advantage of off-the-shelf solutions to problems, overdevelopment, duplicate procurement systems, political interference that resulted in building unneeded facilities, inability to apply business principles, overly bureaucratic and inefficient approval processes, and little client input to help establish priorities.

The labor record at the FAA has also been a problem impacting costs. From the period of the 1960s, some degree of labor unrest has been seen. In 1969, members of the controllers' PATCO union began the strategy of isolated "sick ins," and in 1970 some 3000 controllers took part in an organized "sick in" causing extensive disruption in the nation's air traffic system. These strategies continued through the 1970s, and culminated with the PATCO strike in 1981, discussed in Chapter 29.

Today, FAA employees involved in operations number some 43,000, who are paid a total of $6.5 billion in wages and benefits, or about $151,000 per employee. Controllers, as a group, have compensation packages of about $166,000 each, per year. Labor accounts for two-thirds of the cost of FAA operations.[11]

■ Wendell H. Ford Aviation Investment and Reform Act for the 21st Century (AIR-21)

On April 5, 2000, the far-ranging Wendell H. Ford Aviation Investment and Reform Act for the 21st Century became law. This statute, designed to alleviate many of the intransigent problems faced by the aviation infrastructure arising from deregulation, increased funding for civil aviation in the United States by $10 billion over levels current at the time of its passage. The majority of the increased funding was earmarked for airport construction and improvement and for radar modernization. The major components of the law, broken out into the general categories that are affected, are outlined in the box on page 315.

For the first time, as a result of AIR-21, large and medium hub airports are required to submit Competition Plans to the FAA as a condition of receiving PFCs at those airports. These requirements are designed to assure a competitive environment for all airlines, including gate use monitoring, gate sublease oversight, and procedures for assignment of gates.

When the Deregulation Act was passed in 1978, most airports had in place legally enforceable gate and lease contacts with the airlines that reflected the economic realities of rules imposed by the CAB. Under these rules, as discussed above, airports were happy to have the airlines serving their airports, and the existing contracts reflected this disparity in negotiating position. As we have seen, the beneficial provisions in these contracts to incumbent airlines translated into anticompetitive barriers to new entrant carriers. With the anticompetition provisions in AIR-21, and with the expiration of these pre-deregulation contracts, all airlines, including new entrants, will have a more level playing field.

Aerotropolis—The Evolution of the 21st Century Airport City

Traditionally, airports have been viewed as nuisances and environmental threats that are tolerated in order to accomplish travel purposes and shipping necessities. This thinking has essentially shut down new airport building in the United States and Europe. But a new concept has been articulated for the future: it is called the Aerotropolis.

Coined by John D. Kasarda, Kenan Distinguished Professor of Strategy and Entrepreneurship at the University of North Carolina Business School, it is a concept that is already being built in other parts of the world, like Dubai, Seoul-Inchon, and Hong Kong. The concept describes the creation of airport-linked commercial facilities concentrically arranged around air gateways, and consisting of time-sensitive manufacturing and distribution facilities, hotel, entertainment, retail, convention, trade and exhibition complexes, offices that house professionals and executives, and even permanent dwellings.

While the perfect aerotropolis can only be constructed at newly or recently built facilities, utilizing urban planning and strategic infrastructure, the concept can be approximated at existing airports by urban planners adapting expressway links, express trains, and the addition of special truck lanes to connect airports to major regional business and residential concentrations. While it is without question that aerotopolises will develop around existing major airports, the question is whether they will form in an intelligent manner, minimizing logistical and environmental problems so as to maximize the concept's benefits to the airport, its users, businesses, and surrounding communities.

These results will not come about using current airport area planning and development. A new, synergistic approach is necessary to produce a more economically efficient and aesthetically pleasing business and social community. Kasarda, in his book, *Aerotropolis: The Way We'll Live Next*,[12] suggests that failure to adapt to these coming certainties will spell doom for older cities. This is true, in part, due to the fact that the global network will make communities more relevant to their distant trading and business partners than to their own locale.

Even today airport terminals are evolving into luxurious shopping malls and artistic and recreational areas. Appealing to the volume of business and recreational travelers, airports have gone from offering magazine and newspaper shops to upscale restaurants, brand-name boutiques, cultural attractions, and high-end retail.

The concept is catching on faster in other parts of the world. Hong Kong International has 30 designer clothing shops. Singapore Changi presents theaters, saunas, and a tropical butterfly forest. Frankfurt has the world's largest airport medical clinic, seeing over 36,000 patients annually.

Large airport terminals can boast 85 million passengers passing through annually, while even large shopping malls see only 8 to 12 million people flowing through. On the landside areas of the airport, developers are adding hotel, office, conference and exhibition centers, and facilities for processing time-sensitive products to be shipped from the airport. Nonaeronautical activities at Dallas, Atlanta, Hong Kong, and Schiphol provide some two-thirds of total airport revenues.

Forward-looking airports are changing their management approaches to include the establishment of commercial and real estate divisions to develop landside areas and to promote development beyond airport boundaries.

Asia is leading the world in airport city and aerotropolis development. One reason this is true is that government bodies control the development process and the financing without social or severely restrictive environmental barriers. Hong Kong International, a 2,700-acre site created from two islands and by dredging the bay bottom, and South Korea's Inchon Airport, a 15,000-acre complex set 42 miles from Seoul, are examples. With room to expand landside development, and with high-speed rail connecting the aerotropolis to nearby cities, these may become the paradigm for the future.

In India, the Delhi International Airport spans 5,000 acres and is being developed with a hospitality and retail district composed of a 5-star hotel, premium apartment hotels, condo hotels, office and retail space, and a pedestrian arcade with a metro station surrounded by hotels, offices, and retail shops.

In this new world, businesses will be drawn to developing aerotropolises as multimodal transportation and advanced communications infrastructure are installed. Accessibility to global markets will drive this development, and that will depend on access to the airport and, through the airport, access to those markets.

One intriguing option that has yet to be tried, or even mentioned, is whether the constitutional eminent domain powers of municipalities, states, the federal government, and in some cases the airport authority itself, may not become a way to clear areas adjacent to existing airports by condemnation to facilitate the concepts mentioned here.

Endnotes

1. There has been a downturn in passenger enplanements since 2007 ascribed to the global recession beginning in 2008.
2. U.S. Department of Transportation, FAA/OST Task Force, Airport Business Practices and Their Impact on Airline Competition, October 1999.
3. See pg. 214 for the history of the Airport Improvement Program.
4. PFCs were raised from $3.00 to $4.50 under AIR-21 in the year 2000.
5. With the exception of some small airports that receive subsidies from local governments.
6. This was because of long-standing constitutional principles which limited federal interference with the rights of the states and their subdivisions, as confirmed by the United States Supreme Court case of *Parker v. Brown*, 317 U.S. 341 (1943).
7. Parts of this section are based on the research and writings of Robert Poole, The Reason Institute, and the Cato Institute, with appreciation.
8. Title 49 United States Code section 47134.
9. OIG report discussed in Reuters, "Cost Increases, Delays Cited in FAA Programs," *Washington Post* June 1, 2005, p. A17.
10. McDougall, "Commercializing Air Traffic Control: Have the Reforms Worked?", Legal Studies research Paper Series, Research Paper 09-11, Suffolk University Law School, February 17, 2009.
11. Budget of U.S. Government, Fiscal Year 2011, Appendix—Government Printing Office, 2010—p. 936.
12. Farrar, Straus, and Giroux, New York, 2011.

34 Airports and the Environment

As a result of the industrialization of society and the growth of heavy industry during the late 19th and early 20th centuries, pollution of air and water became a significant by-product of progress. Until the 1950s, prevailing wisdom held that such pollution was the inevitable price of such progress.

Visible air pollution was seen from stationary sources like manufacturing plants and factories and in "smog" accumulations in places like the Los Angeles Air Basin due to automobile emissions. Industrial and municipality discharges into waterways caused widespread prohibitions against swimming and fishing due to health risks. Catastrophes like the Cuyahoga River fire (the river caught fire) and the Love Canal scandal (toxic waste seepage caused a declaration of a federal emergency) were high-profile examples of pollution. When jet transport aircraft were introduced into the air carrier fleet in 1958, the dense, black exhaust emissions created on takeoff at ground level and during climbout were vivid evidence of yet another encroachment on air quality levels.

Prior acceptance of pollution as an inevitable by-product of progress has now been roundly rejected. Current environmental policy is concerned with almost all aspects of the quality of life on earth. In this chapter we will briefly review the evolution of current policy generally, and we will look at how current policy has attempted to address the specific environmental impacts of aviation.

■ The Air Pollution Act and the Clean Air Act

The first attempt by Congress to address the problem of air pollution generally came in the Air Pollution Act of 1955.[1] Subsequent efforts to strengthen controls on pollution occurred in amendments beginning in 1963 in the Clean Air Act, which was amended almost yearly until 1970. That year proved to be a watershed year for environmentalists, with the passage of the Clean Air Act of 1970 (an amendment to the 1963 Act),[2] which created the Environmental Protection Agency as an independent agency reporting directly to the president. Its broad authority is over control of pollution, noise, and radiation.

Although the Clean Air Act mandates a national policy, the statute gives state and local governments primary responsibility for regulation of pollution from power plants, factories, and

0

other stationary sources. The EPA retains primary responsibility for "mobile source" pollution.

The EPA is required to consult with the FAA on any standards sought by the EPA to be made applicable to aircraft engine emissions. The EPA is prohibited by the terms of the Clean Air Act from changing aircraft emission standards if such a change would significantly increase noise or adversely affect safety. The FAA is charged with enforcing EPA standards through FAA regulations.

The EPA coordinates its aircraft engine emission regulation authority with the International Civil Aviation Organization, created by the Chicago Convention in 1944, due to its role to develop international civil aviation in a "safe and orderly manner." ICAO's responsibilities include developing aircraft technical and operating standards and recommending practices. The United States is currently one of 191 participating member States of ICAO. One of the founding principles of ICAO was to create a high degree of uniformity between nations in the interest of global harmonization. Moreover, any participating member may ban the use of aircraft within its airspace that does not meet ICAO standards. EPA standards do not apply to military aircraft.

ICAO's Committee on Aviation Environmental Protection (CAEP) is responsible for the technical work in the environmental field. CAEP is composed of various work groups from many countries who do the technical research and propose solutions and standards. The FAA represents the United States in this committee. This procedure and practice for creating binding U.S. regulatory law has been judicially upheld in *The National Association of Clean Air Agencies v. EPA*, 489 F. 3d 1221 (D.C. Cir. 2007).

The approach taken by the EPA and by ICAO is to regulate nitrogen oxides produced in combustion (and some other pollutants) primarily by imposing standards for new engine designs. The imposition of emissions standards for new engine designs is a complex and cautious undertaking in view of the many other considerations inherent in engine manufacture, such as fuel

efficiency, safety, and cost. The ICAO standards are found in Annex 16, Environmental Protection, Volume II, "Aircraft Engine Emissions."

Aviation Impacts

Aviation activities impact the environment primarily in two ways: (1) engine-generated emissions into the air and (2) noise. Noise legislation has been addressed by the Congress in separate, specific legislation, and we will discuss those statutes later in this chapter. Engine emissions result from both aircraft operations and airport ground operations and are regulated by the EPA under its "mobile source" pollution authority.

The history of EPA regulation of aircraft engine emissions is long-standing:

1974—for engine smoke (revised several times over the years since) and fuel venting;

1984—for hydrocarbon emissions;

1997—for nitrous oxides and carbon monoxide;

2005—for additional nitrous oxides emissions standards;

2012—for additional nitrous oxides emissions standards.

Emissions Generated from Aviation-Related Combustion Processes

Carbon Monoxide (CO) is produced due to the incomplete combustion of the carbon in fuel;

Particulate Matter (PM) consists of small solid or liquid particles that form as a result of incomplete combustion, and are small enough to be inhaled;

Sulfur Oxides (SOx) are produced when small quantities of sulfur, present in essentially all hydrocarbon fuels, combine with oxygen from the air during combustion;

Hydrocarbons (HC) are emitted due to incomplete fuel combustion. They are also referred to as volatile organic compounds (VOCs);

Nitrogen Oxides (NOx) are produced when air passes through high temperature/high pressure combustion and nitrogen and oxygen present in the air combine to form NOx;

Carbon Dioxide (CO_2) is the product of incomplete combustion of hydrocarbon fuels like gasoline, jet fuel, and diesel. Carbon in fuel combines with oxygen in the air to produce CO_2;

Water Vapor (H_2O) is the other product of incomplete combustion as hydrogen in the fuel combines with oxygen in the air to produce H_2O.

Volatile organic compounds (VOCs) are naturally occurring chemical compounds given off by plants and animals, including humans. Some are harmless, some toxic, and others dangerous to human health when combined with other compounds. VOCs are ubiquitous, their concentrations are low, and symptoms they produce are slow to develop. They are regulated by many agencies, especially indoors, and they are characterized by their low boiling point and volatility.

Ozone (O_3) is not emitted directly into the air but is formed by the reaction of VOCs and NOx in the presence of heat and sunlight. Ozone forms readily in the atmosphere and is the primary constituent of smog.

Since 1985, aggregate emissions of the air pollutants the EPA regulates (nitrogen dioxide, ozone, sulfur dioxide, particulate matter, carbon monoxide, and lead) have declined by 25 percent nationally.

Success in reducing particulate matter (PM) in the exhaust of jet engines was realized fairly early. This was due in part to the fact that this type of emission was the most noticeable and a solution was, therefore, quickly sought. In addition, jet-engine-produced black smoke consists of fine carbon particles, partially burned fuel, and raw fuel. These PMs contain carcinogen content and descend to earth, creating health hazards. The reduction of exhaust smoke was accomplished by developing a more complete combustion process whereby the hydrocarbons in jet fuel are converted to carbon dioxide and water. Figure 34-1 shows the decline in air-quality pollutants since 1980. Aircraft emissions have also declined over time but increases in pollution from air traffic are likely to occur as aviation itself increases.

Take off and landing operations produce the highest rates of PMs and NOx. Nitrogen oxides are a primary contributor to the formation of ozone, which is the most significant air pollutant in urban areas and which is a greenhouse gas in the upper atmosphere. Paradoxically, as innovative jet engine designs have produced more power while using less fuel and with lower carbon monoxide emissions, NOx emissions have increased due to their higher operating temperatures. This also accounts for the comparatively high regulatory concern at the EPA

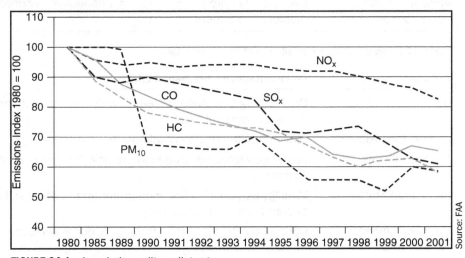

FIGURE 34-1 Local air-quality pollutants.

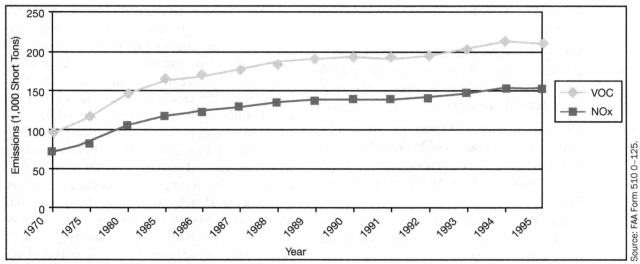

Source: FAA Form 510 0–125.

FIGURE 34-2 U.S. aircraft emission trends, 1970–1995.

Pollutant	Representative Health Effects
Ozone	Lung function impairment, effects on exercise performance, increased airway responsiveness, increased susceptibility to respiratory infection, increased hospital admissions and emergency room visits, and pulmonary inflammation, lung structure damage
Carbon Monoxide	Cardiovascular effects, especially in those persons with heart conditions (e.g., decreased time to onset of exercise-induced angina)
Nitrogen Oxides	Lung irritation and lower resistance to respiratory infections
Particulate Matter	Premature mortality, aggravation of respiratory and cardiovascular disease, changes in lung function and increased respiratory symptoms, changes to lung tissues and structure, and altered respiratory defense mechanisms
Volatile Organic Compounds	Eye and respiratory tract irritation, headaches, dizziness, visual disorders, and memory impairment

TABLE 34-1 Representative health effects of air pollutants.

Pollutant	Representative Environmental Effects
Ozone	Crop damage, damage to trees and decreased resistance to disease for both crops and other plants
Carbon Monoxide	Similar health effects on animals as on humans
Nitrogen Oxides	Acid rain, visibility degradation, particle formation, contribution toward ozone formation
Particulate Matter	Visibility degradation and monument and building soiling, safety effects for aircraft from reduced visibility
Volatile Organic Compounds	Contribution toward ozone formation, odors and some direct effect on buildings and plants

TABLE 34-2 Representative environmental effects of air pollutants.

over NOx in recent years, as shown above. See Figure 34-3 for comparatively high measures of NOx. Since essentially all NOx comes from combustion processes, electric utilities, manufacturing plants and factories, and transportation companies make up the largest share of such emissions. Still, the aviation sector contributes only 0.4 percent of total emissions, which is a miniscule part of the whole. See Figure 34-4 for a graphic comparison of different transportation sources of NOx.

Aircraft idle and taxi operations produce the highest rates of VOCs and carbon monoxide. Ground-operated support equipment is mostly powered by gasoline or diesel engines, which produce VOCs, carbon monoxide, NOx, and PMs.

Carbon dioxide, while not considered a pollutant in the lower atmosphere, can form ozone. Greenhouse gases as a separate measured category are contributed by the transportation sector to the total at 27 percent, but with aviation contributing only 2.7 percent.

Airport operators have no direct control over aircraft emissions, although two foreign countries have imposed landing fees based on the amount of aircraft emissions. Airports are theoretically subject to nationally supervised state control of emissions through State Implementation Plans (SIPs). These plans must be submitted by the states to the EPA for reducing emissions in areas that fail to meet the National Ambient Air Quality Standards set by the EPA under the Clean Air Act. The power of states in controlling pollution at airports is limited, however, since the EPA retains control of regulating mobile sources of emissions and because states are preempted from regulating aircraft operations generally. This is a federal responsibility (in order to maintain a consistent national policy) and the FAA is responsible for enforcing emission standards. For these reasons only three states have even attempted to target airports for emission reductions.[3] Operators of some of the busiest airports in the country have initiated voluntary programs to reduce emissions from sources over which they have control under the Voluntary Airport Low Emission Program (VALE).

VALE is an FAA program established in 2003 under the Vision 100 Century of Aviation Reauthorization Act. It provides funding to be used to reduce ground emissions from static and mobile equipment at airports. It promotes the use of electric-powered ground support equipment, such as baggage tugs, belt loaders, and pushback tractors. It also promotes capital construction projects such as the installation of underground fuel distribution systems to eliminate the need for aircraft fuel trucks.

European Union Carbon Tax on Airlines

The European Union has passed a law, effective as of January 1, 2012, that would expand its pre-existing cap and trade regime to foreign airlines, and which would tax all airlines flying into the EU airspace in 2012 and thereafter based on their carbon emissions. The law is referred to as the Emission Trading System (ETS) and requires all airlines to provide to the EU emission data so that a tax can be calculated and collected beginning in 2013. The tax is said to be applicable not only to flight miles within the EU, but also to the distance over their entire flight path. The tax money would go to all 27 members of the EU as well as to Iceland, Liechtenstein, and Norway. (All of the EU, with the possible exception of Germany, is in dire need of additional cash, without question.)

There has been worldwide opposition to the EU action, with United States airlines requesting President Obama to file an Article 84 complaint with ICAO, which would create a global framework for dealing with carbon emissions and would provide the appropriate forum for the settlement of the dispute. The United States and Canada filed an action in 2011 with the European Court of Justice to block the tax on grounds of sovereignty and treaty, but they were ruled against in December 2011. The U.S. aviation community is also calling on the federal government to challenge the law in international court. The United States has also taken unofficial action in convening two meetings (in Delhi and in Moscow) of opponents of the law

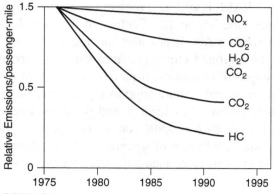

FIGURE 34-3 Relative engine emissions per passenger mile.

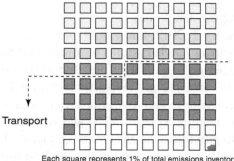

Each square represents 1% of total emissions inventory

Non-Transport	Transport
☐ Electric Utilities	◼ On-Road Vehicles
☐ Industry	☐ Non-Road Vechicles
☐ Commercial/Institutional	◼ Aviation
◼ Misc. area/point sources	
◼ Manufacturing	

Source: FAA

FIGURE 34-4 Emissions generated according to industry. (Note aviation emissions shown in the bottom right hand square.)

and has invoked a resolution in ICAO declaring the EU law illegal. Russia, China, the United States, and India have formed an anti-carbon tax coalition to oppose the law.

In September 2012 both the U.S. Senate and the House of Representatives passed legislation that will make it illegal for U.S. airlines to participate in the ETS scheme. When signed, the head of the Department of Transportation, Ray LaHood, could issue orders to all U.S. airlines not to comply with the EU regimen.

China, which had placed an order for 50 new Airbus airplanes, has cancelled that order and further ordered its airlines to refuse to pay the tax, as well as threatened the EU with a trade war. The Airbus transaction would cost Airbus some $12 billion and cost 1,000 jobs. In March, China stopped Chinese airlines from placing any further orders with Airbus. The Indian government has formally backed its airlines and their decision not to give the EU any carbon data.

Under the ETS law, passengers will be expected to pay a punitive tax on every ticket sold into the EU. This would make Europe a more expensive travel venue. The European Union is standing alone in the world on this issue. Consequences, if the EU persists, could include a worldwide embargo on Airbus aircraft and limitations on flights into Europe.

The United States has consistently refused to join what it has considered ineffective world efforts to lessen carbon emissions; it refused to sign the Kyoto Treaty, for instance. The EU ETS system, as well as any ICAO strategy to be put together to control airline engine emissions, seems like just one more global effort along the same lines, in spite of the miniscule contributions attributed to aircraft engines.

The EU has now deferred application of the emissions system to airlines as of 2012 to allow time to reach agreement between participating countries under the auspices of ICAO. In October 2013, ICAO agreed to develop a global market-based system to address global aviation emissions by 2016, to be applied by 2020. In response, the EU has proposed to tax airlines based only on that part of the flight that takes place in European airspace. No agreement has been reached as of this writing.

Aircraft Noise

While air pollution considerations have become increasingly important in the years since jet transport aircraft were introduced into the civil aviation

Average Emission per Landing/Takeoff Showing Trends

Emission	Older Boeing 737 (pounds)	Newest Boeing 737 (pounds)	Changes
Nitrogen oxides	12.1	17.8	47% increase
Carbon monoxide	16.8	10.7	37% decrease
Hydrocarbons	1.2	1.1	10% decrease

Source: GAO.

Notes: Landing and takeoff data for U.S. aircraft in 2001 obtained from AvSoft. Emissions were calculated using FAA's Emissions and Dispersion Modeling System, version 4.01. The following variables were assumed to be the same for all aircraft: (1) taxi-time: 15 minutes, (2) auxiliary power unit time: 26 minutes, and (3) ceiling height for emissions mixing with local air: 3,000 feet. The model's default was used for takeoff weight.

TABLE 34-3 Additional information on comparison of older and newest model Boeing 737 landing/takeoff emissions.

Emission per Aircraft During Landing/Takeoff Showing Trends

Emission	Boeing 747-400 (pounds)	Boeing B777-200ER (pounds)	Changes
Nitrogen oxides	103.5	124.2	20 percent increase
Carbon monoxide	47.7	30.4	36 percent decrease
Hydrocarbon	4.1	2.4	41 percent decrease

Source: GAO.

Notes: Landing and takeoff data for U.S. aircraft in 2001 obtained from AvSoft. Emissions were calculated using FAA's Emissions and Dispersion Modeling System, version 4.01. The following variables were assumed to be the same for all aircraft: (1) taxi-time: 15 minutes, (2) auxiliary power unit time: 26 minutes, and (3) ceiling height for emissions mixing with local air: 3,000 feet. The model's default was used for takeoff weight. The Boeing B77-200ER data is the weighted average (based on 2001 landings and takeoffs) for three different engines. The nitrogen oxides and other emission characteristics of these engines vary significantly.

The 58 Boeing 747-400s in the 2001 U.S. fleet have PW4056 engines and average 361 seats per aircraft. The 101 Boeing 777-200ERs in the 2001 U.S. fleet have the following engines: PW4090 (37 aircraft averaging 302 seats), GE90-90B (16 aircraft averaging 283 seats), and TRENT 892B-17 (48 aircraft averaging 249 seats). The three engine types for the Boeing 777-200ERs emit 138.6, 123.6, and 112.3 pounds of nitrogen oxide emissions per landing/takeoff, respectively.

TABLE 34-4 Additional information on comparison of Boeing 747 and 777 emissions on a per aircraft basis.

fleet in 1958, noise levels associated with the operation of jet transport aircraft at the nation's airports were an immediate concern to anyone within audible range. Jet noise had previously been limited to military operations, and most people were familiar with jet operations only as they were usually conducted at higher altitudes.

Citizens' groups became quite vocal about this intrusion into what had theretofore been a relatively peaceful coexistence with airport operations. Jet noise brought a new challenge to this attempt at coexistence. It took regulators until 1968 to accumulate enough anecdotal and empirical evidence to bring the matter successfully before the Congress. In that year, the first aircraft noise legislation was passed.

Aircraft Noise Abatement Act of 1968

That year the initial step was taken to confront what was coming to be recognized as not only an environmental issue, but also a health issue. The Aircraft Noise Abatement Act of 1968 required the FAA, in consultation with the new Environmental Protection Agency, to establish noise standards for aircraft and to apply them through issuance of civil aircraft certificates.

Noise Control Act of 1972 and Aviation Safety and Noise Abatement Act of 1979

In 1972, Congress passed the Noise Control Act, which amended the Federal Aviation Act of 1958

Nonattainment area	2008 Total NO$_x$ (tons)	2008 Aircraft percent of mobile source NO$_x$	2020 Aircraft percent of mobile source NO$_x$
Atlanta, GA	5,808	2.6	8.2
Baltimore, MD	1,148	1.3	4.4
Boston—including MA and NH NAAs	2,032	1.0	2.7
Charlotte-Gastonia-Rock Hill, NC-SC	1,917	2.6	10.0
Chicago-Gary-Lake County, IL-IN	6,007	1.8	5.0
Cleveland-Akron-Lorain, OH	680	0.5	1.3
Dallas-Fort Worth, TX	3,880	1.7	6.9
Denver-Boulder-Greeley-Fort Collins-Loveland, CO	2,649	2.5	7.1
Detroit-Ann Arbor, MI	2,312	1.1	3.0
Greater Connecticut, CT	405	0.8	2.4
Houston-Galveston-Brazoria, TX	3,045	1.3	3.4
Indianapolis, IN	1,089	1.4	3.0
Las Vegas, NV	2,308	6.0	15.8
Los Angeles South Coast Air Basin, CA	6,479	1.5	4.5
Louisville, KY-IN	1,211	1.9	6.2
Milwaukee-Racine, WI	557	0.9	3.2
New York-N. New Jersey-Long Island, NY-NJ-CT	10,093	2.3	6.3
Philadelphia-Wilmington-Atlantic City, PA-NY-MD-DE	2,308	1.0	2.8
Phoenix-Mesa, AZ	2,298	1.4	3.3
Pittsburgh-Beaver Valley, PA	480	0.5	1.1
Providence (entire State), RI	232	1.0	2.3
Riverside County (Coachella Valley), CA	70	0.2	0.5
Sacramento Metro, CA	603	1.0	2.0
Salt Lake City, UT	1,235	4.4	14.1
San Diego, CA	1,035	1.4	3.4
San Francisco Bay Area, CA	4,405	2.7	6.7
San Joaquin Valley, CA	74	0.0	0.1
Seattle-Tacoma, WA	1,958	1.4	3.9
St. Louis, MO-IL	810	0.6	1.6
Washington, DC-MD-VA	2,983	2.0	6.2

TABLE 34-5 NO$_x$ EMISSIONS IN SELECTED OZONE AND PM$_{2.5}$ NONATTAINMENT AREAS

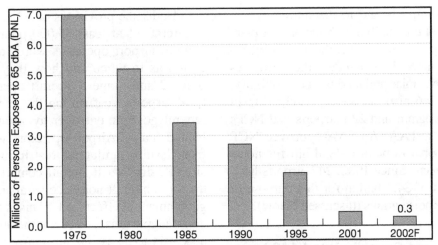

FIGURE 34-5 Significant progress in reduction of aircraft noise.

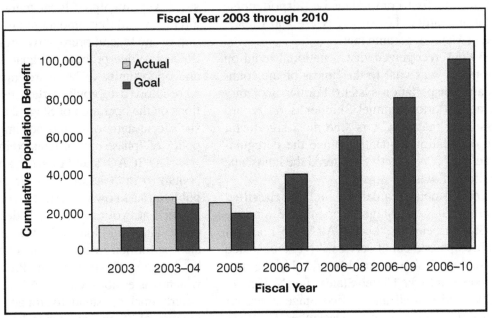

FIGURE 34-6 Populations expected to benefit from noise funding.

to specifically involve the EPA in the regulation of airport noise. This was followed in 1979 by the Aviation Safety and Noise Abatement Act, which authorized the Secretary of Transportation to formulate a national aviation noise policy and authorized the FAA to promulgate regulations pursuant thereto, including "air noise compatibility planning." These regulations are contained in 14 Code of Federal Regulations, Part 150.

The FAA established a program under the 1979 statute to help airport operators develop comprehensive noise reduction programs. Known as the Part 150 program (derived from CFR Part 150), this voluntary program encourages airport operators to develop Noise Exposure Maps (NEM) and Noise Compatibility Programs (NCP). NEMs identify noise contours and land use incompatibilities. NEMS are used to evaluate existing noise impacts and to discourage future development not compatible with the airport plan. If the FAA approves the NEM, the airport operator can submit an NCP, which describes measures that will improve noise and land use compatibility.

In 2005, 266 airports were participating in the Part 150 program and 226 airports had NCPs approved by the FAA. An FAA-approved NCP allows an airport to obtain federal aid for noise mitigation projects. Since 1982, 247 airports have received a total of $4.3 billion for this purpose in addition to AIP noise grants (discussed below).

Airport Noise and Capacity Act of 1990

In 1990, the first comprehensive airport noise regulation statute, the Airport Noise and Capacity Act (ANCA), became law.

ANCA recognized that a national aviation noise policy was vital to the fitness of the country's air transportation system. Former Secretary of Transportation Samuel Skinner is on record as asserting that ANCA is "the most significant piece of aviation legislation since the deregulation act." ANCA effectively altered the landscape in matters of aviation noise.

Federal noise regulations in 1990 classified aircraft as Stage 1, Stage 2, or Stage 3 aircraft, with Stage 1 being the loudest. All Stage 1 aircraft have been phased out of service. ANCA mandated that no Stage 2 aircraft could be added to the fleet or imported into the United States after November 5, 1990, and that all unmodified Stage 2 aircraft be phased out of service by December 31, 1999. Stage 2 aircraft include the 727, DC-9, and early versions of the 737 and 747. These airplanes were developed in the 1960s and 1970s.

Stage 3 aircraft must meet separate standards for takeoff, landing, and sideline measurements, depending on the aircraft's weight and number of engines. Stage 3 aircraft are the newer and quieter 757, 767, and MD-80 series, later versions of the 737 and 747, and aircraft that have been retrofitted with quieter engines by the noise reducing "hush kits."

Under the provisions of ANCA, which apply to aircraft of at least 75,000 pounds certificated weight, airport operators were specifically regulated as to when and how they could restrict Stage 2 and Stage 3 aircraft operations at their local airports, reaffirming the supremacy of the federal government over aviation policy in the United States. Airport operators were prohibited from issuing unilateral restrictions on Stage 3 aircraft, since such aircraft comprise the state-of-the-art in aircraft noise. To paraphrase, the federal government in effect said, "This is the best we can do in engine noise, these are the airplanes that are necessary to be used in air transportation, and they will be allowed to fly no matter what the locals say." Any attempted local regulation of Stage 3 aircraft would thus amount to an unlawful usurpation of the federal prerogatives regarding aviation. Subject to due process safeguards, such as notice and opportunity to be heard, airport proprietors were allowed to apply certain reasonable restrictions on the operation of Stage 2 aircraft as long as such local authorities did not impair the national policy of "phase out" articulated in the statute.

The ICAO standards for aircraft noise are contained in "Chapters" to the above-referenced publication known as Annex 16, Environmental Protection, Volume I, which deals with aircraft noise. The work done at ICAO on aircraft noise is also performed in the aforementioned Committee on Aviation Environmental Protection (CAEP), which was established in 1983. Its Chapters 2 and 3 fairly track the standards found in the FAA's designation of Stage 2 and Stage 3 aircraft.

In June 2001, ICAO adopted new, more stringent noise standards, as recommended by CAEP, which went into effect on January 1, 2006. These standards mandate a noise reduction level of 10 dB below the standards previously required (Chapter 3). These standards are referred to as Chapter 4 standards by ICAO.

These standards were adopted by the FAA by rule on July 5, 2005, designated as Stage 4 standards by the FAA, which also went into effect on January 1, 2006.[4] These noise standards are intended to provide uniform noise certification standards for Stage 4 airplanes certificated in the United States. There is no weight limitation or exclusion for airplane type designs submitted after January 1, 2006; thus, all aircraft types will be subject to the Stage 4 noise standards.

Care should be taken to note the difference between the requirements of ANCA and the new FAA rule. ANCA, which requires compliance with Stage 3 standards, only applies to aircraft with certificated weight of 75,000 pounds and above. The new FAA rule, which requires new type designs to comply with Stage 4 standards, applies to all new airplane type design submissions, regardless of weight.

Although noise control of aircraft is exclusively a federal function, airport authorities and local governments do have the option to mitigate noise effects through land use controls, such as zoning and land acquisition, which the FAA agrees is the exclusive domain of state and local governments. Indeed, federal policy respecting Airport Improvement Program (AIP) funding favors the use of such funds for that purpose. Airport operators applying for funds for these purposes must design noise exposure maps and develop mitigation programs consistent with federal requirements to insure that noise levels are compatible with adjacent land uses. Noise compatibility projects include residential and public building sound insulation. They include land acquisition and relocating residents from noise-sensitive areas. Airports have also installed noise monitoring equipment and noise barriers to reduce ground run-up noise.

ANCA also provides for additional funding sources by permitting the use of passenger facility charges (PFCs) for land use control. Airports have collected and used PFC funds for noise studies and mitigation totaling $15 billion as of 2005.

Overall, ANCA provides a framework for the implementation of a national policy of aircraft noise control, and reaffirms that local governments have the continuing obligation to adhere to that policy and to cooperate with federal authorities to secure the achievement of such national interests. The policy is working. According to statistics supplied by FAA, exposure to airline noise has decreased significantly and consistently from 1975 to 2001. Airline noise levels are calculated using the number of persons exposed to 65 dBA, in millions. In 1975, some 7 million people were subject to noise levels in excess of that number, while in 2001, the number of persons exposed to 65 dBA had declined to just 0.4 million. (See Figure 34-5.)

Through FAA efforts, under the AIP set-aside programs, residential and school populations in the hundreds of thousands are now exposed to reduced aircraft noise (at or below 65 dBA) as of 2010.

Continuous Lower Emission, Energy, and Noise Program (CLEEN)

The CLEEN program was initiated by the FAA in a partnership format with the aviation industry with the objective of reducing aircraft fuel burn by 33 percent and reducing oxides of nitrogen by 60 percent compared to ICAO emissions standards. This voluntary effort attempts to get out in front of the regulatory scheme favored by the EU (and acceded to by the FAA under ICAO guidelines).

The program also seeks to reduce aircraft noise by 32 decibels from the current ICAO standard. Technologies include lighter and more efficient gas turbine engine components, noise-reducing engine nozzles, adaptable wing trailing edges, optimized flight trajectories using NextGen flight management systems, and open rotor and geared turbofan engines. The CLEEN program will accelerate the development of these technologies for potential introduction into aircraft and engines beginning in 2015.

Endnotes

1. Public Law 84-159.
2. 42 U.S.C. section 7401, et seq.
3. California, Massachusetts, and Texas.
4. Aircraft must be built to meet noise certification standards established by ICAO, found in Annex 16, Environmental Protection, V. 1. The first generation of jet aircraft (707, DC-8) preceded the Annex 16 standards. These are Stage 1 aircraft. Chapter 2 of the Annex applied to aircraft built before 1977, and these are referred to as Stage 2 aircraft. Chapter 3 of the Annex covered the latest production aircraft, and are referred to by the FAA as Stage 3.

35 Airlines in the 21st Century

" A recession is when you have to tighten your belt; depression is when you have no belt to tighten. When you've lost your trousers—you're in the airline business. **"**

Sir Adam Thomson

As the airline industry approached the end of the millennium, during the first half of the 1990s, there was no consensus that deregulation was an overall success. Economic deregulation was clearly a boon for mass transit; air fares had plummeted as predicted. But the industry was in disarray. Between 1990 and 1993, airlines in the United States had lost an amount of money equal to all the money that had ever been made in aviation in this country since the first commercial flight. If this was what deregulation had wrought, then deregulation was obviously a tragic mistake.

Deregulation had clearly exposed the sensitive nature of the U.S. airline industry. This sensitivity results primarily from fluctuating economic conditions, often driven by geopolitical factors that affect fuel prices and travel demand. While deregulation gave air travel to the masses, it did so at the expense of the airlines' flexibility and any financial cushion in the industry. Competition had shaved profit margins so razor thin that almost any economic hiccup translated into severe problems for air transportation. The industry has high fixed costs (the cost of labor, aircraft, and facilities) that cannot be reduced quickly during these adverse economic times. Since fuel and labor costs account for over 50 percent of all airlines' expenses, spikes in the cost of fuel are particularly debilitating to the airlines.

The last decade of the 20th century was quite representative of the plight of the airlines: boom or bust. Jet fuel prices doubled in just four months in 1990 due to the invasion of Kuwait by Iraq. Eastern Airlines had been liquidated, followed by Pan American. Thus deregulation had taken out the venerable airline of Eddie Rickenbacker and as well as the "Chosen Instrument" of America. The remaining legacy airlines took on crushing debt trying to stay in business. The economic downturn produced huge losses for the airlines until 1995. The state of the airline industry was so fragile that a presidential commission was established to look into ways to ensure the survival of the industry. There was talk of nationalizing the airlines.

Southwest Airlines

Only Southwest Airlines seemed to understand what was going on. While the major airlines were trying without much success to stop the bleeding, Southwest was raking in record profits; it was also expanding. USAir had acquired PSA in California, and then began to cut back service on the north–south corridor. Southwest came in to fill the void, but at offbeat airports like Oakland and Burbank, and at seemingly ever decreasing fares. Then Southwest entered San Jose to challenge American Airlines. When told that Southwest was coming in, American did not even wait for the discount carrier to arrive; it withdrew, anticipating the losses to come in a one-on-one contest with Southwest.

" If the Wright brothers were alive today Wilbur would have to fire Orville to reduce costs. "

Herb Kelleher, Southwest Airlines, *USA Today*, 8 June 1994

Southwest was also headed east, for the first time in its history. Now Southwest would be in Baltimore (BWI), next to the seat of power in the District of Columbia. Southwest then was the eighth largest airline in the United States (United was first, followed by American, Delta, Northwest, Continental, and USAir), but it was different in at least one highly significant way: it had point-to-point routes (the 100 city-pairs most frequently traveled), and did not waste time getting in and out of large hub terminals.

Code Sharing and Airline Alliances[1]

Deregulation had also produced the practice of code sharing between airlines domestically, in 1983. Code sharing allows an airline to advertise, as its own, a route from an origin to a destination,

even though a part of that route is not actually flown by the advertising airline. Usually unknown to the passenger, a part of the route is flown by a different airline using its own aircraft, its own pilots, and its own support infrastructure and staff, all of which entails utilizing its own procedures and rules. For many reasons, this is information that many travelers would like to know, but a primary reason is that major carriers and regional carriers (who code share) may have significantly different safety records, types of aircraft, and pilot hiring qualifications.

Code sharing also involves airlines jointly setting rates and fares, which is traditionally a big no-no since that kind of action fits exactly the definition of antitrust collusion and anticompetitive behavior. The antitrust laws of the United States apply fully to code-share arrangements, which are administered by the Department of Justice. Over the years, code-share arrangements have gone into effect without interference from the Department of Justice for the simple reason that these arrangements are seen by the DOJ as competitive overall and favorable to the consumer.

Code sharing between domestic airlines and foreign airlines is also subject to the antitrust laws of the United States, unless an express grant of statutory immunity is made by the Department of Transportation. The first foreign code-share arrangement was approved by the Department of Transportation in 1993 to allow KLM Royal Dutch Airlines to infuse capital into financially strapped Northwest Airlines. Although code sharing between airlines does not require a swap of assets or other financial investment between them, approval was initially given by the United States government to these arrangements in part due to the fact that additional financial stability was achieved in the domestic carrier. Following the KLM–Northwest code-share arrangement, approval was given for a United Airlines–Lufthansa pairing, and shortly thereafter British Airways bought into USAir for $400 million and began code sharing. Although these arrangements constituted, in many cases, a deception to the flying public, they were actually a first step in the globalization of the world air transportation market.

Airline alliances are an evolutionary development of code sharing. Beginning with code-sharing arrangements domestically and then internationally, alliances between domestic and foreign airlines have blossomed since the first group, Star Alliance, was founded in 1997. This alliance was followed by two others, One-World and SkyTeam, in 1999 and 2000, respectively. These antitrust immunized arrangements allow the alliance partners to provide a seamless travel experience as if there were a single carrier involved, to include benefits such as coordinated schedules at hubs to expedite interline transfers, integrated frequent flyer programs, and baggage check throughs. These alliances have been greatly facilitated by "Open Skies" treaties.

International alliances and Open Skies treaties, as part of global deregulation, will be further discussed in Part VI.

To the Fin de Siècle

The recession of the early 1990s began to abate toward the middle of the decade. And just as deregulation had produced the greatest losses in the history of the airline business just a few years before, now profits began to rebound under deregulation.

- In 1994, American Airlines saw the highest quarterly profit in its history and in the history of any airline since the beginning of commercial aviation.
- TWA emerged from Chapter 11 and restructured—with a 45 percent employee ownership.
- Northwest avoided bankruptcy with an employee trade-off of stock for concessions.

Beginning in 1995, the financial picture for most airlines markedly improved, and continued to improve through the end of the decade. Net income for many airlines reached its peak that year as traffic figures spiraled upward in a continuation of a good economy and a climate of stable wages and fuel prices. Each year from 1995 through 1999 were profitable ones for the airlines, reaching $5.6 billion that last year. Labor contracts were renegotiated, fleets were expanded, and employment rose. But there was trouble just over the horizon.

Into the New Millennium

The airlines entered the new millennium riding the crest of the same wave that generally took the stock indices and corporate profits to their historical high point. The so-called dot.com computer and technological sector, now seen in context, propelled an economic "bubble" that burst in the year 2000. That year a downturn began in the economy that produced concerns of a "bear" market, then turned to fears of a recession. Although passenger enplanements reached a then all-time high in 2000 of 693 million, the airlines, like everyone else, were now on the backside of the wave.

The year 2000 saw the end of six years of relative prosperity in the air carrier industry. The downturn in air carrier profits actually began in 1998 but it was not until 2001 that adversity took hold. As the year progressed, it was forecast that the industry, as a whole, would experience a loss of perhaps $3 billion. This projected loss was of a magnitude somewhat comparable to the early years of the 1990s, but less than either 1990 or 1992. While this projected loss was substantial, it was still within the bounds of the cyclical nature of the industry since deregulation.

September 11, 2001

The event that will forever be known as "September 11," a terrorist attack on the United

States, occurred on September 11, 2001. It was focused on New York and Washington, D.C., respectively the nation's financial and governmental centers. The perpetrators were members of a fundamentalist Islamic group called Al Qaeda, all followers of a militant Islam sect headed by a man called Osama bin Laden, a member of a wealthy Saudi Arabian family.[2] Bin Laden maintained training camps for militants in Afghanistan, and kept on the move in mountainous areas on the border with Pakistan.

The selection of targets, the World Trade Center in New York, and the Pentagon in Washington, constituted a declaration of war on the institutions and ideals of the free world, and on the free enterprise system that had made possible the unprecedented strides in modern technology that it represented. It is ironic that the tools used by the terrorists to wreck such massive destruction upon that civilization were some of the very tools used to build the system, and which were themselves products of that system, the modern airliner.

American Airlines flight 11 was a Boeing 757 (see Figure 35-1) that departed Boston Logan for Los Angeles and was crashed into the north tower of the World Trade Center; United Airlines flight 175 was a Boeing 767 that departed Boston Logan for Los Angeles and was crashed into the south tower of the World Trade Center. (See Figure 35-2.)

American Airlines flight 77 was a Boeing 757 that departed Washington Dulles for Los Angeles and was crashed into the Pentagon in Washington, D.C.; United Airlines flight 93 was a Boeing 757 that departed Newark for San Francisco and crashed into a field in Pennsylvania. United 93 was the only hijacked airplane that failed to reach its target. Enroute to the target, a small group of male passengers attempted to retake control of the airplane by overpowering the terrorists and storming the cockpit. The airplane crashed during the ensuing fight for control. Although all on board died, there were no casualties on the ground or at the point of the terrorists' target due to this brave action by passengers.

These aircraft were selected by the terrorists because of their size and because each one was scheduled on a planned transcontinental flight heavily loaded with jet fuel which, when ignited upon impact, created an inferno larger than any that could have been accomplished by any transportable bomb available to the terrorists.

Immediately following the September 11 attack, all aircraft within the United States were grounded by federal order. The fact that the weapons used by the terrorists were airplanes caused the government to first ensure that no other aircraft could be used to the same effect. Implementation of the ground stop order was unprecedented in the history of aviation. The mechanism for the

FIGURE 35-1 Boeing 757.

Image courtesy of Corel.

Image © PhotoDisc.

FIGURE 35-2 The Manhattan skyline prior to the terrorists' attacks of September 11, 2001.

order was a relic of the Cold War and was originally conceived to prevent Soviet bombers from surreptitiously entering the United States while in the radar shadow of inbound commercial airliners. Within hours of the issuance of the ground stop order, all flights within the borders of the United States were on the ground, and all inbound international flights had been turned back from America's borders. One of these, incidentally, was the Concorde, which was over the middle of the Atlantic Ocean at the time bound for New York. By the afternoon of September 11, FAA radars were eerily empty, reflecting only patrolling military fighter aircraft, notably above the skies of the Northeastern United States.

Resumption of flight operations occurred incrementally, beginning with the repositioning of commercial aircraft, then resumption of domestic U.S. flag operations, and finally resumption of international flight operations. The federal order grounding all aircraft cost the airline industry over $330 million a day for the duration of the days-long stoppage.

The attacks had a ripple effect on commercial losses, including insurance companies, travel services, the stock market, most commercial transactions and, not least, on the confidence of the world citizen. But of all industry sectors affected, the airlines took the brunt of the blow. The airlines whose airliners were hijacked had to deal with not only the loss of the aircraft and crew, but also with liability issues involving both death and property damage to those passengers on the airplanes and those in harm's way on the ground. The industry as a whole had to deal with the effect of the grounding, and the consequent disruption and loss of revenue while their expenses, including debt service on aircraft, continued unabated.

Congress and the president were quickly convinced that federal intervention was necessary to meet the financial needs of the United States air transportation industry. It was also clear that the nation had to address its overall security posture in the face of a new kind of enemy. A series of legislative initiatives was immediately begun in a Congress united in purpose. Three significant and complex new laws were passed in an almost unprecedented space of time.

The first of these was the Air Transportation Safety and System Stabilization Act. Enacted 11 days later, on September 22, 2001, it (1) provided compensation to the airlines for direct and incremental losses caused by the ground stop order and (2) created a fund to provide loans to qualifying air carriers. The second statute, the Aviation and Transportation Security Act, addressed security upgrades that were needed to strengthen airports and the air transportation system generally. The third, the Homeland Security Act of 2002, created a new Cabinet-level department, the Department of Homeland Security. This statute placed within one executive department responsibility for all planning and procedures deemed necessary to enhance the security of the nation against similar types of threats.

The Air Transportation Safety and System Stabilization Act[3]

The main provisions of the statute provide:

1. Direct payments and loan guarantees
   a. All U.S. air carriers were eligible to share a $5 billion fund to compensate them for direct losses due to the federal ground stop order that resulted immediately after the terrorists' attack, and incremental losses incurred between September 11 and December 11, 2001
   b. Issuance of up to $10 billion in federal loan guarantees and credits to air carriers, subject to terms and conditions set by the president
2. Insurance and liability
   a. Limited the liability of air carriers, certified by the DOT as victims of an act of terrorism, for losses suffered by third parties to $100 million in the aggregate (due to the terrorist act) with provisions for the government to assume all liability over that amount

   b. Prohibited the imposition of punitive damages against either the carrier or the government as a result of the terrorist act
   c. Granted the DOT authority to reimburse air carriers for insurance premium increases due to September 11
3. Tax provisions extending certain tax due dates for air carriers
4. Creation of a victim compensation fund to compensate individuals (or their survivors) for injuries or death caused by terrorist-related aircraft crashes on September 11

The Act established the Air Transportation Stabilization Board, whose function was to administer the issuance of the $10 billion in federal loan guarantees to affected airlines. As a precondition to the issuance of any guarantees, the Board had to determine that:

1. Credit was not reasonably available to the airline at the time of the issuance
2. The intended obligation (the loan and the purpose for the loan) was prudently incurred
3. The transaction was a necessary part of maintaining a safe, efficient, and viable commercial aviation system in the United States

By the middle of 2002, some 400 air carriers had applied for compensation for *direct losses* as a result of September 11. The government had approved and paid $4.3 billion to 382 different carriers. The largest payments went to the largest airlines. United received almost $725 million, American received $656 million, and Delta got $595 million.

At the same time, the Stabilization Board continued to work through applications for *loan guarantees*. It quickly became clear that the Board was not going to rubber-stamp applications for the airlines. America West, the first to receive guarantees, was required to rework its application several times in order to satisfy the Board, and the guarantees were conditioned on the airline granting to the government a form of collateral to guarantee repayment, warrants on one-third of the airline's stock. Warrants are options to purchase stock at a predetermined price.

The Board rejected other applications, including Vanguard Airline's request for just $7.5 million in guarantees. Eleven other small airlines made applications, with varying results.

Major airlines were slow to apply, primarily because of the rigid stance taken by the Board in evaluating applications. In addition to requiring security for the government guarantees, the Board also required the airlines to make operating changes designed to increase the likelihood of repayment. US Air, for instance, received conditional approval for $900 million in guarantees dependent on the airline securing sizeable concessions from its employees. The labor unions would not agree, and U.S. Air went into Chapter 11 in August 2002. United Airlines also applied for guarantees in an amount of $1.8 billion. Again, labor would not agree to the concessions required by the government. In December 2002, UAL filed for bankruptcy protection under

Chapter 11 of the Act. The other legacy carriers were just barely hanging on. Later in this chapter we will review the record of all remaining legacy carriers' use of Chapter 11 since 2001.

Aviation and Transportation Security Act[4]

The president of the United States signed the Aviation and Transportation Security Act on November 19, 2001. The Act created the Transportation Security Administration (TSA) (see Figure 35-3), which was originally placed in the Department of Transportation, and which is charged with insuring the implementation of a sequenced series of enhanced security measures applicable to both aircraft and airports. These measures include installation of fortified cockpit doors on aircraft, implementation of new standards for airport baggage screeners, revitalization of the federal air marshal program, and the strengthening of airport perimeter areas. The TSA was moved to the Department of Homeland Security in 2003.

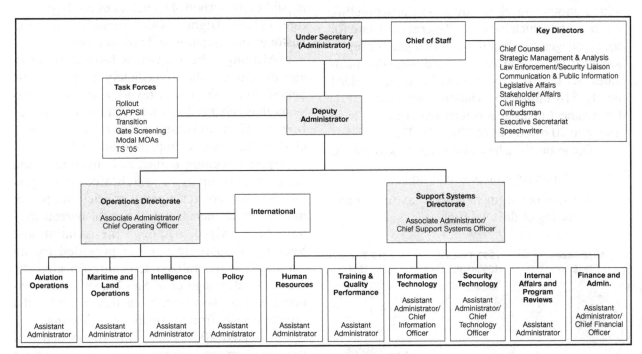

FIGURE 35-3   Organization of the Transportation Security Administration (TSA).

Fiscal year 2011 collections ($ millions) from airlines

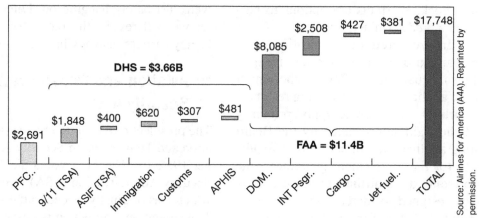

FIGURE 35-4 Special aviation tax burden.

Passenger screening was previously the responsibility of the FAA, which was carried out by the airlines under FAA guidelines. The Act transferred this function to the TSA, which had to be organized, staffed, and trained at significant expense. The Act authorizes the TSA to impose user fees on both passengers and air carriers to help pay for these new security efforts, which added another level of stress on the struggling airlines, and which increases the cost of airfare for the passenger. See Figure 35-4 for a graphic representation of these taxes, fees, and unfunded mandates. As of 2011, these impositions have added nearly $18 billion to aviation costs since 2001. Government taxes as a percentage of airfare have grown to 20 percent as of 2012. See Figure 35-5.

Domestically, a base airfare has tacked onto it:

1. A 7.5 percent federal excise tax,
2. A $3.80 per segment federal tax (a segment is one leg of the total flight),

3. A $2.50 September 11 federal tax per segment (to pay for security screening), and
4. A $4.50 passenger facility airport charge per departure.

The base fare is retained by the airline. The excise tax, the segment tax, and the 9/11 tax are paid to the federal government. The PFC charge is paid to the airport. Federal taxes are higher for international flights, which include departure, customs, immigration, and arrival taxes.

Although the idea of a federal security agency was popular immediately after 9/11 (the Senate voted 100 to 0 in favor), over the 10-plus years that enhanced federal aviation security has been in effect, mounting criticism has been leveled at the TSA. Complaints about long lines at airport screening points, rude treatment, and unnecessarily invasive searches of passengers by TSA workers, reactionary policies and procedures, and an increasingly wasteful bureaucracy have been lodged. Although the Aviation and Security Transportation Act provided for an "opt out" of federalized screening for airports, few took advantage of it. San Francisco International Airport, however, is one that did; it hired a privatesecurity firm to conduct its screening.

A leaked 2007 TSA study found that San Francisco's private screeners were twice as good at detecting fake bombs as TSA screeners. The private screeners were "friendlier" and "more helpful."

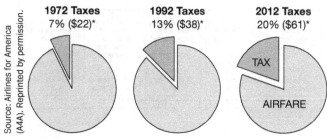

FIGURE 35-5 Tax bite on $300 fare.

Their lines were shorter and the private company used procedures to minimize wait times. A House Transportation Committee in 2011 found that the San Francisco screeners could process 165 passengers in the same time that it took TSA screeners in Los Angeles International Airport to process 100 passengers. Scores of other airports have petitioned the TSA to allow them to switch to private screeners, without success. The TSA has responded exceptionally slowly, and when it has responded, it has denied the applications on the stated basis of "no benefit to the federal government." New legislation is pending in an attempt to provide more transparency to such TSA decision-making.

There are good reasons to question the efficacy of TSA procedures. Richard Reid, the "shoe bomber" who attempted to bring down a transatlantic flight in 2002, was stopped by passengers on the airplane, not security forces. Yet, ever since this episode, all passengers have been required by the TSA to take off their shoes for x-ray inspection. The "New York Times Square bomber," who botched his car bombing attempt in 2010, left the area and "ordered his ticket on the way to JFK, went through TSA, and got on the plane."[5] In 2011, a House Oversight and Government Reform Subcommittee found that there had been more than 25,000 documented airport security breaches under TSA auspices.

The TSA also installed nearly 100 explosive detection machines at airports at a cost of $150,000 each, only to discover that they do not work. The TSA paid the Department of Defense $600 each to destroy them.[6]

◼ Homeland Security Act of 2002[7]

Congress passed the Homeland Security Act in November 2002, creating a new department in the executive branch at the cabinet level known as the Department of Homeland Security (DHS). The primary missions of the Department are preventing terrorist attacks in the United States, reducing the country's vulnerability to terrorism, and minimizing damage in the event such attacks occur. Specifically, the scope of DHS activities includes border

security, intelligence collection and analysis, emergency preparedness and response, and detection of chemical, biological, and radiological threats.

This statute combined over 22 existing federal agencies previously scattered throughout the government into one cohesive organization. DHS includes not only the TSA, but also U.S. Customs and Border Protection (CBT), the Federal Emergency Management Agency (FEMA), U.S. Immigration and Customs Enforcement (ICE), the Secret Service, the U.S. National Guard, and the U.S. Coast Guard. Some agencies and departments involved in national security that are not in DHS include the FBI, the CIA, and the Department of Defense.

The Act provides for the training of air carrier pilots in the use of firearms to be carried in the cockpit. In April 2003, the first 44 airline pilots certified as Federal Flight Deck Officers were graduated from the Federal Law Enforcement Center in Glynco, Georgia.

Third-party liability insurance (insurance to cover airlines for losses of those airlines to third parties, such as passengers, persons on the ground, and others) ordinarily does not cover risks of damage caused by war, sabotage, civil unrest, or terrorism. After 9/11, this specific kind of war risk insurance became prohibitively expensive for airlines to obtain, causing the issuance of Presidential Determination No. 01-29 on September 23, 2001. This Determination, which authorizes the issuance of war risk coverage to U.S. flag air carriers for such loss or damage, and/ or the reimbursement of insurance cost increases to such carriers, was carried over into and as one of the provisions of the Homeland Security Act.

◼ Aftermath

Still, the nation's airlines faced many challenges after September 11. The extraordinary provisions of the supportive legislation passed by Congress in 2001 and 2002 certainly went far in preventing the collapse of segments of the air carrier industry, but much damage had been done. Projections made at the beginning of 2001 forecast a $3 billion loss for the airline industry for the year. As a result of 9/11, that loss quickly became more than twice that figure, $7.7 billion.

Added to this were the U.S. invasion of Afghanistan in October of 2001, the beginning of the Iraq War in March 2002, and the SARS epidemic (severe acute respiratory syndrome) in early 2003.[8]

The air transport industry was in for a very hard time during this turbulent period.

Airline Adjustments Due to September 11 and Its Aftermath

The combination of adverse effects due to September 11 and its aftermath bore down heavily on the airlines. The domestic air carrier industry was in for five years of negative profitability beginning in 2001. Through 2005, the airlines lost $35.1 billion just for that five-year period. The airlines were also deeply in debt.

Labor

Aside from low passenger traffic counts, the plight of the airlines was complicated by increased labor costs that were the result of protracted negotiations with their labor groups from the period

of profitability during the late 1990s. Labor had pushed to make up for some of the concessions that had been granted management to keep the airlines afloat during the dark days of the early 1990s, and now the cost of those new labor agreements were coming due. Labor costs have traditionally been the largest single expense factor faced by airlines, historically amounting to some 35 percent of total operating costs. The average airline employee in 2002 made $73,000 a year, including pension and insurance benefits. Because airlines require the services of highly skilled employees, their employees historically are highly paid. Airline wages were 53 percent higher than national averages.

Following September 11 the airlines were forced to reduce their workforces significantly, on average among the 13 largest carriers by 14 percent, although at United the reduction was 20 percent and at US Airways it was an even greater 24 percent. In numbers, there were over 80,000 layoffs immediately. By 2003, that number was 140,000. See Figures 35-7 through 12 and Table 35-1.

Fuel

Fuel prices are inextricably interwoven with overall economic conditions. A close correlation

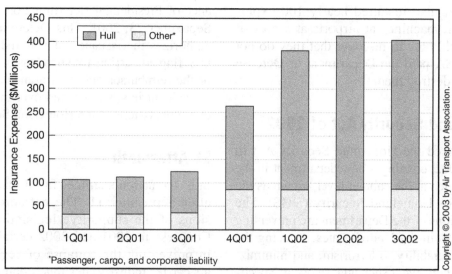

FIGURE 35-6 Airline insurance costs.

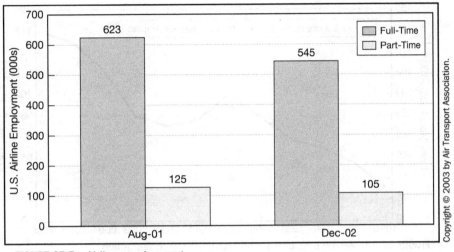

FIGURE 35-7   Airline employment.

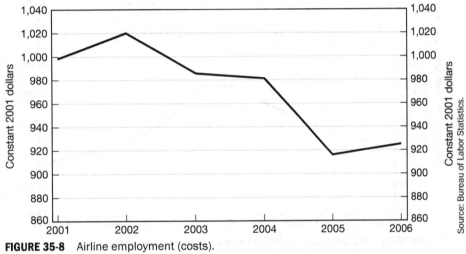

FIGURE 35-8   Airline employment (costs).

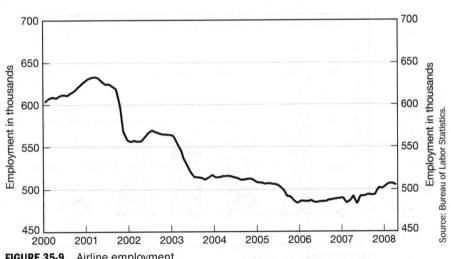

FIGURE 35-9   Airline employment.

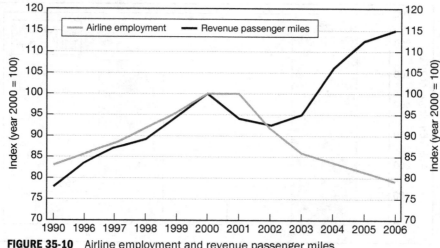

FIGURE 35-10   Airline employment and revenue passenger miles.

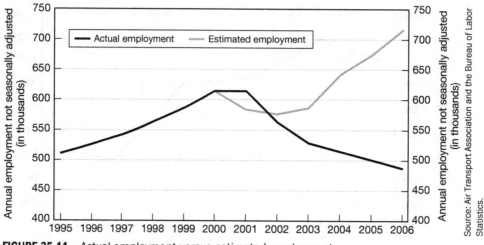

FIGURE 35-11   Actual employment versus estimated employment.

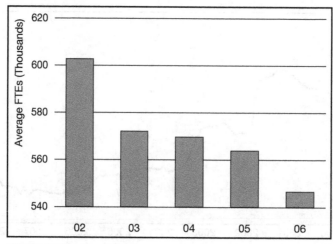

FIGURE 35-12   Employees.

U.S. Airlines—Average Full-Time Equivalents (FTEs)

	2005	2006	Change (%)
Pilots and Copilots	74,478	**69,181**	(7.1)
Other Flight Personnel	5,440	**4,824**	(11.3)
Flight Attendants	70,173	**76,919**	9.6
Mechanics	51,469	**47,335**	(8.0)
Aircraft and Traffic Service Personnel	288,542	**275,523**	(4.5)
Office Employees	36,537	**34,876**	(4.5)
All Other	35,827	**35,882**	0.2
Total Employment	562,467	**544,540**	(3.2)
Average Compensation[1]			
Salaries and Wages	$52,374	**$52,830**	0.9
Benefits and Pensions	15,931	**16,268**	2.1
Payroll Taxes	4,126	**4,100**	(0.6)
Total Compensation	$72,431	**$73,197**	1.1

[1]Passenger airlines only.

TABLE 35-1 Employment.

can be observed between periods of recession and increased energy prices. (See Figure 35-13.) In spite of advances in fuel-efficient aircraft engines (the aircraft fleet in 2002 was twice as fuel efficient than 30 years before), fuel prices continued to contribute heavily to the airlines' financial woes. During the first 11 months of 2002, jet fuel prices rose 27 percent, and from December 2002 to February 2003, those prices rose an additional 55 percent. Jet fuel prices more than doubled in the one-year period February 2002 to February 2003. Crude oil prices increased by 60 percent in

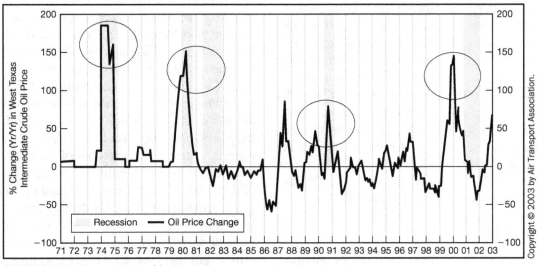

FIGURE 35-13 Comparison of fuel spikes.

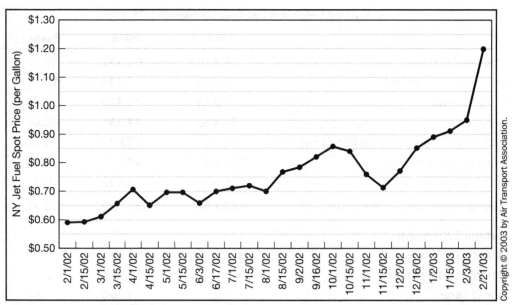

FIGURE 35-14 Market price of jet fuel.

2004, and in 2005 the airlines' fuel costs doubled over that in 2003. (See Figure 35-14.)

Southwest Airlines, exhibiting another facet of original thinking, began hedging its fuel costs.[9] In 2004, Southwest's fuel costs were much lower than its competitors' costs for this reason. Southwest continued to demonstrate profitability even under these trying circumstances.

Fleet

Airlines reduced the number of aircraft in their fleets by retirement, sale, or simply parking the airplanes. Especially targeted were less fuel-efficient and maintenance-intensive aircraft. The overall U.S. fleet was over 5,600 airplanes in 2000, but by 2003 there were only 4,479, a 20 percent reduction. Orders on new aircraft were reduced, down by over 100 airplanes at the end of 2002 as compared with the end of the second quarter of 2001. (See Figures 35-15 through 35-16 and Table 35-2.) At the end of 2006, the fleet still comprised only 4,339 aircraft.

Restructuring

At the end of 2002, only two major airlines ended up in the black. Southwest reported

profits of $241 million, and JetBlue reported $55 million. The remainder of all major U.S. airlines reported substantial losses: American, $3.5 billion; United, $3.33 billion; Delta, $1.3 billion; Northwest, $766 million; Continental, $451 million; U.S. Airways, $1.66 billion. The combined losses of the industry exceeded $10 billion. It was no coincidence that the profitable airlines were the "no frills" low-cost carriers, and the unprofitable ones were the legacy airlines.

Traditionally, the legacy airlines' largest cost of doing business has been wages and benefits of the rank and file employee, almost all of whom are represented by labor unions. The terms of union contracts control both wages and work rules, neither of which can be unilaterally changed by airline management. Yet, these were exactly what the airlines needed to change before any significant or long-lasting recovery could be expected. This was especially true since the cost of fuel, which has traditionally been the airlines' second highest cost of doing business, continued to spiral upward.[10]

Beginning in 2002, the legacy airlines again resorted to the Bankruptcy Code as their last hope of survival. As the decade progressed, some critics said that Chapter 11 was becoming a management tool, but the fact is that restructuring

Fleet	6/30/01	12/31/01	6/30/02	12/31/02	Change
B727	480	333	259	224	(256)
MD80	631	573	561	554	(77)
DC10	133	111	96	72	(61)
DC9	311	274	272	268	(43)
DC8	118	80	78	77	(41)
F100	114	96	74	74	(40)
B717	28	43	13	13	(15)
L1011	20	15	13	13	(7)
B747	174	174	170	168	(6)
B737	1,296	1,277	1,303	1,294	(2)
A330	9	9	9	9	–
MD90	16	16	16	16	–
A310	41	43	46	45	4
A321	19	23	28	28	9
MD10	12	12	16	22	10
MD11	51	53	56	62	11
A300	89	94	101	104	15
B777	110	119	129	129	19
B767	333	344	359	363	30
B757	579	600	615	623	44
A319	158	177	196	210	52
A320	228	251	267	284	56
TOTAL	**4,950**	**4,717**	**4,677**	**4,652**	**(298)**

FIGURE 35-15 Airline fleet by type.

of the type that had to be done could only be accomplished in reorganization in a bankruptcy court. Before it was over, every legacy airline would enter Chapter 11 bankruptcy.

The air carrier industry briefly returned to profitability in 2006. By then airline employment had declined to 544,540, down from a high of 680,000 in the year 2000. Airline capacity, measured in available seat miles, had been reduced by more than 25 percent by aircraft retirements. But profitability since then has been elusive. Next we will take a look at the airlines in bankruptcy,

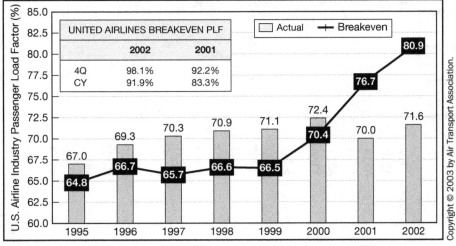

FIGURE 35-16 Load factors.

TABLE 35-2 ATA member airline operating fleet—2006.

		ABX (GB)	Alaska (AS)	Aloha (AQ)	American (AA)	ASTAR (ER)	Atlas/Polar (5Y/PO)	Continental (CO)	Delta (DL)	Evergreen Int'l (EZ)	FedEx Express (FX)	Hawaiian (HA)	JetBlue (B6)	Midwest (YX)	Northwest (NW)	Southwest (WN)	United (UA)	UPS (5X)	US Airways (US)	Total
Airbus	A300				34	6					56							53		**149**
	A310										66									**66**
	A319														66		55		93	**214**
	A320												96		73		97		75	**341**
	A321																		28	**28**
	A330														24				9	**33**
Boeing	B-717											11		25						**36**
	B-727					29					104							31		**164**
	B-737		91	24	77			264	71							481	94		96	**1,198**
	B-747						38			13					33		30	11		**125**
	B-757				142			58	121						66		97	75	46	**605**
	B-767	33			73			26	104			18					35	32	10	**331**
	B-777				46			18	8								52			**124**
	DC-8	5				9												46		**60**
	DC-9	61													107					**168**
	DC-10										31				2					**33**
	MD-10										52									**52**
	MD-11										58							34		**92**
	MD-80		23		325				120					11						**479**
	MD-90								16											**16**
Embraer	E190												23						2	**25**
Total		**99**	**114**	**24**	**697**	**44**	**38**	**366**	**440**	**13**	**367**	**29**	**119**	**36**	**371**	**481**	**460**	**282**	**359**	**4,339**

Note: Values reflect mainline aircraft counts as of December 31, () Airline code

Source: Air Transport Association.

and how mergers have shaped the industry. But to put things in perspective, we need to briefly review how the airlines got to this point.

Taking Stock

In the over 30-year period since deregulation, the existence of the air carrier industry has been characterized by a cyclical "feast or famine" roller coaster ride. Short periods of prosperity have always been followed by periods of stress and financial loss. Each one of these cycles has been precipitated by overriding economic and political conditions, punctuated by high fuel costs, all of which have been largely beyond the control of airline management.

The business model that existed during the period of CAB control beginning in the 1930s, the model the legacy airlines operated under when deregulation began, has been tested and has now been found to be unworkable in the new competitive environment of deregulation. This was not true during the early years of deregulation, when the incumbent airlines' economies of scale (size, experience, computer reservation systems, gate and slot ownership, and control of the hub and spoke system) did, in fact, inhibit the success of new entrant airlines.

The predominance of the legacy airlines during the years immediately following deregulation turned out to be a transitional phase in the progression of the industry away from government control. But the challenges of a never-ending stream of new entrant airlines continued to apply pressure to the business model of these airlines, which were still constrained by high labor costs, high fixed costs, low fares, and ever-increasing debt incurred in an effort to continue to exist.

Southwest Airlines brought to the contest a new business model, one which during the more recent period of commercial aviation experience has provided an example to new entrant airlines, and has been instructive to the legacy carriers as well. The "Southwest Effect," as its way of doing business and culture have been termed, has come to define how an airline can be run profitably in the deregulated world.[11]

Although Southwest is 82 percent unionized, its employees do not belong to the same unions as the legacy airlines, whose labor contracts are the product of adversarial negotiations of long standing. Southwest's employee relations are

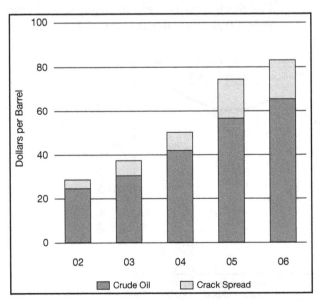

FIGURE 35-17 Differential between the price of crude oil and the price of petroleum products extracted from it.

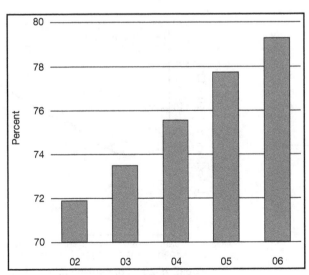

FIGURE 35-18 Passenger load factor.

349   P A R T   5   Deregulation

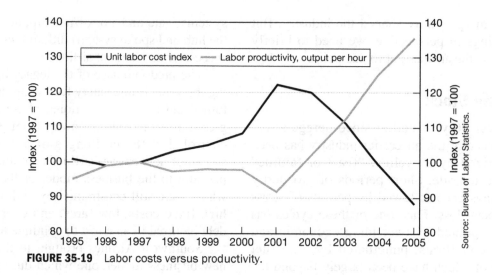

FIGURE 35-19   Labor costs versus productivity.

more personal and informal, and have produced a loyal workforce that views the airline's success as its own. But perhaps most important is the fact that the various classes and crafts of workers are permitted under their labor contracts to perform cross-functional tasks. One of the sacred cows of railroad style union contracts is that employees are prohibited from performing work that belongs by contract to others' crafts. A mechanic may not change a light bulb. A clerk may not use a broom. At Southwest, with the use of an incentivized pay structure, everyone pitches in to get the job done in the quickest and most efficient way possible. This results in much higher productivity. As an example, in 2000 the total labor expense at Southwest, measured per available seat mile, was 25 percent lower than at American and 58 percent lower than at USAir. This business model has produced the lowest operating expense in the industry, calculated on cost per available seat mile, 12.96 cents, compared with Delta Airlines' 14.76 cents. But the gap is beginning to narrow.

The Southwest model has always used only one type of aircraft, the Boeing 737, which has

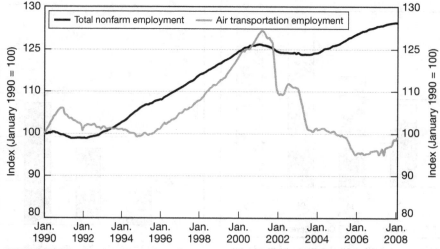

FIGURE 35-20   Comparison of nonfarm employment and employment in air transportation.

resulted in reduced maintenance costs and training costs of pilots and mechanics. Southwest flies into secondary airports rather than primary airports where possible, which lowers airport landing fees and costs and, along with a non-standard general boarding procedure, results in a comparatively low turn-around time. It has avoided hub and spoke costs and delays by employing a point-to-point networking system. This allows much higher equipment utilization.

The "no frills" airline group that has emulated many of the practices modeled by Southwest has come to be known as the "low-cost carriers" (LCCs). There have been many new entrants in this category into the domestic air carrier community since deregulation in 1978, but at least 20 have failed, including People Express, ATA Airlines, and MetroJet. Among the survivors of this group are AirTran, Allegiant Air, Frontier, JetBlue Airways, Spirit Airlines, and Virgin America. Some of these airlines fly only domestically, and some both domestically and internationally.

Primary among this group is JetBlue, which was founded by a nucleus of former Southwest Airlines employees. While following the basic low-cost model of Southwest, JetBlue offered some distinguishing amenities such as television monitors at every seat and satellite radio. It was kick-started in 1999 when the FAA awarded it 75 slots at its home base at JFK, and it began service in February 2000. As mentioned above, JetBlue was one of the few airlines that recorded a profit during 2001. JetBlue has not been as consistently profitable as Southwest, but it does maintain a certain cache among flyers and the airline community. It has also received high passenger satisfaction awards.

The other notable among the LCCs was AirTran, which operated Boeing 717 and 737 aircraft, headquartered in Orlando, Florida. In March 2012 the government approved the purchase of AirTran by Southwest and the merger process is under way. Since Southwest prides itself on operating only the Boeing 737, one of the initial problems with the merger was that AirTran flew both the Boeing 737 and the 717.

Latest developments indicate that all of the AirTran 717s will be leased to Delta Airlines. Thus Southwest is intent on keeping its operations limited to the Boeing 737.

◼ The Travails of the Legacy Airlines—Bankruptcy

The survival of the air carrier industry in the days after 9/11 was no sure thing. Passenger volumes plummeted. Fares were lowered in an intensified competition for what traffic there was. Enhanced airport security procedures, with attendant delays, contributed to the problem. Added costs to the airlines included cost of security (e.g., fortified cockpit doors), increased insurance premiums, and increased taxes. Fixed airline costs, like airplane lease payments and debt service, ran on. There was talk of nationalization of the industry or, at least, re-regulation. Gloom prevailed.

The airlines did what they could within the limits of management discretion, but that generally was not enough. It was not enough even with the payouts made by the Air Transportation Stabilization Board, which paid out $7 billion in direct assistance to the airlines and many billions more in indirect assistance in the form of loan guarantees to selected airlines. Aid included a tax holiday and pension relief. Still, it was not enough.

US Airways

On August 11, 2002, US Airways was the first carrier after 9/11 to seek bankruptcy protection. US Airways was the largest carrier at Washington Reagan Airport, and as such was severely impacted by the airport's closure for an extended period of time. In Chapter 11, U.S. Airways made significant changes to its operating model. It became the first U.S. airline to eliminate the pensions of its pilots, affecting some 6,000 employees. It became the first legacy carrier to eliminate complimentary meal service on domestic flights. As a part of its reorganization, it began a process of de-emphasizing its hub and spoke system, particularly in the Eastern United States, in favor of point-to-point service similar to Southwest's successful model. While in bankruptcy, the airline received a government-guaranteed loan under the Air Transportation Stabilization Board.

United Airlines

After 9/11, then the sixth largest airline in the country, United applied for a government-guaranteed loan from the Air Transportation Stabilization Board. In December 2002, the Board voted to deny the application in spite of concessions previously given by its flight attendants and its pilots. The Board believed that United's labor burden was still too bloated to allow it to compete in the existing business environment. United filed for bankruptcy protection on December 9, 2002. In 2003, in bankruptcy court, United cut pilots' wages 30 percent. Pilots pay then ranged between $33,000 for new hires to a high of $195,000. It also terminated its employee pension plan, the second airline to do so. Both of these pension plans were transferred to the Pension Benefit Guaranty Corporation, a federal agency set up to protect, at tax payer expense, employees' pensions.[12]

Delta Airlines

After 9/11, Delta Airlines continued its downward spiral, losing $10 billion between 2001 and 2005. The third largest carrier in the United States, Delta entered Chapter 11 on September 14, 2005. Although Delta had been in financial straits for some time, its pilots pay ranged from $48,000 for beginning pilots to $275,000 for Boeing 777 captains. Delta froze its employee pension plan (which allowed Delta to forego any further contributions to the plan) by agreement with its unions. In September 2006, the Bankruptcy Court approved termination of Delta's pilot pension plan. Delta has preserved ground and flight attendants' pension plans based on the passage of the Pension Protection Act by Congress in 2006. This statute gives Delta (and Northwest) a period of 17 years to fund the employee plans.

Northwest Airlines

Northwest, the fourth largest U.S. carrier, entered Chapter 11 on the same day as Delta, September 14, 2005. Precipitating the filing, Northwest had been unable to win necessary wage concessions from its unions. In fact, Northwest had been operating for almost a month prior to filing with its unionized mechanics on strike. Like Delta, Northwest froze its employee pension plan in bankruptcy. Unlike other airlines in bankruptcy, Northwest preserved all of its pension plans.

As of September 14, 2005, four of the top seven carriers in the United States were in bankruptcy. They were all legacy airlines. See Figure 35-21.

ATA Airlines

ATA was a new entrant airline, receiving its air carrier certificate in 1981, post deregulation. As the country's 10th largest air carrier, it filed for protection on October 22, 2004, citing fuel prices, competition, and lease payments on aircraft. This was necessary in spite of receiving an ATSB loan guarantee in the amount of $168 million in 2002. As part of its restructuring under bankruptcy protection, ATA agreed to sell its hub operation at Chicago Midway to AirTran, one of its major competitors. It also sold its slots at LaGuardia and Reagan National to AirTran.

Hawaiian Airlines

Founded in 1929 as Inter-Island Airways, Hawaiian Airlines had the distinction of being the oldest U.S. carrier never to have had a fatal accident in its history. Conditions after 9/11 forced HAL to begin a restructuring process, in which it negotiated significant concessions from its labor forces. The company was unable to satisfactorily

Airlines Filing Chapter 11

		2011 revenue passenger miles
United Continental	Continental became part of United in 2010	175.1 billion
Northwest Delta	Northwest became part of Delta in 2008	163.8
US Airways America West	America West became part of US Airways in 2005	53.1
TWA American	TWA became part of American Airlines in 2001	106.5

2000 2001 2002 2003 2004 2005 2006 2007 2008 2009 2010 2011

2011 revenue passenger miles-one passanger flown one mile

In August 2002, American announces a reorganization amid an industry-wide recession. It laid off staff, grounded jets, and changed how it connected passengers at its hubs.

In 2003, American Airlines workers took some $1.8 billion in concessions to help avoid Chapter 11 bankruptcy.

In January 2007, AMR posted a small profit in the fourth quarter due to lower fuel prices, continued cost-cutting, and higher ticket prices.

In July 2010, AMR secured antitrust approval for its trans-Atlantic alliance with British Airways and others.

In November 2011, AMR filed for Chapter 11 bankruptcy protection and Thomas Horton became CEO, replacing Gerard Arpey.

FIGURE 35-21   Airline bankruptcy chart.

restructure its aircraft leasing contracts, and entered bankruptcy on March 21, 2003.

Aloha Airlines

Aloha Airlines received its operating certificate in 1949. The company went private in 1986 with 100 percent ownership in two Hawaiian families. Aloha received a $45 million loan guarantee from the Air Transportation Stabilization Board in 2002, but by December 30, 2004, it was unable to continue operations outside of Chapter 11 bankruptcy. When it entered bankruptcy protection, it had repaid about half of the government-backed loan. The filing was attributed to competition factors, likely including its chief competitor, Hawaiian Airlines, which had

already secured creditor relief from bankruptcy protection.

Mesaba Airlines (a Northwest link airline)

Mesaba began operations in 1944 as a feeder route in Minnesota. In 1984, it began flying exclusively for Northwest Airlines as a regional carrier. Mesaba depended on Northwest for all of its passengers and its entire schedule. When Northwest filed for bankruptcy protection on September 14, 2005, cash shortages, fleet changes, and other uncertainties were imposed on Mesaba by Northwest. It is not surprising, then, that Mesaba followed Northwest into Chapter 11, which it did on October 13, 2005. Mesaba was owed $30 million by Northwest when Northwest filed in September.

Between 2002 and 2005, eight major carriers had entered bankruptcy. By 2007 all major airlines that had entered Chapter 11 post 9/11 had emerged from bankruptcy:

- June 2, 2005: Hawaiian Airlines
- September 27, 2005: US Airways. In Chapter 11, it merged with America West.
- February 1, 2006: United Airlines
- February 17, 2006: Aloha Airlines
- April 30, 2007: Delta Airlines
- May 31, 2007: Northwest Airlines

These transitions through reorganization have been largely at the cost of air industry labor groups and employees, as well as the stockholders of the companies. The one consistent winner through the years since deregulation has been the consumer. Domestic airfares had fallen 50.5 percent since 1978, adjusted for inflation. This phenomenon explains, in large part, the explosive growth that has been seen in air travel.

In 2005, the U.S. air carrier industry reported its first operating profit since 2000. Yet interest expense and other nonoperating costs left the airlines with a net loss of $5.7 billion.

By the end of 2006, for the first time since the turn of this century, U.S. air carriers had recorded a net profit. That year the airlines posted net income of $3 billion on $163.8 billion in revenues. Although fuel prices continued to increase (see Figure 35-17), fuel efficiency also increased, by 22 percent over the year 2000. Passenger load factor increased to 79 percent. (See Figure 35-18.) The airlines carried 12 percent more passengers in 2006 than in 2000, and they used 719 million fewer gallons of fuel in doing so. And they did it with fewer employees. (See Figure 35-12 and Table 35-1.) The airline fleet continued toward modernization. (See Table 35-2.)

"Since 1978 the record pretty well shows that no start-up airline . . . has really been successful, so the odds of JetBlue having long-term success are remote. I'm not going to say it can't happen because stranger things have happened, but I personally believe P. T. Barnum was, in that respect, correct."

(Ed. Note: P. T. Barnum, a 19th century showman and circus owner, is supposed to have famously said, "There is a sucker born every minute.")

Gordon Bethune, CEO Continental Airlines, commenting on the 70% rise in JetBlue's stock price in the days after its IPO. Continental's annual shareholder meeting, 17 April 2002.

Fleeting Profits, Mergers, and More Bankruptcy

A fleeting two years of profitability in the nation's airlines during 2006 and 2007 ended in 2008 with an industry operating loss of $3.6 billion.[13] In that year began a global recession of large dimensions, precipitated by a burst housing bubble caused by defaults on subprime mortgages (which began in 2007), largely due to loose credit policies of government backed mortgages. Stated differently, many people were encouraged by government policy to buy houses that they could not afford. As defaults increased due to homeowners' failure to make mortgage payments, banks and hedge funds that had bought these worthless mortgages packaged up as tradable securities bearing high credit ratings by Moody's and Standard and Poor's, began to face huge losses. Bankruptcies and government intervention in such institutions as Bear Stearns, AIG, Fannie Mae, Freddie Mac, IndyMac Bank, and Washington Mutual caused a drying up of credit that precipitated a widespread decline in employment. Unemployment rates nationally exceeded 10 percent. Unemployment rates for years 2003 to 2007 were between 6.3 and 4.4 percent.

At the same time, in 2008, the price of a barrel of crude oil oscillated wildly between $145 and $33 within a few months, causing the price of jet fuel to range between a low of $1.26 to a high of $4.26 a gallon. Fuel was now not only the highest cost factor in airline operations; it was also the most volatile. Revenues plunged 17 percent in 2009, which caused the largest two-year contraction in the history of aviation, and which resulted in a loss of $2.5 billion for the year. Over the nine-year period ending in 2009, the air transport industry lost $58 billion dollars.

Between 2002 and 2007, Chapter 11 bankruptcy reorganization had helped slim down four of the largest legacy airlines (US Airways, twice—in 2002 and again in 2004; Northwest and Delta, which filed on the same day in 2005; and United, which filed in 2002). These airlines had used Chapter 11 to renegotiate their union contracts for lower wages and more flexible union work rules, eliminate jobs, reduce capacity, and increase fares. These airlines were in a much better position to weather the economic turbulence of the late 2000s because of restructuring in Chapter 11.

During the first decade of this century, merger was also employed by all airlines in addition to bankruptcy as a corporate tool to consolidate resources and to try to advance profits. TWA was absorbed into American Airlines in 2001, before 9/11. America West Airlines was merged into US Airways in 2005, as a part of the Chapter 11 process of US Airways. Northwest merged with Delta in 2008, and the airline continued operation under the name of Delta. In 2010, Continental became a part of United. Southwest acquired AirTran in March 2011. All of these mergers were approved by the Department of Justice and were deemed not to violate any of the constraints of the antitrust laws.

During the first part of the 21st century, the legacy airlines were reinventing themselves from a historical perspective through the use of bankruptcy and merger. Although there were no bankruptcies of any airline during the days of economic regulation, there were a few mergers. These mergers were facilitated by the CAB, in order to maintain service and rates as prescribed, by requiring successful airlines to absorb the less

successful ones. That is the reason that the 16 airlines grandfathered under the Civil Aeronautics Act of 1938 had contracted to 10 airlines by 1978.

All of the legacy airlines, except American, had slimmed down through bankruptcy, and all had combined through merger with another carrier during the first decade of the 21st century. In 2011, not having been "cleansed" through bankruptcy, American had lost $11 billion since 2001. American Airlines faced labor costs that were significantly higher than any of its competitors and pensions that were the richest in the industry. Its labor and operating costs in 2011 were about 10 percent higher than Delta's. In fact, in 2011 American was the only major airline to lose money.

To further complicate the picture, American owns and operates American Eagle, a regional carrier that uses small, 50-seat aircraft that other airlines have been shedding (most other major carriers contract out their regional connections to independent regional airlines and have moved a bigger risk share to them). It is the only major airline that still performs most maintenance in-house. It also flies obsolete MD-80s, which are not fuel efficient, and are a big liability in these times of spiraling fuel prices.

In spite of years of negotiations with its unions, there was little progress in moving the issue forward, so in November 2011 the last holdout of the legacy airlines, American, capitulated and filed for Chapter 11 protection.[14] At that time, there had been 178 bankruptcy proceedings filed by domestic airlines since 1978, 46 of which had been in Chapter 11.[15]

American Airlines

Shortly after American entered Chapter 11, US Airways launched a hostile bid to cause a merger of the two airlines while American is under bankruptcy protection. While management at American initially resisted this move, the unions of both airlines, the creditors of American, and the stockholders of both airlines ultimately came out in favor of it. In February 2013, the companies announced agreement to the plan of merger, subject to the approval of the Bankruptcy Judge and the Justice Department.

The merger plan agreed to by the companies' boards of directors includes combining the airlines under the American Airlines brand, but with the US Airways management team in charge. The US Airways name would cease to exist. Creditors of American would receive the largest part of the stock of the new company, which is expected to reimburse them in full, with interest. US Airways stockholders would receive the balance of new company stock, except for a carve out of 3.5 percent for existing stockholders of American Airways.[16]

If approved, the new American Airlines company would be the largest airline in the world and would be a commanding presence in eight of the busiest airports in the United States. (See Fig. 35-22.) It would also remain a member of the Oneworld global airline alliance. The new arrangement would give American Airlines a 26 percent U.S. market share, with United at 19.3 percent, Delta at 19.2 percent, Southwest at 18.2 percent, and all other airlines combining for 17.3 percent.

Informed sources uniformly predicted government acceptance of the proposed merger plan based on prior merger approvals of United-Continental, Delta-Northwest and Southwest-Air

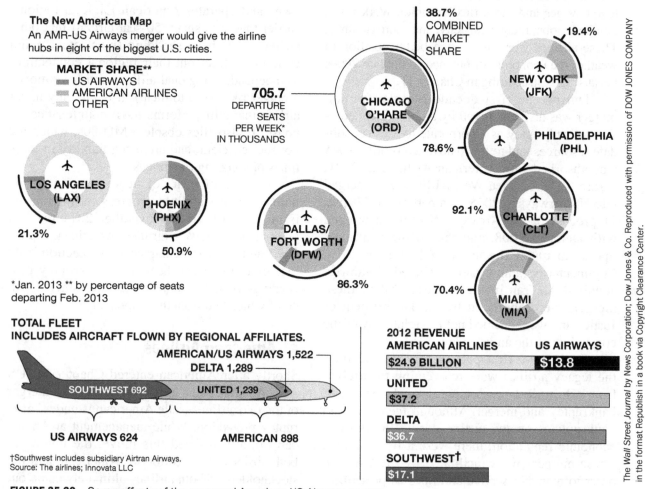

FIGURE 35-22 Some effects of the proposed American-US Airways merger.

Tran. But on August 13, 2013, the Department of Justice, joined by six states and the District of Columbia filed suit to block the merger. This action came as a particular surprise since the European Commission had approved the basic plan only a week earlier. The proposed merger partners announced their full intention to fight the lawsuit and they expect to prevail. The most recent conventional wisdom is to expect some sort of compromise with the DOJ to lessen any anti-competitive effects of the proposed merger.

During the period 2000 through 2012 the domestic airline industry went through significant consolidation, yet airline fares rose at a rate less than food (27 percent), beverage prices (38 percent), and housing costs (30 percent). The average increase in prices of all items monitored by the federal government increased 32 percent. The monitored airline fares, however, do not include the add-on fees that airlines have increasingly imposed on travelers in recent years.

◼ Convergence of Operating Practices

The overall result of these changes in the legacy carriers' structure is to make them look more like the low-cost carriers with which they have competed under deregulation. Not only are the legacy carriers structured more like the LCCs, they are beginning to adopt their operating practices as well. The lower fare structure of the new legacy airlines removes a major advantage previously held by the low-cost carriers. At the same time, the low-cost carriers are beginning to look more like the legacy carriers, causing a convergence between the two groups as they pursue the airline traveler dollar under a maturing deregulated air transportation system. The third group that makes up what comprises the majority of the domestic air transport system, the regional carriers, have also gone through a transformation as these changes roll downhill.

While the DOT classifies airlines as "majors" (20), "nationals" (33), or "regionals" (31) based strictly on revenues, this classification is not helpful in differentiating between the actual functions of the various groups. For instance, American Eagle is classified as a "major" airline due to its revenue, but its operations conform to what a regional or feeder airline does. A more practical classifying of airlines would separate them into legacy (or network or incumbent) airlines, low-cost carriers (LCCs), and regional airlines. By now, we know that the legacy airlines are the surviving carriers that operated during the period of CAB regulation; the LCCs are the "no frills" airlines that are either new entrant airlines (since 1978) or airlines that operated wholly intrastate during the CAB period; and regional airlines are those airlines that now operate as feeder airlines, mainly to the legacy carriers. Legacy carriers and LCCs are sometimes referred to as "mainline" carriers. A fourth group of carriers, not discussed here, are "commuters" (61), which operate aircraft of 60 or fewer seats or have a maximum payload of 18,000 pounds or less.

◼ The New Legacy Airlines

As a result of the bankruptcies and mergers of the legacy carriers beginning in 2002, this group of airlines has emerged as viable contenders with the LCCs. The new legacy airlines are United, Delta, US Airways (before the pending merger with American), and American Airlines. During the first decade of the 21st century, these airlines (representing also the absorbed Continental, Northwest, TWA, and America West) contracted their networks, route miles, number of employees, and number of aircraft, while focusing on down-sizing, cost-cutting, and improving productivity.

They began to emphasize Internet ticket purchasing and distribution and web check-in. These newly oriented carriers began to mimic other LCC practices by eliminating or reducing services and amenities that had come to be standard as the legacy brand, such as meals, soft drinks, snacks, and pillows.

By 2008, these airlines began to levy fees, in addition to the base airline fare, for services and amenities that had always been complimentary to their passengers. These add-on fees include, depending on the airline, ticket change fee, ticket cancellation fee, booking fee for phone or in person, seat selection fee, unaccompanied minor fee, pet in cabin fee, fees for checked bags, oversized bags, and overweight bags, early boarding fee, seat selection upgrade fee, wireless Internet fee, blanket and pillow sets fee, inflight entertainment fee, and inflight food and beverage charges. See Figure 35-23 for a depiction of select fees and the locations where offered for purchase. See Tables 35-3 and 35-4 for a listing of airlines and airlines' imposed fees for optional services.

The legacy carriers have, however, maintained business and first class services, which render much higher yields than standard. The legacy carriers also have the advantage of flying more profitable international routes as a result of global deregulation and Open Skies agreements.

■ The Low-Cost Carriers

Led by Southwest Airlines, a class of new entrant discount airline began entering the industry shortly

FIGURE 35-23 Ways added airline fees increase the cost of travel.
Source: GAO-10-785 Commercial Aviation

Airline	First bag (airport/online)	Second bag (airport/online)	Additional bags (each)	Overweight bags	Oversized bags
Air Tran	$15	$25	3+: $50	51–70 lbs: $49 71–100 lbs: $79	$49–$79
Alaska[a]	$20	$20	3: $20 4+: $50	51–100 lbs: $50	$50–$75
Allegiant	$35/$15–$30	$35/$25–$35	$35/$50	51–74 lbs: $50 75+ lbs: $100	$35
American	$25	$35	3–5: $100 6+: $200	51–70 lbs: $50 71–100 lbs: $100	$150
Continental	$25/$23	$35/$32	3+: $100	51–70 lbs: $50	$100
Delta	$25/$23	$35/$32	3: $125 4–10 $200	51–70 lbs: $90 71–100 lbs: $175	$175–$300
Frontier	$20	$30	3+: $50	51+ lbs: $75	$75
Hawaiian	$25/$23 inter-island: $10	$35/$32 $17 inter-island $17	3–6: $125 7+: $200 inter-island: $25	51–70 lbs: $50 inter-island: $25	$100 inter-island: $25
Jet Blue	$0	$30	3: $75	51–70 lbs: $50 71–100 lbs: $100	$75
Midwest	$20	$30	3+: $50	51–100 lbs: $75	$75
Southwest	$0	$0	3–9: $50 10+: $110	51–100 lbs: $50	$50
Spirit[b]	$25/$19	$25	3–5: $100	$51–70 lbs: $50 71–99 lbs: $100	$100–$150
Sun Country	$25/$20	$35/$30	$75	51–100 lbs: $75	$75
United[c]	$25	$35	3+: $100	51–100 lbs: $100	$100
USA3000	$25/$15	$25	$25	51–70 lbs: $25	$25–$50
US Airways	$25/$23	$35/$32	$3–9: $100	51–70 lbs: $50 71–100 lbs: $100	$100
Virgin America	$25	$25	3–10: $25	1st <70 lbs: free 51–70 lbs: $50 71–100 lbs: $100	$50

Source: GAO review of airline Web Sites and interviews with airline officials.

[a]Alaska Airlines does not charge for the first 3 checked bags for trips wholly within the state of Alaska.

[b]Spirit revised its checked baggage fee for travel on or after August 1, 2010 to $25 for each of the first two bags, and $85 for each of the 3rd, 4th and 5th bags.

[c]United also offers a $249 annual fee to check one or two bags per flight without charge.

TABLE 35-3   Domestic Checked Baggage Fees of 17 U.S. Airlines as of July 1, 2010

Airline	Ticket change or cancellation (domestic ticket)	Booking phone/ in person	Unaccompanied minor	Pet in cabin	Seat selection	Inflight food and beverage	Blanket and pillow
Air Tran	$75	$15/$0	$39 direct/ non-stop $59 connecting	$69	$6 advance $20 exit row	F: NA B: $6	NA
Alaska	$100 ($75 online)	$15/$15	$25 direct/ non-stop $50 connecting	$100	NA	F: $3.50–$7 B: $6	NA
Allegiant	$50 per segment	$15+$14.99 per segment/ $0	NA	NA	$4.99–$24.99 varies by flight length and seat.	F: $2–$5 B: $2–$7a	NA
American	$150	$20/$20–$30	$100	$100	NA	F: $3–$10 B: $6–$7	$8
Continental	$150	$20/$20	$100	$125	NA	F: $0 B: $6	NA
Delta	$150	$20/$35	$100	$125	NA	F: $2–$8 B: $5–$7	NA
Frontier	$50–$100	$0/$0	$50 direct/ non-stop $100 connecting	$75	$15–$25	F: $3–$7 B: $2–$5a	NA
Hawaiian	$100–150 inter-island: $25–$30	$25/$35 inter-island: $15/$35	$100 inter-island: $35	$175	NA	F: $5.50–$10 B: $6.50–$14	NA
Jet Blue	$100	$15	$75	$100	$10 extra legroom	F: $0 B: $6	$7
Midwest	$100	$0/$0	$50 direct/ non-stop $100 connecting	$75	NA	F: $3–$7 B: $2–$5a	NA
Southwest	$0	$0/$0	$50	$75	$10 priority boarding	F: $0 B: $3–$5	NA
Spirit	$110 ($100 online)	$5/$0 ($5 each way online)	$100	$100	Varies based on location.	F: $2–$5 B: $2–$6a	NA
Sun Country	$75	$15/$0	$75/ segment	$100	$8	F: $3–$6 B: $5	$5

TABLE 35-4 Partial List of Add-on Fees Charged by 17 Carriers

Airline	Ticket change or cancellation (domestic ticket)	Booking phone/ in person	Unaccompanied minor	Pet in cabin	Seat selection	Inflight food and beverage	Blanket and pillow
United	$150	$25/$30	$99	$125	$9/$109	F: $3–$9 B: $6	NA
USA3000	$75	$0/$0	$50	$75	$9–$25	n/a	NA
US Airways	$150	$25–$35	$100 (non-stop flights only)	$100	$5+ Varies by location.	F: $3–$7 B: $7–$8	$7
Virgin America	$100 ($75 online)	$15/$10	$75	$100	NA	F, B: $2–$10	$12

Source: GAO analysis

ᵃFee for some nonalcoholic beverages.

TABLE 35-4 Continued

after 1978. Their distinguishing characteristic has been to provide a no frills, basic transportation service at the cheapest fare possible. They have sought to do this by concentrated efforts to reduce their operating and marketing costs by various means and practices uncommon in the traditional airline business. Primary among these airlines currently are Southwest, JetBlue, AirTran (prior to merger with Southwest), Spirit, Frontier, Allegiant Air, Sun Country Airlines, and Virgin America.

Contrary to most airlines and to emerging trends, Southwest does not charge for baggage. It is also contrarian by the fact that it has never furloughed any employees and has never asked its labor workforce for wage concessions. It has, therefore, a high wage structure compared to other airlines. It has been able to maintain consistent profitability through the utilization of the various efficiencies discussed above. As the unit cost gap between the new legacy carriers and Southwest and the other LCCs narrows, it will be interesting to see how Southwest, in particular, is able to continue its labor practices into the future competition.

The evolution of Southwest is further marked by its purchase of AirTran in 2011. AirTran has service to Mexico and the Caribbean, so part of the process of combining operations and expanding their route systems will involve

Southwest becoming an international carrier. This is far removed from the original discount carrier concept that Southwest pioneered and then carefully honed. In the process Southwest is becoming increasingly larger; as of 2102 it operated scheduled service to destinations in 42 states. Its size, number of enplanements (it carries more passengers than any domestic airline), and increased number of destinations, has caused it to change from a primarily point-to-point airline to one that must facilitate connections.

It now practices the "rolling hub" concept, which schedules a majority of flights into certain designated airports for connection purposes, but it avoids arrival "banks" of aircraft at the same time to lessen congestion, rather scheduling arrivals over longer periods of time. With Phoenix having 181 daily departures, you might say that this is Southwest's largest rolling hub, but it also has extensive departures from Las Vegas, Baltimore-Washington, Houston, Chicago-Midway, and many others. The AirTran merger will carry it into Atlanta in a big way.

Southwest pioneered the Internet reservation system in the 1990s and in the process personalized its service, made it transparent and readily accessible, and saved a lot of money. Now, with its excursions into international passenger service (which is more lucrative than domestic service), it has partnered with a European global distribution firm known as Amadeus, which is seen as a major move toward transforming itself from a low-cost domestic carrier into a large airline in the global airline industry, probably expanding into South America.

The other primarily notable LCC is Jet-Blue Airways which, while still classified as a low-cost carrier, differs significantly from the Southwest model. JetBlue, for instance, began operations in 2000 at John F. Kennedy International airport, a busy international hub centered in the most congested area of the country. It had to have slots to operate (which it got from the FAA) and it flew into other large airports, originally serving the east coast of the United States and then spreading across the country and internationally to Puerto Rico and 11 countries in the Caribbean and Latin America. While offering services at a discounted price, it differentiated itself by offering amenities like leather seats and DirecTV at every seat, and a personalized customer experience that has resulted in high satisfaction and a loyal customer base.

JetBlue sells only electronic tickets, primarily through its website. So far its workforce is entirely nonunion, so it has flexible work rules and effectively uses part-time employees. Its relatively new fleet consists entirely of two types of airplanes, the Airbus 320 and the Embraer 190. JetBlue carries high debt due to new aircraft acquisition, on a debt-to-value ratio between 65 and 75 percent, compared to Southwest's 20–40 percent.

The company has a marketing program that is innovative yet inexpensive, using social media such as Facebook and YouTube at very little cost.

Head to Head Comparison of Legacy Airlines and LCCs

Market Entry and Exit: Legacy airlines have entered new markets at a reduced rate and have exited markets at an increased rate since 2004, just the opposite of LCCs.

Route structure: Route overlap between the two sets of carriers was 13 percent in 1997 but had risen to 31 percent in 2009, indicating an increasing competitive challenge to the legacy airlines.

Fleets: Legacy airlines reduced their fleets from 1995 to 2009 while LCCs increased their fleets from 257 in 1995 to 911 in 2009. The legacy airlines' fleet is still about three times larger than the LCC fleet.

Employees: LCC employee numbers have increased and legacy airlines' have decreased.

Fares: The fare differential between legacy carriers and LCCs is lessening, partly due to increased market pressure and competition from the LCCs. Fare premiums due to hub concentrations (hub premiums) by the legacy carriers was 24.9 percent in 1995 but had dropped to 6.6 percent in 2009 (greater N.Y. area) and respectively from 18.6 percent to 6.4 percent in Chicago and Dallas.

Customer Satisfaction: An objective criteria standard called the "Airline Quality Rating" was created in 1991 by Wichita State University (now in cooperation with Purdue University), to report passenger satisfaction levels. It is based on 15 criteria, including on-time performance, denied boardings, mishandled baggage, and customer complaints. See Figures 35-24, 35-25, and 35-26.

Regional Airlines

Regionals are a mixed bag. Regionals can be large or small; they can be independently owned or owned by larger carriers; they can operate jets (30–108 seats) or turboprops (9–78 seats). Most operate under contract to mainline carriers called "pro-rate agreements" or "capacity agreements" and they all serve the function of feeding passengers from smaller airports to larger ones and back. At 498 airports in 2010, regional airlines provided the only service. Stated differently, 72

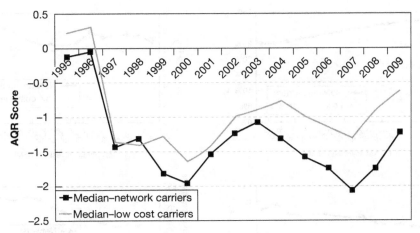

FIGURE 35-24   Airline quality rating (customer satisfaction) comparison between legacy carriers and LCCs.

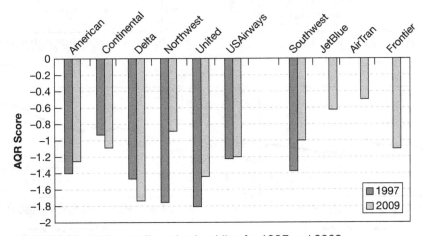

FIGURE 35-25   Airline quality rating by airline for 1997 and 2009.

percent of U.S. communities rely exclusively on regional airlines for all scheduled air service.

In 2012, the FAA said that the U.S. commercial aviation industry at the end of FY 2011 consisted of 16 scheduled mainline air carriers that used large passenger jets (over 90 seats) and 68 regional carriers that used smaller piston, turboprop, and regional jet aircraft (up to 90 seats). Regional carrier international service is confined to the border markets in Canada, Mexico, and the Caribbean.[17]

Under a pro-rate or revenue-sharing agreement, ticket revenues are shared according to a proration formula. All costs incurred in the regional airline portion are borne by the regional airline, and it is responsible for pricing, scheduling, and ticketing. The regional airline assumes the risk of its operation, but also presumes to benefit from declines in fuel prices and increased passenger counts and ticket prices. While the risks are greater under these agreements, so can be the profits.

Under a capacity purchase or fixed-fee agreement, part or all of a regional's seat capacity is purchased by a mainline partner. The regional carrier is paid a fixed fee for each block hour of aircraft operation. The mainline carrier assumes the cost of ground support and gate access, as well as operating expenses. The regional airline

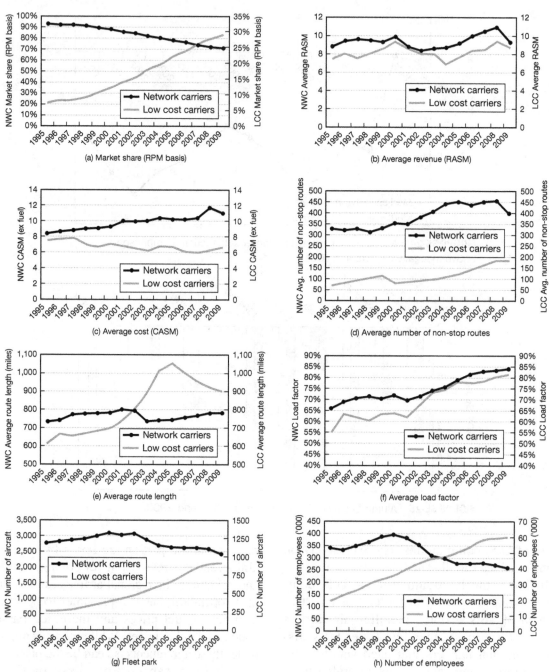

FIGURE 35-26 Head to head comparisons between legacy carriers and LCCs.

is responsible for labor costs, aircraft maintenance, and ownership or lease expense. Under this arrangement, the regional carrier is protected from fluctuations in load factors, cost of fuel, and ticket prices.

Under either contractual arrangement, the regional airline is an independent contractor and the mainline carrier assumes no third-party liability for the regional's acts, including liability for aircraft accidents.

As the larger new legacy carriers have cut back on route mileage and networks, regionals have increased their percentage of total miles flown. While the number of regionals has diminished from 247 carriers in 1980 to 61 carriers in 2010, they have flown increasing numbers of passengers, longer distances, and in larger aircraft over that period. In 2010, regionals carried over 163 million passengers and operated almost half of all scheduled airline flights in the United States, a 40 percent increase since 2003 at a time when traffic volumes have remained static. Code sharing with larger airlines accounts for 99 percent of all regional traffic, and the regional aircraft may fly the livery of its larger contracting carrier or it may fly its own.

1. **United/Continental** has contractual relationships with Atlantic Southeast Airlines, Chautauqua Airlines, Colgan Airlines, CommutAir Airlines, ExpressJet Airlines, GoJet Airlines, Mesa Airlines, Shuttle American, SkyWest Airlines, and Trans States Airlines.
2. **Delta** has contractual arrangements with nine regional carriers: Comair is wholly owned. The others are Atlantic Southeast Airlines, SkyWest Airlines, Chautauqua Airlines, Shuttle American, Compass Airlines, Pinnacle Airlines, Mesaba Aviation, and American Eagle.
3. **American** has capacity agreements with two wholly owned subsidiaries of AMR: American Eagle Airlines and Executive Airlines, and also has a capacity agreement with Chautauqua Airlines.
4. **Alaska Airlines** has a capacity agreement with its wholly owned subsidiary Horizon Air.
5. **US Airways** has capacity agreements with two wholly owned subsidiaries: PSA and Piedmont. It also has agreements with Air Wisconsin Airlines, Mesa Airlines, Chautauqua Airlines, and Republic Airways.

Some of the largest regionals are combined in corporate ownership groups.

Regional Airline Operating Practices

As a result of high-visibility air crashes involving regional airlines, regional airlines staffing and operating practices have recently come under renewed and intensive review. While regional airlines fly one out of four airline passengers today, they usually do so under the brand of the mainline carrier that conducts the majority of the flight segments. Many, if not most, of the passengers who board the regional carrier aircraft will not be aware that the mainline carrier is not operating the aircraft that they are boarding. They will not realize that pilot hiring requirements, pilot flight experience, pilot training procedures, and pilot pay scales will be very different from mainline carriers, even though the same FAA requirements apply to both types of carriers.[18] Regional pilots are paid much less than their counterparts in the mainline carriers, sometimes even less than TSA screeners.

There were six fatal domestic airline accidents between 2003 and 2009, all involving regional airlines.[19]

* Jan. 8, 2003: Air Midwest flight 5481, flying as US Airways Express, crashed in Charlotte, N.C., killing 21. The NTSB investigation cites deficiencies in Air Midwest's oversight of outsourced maintenance as a contributing cause.
* Oct. 14, 2004: Pinnacle Airlines flight 3701, operating under a code share as Northwest Airlink, crashed in Jefferson City, MO, killing two crew members who were repositioning the plane to another airport after routine maintenance. The NTSB cites poor airmanship, unprofessional behavior, and deviation from standard operating procedures as probable causes.
* Oct. 19, 2004: Corporate Airlines flight 5966 crashed in Kirksville, MO, killing 13. NTSB investigators cite pilots' failure to follow established procedures as a probable cause and pilot fatigue as a contributing cause.
* Dec. 19, 2005: A seaplane, operated by Flying Boat Inc., but flying as Chalks Ocean

Airways flight 101, crashed in Miami, killing 20. The NTSB cites Chalks' inadequate maintenance program and the FAA's failed oversight of the airline as probable causes.

- Aug. 27, 2006: Comair flight 5191, operating under a code share as Delta Connection, crashed in Lexington, KY, killing 47 passengers and 2 crew members. One crew member survives. The final NTSB report cites pilot performance as the probable cause and non-relevant conversation by crews as a contributing cause.
- Feb. 12, 2009: Continental flight 3407, a Colgan Air-operated plane flying under a code share as Continental Connection, crashed outside of Buffalo, N.Y., killing all 49 on board and 1 on the ground. NTSB cites the captain's inappropriate response to a stall, unprofessional pilot behavior, and Colgan Air's inadequate procedures for flying in icing conditions as probable causes.

The last accident, Colgan Air flight 3407, was highly publicized in the news media and in aviation circles. The issues raised by this event concerned the adequacy of entry-level flight qualifications of pilots, the airline's training standards for all pilots, the acceptable level and quality of crew rest, and pilots' pay levels. The first officer of flight 3407, for instance, was paid a salary of $16,000 per year, lived with her parents in Seattle, Washington, and commuted to her home base at Newark by overnight deadheading, at least partially due to financial constraints. It was said that she also had a part-time job in a coffee shop.

The airplane flown by Colgan Air was painted in Continental's livery, including Continental's trademark globe on the tail, and only the fine print on the ticket gave any indication that this was not a Continental operation.

In February 2012, the FAA proposed to substantially increase the qualification requirements for first officers consistent with a mandate in the Airline Safety and Federal Aviation Administration Extension Act of 2010. The proposed rule is entitled "Pilot Certification and Qualification Requirements for Air Carrier Operations." Among other things, this proposal would require an Airline Transport Rating for first officers, completion of a new FAA-approved program for the ATP certificate with enhanced training requirements, but contain allowances for reduced minimum flight time to qualify for the ATP rating under certain circumstances, including military training or a four-year baccalaureate degree program.

This rule seems to have stirred some controversy, with even the former FAA administrator Randy Babbitt on record as saying he does not think this is the best solution to the problem, citing overall safety statistics. It must also be recognized that the kind of flying that the regionals have to perform is not comparable with that of the mainline carriers. Regionals perform many more takeoffs and landings, thus more instrument approaches in IMC, fly at lower altitudes, use shorter and narrower runways at outlying airports, and often fly turboprop equipment.

Overall, according to the NTSB, from 2000 to 2009, it was more than twice as safe to fly as it was in the preceding decade, and more than seven times safer than in the 1970s. While these are impressive and reassuring statistics, unanswered questions implicit in the foregoing illustrations of regional practices remain.

Domestic Airlines in the 21st Century

A deregulated air transport system driven by consumer demand based primarily on price has emerged in the 21st century. It is a system that tends toward a low-cost approach as its first goal, and then tries to find ways to survive while providing it. Airlines have not proven to be good investments in an economically deregulated world. As of 2012, there is only one domestic airline that possesses investment grade credit, the minimum rating of BBB–, and that airline is the only airline that has been consistently profitable under the deregulated system. See Figure 35-29 for a comparison of corporations and their credit ratings.

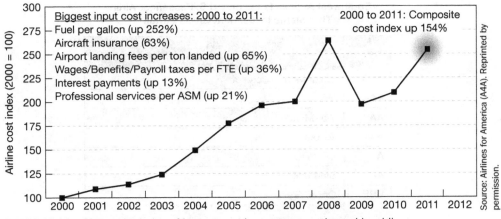

FIGURE 35-27 Composite index of largest cost increases experienced by airlines.

Biggest input cost increases: 2000 to 2011:
Fuel per gallon (up 252%)
Aircraft insurance (63%)
Airport landing fees per ton landed (up 65%)
Wages/Benefits/Payroll taxes per FTE (up 36%)
Interest payments (up 13%)
Professional services per ASM (up 21%)

2000 to 2011: Composite cost index up 154%

Source: Airlines for America (A4A). Reprinted by permission.

Price per Gallon (Gulf Coast Jet Fuel)

Year	Total fuel cost
YTD 2012	$3.12
2011	$3.00
2006–2010	$2.17
2001–2005	$1.02
1996–2000	$0.58
1991–1995	$0.54

(a)

Fuel Impact on Operating Costs

Year	% of operating costs	Average price per barrel of crude	Break-even price per barrel	Total fuel cost
2003	14%	$28.8	$23.4	$44 billion
2004	17%	$38.3	$34.5	$65 billion
2005	22%	$54.5	$51.8	$91 billion
2006	26%	$65.1	$68.3	$117 billion
2007	28%	$73.0	$82.2	$135 billion
2008	33%	$99.0	$82.5	$189 billion
2009	26%	$62.0	$58.9	$125 billion
2010	26%	$79.4	$89.6	$139 billion
2011 F	30%	$111.2	$116.1	$176 billion
2012 F	33%	$110.0	$111.9	$207 billion

(b)

Data source: Airlines for America (A4A).

FIGURE 35-28 Airline fuel cost analysis.

The legacy airlines have been reduced in number significantly through consolidation since the turn of the century, although their resulting, consolidated market share has remained about the same. They have shed much of the drag previously generated by old labor contracts, excess employment, excess capacity, and antiquated fleets. Southwest now has the highest labor cost based on available seat miles other than American Airlines, which entered Chapter 11 in November 2011 in large part *because* of its high labor cost. The other legacy carriers all have less cost attributable to

labor as of the end of 2011 than the original discount carrier, Southwest. They are in much better shape to take on the low-cost carriers because, in a sense, they themselves have adopted many of the LCC attributes.

The low-cost carriers have found a firm footing in the industry and have shown that they can compete within the industry and that they have some staying power. Southwest, in particular, has shown an inclination to grow and to expand, although all LCCs have increased market share.

**Southwest Airlines Is the only U.S. Passenger Airline
That Merits Investment Grade Status**

Grade	Airlines	
AAA	ExxonMobil, Microsoft	
AA+	GE	
AA	Wal-Mart	
AA–	Toyota	
A	BP, eBay	
A–	Starbucks	
BBB	QANTAS	
BBB–	Lufthansa, Southwest	>= BBB– (investment grade) < BBB– (speculative grade)
BB–	Alaska, Allegiant, British Air	
B+	GOL, TAM	
B	Delta, United	
B–	Air Canada, JetBlue, SAS, US Airways	
D	American	

FIGURE 35-29 Credit rating comparisons among certain industries and airlines.
Source: Airlines for America and Standard & Poor's.

During the last half of the first decade of the new century, hard times have again beset the air transport industry because of a severe recession beginning in 2008 and because of the volatility and high price of jet fuel. These adversities affect all airlines, as they continue to try to eke out an existence.

Now What?

There has been an on-going shake-out in the air transportation business for 35 years. We have attempted to trace the progress of this evolution in the preceding chapters and what we have seen is not pretty. Economic deregulation has brought chaos to the airline industry.

The air carrier industry has become just about as lean as it is possible to get, mostly at a cost to the airline employee and the comfort of the traveler, yet profits are scarce and undependable. Capacity has decreased. Air fares are rising. The last legacy airline has gone into Chapter 11.

There can be no question that the consumer has benefitted greatly—but at what cost? The entire sector is barely hanging on, trying to survive between one uncontrollable externality and the next. Under deregulation, unfettered competition has taken the place of any discernible national transportation policy. Is this sustainable?

One authority on the subject, Robert Crandall, former American Airlines CEO, thinks not:

" Three decades of deregulation have demonstrated that airlines have special characteristics incompatible with a completely unregulated environment. To put things bluntly, experience has established that market forces alone cannot and will not produce a satisfactory airline industry, which clearly needs some help to solve its pricing, cost, and operating problems."

The airline industry is composed of or affected by at least four main entities: airline labor, airline passengers, airline management, and airline company shareholders. Their individual interests are vastly disparate, but their one common interest is airline profitability. Yet, airlines are not reliably profitable; in fact, they are rarely profitable. Under the private enterprise system, a corporation will not long exist if it does not make a profit.

As legacy airlines have slimmed down under Chapter 11 or gone out of business, and as new entrant airlines have picked up the slack in capacity and service abandoned by the legacy carriers, a tentative status quo has been maintained. But at some point this process as a means of maintaining an air carrier system must cease, and a sustainable model for a profitable and durable airline system must emerge. Whether this can be done without at least some form of governmental control or economic re-regulation is now an open question. But there are powerful interests that now suggest that some sort of re-regulation, different from the kind of onerous and inclusive CAB regulation previously in place, must be entertained.

Endnotes

1. Discussed more at length in Chapter 40.
2. Bin Laden was killed by members of United States Navy Seal Team 6 on May 1, 2011 in Pakistan.
3. Pub. L. No. 107-42; 115 Stat. 230.
4. Pub. L. No. 107-71; 115 Stat. 597 (2001).
5. Representative John Mica, Chairman of the House Transportation Committee.
6. *Wall Street Journal*, April 9, 2012.
7. Pub. L. No. 107-296; 116 Stat. 2135 (2002).
8. The SARS epidemic was the outbreak of a viral respiratory disease in Hong Kong in late 2002, which spread worldwide during the ensuing months, causing over 900 deaths. Although the death rate of SARS is only 1 percent for people aged 24 or younger, it is 50 percent for those 65 or older. SARS caused a worldwide reduction in airline traffic volumes.
9. Hedging refers to the practice of buying crude oil futures contracts. Prices can be locked in at a predetermined (current) price even as the price of oil goes up. Hedging does carry some risk since to buy a futures contract assumes that the price will rise in the future. If it does not, then the owner of the futures contract will either make no profit or will lose money. Given the history of oil prices, hedging has been a lucrative practice in recent years.
10. Fuel would soon surpass wages as the largest airline cost of doing business.
11. In January 2012, Southwest reported its 39th consecutive year of profitable operation.
12. The Pension Benefit Guaranty Corporation's (PBGC) single-employer insurance program is a federal program that insures certain benefits of the more than 34 million worker, retiree, and separated vested participants of over 29,000 private sector defined benefit pension plans. Defined benefit pension plans promise a benefit that is generally based on an employee's salary and years of service, with the employer being responsible to fund that benefit, invest and manage plan assets, and bear the investment risk. A single-employer plan is one that is established and maintained by only one employer. It may be established unilaterally by the sponsor or through a collective bargaining agreement.
13. Operating loss does not include interest expense and other allowable expenses. The net loss was $23 billion total for all airlines.
14. Alaska Airlines is part of a system of airlines that originated in 1932 and existed as a feeder airline during the period of regulation. It took the name "Alaska Airlines" in 1944. It is the only pre-1978 intrastate airline not to have sought bankruptcy protection.
15. Air Transport Association. "List of Bankruptcies." http://www.airlines.org/economics/specialtopics/USAirlineBankruptcies.htm.
16. This is an unusual result since stockholders of a bankrupt company, even in Chapter 11, usually get wiped out.
17. U.S. Department of Transportation, FAA Aerospace Forecast, Fiscal years 2012–2032.
18. In 1995, the FAA brought regionals flying aircraft with 10 or more seats under the same regulatory scheme as the major airlines.
19. These incidents are taken from Public Broadcasting Corporation website *Frontline* http://www.pbs.org/wgbh/pages/frontline/flyingcheap/etc/cronfaa.html#six).

36

Something New Under the Sun: Next Generation Air Transportation System (NextGen), the National Airspace System, and Unmanned Air Vehicles

The National Airspace System (NAS) is defined as the network of United States airspace: air navigation facilities, equipment, services, airports, aeronautical charts, rules, regulations, procedures, technical information, manpower, and material. The NAS is a product of the evolution of aviation, including the incorporation of technology as it evolved, the establishment of airspace classifications, the promulgation of regulations and procedures, and the development of airports and facilities, all for the purpose of transporting people and cargo as safely and efficiently as possible.

The National Airspace System has become inadequate to fulfill its function in air transportation. The technology that is used to control movement within the system is basically 1950s technology, largely ground-based radars and navaids, and the ground-based equipment that uses the system is essentially worn out. Congestion and weather externalities cause substantial delays. Fuel conservation cannot be optimized even as the price of fuel surges. Environmental concerns from air transportation operations are not being assuaged. There

is little coordination between airport operations and airborne operations. Further evolution of the same technology will not serve the needs of the NAS and the traveling public in the future. A new technology and a new way of doing things are needed.

Vision 100—Century of Aviation Reauthorization Act of 2003[1]

After many years of anguished discussion concerning the state of U.S. air traffic control, FAA equipment problems, and the burgeoning volume of air traffic following economic deregulation of the airlines, Congress passed legislation in 2003 that will, in stages, revamp the way aircraft, passengers, and cargo are moved from airport to airport, and in the process will coordinate airport functions and ground operations with air segments.

This comprehensive and far-reaching statute encompasses many areas of the air transportation system, but most importantly it authorizes the development and implementation of a new and modernized National Airspace System. Labeled "The Next Generation Air Transportation System," or NextGen, it proposes to transform the air transportation system from one based on ground radars to one based on precision satellite-based navigation, with comprehensive changes in virtually every aspect of movement by air. This undertaking is so vast that it is best described as an evolution of ideas and technologies that are developing even as it is being put in place. The process contemplates a 20-plus year time frame for completion, projected for the year 2025.

NextGen is a transformative change in how we fly. It will change the management and operation of the NAS, while enhancing safety, reducing delays, saving fuel, and reducing adverse environmental impacts. It will integrate satellite navigation with advanced digital communications and it will incorporate the airport environment into the overall planning and functionality of the National Airspace System. It will change the way weather information is provided to pilots, controllers, and airline dispatchers.

Development and implementation of NextGen is a daunting task for many reasons, including:

1. It must be developed and implemented at the same time that the present radar-based system is running full tilt.
2. It proposes technology that has yet to be perfected.
3. It requires significant financial investment in new ground-based equipment by government and new onboard equipment by flying users of the new system, estimated to be in excess of $40 billion.
4. Airlines are reluctant to invest in the required onboard equipage until the FAA can demonstrate with some confidence when the government-funded technologies will be available for use in the new system.
5. It requires training in the use of new equipment and in procedures by government, military, and civilian users of the new system.

6. It requires the building of more than 700 new ground stations and facilities around the country to implement the new technology.
7. It requires the promulgation of new rules and procedures, and the publication of new charts and approach plates to use the new system.
8. The system must be integrated on a global basis.

The development and implementation of the new system, therefore, involves every entity that is in the production chain of development and every entity that is affected or will be affected by the implementation of the system, which includes virtually everyone involved in the air transportation community. Collaboration among these stakeholders is being facilitated by several organizations or relationships, including:

1. The Joint Planning and Development Office (JPDO), which was authorized in the statute, and which coordinates among the FAA, NASA, the Departments of Defense, Commerce, and Homeland Security and which has laid the groundwork and plans for the future vision for NextGen.
2. RTCA, which is a private, not-for-profit corporation that functions as a Federal Advisory Committee and includes some 400 industry and academic organizations from the United States and other countries. RTCA was organized in 1935 as the Radio Technical Commission for Aeronautics and develops consensus-based recommendations regarding communications, navigation, surveillance, and air traffic management.
3. The NextGen Mid-Term Implementation Task Force, which is a consortium of over 300 representatives of the aviation community who provide recommendations to the FAA as it moves forward on NextGen implementation.

4. The FAA, which is collaborating with the Department of Defense and Homeland Security to facilitate the entry of unmanned aircraft systems (UAVs) into the NAS.

5. The FAA, which is collaborating with the military, NASA, and NOAA's National Weather Service to incorporate weather data into the system.

6. The FAA, which is working through ICAO with international partners in Europe, Japan, and Australia to ensure compatibility with global standards.

Performance-Based Navigation

The NextGen system is based on the concept known as Performance-Based Navigation (PBN). PBN is basically a system of aircraft movement that maximizes on board navigation capabilities and options while reducing ground-based control personnel and Navaids. PBN is based on two fundamental elements: Area Navigation (RNAV) and Required Navigation Performance (RNP).

RNAV as a general concept has been around for a long time. It was first implemented by using the Navaid system of VORs and other ground-based facilities now in place. Avionics onboard aircraft could "move" Navaids to any point in two-dimensional space, thus creating "waypoints" which could be used to fly direct routes. It was also subsequently used with LORAN airborne receivers in a similar manner for direct route navigation. The new RNAV system proposed in PBN uses satellite-based navigation and is much more sophisticated than previous concepts of RNAV.

Required Navigation Performance is a set of standards or parameters by which departure, en route, approach, and landing must be accomplished by aircraft in the National Airspace System, and which requires the aircraft and its equipment to meet those associated performance standards. RNP contemplates a "trajectory" profile that will maximize the performance characteristics of jet aircraft and allow immediate climb to altitude and delayed, continuous descent to landing instead of the "stair-step" procedures currently in use for both climb and descent.

ADS-B Out

RNP requires the use of a new technology called Automatic Dependent Surveillance-Broadcast (ADS-B). ADS-B is a replacement for traditional radar-based surveillance of aircraft. Instead of using ground-based radar to interrogate aircraft and determine their positions, each aircraft will use Global Navigation Satellite System (GNSS) technology (GPS in the U.S.; Galileo in Europe) to find its own position and then automatically report it to ground stations (FAA stations in the United States) and to other aircraft equipped to receive it. At the same time, it reports the aircraft's speed, heading, altitude, and flight number. This function is called ADS-B Out.

The FAA has mandated that all aircraft must have the ADS-B Out equipment installed by 2020. It is surmised that this equipment capability will be needed in areas where transponders are now required.

ADS-B In

The function of an aircraft receiving the reported position of other aircraft is called ADS-B In. There is no requirement yet for the installation of ADS-B In capability, primarily because there has been no consensus that this technology has proven its value relative to its cost.

TIS-B and FIS-B

The FAA ground station receiving the airborne data rebroadcasts back to the sky once every second. This data broadcast is called TIS-B. The ground station also broadcasts additional flight information such a graphical weather display and NOTAMS. This data is called FIS-B.

There are three distinct benefits of ADS-B over radar:

1. GPS reported positions are more accurate than radar and more frequently reported. Unlike radar, ADS-B accuracy does not seriously degrade with range, atmospheric conditions, or target altitude. Update intervals do not depend on the rotation speed or reliability of mechanical antennas. This means that closer spacing can be used than presently, and this provides much needed capacity improvements in congested airspace.

2. ADS-B is less expensive to deploy than ground radars. ADS-B can also be deployed in areas where there was previously no coverage by radar, for instance, ocean routes and the Gulf of Mexico, where only procedural separation could be employed. These areas can now receive air traffic control separation and free up needed airspace.

3. Other aircraft with ADS-B In equipage can receive the ADS-B broadcast to facilitate aircraft avoidance.

The totality of NextGen benefits will depend on the successful development of FAA ground-based systems, space-based systems, alternative fuels, engine and airframe improvements, advanced avionics capabilities, and airport infrastructure.

Implementation Process

The FAA published its Roadmap for Performance-Based-Navigation in order to detail three periods of implementation: Near Term (2005–2010); Mid Term (2011–2015); and Far Term (2016–2025).

By 2012, most of the Near Term objectives for implementation had been achieved. The ADS-B ground-based infrastructure had more than 400 ground stations operational. These stations were providing satellite-based surveillance coverage for the east, west, and Gulf Coasts and most of the area near the U.S.–Canadian border (see Figure 36-1). ATC is already using this foundation NextGen technology to separate equipped aircraft at several areas, including Louisville, Kentucky; Juneau, Alaska; Houston; and Philadelphia. The total complement of 700 ground-based stations is expected to be operational by 2014 and will allow controllers to use the airspace more efficiently.

A significant volume of PBN arrival and departure procedures for commercial airports, as well as high and low altitude en route charts, have been published. Access to general aviation airports has been improved through the publication of PBN approach procedures using Area Navigation Wide Area Augmentation System (WAAS) Localizer Performance with Vertical Guidance (LPV) charts. LPVs are operationally equivalent to Instrument Landing System (ILS) approaches but require no costly infrastructure or maintenance. As of February 2011, there were 2,772 LPVs at 1,400 airports nationwide.

Metroplex Initiative

A metroplex is a metropolitan area where multiple airports are located. The Southern California metroplex, for example, contains more than a dozen general aviation airports as well as large commercial airports such as Los Angeles International Airport (LAX). The FAA has undertaken studies to identify PBN improvements that can be completed within three years, followed by the design phase to implement these changes, at 5 metroplex locations: Washington, D.C., North Texas, Northern California, Southern California, Houston, Atlanta, and Charlotte. Work of various kinds to advance the program is ongoing at a number of other locations at the same time. (See Figure 36-2.) Some 21 metroplex areas have been designated in this program,[2] adding 5 per year for studies and design work. These efforts include both airspace and airport surface improvements and coordination.

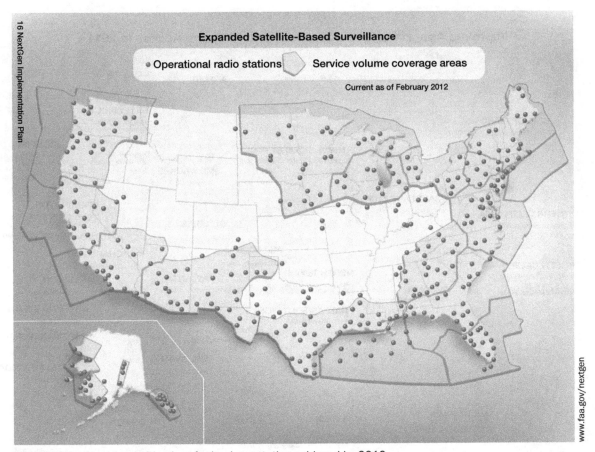

Expanded Satellite-Based Surveillance

• Operational radio stations ⬡ Service volume coverage areas

Current as of February 2012

16 NextGen Implementation Plan

www.faa.gov/nextgen

FIGURE 36-1 Near term objectives for implementation achieved by 2012.

Government–Industry Cooperation

Input from all stakeholders is necessary to design the NextGen system so that it will work for everyone and provide the most benefits.

The FAA is also working with selected air carriers to obtain ADS-B data for operational, training, and experience purposes, including JetBlue along the east coast and United Airlines over the Pacific Ocean. Tests, trials, and experiments are on-going at all times in various places in a joint effort between the FAA and stakeholders, particularly the airlines, to find better and new ways to utilize the new technology.

Commercial air carriers and the FAA have established an unprecedented system of sharing proprietary information (from the airlines) and internal data from the FAA under the acronym

ASIAS (Aviation Safety Information Analysis and Sharing), from which 65 databases have been created from 43 commercial carriers, accounting for more than 95 percent of commercial operations in the NAS. These databases are used to evaluate safety in emerging systems, and point to the cooperative and joint effort of government and private enterprise to enhance safety in the air transportation system.

Concepts are evaluated and tested for integration at the William J. Hughes Technical Center in Atlantic City using simulators for aircraft cockpits, air traffic control tower interiors, airline operations centers, and unmanned aircraft system ground control centers. Test bed facilities, which is a term used to describe a platform for experimentation, have been established in Florida and

FIGURE 36-2 FAA-designated Metroplex areas.

North Texas, with the Department of Defense Research and Engineering Network being added in 2012. The training of the FAA workforce is also in process.

Airport Surface Safety and Efficiency Improvements

Safe and efficient runway and taxiway use is an integral necessity to the effectiveness of NextGen. The FAA is currently monitoring ground movements at 35 major airports using Airport Surface Detection Equipment-Model X (ASDE-X), which tracks surface movement by radar, multilateration,[3] and ADS-B. Beginning in 2014, the FAA will provide surface data sharing at nine additional complex airports[4] using Airport Surface Surveillance Capability (ASSC), which collects data from multilateration and ADS-B only. The FAA is working on the best means to use these data and how to convey the information to those who need it, including ATC, flight operations, dispatchers, and ramp operators. This technology will make an unprecedented amount of data available to facilitate movement and safety,

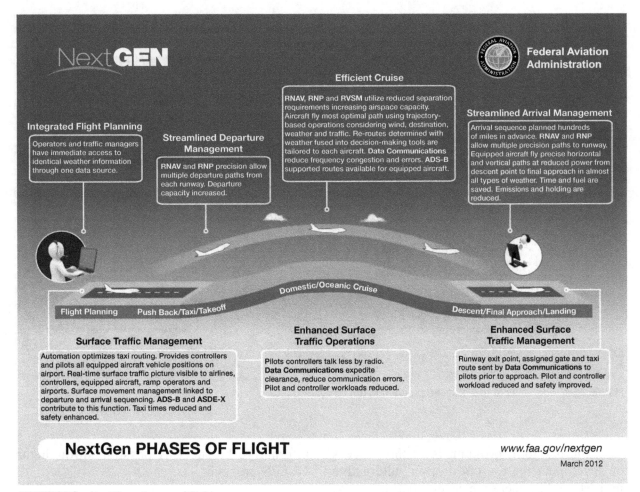

FIGURE 36-3 NextGen phases of flight.

including hazards involving runway incursions (see Figure 36-3).

Data Communications

Data Communications (Data Comm) is a new information sharing digital technology for use in both the surface and airborne environments. It represents the first phase in the transition from a voice communication system to a predominately digital textual mode of communication. Data Comm will enable faster departure clearances, trajectory-based routing, and optimized profile descents (see Figure 36-4).

Environmental Initiatives

As mentioned in Chapter 34, an FAA-industry program called Continuous Lower Energy, Emissions, and Noise (CLEEN) is underway to reduce aircraft fuel burn by 33 percent and to reduce oxides of nitrogen by 60 percent, while reducing aircraft noise by 32 decibels, all from the current ICAO standard. CLEEN technologies include alternative fuels, noise reducing engine nozzles, adaptable wing trailing edges, optimized flight trajectories using onboard flight management systems, and open rotor and geared turbofan engines. Target date for beginning implementation is 2015.

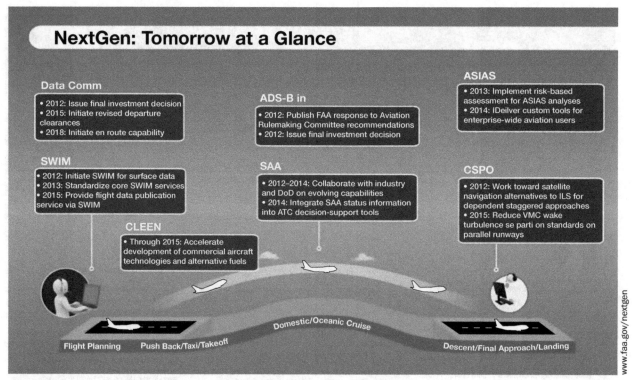

NextGen: Tomorrow at a Glance

Data Comm
- 2012: Issue final investment decision
- 2015: Initiate revised departure clearances
- 2018: Initiate en route capability

ADS-B in
- 2012: Publish FAA response to Aviation Rulemaking Committee recommendations
- 2012: Issue final investment decision

ASIAS
- 2013: Implement risk-based assessment for ASIAS analyses
- 2014: IDeilver custom tools for enterprise-wide aviation users

SWIM
- 2012: Initiate SWIM for surface data
- 2013: Standardize core SWIM services
- 2015: Provide flight data publication service via SWIM

SAA
- 2012–2014: Collaborate with industry and DoD on evolving capabilities
- 2014: Integrate SAA status information into ATC decision-support tools

CSPO
- 2012: Work toward satellite navigation alternatives to ILS for dependent staggered approaches
- 2015: Reduce VMC wake turbulence se parti on standards on parallel runways

CLEEN
- Through 2015: Accelerate development of commercial aircraft technologies and alternative fuels

Domestic/Oceanic Cruise

Flight Planning   Push Back/Taxi/Takeoff

Descent/Final Approach/Landing

www.faa.gov/nextgen

FIGURE 36-4 Elements of the NextGen program in the works.

Another joint program is in the process of developing the use of "drop-in" alternative jet fuels. While there are several definitions as to what constitutes a "drop-in" alternative jet fuel, one popular one says that it is any renewable fuel which can be blended with petroleum products and utilized in the current infrastructure of pumps, pipelines, and other existing equipment. They are functionally identical to conventional jet fuel and do not differ in performance or operational capability. ASTM International has so far approved two drop-in alternative jet fuels.[5]

There is no single renewable jet fuel that will meet all of aviation's needs because of the lack of predictable availability, which is a function of crop availability, climate factors, and related variables. The FAA, therefore, is working to secure ASTM approval for as many

alternative biofuels as possible through the CLEEN program.

Special Activity Airspace (SAA)

Special activity airspace is designated airspace wherein limitations may be imposed on aircraft operations, including restricted, prohibited, and military operations areas. This airspace is scattered throughout the NAS and poses potentially blocking areas to direct flight. Most of these areas have non-active periods that permit commercial and general aviation aircraft to transit them, but their activity schedules are often difficult to determine for flight planning and flight operations. The FAA has published a concept of operations for SAA data automation, including a system of electronic schedules and updates of SAA operations, to provide real-time information of the status of SAAs for flight planning and en route use.

Global Integration

As the FAA moves forward to develop and implement NextGen capabilities in the United States, similar systems are being put in place around the world. It is necessary that these systems and procedures be coordinated so as to provide seamless and efficient operations globally, and that the same avionics are approved to be able to conduct similar operations everywhere. To that end, the FAA works with governments and representative groups worldwide, including the European equivalent of NextGen, Single European Sky Air Traffic Management Research (SESAR) and ICAO.

▓ Why NextGen Matters

By some projections, passenger demand is expected to increase by 25 percent this decade. General aviation piston aircraft are projected to increase at an annual rate of 1.4 percent, while business jets are expected to increase at the rate of 4 percent. Very Light Jets (VLJs) will add hundreds of aircraft to the NAS per year. Unmanned Aircraft Systems will become routine in the NAS.

NextGen will help communities make better use of their airports. Flying will be quieter, cleaner, more efficient, and safer. Travel will confront fewer delays with less time sitting on the ground or holding in the air, and with more flexibility to deal with weather.

▓ Unmanned Aircraft Systems (UAS)

The FAA defines UAS as an unmanned aircraft (UA) and all of the associated support equipment, control stations, data links, telemetry, communications, and navigation equipment, etc., necessary to operate the unmanned aircraft. The UA is the flying portion of the system, flown by a pilot via a ground-control system, or autonomously through use of an on board computer with associated equipment necessary for the UA to operate safely. UAS are also referred to variously as drones or unmanned aerial vehicles (UAVs).

We saw in Chapter 22 how UAS in the United States National Airspace System (NAS) has been certificated and controlled by the FAA during its short and recent history of authority over these aircraft. The first priority of the FAA being safety, the agency has moved slowly and cautiously in granting certificates for UAS operations within the NAS. While the FAA does not disclose the exact nature of UAS certifications within the NAS (which policy has prompted lawsuits under the Freedom of Information Act), certain UAS authorizations are known.[6] For example, the Department of Homeland Security uses UAS for surveillance of borders and port facilities. NASA and NOAA are engaged in research and environmental monitoring using UAVs. Local and state law enforcement agencies also have been certified to use drones. The FAA issued 313 certificates in 2011.

While UAS have been primarily used by the U.S. military overseas in war zones for both surveillance and offensive military strikes, there has been a steady growth of interest in their use here at home. Civil uses include aerial mapping, crop monitoring, forest fire detection, and rescue operations. Development of UAS is ongoing worldwide, but in the United States alone some 50 different groups ranging from universities, private companies, and government organizations are developing and producing numerous and varied unmanned aircraft designs. This has created a powerful lobby for the proliferation of UAS uses in the NAS.

In February 2012, Congress mandated the FAA, in the FAA Reauthorization Act of 2012, to develop regulations and procedures to permit, by 2015, widespread use of UAS in the National Airspace System by both government and commercial operators. The purpose of this mandate is to expedite and streamline the certification process and to develop means whereby they may be safely integrated into the NAS. The present certification of drones precludes their use in airspace occupied by civil aircraft due to the inability of UAVs to "sense and avoid" other aircraft.

The fact that UAS are of varying degrees of size and sophistication adds to the problem of integrating them into the NAS where they will be required to mix and assimilate with manned aircraft. Some UAVs have the wing span of a Boeing 737 and are powered by turbojets. At the other extreme, there are very small UAVs weighing less than one pound with wing spans (or rotors) of six inches or less and powered by a lithium-ion battery (micro aerial vehicle). Some are even designed in the form of hummingbirds with flapping wings.

Posse Comitatus Act of 1878

This new legislation has also raised the prospect of federal government involvement in state and local law enforcement issues, which may violate long-standing federal law. The Posse Comitatus Act of 1878 is an arcane statute passed by Congress toward the end of the Reconstruction Era after the Civil War. The Reconstruction Era refers to the period after the defeat of the Confederate states during which the former rebellious states were reincorporated into the Union. Federal troops had occupied the former Confederate States to enforce federal law and to police state and local elections.

Posse Comitatus is Latin for "power of the county" and the doctrine arose in England in the 15th century to support the common law right of local sheriffs to impress citizens into a posse to enforce the law. In the American colonies, the doctrine referred to the military enforcement of civil or state laws, which was anathema to the colonists due to the use of British military forces in the colonies to enforce laws passed by the English Parliament prior to the American Revolution.

The Constitution of the United States specifically limits the role of the military in civil matters, and makes the military at all times subject to the oversight of civilian elected authority. The Constitution also limits the role of the federal government generally, reserving unto the states all powers not specifically granted by the Constitution to the federal government. During the Civil War some constitutional protections, like habeas corpus (which is a constitutional safeguard and mechanism to prevent unlawful or secret imprisonment of citizens) were suspended by President Lincoln under claim of "war powers." After the Civil War ended, the federal military occupied the South as a conquered territory and became the primary tool of law enforcement.

The Posse Comitatus Act of 1878 was designed to remove federal military authority over the state and local governments of the southern states after 13 years of Reconstruction. The original law specifically prohibits the Army from enforcing civilian law, and by amendment in 1956, it also includes the Air Force. By a directive of the Department of Defense, the Navy and the Marines are also prohibited from interfering with or participating in state and local law enforcement. The Coast Guard, which is now lodged in the Department of Homeland Security, is not covered by the Act or by any federal directive because the Coast Guard is actively involved in coastal law enforcement and has a federal complementary mission with the states.

The use of military or federal government drones within the United States, therefore, will be a subject of constitutional and judicial scrutiny because of the Posse Comitatus Act as well as the Fourth Amendment to the Constitution.

The Fourth Amendment and Case Law

The Fourth Amendment to the United States Constitution also had its genesis in the British occupation of the American colonies. The Amendment provides, in relevant part, that the people have a right "to be secure in their persons, houses, papers, and effects, against unreasonable searches and seizures . . ." and that such right "shall not be violated and no Warrants shall issue, but upon probable cause . . .".

Since the adoption of the Bill of Rights in 1791, a large body of law has grown up around the interpretation in various fact situations of what "unreasonable" means, and what "probable cause" means, including opinions of the United States Supreme Court and lower federal and state courts. By prior law, property taken by the police to be used in evidence is not admissible in a criminal proceeding against the accused if the seized evidence has been taken in contravention of the Fourth Amendment or the cases interpreting it. A number of exceptions to the requirement of having a warrant to search have been articulated by the courts (for example, no warrant is necessary to search a person who commits a crime in the presence of an officer of the law, or a person who is under arrest). Similar types of exceptions have been articulated to the question of the sufficiency of the facts necessary to secure a warrant, where a warrant is required before a search of premises can be lawfully made. If the facts supporting the warrant are not legally sufficient, then the warrant is unlawful and anything seized is inadmissible in a criminal proceeding.

The question arises, then, whether drones may be used in law enforcement to fly over a person's property to view what is on the property, for instance, as a basis to secure a warrant to enter the property in order to seize evidence to be used in a criminal proceeding. There have been two cases that bear on this question.

In *Summers of California v. Ciralo*, 487 U.S. 207 (1986), the Supreme Court had before it a case where the police had received an anonymous tip that the accused was growing marijuana in his back yard. The back yard was enclosed by a high fence that precluded viewing what was in the back yard from ground level. A police officer in an airplane flew over the property from a 1,000 foot altitude while in navigable airspace

and was able to clearly identify the marijuana from the air. A search warrant was obtained and executed the next day, seizing the marijuana plants on the private property.

Prior law had established that a police officer may look and see whatever is in plain view, and he may use this as a basis to either seize unlawful contraband or as a basis for a lawful search warrant. The court held that since the marijuana was in plain sight, using the naked eye, from a place in the navigable airspace (the NAS, which is in the public domain), the accused had no reasonable right of privacy. The view by the naked eye of the backyard was reasonable (as the same would be from a high truck or double decker bus from the street). Other specific legal analyses of the case are not permissible here, but suffice it to say that the court held that the over flight of the accused's back yard and the viewing of it from 1,000 feet in the NAS, was a legitimate basis for the search warrant.

In the second case, *Florida v. Riley*, 488 U.S. 445 (1989), a similar situation was before the Supreme Court. The accused had a greenhouse on his private property, the contents of which could not be viewed from any ground level public place. Relying on an anonymous tip that marijuana was being grown on the property, a county sheriff using a helicopter circled twice over the subject's property at 400 feet. Through openings in the roof of the greenhouse, the officer could see with the naked eye growing plants that he identified as marijuana. A search warrant was obtained and the premises were searched, and the marijuana plants were seized as evidence.

The court held, along the lines of *Ciralo* above, that helicopter flights at 400 feet above people's property are routine, and that what is viewable from that position in the NAS is not protected under the Fourth Amendment, in spite of FAA regulations limiting low flight for fixed-wing aircraft in the navigable airspace. The FAA limitation is based on safety considerations, not privacy expectations, and does not necessarily apply to helicopters.

Both of these cases rely on the police being where they were legally allowed to be, on the "plain view" doctrine that allows police to see what is there to be seen using the naked eye, whether through a window or otherwise, and that they were using normal and routinely used aerial vehicles from which the sightings were made. The use of drones, however, is not normal or routine in many venues, and drones frequently use specialized imaging and sophisticated technologies, like infrared and thermal applications, to view the ground. There will no doubt be many other distinctions that will be argued under Fourth Amendment principles as UAVs become more prevalent and are increasingly used by the government. At this point, it is still safe to say that the incorporation of UAV technology in the NAS, as projected by the recent statutory law and by the plans of the FAA, will result in many legal contests between citizens and the government.

Endnotes

1. P.L. 108–176.
2. Atlanta, Boston, Charlotte, Chicago, Cleveland, DC Metro, Denver, Detroit, Houston, Las Vegas Valley, Memphis, Minneapolis-St. Paul, New York/Philadelphia, Northern California, North Texas, Orlando, Phoenix, Seattle, Southern California, South Florida, Tampa.
3. Multilateration is a means of navigation using the measurement of the difference in distance between two or more stations at known locations that broadcast signals, enabling the determination of a "fix."
4. Portland, OR; Anchorage; Kansas City, MO; New Orleans; Pittsburgh; San Francisco; Cincinnati; Cleveland; and Andrews Air Force Base.
5. In 2009, 50 percent synthetic fuel blends were created from a process known as Fischer-Tropsch synthesis. In 2011, a biofuel known as Hydroprocessed Esters and Fatty Acids (HEFA) can be mixed up to 50 percent with standard kerosene.
6. As a result of the Freedom of Information suits filed against the DOT, the FAA released information in April 2012 disclosing the identities of holders of Certificates of Authorization (COAs) and Special Airworthiness Certificates in the Experimental Category (SAC-EC).

PART VI

International Civil Aviation

37 Treaties and International Civil Aviation Organizations

The concept of international air transportation emerged almost immediately with powered flight itself. Flight in lighter-than-air craft had been an international affair from the start. As the reality of powered flight neared, activity in both North America and Europe proceeded simultaneously. After the Wright brothers' success in 1903, Europeans immediately followed, developing their own brands and models of airplanes.

International flight in heavier-than-air machines first occurred on July 25, 1909, when Louis Bleriot flew his monoplane across the English Channel from France to England. William Boeing was carrying airmail between Seattle and Vancouver in his Boeing B-1E seaplane in 1919 under agreement with both the United States and Canada. The International Air Traffic Association was organized in 1919 by six European air transport companies. It was obvious that mere boundaries could not contain the airplane and those who would use it in commerce. Still, under international law, borders could not be transcended with impunity, and it was clear early on that some kind of structure would have to be put in place to deal with the interaction between peoples of different cultures and different laws.

■ International Aviation Relations

Beginning in 1910 in Paris, international conferences between nations, attended by their appointed representatives, convened for the purpose of discussing and resolving issues related to international civil aviation. Representatives from 19 European countries assembled that year in a meeting, now known as the Paris Conference, to consider the legal and practical requisites for international air commerce. Although little was immediately accomplished, a start had been made, and much of the work of that first conference resurfaced in the conferences of the future.

It is important to note the international legal distinction between the words *conference* and *convention*. A convention, as used in international civil aviation, means an agreement between nations, not yet rising to the status of a treaty, the latter of which only occurs upon ratification by the signatory nations. The word *conference* is used to describe the assembly or gathering where a convention might be agreed on. A protocol is a major amendment to the regulations of the convention. An amendment is a minor change in the regulations enforced by the convention.

In 1919, after World War I, representatives of the victorious nations, as well as Brazil and Cuba, adopted the Paris Convention, which established for the first time several important foundations for civil aviation. First, the Convention recognized that each nation has sovereignty over its own airspace, including its territories and colonies. Second, it followed the maritime law principle that each aircraft must have a national registration. Third, it established certain basic rules regarding the airworthiness of aircraft. Fourth, it adopted rules regarding the certification of pilots. Although the United States signed the Convention, it was not ratified. It would, however, become a model for the later enactment of statutes in the United States regarding the same subject matters.

In 1926, representatives from countries left out of the Paris meeting in 1919 adopted the Madrid Convention, which basically was the same agreement adopted in Paris in 1919. This agreement would have no substantial effect on later agreements in the field of civil aviation.

The Havana Convention of 1928 was an agreement between nations of the Western Hemisphere, and grew out of the Pan American Conference held in Santiago, Chile, in 1923. The provisions of this Convention were similar to those of the Paris Convention, but due to variations between the two, this Convention caused some commercial and operating uncertainties in the international community until the differences were finally resolved in 1944 at the Chicago Convention.

Treaties Dealing with the Issue of Liability of Airlines

There has been a succession of treaties and agreements between nations, beginning in 1929, dealing with the issue of liability of airlines to their passengers and shippers. The reason for this progression of agreements concerns the way in which airlines themselves were viewed during the early years of their existence. We have previously seen how the attempt to establish and maintain a viable airline business was as risky as, and often directly proportional to, the dangers of flying itself. Flying was dangerous and aircraft were relatively primitive and unreliable. Since commercial aviation was considered by most governments to be a national resource and its promotion to be a government responsibility, the laws governing the liability of such companies reflected their inherent financial frailty.

As air travel became progressively safer and more reliable over the years, the concern of government shifted from promoting aviation for its own sake to concerns over the way and manner that the airline business was conducted, and to the protection of the people who used the airlines for personal travel or shipping cargo.

Below we will consider each of these agreements, culminating in the Montreal Convention. All of these agreements were important during the time that they were in effect, but all except the last, the Montreal Convention, are now relegated to historical significance only. The Montreal Convention, like all other international treaties, had to go through a ratification process to become binding upon those countries that subscribe to it. This process began in 1999 and has now about run its course as most civilized countries on earth have signed on. It is to be considered the law for all purposes in this course.

The Warsaw Convention—1929

At the same time that the hemispherical conferences were going on in the West, conferences were held in Europe, first in Paris in 1925 and then in Warsaw in 1929. Commercial air transportation between far-flung nations, including Europe and the United States, was being recognized as a probability since the significant aerial accomplishments of 1919. In that year the first transatlantic flight had been completed by the United States Navy in a Curtiss flying boat,

NC-4, from North America to Lisbon via the Azores (requiring 57 hours of actual flying time). Englishmen Captain John Alcock and Lieutenant Arthur W. Brown made the first nonstop crossing from Newfoundland to Ireland (completed in just over 16 hours flying time). The English dirigible R-34 made a round trip from Scotland to Roosevelt Field, Long Island (between July 2 and July 8), and the first scheduled airplane passenger service was inaugurated between London and Paris. The primary concerns at the Paris and Warsaw conferences related to the lack of uniformity in commercial and legal transactions in international civil aviation. In 1929, the signatory nations established through the Warsaw Convention, effective on February 13, 1933, the first rules relating to carrier liability for passenger and cargo interests in international air transportation. The Warsaw Convention (Warsaw) provides the legal framework for the payment of claims for personal injury and death of passengers, claims for damaged goods, cargo and baggage, and claims for delay. Simply put, airlines must pay regardless of fault (strict liability) up to the limits of liability prescribed, subject to certain defenses set out therein. Warsaw also prescribed form and content for tickets, air waybills, and other lading documents.

The Hague Protocol and the Montreal Agreement

Warsaw has been amended over its history, and its legal effect has been modified by separate agreements between nations. The original limitation of liability set forth in Warsaw was $8,300 per passenger for personal injury or death. This amount was doubled by operation of the Hague Protocol of 1955, effective in 1964. As inflation eroded the value of currencies the world over, the limitations of liability contained in Warsaw became effectively lower and lower. The United States, in 1965, let it be known that it would consider withdrawing from Warsaw if liability limits were not raised. This led to a voluntary accord,

known as the Montreal Inter-Carrier Agreement, being signed in 1966 by all major foreign and U.S. carriers serving the United States. Under this agreement, limits of liability were raised to $75,000 per passenger for death or injury. This agreement was not an amendment of Warsaw, but a voluntary acceptance by the airlines of an increase in their potential liability. Any carrier desiring to fly into the United States was required to join the agreement. The Montreal Agreement was followed by a similar agreement between European civil aviation authorities, called the Malta Agreement, which increased those airlines' liability in such cases on international flights between their nations.

The Montreal Agreement was seen as an interim fix, and the United States continued efforts to have Warsaw formally amended or replaced. This led to two subsequent formal agreements, the Guadalajara Convention in 1961 and the Guatemala Protocol in 1971, but neither of these was ratified by the United States.

The Montreal Protocols in 1975 dealt with cargo issues arising under Warsaw, provided for increased liability limits and, importantly, eliminated the outmoded cargo documentation provisions of Warsaw. This step allowed the use of electronic commerce in international cargo transactions, eliminating the necessity of providing detailed air waybills and the like. This agreement was ratified by the United States in 1998.

IATA Inter-Carrier Agreement and IATA Measures of Implementation Agreement

In 1995, at the urging of the Department of Transportation, discussions were initiated between foreign and U.S. carriers under the auspices of IATA and ATA, to reach voluntary agreement to waive the limitations of liability set out in Warsaw. Later that year, these carriers signed the IATA Inter-Carrier Agreement (IIA) that committed the airlines to take action to waive the limitation of liability provisions of the Warsaw Convention. In 1996, the second step was taken when many of them signed the IATA Measures of Implementation Agreement (MIA), which waived the Warsaw limitations up to 100,000 Special Drawing Rights (SDRs). SDRs are monetary units representing an artificial "basket" currency developed by the International Monetary Fund to replace gold as a world standard. Recently 100,000 SDRs represented approximately $130,000. By the middle of the year 2000, 122 international carriers, comprising more than 90 percent of the world's air transport industry, had signed IIA, with most of those also signing MIA. The effect of these developments was that any international passenger who qualified would have an absolute right to receive a payment of approximately $130,000 regardless of airline fault.

The Montreal Convention—1999

As a result of the band-aid approach to fixing the deficiencies of Warsaw, the world international transportation community operated under a patchwork of rules governing liability and compensation in cases of loss. Under the auspices of ICAO, an international conference was convened in Montreal in 1999 and adopted what is now referred to as the Montreal Convention of 1999 (Montreal 99). The basic provisions of the Convention (Montreal 99) include: (1) imposition of strict liability for the first 100,000 SDRs of proven damages for passenger death or injury, (2) removal of all arbitrary limits of liability for amounts in excess of 100,000 SDRs for passenger death or injury (assuming there is carrier negligence), (3) increases the number of jurisdictions (countries) where suits may be brought than was allowed under Warsaw, and (4) clarifies carrier responsibilities under code-sharing arrangements.

Montreal 99 was ratified by the United States on May 9, 2003, and entered into force as of November 4, 2003, as the Montreal Convention—1999. As of 2012, the Convention had been ratified by 102 countries and is considered the law of most of the civilized world in airline liability.

The Chicago Conference

Toward the end of World War II, the United States invited representatives from the countries allied in the war effort against the Axis countries, as well as representatives from some of the neutral countries, to participate in an international conference on the subject of civil air transportation. World consensus was that there would be a mighty surge of international civil aviation and commerce after the expected end of hostilities. The United States at that time was in a preeminent position, vis-à-vis the rest of the world, to extend its influence all over the globe, and to capitalize on the great advantage that it held in international aviation as a result of the American air fleet produced during the war. American airplanes of the transport category had proliferated after wartime production began in 1941, and they had pioneered intercontinental routes in support of United States ground and naval personnel dispatched to all corners of the globe to meet the aggression of the Axis Powers. America, in fact, held a virtual monopoly on transport aircraft capable of intercontinental reach.

The Chicago Convention—1944

In November 1944, representatives from 54 countries attended the conference, since known as the Chicago Conference, at the end of which 32 countries signed a convention, the Chicago Convention, 1944, which established the International Civil Aviation Organization (ICAO) upon ratification of the convention by the required number of 26 countries. Ratification was accomplished on April 4, 1947, and at the invitation of the Canadian government, headquarters were established in Montreal. Legally, ICAO became a specialized agency linked to the Economics and Social Council of the United Nations.

The stated purposes of the Convention, to be administered and facilitated by ICAO, included (1) providing for the adoption of International Standards and Recommended Practices regulating international navigation, (2) providing recommendations for the installation of navigational facilities by the Contracting States, and (3) suggesting ways for the reduction of customs and immigration formalities. These purposes were to establish the fundamental basis for the safety, efficiency, and regularity of international civil aviation in the years to come.

The International Air Transport Agreement

During the Chicago Conference the United States pressed its view that international civil aviation would be served by adoption of "Open Skies," the concept of free flight over, to and from, and within the borders of the sovereign states represented at the Conference. It should be noted that "countries," in international treaty parlance, are known as "states," and exclusively referred to in that way. Of all the countries represented, only the United States was in a position to do any such flying. Known as the "Five Freedoms," this concept is outlined in the following box.

The Five Freedoms

1. Freedom One—The right of overflight without landing

2. Freedom Two—The right to land for reasons other than loading or unloading traffic, such as maintenance, fuel, or emergencies

3. Freedom Three—The right to carry traffic from a home country to a foreign country

4. Freedom Four—The right to carry traffic from a foreign country back to a home country

5. Freedom Five—The right to carry traffic between two foreign countries, as a part of an overall itinerary from or to a home country

---

The opposing view to Open Skies in 1944 was most forcefully stated by representatives of the United Kingdom. Britain believed that free and unlimited access by a foreign power to one's country and its markets was premature. England had no significant number of transport aircraft with which to take advantage of the Open Skies concept. Given the physical and financial state of its war-torn country, it was realized that it might take some years to be in a position to compete with the United States on any kind of a level playing field. The proposed agreement that would implement the Five Freedoms, officially known as the International Air Transport Agreement, informally referred to as the "Five Freedoms Agreement," was not generally acceptable to the main body of representatives present at Chicago, and only 19 countries were willing to sign it. It was not, therefore, effective, and is even less so today as many of the original signatories have withdrawn from it.

The Transit Agreement

The second agreement entered into at Chicago is known as the International Air Services Transit Agreement, or "Two Freedoms Agreement." This agreement embodies the first two freedoms, that is, overflight rights and landing rights for nontraffic reasons. Although signed by less than all conferees (100 nations had signed the "Transit Agreement" by 1992), this agreement became the basis upon which all future transit agreements would rest, and it established at least a minimum interactive relationship between the signatories. This agreement, therefore, may be considered to be one of the most significant results of the Chicago Conference.

The Bermuda Agreement

While the United Kingdom was not amenable to a multilateral treaty arrangement granting access to its markets, it was realized that the relationship between the United States and England was such that some sort of commercial aviation mutuality was in the interest of the United Kingdom. As the two most powerful leaders in the West to come out of World War II, the two governments agreed to have representatives meet in Bermuda in 1946 in an effort to reach an accord. The agreement that was reached was a compromise between the two positions previously articulated, and constituted the most important of the early bilateral (instead of multilateral) agreements to affect international civil aviation. The agreement essentially provided that

1. Fares and rates would have to be mutually acceptable to the two governments
2. Routes would have to be mutually agreed, and implicitly that there would be a *quid pro quo* for each route
3. Fifth Freedom rights (the carriage of traffic between two foreign countries without return to the home country) would be agreed on a case-by-case basis

The Bermuda Agreement became the model for future bilaterals between the United States and England and formed the model that would be used in other agreements between the United States and other foreign countries. Bilateral agreements have covered a variety of subject matters, including reciprocal recognition of pilot licenses, airworthiness standards for export aircraft, and radio communications.

■ Additional Conventions

International Recognition of Rights in Aircraft (Geneva Convention—1948)

Ninety-four countries had ratified this Convention as of 2002. The purpose of the treaty is to protect the rights of aircraft owners and others holding legal rights to the aircraft (such as security interests) when the aircraft crosses the borders of a signatory nation. One of the intended effects of the Convention was to encourage investors or financial institutions to more freely provide financing in the purchase of aircraft. Although a signatory to the Convention, Mexico filed a reservation to the effect that priority would be given by Mexican laws to "fiscal claims and claims made for work contracts" over claims asserted under the Convention. Sad stories are legend concerning the recovery of aircraft from Mexico.

Damage to Third Parties on the Surface Caused by Foreign Aircraft (Rome Convention—1952)

This Convention provides for the imposition of strict liability of the aircraft operator for damage caused to third parties on the ground, but places a limitation on the amount of compensatory damages. It also provides for the compulsory recognition of foreign judgments against the aircraft operator, so that a judgment secured in the injured parties' home jurisdiction may be enforced against the aircraft operator in the same manner as a domestic judgment.

Air Offenses Convention (Tokyo Convention of 1963)

This Convention is designed to insure that offenses committed on board an aircraft may be punished by authorities in the jurisdiction of the registration of the aircraft, no matter where the location of the aircraft may be when the offense is committed. The aircraft commander or his designees are empowered to prevent the commission of such acts and to take the offender into custody, and authorized to remove the offender from the aircraft. Signatories to the Convention are obligated to take all appropriate measures to prevent unlawful and forcible seizures of aircraft by persons on board and to restore control of the aircraft to the lawful commander of the aircraft.

Hijacking Convention (Hague Convention for the Suppression of Unlawful Seizure of Aircraft—1970)

As has been described, the rash of hijackings that occurred in the 1960s caused international concern. Representatives met at The Hague to consider the problem and underscored international determination to do everything possible to prevent such actions and to ensure the severe punishment of perpetrators. Detailed provisions are set forth in the Convention concerning the establishment of jurisdiction by signatory nations in order to prosecute such offenses, including rights of nations to take offenders into custody and to prosecute or extradite them according to its provisions.

Convention for the Suppression of Unlawful Acts against the Safety of Civil Aviation (Montreal Convention—1971)

This Convention is concerned with unlawful acts other than those relating to the seizure of aircraft. The treaty defines a variety of acts deemed to constitute prohibited acts and makes those acts punishable by severe penalties. By a supplementary Protocol in Montreal in 1988, the enumeration of prohibited acts was expanded to include specific acts committed at airports serving international civil aviation.

Plastic Explosives Convention (Convention on the Marking of Plastic Explosives for the Purpose of Detection—1991)

The aim of this Convention is the prevention of unlawful acts involving the use of plastic explosives. Signatory nations are required to adopt measures to ensure the marking of plastic explosives that will assist in detecting such explosives. Specifically, the manufacture of plastic explosives is to be regulated to prevent the distribution of unmarked explosives, to provide for control of the transfer of marked explosives, and for their destruction under time limitations. The Convention contains specific descriptions of the concerned explosives, the detection agents to be used in marking them, and it creates an International Explosives Technical Commission to keep track of developments in the manufacture, marking, and detection of the explosives.

The Cape Town Convention on International Interests in Mobile Equipment and Related Aircraft Protocol—2001

This treaty relates to the financial transactions involving certain aircraft, airframes, engines, and helicopters and provides for a registration system that tracks ownership and security interests in such mobile equipment on an international basis. The FAA registry is concerned with United States aircraft and registry, while the Cape Town Convention and the International Registry it created effectively deal with the problems related to the international movement, sale, leasing, and recordation of such interests. The law created by these international instruments coexists with the law of the United States regarding these interests.

Beijing Convention—2010 (Convention on the Suppression of Unlawful Acts Relating to International Civil Aviation)

Beijing Protocol (Protocol to the 1971 Hague Convention on the Suppression of Unlawful Seizure of Aircraft)

Following the attacks of September 11, 2001, member states of ICAO endorsed a global plan for strengthening aviation security, to include a review of legal instruments in aviation security to identify gaps and inadequacies in relation to emerging threats. It was concluded that the use of aircraft as weapons, suicide attacks, electronic and computer-based attacks, chemical, biological and radioactive attacks, were not adequately covered by existing agreements.

It was also concluded that existing law focused mainly on persons who actually perpetrated the attacks, usually on board the aircraft or at the airport, without considering the people who might be responsible for organizing, directing, or financing the attack.

The Beijing Convention and the Beijing Protocol may be considered together as two new counterterrorism treaties that promote and improve aviation security. These agreements criminalize the act of using civil aircraft as a weapon, and of using dangerous materials to attack aircraft or other targets on the ground. The unlawful transport of chemical, biological, or nuclear weapons is a punishable offense, as well as conspiracies to carry out such attacks. Making threats against civil aviation is also covered. The effect of these provisions is to require signatories to criminalize these acts.

After entry into force, the Beijing Convention of 2010 will prevail over the Montreal Convention of 1971 and the Protocol signed in Montreal in 1988.

■ The International Civil Aviation Organization (ICAO)

ICAO officially came into being in 1947 as a result of the Chicago Convention, upon ratification by the requisite number of states. According to the mission statement of the organization, its aims and objectives are to develop the principles and techniques of international air navigation and to foster the planning and development of international air transport, so as to meet the needs of the international civil aviation community. The organization emphasizes its commitment, among other things, to facilitate:

1. The safe and orderly growth of civil air transportation
2. Aircraft design and operation for peaceful purposes
3. The development of airports, airways, and air navigation facilities for international civil aviation

Specifically, ICAO undertook to:

1. Establish international standards for aircraft airworthiness certification, flight crew certification, communications, and radio aids to navigation
2. Establish principles and procedures for the economic regulation of international routes, fares, frequency, and capacity

The use of English as the required language for communication between aircraft and air traffic control authorities in international civil aviation all over the world is an example of ICAO work.

ICAO adopts and publishes technical standards referred to as Standards and Recommended Practices (SARPs) that govern the interaction of civil air transportation the world over. These international standards are incorporated into 18 technical annexes to provide uniformity and consistency that contribute to the safety and smooth operation of international civil aviation. ICAO proposes amendments and additions to SARPs as technology advances and conditions change. ICAO is essential in the coordination of the United States' NextGen program and the European Union's complementary SESAR innovations, and with the spreading of compatible technology throughout worldwide civil aviation. The human element component of the equation is addressed through its TRAINAIR PLUS program, which is aimed at improving the quality and efficiency of aviation training, and the Human Factors program, which is directed toward reducing the impact of human performance limitations.

Other programs and efforts of the organization relate to education, the environment, including noise issues and emissions affecting the ozone layer, problems involving multiple taxation, airport and route facility management, statistics, economic analysis, legal matters including treaty drafting and interpretation of law, and security.

Security has been a subject of ICAO action since the early 1970s as a result of the hijacking of aircraft beginning in the 1960s. In 1974, ICAO adopted its Standards and Recommended Practices (SARPs) on Security, designated as Annex 17. The Annex is under constant review, and it has been amended multiple times in order to respond to changing needs. The progression of emphasis in Annex 17 has been from hijacking, to sabotage, to baggage reconciliation with passengers, to screening of passengers and baggage and carry-on luggage, and the prevention and suppression of unlawful acts generally against civil aviation worldwide. The latest revision was effective on July 1, 2011.

Another example of ICAO commitment to global civil aviation relates to aviation safety in underdeveloped nations and regions. Due to the disproportionately high aviation accident rate in Africa, beginning in 2008, ICAO began adopting a "new approach" toward carrying out its mandate to improve worldwide aviation safety as it relates to that region. Designated the Comprehensive Regional Implementation Plan for Aviation Safety in Africa (AFI Plan), ICAO developed a work program to enhance the aviation safety culture of African aviation service providers, to enable African countries to establish and maintain a safety oversight system, and to assist them in identifying and resolving deficiencies in a reasonable manner.

The International Air Transport Association (IATA)

The roots of IATA go back to 1919, the year that saw the world's first scheduled air transport service, when six "air transport" companies formed the organization known as the International Air Traffic Association. Membership comprised solely European carriers until Pan American joined in 1939. The present organization was founded in Havana, Cuba, in 1945, and was originally composed of 57 airlines mostly operating in Europe and North America. The purposes of the new organization were to promote safe and

economical international air transport, to provide a means for collaboration of airline companies, and to cooperate with the newly formed International Civil Aviation Organization (ICAO) as the representative of member airlines. As liaison to ICAO, through its members IATA supplied technical input for the Standards and Recommended Practices (SARPs) found in the Annexes to the Chicago Convention. IATA contributed to documentation and procedures standardization that has allowed countries with differing languages and cultures to commercially interact with little difficulty. It also assisted in structuring a sound legal basis for international commercial transactions, meshing treaty law with existing air transport law of the United States. Ongoing work involves revision and modernization of the legal basis of carriage of persons and cargo in international aviation, as liability provisions of the Warsaw Convention have given way to subsequent amendments and superseding agreements.

After World War II, IATA began developing tariffs containing fares and rates (Traffic Coordination) for international carriage of passengers and cargo at meetings called Traffic Conferences, subject to the approval of the governments involved. A consistent schedule of rates and fares was also established, allowing airlines to accept each other's tickets on multisector itineraries, which in turn led to interlining between the world's airlines. It had been argued for years that IATA was, through its Traffic Coordination practices, engaged in price fixing that would normally be in violation of antitrust laws and in derogation of competition. Yet the United States, and other countries having similar laws, routinely granted antitrust exemptions for the activity. The truth was that international air transportation was among the least competitive industries in the world.

With the "father of deregulation," Alfred Kahn, at the helm of the CAB when deregulation was enacted in 1978, the deregulators turned their attention to international aviation. In 1979, hearings were conducted by the CAB in the United States to ascertain whether antitrust immunity should be removed from the Traffic Coordination activities of IATA. The world's airlines lined up in uniform opposition. The hearings concentrated on the North Atlantic routes, which were served by 40 airlines. The Justice Department supported the CAB, but the Department of Transportation urged a "go slow" position. Nevertheless, on May 5, 1981, the CAB issued a "show cause" order that raised the issue of whether antitrust immunity should be removed from IATA Tariff Coordinating Conferences. No decision was reached by the CAB prior to its demise at the end of 1984 pursuant to the "sunset" provisions of the Airline Deregulation Act. The Department of Transportation, having inherited the antitrust responsibilities of the CAB beginning in 1985, terminated the proceeding that year.

IATA, taking its cue, then reorganized itself into two parts, a Trade Association and a voluntary Traffic Conference, the latter dealing with the controversial issues of fare setting. In this way, IATA members sought to avoid further antitrust scrutiny of the United States antitrust regulators. No further proceedings have been initiated by the United States on this issue. IATA is still an influential trade association.

The organization has also served since the early days as the clearinghouse for interline accounting, and today services the accounts for 240 airlines in over 115 countries. Multilateral Interline Traffic Agreements have been signed by most of the international carriers, which facilitates the seamless flow of passengers and cargo throughout the world.

38

Europe after World War II—The Rise of the European Economic Community

Since the 1950s, Europe has been on a journey to consolidate its economic power through a close association of its several states. Significant developments during that period are now having an important impact on the evolving global market. Specifically, the evolving equality between Europe and the United States, and the resulting competition between European and American commercial interests in international civil aviation, is a direct result of these developments. It is important, therefore, that we understand something of the history of the relationship between these two great areas of commerce.

■ The European-American Relationship

The primary advances in commercial aviation during the first part of the 20th century were made in Europe. The French builder Deperdussin, for example, flew a 100-mile per hour airplane in 1912, a feat technologically far ahead of the Americans. European manufacturers supplied essentially all of the military aircraft used in World War I. French, German, and English manufacturers produced the world's most advanced aircraft designs and the most powerful aircraft

engines. Further, the countries of Europe led the way in creating, organizing, and funding commercial passenger aviation immediately after World War I and began scheduled international aviation transportation as early as 1919. America had to play catch up during the 1920s, and American business interests had a hard time trying to figure out how the airplane could make any meaningful contribution to the progression of commerce in the United States.

The first airlines in the United States during the 1920s often looked to Europe to supply their aircraft needs. Juan Trippe, for example, began Pan American service in 1927 with Fokker Trimotors, as that airplane set the standard with its cantilevered, monowing design. The Fokker departed from the biwing, wire-and-fabric airplanes of that and prior decades. This design was largely emulated in the Ford Trimotor in the 1920s.

But the pendulum began to swing in favor of the Americans about this time when Fred Rentschler and Pratt & Whitney developed the powerful Wasp radial engine, which would supply the motive power for the newest and most advanced designs of aircraft in the world beginning in 1927. In fact, aircraft would begin to be designed around the new radial engines.

The work of the small group of engineers at the National Advisory Committee on Aeronautics would produce cowl designs and other innovations that would lead to the introduction in 1933 of the twin-engine Boeing 247, broadly acknowledged as the first modern airliner with its low monowing, retractable landing gear, and stressed all-metal skin design. At the same time, the fortunes of the leading European aircraft manufacturer, Fokker, went into decline due to design failures that resulted in stress fractures in its wooden wing. The first known failure of this wing caused the highly publicized crash of a Fokker Trimotor in 1931, resulting in the deaths of all passengers, including Notre Dame coaching legend Knute Rockne.

In addition, the vast geographical area of America proved to be a fitting laboratory for the evolution of the commercial airliner. Navigational developments in the United States, beginning with its beacon system and followed by radio navigation, would lead the world in aviation technology as the airlines of America took to the skies. Beginning with the radial engine, the United States would take the lead in civil aviation technology and never look back.

Production of state-of-the-art transport aircraft intensified in the United States during the 1930s as Douglas inaugurated the highly successful Douglas Commercial (DC) series of airplanes. Lockheed joined the contest with the Constellation, Boeing countered with the first pressurized passenger airplane (the 309), and then came World War II.

The consolidation of military and political power by Germany during the 1930s, and the resulting devastation visited on the countries of Europe during the six years of World War II left the United States in a position of preeminence in all things relating to commercial aviation by 1945. America had a ready-made fleet of commercial-type aircraft, the most advanced of which included the Douglas DC-4 and the Lockheed Constellation. Immediately after the end of the war, advanced types of even larger aircraft began rolling off the American assembly lines, lines that had been set up during the war to produce the massive military airlift capacity of the Allies. The entire war production plant of the United States was now turned to peaceful and commercial ventures. At the same time, Europe lay in ruins.

In 1945, there were widespread hunger, unemployment, and housing shortages throughout the continent of Europe. Raw materials and foodstuffs were in short supply. Industries lay idle, or almost so, as much-needed machinery and capital proved elusive. European cities were little more than acres of rubble, an estimated 500 million cubic tons of it in Germany alone. A breakdown of moral, social, and commercial life was threatened. The occupying forces of the Soviet Union were entrenched in much of Europe, and the expansionist Stalin government in power in the U.S.S.R. after World War II cast a covetous eye over the continent.

The Marshall Plan

Two years after the end of World War II, the situation in Europe was not much improved—in fact, whole segments of populations faced starvation. An economic depression loomed for the entire continent. Serious concerns were voiced in the United States over the deteriorating economic condition of Europe, and ideas were debated in foreign policy circles as to the best way to meet these concerns. By early 1947, preparations were complete for the initiation of a European economic recovery, a program that would come to be known as the Marshall Plan.

George C. Marshall was the Secretary of State in the Truman Administration in 1947. During the war he had been Army chief of staff and central to the military planning that had led to the defeat of the Axis Powers, particularly in Europe. He was considered indispensable in European affairs and he enjoyed considerable prestige with the United States Congress. In a speech to the graduating class at Harvard University on June 5, 1947, he proposed a solution for the European economic situation that was centered on the concept that the European countries would themselves set up a program for reconstruction, with the assurance of American assistance. The problem, he said, was:

> The truth of the matter is that Europe's requirements for the next three or four years for foreign food and other essential products—principally from America—are so much greater than her present ability to pay that she must have substantial additional help or face economic, social, and political deterioration of a very grave character.
>
> The remedy lies in breaking the vicious circle and restoring the confidence of the European people in the economic future of their own countries and of Europe as a whole.[1]

European response to this U.S. proposal of assistance was immediate and positive. A conference of 16 European countries arranged to meet in Paris in 1947. Twenty-two countries were invited to participate and all of those invited, except the Soviet Union and those countries under its control, attended. The Soviet Union, in fact, vigorously opposed the plan. The Paris conference led to the establishment of the Committee for European Economic Cooperation, and it was the forerunner of successive organizations that ultimately led to the existence of the European Union today.

In the United States, Congress passed the Economic Assistance Act of 1948, which became known as "The Marshall Plan." Congress appropriated in excess of $13.3 billion over the next four years and applied it to the European recovery plan. The plan has become known as the costliest, most successful, and arguably the most visionary international cooperative plan ever conceived in peacetime. It averted a postwar European

depression and led to the economic recovery of the Western European countries, allowing an economic independence along with political stability that has endured. In addition to leading to the creation of the European Union, in due course it led to the creation of the Organization for Economic Development and Cooperation and to the North Atlantic Treaty Organization (NATO).

The Plan was amended in 1949 to include West Germany, the western part of the former German National Socialist State that had been the former foe of the United States and the other countries in Europe, which was a marked change from the victors' treatment of Germany after World War I. The inclusion of West Germany was not only a benevolent and humanitarian act, it was a far-sighted move that quickly contrasted the free West German economy with that of the communist Soviet-controlled East Germany, and led to the establishment of a lasting progressive, free, and dynamic German economy. The Plan did not include Spain, which in 1948 was a dictatorship under Franco, and Spain was not invited to participate. At the same time, Spain had not been a combatant against Germany, and its economy and commercial infrastructure were relatively intact. (See Figure 38-1.)

To say that the Marshall Plan was a success would understate the facts. Europe gradually rebuilt, and its countries set about consolidating their common interests and strengths. The economic cooperation that spawned the European Community has gradually evolved into a legal, political, commercial, and social phenomenon.

In 1971, President Richard M. Nixon prophetically said of the American relationship with Europe:

> The program which Secretary Marshall announced in 1947 served as a catalyst in helping the peoples of Western Europe release their boundless energies and express their abundant creativity. The Marshall Plan also created an environment in which the growth of

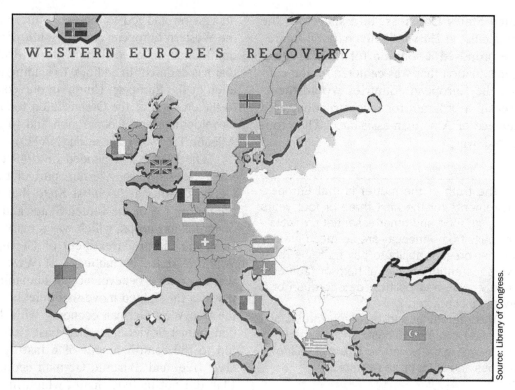

FIGURE 38-1 Western Europe after World War II, showing countries that received aid under the Marshall Plan.

Source: Library of Congress.

strong ties within the Atlantic Community could be continually nourished.

The relationship between the United States and Europe is a dynamic one, susceptible, as we have seen, to constant, constructive change and thus touches on almost all aspects of our national well-being. This relationship is too critical to be taken for granted, too complex to be easily understood. We believe there is a great need for continuing study to enhance understanding of the relationship among all of our peoples.[2]

■ The Evolution of the European Community

In 1948, the major free nations of Europe created the Organization for European Economic Cooperation for the purpose of coordinating and administering the Marshall Plan for the economic recovery of Europe as a result of the devastating effects of World War II. Two years later, in 1950, the first significant step toward economic unification occurred with the agreement to pool coal and steel resources, which was entered into by those countries thereafter known as the "Six," and who were the original members of the European Community.[3] This was followed in 1951 with formalization in the Treaty of Paris, which established the European Coal and Steel Community. In 1953, the Six agreed to remove customs duties and quantitative restrictions on these raw materials, thus establishing for the first time a Common Market for coal and steel among those six countries.

In 1957, the Six signed the Treaty of Rome (amended in the Treaty of Lisbon, signed in 2007 and entered into force on December 1, 2009), establishing the European Economic

Community (EEC). This agreement was to become the cornerstone of the present European Union, and is sometimes referred to as its "constitution." The Treaty of Rome is a comprehensive undertaking, articulating monetary policy, broad economic policy, and common commercial policy. It set goals for research and development, and for dealing with the environment, employment, discrimination, competition, and transportation. The Treaty also established the four governing bodies of the EEC: the Council, the Commission, the Parliament, and the European Court of Justice.

Institutions of the EEC

The governmental entities created by the Treaty of Rome were entities in name only. They had been created and their responsibilities had been generally articulated. But boxes on an organizational chart must be given life by those who will take up the duty of beginning to perform the responsibilities assigned to them. The jurisdictional limits of each had to be established, and then tested one against the other. A pecking order had to be worked out. Bureaucratic motivations, goals, and energies had to be demonstrated. Results were measured. In the course of starting up a program as ambitious and unique as the European Economic Community, monumental uncertainties were expected and experienced, but they gradually gave way to a semblance of purpose and order. We will next review these governing entities and their duties, and we will then see how they came together to perform their difficult joint function of pulling together the various disparate Member States into one cohesive, cooperative, and effective unit.

The **Council,** composed of representatives appointed from the Member States (one representative from each Member State), has both executive and legislative functions. It is charged with responsibility for ensuring that the objectives of the EC, as an entity, are realized and put into

practice. It may issue regulations and directives that are binding on Member States. Regulations are normally adopted based on recommendations of the Commission or Parliament. Work of the Council was compromised, particularly early on, by representatives' allegiances to their own government's interest, rather than to the collective interests of the EC. National governments still retain some powers not delegated to the EU.

Parliament is composed of elected representatives from the Member States (754 representatives elected by citizens of Member States). From the first elections held in 1979, the Parliament has assumed a larger and more powerful role in the EU as a result of the 1992 Maastricht Treaty (amended in the Treaty of Lisbon, signed in 2007 and entered into force on December 1, 2009) and the 1997 Amsterdam Treaty. The European Parliament, through these treaties, has progressed from a consultative body to a true legislative assembly. The Parliament is the only EU body that meets and debates in public, and it enacts the majority of European laws today. The legislative procedure for enacting legislation depends on a "co-decision" process through which the Parliament and the Council are put on an equal footing, and together they enact laws proposed by the Commission. Unlike similar legislative bodies, the Parliament does not possess the right of legislative initiative or the proposing of law. The members of Parliament are committed to act on behalf of the EC rather than at the behest of their constituency or their home governments, and sit in political groups instead of national delegations. Examples of European political groups that represent a particular political allegiance are: (1) European Conservative and Reformists, (2) European People's Party, and (3) Alliance of Liberals and Democrats for Europe.

The **Commission** is headquartered in Brussels and is composed of 27 representatives appointed by the Member State governments (one commissioner per State). Due to the breadth of its administrative duties, it is the largest of the

EU institutions, employing about half of all EU employees. The Commission is unique in that it is responsible for proposing all legislation to the European Parliament (for co-decision with the Council). The Commissioners all swear an oath of independence, disclaiming any partisan influence from any source, and undertake to protect the interests of the European citizen, not the national citizen.

The Commission is in the nature of a Secretariat, or executive body, having primarily executive duties, and its purpose is to see to it that the development of the EC conforms to the requirements of the Treaty of Rome. It has considerable autonomy in matters of competition, trade policy, and agriculture. It issues recommendations and opinions to the Council with the view to having the Council adopt binding regulations or directives to enforce compliance, specifically with regard to competition issues. The Commission has taken the lead in forcing compliance with the objectives of the Treaty of Rome (e.g., that the EC act as a cohesive force for the common good of the Member States rather than in their own national interests). The Commission has gradually accrued more power and responsibility since the 1980s, primarily as a result of decisions of the Court of Justice.

The foregoing were the original political institutions of the EEC, and remain as such in the European Union.

The **European Court of Justice**, although not political, was an original institution of the Treaty of Rome. It sits in Luxembourg and is the highest court in the EC. It is responsible for interpreting the treaties that established the EU and its predecessors and the laws, regulations, and directives emanating from its institutions.

The Continuing Evolution of the European Union

From the basic idea and structure set forth in the Treaty of Rome, the European Union has created itself and its actual structure and composition through a painful process of evolution. The original idea of union from such a diverse population and separate systems of government, with its violent history, was bound to be difficult. Yet, it is said that "nobody would have deliberately designed a government as complex and as redundant as the EU.[4]"

By 1986, the EC had grown to 12 member states.[5]

The **European Union** came into existence with the Treaty of Maastricht, signed in 1992. By 1995, the addition of Austria, Sweden, and Finland brought the number of countries in the EU to 15. In 2004, 10 more countries were admitted.[6] By 2007, the total membership had risen to 27 with the addition of Bulgaria and Romania.

Along the way came the **European Central Bank**, which is the central bank for the countries that have adopted the Euro, the EU's common currency. It controls monetary policy for that currency and its subscribing countries. It has inherited a central and very important role as certain Member States of the EU have demonstrated financial instability and weakness that threatens the very existence of the EU. This instability pits the more "industrious" Member States against those that might be termed "profligate" by some, the most glaring extremes of which are Germany (the world's fourth largest national economy) and Greece.

Although the purposes of the community are increased economic stability, expansion of economic activities, securing an improved standard of living, and the creation of a genuine, barrier-free internal market, the nature of the culture and the people of the various countries in the Union are playing a divisive role as the EU attempts to accomplish its original goals. The result appears to be that some of the more industrious and efficient countries are being called upon to "bailout" other Member States that have accumulated significant debt and that do not have the financial strength to continue to operate their governments, given their obligations. As of 2013, the EU is in crisis.

The Treaty of Rome and Air Transportation

A cornerstone of the dream of a unified Europe was that a reliable, common transportation system exist for the moving of people and goods. The Treaty of Rome incorporated this realization into Articles 85 and 86, which required the implementation of a common transport policy within the Community. Nevertheless, when the Council in 1962 adopted Regulation 17, which implemented those provisions of the Treaty, both air and sea transport were exempted.

The EC went further in 1968 and adopted a broad transportation policy applicable to commercial rail, road, and inland waterways, but not to sea and air transport. Air transportation policy within the EC was a difficult issue since each of the member states had, since the Chicago Convention of 1944, regularly entered into bilateral agreements with other countries around the world. In addition, the airlines of Europe were heavily subsidized by their separate governments. They were generally understood to be and were treated as public utilities, and were considered part and parcel of the national image projected by the government. There was, therefore, very little progress made in the area of air transportation policy prior to 1986.

The Treaty of Rome also incorporated into Articles 85 and 86 specific provisions prohibiting anticompetitive activities and policies in the field of transportation by Member States. It was realized that any true integration of European economies would be impossible unless and until barriers to the smooth flow of commerce between them were removed.

By the middle of the 1980s, the competition rules of the Treaty of Rome had been applied to other forms of transportation and to virtually all other areas of commerce. Within the international aviation community, pressure had been building for some time to apply these rules to commercial aviation. The fact was that commercial aviation in the European Community had been left out of the integration that had proceeded with all other forms of commerce. At the same time, the Community found it hard to ignore the competitive effects of deregulation in the United States as U.S. airlines adopted policies and procedures in the running of their companies that produced more efficient operations, reduced overhead, and allowed reduced rates and fares. While some of the harsher realities of deregulation that had occurred in the United States were closely evaluated in Europe, it was realized by all concerned that Europe was going to have to compete with these American airlines on the international scene sooner or later. Next, we will look at the effect that American deregulation had on the European Union.

Endnotes

1. http://www.loc.gov/exhibits/marshall/m9.html.
2. http://www.loc.gov/exhibits/marshall/m12.html.
3. France, Luxembourg, Italy, West Germany, Belgium, and the Netherlands.
4. Tom Reid, *Washington Post*.
5. In addition to the Six, there now were Ireland, Greece, Denmark, the United Kingdom, Spain, and Portugal.
6. Cyprus, Czech Republic, Estonia, Hungary, Latvia, Lithuania, Malta, Poland, Slovakia, and Slovenia.

39 American Deregulation and the European Union

The sudden abrogation by the United States Congress of economic regulation of American airlines in 1978 caught the world by surprise. The air carrier industry worldwide, for practically its entire existence, had been operating under the benevolent supervision of national governments. But in the United States, although air carriers were subject to the economic control of the Civil Aeronautics Board, they operated within a greater free enterprise system that reflected the philosophy of the national government and American heritage. In Europe, governments after World War II largely embraced socialist economic philosophy and policies. Conceptually, the complete removal of all government economic control of the air carrier industry was a more difficult hurdle for Europeans than for Americans.

Airline management in the United States after deregulation was quick to embrace the competition of the free market. The competitive spirit had been there all along, as demonstrated by the rivalry between American Airlines and United Airlines during the 1970s, as they fought for market share even under CAB constraints. After deregulation, U.S. airlines simply joined the ranks of most other American businesses and operated under the same national laws that governed everybody else. Competition, after all, was what the American economy was all about.

In Europe, on the other hand, national governments were quite less ready to accept full free market principles in most economic endeavors. Philosophical concerns of government typically ran to issues of citizen welfare, access to medical treatment, worker benefits, and other social entitlements, not to the state of competition in routine business affairs. With the prospect of privatization of air transport, all of these social concerns were present. Added to these concerns was anxiety over the loss of government control in directing the future of their airlines as organs of national influence.

Moreover, the demonstrated economic turmoil, bankruptcy, and labor strife that American deregulation had unleashed in the United States presented a foreboding view of the future under deregulation, and constituted another justification for European pause. The countries of Europe and the institutions of the EC debated the pros and cons of deregulation and its effect on the greater economy. Their approach was one of caution. The consensus generally formed was that air transport should be more the object of a policy of "liberalization" of regulation than an "abrogation" of regulation.

Then there was the matter of national diversity. The history of Europe through the first half of the 20th century is a history of conflict based largely on nationality or allegiances. European wars were the historical rule, not the exception. But after World War II, Europeans began to believe that things could be different. The countries that made up the EEC had agreed in the Treaty of Rome to embark on a more enlightened path for the future of Europe; cooperation and free competition, without national constraints, was the course set to be followed. But when it came to implementing the vision, old habits proved hard to break. National interests were difficult to ignore, particularly given the history of the continent. Progress was slow.

In short, the United States was far more prepared to deal with the radical idea of economic deregulation of the airlines (free competition) than were the states of Europe. Still, the Treaty of Rome had been signed and ratified; it was the law. It had been the law, in fact, for over 20 years when American deregulation came along in 1978. The institutions of the European Community had been set up, and they were staffed and operating. Many of those who had been charged with making the EC a reality were serious about their charge, and none more so than those within the European Commission.

Liberalization of Air Transport in the European Community

During the first 20 years of the EC, the European Council was unable to come to any consensus as to how to break down the State-sponsored anticompetitive barriers and practices that characterized European airlines, even though this was clearly its mandate. The European Commission, chafing at the lack of movement in this area, began the "liberalization" process with its Memorandum No. 1 in 1979, which dealt primarily with the existence of high tariffs between Member States. The Commission does not have

authority to enact binding regulations, but only proposes to the Council, which has that authority. The Commission, therefore, used the "Memorandum" vehicle as a gentle prod to the Council.

When the Council had failed to take action by 1984, the Commission published its Memorandum No. 2. This position paper was an expansion of the positions taken in Memorandum No. 1, and contained further, comprehensive proposals aimed at breaking down anticompetitive practices in air transportation among the Member States. The paper dealt with the intransigence of Member States in implementing Common Market unification strategies required by the Treaty of Rome, and emphasized the need for a unified European Community position in view of the effects of deregulation in the United States.

Further, between the Commission's Memorandum No. 1 and Memorandum No. 2, the Parliament brought an action against the Council in the European Court of Justice seeking a declaration that the Council had failed in its duty to act in promoting a common transportation policy. While the decision of the Court of Justice was wide-ranging, the decision did agree that the Council had effectively eschewed its responsibilities regarding air transport. With the rendering of this opinion of the Court of Justice, the Council had effectively been chastised by all three of the other EC institutions.

In April 1986, the European Court of Justice rendered its decision in the case of *Nouvelles Frontieres*.[1] This decision removed any remaining doubt that air transport was subject to the competition rules of the Treaty of Rome. The court held, in effect, that if the Council failed to act on competition issues, the Commission could issue a "reasoned decision" under Article 89 that would have the effect of putting competition issues into litigation for resolution. This decision constituted an "end run" around the Council, giving the Commission direct means to address the issue of competition in air transport matters.

Strengthened by *Nouvelles Frontieres*, later in 1986 the Commission sent letters to

10 European airlines alleging that they had violated the anticompetitive provisions of the Treaty of Rome by price fixing, capacity limitations, and various other practices. In due course, negotiations between the carriers and the Commission led to the implementation of restrictions of some of these anticompetitive practices for the first time.

After years of stagnation regarding the question of "liberalization" in the European air transport industry, things were now beginning to happen. The Single European Act,[2] an agreement ratified by the Member States in February 1986, and which went into force on July 1, 1987, effectively laid the necessary groundwork for the creation of the European Union. Its intention was finally to create a true internal market in the Community, one in which restrictions on the movement of goods, services, people, and capital were eliminated. Additionally, by its amendment of the voting procedures used within the European Council (it eliminated single state veto and mandated majority vote), the Council was freed from its preexisting paralysis on a number of issues, including the issue of a common transport policy regarding aviation. No longer could one Member State veto action by the Council. No longer could minority bickering between nations within the 12-member Council thwart the efforts of the majority toward full integration of Member States and the elimination of frontiers. At last, the Treaty of Rome had teeth.

■ Advent of the European Union

Although it had taken 30 years to accomplish, by 1987 the basis for broad European cooperation had finally been achieved. It had taken the separate efforts of all of the EC institutions to make it happen: the Commission, by its Memorandum No. 1 and Memorandum No. 2; the Parliament, by its civil action against the Council; the European Court of Justice, by its decision in the *Nouvelles Frontieres* case; and finally, the Single European Act. Henceforth, national autonomy would take a back seat to the unity of the European Union.

Competition Rules in Air Transport

Now it was the turn of the Council to take the leading role in implementing the goal of full economic integration by restructuring air transport policies. The Council, in 1987, adopted regulations (the Competition Rules) designed to apply the rules of competition, mandated by the Treaty of Rome, to scheduled air transport. These regulations applied only between Member States, not to internal domestic traffic nor to operations between a Member State and a non-Member State. Air transport operations to third-party states were, and had been, controlled by bilateral agreement beginning after the Chicago Convention in 1944.

The Council regulations came in three phases, or "packages" as they were called, between 1987 and 1993. The third set of regulations, effective on January 1, 1993, effectively satisfied the goal of air transport liberalization mandated by the Treaty of Rome. This group of regulations dealt with the important issues of fares, market factors (slot allocations, capacity, etc.), computer reservation systems, ground handling, cargo services, mergers, and subsidies.

In addition, by 1993 there had already begun a trend toward privatization of national airlines. British Airways was the first of the national airlines to privatize, in 1987, followed by Icelandair, and others were well on the way to privatization, like KLM (39 percent government owned), Sabena (53 percent), SAS (50 percent), Lufthansa (48 percent). Still others, like Air France, Iberia, and Olympic remained wholly government owned, but the trend toward privatization had been started. By the end of 2002, KLM and Iberia were fully privatized. Privatization among other international airlines is shown in Figure 39-1.

Predation and Merger

The Council's competition rules are mainly enforced by the Commission. Commission investigations of predation and mergers can be compared to those of the United States Department of Justice. With respect to mergers, the EU and the United States agreed in 1991 to coordinate their activities so as to reduce the likelihood of significant discrepancies existing in their anti-competition rules and policies regarding transatlantic mergers and acquisitions.[3]

Government Subsidies

Economic Issues Affecting Competition

National airlines of the European countries had been the object of national pride, support, and ownership for many decades, as discussed above. Under the new regulations of the Council effective in 1993, however, subsidization of national

airlines was recognized to be a major problem and impediment to the goal of free competition within the EU. Still, such a long-standing and venerable practice was a difficult subject for the Commission to approach. In 1994, the Commission adopted a complex set of "guidelines" as a statement of policy, and a basis for potential enforcement, on the subject of government aid of airlines.

The guidelines apply not only to carriers but to the operations "accessory to air transport." These activities would include flight schools, duty-free shops, and airport facilities. **Notably, aircraft manufacturing subsidies were not included in the guidelines, an omission that effectively removed any consideration of the**

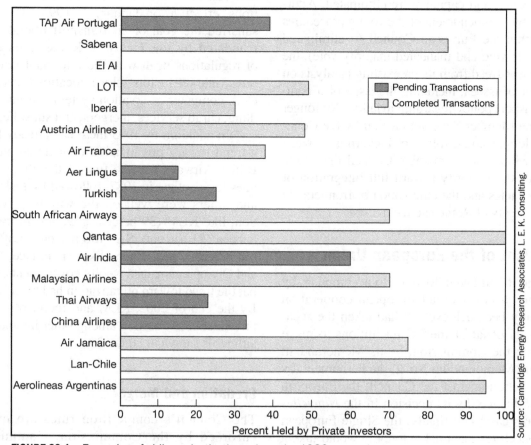

FIGURE 39-1 Examples of airline privatizations since the 1980s.

consortium Airbus Industrie from the policy of non-subsidy. State aid to airports and funds for new airport construction were also not included in the scope of the guidelines.

The thrust of the rules governing subsidies is to prevent any operator from achieving a competitive advantage over any other operator based in the EU countries by subsidy. The guidelines recognized at least five types of government aid that would be objectionable and contrary to the purpose of the EU. Direct operational subsidies are the most obvious and flagrant form of state aid. State "investment" came under scrutiny by the Commission and became subject to evaluation using certain tests and criteria to determine if the aid is really "direct subsidy" in disguise. Other forms of state assistance may include:

- Capital injection
- Loan financing
- Loan guarantees
- The granting of exclusive rights

Noneconomic Issues

The EU institutions have also assumed responsibility for certain noneconomic issues that have direct bearing on air transport. Included in these issues are:

- Air traffic control
- Noise
- Carrier liability
- Accident investigation

Air Traffic Control

In 1961, the European Economic Community (EEC) was composed of just the original six members. Air traffic control after World War II had been the responsibility of each of their individual national governments. One of the first attempts at consolidation by the EEC was the coordination of air traffic within their severely restricted airspace. Beginning that year, the EEC created the agency known as Eurocontrol, which took charge of air traffic control over the greater part of Europe.

In 1999, almost 40 years after establishment of the EEC, the European Commission recommended changes to Eurocontrol that would bring about a more unified and efficient air traffic control system. By 1999, the organization had grown to 15 Member States, and the EEC had become the substantial sovereign entity known as the European Union. One of the recommended changes to the operation of Eurocontrol was the creation of the concept known as "Single European Sky."

Later in this chapter we will review the historical evolution of Eurocontrol, the transition of air traffic control under the Single European Sky concept, and the proposed development of a satellite-based air traffic control system.

Noise Limitations

Reduction of noise levels on and around airports worldwide has received much attention. Excellent progress has been made in this area as decibel levels of operating aircraft have progressively been reduced and as land use management and other methods of noise reduction have been adopted. Europe's urban concentrations have made airport noise limitation a critical issue, and the EU has been aggressive in this area. Some EU practices, however, have caused consternation to foreign carriers and their governments. It is alleged, for instance, that the EU noise restrictions adopted by the Council have been applied in order to manage and restrict market access to foreign aircraft manufacturers, notably in the United States (Boeing). The argument is made that such restrictions are actually a form of "protectionism" for Airbus Industrie. These arguments note that EU noise limitations are significantly more limiting than ICAO standards.

Air Carrier Liability

Until recently, air carrier liability was governed by the terms of the Warsaw Convention of 1929, as modified by subsequent protocols and voluntary carrier agreements. A complete overhaul of the system was completed in 1999 (the Montreal Convention of 1999), and it entered into force as of November 4, 2003, among ratifying nations.[4] In 1997, the European Council adopted regulations that defined carrier liability of EU operators, increasing their potential liability (100,000 SDRs). These regulations are mandatory for EU-based operators but non-EU operators may exempt themselves from their operation through tariff clauses if notice to passengers is properly given.

Accident Investigation

In 1994, the Council adopted regulations designed to harmonize accident investigations within the EU, and outside the EU in some circumstances, by providing guidelines and requirements to be observed by Member States. National governments have had responsibility under the Chicago Convention for coordinating investigations of air crashes and incidents for 50 years. The action by the Council standardizes the procedures and requires reports to be filed with the Commission.

■ Aviation Agencies of the European Union

The European Civil Aviation Conference (ECAC)

The European Civil Aviation Conference is an independent body of 42 Member States that is closely integrated with ICAO, as anticipated by Article 55 (a) of the Chicago Convention. ECAC was founded in 1955 at the behest of the fledgling European Council to be to the pan-European states what ICAO is to the entire world. As ECAC has matured over the period of one-half century, its functions have been expanded, and it has become the only Europe-wide organization with the membership and expertise capable of responding to the complex needs of the European air transport industry.

ECAC's stated objectives include the promotion of continued development of a safe, efficient, and sustainable European air transport system that seeks to harmonize civil aviation policies and practices among its member states and the major industrialized countries of the world. It has become the essential forum for discussions of every major civil aviation topic and regularly conducts seminars and international symposia on various issues. It concerns itself with the environment, noise, accident investigation, security, immigration, certification, airport policy, and land-use management.

ECAC works closely with the European Commission in aviation affairs and is funded by the European Council. The aviation safety responsibilities of ECAC are currently carried out by the Joint Aviation Authorities and by its successor organization, the European Aviation Safety Agency (EASA).

The European Joint Aviation Authorities (JAA)

JAA was organized in 1970 as a group of civil aviation authorities from separate European states, formed to cooperate in producing "Joint Airworthiness Requirements" (JARs) for certification of aircraft and other products jointly produced in Europe and to facilitate the export and import of such products between European States. Beginning in 1989, JAA as an organization was cohesively associated as a body with ECAC and was charged with taking care of the regulatory activities in aviation safety under the oversight of ECAC. The ECAC itself concentrates on policy issues, security, and the environment as they relate to civil aviation.

JAA's primary function was to ensure that JAA Member States achieved a consistent level of aviation safety through the cooperation of its members. There has been a transition of these activities from JAA to the permanent European Union agency responsible for all civil aviation safety known as the European Aviation Safety

Agency (EASA). EASA became operational in 2003 and is now responsible for rule-making, certification, and standardization of rules to be applied by the national aviation authorities.

JAA developed and adopted JARs in the areas of aircraft design and manufacture, aircraft operations and maintenance, and the licensing of aviation personnel. It also developed administrative and technical procedures for the implementation of JARs once they were adopted. Since 1996, for instance, JAA had the responsibility of running the Safety Assessment for Foreign Aircraft (SAFA) program for ECAC. While ICAO has undertaken the overall role of developing and implementing safety standards worldwide, SAFA is an ECAC program that complements ICAO based on a "bottom up" approach. Under this program, JAA conducted ramp inspections of aircraft throughout its Member States utilizing Standards of ICAO Annexes 1 (Personnel Licensing), 2 (Operations of Aircraft), and 3 (Airworthiness of Aircraft).

Beginning in 2000, JAA had developed a fully operational database, completely computerized, which is the repository for all reports completed as a result of the ramp inspections Europe-wide. In 2001, 25 states performed 2,706 inspections, up from 75 inspections in 1996. JAA action taken as a result of these inspections ranged from simple discussions with aircraft commanders concerning minor items to grounding of the aircraft until corrective action is taken for serious violations. Notification of the responsible Civil Aviation Authority of the aircraft's home country usually followed the notation of a violation. In repeated or egregious cases, entry permits of the aircraft operator were revoked.

JAA has sought to maintain a high level of cooperation and coordination with the FAA in the United States and, more recently, with the appropriate safety regulatory authorities of Russia and other former communist countries that joined the JAA, as well as with Canada, Japan, Australia, and others. With respect to the FAA, JAA sought to harmonize the relationship between FARs and JARs as they relate, particularly, to:

1. Design and manufacture, operation, and maintenance of civil aircraft and related products and parts
2. Noise and emissions from aircraft and aircraft engines
3. Flight crew licensing

JAA was widely regarded as the European equivalent of the FAA, and, in many respects, that is an accurate comparison.[5] The JAA was criticized by the United States, however, as having a protectionist agenda, that is, it adopted regulations for the express purpose of promoting European aviation to the detriment of competitors from outside of the EU, particularly the United States. In June 1997, for instance, the JAA attempted to adopt rules that would have required flight training for European pilots to be conducted at flight schools that are 51 percent owned by Europeans. Although this requirement was dropped after objection by United States interests, the new regulation still severely restricts flight training at facilities outside of the EU countries, and makes it difficult to convert a license issued by the FAA into one acceptable under the JAA regulation. This regulation was justified by the JAA on the basis of safety, although even a cursory analysis of the rationale will disclose that basis to be a sham. It is a unilateral trade restriction designed to promote European flight schools to the detriment of similar schools located in the United States.

As to the function of JAA coordinating with foreign safety regulatory authorities, like the FAA, on the certification of products and services, JAA made the process of securing its approval of U.S. manufactured products very difficult. Approval by JAA was a requirement before any such American product could be exported to Europe. The approval was designed to be a validation of FAA or other certification, not a new and complete recertification regimen imposed by the JAA. Allegations were lodged that JAA abused this validation process to delay or prevent sales of U.S. aviation products in Europe. One example cited is the difficulty the Gulfstream V has had in securing JAA approval for sale in Europe, difficulty that resulted in years of delay and the expenditure of millions of dollars. Another example is the Cessna X, which required in excess of four years and the expenditure of $3 million to secure JAA approval. In order for a new aircraft type manufactured in the United States, and certified by the FAA, to be approved for export to Europe, JAA review required as much as an additional 52 percent of the time it took the FAA to certify the new type in the first place. This compares with 15 to 17 percent of the time the FAA takes to certify foreign aircraft for sale in the United States.[6]

These European practices may create trade issues that transcend anything previously experienced in world aviation commerce, and may have ramifications that affect the overall global aviation market. At a minimum, these practices violate the spirit of international trade agreements and impair the promise of the global marketplace. These practices by the EU, termed "Regulatory Nationalism," are receiving increasing scrutiny by United States government authorities.[7]

On January 1, 2007, the JAA entered an official "transition" phase designed to mark the absorption of JAA functions into EASA. Combining the offices of JAA with EASA in Cologne, Germany, began on March 1, 2007. The JAA system was disbanded effective June 30, 2009.

European Aviation Safety Agency (EASA)

EASA became operational in 2003 under European Parliament and Council authority. It is an independent EU body accountable to the Member States and the EU institutions. Its responsibility is aviation safety and aviation's impact on the environment. It reached full functionality in 2008 when the functions of the former JAA were incorporated into EASA.

While EASA has taken over the responsibilities previously performed by JAA, there are differences. EASA has regulatory authority from the European Commission, the Council, and the Parliament, while JAA's operations were conducted under coordinated laws of the several Member States of the EU. EASA regulations have the direct force of law.

EASA's main tasks include:

* Rule-making, that is, drafting safety legislation for the European Commission
* Standardization programs and inspections to insure uniform implementation of EU aviation safety legislation in all Member States
* Type certification of aircraft, engines, and parts
* Data collection, analysis, and research to improve aviation safety
* Licensing of crews within the EU, certification of non-member States' airlines, as well as playing a key role in the safety regulation of airports
* The agency is also developing close working relationships with safety organizations in other countries (like the FAA) and with ICAO with the goal of harmonizing safety standards and procedures.

■ European Air Traffic Control

European air traffic control after World War II was similar to jurisdiction of everything else in Europe, a matter of the sovereign control of each separate government, with interaction between nations being dictated by treaty. The same impediments to unification seen elsewhere prevailed in attempts to create a system of air traffic control for the European continent. Movement of aircraft across borders involved air traffic control of both countries, with no central flow system.

Centralization of air traffic control was the beneficiary of advances made in other sectors of the growth of the EEC, which ultimately culminated in the formation of the European Union. As advances were made in those other sectors, an infrastructure for air traffic control was also being built. Navaids were installed, routes were created, rules and regulations for flight and control authority were established. The separate States relied on past treaties (Paris Treaty of 1919), the First Convention Relating to the Regulation of Aerial Navigation (signed by 27 States in 1919), the International Civil Aviation Conference, and then NATO to coordinate military use of the airspace.

In 1958, seven States[8] set up the Technical Working Group "Eurocontrol" composed of civil and military representatives. Basically filling a vacuum due to the absence of any orchestrated plan between the States of Europe, Eurocontrol grew, receiving authority to establish centers, facilities, data processing, establishing communications networks between States and their governing authorities, and generally building other necessary infrastructure to handle air traffic management over and beyond the borders of Europe.

Harmonization and integration was facilitated under the auspices of ECAC during the 1980s and by the creation of the Central Flow Management Unit (CFMU). That system under Eurocontrol became responsible for all traffic control flow management for the entire continent in 1996.

In 1999, the European Commission announced the creation of the "Single European Sky" (SES), requiring a developmental approach involving Eurocontrol interim cooperation and assistance and the preparation for the assumption of a primary role in the "Single European Sky" concept. Traffic handling was still very much a national, sovereign affair, and Eurocontrol operation was separated among five regional flow management centers, all operated by their own national administrations.

SES is an ambitious initiative to reform the architecture of European air traffic control and to meet future capacity and safety needs.

In 2004, the Council and the European Parliament endorsed the Single European Sky legislation that will integrate all European air traffic control in the European Community. A package of four regulations is included in this enabling legislation.

1. The framework regulation: This sets out the overall objectives for the Single European Sky initiative—"to enhance current safety standards and overall efficiency for general air traffic in Europe, to optimize capacity meeting the requirements of all airspace users and to minimize delays."

2. The airspace regulation: This concerns the use and organization of airspace, both for the civil and military requirements of Member States.

3. The service provision regulation: This mandates that common standards are to be applied for all navigation services provided.

4. The interoperability regulation: This looks to insure the integration of all systems from whatever source. The systems include eight areas: airspace management, air traffic flow management, air traffic services, communications, navigation, surveillance, aeronautical information services, and meteorological information.

This is a work in progress. The final product will include the standardization of air traffic systems across Europe, the common licensing of air traffic controllers, and the reconfiguration of European airspace into functional blocks irrespective of national borders. The original concept of SES has been reformed (amended) in a communication known as Single European Sky II (2008), which more clearly defines the goals of SES to be based on four pillars:

1. Performance, to include reductions in delays and shortening of routes, creation of functional airspace blocks (FABS) designed to

meet these performance objectives, slot allocation and deployment of the SESAR (like NextGen performance-based navigation).

2. Safety, to extend EASA authority to aerodromes, air traffic management, and air navigation services.

3. New technologies, or the implementing of SESAR and its benefits.

4. Managing capacity on the ground to insure airports' capacities comport to ATM capacity.

The intent is to perform an internal reform of Eurocontrol to align it with the government structures of Single European Sky. Assuming this can be done, Eurocontrol will proceed to implement these policies.

SESAR (Single European Sky ATM Research Program)

As a part of the SES initiative, SESAR represents the technological dimension of the plan, which will incorporate state-of-the-art innovative technology.

SESAR might be compared to the NextGen program in the United States and, like the Joint Planning and Development Office (JDPO), the planning segment of NextGen in the United States, it is a forward-looking program that involves all of the entities that operate within the air transport system. These include civil and military agencies of government, legislators, industry, operators, and users. These entities will be central to the defining, committing to, and implementing of a pan-European ATM system.

The SESAR program is separated into three sequential phases:

Definition Phase (2005–2008), now completed

Development Phase (2008–2013), like Next-Gen, under development.

Deployment Phase (2014–2020), like Next-Gen, under development.

During the first phase, a European Master Plan was presented, bringing European ATM stakeholders together to produce and validate a common view of the future of European ATM. The updated second phase takes into account the global financial crises that began in 2008 after the Master Plan was published. It proposes to seek an impact statement to confirm that the Master Plan is affordable and can be done and to update the Plan in light of developments. This is a work in progress, as is the remainder of the SESAR program. Fast-moving technological developments, as well as global financial developments, will affect the deployment effort. The implementation phase will depend on accomplishing the goals of the second phase.

SESAR will incorporate the European Global Navigation Satellite System (GNSS) known as Galileo, into the ATM system to be launched. Details of the manner and means by which the new system will operate have not been disclosed, but it might be presumed that it will evolve in a similar manner to the NextGen plan in the United States. Part of the U.S. plan, in fact, is to reach out to the global community so that the several systems now on the drawing boards might be developed with the requirements of the others in mind. It makes sense that these satellite-based air traffic control systems be compatible to the extent possible so that the globalization of the air transport system will extend, not only to marketing and governmental policy developments, like deregulation and Open Skies, but to operational considerations, like air traffic control, to enhance the seamless transition of air transport operations over the globe.

Harmonic Convergence

The United States and the EU are working simultaneously on the complete transition of their air traffic control systems from land-based navigation to satellite navigation. The fact is that these programs are being carried out separately, under separate management and with distinct challenges; yet the hundreds of flights that travel between the two continents daily demand that these separate systems be compatible and that the flights be operationally seamless and safe.

There are also distinctions between the two systems that reflect the political and cultural differences between the United States and the countries of Europe. The U.S. system is a federal one, while the EU must still deal with the concerns of 27 sovereign states. The controlling governmental entity for the United States is the FAA, while that for the EU is the SESAR Joint Undertaking (SJU), which consists of Eurocontrol, the European Commission, and 15 more member organizations.

The tentative nature of some aspects of each of the programs, partially because of still undeveloped technological systems, unknown pricing, and even undetermined commitment, have caused skepticism and doubts among stakeholders (primarily airlines, on both sides of the Atlantic, who must equip their aircraft). All of this has been exacerbated by the global financial crisis, which has manifested itself in a very divisive manner in the EU and its separate Member States.

The uncertainties inherent in each of the programs contribute to difficulties in harmonization. There can be no doubt that each side understands that the systems must, in fact, be compatible and consistent, but both programs at this point still involve a lot of theory, unproven development, and the possibility of a change in course that will affect the financial conditions of both the private and governmental sectors.

Final developments cannot be stated with certainty under these conditions. There appears to be a bona fide commitment to accomplish the stated goals of both the United States and the EU, and hard work is proceeding in many quarters in the United States and in Europe; indeed, including private enterprise all over the world. Air traffic management systems are obsolete and must be fixed. Exactly what will develop, and when it will develop, remains to be seen.

Endnotes

1. *Ministere Public v. Lucas Asjes*, 3 C.L.R. 173, Eur. Ct. R. 1425.

2. Common Mkt. Rep. (CCH) p. 202.7 (1978).

3. Agreement between the government of the United States of America and the Commission of the European Communities regarding application of their Competition Laws, 1995 O. J. (L95) 47.

4. See discussion in Chapter 37.

5. Most developed countries have their own regulatory authority that is equivalent to the FAA. Here are some worldwide certification agencies: Canada—Transport Canada; Brazil—CTA; EU—EASA (27 countries); Kenya—KCAA; Russia—Aviation Register; China—CAAC; Japan—JCAB; Australia—CASA.

6. Lipinski, William O., An Evaluation of the U.S.–EU Trade Relationship <http://www.house.gov./lipinski/aviation.htm>.

7. *Competition in the U.S. Aircraft Manufacturing Industry.* Testimony before the Subcommittee on Aviation of the Committee on Transportation and Infrastructure, U.S. House of Representatives, July 26, 2001, U.S. Government Printing Office.

8. Belgium, France, Luxembourg, the Netherlands, Federal Republic of Germany and the United Kingdom.

40   Global Deregulation Takes Off

Worldwide, the air transport industry is a major factor in the economic health of nations.

There are hundreds of airlines the world over, and they operate tens of thousands of aircraft. Over 2 billion passengers travel on the world's airlines, with projected increases worldwide in the coming years. Over 40 percent of the world's manufactured exports travel by air, and in 2006 the air transport industry provided, directly and indirectly, 29 million jobs for the global workforce.[1] North American airlines carry about 40 percent of the world's air passengers, with European carriers accounting for 26 percent, and the Asia/Pacific region's airlines at 24 percent. Latin American, Middle Eastern, and African carriers account for the remainder.

The aviation transport industry generates wealth, employment, taxes, tourism, and related benefits for each nation with a viable air transport system. It is obvious, therefore, that it is in the national interest of such countries to be and remain competitive in the global air transport market. As we have seen, the airline industry has historically been regulated internally by their home governments and, except for the United States, state-owned airlines have been the general rule. Regulation of international air transport has been accomplished as a part of international relations primarily by means of the bilateral agreement format between nations. Prior to the Airline Deregulation Act of 1978 in the United States, therefore, regulation by governments around the world, supplemented by the traffic coordination activities of the International Air Transport Association (IATA), had maintained a more or less stable marketing environment in international aviation.

For more than a third of a century in the United States, the cost benefits to air travelers and shippers directly attributable to the competitive influences of deregulation have been apparent. The number of enplanements and the number of flights have greatly increased as many more people have taken to the air as the primary means of travel. Although not all of the changes produced by deregulation have been positive (notably the lowering of airline employee wages, crowded airplanes, and long lines) competition in the airlines is here to stay.

We saw in the last chapter how the Airline Deregulation Act has had a ripple effect throughout the world, with the new competitive system brought by the American statute becoming a fact of life for airlines to be dealt with on an international basis. We saw also how difficult it was for the Europeans to break away from their long-held belief in the state-ownership of domestic airlines and how painful it was to come to grips with the practicalities of global competition, in spite of the fact that this is what their own law required under the Treaty of Rome.

While this was going on in Europe, the United States in 1992, took measures, to force the issue internationally. The United States Department of State announced the policy of "Open Skies," which is designed to make international travel more seamless and less controlled by nation-states.

Open Skies embraces full deregulation of international air transportation. This concept includes:

1. Unrestricted access to airlines to operate between international gateways by way of any point and beyond to any point (outside of the destination country) at the discretion of airline management

2. Unrestricted service opportunities, so that airlines are free to decide the frequency, capacity, and equipment necessary to service market demand

3. Freedom of airlines to set prices

Still not included as a part of Open Skies are cabotage rights (freedom to serve domestic traffic within the United States from another U.S. city) and foreign control of U.S. airlines (this maintains the current limitation of foreign ownership of U.S. carriers).[2]

The policy of the United States, as established by the Department of Transportation and the State Department, does support liberalization of long-standing cabotage rules and the long-standing policy restricting foreign ownership of U.S. airlines. The U.S. Congress, on the other hand, has failed to approve any change in these constraints to full deregulation. In 2006, in fact, the United States Congress was opposed to increasing foreign ownership of U.S. airlines,[3] and still is today. This disagreement over the future of airline deregulation is an example of the Constitutional separation of powers. In this case, the rift pits the policy-making prerogatives of the Executive Branch against the law-making

prerogatives of the Legislative Branch and the requirement that the Senate ratify all treaties.

The policy of the United States also calls for the end of subsidies by foreign governments to national airlines, including state ownership, protectionism, or financial assistance of any kind, since these activities produce market-distorting results in a competitive system.

Within the European Union, the separate governments of the Member States historically insisted on retaining their individual rights to negotiate and enter into old-style bilateral traffic agreements as they chose, particularly with the United States. The European Commission, on the other hand, insisted that the right to negotiate and sign international traffic agreements lay with the EU, not the individual Member States.

Relying on its prior success at consolidating powers, the Commission in 1995 began to lobby hard for authority to regulate all bilaterals affecting the EU nations. The Transport Commissioner of the EU threatened to bring the issue before the European Court of Justice. When that threat failed, the Commission sued six Member States.[4] That litigation was halted by agreement between the Commission and the defendants, but when Member States continued to pursue unilateral talks with the United States on the terms of bilaterals, the Commission again sued, this time adding Germany and the United Kingdom to the original six defendants.[5]

A standoff ensued on this issue in the EU. For a time the issue appeared to have been relegated to secondary importance, and EU Member States continued to negotiate directly with the United States in Open Skies bilaterals. France and the United States, for instance, signed an Open Skies agreement in January 2002, which contained the standard freedoms enumerated above.

In 2002, however, the European Court of Justice ruled that the practice of EU Member States separately negotiating bilaterals directly with the United States was incompatible with EU law. The Court did not, however, strike down the existing bilaterals, so international traffic continued under those preexisting agreements.

This uneasy situation persisted until the "break-through" occurred in 2006, discussed below.

The First Multilateral Open Skies Agreement

On November 15, 2000, agreement was reached between the United States and four of its aviation partners for a comprehensive liberalization of aviation services: the first multilateral Open Skies agreement. Brunei, Chile, New Zealand, and Singapore, countries from diverse areas of the globe, agreed with the United States to unrestricted service by the airlines of each country to, from, and beyond the other's territory, as well as unrestricted destinations (except cabotage), routes, number of flights, and prices charged. This multilateral accord was finalized in 2001 and it has been subsequently joined by Samoa, Tonga, and Mongolia.

Deregulation and the United Kingdom

In contrast to the apparent worldwide move toward liberalization, efforts to secure agreement with the U.K. failed, and the restrictions in the current bilateral agreement between the United States and Britain, known as Bermuda 2, are severe. Bermuda 2 was signed 30 years after the original agreement between these countries,[6] and while the new agreement relaxed some of the requirements and restrictions of the original pact, air transportation between the two countries remained heavily constrained. This "anachronistic agreement," as labeled by the Secretary of Transportation,[7] still limited the number of cities in the two countries that can be served, the number of airlines that can serve the market, the fares that can be charged, and the level of service that can be provided. Under Bermuda 2, for instance, only American Airlines and United Airlines were allowed to serve Heathrow airport.[8]

According to the DOT, the U.K. position is nothing other than protectionism of British Airways, which opposes entry into the world of free and fair competition. The effect of the British position has created a degree of British isolation in an increasingly progressive European aviation community.

Breakthrough—Open Skies Agreement between the United States and the European Union

The decision of the European Court of Justice in 2002, holding that bilaterals between Member States and the United States were in violation of EU law, posed a significant problem for the EU States, as well as for the United States. It did, however, provide an opportunity to pressure the United Kingdom into finally seriously addressing the issue of globalization and relaxation of the constraints imposed by Bermuda 2.

In 2006, agreement was reached between negotiators for the U.S. and the EU for an Open Skies agreement for all EU Member States, including the U.K. Open Skies agreements are, technically, treaties between nations and, as such, in the United States these agreements must obtain Senate approval. The Senate that year refused to approve the Open Skies agreement that had been negotiated, primarily on the basis that the agreement would have relaxed the law (enacted by the entire Congress) applicable to foreign ownership of U.S. airlines.

The negotiating teams went back to work, and in 2007, a new Open Skies agreement was reached, but this time the ownership rules were preserved, as well as historical cabotage restraints.[9] This new Agreement was signed on April 30, 2007, by the representatives of the EU and by the U.S. Department of State. The Agreement was originally slated to go into effect in October 2007 but, due to objections posed by the U.K., the effective date was moved back to March 30, 2008. This was, in part, to allow Heathrow airport to complete new terminal construction to enlarge its facilities in anticipation of the significant increases in traffic that the Agreement will cause.

The Agreement also contained exit provisions that allowed the EU to renounce the agreement in 2010 if the issues of cabotage and airline ownership had not been liberalized. This Agreement went into effect in March of 2008.

The EU has voiced one additional complaint. They say that the United States has the better part of the deal since U.S. airlines are permitted to fly into any EU country and then fly from that country into any other EU country. Although U.S. airlines may not fly from one point in any one EU country to another point in that same country, U.S. airlines do have a sort of cabotage right if the EU is considered a single sovereign entity. For instance, a U.S. airline will be permitted to land at Heathrow, pick up passengers and fly on to Paris, while an EU airline, landing at JFK, will not be permitted to proceed with passengers to Dallas, or any other U.S. city.

The right of the EU to renounce the Agreement in 2010 gave rise to continued negotiations on the issues that remained unresolved in the 2008 Agreement. The EU wanted unlimited rights to fly intra-United States (cabotage) and they wanted liberalization of ownership rights in U.S. airlines to allow foreign majority ownership. Although there are good arguments on both sides, no agreement has been reached.

Some believe that foreign investment in U.S. airlines could enhance the financial condition of domestic airlines, take advantage of larger route networks and their economies of scale, as well as improve the level of service. Others fear that foreign ownership would bring a loss of jobs and control, and perhaps the disappearance of some U.S. airlines. Such a revision of United States law would certainly alter or eliminate cabotage and would seriously affect the ability of the country to command the participation of U.S. airlines in times of emergency or national need. Bob Crandall, formerly CEO of American Airlines, poses the question of why any foreign airline or group would actually want to own an American airline, given their proven poor financial track record, the high level of competition, and the slim profit margins that exist for even profitable airlines in this country. He also poses the answer: Foreign ownership would be used by foreign interests only for the purpose of access to U.S.

markets, which doubtless are vast, and to control airline transportation to and from the United States. Under his view, domestic airline service would significantly deteriorate under such a system.

A second-stage EU-U.S. Open Skies Agreement was signed in March 2010, but it did not contain the cabotage and airline ownership rights sought by the EU. The new arrangement does provide means for cooperation on competition, environmental issues, labor standards, safety, and security. It will also give airline alliance partners greater flexibility in service areas.[10] The Fly America Act which requires all travel funded by the United States government to be on a domestic airline, is not applicable since it contains an exception for flight on airlines associated with nations that have a bilateral or multilateral agreement with the United States.

The 2010 amendment goes only so far as to commit the parties to engage in a process of reforming airline ownership and control rules, promising a quid pro quo for allowing majority ownership in each group's airlines.

By 2011, the United States had concluded Open Skies agreements with over 100 countries. Although global liberalization began with the Airline Deregulation Act of 1978, it was difficult to actually achieve a common policy of liberalization within Europe, even after the founding of the European Union. Through steady pressure by the institutions of the EU, and the Open Skies accords that have been put in place by the United States and the EU, there is a shared appreciation for the benefits that accrue from the elimination of trading and operating constraints.

Traffic growth after liberalization averages between 12 percent and 35 percent according to a recent study,[11] and in some cases has reached nearly 100 percent of the pre-liberalization rates. As an example, liberalizing 320 specific country pair bilateral contracts specified in the study would produce 24.1 million full-time jobs and generate an additional $490 billion in GDP (corresponding to an economy almost the size of Brazil).

While we have analyzed the results of these policies within the United States as a result of

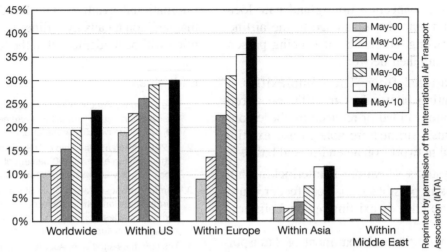

FIGURE 40-1 LCCs now supply a quarter of scheduled seats worldwide.

deregulation, examples of similar global effects include the growth of international services to secondary airports in the United Kingdom (Manchester, Birmingham, and Glasgow), the growth of Dubai as a major international hub, domestic deregulation in India, and the putting in place of the EU's Single European Market, resulting in the growth of low-cost carriers such as Ryanair and Easyjet. Significant examples of other symbiotic traffic relationships include United Arab Emirates and Europe, Malaysia and Thailand, and Australia and New Zealand. Please refer to Figure 40-1 for a chart depiction of the number of seats worldwide supplied by low-cost carriers. Cooperation between countries utilizing these anticompetitive techniques also results in sharing the ideas and effects of improved environmental measures, such as noise reduction, improved fuel efficiency, and reduction of emissions, as well as efficient air traffic management.

Airline Alliances

In addition to Open Skies bilateral and multilateral agreements between countries, the United States advocates and approves strategic sharing alliances between U.S. carriers and foreign carriers under "antitrust immunity" agreements with those carriers. Under this arrangement, the alliance partners are free to set prices and to otherwise combine their resources in order to maximize marketing strategies that inure to the benefit of the international traveling public and to themselves. These alliances have produced significant results.

According to an early report of the DOT,[12] implementation of alliances under Open Skies agreements resulted in increases in passenger traffic numbers, decreases in prices, and the tapping of entirely new segments of populations that are now availing themselves of international air travel for the first time. Travelers from "behind European gateways" who had never before been serviced in the transatlantic market were of particular note.

The three largest airline alliances are Star Alliance, SkyTeam, and OneWorld.[13] These Alliances combine to carry over 82 percent of transatlantic traffic. Alliances have extended to the world of cargo airlines as well, including ANA/UPS Alliance, SkyTeam Cargo, and WOW Alliance.

Similar to code-sharing arrangements, these alliances provide on the international level many of the benefits of standard code sharing but go a step beyond because of international complications:

1. Joint booking systems. Airlines are able to sell seats through to the passenger's destination with all the passenger advantages of a seamless journey with ticketing, baggage

handling, connection timing and gate location, and with the advantage to the airlines of increasing the chance of keeping passengers within their network.

2. International flow. The complexities of negotiating bilateral or multilateral agreements are avoided or reduced by these combinations. Airlines are able to use existing national networks on an end-to-end basis.

3. Hub systems. Creation of interlocking hub systems is possible with local feeder routes being provided by existing regional airlines.

The United States Department of Transportation has the statutory authority to approve and immunize from the U.S. antitrust laws agreements relating to international air transportation.[14] The DOT has granted over 20 international alliance agreements since the early 1990s, which allows those airlines to collude on prices, schedules, and marketing. Exemptions are granted provided that "the exemption is required by the public interest."[15] Exemptions granted by the DOT, therefore, are based on considerations other than fare or price.

The DOT states the U.S. foreign policy goals are a key element of these public benefits. Recognized as a primary policy goal of the country is the "Open Skies" initiative announced in the early 1990s to complement and extend the effects of the economic deregulation of domestic airlines. In approving immunizations of airlines within alliances, the DOT highlights the importance of strong competition between the alliances, which can better discipline the fares and services offered to consumers. The correlation between the "Open Skies" announcement and the immunization of airline alliances can be easily seen.

Yet, the DOT has found from recent evidence that alliances do, in fact, decrease competition over the North Atlantic, resulting in higher fares for consumers. As airline practices are modified and as new data reveal the results of regulatory practices, the regulators at the DOT will be called upon, in spite of Open Skies agreements, to determine how much competition will need to be preserved in international aviation. The DOT is telegraphing that additional calls by airlines to decrease competition will be harder to sell in the future.

Endnotes

1. The Economic Benefits of Air Transport, 2000 edition, The Air Transport Action Group, 33 Route de l'Aeroport, P.O. Box 49, 1215 Geneva 15, Switzerland.
2. In 2007, foreign ownership of U.S. airline companies is permitted to be in excess of 50 percent of voting and nonvoting stock, but only 25 percent of voting shares.
3. The first proposal for an Open Skies agreement with the European Union, which contained liberalization of foreign ownership rules, was voted down in the Congress even though it was supported by the Administration.
4. The countries sued were Austria, Belgium, Denmark, Finland, Luxembourg, and Sweden. Bruce Barnard, Kinnock Perseveres in Fight for EU-Wide Air Talks with U.S., J. Com., June 20, 1995, at 2B.
5. Dempsey, Paul, Competition in the Air: European Union Regulation of Commercial Aviation, Journal of Air Law and Commerce, Summer 2001.
6. The original Bermuda Agreement was signed in 1946.
7. Slater, Rodney, Testimony before the Aviation Subcommittee, U.S. House of Representatives, February 15, 2000.
8. United's transatlantic routes to Heathrow dated back to the days when Pan American was the only international U.S. carrier. These routes were sold by Pan American to United in 1989, just before Pan Am's liquidation.
9. Ownership of U.S. airlines is limited to 25 percent of voting stock in the airline. Cabotage, the prohibition for foreign airlines to carry revenue traffic between two U.S. cities, was also preserved.
10. 49 U.S.C. section 40118.
11. The Economic Impact of Air Service Liberalization, see the IATA website.
12. U.S. Department of Transportation, International Aviation Developments—Global Deregulation Takes Off (First Report) December 1999; U.S. Department of Transportation, International Aviation Developments, Second Report—Transatlantic Deregulation—The Alliance Network Effect, October 2000.
13. Members of these three Alliances are as follows: Star Alliance—Adria Airways, Air Canada, Air New Zealand, All Nippon Airlines, Asiana, Austrian, Blue1, British Midland International, Croatia Airlines, LOT Polish, Lufthansa, SAS Scandinavian, Singapore, South African, Thai Airways, Swiss, TA Portugal, Spanair, United, US Airways, Varig; OneWorld Alliance—Aer Lingus, American Airlines, British Airways, Cathay Pacific, Finnair, Iberia, LAN Airlines, Qantas; SkyTeam Alliance—Air France-KLM, Delta Airlines, Northwest, Continental, Korean Air, Alitalia, Aeroflot, Aeromexico, CSA Czech.
14. 49 U.S.C. sections 41308-41309.
15. 49 U.S.C. section 41308 (b).

41   Beyond Earth

"The Earth is the cradle of humanity, but mankind cannot stay in the cradle forever."

Konstantin Tsiolkovsky

Thirty-eight years before the Wright brothers' first flight, and two years before even the transcontinental railroad was completed, wild fantasies of space exploits, a genre later to be known as "science fiction," hit the presses. In Jules Verne's *From Earth to the Moon*, published in 1865, three members of an American gun club travel to the moon aboard a spaceship launched from a columbiad[1] located in Florida. The story bears an uncanny parallel to the U.S. Apollo program that operated from Cape Canaveral, Florida, to the moon 100 years later.

Between Jules Verne and Apollo, however, there was much work to be done.

■ The Founding Fathers of Rocketry

The progression of rocketry from literary fancy to scientific reality is generally credited to three men, all of whom worked separately from each other at about the same time. All were inspired by Jules Verne.

Konstantin Tsiolkovsky (1857–1935) was a provincial math teacher who spent most of his life in the small Russian town of Kaluga. Tsiolkovsky was a theoretician in aerodynamic flight, working through some of the same problems the Wright brothers did at about the same time. His theories extended into jet propulsion and rocketry, as well as to the mechanics of living in space. In 1895 he published *Dreams of the Earth and Sky*, in which he described the mining of asteroids.

Tsiolkovsky's primary work, *Exploration of the Universe with Reaction Machines*, was published in 1903 and is generally recognized as containing the first scientifically provable theories on the use of rockets in space. His writings are very detailed, including his specification for a mix of liquid oxygen and liquid hydrogen to fuel the engine of his theoretical spacecraft. Hydrogen was first liquefied in 1898, and it is nothing short of amazing that this mixture propels the Space Shuttle today. Tsiolkovsky was a true theoretician, never attempting to prove his theories by practical applications, like building models or attempting motor or flight tests. In spite of the volume of his publications, his work was not widely known outside of Russia.

FIGURE 41-1   Konstantin Tsiolkovsky.

Robert Goddard (1882–1945) was inspired not only by Jules Verne's writings but also by another science fiction tome, H. G. Well's *The War of the Worlds*. He dedicated himself to aeronautics and space issues from an early age, and his first article, "The Use of the Gyroscope in the Balancing and Steering of Airplanes," was published by *Scientific American* in 1907.[2] After earning a Ph.D. in physics in 1911, he registered two patents describing multistage launchers and liquid and solid propellant rockets, which became central to the progression of rocket science. By 1916, his work was being partially subsidized by the Smithsonian Institution.[3]

Goddard's 1919 manuscript entitled *A Method of Reaching Extreme Altitudes*, published by the Smithsonian in 1920, is regarded as a seminal work in the pioneering of rocketry. He continued his experimentation with rockets, launching the first liquid-fueled rocket on March 16, 1926, in a cabbage patch near Auburn, Massachusetts. Although it rose only 184 feet in 2.5 seconds, it proved the workability of liquid-fuel propellants in rockets.

Like many who had gone before, much of Goddard's work was met by mocking and scorn, particularly by the press, and most particularly by *The New York Times*.[4] Although he withdrew from public view and conducted his experiments in as much privacy as possible, Goddard still attracted notoriety with each rocket launch. Launch failures and ensuing ground fires caused the Massachusetts State Fire Marshal to prohibit Goddard from conducting any further tests in the state.

Charles Lindbergh found Goddard's work fascinating and full of promise, and contacted him in November 1929. Lindbergh was famous by this time, and the lending of his name and credibility to Goddard's experimentation was invaluable. Through the influence of Lindbergh, Daniel Guggenheim agreed to fund Goddard's research in the amount of $50,000 beginning in 1930. Goddard continued to receive support from the Guggenheim Foundation in the ensuing years.[5]

Seeking open space and relative solitude, in July 1930, Goddard relocated to, of all places, Roswell, New Mexico,[6] where he continued his research and experimentation until the beginning of

FIGURE 41-2   Robert Goddard on March 16, 1926 with the first liquid-fueled rocket.

World War II. He experimented with rocket control through movable vanes and rudders, as well as the use of gyroscopes. His rockets carried aloft the first payload, a barometer and a camera. Details of all of his work were published in 1936 in the treatise, *Liquid Propellant Rocket Development*.

Efforts to interest the United States government in his work were unsuccessful. But not everyone was unable to grasp the potential of his work. The new government of Germany, which took power in January 1933, was highly interested in Goddard's work. The National Socialist German Workers Party, also known by its acronym, the "Nazi Party," led by Adolf Hitler, was very interested indeed.

Hermann Oberth (1894–1989) was born in Romania but lived his life in Germany. He was one of the first to discover the works of Konstantin Tsiolkovsky, during the 1920s. He published the book, *The Rocket into Interplanetary Space*, in 1923. This book presented theories very similar to Goddard's, but Oberth denied that he had had the benefit of Goddard's work beforehand.[7] Oberth conducted his own experiments during the 1920s, and in 1929 published an updated version of his previous book under the title of *The Road to Space Travel*.

Largely due to Oberth's efforts, rocketry became popular in Europe during the 1920s. In 1928, Wernher von Braun, while attending a boarding school in northern Germany, happened on Hermann Oberth's book (*The Rocket into Interplanetary Space*). Fascinated, he launched himself into a program of physics and mathematics that would prepare him for the fledgling science of rocketry. By 1930, von Braun was a student at the Technical University of Berlin, where Oberth was an instructor. An amateur rocketry group inspired by Oberth's book, known as the "Spaceflight Society," held meetings on the Berlin campus, and von Braun became a member. It was here that he met Oberth, and as a result von Braun was selected to assist Oberth in his liquid-fueled rocket motor tests. At this time

von Braun was introduced to Goddard's work, and he followed up with his own research into Goddard's publications through scientific journals and publications.

The German Army began its rocket program in 1931. When it came to power in 1933, the Nazi government placed the advancement of rocketry high on its military "want list." At the time, the terms of the Versailles Treaty (the 1918 agreement that ended World War I) prohibited Germany from developing military aircraft, but it said nothing about rocketry, mainly because practical rocketry was unknown to anyone except to a handful of engineers. The German Army began recruiting bright university students with credentials and interest in rocket science.

By 1933, von Braun was working on his doctoral dissertation in physics. Because of a research grant from the German Army, von Braun began collaborating on a secret solid-fuel

FIGURE 41-3   Hermann Oberth (foreground) and Wernher von Braun (near right).

program at the ballistic weapons center at Kummersdorf. The Kummersdorf site was moved to Peenemunde on the Baltic coast in 1936. Peenemunde was the secret laboratory and test site for the development of the V-2 rocket, which is recognized as the immediate precursor of the launch vehicles later used in the U.S. space program. The V-2 was the first practical rocket, 46 feet in length and weighing 27,000 pounds. It flew at speeds in excess of 3,500 miles an hour and delivered a 2,200-pound warhead 500 miles away. It was put to use against Allied targets, including London, in September 1944.

With the approach of Allied forces toward the end of World War II, von Braun arranged the defection of about 125 of his top rocket scientists and engineers, who brought with them their plans, drawings, and test results. Von Braun and his "rocket team" became the backbone of the United States' ballistic missile program after World War II, and ultimately were largely responsible for the development of the Saturn V super launch vehicle that propelled the Apollo modules to the moon. Although von Braun was central to the perfection of rocket science in its practical aspects, he is considered in the "second generation" of rocket pioneers.

■ Space: The New Frontier

From a technical perspective, atmospheres have no "end"; they just get progressively thinner. During the 1950s, it was generally known in the scientific community that, beyond some altitude, the physics of flight changed drastically. The principles for flight in the atmosphere, or the science of aeronautics, were fairly well understood. The principles for flight without an atmosphere, or the science of astronautics, were less understood. Some believed that these two disciplines needed some definition as to their separation.

There is no "bright line" that determines where outer space begins. NASA accords astronaut status to any individual who travels above

80 kilometers (50 miles). Yet atmospheric drag becomes evident on reentry at 75 miles above the earth's surface.

The venerable Fédération Aéronautique Internationale,[8] which was founded in 1905, has ever since that time been accepted worldwide as the arbiter of aeronautical records. Through this private organization, the physicist Theodore von Kármán in 1957 proposed a formula for the calculation of a boundary that would establish the beginning of space. One of the characteristics of aeronautical flight is the concept of lift, which is a function of speed through the atmosphere, among other things. The thinner the atmosphere, the faster the airplane must fly in order to gain the lift necessary to remain aloft. Kármán proposed an altitude of approximately (the exact altitude depends on certain variables) 100 kilometers (62.1 miles) as the separation point based on his calculations that a space vehicle would have to travel faster than the speed necessary to obtain orbital velocity in order to maintain aeronautical lift. In other words, aerodynamic lift becomes less than centrifugal force.

This became the internationally accepted boundary to space, and it is known as the "Kármán line." The Fédération Aéronautique Internationale is now the recognized keeper of all records that are established in astronautics.

■ Sputnik

Before October 4, 1957, humankind had always conducted its affairs below this boundary. On that date, the Space Age began with the orbiting of the artificial earth satellite known as "Sputnik," which was launched by the Soviet Union (Union of Soviet Socialist Republics, or U.S.S.R.) on a military rocket. This accomplishment, while heralded by the scientific community, caused considerable distress in the nations of the West.

After World War II, the Soviet Union had asserted dominion over the countries of Eastern

Europe, and it was the titular head of the Communist World. The People's Republic of China, the name of the communist government that controlled that country beginning in 1949, and the People's Republic of North Korea also fell into this camp. Communist-controlled governments, considered by the West to be bent on world domination, extended from Northern Europe to the Pacific Ocean. The hostile relationship that emerged after World War II between the nations of the West and the Communist Bloc countries had been termed the "Cold War" by Winston Churchill in 1948, but there had been a shooting war on the Korean Peninsula between these factions from 1950 to 1953, and millions of people, both civilians and combatants, had died.

The Soviet Union had perfected nuclear weapon capability well before 1957, and with the launch of Sputnik, it was clear that the U.S.S.R. now had the capability to deliver these weapons on intercontinental ballistic missiles. Now also, for the first time since Roman law had established that national sovereignty extended from the ground upward to infinity, the sovereign skies of the Western countries were being violated every 90 minutes by the unauthorized passage overhead of the Russian satellite. Its "beeping" radio signal every few seconds only punctuated their helplessness.

The geopolitical contest between the Western powers and the Communist Bloc countries was one of brutal competition, and it was considered a philosophical, social and, if necessary, a military fight to the death. But in the midst of this perilous world scene, there was some precedent for cooperation and good will among nations, based on scientific inquiry. Worldwide cooperative endeavors known as the International Polar Year in 1884, the Second International Polar Year in 1934, and the International Geophysical Year beginning in 1957 stood as hopeful examples of the advancement of humankind through peaceful cooperation.

People worried which way the Space Age would take them.

Scientific Cooperation— Precedent for Space

The Space Age arrived during the International Geophysical Year (IGY), which was actually an 18-month period that extended from July 1, 1957 to December 31, 1958. The IGY was an international effort to coordinate worldwide measurements and data collection of geophysical (earth, oceans, atmosphere) properties, as well as to investigate an expected peak of sunspot activity and a number of solar eclipses. It was apolitical and non-nationalistic, coordinated by the International Council of Scientific Unions, and 67 nations participated.

The American participation was done under the auspices of the National Academy of Sciences, with the stated goal: ". . . to observe geophysical phenomena and to secure data from all parts of the world. . . ." The IGY sought to capitalize on the many innovative technologies that were appearing after the Second World War, including computers, rocketry, and radar.

The International Geophysical Year was patterned on two previous international scientific undertakings. The first was the International Polar Year (IPY), which took place from 1881 to 1884, now known as the 1882 IPY. It was the first series of coordinated international expeditions ever undertaken to the Polar Regions. The project was inspired by the Austrian explorer, Carl Weyprecht, who believed that nations should put aside their competition for geographical dominion and, instead, fund a series of coordinated expeditions dedicated to scientific research. Eleven nations participated in the effort, and 12 stations were established and maintained in the Arctic for the three-year period.

A second expedition was conducted on the 50th anniversary of the first, and it became known as the 1932 Polar Year, or the Second

International Polar Year. The Second IPY was promoted by the International Meteorological Organization to take advantage of several new technologies, such as precision cameras and high frequency radio, and to investigate the newly discovered "jet stream." Forty countries participated and 40 permanent observation stations were established in the Arctic. The contribution of the United States was the establishment in Antarctica of the meteorological station on the Ross Ice Shelf during the second Byrd expedition. The Second IPY was primarily concerned with the investigation of meteorology, magnetism, atmospheric science, and the mapping of ionospheric phenomena that advanced radio science and radio technology.

Many scientific accomplishments have been recorded through these three international cooperative endeavors. Because of the IGY, for example, scientists defined the mid-ocean ridges (furthering the understanding of the effects of plate tectonics and verifying the formation of continental shapes), discovered the Van Allen radiation belts, charted ocean depths and currents, studied earth's magnetic field, measured upper atmospheric winds, and studied Antarctica in great detail.

The Antarctic Treaty

The work of the IGY led directly to the Antarctic Treaty of 1959, which regulates international relations concerning Antarctica. Antarctica is the only continent on earth without a native human population, and none of the continent has been appropriated under claim of right of discovery. The treaty's main aim is to establish Antarctica as a continent to be used by all nations for peaceful purposes and for cooperative scientific research. Military activity, weapons testing, nuclear testing, and radioactive waste disposal are prohibited. The Treaty went into effect on June 23, 1961, and over 40 nations are signatory to it.

The Antarctic Treaty is a singular achievement by the governments on earth, and it stands in stark contrast to the history of nationalistic exploration and colonization that began with the Spanish expeditions led by Columbus in 1492. One of the reasons that Antarctica was never colonized, of course, is the fact that its climate has been inhospitable to long-term human presence. It is obvious that outer space possesses the same characteristics, even more so. The existence of the Antarctic Treaty, then, held out some hope in many quarters of the world that the Space Age might bring a more hopeful future to humankind.

The Space Race Begins

Compounding the frustration of the United States over Sputnik, the Soviets launched a second, and larger, satellite (Sputnik 2) on November 3, 1957. This one carried a live animal, a dog named Laika, into orbit. Laika is believed to have survived only for a few hours due to an inability to properly regulate temperature in the capsule. But the Soviets were obviously making strides in space. The propaganda value to the U.S.S.R. was significant.

On January 31, 1958, the United States finally launched its first earth satellite, Explorer 1. Although smaller than either Sputnik 1 or Sputnik 2 (Explorer 1 weighed 30.8 pounds compared to 184 pounds for Sputnik 1 and 1,120 pounds for Sputnik 2), it accomplished more than the Sputniks; its mission payload Geiger counter was responsible for the discovery of the Van Allen radiation belts.[9]

While the launch of Explorer leveled the playing field, it also launched the contest that would preoccupy the world for the next 30 years, the Space Race. The shock of Sputnik also caused the United States to swiftly create a permanent federal agency dedicated to the exploration of space. All U.S. nonmilitary space activities were placed in the venerable, prestigious National Advisory Committee on Aeronautics (NACA).[10] In 1958, Congress passed the National Aeronautics and Space Act, which converted NACA into NASA, and charged the agency with the broad mission to plan, direct, and conduct aeronautical and space activities, to involve the nation's scientific community in its mission, and to disseminate information about its activities.

The stage was now set; the actors (the United States and the Soviet Union) took their places on the stage; the world audience looked on; the only trouble was nobody had a script.

Who Owns Outer Space?

Like the crossing of the Rubicon, traversing the Kármán line marked a point of no return for humanity. In the context of the Cold War, the potential for disaster was palatable. ICBMs were now a reality, and there was no defense. Mutually Assured Destruction (MAD) was the acronym of the day, and it was a chillingly accurate description of what any miscalculation by either (later any) nuclear power would bring. This was the Wild West on an international level, without a sheriff.

In the context of international civil law, however, many people held out hope. It had been remarked by both astronauts (American) and cosmonauts (Soviets) that national boundaries on earth were not discernable from space. Boundaries on earth, of course, imply the sovereignty of nation-states, and they have been the cause of wars since time immemorial. But there was something about being in space that seemed to strike a humanistic, rather than a nationalistic, chord in those first space travelers.

In 1945, the United Nations was founded among the world's sovereign states in the hope that it could provide a forum for the peaceful consideration of issues between states as an alternative to war. The United Nations is large, and through its organizations (its committee structure), programs (such as trade and food programs), and specialized agencies (such as WHO, the World Health Organization), it has assumed many and varied roles in the international community.[11]

In 1958, the United Nations set up an ad hoc committee called the Committee on the Peaceful Uses of Outer Space (COPUOS) consisting of 11 Member States. COPUOS became a permanent committee in the U.N. in 1959, with 24 members. Among the purposes of this body were the promotion of international cooperation in space, the encouragement of continued research and dissemination of information concerning space, and the study of legal problems arising relating to the exploration of outer space.

The main question confronting CUPUOS was whether a coherent form of international law could be brought to govern human interaction in outer space. If so, what form should it take? In view of international tensions at the time, this was a daunting task.

Terrestrial Precedents

It had been proposed, prior to Sputnik, that international relations with respect to the high seas should be precedent for space. To understand why, we will take a quick look at the concept of national sovereignty and how it relates to the high seas.

National sovereignty implies complete legal authority over an area or a population, which is defined by established national boundaries. Nations that bound the oceans have historically extended their sovereignty from their coastlines into the oceans for a defined distance. These areas are known as "territorial waters" and for many years the standard limit was three miles.[12] The high seas begin at the point territorial waters end.

Since Roman times, national sovereignty also extended *ad coelum*, the Latin phrase meaning "to the sky." With the advent of airplanes, this doctrine was applied by international law above the territory of all nations, for as high as airplanes could fly. In all cases, that was in earth's atmosphere. It continued to be applied to the sky, at least within earth's atmosphere, even after the launch of the first artificial earth satellites,[13] but by custom and acceptance, it has not been applied to flights above the Kármán line.

The legal relationships between sovereign nations are governed by international law. As we saw in Chapter 36, international law has developed primarily through the agreement of two or more nations in the form of treaties, which become binding upon ratification and entry into force. In addition, sources of international law derive from "customary international law," which is based on universally accepted principles and general practice. These principles are often based on concepts of right and wrong, ethics, and responsibility.

All land masses on earth are "owned" by sovereign nations with the exception of Antarctica. As we have seen, international law concerning that continent is now the subject of treaty. The other 70 percent of the earth, known alternatively as "international waters" or the "high seas," since the early 18th century, has universally been accepted by custom as "free seas." Hugo Grotius[14] in 1609 set out in a dissertation called *Mare liberum* (free seas) the logical premise and argument for a natural right residing in all nations and in all peoples to have free access and use of the seas. The concept of free seas implies the right of passage, the right of navigation, the right to fish, and the right to trade. The seas, being unbounded by man and incapable of possession, constitute an equitable, common benefit to the human race.[15]

Although it was a shock to the average citizen, the orbiting of Sputnik came as no surprise to either the scientific or legal community. In the scientific world, in fact, it had been an advertised feature of the International Geophysical Year that an artificial earth satellite would be launched before December 31, 1958, but it had always been assumed that it would be launched by the United States. In the international legal community, debate and discussion had been occurring for some years on many of the questions that were expected to arise once orbiting satellites were a reality.

There had been significant discussion, for instance, of whether the *ad coelum* doctrine would or should apply in outer space, but there was no agreement. Persuasive arguments were made for each position. But when Sputnik was launched, all of the sterling legal arguments were suddenly rendered irrelevant. Sputnik was a scientific and technological fact, and there was nothing anyone could do about it. It became clear that law was going to have to follow science.[16]

There was not one objection by any nation that its national sovereignty was being violated by Sputnik's transits overhead. There was now an acceptance of a limit to national sovereignty somewhere around the Kármán line. But more importantly, the conclusion was compelling that outer space was, indeed, like the high seas. As Grotius had said, "What cannot be possessed is necessarily free for all to use."

The precedent of international maritime law influencing space law was a good thing. Since nations had been sharing the seas for millennia, there was now some basis to believe that the earth-based international community might, after all, be able to agree on how to use outer space in a peaceful way.

Another terrestrial precedent is aviation law. When airplanes became capable of overflying borders into another country's airspace, leaders of those countries sat down together and worked out the details that extended maritime law principles to aviation and devised new rules required by the new aviation technology. Examples of these include the Paris Conference of 1910 and the Paris Convention of 1919. (Refer to Chapter 37.) As aircraft became capable of longer range and higher flight, international civil aviation was born to replace, in large part, the maritime passenger industry and to supplement the maritime shipping trade.

The future for international civil aviation was set by the Chicago Convention of 1944. Recognizing the increasing importance to the world of aviation after World War II, contracting nations agreed to set up a structure for the adoption of international regulations, standards, and procedures that would govern and control essentially all aspects of international flight.[17]

But in the years just after the first launches of artificial earth satellites, there were still only two participants in outer space, the United States and the U.S.S.R., and they were still engaged in the "Cold War." It was obvious that some bilateral accommodation between these two powers would have to accompany, if not precede, any effective peaceful solution to the problems of outer space.

Treaties Affecting Outer Space

The Limited Test Ban Treaty of 1963

Escalating tensions and the growth of nuclear armaments during the 1950s had caused talks between the United States and the U.S.S.R to commence in 1955 over the issue of the testing of such weapons. Radiation fallout from atmospheric tests by both sides had accidentally contaminated people and areas far removed from the test sites. Apprehension over the cumulative effect of contamination of the environment and possible genetic damage to the population was shared by most civilized countries.

The United States and the Soviet Union both had actually detonated nuclear devices above the Kármán line, the highest at 540 kilometers (335 miles). The effects of these explosions were varied, and their visual effects were quite spectacular, but the destruction of the electronic components of satellites in low earth orbit by electromagnetic pulses was a common result. During the Cuban missile crisis in October 1962, both the United States and the Soviet Union detonated several high altitude devices as a show of force. The most significant, destructive effects of nuclear detonations in space occurred during this time, on October 22, 1962, when the Soviets exploded a device at an altitude of 290 kilometers. Electromagnetic impulses at ground level in Kazakhstan fused 570 km of overhead telephone line, started a fire that burned down a power plant, and shut down 1,000 km of buried power cables.

The next year, in 1963, the United States and the Soviet Union agreed to prohibit nuclear weapons tests "or any other explosion" in the atmosphere, under water, or in outer space. The inclusion of outer space in this essentially terrestrial agreement created a benchmark for future agreement on outer space.

The General Assembly of the United Nations created the Committee on the Peaceful Uses of Outer Space, COPUOS, in 1959. Although it was not involved in the bilateral Limited Test Ban Treaty of 1963 between the United States and the U.S.S.R., its purpose was to review the scope of international cooperation in peaceful uses of outer space. It has two subcommittees, the Scientific and Technical Subcommittee and the Legal Subcommittee.

COPUOS has been central to the development of existing international law regarding space. It has, in fact, drafted all international treaties that now exist dealing with outer space, some five in number that were adopted between 1967 and 1979. The Committee was composed of just 24 members when it was created as a permanent body in 1959, which facilitated its work since the Committee is operated on the basis of consensus (agreement), not majority vote. It is now composed of 71 members. We will now look at the five treaties that have been adopted out of COPUOS.

The Outer Space Treaty of 1967

The cumbersome title, "The Treaty on the Principles Governing the Activities of States in the Exploration and Use of Outer Space, Including the Moon and Other Celestial Bodies," is commonly called the Outer Space Treaty. This treaty is to space law what the Magna Carta is to English Common Law, and what the Treaty of Rome is to the European Union. It is the most inclusive and authoritative document for human governance in space, and it is the basis for all treaties that have come after it. It is modeled on the Antarctica Treaty, which was drafted for much the same reason in 1959, as was the Outer Space Treaty in 1967.

Like the Antarctica Treaty, it is a "no armament" treaty. It seeks to prevent a new form of colonial competition in outer space. The treaty covers the entire outer space environment, including the moon and other celestial bodies. It entered into force on October 10, 1967.

The main provisions of the Outer Space Treaty provide:

- The use and exploration of outer space is to be carried out for the benefit of all.
- Outer space is not subject to national appropriation by claim of sovereignty.[18]
- Activities in outer space are to be in accordance with international law.
- Outer space is to be free of nuclear weapons or other weapons of mass destruction.
- Military bases and testing of weapons are forbidden, although military personnel may be used for scientific research and other peaceful purposes.
- Astronauts are envoys of mankind and shall be rendered all possible assistance in the event of accident, distress, or emergency landing on any state's territory or on the high seas.
- States launching objects into outer space are liable for any damage caused.
- Launched objects shall remain the property of the state or party that launched it.
- Use and exploration of outer space is to be carried out without interference to other states, and a procedure for consultation between states is provided for this subject.
- States will inform all concerned, including the public, of intended space activities.

The treaty is broadly worded and, therefore, does not purport to provide definition on many issues. Implicit in the drafting is the expectation that other, more specific agreements would be crafted in the future to address specific concerns as needed.

The United States is a signatory to this treaty.

◼ The Rescue Treaty of 1968

The full title is "The Agreement on the Rescue of Astronauts, the Return of Astronauts, and the Return of Objects Launched into Outer Space."

Its purpose is to give specificity to the provisions of the Outer Space Treaty that call for the rendering of aid to astronauts and the return of space crews and property launched into space.

The Rescue Treaty creates obligations on contracting parties, both as to crew and as to objects launched into space, who learn of any accident, unintended landing, or crew distress, to immediately:

- Notify the launching authority or make a public announcement, and notify the Secretary-General of the UN.
- Rescue crew and render assistance, even if on the high seas.
- Return the crew to the launching authority.
- Return the space object to the launching authority.

The words of the treaty express the sentiment that astronauts are the "envoys of mankind," and that all nations shall have the attitude toward them that reflects the spirit of international cooperation and assistance.

The United States is a signatory to this treaty.

The Liability Treaty of 1972

This treaty is fully titled as "The Convention on International Liability for Damage Caused by Space Objects." It recognizes one of the truisms of human existence, that there can and will be unintended consequences attached to human endeavors, and when those consequences result in damage to others, there should be a defined process to address those consequences by the payment of money damages.

The Liability Treaty sets out a complex regimen designed to cover essentially every possible scenario in which damage results from the launch of any space object. It incorporates principles of tort law, contract law, strict liability, indemnity, and other legal concepts that are beyond the scope of our discussion. The basic operation of the treaty, however, follows.

The treaty makes the launching state (or any state that procures a launch by another state) absolutely liable for any damage caused by the launched object that occurs either on the surface of the earth or to aircraft in flight. The liability is on the contracting party (the country that signs the treaty) even though the launch may be made by a private company. The liability attaches to the state even though there is no fault, or negligence, connected with the launch in any way. This is known as "strict liability."

By way of example, assume that the country of Malaysia contracts with Boeing Launch Services to launch a satellite from Cape Kennedy. The launch results in a collision with an Airbus 300 operated by Air France, killing all foreign passengers and crew and destroying the aircraft. The debris falls in the ocean on the high seas and damages a Russian warship and members of its crew. Who is liable?

The short answer is that the United States, as the signatory country to the treaty, would bear the liability in the first instance. The liability would be to Air France for the value of the Airbus, for damages to the families of the passengers and crew for loss of life, for damages for the value of onboard baggage and cargo, for damages to the warship to the state of Russia, and for damages to sailors aboard the Russian ship.

If neither the United States nor Malaysia (which procured the launch) is guilty of any fault or negligence, then the United States would have an action under the treaty to recover half of its payout from the state of Malaysia, assuming it was also a signatory to the treaty. The United States (and Malaysia) would have a possible right of indemnity against Boeing Launch Services, under the laws of the United States, for which the United States would be made whole for all payments made.

The treaty separately addresses the situation where a space object belonging to a launching state (State A) is damaged by a space object belonging to a second launching state (State B). If the space object that is damaged is on the surface of the earth, the rules are the same as stated above, that is, strict liability. But if the damaged space object is anywhere else (in the atmosphere or in outer space), then the state that launched the damaging space object (State B) is liable to State A only if State B is somehow at fault, or negligent, which causes the damage. This distinction recognizes, for example, that a collision of satellites or launch vehicles in motion may be the fault of either one or the other launching states, or both, and that proof of that fault should be a precondition to liability.

Liability may be avoided by the launching state, even under strict liability, if the launching state can prove that the damage was caused by the claimant's gross negligence or intentional act.

The treaty also does not apply to claims made by citizens of the launching state against the launching state (for example, an American against the United States), since that would be a matter of national, not international, law.

Claims for compensation are presented through diplomatic channels, or through the United Nations.

The Registration Convention of 1976

Officially termed "The Convention on the Registration of Objects Launched into Outer Space," the Registration Treaty requires launching states to maintain a register of launched objects, and to

Box 41-1 The Cosmos 954 Incident

There have been only a few claims made under the Liability Treaty since it entered into force. The first, and perhaps the most notable, was Cosmos 954. Cosmos 954 was a 46-foot-long, 5-ton Soviet reconnaissance satellite powered by a nuclear reactor. The "spy satellite" was on a sensitive and secret mission designed to locate and track U.S. nuclear submarines. The reactor core failed to attain nuclear-safe orbit (800 miles high) and remained in a lower orbit that decayed within a year to re-entry in 1978.

The United States had begun tracking the satellite from the time of its launch, September 18, 1977, and was aware of its sagging orbit by December 1977. The United States began diplomatic conversations with the Soviets to try to determine the extent of the risk, such as a critical mass explosion on reentry or on impact with the ground. The Soviets cooperated, but were circumspect due to the satellite's mission. The United States wanted answers about the enrichment of the uranium on board.[19]

The trajectory for reentry placed the satellite over North America, possibly near New York City. U.S. and Canadian technical forces stood by awaiting the event. The satellite actually crashed into the Northwest Territory of Canada, spreading radioactive fuel over a large area.

A joint American–Canadian effort was undertaken to recover radioactive material, the search covering over 48,000 miles in area. The United States sent a U-2 and a KC-135 to check for high-altitude radiation, along with a 44-man team of military technicians. The Canadians sent in a nuclear-accident team of 22 people in radiation suits to find and collect debris. The Soviets naturally offered to help, but Canada declined the offer.

The cleanup continued into October 1978 and consisted of locating, recovering, removing, and testing the debris and normalizing the affected area. Most of the recovered debris was radioactive, some to a lethal degree. The government of Canada presented to the U.S.S.R. its claim in the amount of $6,041,174.70 relying on the Liability Treaty, the Outer Space Treaty, and general principles of international law dealing with the violation of national sovereignty.

The claim resulted in extended negotiations over the course of the next three years between Canada and the U.S.S.R., resulting in a settlement of the claim for a total of just $3 million. The nature of the defense presented by the U.S.S.R that would cause the Canadian government to accept less than half its claim is not known, but it is likely related to the fact that Canada refused the offer of assistance made by the U.S.S.R. before the cleanup began. In law, this is known as a failure to mitigate (or lessen) one's own damages.

furnish to the United Nations certain basic information, including:

- The name of the launching state
- The designator of the space object or its registration number
- Date and territory or location of the launch
- Basic orbital parameters, including nodal period, inclination, apogee, and perigee
- General function of the space object

- A registration list of space objects that are no longer in orbit

In addition to providing a launch registry for general housekeeping purposes, it is expected that the registry will assist in identifying space objects that are involved in claims of liability and also serve as a basis for helping to clean up space debris.

The United States is a signatory to this treaty.

Box 41-2 The Collision of Cosmos 2251 and Iridium 33

The first-ever collision between two intact satellites in orbit occurred on February 10, 2009 between Iridium 33 and Cosmos 2251 over northern Siberia. Both satellites were launched from Russia: Cosmos 2251 was a military communications satellite launched from the Plesetsk Cosmodrome, 600 miles north of Moscow, on June 16, 1993 and Iridium 33 was an American commercial telecommunication satellite launched from the Tyuratam Cosmodrome some 1,400 miles southeast of Moscow on September 14, 1997.

Cosmos 2251 was deactivated in 1999 and became non-functioning, while remaining in a generally east–west orbit. Iridium 33 was a working satellite that was part of the worldwide Iridium satellite telephone service, on a general north–south orbit. The orbits of the two satellites intersected at a 103 degree angle at 788.6 kilometers above earth and at a speed of 26 times the speed of sound.

The collision was an unthinkable surprise to all parties. Even though there was no damage to person or property on earth, the loss of the Iridium satellite was substantial. This scenario is covered under the second part of the Liability Treaty, section 2 above, dealing with the collision of satellites in space in which a showing of fault is required before liability attaches. Although Russia launched both satellites, it denied liability on the basis that there was no showing of fault on its part. It pointed out that Cosmos 2251 was a derelict incapable of maneuvering and that it had no obligation under the law to dispose of the satellite after it became non-functioning.

Although this incident remains unresolved from a legal point of view under the Liability Treaty of 1972, is has spurred an awareness of the very real possibility of substantial loss in space and has resulted in a cooperative agreement between Russia and the United States. Under the auspices of the Joint Space Operations Center, orbital information is now shared among concerned parties so that trajectories are known by all affected parties and avoidance measures can be implemented.

The United States is a signatory to the Liability Treaty of 1972.

The Moon Treaty of 1979

"The Agreement Governing the Activities of States on the Moon and Other Celestial Bodies," or the Moon Treaty, is yet another follow-on treaty that proceeds from the first space treaty, the Outer Space Treaty. Each of the treaties that have been adopted since the Outer Space Treaty has added more detail and definition to the general principles enunciated in the first treaty. The Moon Treaty, however, is considered by most as a "failed" treaty because the specific, additional language used has met with opposition from the major space-faring countries.

The basic stumbling block in the treaty is the use of the words "common heritage of mankind" to describe the nature of the moon and its resources, as well as the other celestial bodies. The treaty provides for the establishment of an international regime to govern the exploitation of these resources when such exploitation becomes feasible.

The general interpretation of this language is that all nations of the world have equal rights to the resources of the heavens, irrespective of whether or not they put forth any effort or incur any risk, financial or otherwise, in development of ways and means to recover those resources. Any plan to develop these resources would ostensibly require approval of all nations on earth, which would be impracticable.

The rejection of the Moon Treaty follows a similar rejection of the terrestrial Law of the Sea Treaty (referred to gleefully by its detractors as LOST). In 1982, the United Nations conceived the Law of the Sea Treaty as a means of control and governance of the world's oceans. The breadth of the treaty was such that it sought to regulate deep-sea mining, as well as such controversial areas as the ocean environment. Like the Moon Treaty, LOST failed to gain support from the major developed nations since it was viewed as an attempt to create a new world order based on a system for the redistribution of the world's wealth. This new system rejects the free-market system of risk and reward for a global collectivist regimen like socialist central planning. Under this scheme, ocean resources would necessarily have to be shared among all mankind. This approach is seen mainly as a benefit to third-world countries.

Most knowledgeable people feel that the provisions of the Moon Treaty materially narrow the intent and provisions of the Outer Space Treaty, although the latter uses similar words of description, "the common Province of all mankind." The meaning of the latter phrasing, found in the Outer Space Treaty, was that no single country could claim outer space or other celestial bodies as its own in the colonial sense, but it did permit the extraction of resources. The "common heritage of mankind" language and related provisions of the Moon Treaty mean that the celestial resources may not be extracted unilaterally by any single nation.

The United States is not a signatory to this treaty.

The International Space Station Agreement

The competitive aspects of the space race resulted in much duplication of effort and fiscal waste. During the 1980s, the Soviets had the Salyut and Mir space stations, the U.S. had planned Space Station Freedom, the European Union had planned Columbus, and the Japanese, Kibo. With the demise of the U.S.S.R., the United States initiated discussions with the EU, Russia, Japan, and Canada in the early 1990s concerning a joint effort to build a significant, lasting international space station. The project, named the International Space Station (ISS) was jointly announced in 1993, and it attempted to combine the best features of all of the existing or planned national space stations.

The primary agreement authorizing the ISS is a treaty signed on January 28, 1998, by the 15 participating countries[20] known as the Space Station Intergovernmental Agreement (IGA). The IGA provides for a long-term cooperative framework for the design, development, operation, and utilization of the ISS.

In addition to the IGA, there are two additional levels of agreement contemplated, called "Memoranda of Understanding." The IGA designates NASA as the Manager of the ISS, and these additional agreements are between NASA and the space agencies for the other participating partners[21] or with agencies of countries other than the original 15 participants.[22] These supplementary agreements deal with the specifics of the management and operation of the ISS, including criminal jurisdiction and codes of behavior.

The IGA provides for the participating countries to extend their jurisdiction into outer space with the ISS. Each country, therefore, will retain jurisdiction and responsibility for the parts of the ISS it registers and for its nationals who are on board. This aspect of the IGA establishes that, for instance, the law of the EU will apply to activities within the European Columbus Laboratory module. Thus, national law applies to criminal and liability issues, and is the basis for the protection of intellectual property rights arising on the ISS.

The first section of the ISS was placed in orbit in November 1998, followed by two additional sections soon after. The ISS is in low earth orbit, which ranges from 199 miles to 215 miles above the earth. On November 2, 2000, the first crew, consisting of two Russians and one American, took up residence. The ISS is powered by electricity generated by the sun, it generates its own oxygen on board, and recycles waste and water. The ISS is still being assembled and, when complete, it will have 1,200 cubic meters of pressurized space, or about the size of the interior of a Boeing 747.

Activity aboard the ISS centers on research in "experiment modules," which by 2010 were all in place. Research fields include biology (including biomedical research and biotechnology), physics (including fluid physics, materials science, and quantum physics), astronomy, and meteorology. The goals of this research include developing an understanding of, and the technology to deal with, long-term human presence in space, developing methods for the more efficient production of materials, developing new ways to treat disease, achieving more accurate measurements than is possible on earth, and a better understanding of the universe.

NASA and the United States Space Program—A Review

Created by the National Aeronautics and Space Act on July 29, 1958, during the Eisenhower Administration, the National Aeronautics and Space Administration replaced the National Advisory Committee for Aeronautics (NACA) which had been researching flight technology for more than 40 years. NASA's mission continued the work of aeronautics research, but also specifically assumed the responsibility for research in aerospace and for the overall civilian space program for the nation, including the human space flight program.

The United States space exploration and development program has included both manned and unmanned launches, and unmanned launches designed specifically as precursors of human space flight. Included in these are Mercury, Gemini, Apollo, Apollo-Soyuz, the Space Shuttle, Skylab, and the International Space Station.[23]

Mercury

It was only in 1958 that studies and tests conducted by government and industry indicated the feasibility of manned space flight. America's first manned space flight program was named Mercury on October 7, 1958 with the objectives of placing a manned spacecraft in orbital flight around the earth, to investigate man's capabilities and ability to function in space, and to recover the man and spacecraft safely from space.

The American space program, like that of the U.S.S.R., had to begin from a standing start. This meant that all aspects of the program had to be originated, tested, and approved, including the selection of the launch vehicle, the spacecraft, and the selection of the men who were to participate in the program. After the completion of a pervasive and exhausting testing regimen and selection process, seven military pilots were chosen as the original participants in the program and were introduced to the Congress as astronauts on May 28, 1959. They were quickly accepted as a new kind of hero.

The initial flights for the Mercury mission were conducted on Redstone rockets (suborbital flights of Shepherd and Grissom in 1961). A modified Atlas rocket carried John Glenn to America's first manned orbit on February 29, 1962 and to the following orbital missions of the program, ending with Gordon Cooper's 34-hour, 19-minute final Mercury mission on May 16, 1963.

The project was terminated in 1963.

Gemini

Gemini was the second manned space program, begun in 1962. Its name derived from the third constellation of the Zodiac (the Twins), since the capsule was designed to carry two astronauts into space. Its mission included launching men and equipment for up to two weeks in low earth orbit, to rendezvous and dock, and to refine a system for maneuvering the docked combination by using the target vehicle's propulsion system. The program's launch vehicle was the Titan II rocket. The project successfully flew 10 manned missions, achieved the first extra vehicular activity in space (EVA) and a record altitude of 739.2 miles. This project was canceled in 1964.

Apollo

The Apollo Program was designed for lunar exploration using a three-man spacecraft and lunar orbiter and a serially developed Saturn rocket.

The Apollo Program consisted of 33 flights, of which 11 were manned. The 22 unmanned flights were conducted to qualify the launch vehicle and spacecraft for manned space flight. Four of the manned flights were also conducted to man-rate the overall vehicle for lunar exploration. The final 7 flights were conducted to explore the lunar environment and lunar surface. During the program, no launch failure occurred to prevent a mission and only one in-flight failure (Apollo 13) occurred to prevent the intended mission from being accomplished.

Testing Phase: The original launch vehicle for the Apollo program was the Saturn I missile, first tested in October 1961 in a suborbital trajectory. The first orbital mission (unmanned) occurred on January 29, 1964 on the Saturn's fifth launch. Testing progressed using the Saturn 1B launch vehicle and an unmanned Apollo spacecraft. November 9, 1967 marked the first flight of the Saturn V three-stage rocket, which was to be used for lunar missions.

Manned Phase: On January 27, 1967, a flash fire occurred in the Apollo spacecraft (denominated command module 012) while positioned on the launch vehicle and during a launch pad test of the vehicle for the first manned flight, killing three astronauts. Dead were Lt. Col. Virgil I. Grissom, one of the original seven and a veteran of flights in the Mercury and Gemini programs; Lt. Col. Edward H. White, the first astronaut to conduct an EVA (Gemini Program); and Roger B. Chaffee, who was prepping for his first space flight. As a result of a comprehensive investigation, which caused an 18-month delay in the first manned mission, significant design and engineering modifications were made to the spacecraft.

The first manned mission, known as Apollo 7, flew on October 11, 1968 and began the series of missions that would land men on the moon. Apollo 8 was the first mission designed to leave earth orbit and to circle the moon, and the first manned flight to be launched using the three-stage Saturn V rocket. Aboard this flight were Frank Borman, Commander; James A. Lovell, Command Module Pilot; and William A. Anders, Lunar Module Pilot.

The mission of Apollo 11 was to land Neil A. Armstrong and Edwin E. Aldrin, Jr. on the surface of the moon, have them exit the lunar module and perform certain minimum tasks, and return safely to the command module for the return to earth. Ed Collins remained in lunar orbit in the command module. The lunar module successfully landed on the lunar surface on July 20, 1969 and six hours later, at 0256 UTC on July 21, Neil Armstrong became the first human to set foot on the moon, followed by Ed Aldrin. Together they spent over 21 hours on the moon's surface and collected over 47 pounds of lunar material for return to earth. Most of their activities were seen by a live television feed broadcast to a world-wide audience. All three astronauts returned to earth on July 24, 1969.

Subsequent missions in the program, with the exception of Apollo 13, were carried to successful conclusion, ending in the mission of Apollo 17 (launched on December 7, 1972). Apollo 17 brought to a close one of the most ambitious and successful endeavors ever attempted by man.[24]

Skylab

The Skylab space station was launched on May 14, 1973 in the program designed for the conduct of scientific experiments in zero gravity, earth resources experiments, and solar observations in long-duration missions. Three separate crews were launched in Apollo-type command modules on May 25, July 28, and November 16, 1973. These crews remained, respectively, for mission periods of 28 days, 59 days, and 84 days. The Skylab mission also proved that humans can remain for extended periods of time in space without adverse health or psychological consequences and that resupply of space vehicles is workable.

Skylab's orbit deteriorated because there were no spacecraft, nor any program ready (the Space Shuttle had been delayed), to boost its orbit. On July 11, 1979, Skylab reentered the earth's atmosphere and disintegrated over the Indian Ocean and across Western Australia.

Apollo-Soyuz Mission

This mission was the first international manned space flight and had as one of its main goals the proving of the reliability of rescue plans of international crews. The Apollo spacecraft used was essentially the same as that used in the lunar program and the Soviet Soyuz was the same that had been in use since 1967. The flight was conducted between July 15 and July 24, 1975, with launches in the United States and the Soviet Union, docking over a two-day period, and return of the spacecraft to their respective countries after separation.

The return of Apollo marked the beginning of a six-year hiatus in the American manned space flight program. In addition to the human space flight program, NASA also maintained a small aeronautics research program, a space science program (including deep space and interplanetary exploration), and an earth observation program.

The Space Shuttle—Space Transportation System (STS)

The Space Shuttle Program arose from discussions about what should follow Project Apollo and the lunar explorations and landings. In the 1960s, NASA's grand vision for the future advocated placing increasingly large outposts in earth orbit, lunar orbit, and even on the moon itself. With the development of the Saturn V, these ideas became possible, and earth orbit stations holding 12, 50, and even 100 people were expected. Mars would be explored by human crews. The need for crew changes and for supplies for the stations in low earth orbit is where the idea of the Space Shuttle first developed. The concept was to minimize costs by developing a reusable vehicle.

As is often the case, dreams of engineers and planners frequently do not match those of earth-bound politicians and their constituents. President Johnson's Great Society programs, followed by the exigencies of the Vietnam War, took precedence. The Department of Defense had its own priorities for space assets in orbit. The Nixon White House rejected NASA's grand plans; the Space Shuttle for low earth orbit became the only feasible alternative, which was a compromise for all interests. Planned commercial, scientific, and national security payloads visualized 50 STS missions every year.

As each interest's needs were realized and as designs were fleshed out, the Shuttle took form. The 60-foot-long bay, payload weight requirements, delta wings to allow maneuvering, and the reusable thermal shield for reentry were developed to accommodate those interests. The Shuttle would be the first reusable spacecraft, the first to have wings, and the first to land on a runway. But budget constraints in 1971 doomed plans for a completely reusable vehicle. Modified designs were searched out. Nevertheless, NASA claimed in 1972 that for the $5.5 billion funded for the project, the Shuttle would meet all performance requirements, would perform 100 missions for each successive vehicle, and each mission would cost $7.7 million. The program was launched to great fanfare during the election year of 1972.

The promised delivery date of March 1978 came and went. So did the next one, 1979, when the program was fully reviewed by the Jimmy Carter White House. One of Carter's priorities was the need for a space platform to verify compliance with the Salt II arms treaty by the Soviet Union, which, among other things, assured the continuation of the program of development to flight status. Problems with the Shuttle's main engines and the reentry tile structure resulted in two more years of delay.

The first STS was named *Columbia*, completed after nine years of development. It was launched for its first test flight from Cape Canaveral on April 12, 1981 for a two-day orbit and returned for landing to Edwards Air Force Base. Four more test flights were made and, in 1982, the Shuttle was made fully operational "for economical and routine access to space for scientific exploration, commercial ventures, and for tasks related to the national security."[25]

As finally configured, the Space Shuttle, mission-designated as STS with mission number, consisted of the Orbiter, which in common usage became the "Space Shuttle," the Shuttle's three main engines, the external tank, and the two solid rocket boosters. The Orbiter carried a maximum crew of seven, a payload of up to 56,300 pounds depending on the orbit, and an airlock for exiting either on the ground or in orbit. The main engines burned a mixture of oxygen and hydrogen at a rate of half a ton per second, each engine producing 375,000 pounds of thrust, four times that of the largest commercial jet; the large bell-shaped nozzles swivel for steering control during ascent. The burn rate of the main engines would empty a normal-sized swimming pool in twenty seconds. The external tank carried over 143,000 gallons of liquid oxygen and over 385,000 gallons of liquid hydrogen, stored at minus 297 degrees and 423 degrees Fahrenheit, respectively; the external tank was not reusable. The solid rocket boosters provided 85 percent, or six million pounds, of the necessary thrust for the STS. These motors burned for two minutes each, then separated and were pushed away from the array by small rocket motors; parachutes deployed from their nose cones returned them to earth 120 miles downrange in the Atlantic Ocean.

Declaring such first-generation technology operational after only five test flights was considered risky and unusual by many informed observers. That decision has been laid over to NASA's desire to secure Presidential approval of its next manned program, the Space Station, which would necessarily depend on a credible Shuttle, and to the appearance of the European Space Agency's "Ariane" expendable launch vehicle. Ariane was already competing for commercial launch contracts as early as 1982. The appearance of Ariane greatly conflicted NASA's expectation of off-setting the Shuttle's operating costs with commercial contracts. As a result, even though launch costs were running at the time over $120 million dollars each, NASA offered commercial launches for just $42 million.

The Shuttle Story was not all negative. Between 1982 and 1986 it retrieved two communications satellites, repaired another in orbit, and launched 24 more. It visited the European-built Spacelab, carried citizens of Germany, Mexico, Canada, Saudi Arabia, France, and the Netherlands into space, as well as two members of Congress. By 1985, four Orbiters were in operation. Yet, that year the Space Shuttle flew just nine missions.

The goal was no longer 50 flights each year as originally predicted; the goal in 1985 was 24 flights, but even that was unattainable. The cost of each mission was over $140 million, seven times greater (adjusted for inflation) than that projected the previous decade. The interim preparation period for each mission had grown from a projected 10 days to an average of 67 days. Worse, pressure on maintaining the flight schedule caused NASA to begin to accept less than specification performance of shuttle components.

The 25th mission of the Shuttle, flown by *Challenger* on January 28, 1986, abruptly terminated 73 seconds after launch, killing all seven crew members on board. No Shuttle was launched thereafter for 32 months. The Department of Defense decided to launch all future military payloads on expendable rockets (excepting a few in progress). President Reagan announced the termination of all commercial launches via the Shuttle. The abandonment of the proposed

Shuttle launch site at Vandenberg Air Force Base was announced. This event, and these decisions, greatly reduced the effectiveness and glamour of the Shuttle and increased its net costs, and there was yet to be further tragedy.

The next mission was not launched until September 29, 1988, and the Shuttle was no longer described as "operational." It was, in fact, thereafter treated like an R&D test program, according to NASA Associate Administrator Richard Truly.[26] Yet, the Shuttle accomplished many objectives before the loss of *Columbia* in 2003. During that 15-year period, the Shuttle flew 87 missions, compared with 24 before the *Challenger* accident. It launched the Hubble Space Telescope in 1990, its repair in 1993, and its servicing in 1999 and 2002. It returned America's first orbiting astronaut, John Glenn, to orbit again in 1998, and it delivered America's contributions to the International Space Station. It launched several planetary probes and participated in a number of Shuttle–Spacelab missions devoted to scientific research. It conducted nine missions to rendezvous with the Russian space station *Mir*. For a time, the Shuttle was the only vehicle that could launch the ready-built constituents needed to complete European and Japanese contributions to the ISS and to supply access to and from the ISS for scientific experiments. It was this ISS-Shuttle symbiosis, in fact, that justified the Shuttle's existence.

The White House made a change in 1992 in NASA leadership with the appointment of Daniel S. Goldin as Administrator. Goldin brought Russia into partnership in the International Space Station, and the ISS became his (and NASA's) main program with the Shuttle playing a subordinate role. He transferred engineering talent and workforce from the Shuttle to the ISS and to his pet project, the exploration of Mars. This also transferred the emphasis of the NASA mission from the Shuttle to its original mission of exploration.

During the middle of the 1990s, the emphasis centered on ways to make public-sector programs more efficient and less costly. Transferring government operations to the private sector (privatization) was a preferred way of doing this. At the time, NASA was managing 86 separate contracts with 56 different firms in order to keep the Shuttle going. In 1995, a joint venture of Lockheed Martin and Rockwell won the Space Flight Operations Contract and formed a new corporation known as United Space Alliance to run the Shuttle program, with NASA oversight. Boeing soon replaced Rockwell.

Although by some estimates this development saved NASA some $1 billion over six years, the split of authority between NASA and United Space Alliance was not optimal. Plans for complete privatization were discussed along with a replacement for the Shuttle, which was recognized as approaching obsolescence. The X-33 program with Lockheed Martin and the X-34 program with Orbital Sciences were floated with the hope that the next generation of human space flight could be privately funded with little government spending.

These programs did not mature, despite significant spending to find a Shuttle replacement between 1986 and 2002. In the meantime, the Shuttle ground infrastructure was deteriorating dangerously and the Shuttle itself required costly safety upgrades. When the Bush Administration took over in 2001, the International Space Station was $4 billion over budget. Discussions about what to do about the situation continued without result into 2003. The workforce was depicted as "The Few, the Tired," also an apt description of the entire Shuttle Program when the *Columbia* reentry accident occurred in 2003, according to the Accident Board investigating that tragedy.

In its final report in August 2003, the Board stated what it called "an inescapable conclusion: *Because of the risks inherent in the original design of the Space Shuttle, because that design was based in many aspects on now-obsolete technologies, and because the Shuttle is now an aging system but still developmental in character, it is in the nation's interest to replace the Shuttle as soon as possible as the primary means for transporting humans to and from Earth orbit.*"[27]

In January 2004, President George W. Bush announced the mandatory retirement of the Space Shuttle, to take place in 2010. The Shuttle next flew after the *Columbia* accident some two and a half years later, when *Discovery* was launched on July 26, 2005. Congressional funding for the Shuttle allowed flights into 2011, with the final launch occurring on July 26, 2011, of the STS *Atlantis*.

Although in 2004 President Bush had announced a subsequent space program known as "Constellation" in his Vision for Space Exploration, which would have sent astronauts first to the ISS, then to the Moon, and then to Mars, in 2010 the Obama Administration canceled the program.

In all, there were five Shuttles: *Columbia*, *Challenger*, *Discovery*, *Atlantis*, and *Endeavor*. Two of these were destroyed during Shuttle missions, a 40 percent vehicle failure rate, with the loss of 14 lives onboard. Compared with other space programs, this loss rate was extraordinary. The Mercury and Gemini Programs had no fatalities. Apollo had three fatalities, which occurred in the capsule during a test while on the launch pad at Cape Canaveral. While there is no verifiable data, the Russian space program admits one cosmonaut death during reentry (Soyuz 1) and three cosmonaut deaths during Soyuz 2 when they were exposed to space vacuum. There are unverified reports of other casualties during the early days of that space program. To date, there have been no reported Chinese space program fatalities.

NASA says that it cost $450 million to launch one STS mission. There were 135 missions in total. It was independently reported in 2011 that NASA spent more than $192 billion on the Shuttle Program from 1971 to 2010 (in 2010 dollars), and that during the period 1982 to 2010, the average cost per launch was about

$1.2 billion.[28] The Russian Space Agency does not advertise its launch costs, but it is reliably rumored to be around $45 million per launch. They started out selling tickets to the public for orbital flights at $20 million a seat. The price lately has risen to $63 million.

The legacy of the Space Shuttle will be a subject of discussion for years to come.

■ Commercial Space Transportation— End of a Government Monopoly

For many years after the launch of *Explorer I* in 1958, conventional wisdom and generally held perception was that space activities were, and should be, the exclusive domain of national governments. Only NASA, the military services, and the National Reconnaissance Agency[29] were permitted or able to engage in launch activity. Although some commercial payloads were placed in orbit as early as the 1960s, the launching of them was strictly a government business. This view prevailed in spite of the fact that the United States has long based its successful economic system on private enterprise, with the role of government being limited and supportive of the private engines of commerce. This government–private sector symbiosis was the dynamic partnership that we described at the beginning of this book, and it has been the norm in every industrial, technical, and a scientific advance seen in the United States. We will first look at the development of the law that is making this transition possible.

The Communications Satellite Act of 1962

When Sputnik was launched on October 4, 1957, telephone communications across the oceans were sent through large undersea copper cables. Television transmissions were sight limited and unavailable for overseas transmissions (or other long distances) due to the curvature of the earth's surface. In the United States, American Telephone and Telegraph (AT&T) advanced the idea in the early 1960s of its funding a communications satellite that could be used to relay television signals across great distances, including the Atlantic Ocean to Europe.

While the promise of this great technological advancement was intriguing, the anticompetitive aspects of such an arrangement were daunting and, under American law, possibly illegal. There was also the matter of private enterprise now being inserted into space operations that had always been reserved for government function worldwide (the United States and the U.S.S.R.).

The solution was to create a quasi-public corporation to own the satellite under government regulation. This was accomplished by passage of the Communications Satellite Act of 1962, and it created Comsat Corporation as the owning and operating entity. The Telstar satellite, built by AT&T and launched by NASA on July 10, 1962, became the first direct-relay communications satellite. While AT&T owned 29 percent of the corporation, the majority of shares were distributed so as to insure independence. AT&T controlled six directors, the other shareholders an additional six, and three were appointed by the president of the United States.

One of the problems with Telstar was that it had been placed in low earth orbit, which required movable receptor dishes to track the satellite in order to pick up its signals as it traversed the sky. Hughes Aircraft was a competitor of AT&T and suggested placing one of its satellites in geostationary orbit (GSO), which would eliminate tracking requirements of the satellite by receivers. NASA approved and the first Syncom satellite reached high orbit in 1963.

The geostationary orbit is a unique, circular orbit plane directly above the earth's equator. By "unique" is meant that there is only one GSO, which is the orbital plane at zero degrees inclination. A satellite placed in this orbit will appear to hover directly over the same point on earth above the equator at all times.[30] A GSO satellite orbits at an altitude of about 22,236 miles above earth.

Since GSO is unique, the number of satellites that can be placed in it is limited. A system of slots is being monitored by the United Nations to insure fairness in allocation of GSO participation among nations.

In August 1964, a second organization was formed for the propagation of international satellite telecommunications. The International Telecommunications Satellite Organization, or Intelsat, was created by 11 separate nations with control in its board of directors weighted to reflect the member nation's volume of communications. Comsat controlled over half the board of directors. Its first satellite, known as Early Bird, was purchased from Hughes Aircraft and was launched into GSO orbit in 1965.

By 1969, global coverage had been achieved by Intelsat by the placing of three satellites over the Atlantic and three over the Pacific. A seventh, in GSO over the Indian Ocean, linked London and Tokyo and completed the system.

Before the Europeans developed their own satellite launching systems, NASA launched foreign telecommunications satellites known as Symphonie in 1974 and 1975, owned by France and West Germany. Intelsat was by now serving some hundred different countries, some of whom had never even had local television service or had ever laid any significant telephone lines within their own borders, such as Bangladesh and large portions of Africa.

The Commercial Space Launch Act of 1984

Aside from telecommunications, private enterprise remained largely on the sidelines of space operations. The "government only" perception began to change during the 1980s. Europe's Arianespace began offering launch services in 1983. This was followed by President Reagan's Executive Order 12465 signed in 1984, which authorized U.S. commercial space launch activity with the words "in order to encourage, facilitate, and coordinate the development of commercial expendable launch vehicle (ELV) operations by private United States enterprises." Up to that time, all U.S. commercial satellites had been launched on rockets owned and operated by the United States government. The Executive Order was followed by passage in Congress of the Commercial Space Launch Act that same year, which directed the Department of Transportation to "encourage, facilitate, and promote commercial space launches." The DOT set up the Office of Commercial Space Transportation to address the transition from government to commercial operations. In 1989, the U.S. government decided to stop launching commercial payloads on the Space Shuttle, in part because of the *Challenger* disaster that occurred in 1986. This spurred commercial launch interest even more.

The Commercial Space Launch Act established a comprehensive licensing structure that enabled launch operators to comply quickly and efficiently with existing federal regulations. The statute also authorized the licensing of nonfederal launch sites, from which commercial space launches would occur, in addition to commercial launches from federal sites. In 1995, the licensing responsibility was transferred from the DOT to the FAA's Office of Commercial Space Transportation (FAA/AST), which now licenses and regulates U.S. commercial space launch and reentry activity, including launch vehicles. It also licenses nonfederal launch sites. But even with the mandate given to FAA/AST, there were at least 12 other federal bureaus identified that could have some jurisdiction in regulating space activities. In fact, it was not clear under existing law that a private company could legally land a launched vehicle back in the United States. There was clearly a need for clarification of the limits of commercial space law and its regulation by FAA/AST.

The Commercial Space Act of 1998

The Commercial Space Act resolved the confusion. It also specifically approved the development and use of commercial reusable launch vehicles (RLVs) for launch and landing within the United States. In addition, the fledgling commercial space launch effort received a significant boost by the law directing NASA to use commercial launch services "when required in the course of its activities" and to "plan missions to accommodate U.S. commercial providers." The statute prohibited the government from using any missile that was formerly used by the Department of Defense for national defense purposes as a space transportation vehicle, which effectively took the government out of the satellite launch business. The statute did provide for seven exceptions to be used in the case of national defense overrides.

The Commercial Space Launch Amendments Act of 2004 (CSLAA)

This legislation was passed by Congress in December 2004. The law is "designed to promote the development of the emerging commercial human space flight industry" and creates the structure for the regulation of private space activities. It also frees the fledgling industry from the patchwork of regulations that had been applied to it.

Its overriding premise is that the federal government should not "over regulate" this new industry for fear that, in so doing, it will stifle the innovation necessary to make the concept succeed. Those now in the forefront of experimentation are compared to the early pioneers in aeronautical flight at the beginning of the last century. These current pioneers need a regulatory environment that will allow them room to experiment and take chances as they develop the space concepts of the future.

The government has decided that regulation will not be the enemy of innovation. Remembering the early days of aviation presented earlier in this book, we saw that the first regulation of aviation by the federal government occurred in 1926, some 23 years after the Wright brothers' first flight. As with the development of law after the first Sputnik orbited earth, it was clear that law must follow, not lead, technology. Just as government oversight of aviation safety gradually developed as aviation itself developed, so too will government oversight of the commercial space industry evolve.

According to statements made by FAA representatives to Congress, the government is placing its oversight emphasis on the protection of the public, not the participants. Given the experience of the industry regarding the failure rate of expendable launch vehicles, which is about 10 percent of all attempts, it is recognized that space launches are a relatively dangerous activity. FAA efforts are directed, therefore, not to the over-protection of those who voluntarily place themselves in harm's way as a part of the industry itself, but to the bystanders of the process, the public. In this regard the oversight process employed by the FAA has been successful. There have been no deaths or serious injuries, nor any significant property losses, as a result of FAA-monitored commercial launch activity.

It may be expected, however, that once commercial launch activity is removed from federal launch sites, with their isolated locations and ranges, and with their strict safety regulations and controls, there may be greater likelihood of harm to the general public. The regulatory regimen of CSLAA provides for launch operators to maintain an under-layer of liability insurance, but also requires the federal government to indemnify or reimburse operators for losses to third parties in excess of that insurance up to the sum of $1.5 billion. The removal of this financial risk is important to private investment.

Commercial Orbital Transportation Services (COTS) and Commercial Crew Development (CCDev/2) NASA Programs

On January 18, 2006, NASA announced a new program to encourage the development of new spacecraft and launch systems designed to be able to supply the delivery of crew and cargo to the International Space Station. This need, of course, is due to the cancellation of the Shuttle program, which formerly performed that function, among others.

The COTS program anticipates an extra dimension of precision needed by participants since delivery to the ISS requires exact orbit insertion, rendezvous, and docking with or proximity to the ISS or other spacecraft. The program includes the award of financial contributions and the transfer of proprietary NASA technical data to assist in the development of the participants' vehicles.

More than 20 companies submitted proposals under the COTS program in March 2006 and an additional seven by November 2007. The primary recipients of COTS awards have been Space Exploration Technologies Corporation (Space X) and Orbital Sciences Corporation. Space X has achieved success in reaching its milestones under the program (see below) and has received some $500 million from NASA.

Commercial Space Launch Activity

The first licensed commercial space launch occurred in the United States in March 1989 when a Starfire suborbital vehicle carried aloft the Consort 1 payload from White Sands Missile Range in New Mexico. By the end of 2011, the DOT/FAA had licensed 205 orbital and suborbital commercial launches. From 1989, the number of annual launches increased each year through 1997 with a high that year of 24 launches. Beginning in 1998, launch activity leveled off, and even began to decline on an annual basis. Launches peaked again during the 2007–2008 period. For historical and forecast launch and satellite data, see Table 41-1 and Figures 41-4, 41-5, and 41-6.

Until the 1990s, most commercial satellites were telecommunications orbiters that were placed in geostationary orbit (GSO). Since 1997,

2007	2007	2008	2009	2010	2011	2012	2013	2014	2015	2016	Total	Average
GSO Forecast (COMSTAC)	23	22	21	23	19	22	21	21	19	19	210	21.0
NGSO Forecast (FAA)	34	18	34	30	22	14	13	10	8	8	191	19.1
Total Satellite	**57**	**40**	**55**	**53**	**41**	**36**	**34**	**31**	**27**	**27**	**401**	**40.1**
GSO Medium-to-Heavy	17	18	16	17	13	16	15	15	13	13	153	15.3
NGSO Medium-to-Heavy	11	8	8	5	4	3	2	4	2	2	49	4.9
NGSO Small	6	5	5	4	2	2	2	2	2	2	32	3.2
Total Launches	**34**	**31**	**29**	**26**	**19**	**21**	**19**	**21**	**17**	**17**	**234**	**23.4**

TABLE 41-1 Commercial space transportation payload and launch forecasts.

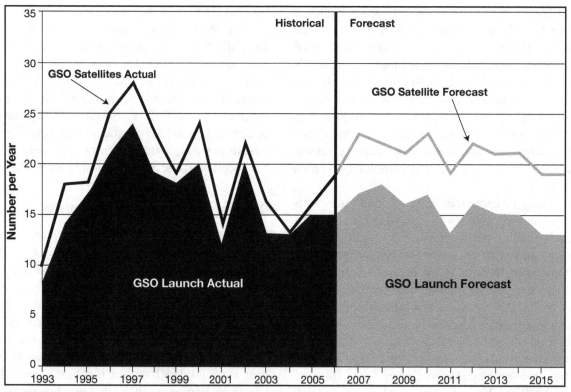

FIGURE 41-4 2011 and historical GSO payloads and launches.

satellites have also been placed in low earth orbit (LEO) or nongeosynchronous orbit (NGEO)[31] in order to serve new markets in commercial mobile telephones, data messaging, and remote sensing.

Launch forecasts consider five payload categories, defined by the type of service the spacecraft are designed to offer:

1. Commercial telecommunications;
2. Commercial remote sensing;
3. Science and engineering;
4. Commercial cargo and crew transportation services;
5. Other payloads launched commercially.

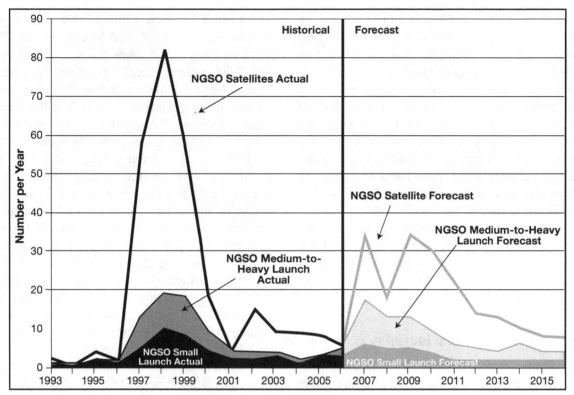

FIGURE 41-5 2011 and historical NGSO payloads and launches.

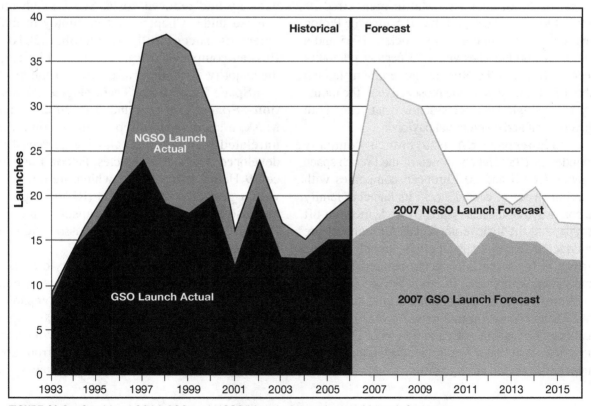

FIGURE 41-6 Combined 2011 GSO and NGSO historical launches and launch forecasts.

Commercial launch demand is driven by activity in the global satellite market, ranging from customer needs and the introduction of new applications to satellite lifespan and regional economic conditions. The GSO market is served by both medium and heavy lift launch vehicles, for which there is a constant commercial customer demand for telecommunications satellites. The NGSO market is served by small, medium, and heavy lift launch vehicles and has a wider variety of satellite and payload missions, but also has more demand fluctuation.

Globally, the United States lags both Europe and Russia in commercial launches. In 2010, for instance, there were 23 launches worldwide: 13 in Russia (57%), 6 by Europe (26%), and 4 for the United States (17%).

Primary Launch Service Providers[32]

International Launch Services (ILS) has experience dating back to 1995 when it was a partnership between Lockheed Martin and several Russian firms. In 2006, Lockheed Martin transferred its interest to Space Transport, Inc. ILS uses the Proton heavy-lift rocket with a history back to 1965 and a record of 360 launches and a 95 percent reliability record. ILS and the Russian government launch about 12 flights a year, the most active in the industry for a single-launcher system. It launches both government and commercial payloads.

Arianespace SA is a French company founded in 1980 and composed of the French space agency CNES and 20 European companies with varying shares of capital stock. Its launcher family is composed of the heavy-lift Ariane 5, medium-lift Soyuz, and the lightweight Vega. All launches are conducted from its spaceport in French Guiana. Soyuz is the world's longest-operated launcher and joined Arianespace in 2011. Soyuz is used for medium-weight telecommunications, scientific, and earth observation missions. As of 2012, there had been 61 launches of Ariane 5, with 47 consecutive successful launches. It launches both government and commercial payloads.

United Launch Alliance (ULA) is a joint venture between Lockheed Martin and the Boeing Company. ULA uses the successful Atlas and Delta rocket programs (Evolved Expendable Launch Vehicles) to provide launch services to the United States government, including the Department of Defense, NASA, and the National Reconnaissance Office. ULA primarily uses the Atlas V (100 percent mission success rate) and Delta IV (used in five configurations from medium to heavy). ULA launches are conducted from Canaveral Air Force Station, Florida and Vandenberg Air Force Base, California. It launches mostly government payloads (commercial customers have comprised less than 20 percent since 2006).

Sea Launch Co. LLC was established in 1995 as a combination of companies from Norway, Russia, Ukraine, and the United States, managed by the Boeing Company. It uses a mobile sea platform to allow equatorial launches of commercial satellites on Zenit 3SL rockets. The equatorial launch capability allows for optimum earth positioning for increased payload capacity and reduced costs. Sea Launch reorganized under Chapter 11 bankruptcy in 2009, emerging successfully in October 2010. A Russian company, Energia Overseas Limited, is the majority stockholder after reorganization.

Space Exploration Technologies Corporation—Space X, was founded in 2002 by Elon Musk, a successful entrepreneur in completely unrelated technologies, and has successfully developed two launch vehicles, Falcon 1 and Falcon 9 Heavy Lift, both of which are developed with a goal of being reusable (RLVs). Space X has also developed a space capsule called the Dragon Spacecraft to be used in association with the Falcon rockets.

Space X is a Silicon Valley-style corporation, building most of its components in-house with a paltry 1,800 employees when compared to a competitor like Boeing, with 170,000 employees in 70 countries. Space X is moving ahead under a stiff headwind of resistance from some industry and government officials who had ridiculed the notion that a startup without contacts with proven aerospace firms could compete in this very small and specialized market.

Space X first made history in December 2010 when it became the first private company to send a spacecraft into earth orbit and retrieve it successfully. Again, on May 25, 2012, Space X became the first privately held company to successfully send a cargo payload to the International Space Station. It used its Falcon 9 launcher and its Dragon Spacecraft. Space X is expected to begin making regular runs to supply the ISS. This is a breakthrough into government business, which has been basically controlled by United Launch Alliance. It is also in competition with Boeing's private space capsule in development called the CST-100, said to be launchable on the Atlas 5 rocket. Space X has NASA contracts in the $1.6 billion range.

The Dragon Spacecraft is also being reconfigured to carry up to seven astronauts into orbit. It will be equipped with the NASA Docking System for manned flights.

In addition to its government efforts, it has dozens of commercial contracts worth more than $4 billion to launch satellites for various countries and telecommunications companies.

Orbital Sciences Corporation was founded in 1982 and has heavy experience in the missile defense realm and in the manufacturing and launch of satellites for both commercial and military customers. It has successfully completed milestones in the NASA-run COTS program with its Cygnus Spacecraft and Antares-Taurus II rocket and has NASA contracts in the $1.9 billion range. It plans launches using these launch and space vehicles from Wallops Island, Virginia in 2013.

U.S. Spaceports

By June 2012, the following spaceports were approved or active.

U.S. Federal Launch Sites

Cape Canaveral Air Force Station
Vandenberg Air Force Base

List of active Launch Service Providers

- Earth2Orbit (E2O) http://www.earth2orbit.com/ (PSL V/GSL V)
- Antrix Corporation (PSL V/GSL V)
- Arianespace (Ariane 5/Vega)
- COSMOS International (Kosmos-3M)
- Eurockot (Rockot)
- Great Wall Industial Corporation (Long March) [citation needed]
- International Launch Services (Proton-M)
- ISC Kosmotras (Dnepr)
- Land Launch (Zenit-2SLB/Zenit-3SLB)
- Mitsubishi Heavy Industries (H-IIA)
- Orbital Sciences Corporation (Minotaur/ pegasus/Taurus)
- Sea Launch (Zenit-3SL)
- SpaceX (Falcon 1/Falcon 9)
- Starsem (Soyuz-FG/Soyuz-2)
- United Launch Alliance (Atlas V/Delta IV)
- Alcântara Cyclone Space (Tsyklon-4)

FIGURE 41-7 Full list of launch service providers.

Edwards Air Force Base
Wallops Flight Facility
White Sands Missile Range
Reagan Test Site

Non-Federal FAA-Licensed Launch Sites

Spaceport Florida–Cape Canaveral
Cecil Field Spaceport–Florida
Mid-Atlantic Regional Spaceport–Virginia
Oklahoma Spaceport
Mojave Spaceport–Edwards AFB
Spaceport America–White Sands
California Spaceport–Vandenberg AFB
Kodiak Launch Complex–Alaska
Poker Flat Research Range–Alaska
    Geophysical Institute
Sea Launch Platform–California-Equatorial
    Pacific Ocean

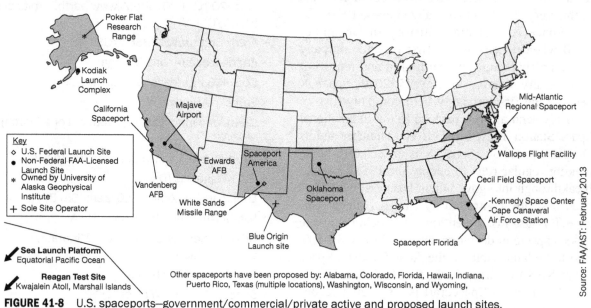

U.S. Spaceports
Commercial/Government/Private Active and Proposed Launch Sites

Poker Flat Research Range

Kodiak Launch Complex

California Spaceport

Majave Airport

Mid-Atlantic Regional Spaceport

Key
◇ U.S. Federal Launch Site
● Non-Federal FAA-Licensed Launch Site
✳ Owned by University of Alaska Geophysical Institute
+ Sole Site Operator

Wallops Flight Facility

Edwards AFB

Spaceport America

Cecil Field Spaceport

Vandenberg AFB

White Sands Missile Range

Oklahoma Spaceport

-Kennedy Space Center
-Cape Canaveral Air Force Station

Blue Origin Launch site

Spaceport Florida

Sea Launch Platform
Equatorial Pacific Ocean

Reagan Test Site
Kwajalein Atoll, Marshall Islands

Other spaceports have been proposed by: Alabama, Colorado, Florida, Hawaii, Indiana, Puerto Rico, Texas (multiple locations), Washington, Wisconsin, and Wyoming,

Source: FAA/AST: February 2013

FIGURE 41-8   U.S. spaceports—government/commercial/private active and proposed launch sites.

U.S. commercial launches to GSO are made from either Cape Canaveral Air Force Base or from the platform operated by Sea Launch in the Pacific. Launches to NGSO can occur from any U.S. launch site. The legislatures of the states of Florida and Virginia have passed legislation granting certain tax exemptions for investment in space assets and activities within those states.

Spacecraft Systems and Suborbital Launch Systems

Boeing is in the process of developing a spacecraft known as the CTS-100 (Commercial Crew Transportation System) for use with the Atlas V rocket. Boeing says that the spacecraft will be operational by 2015 as a part of a complete transportation system, consisting of spacecraft, launch vehicle, ground operations, mission operations, and recovery. It will utilize the Apollo-proven parachute landing system after reentry.

Sierra Nevada is an electronics systems and integration company involved with telemedicine, navigation and guidance systems, space, and other

cutting edge technologies. Its Dream Chaser concept of reusable spacecraft is being designed to be launched on the Atlas V rocket for low earth orbit access. It is a lifting body design that will carry up to seven passengers or cargo, can be crewed or autonomous, will feature low gravity reentry (1.5 G) pressures, and will have quick turnaround. The craft is in the aerodynamic testing phase in 2012.

Blue Origin is a startup private aerospace company that has received some funding from NASA under the Commercial Crew Development Program. The company was formed originally to develop means to provide suborbital tourist spaceflights, but has also indicated that it is in development of an orbital space vehicle that can be launched on an Atlas V rocket. It has also contracted with NASA for developmental work on a launch escape system.

Bigelow Aerospace was founded in 1998 for the production of expandable space modules to house space travelers in earth orbit. Due to the cancellation of the Space Shuttle and the lack of any reliable, affordable technology to replace it, the company instituted drastic cutbacks of staff and operations in 2011. It claims technology that is superior to metallic capsules that will withstand micrometeor impacts safely.

SpaceShipOne (SS1)—A Different Kind of Space Flight

April 1, 2004, FAA/AST granted the first license ever issued for a private, crewed, suborbital flight. The award went to a company founded by aeronautical pioneer Burt Rutan, Scaled Composites, in conjunction with joint venturer Paul Allen. Rutan, an aerospace engineer, gained a reputation for developing new, unconventional airplane designs built of strong, light, composite materials. In 1986, his *Voyager* aircraft was the first to fly around the world without refueling.

Just one year before being awarded the federal license, Scaled Composites revealed that it was working on a spacecraft design to compete for the Ansari X Prize.[33] At the time, there were 27 announced competitors for the prize. The Ansari X Prize, in the amount of $10 million, was offered by the X Prize Foundation for the first private, nongovernmental launch of a reusable manned spacecraft, capable of carrying three people into space with safe return, twice within a two-week period. The Ansari X Prize is patterned after the early 20th century practice of awarding monetary prizes to aviators in order to spur greater achievements in the then-nascent aviation field. In particular, it is reminiscent of the Orteig Prize of $25,000 that was posted by Ray Orteig in 1919 for anyone who successfully completed a nonstop flight between New York and Paris. The Orteig Prize was claimed by Charles Lindbergh in 1927. (See Chapter 13. See also the NASA Centennial Challenges below.)

The Ansari X Prize stipulated that the spacecraft exceed 100 kilometers as the

FIGURE 41-9 White Knight lifting SpaceShipOne.

© Jim Sugar/Corbis

© Jim Sugar/Corbis

FIGURE 41-10 SpaceShipOne.

required threshold of space (the Kármán line) at 62.1 miles above the earth. The SS1 flights originated from the Mojave Airport Civilian Flight Test Center (now Mojave Spaceport) in California. SpaceShipOne was aerially launched from a specially Rutan-designed carrier jet called "White Knight." The spacecraft was powered by a hybrid rocket engine that used nitrous oxide (laughing gas) as the oxidizer and synthetic rubber as the fuel. (See Figures 41-9, 41-10, and 41-11.)

The first competitive flight in the Ansari X Prize competition occurred on September 29, 2004, achieving an altitude of 102.9 kilometers and a maximum speed of 2.92 Mach. On October 4, 2004, SpaceShipOne duplicated its earlier successful suborbital flight, this time to 111.996 kilometers and a maximum speed of 3.09 Mach, thereby completing all requirements for the Ansari X Prize. That date was the 47th anniversary of the first Sputnik flight.

SpaceShipTwo is a follow-on suborbital, air-launched space vehicle being developed by a joint venture between Scaled Composites and the Virgin Group (Virgin Galactic). The vehicle was introduced to the public in December 2009 and, as of July 2012, is undergoing glide tests. The company is taking bookings for suborbital flights set to start late in 2013 at a price of $200,000.

The joint venture plans orbital flights using its planned SpaceShipThree, assuming success in its Virgin Galactic project. Orbital flight is much more difficult to achieve than is suborbital flight since the speed necessary to gain escape velocity is on the order of 7 to 8 times that required to reach suborbital altitudes. While SpaceShipOne reached the Kármán line by accelerating to a little over 3 Mach, orbital vehicles will require 25 Mach to achieve escape velocity. Reentry is also much more complex, since all of the excess speed must be dissipated on reentering earth's atmosphere.

■ The NASA Centennial Challenges

In 2003, NASA started a new program known as "The Centennial Challenges" based on a recommendation of the National Academy of Engineering in 1999. This recommendation was that Congress should encourage federal agencies to experiment more extensively with inducement prize contests in science and technology. The NASA Centennial Challenges were named in recognition of the Wright brothers' first flight 100 years before.

The "Challenges" set up a monetary prize format similar to that discussed above, and which actually relates back to the British prize of 20,000 pounds sterling offered in 1714 for a reliable method of determining longitude on a ship at sea. (See Chapter 1.)

The NASA Challenges typically coordinate the competitions with private foundations, like the X Prize Foundation, the Spaceward Foundation, or others, which actually run the events. The Challenges are announced annually and range over a wide spectrum of scientific and technical issues. Examples from past competitions include the Astronaut Glove Challenge (to devise the best performing glove for space use), the Moon Regolith Oxygen Challenge (the extraction of oxygen from lunar soil), and the Suborbital Payload Challenge (to achieve suborbital altitudes that provide enough linger time for the kind of microgravity research NASA needs).

The Strong Tether Challenge and the Power Beaming Challenge are designed to produce

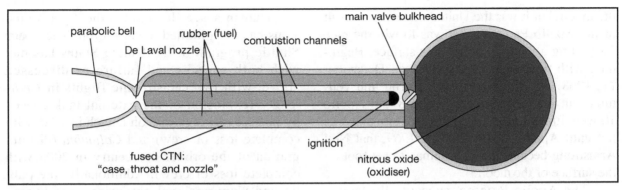

FIGURE 41-11   Hybrid rocket engine used by SS1.

technology that will put humans and objects into space without the use of rocket propulsion. These Challenges are subparts of the larger "space elevator" concept that was first mentioned by Konstantin Tsiolkovsky in the late 19th century, and then more specifically proposed by a Russian engineer (Yuri Artsutanov) in the 1960s. The basic idea is to anchor a tether (a ribbon with a diameter half that of a pencil) at a point on earth that will extend into outer space, to a point beyond the geosynchronous orbit. A counterweight positioned at the space end of the tether would provide enough inertia through the rotation of the earth (centripetal force) to keep the length of the tether taut. Payloads would be attached to the tether for delivery into space.

When first proposed, and even in 1960, the idea was assigned to science fiction because there existed no material strong enough to construct a workable tether. In 1991, science discovered a new class of molecule known as the carbon nanotube, which possesses over twice the strength necessary to make the tether work.

The Strong Tether Challenge is held at the Space Elevator Conference sponsored by Microsoft, The Leeward Space Foundation, and the International Space Elevator Consortium. Although as of 2011 there has been no winner, the strength of the tethers has continued to increase for the five years of the competition. The prize purse has continued to increase over the years and is now at $2 million.

The Power Beaming Challenge is a competition to build a wireless lifting mechanism, called a climber system, powered by electricity from a ground electrical outlet that is "beamed" (wirelessly) to the climber apparatus. The beam is a high-power low-intensity laser. The lifting mechanism must lift a payload a prescribed height within a prescribed time. Beamed power competitions held since 2005 finally resulted in a winner in 2009. LaserMotive LLC was awarded $900,000 that year for successfully driving the climber up a cable one kilometer high, suspended from a helicopter.

A Confusing Vision for Space Exploration—A Statement of National Purpose?

For many years after the launch of Sputnik, the competitive aspects of the space race between the United States and the U.S.S.R. spurred space advances and development. These were the days of setting new records over the whole spectrum of space activity. These "firsts" included the first human in space, the first woman, the longest human time-period in space, and the first "spacewalk."

A Brief History

During these early years, the space race included the race to the moon. Both the U.S. and the U.S.S.R. successfully sent unmanned probes to the moon, but it was the United States, as a result of the Apollo Program, that was to win the race for putting a man on the moon's surface. Beginning with the launch of Apollo 8 on December 21, 1968, Americans left earth's orbit and ventured out into deep space. Apollo 8 and Apollo 10 were limited to lunar orbiting missions; it was not until Apollo 11, on July 21, 1969, that Neil Armstrong became the first human to set foot on the surface of the moon.[34]

The Apollo Program successfully landed six missions on the surface of the moon. Apollo 11 through Apollo 17 were landing missions to the moon, but due to a life-threatening explosion of an oxygen tank aboard the command module of Apollo 13, on April 13, 1970 en route to the moon, that lunar landing mission had to be scrapped. Only through superior scientific and engineering skill, and determination by NASA personnel and the onboard crew, with a bit of luck thrown in, was the Apollo 13 crew successfully retrieved from space to a safe landing. The details of this extraordinary feat are well worth reading.

The Soviet Lunar Program had 20 successful missions to the moon, including the first flyby, first soft landing on the moon, and the first circumlunar probe to return to earth. Although denied by the Soviet government at the time, the U.S.S.R. had two manned lunar programs in progress in competition with the United States during the 1960s and 1970s. Due to several launch vehicle failures, these programs were canceled by 1976.

To date (circa 2013), only three countries have placed humans into space utilizing their own launching systems. In addition to the United States and the U.S.S.R., in October 2003, the People's Republic of China successfully launched its first astronaut into orbit on the Shenzhou 5 launch vehicle. China has also announced its intention to put astronauts on the moon by 2025. All other countries' programs, including the European Hermes and the Japanese Hope-X programs, have been canceled.

Human space flight since the Apollo missions has been limited to earth orbit. The Space Shuttle program in the United States has met with both success and failure as discussed above, with two catastrophic flights in *Challenger* (explosion of the external tank caused by booster rocket failure on launch in 1986 with complete loss of crew) and *Columbia* (disintegration of the orbiter on reentry in 2003 with complete loss of crew). Additionally, the public and Congressional enthusiasm for human space flight seemed to wane as the space program became more mundane and as costs for the program came under greater Congressional scrutiny.

The Vision—2004

In 2004, President Bush announced a new space policy for the country termed "Vision for Space Exploration" which included a NASA initiative called the Constellation Program, centering on future human space flight. Its purpose was to give new direction to the American space program and regain public enthusiasm for space exploration. The new program set out an ambitious agenda:

- The International Space Station was to be completed by 2010.
- The Space Shuttle was to be retired by 2010.
- Replacement of the Space Shuttle, by a program called Orion (successor to the Crew Exploration Vehicle), was slated to be operational by 2014.
- A new generation of reusable and partially reusable launch vehicles was to be developed using some Space Shuttle technology, called Shuttle-Derived Launch Vehicles. These launchers included the Ares I, Ares IV, and the Ares V. The new concept was to use the Ares I for crew lift and the bigger, more expensive Ares V for cargo lift. These were to be the launchers for further moon exploration. (See Figure 41-12.)

- Renew moon exploration by launching robotic missions to the moon by 2008 (which never evolved) and crewed missions to the moon by 2020.
- Continue the exploration of Mars with robotic missions to be followed by crewed missions.

The Reality—2010

Although presidential candidate Barack Obama campaigned on a positive NASA platform, including human launches to the moon by 2020, the Obama White House has maintained no consistent position on space development. By 2010, the Constellation program had been canceled, except for a modified version of the Orion space vehicle. The Ares launch vehicle program had been converted into a "Shuttle-Derived Heavy Launch Vehicle," effectively replacing the Ares V. It appears that the International Space Station is being approved for funding for an additional five years, through 2020—the ISS has been continuously manned since the year 2000.

The Obama White House also seems to favor the use of commercial launch vehicles and spacecraft as the basis for future U.S. civil space policy. This has brought many powerful Congressmen, who favor stronger government control in manned space flight, and important former astronauts, including Neil Armstrong, into conflict with the administration. Congress has provided no money for the COTS program in the NASA budget for 2013. The conflict is over whether there should remain funding for several of the top-ranked commercial launch and spacecraft upstarts (like Space X and Orbital Services) or whether a tried and proven commercial launch and services program (like Boeing, Lockheed, United Launch Alliances) should be funded alone. The argument against funding several companies in a competitive atmosphere is that there is no proven track record (other than the one-time Space X orbit

rendezvous with the ISS in 2012), that it would be more costly to fund the competition, and the satellites and other payloads that must be put in orbit are so expensive that launch customers will be hesitant to trust upstarts. Many think that this is a short-sighted view since competition has been historically proven to provide creativity and innovation. It is also contrary to the concept of the NASA Centennial Challenges, to the spirit of the Commercial Space Launch Amendments, and to the history of pre-space flight innovation.

While the debate continues as to the country's future in space, American astronauts must be launched to the International Space Station aboard Russian Soyuz spacecraft, since the United States has no human space launch program. And we have the rather puzzling declaration by newly Obama-appointed NASA Chief Charles Bolden that he has been tasked by the White House with a new mission that has nothing to do with space. According to an interview given by Bolden to Al Jazeera while in the Middle East,[35] his "foremost" mission as the head of American's space exploration agency is to improve relations with the Muslim World.[36] Specifically, (Bolden said that Obama charged him with three specific assignments: "When I became the NASA administrator—or before I became the NASA administrator—he charged me with three things. One was he wanted me to help re-inspire children to want to get into science and math, he wanted me to expand our international relationships, and third, and perhaps foremost, he wanted me to find a way to reach out to the Muslim world and engage much more with dominantly Muslim nations to help them feel good about their historic contribution to science . . . and math and engineering.").

At the same time, NASA is moving ahead in unmanned, robotic space exploration. In August 2012, a one-ton, four-wheeled vehicle was successfully landed on Mars. Known as the "Curiosity Rover," it is a full-fledged geochemical laboratory equipped with lasers, video cameras, and measuring instruments, and it has the capability of analyzing soil and air samples and then sending the results back to earth. Its main function is to search for evidence of microbial life. "Curiosity" follows the much smaller and simpler Sojourner rover, which landed on Mars in the 1997 Pathfinder mission. "Curiosity" represents the 40th mission to explore the Red Planet over the last 50 years.

There are also currently satellites orbiting the Sun, Mercury, the moon, the asteroid Vesta, Mars, and Saturn, which provide an on-going flow of information, as well as missions now en route to Jupiter and Pluto. Sixteen earth observation satellites are currently studying various systems of the earth, including climate, the oceans, and the Polar Regions.

The Role of Government

At the beginning of the space age, while it assumed complete control of space activities, the government partnered with private industry to provide for the nation the best and safest space program in the world. As space technology and experience evolved, the government once again stepped aside as the commercial opportunities manifested themselves, and during the Reagan years it invited the great American enterprise system to take over. American business and technology

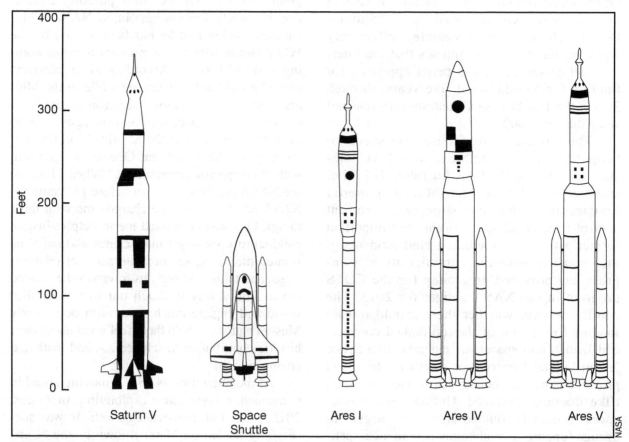

FIGURE 41-12 Saturn V, space shuttle, and shuttle-derived launch vehicles (Ares I, Ares IV, and Ares V) shown by relative size.

have responded in a resounding fashion, as the launch industry has promoted the evolution of new markets. At first these markets were communications, requiring communication satellites, then came direct television, bringing satellite television into homes, then came data services, and then satellite radio. The commercial remote sensing industry was born, and with all of these came the need for more satellites and ground-support equipment.

The federal government has now shifted from providing the only launch capability in the country to becoming a customer for private commercial launch providers. The current heavy-lift evolved expendable launch vehicles, the Delta IV and Atlas V rockets, were developed hand in glove with government space programs. Now government has provided a program of funding for the private development of reusable launch and spacecraft systems of different kinds. The enabling statutes and programs discussed above have set the private enterprise system on course to provide the future of American space flight. The primary missing link at the beginning of 2013 is a definitive national space policy: the orderly progression of exploration for the nation of the "fourth environment" of space.[37]

Endnotes

1. A large-caliber muzzle-loading gun able to fire heavy projectiles.
2. Refer to Chapter 8 for a review of the impact of *Scientific American* on the early aviation community.
3. Refer to Chapters 6 and 7 for a review of the Smithsonian's impact on the early work in aeronautics by Samuel Langley and the Wright brothers, and to Appendices 1 and 2 for comments by Dr. Alexander Graham Bell at the Smithsonian in 1913 about their experiments.
4. On July 17, 1969, the day after the launch of Apollo 11 for the moon landing, the *Times* issued a "correction" to its 1920 mocking editorial of Goddard's 1919 treatise. It concluded: "The *Times* regrets the error."
5. Refer to Chapter 13 for a discussion of the Guggenheim family and their contributions to early aviation and research in the United States.
6. Roswell would become famous as the site of the alleged alien space ship crash in 1947.

7. It is known that several score of the 1,750 copies of Goddard's 1920 Smithsonian Report did reach Europe.
8. The F.A.I. awarded Amelia Earhart a "flying certificate" before the U.S. began licensing pilots. See Chapter 13.
9. The Van Allen radiation belts are bands of trapped plasma (charged particles) radiation that surround the earth along the magnetic field. The belts are closely related to the aurora borealis and are capable of damaging earth satellites.
10. Formed in 1915, we first encountered NACA back in Chapter 9.
11. For instance, the International Civil Aviation Organization (ICAO) is a specialized agency of the U.N. Refer to Chapter 37 for the discussion on the creation of ICAO as a result of the Chicago Convention of 1944.
12. The three-mile limit was established by custom and acceptance because that was the distance that a nation could defend its territory from shore by the use of cannon in the 18th century. By the middle of the 20th century, most maritime nations claimed a 12-mile limit in order to extract mineral resources, to protect fish stocks, and as a means to enforce pollution controls.
13. The Soviets shot down the U.S. U-2 reconnaissance aircraft flown by Francis Gary Powers over Soviet territory on May 1, 1960.
14. Grotius was a Dutch philosopher and legal theorist who became known as the "father of international law."
15. At various times, a few nations have attempted to lay claim to the high seas. The Romans claimed the waters of the Mediterranean Sea, the English claimed the North Sea and the English Channel, and Denmark claimed the Baltic Sea. None of these claims could be sustained.
16. COPUOS has never adopted a legal or a scientific definition for "outer space." The scientific evidence is that the maximum altitude of stable aerodynamic flight is considerably lower than the minimum altitude for stable orbital flight. This band of "no man's land" is so wide that a specific altitude denoting the boundary between the atmosphere and outer space would necessarily have to be arbitrary.
17. Refer to Chapter 37 for a review of the Chicago Convention.
18. The South American country of Colombia, on behalf of equatorial states, in 1975 claimed sovereignty over a 5.5 degree segment of the geostationary orbit (GSO). The GSO is the circular orbit in which a spacecraft has an orbital period exactly equal to the period of rotation of the earth. This period, 23 hours, 56 minutes, allows the spacecraft to remain in the same place relative to the earth at all times. The claims of the equatorial countries have been rejected by COPUOS.
19. Uranium 235 and Plutonium 239 are the most practical fuels for space reactors. U-235 is much less harmful than Plutonium 239.
20. The U.S., Canada, Japan, the Russian Federation, and 11 Member States of the European Union (Belgium, Denmark, France, Germany, Italy, the Netherlands, Norway, Spain, Sweden, Switzerland, and the United Kingdom).

21. ESA, the European Space Agency; CSA, the Canadian Space Agency; RKA, the Russian Federal Space Agency; and JAXA, the Japanese Aerospace Exploration Agency

22. NASA contracted with the Brazilian space agency, AEB, for the use of Brazilian equipment on board ISS.

23. For more complete information on all NASA manned space missions see http://history.nasa.gov/humansp.html.

24. Much of the information and text used in this synopsis of the Apollo Program comes from the Apollo Program Summary Report, NASA History Program Office, Part 1 and Part 2, pages i to 2-28 and 2-29 to 3-32, available from the NASA website.

25. Report of the Columbia Accident Investigation Board, from which much of the information of the Shuttle Story is taken.

26. Quoted, John M. Logsdon, "Return to Flight: Richard H. Truly and the Recovery from the *Challenger* Accident."

27. *Columbia* Accident Investigation Board, V. 1, Chapter 9, p. 211, CAIB_medres_full[1].pdf.

28. *Nature*, Volume 472, Issue 7341, April 2011.

29. The NRO is an agency of the Department of Defense and builds and operates the nation's reconnaissance satellites.

30. A geostationary orbit must first be geosynchronous, that is, equal to the earth's rotational period. The difference is that a geosynchronous orbit may or may not be in the equatorial plane. If it is not, it will appear to move above and below the equator (changing latitude location) as viewed from earth, although it will remain at the same line of longitude at all times. A geostationary satellite, however, will remain in the equatorial plane at all times and over the same point on earth at all times. Geostationary satellites have a zero inclination. These two types of orbits are often referred to interchangeably, but incorrectly.

31. NGSO or NGEO satellites are all satellites not in GSO or GEO. LEO satellites orbit from lowest achievable orbit to about 2,400 km, medium earth orbit (MEO) satellites orbit from 2,400 km to GSO.

32. See Figure 41-7 for a full list of launch service providers.

33. The X Prize is titled after Anousheh Ansari, a female Iranian who immigrated to the United States as a teenager, unable to speak English. She gained financial success through her own superior efforts in the computer and technology fields, founding Telecom Technologies in 2001. She became a member of the X Prize Foundation Vision Circle, and in 2006 became the first female private space explorer when she traveled to the International Space Station as part of the Expedition 14 crew.

34. Neil Armstrong was the first human to stand on the moon. Jim Lovell, also on the Apollo 11 crew, was the second.

35. As reported by Fox News on July 5, 2010.

36. http://www.foxnews.com/politics/2010/07/05/ nasa-chief-frontier-better-relations-muslims/ #ixzz24sPua6tq

37. The first three "environments" are land, sea, and air.

APPENDIX 1

Excerpts from the Address of Dr. Alexander Graham Bell in Presenting the Langley Medal to Mr. Gustave Eiffel and to Mr. Glenn Curtiss in 1913

On the sixth of May 1896 a steam engine provided with wings made a successful flight in the air over the Potomac River at Quantico, Virginia about sixty miles from Washington, D.C. There was no man in the machine, yet it pursued its way steadily through the air, continually rising until its power gave out, when its propeller stopped and it descended so gently to the water that it was immediately ready for another flight.

The second flight was equally successful, and though the total distance was not great, barely exceeding one half mile, it succeeded in demonstrating to the world the practicability of mechanical flight by machines heavier than the air and driven by their own motive power.

The production of this machine was really the culminating point of the researches of the late Secretary of the Smithsonian Institution, Dr. Samuel Pierpoint Langley, and the Smithsonian Institution very properly celebrates the sixth of May as "Langley Day."

For many years before 1896 Professor Langley, being assured in his own mind of the practicability of mechanical flight had devoted himself to scientific experiments with aeroplanes, that is, with flat surfaces or planes driven edgeways through the air, at varying angles of incidence to the horizon. In his usage the aeroplanes, while applicable to the wings of a flying machine, was not applicable to the machine itself. The machine as a whole he called an aerodrome, from the Greek work aerodromos, "traversing the air." In the terminology employed by him aerodromics is the art of traversing the air—the art of aerial locomotion; and an aerodrome was a machine for traversing the air.

The knowledge that so eminent a man as the Secretary of the Smithsonian Institution, believed in the possibility of mechanical flight and was carrying on scientific experiments to attain that end, proved a great stimulus and encouragement to many less eminent men who were working along the same lines under the discouragement and ridicule from the incredulous world . . . I was the only witness of this remarkable flight outside of the workmen employed. I may perhaps be pardoned for saying a few words about it. Professor Langley had met with so many failures that, though hopeful, he was somewhat doubtful of the result, and he invited me to witness the experiment on the condition that I was the only man he knew whom he could bear to be a witness of a failure.

I found a houseboat containing all his apparatus anchored in the little Bay of Quantico and, on the roof, his machine was arranged ready to be shot off by a huge catapult. It was a huge model, thirteen feet from tip to tip, . . . and sixteen feet from head to tail, the whole propelled by a wonderfully light steam engine of Professor Langley's own design.

I had a boy row me out on the bay where I thought I could get a good snapshot of the machine when it leaped into the air, while Professor Langley, too nervous to be close to the scene of operations, retreated to the shore, and I saw him standing lonely on the end of a little pier with the wooded shore behind him.

Then the whirr of the propellers was heard and the catapult was released causing the machine to shoot out into the air almost horizontally. Then came the critical moment. Would it fall into the water? Would it strike against the trees that surrounded the bay? Or would it ascend and clear them? The queries were soon answered. For the huge bird-like machine gracefully soared from twenty to thirty feet above the tops of the trees, turning slightly as it rose, and made a beautiful flight of over half-a-mile, when the steam was exhausted the propellers stopped and it began to come down.

The descent was as fascinating as the ascent, and it glided gracefully to the surface of the water. The workmen employed hailed the success of the experiment with loud cheers, in which I joined. It was picked up and found to be practically uninjured except for a wetting. The experiment was then repeated with even greater success than before.

The prophecy received its fulfillment but not until the beginning of the twentieth century. In 1898 the Board of Ordinance & Fortification, after carefully studying the flight of 1896, appropriated $50,000 to enable Langley to experiment with a full sized aerodrome carrying a man. This was not completed until 1903, and on August 8 of that year a quarter-sized model of it propelled by a gasoline engine made a beautiful public flight.

On September 7, 1903, the full-sized aerodrome, carrying Mr. F. W. Manley, as aviator, was tried on the Potomac, but when the catapult was released, the aerodrome sped along the track on the top of the houseboat attaining sufficient headway for normal flight; but at the end of the rails it was jerked violently down at the front, and plunged headlong into the river. It was subsequently discovered that the guy post that strengthened the front pair of wings had caught in the launching ways, and bent so much that those wings lost all support.

A second launching was attempted on the Potomac River near Washington, on December 8, 1903. This time the rear guy post was injured, crippling the rear wings, so that the aerodrome pitched up in front and plunged over backwards into the water. Fortunately the aviator, Mr. Manly, received no injury in either case.

It will thus be seen that Langley's aerodrome was never successfully launched, so that it had no opportunity of showing what it could do in the air. The defect lay in the launching mechanism employed and not in the machine itself, which is recognized by all experts as a perfectly good flying machine, excellently constructed and made long before the appearance of other machines.

Langley's efforts at aviation were received with public ridicule, and he found it impossible to obtain the necessary funds to try the experiment again. Professor Langley was of a very sensitive nature and the public ridicule with which his efforts were received had a good deal to do with the illness which caused his death. Not very long after the accident he received a paralytic stroke, and after partially recovering from this, another stroke ended his life in 1906. . . .

The second and last trial of Langley's aerodrome occurred December 8, 1903, and on December 17 of that same year, the Wright brothers made their first flight in their gliding machine provided with a 16 HP engine and two screw propellers. Little or nothing was known of this flight by the general public. The Wright brothers removed their machine to Dayton, Ohio. During 1904 and 1905 numerous flights were made in Dayton, Ohio, culminating in a flight of eleven miles on September 26, 1905. These were all in secret. After this, field practice with them ceased for more than two years to enable them to preserve the secrecy which they had hitherto maintained.

A few statements concerning their success leaked out into the public press, but were generally received with incredulity and unbelief.

A competent scientific investigator was sent from France to Dayton, Ohio to investigate the truth of the rumors that had appeared in the newspapers of success that had found their way into the press. He was unable to obtain any definite information concerning the trials that had been made, but by interviewing the neighboring farmers he was able to satisfy himself that flights had actually been made, and so reported to his principals in France, and it was from France that America received the first authentic news that the Wright brothers had actually flown.

Then M. Archdeacon stirred up the patriotic spirit of the French, not to be beaten by America, and offered his prize . . . of FF3000 to be awarded to the first person who should sail or fly twenty-five meters, under certain conditions.

The whole art of aerial locomotion originated in France. In 1783, the Montgolfiers produced the balloon, their hot air balloon, and in the same year M. Charles and the Brothers Roberts gave us the hydrogen balloon. After the lapse of 100 years, Nadar issued his celebrated manifesto in which he advocated the heavier than air flying machine, rather than the balloon, and started the controversy between the lighter-than-air and the heavier-than-air camps, which has lasted to our day, and is not settled yet. . . .

On August 22, 1906, M. Santos-Dumont made a tentative flight in his new "aeromobile," and on October 23, 1906 he ran this strange machine swiftly over the ground and glided boldly into the air, flying above the excited spectators at a speed of twenty-five miles an hour, and covering a distance of two hundred feet, thus gaining the Archdeacon Cup.

This was the first public flight in the world, made without any certain knowledge of the previous secret flights made by the Wright brothers in America.

From this time the French have been feverishly active in the field of aviation. In October 1907 the Aerial Experiment Association was organized with the object of constructing a practical aerodrome, driven through the air by its own motive power, and carrying a man. This was a mere experimental association, financed by my wife, and consisting of the late Lt. Selfridge, Mr. F. W. Baldwin, Mr. Glenn H. Curtiss, Mr. J. A. D. McCurdy and myself. On March 12, 1908, the Association succeeded in raising its first aerodrome, the Red Wing, into the air from the ice on Lake Keuka, near Hammondsport, N.Y. Mr. F. W. Baldwin was the aviator on this occasion, which constituted the first public flight of an aerodrome in America. The Wright brothers, of course, had previously flown, but nothing was known with certainty at that time concerning their achievements. Then in that same year, 1908, the Wright brothers for the first time appeared publicly in flight. Wilbur Wright in Europe, and Orville Wright in America, startled the world with their achievements, and proved themselves to be the master of their art. . . .

APPENDIX 2

Excerpts from Remarks of Dr. Alexander Graham Bell before the Board of Regents of the Smithsonian Institution on February 13, 1913 on the Award of the Langley Medal

Since the award of the Langley Medal to the Wright brothers three years ago, there has been great activity in the field of aviation. The war departments of the different nations have been constantly at work, but little is known concerning the character of the advances made. So far as the public are aware the chief progress has related to details of construction and improvement in motive power. The advance has been much greater in the *art* than in the *science*.

There has, however, been considerable advance in the science of aerodromics along the lines laid down by our late Secretary, Dr. S. P. Langley, and by M. Gustave Eiffel, Director of the Eiffel Aero-Dynamical Laboratory in Paris.

In 1907 M/Eiffel published the results of experiments made at the Eiffel Tower; in 1911, he published the results of his experiment at the aerodynamic laboratory in Paris on the resistance of the air in connection with aviation, and these results have been of great value to aerial engineers in designing and construction flying machines. Indeed his works upon the subject have already become classical. . . .

In spite of the great advances that have been made in the art of aerodromics we are confronted with a long list of fatalities to aviators, for whose protection there remains a great deal yet to be done. There has been one very notable development in this direction, made by an American, Mr. Glenn R. Curtiss of Hammondsport, N.Y.

In 1908, the Aerial Experiment Association, of which Mr. Curtiss was a member, discussed the advisability of have flying machines so constructed as to enable them to float, and to rise from the water into the air, as an element of safety. In pursuance of these ideas, the Association's aerodrome No. 3, the "Curtiss June Bug" was attached to pontoons and an experiment was made on Lake Keuka on November 6, 1908. Although the speed on the water appeared to be satisfactory, the machine failed to rise in the air, but the occasion formed the starting point for Mr. Curtiss' independent researches.

After the dissolution of the Association, March 31, 1909, Mr. Curtiss continued his experiments to find a practical solution of the problem, and in May 1910, he made that remarkable flight from Albany to New York City over the Hudson River, a distance of 152 miles in 2 hours 52 minutes, with two light pontoons attached to his machine, to enable it to float should it come down into the water.

In 1911 Mr. Curtiss continued his efforts to construct a machine that would not only float, but would rise from the water into the air, and in January 1912, he succeeded in doing this in San Diego Bay, California. "On January 26, 1912" he says "the first success came": and on January 27, 1912, the Aero Club of America awarded him the Collier Trophy for his accomplishment.

In February 1912, he demonstrated the use to the Navy of such machines by flying to the U.S. Armored Cruiser "Pennsylvania" . . . alighting in the water beside the vessel. The machine was hoisted up on the vessel's deck, and then again lowered into the water without damage, showing the possibility of handling such machines without special equipment. He then rose from the water and flew back to the starting point.

By July 1912, he had developed the remarkable machine he calls "the flying boat," which represents the greatest advance yet made along these lines. It develops great speed upon the water and also in the air, and is equally at home in either element. The world is now following Mr. Curtiss' lead in the development of flying machines of this type.

Great experience in the handling of aerial machines is necessary before aviators can safely make extended flight over land, where a fall might be fatal. The successful development of the hydro-aerodrome now enables this experience to be gained over water without serious danger to life or limb; and marks a notable advance in the direction of safety that might well be recognized by the Smithsonian Institution by the award of a Langley Medal to Mr. Glenn M. Curtiss.

APPENDIX 3

The 1914 Tests of the Langley "Aerodrome"[1]

By C. G. ABBOT
Secretary, Smithsonian Institution

NOTE—This paper has been submitted to Dr. Orville Wright, and under date of October 8, 1942, he states that the paper as now prepared will be acceptable to him if given adequate publication.

It is everywhere acknowledged that the Wright brothers were the first to make sustained flights in a heavier-than-air machine at Kitty Hawk, North Carolina, on December 17, 1903.

Mainly because of acts and statements of former officers of the Smithsonian Institution, arising from tests made with the reconditioned Langley plane of 1903 at Hammondsport, New York, in 1914, Dr. Orville Wright feels that the Institution adoped an unfair and injurious attitude. He therefore sent the original Wright Kitty Hawk plane to England in 1928. The nature of the acts and statements referred to are as follows:

In March 1914, Secretary Walcott contracted with Glenn H. Curtiss to attempt a flight with the Langley machine. This action seems ill considered and open to criticism. For in January 1914, the United States Court of Appeals, Second Circuit, had handed down a decision recognizing the Wrights as "pioneers in the practical art of flying

with heavier-than-air machines" and pronouncing Glenn H. Curtiss an infringer of their patent. Hence, in view of probable further litigation, the Wrights stood to lose in fame and revenue and Curtiss stood to gain pecuniarily, should the experiments at Hammondsport indicate that Langley's plane was capable of sustained flight in 1903, previous to the successful flights made December 17, 1903, by the Wrights at Kitty Hawk, N. C.

The machine was shipped to Curtiss at Hammondsport, N. Y. in April. Dr. Zahm, the Recorder of the Langley Aerodynamical Laboratory and expert witness for Curtiss in the patent litigation, was at Hammondsport as official representative of the Smithsonian Institution during the time the machine was being reconstructed and tested. In the reconstruction the machine was changed from what it was in 1903 in a number of particulars as given in Dr. Wright's list of differences which appears later in this paper. On the 28th of May and the 2d of June, 1914, attempts to fly were made. After acquiring speed by running on hydroplane floats on the surface of Lake

Abbot, C. G. 1942. *The 1914 Tests of the Langley "Aerodrome."* Smithsonian Miscellaneous Collections, 103:8. Washington, D.C.: Smithsonian Institution. (Document supplied to the author by Dr. Larry Jenkins.)

Keuka the machine lifted into the air several different times. The longest time off the water with the Langley motor was approximately five seconds. Dr. Zahm stated that "it was apparent that owing to the great weight which had been given to the structure by adding the floats it was necessary to increase the propeller thrust". So no further attempts were made to fly with the Langley 52 HP engine.

It is to be regretted that the Institution published statements repeatedly[2] to the effect that these experiments of 1914 demonstrated that Langley's plane of 1903 without essential modification was the first heavier-than-air machine capable of maintaining sustained human flight.

As first exhibited in the United States National Museum, January 15, 1918, the restored Langley plane of 1903 bore the following label:

The Original, Full-Size Langley Flying Machine, 1903

For this simple label others were later substituted containing the claim that Langley's machine "was the first man-carrying aeroplane in the history of the world capable of sustained free flight."

Though the matter of the label is not now an issue, it seems only fair to the Institution to say that in September 1928, Secretary Abbot finally caused the label of the Langley machine to be changed to read simply as follows:

Langley Aerodrome

The Original Samuel Pierpont Langley Flying Machine of 1903, Restored

Deposited by The Smithsonian Institution

301,613

This change has frequently been overlooked by writers on the controversy.

In January 1942, Mr. Fred C. Kelly, of Peninsula, Ohio, communicated to me a list of differences between the Langley plane as tested in 1914 and as tested in 1903, which he had received from Dr. Wright. This list is given verbatim below. The Institution accepts Dr. Wright's statement as correct in point of facts. Inferences from the comparisons are primarily the province of interested experts and are not discussed here.

Comparison of the Langley Machine of 1903 with the Hammondsport Machine of May-June, 1914

Langley, 1903.	Hammondsport, 1914.
Wings.	
1 SIZE: 11'6" × 22'6" (L.M. p. 206)	SIZE: 10'11¾" × 22'6"
2 AREA: 1040 sq. ft. (L.M. p. 206)	AREA: 988 sq. ft.
3 ASPECT RATIO: 1.96	ASPECT RATIO: 2.05
4 CAMBER: 1/12 (L.M. p. 205)	CAMBER: 1/18
5 LEADING EDGE: Wire 1/16" diameter (L.M. P1.66)	LEADING EDGE: Cylindrical spar 1½" dia. at inner end, tapering to 1" dia. at outer end.
6 COVERING: Cotton fabric, not varnished.	COVERING: Cotton fabric, varnished.

Langley, 1903.	Hammondsport, 1914.

Wings.

7 CENTER SPAR: Cylindrical wooden spar, measuring 1½" dia. for half its length and tapering to 1" at its tip. (L.M. p. 204). Located on upper side of wing.	CENTER SPAR: Cylindrical spar about 1½" dia. at inner end, tapering to about 1" dia. at outer end. Located on upper side of wing. This center spar was reinforced (1) by an extra wooden member on the under side of the wing, which measured 1" × 1½" and extended to the 7th rib from the center of the machine; and (2) by another wooden reinforcement on the under side extending out about one-fourth of the length of the wing.
8 RIBS: Hollow box construction. (L. M. Plates 66,67)	RIBS: Most of the original Langley box ribs were replaced with others made at Hammondsport. (Manly letter, 1914). The Hammondsport ribs were of solid construction and made of laminated wood. That part of the rib in front of the forward spar was entirely omitted.
9 LOWER GUY-POSTS: A single round wooden post for each pair of wings (see Fig. 3), 1¼" in dia. 6½' long. (L.M. Plate 62, p. 184).	LOWER GUY-POSTS: Four for each pair of wings (see Fig. 4), two of which were of streamline form measuring 1¼" × 3½" × 54" long; and two measuring 2" × 2" with rounded corners, 3'9" long.
10 The front wing guy-post was located 28½" in front of the main center spar. (L.M. Plate 53).	The front wing guy-posts were located directly underneath the main center spar, 28½" further rearward than in 1903.
11 The rear wing guy-post was located 31½" in front of the main center spar. (L.M. Plate 53).	The rear wing guy-posts were located directly under the main center spar, 31½" further rearward than in 1903.
12 UPPER GUY-POSTS: For each pair of wings a single steel tube ¾" dia., 43" long. (L.M. p. 184, pl. 62).	UPPER GUY-POSTS: For each pair of wings, two streamline wooden posts each 1¼" × 3½", 76" long, forming an inverted V. (See Fig. 4).
13 Front wing upper guy-post located 28½" in front of the main center spar. (L.M. pl. 53).	Front wing upper guy-posts located directly over main spar, 28½" further rearward than in 1903.
14 The rear wing upper guy-post was located 31½" in front of the main center spar. (L.M. pl. 53).	The rear wing guy-posts were located directly over the main center spar, 31½" further rearward than in 1903.
15 TRUSSING: The wing trussing wires were attached to the spars at the 5th, 7th and 9th ribs out from the center (L.M. pl. 54). The angles between these wires and the spars to which they were attached are shown in Fig. 3.	TRUSSING: A different system of wing trussing was used, and the wing trussing wires were attached to the spars at the 3rd, 6th and 9th ribs from the center. The angles between these wires and the spars to which they were attached were all different from those in the original Langley machine. (See Fig. 4).

(continued)

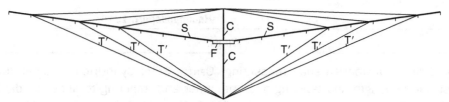

FIGURE 1 Langley Wing Trussing 1903.

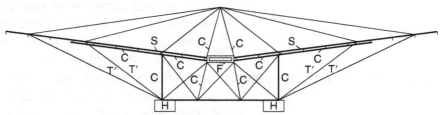

FIGURE 2 Hammondsport Wing Trussing 1914.

Langley, 1903.   **Hammondsport, 1914.**

Control Surfaces.

16 VANE RUDDER: A split vane composed of two surfaces united at their leading edges and separated 15" at their trailing edges, thus forming a wedge. Each surface measured 2'3" × 4'6", with aspect ratio .5. (L.M. p. 214, pls. 53,54).

VERTICAL RUDDER: The Langley vane rudder was replaced by a single plane vertical rudder which measured 3'6" × 5', with aspect ratio of .7.

17 Operated by means of a wheel located slightly in front of the pilot at his right side and at the height of his shoulder (L.M. p. 216, pls. 53,54).

Operated at Hammondsport through the Curtiss steering wheel in some tests, (Zahm affidavit pp. 5, 6), through the Curtiss shoulder yoke in some others (Manly letter, 1914), and fixed so as not to be operable at all in still others, (Zahm affidavit p. 7).

18 Used for steering only. (L.M. p. 214).

Used "as a vertical aileron to control the lateral poise of the machine", (Zahm affidavit p. 6) as well as for steering, (Zahm affidavit p. 7).

19 PENAUD TAIL: This was a dart-shaped tail having a vertical and a horizontal surface (Penaud tail), each measuring 95 sq. ft. It was located in the rear of the main frame.

TAIL RUDDER: Same size and construction as in 1903.

20 Attached to a bracket extending below the main frame.

Attached to same bracket at a point about 8" higher than in 1903.

21 "Normally inactive", (L. M. p. 216) but adjustable about a transverse horizontal axis by means of a self-locking wheel located at the right side of the pilot, even with his back, and at the height of his shoulder. (L.M. pls. 51, 53).

Operable about a transverse horizontal axis and connected to a regular Curtiss elevator control post directly in front of the pilot (Zahm affidavit p. 5).

Langley, 1903.	Hammondsport, 1914.

Control Surfaces (continued).

22 Immovable about a vertical axis. (L.M. p. 214, pl.56, Fig. 1). No means were provided for adjusting this rudder about a vertical axis in flight. "Although it was necessary that the large aerodrome should be capable of being steered in a horizontal direction, it was felt to be unwise to give the Penaud tail and rudder motion in the horizontal plane in order to attain this end". (L.M. p. 214).

Immovable about a vertical axis on May 28, 1914, only. Thereafter it was made movable about a vertical axis and was connected through cables to a Curtiss steering wheel mounted on a Curtiss control post directly in front of the pilot.

23 Keel: A fixed vertical surface underneath the main frame measuring 3'2" in height by 6' average length. Area 19 sq. ft. (L.M. pl. 53).

Keel: Entirely omitted.

System of Control.

24 Lateral Stability: The dihedral only was used for maintaining lateral balance. (L.M. p. 45).

Lateral Stability: Three means were used for securing lateral balance at Hammondsport: The dihedral angle as used by Langley, a rudder which "serves as a vertical aileron" (Zahm affidavit p. 6), and the Penaud tail rudder. The last two constituted a system "identical in principle with that of Complainant's [Wright] combined warping of the wings and the use of the vertical rudder". (Zahm affidavit p. 6).

25 Longitudinal Stability: Langley relied upon the Penaud system of inherent stability for maintaining the longitudinal equilibrium. "For the preservation of the equilibrium [longitudinal] of the aerodrome, though the aviator might assist by such slight movements as he was able to make in the limited space of the aviator's car, the main reliance was upon the Penaud tail." (L.M. p. 215).

Longitudinal Stability: At Hammondsport the Penaud inherent longitudinal stability was supplemented with an elevator system of control.

26 Steering: Steering in the horizontal plane was done entirely by the split-vane steering rudder located underneath the main frame. (L.M. p. 214).

Steering: On one day, May 28, 1914, steering in the horizontal plane was done with the vertical rudder which had been substituted for the original Langley split-vane steering rudder. After May 28th the steering was done by the vertical surface of the tail rudder (Zahm affidavit p. 7), which in 1903 was immovable about a vertical axis, (L.M. p. 214).

(continued)

Langley, 1903.	Hammondsport, 1914.
Power Plant.	
27 MOTOR: Langley 5 cylinder radial.	MOTOR: Langley motor modified.
28 IGNITION: Jump spark with dry cell batteries. (L.M. p. 262).	IGNITION: Jump spark with magneto.
29 CARBURETOR: Balzer carburetor consisting of a chamber filled with lumps of porous cellular wood saturated with gasoline. The air was drawn through this wood. There was no float feed. (L.M. p. 225).	CARBURETOR: Automobile type with float feed.
30 RADIATOR: Tubes with radiating fins.	RADIATOR: Automobile radiator of honeycomb type.
31 PROPELLERS: Langley propellers (L.M. pl.53, pp. 178–182).	PROPELLERS: Langley propellers modified "after fashion of early Wright blades".
Launching and Floats.	
32 LAUNCHING: Catapult mounted on a houseboat.	LAUNCHING: Hydroplanes, developed 1909-1914, attached to the machine.
33 FLOATS: Five cylindrical tin floats, with conical ends, attached to underside of main frame at appropriate points, and about six feet above lowest part of machine.	FLOATS: Two wooden hydroplane floats, mounted beneath and about 6 feet to either side of the center of the machine at the lateral extremities of the Pratt system of trussing used for bracing the wing spars of the forward wings; and one (part of the time two) tin cylindrical floats with conical ends, similar to but larger than the Langley floats, mounted at the center of the Pratt system of trussing used for bracing the rear wings. All of the floats were mounted from four to five feet lower than the floats of the original Langley, thus keeping the entire machine above the water.
Weight.	
34 TOTAL WEIGHT: With pilot 850 pounds (L.M. p. 256).	TOTAL WEIGHT: With pilot, 1170 pounds.
35 CENTER GRAVITY: 3/8" above line of thrust.	CENTER GRAVITY: About one foot below line of thrust.

Since I became Secretary, in 1928, I have made many efforts to compose the Smithsonian-Wright controversy, which I inherited. I will now, speaking for the Smithsonian Institution, make the following statement in an attempt to correct as far as now possible acts and assertions of former Smithsonian officials that may have been misleading or are held to be detrimental to the Wrights.

1. I sincerely regret that the Institution employed to make the tests of 1914 an agent who had been an unsuccessful defendant in patent litigation brought against him by the Wrights.

2. I sincerely regret that statements were repeatedly made by officers of the Institution that the Langley machine was flown in 1914 "with certain changes of the machine necessary to use pontoons", without mentioning the other changes included in Dr. Wright's list.

3. I point out that Assistant Secretary Rathbun was misinformed when he stated that the Langley machine "without modification" made "successful flights".

4. I sincerely regret the public statement by officers of the Institution that "The tests" [of 1914] showed "that the late Secretary Langley had succeeded in building the first aeroplane capable of sustained free flight with a man."

5. Leaving to experts to formulate the conclusions arising from the 1914 tests as a whole, in view of all the facts, I repeat in substance, but with amendments, what I have already published in Smithsonian Scientific Series, Vol. 12, 1932, page 227:

    The flights of the Langley aerodrome at Hammondsport in 1914, having been made long after flying had become a common art, and with changes of the machine indicated by Dr. Wright's comparison as given above, did not warrant the statements published by the Smithsonian Institution that these tests proved that the large Langley machine of 1903 was capable of sustained flight carrying a man.

6. If the publication of this paper should clear the way for Dr. Wright to bring back to America the Kitty Hawk machine to which all the world awards first place, it will be a source of profound and enduring gratification to his countrymen everywhere. Should he decide to deposit the plane in the United States National Museum, it would be given the highest place of honor, which is its due.

Endnotes

1. For an account of early Langley and Wright aeronautical investigations, see Smithsonian Report for 1900 and The Century Magazine of September 1908.

2. Smithsonian Reports: 1914, pp. 9, 219, 221, 222; 1915, pp. 14, 121; 1917, p. 4; 1918, pp. 3, 28, 114, 166. Report of U. S. National Museum, 1914, pp. 46 and 47.

APPENDIX 4

Blazing the Trail to Chicago

The first person account of the original survey flight from New York to Chicago on September 5, 1918, made to determine the feasibility of carrying airmail between those two cities, by Max Miller, Aerial Mail Pilot No. 1. Miller died on September 1, 1920 when his mail plane caught fire in the air and crashed.

Blazing the air trail to Chicago would have been a "cinch" if I had started at 6 A.M. on September 5th, as had been planned. This would have enabled me to start one hour ahead of the storm, and I could have reached Chicago by evening without trouble.

I left Belmont Field, Long Island, at 7:08 A.M., with a good wind in back of me, flew over the City of New York, the Hudson River and Hoboken, and headed west 284 degrees.

There was a bank of low clouds near the ground and another layer of clouds at a high altitude. I kept right between them and flew on my compass course. I could not see the ground, but ran for about two hours and at ten o'clock I came down through the lower strata of clouds and landed one mile from Danville, N.Y., about 155 miles from New York City. There I inquired to find out my bearings and found that I was not more than two miles out of my course. I did not kill the motor, but left it running, and after five minutes started up again and headed for Lock Haven.

I entered the fog which hung low over the ground and over the tops of the mountains, and I figured that it would take me about three-quarters of an hour to make Lock Haven. I came down and saw the field through a notch in the mountains and made a good landing. My motor was missing, so I changed spark plugs which took me about an hour, filled up with oil and gas, got a couple of sandwiches, and left about 11:45 A.M.

I climbed up through the fog again and went on over the mountains. I sailed on my compass course for an hour, 283 degrees, and I figured I was about 100 miles further on. Then I came down to see where I was and get my bearings, and the first thing I knew I hit the top of a tree. That sure gave me a good scare. I hustled back up again into the fog, determined to get plenty of altitude and keep on going as long as my gas held out.

I went fifty miles, and then I found my radiator was leaking and I came down and I saw a town with a fair going on. There was such a mob of people that I did not land there, but went on about twenty miles to a town named Cambridge. I inquired where I was and was told "Jefferson." On looking on my map I found a town called Jefferson lying to the north of my route, so on leaving I headed toward the south in order to cross the route again; but I found that it was Jefferson Country, PA, instead of the town of Jefferson, Ohio, and I went about 150 miles out of my way before reaching Cleveland, where I had to remain all night on account of darkness.

The next morning I got my radiator fixed and rested up after being buffeted about by the storm and rain, and got away at 1:35 P.M. for Bryan on the compass course of 275 degrees, a little south of due west about 140 miles. I had to stop several times to fill up my radiator with water. The weather was very much better, and I was able to make Bryan, where I was received by Postmaster Jordan and got away at 4:35 P.M. I skirted the southern shore of Lake Michigan and arrived over Grant Park at an altitude of 5,000 feet at 6:55 P.M.

I circled around and made a good landing and was received by Postmaster Wm. B. Carlile, Mr. Chas. Dickenson, President of the Aero Club of Illinois, Capt. B. B. Lipsner, Superintendent of Aerial Mail Service, Mr. Thos. Downey, Assistant Superintendent of Mails, Mr. James O'Conner, Director of the U.S. War Exposition, Mr. James Stevens, Secretary of the Aero Club of Illinois, and Mr. Augustus Post, Secretary of the Aero Club of America, who had come on from New York to witness the inauguration of the first aero mail service between New York and Chicago.

The weather on the return trip was much better. I started from Chicago on September 10, at 6:26 A.M. I carried about three thousand pieces of mail. The weather looked so good that I expected to make a record trip. There was some haze on the ground, but not nearly enough to prevent landmarks being distinct. Just as I was over Cleveland, I found a broken connection in the radiator and I landed there to get it repaired.

This took some time, but I got away from there by 4:30 P.M., in time to make a pleasant flight to Lock Haven, one of the scheduled stops, before dark, a distance of 210 miles. I stayed at Lock Haven all night, leaving there at 7:20 A.M. As a path finding trip it was an immense success. We gathered a lot of information which will be very valuable in the future trips.

The radiator trouble was the only thing that prevented me from making the trip within the ten hours set. If I had had a spare aeroplane even, I could have done it. We will, of course, have spare machines for the permanent route, so it will not happen again.

APPENDIX 5

Excerpts from Lindbergh's Log of His Solo Flight from New York to Paris

◼ New York to Paris

Charles Lindbergh was already being treated like something of a celebrity even before he departed New York for Paris. He and the Spirit of St. Louis had been ready to fly since Monday, May 16, 1927, but the weather was dreadful in New York and points north. Since his arrival in New York he had been feted and greeted by dignitaries ranging from William McCracken, the Assistant Secretary of Commerce for Aeronautics to Harry Guggenheim, Tony Fokker, Rene Fonck, C. M. Keyes of the Curtiss Company, Charlie Lawrance, the air-cooled radial engine pioneer, and Theodore Roosevelt, Jr.

The press had been pushy and ever-present, and the week had been very tiring. On Thursday, the 19th, Lindbergh visited the Wright factory in Paterson, New Jersey, and attended the theater that night, including a trip backstage. He did not arrive at his hotel until after midnight, and he was scheduled to arise at 3:00 A.M. to go out to Roosevelt Field to make the final decision for takeoff as weather had been reported improved. He was too keyed up to sleep.

In the pre-dawn gloom of Roosevelt Field on Friday, May 20, 1927, the clouds hung low and a light rain was falling. The weather was reported as still improving, and a high-pressure area is moving in over the North Atlantic. After the Spirit of St. Louis is towed into takeoff position and fueled, the wind shifts to a tailwind. The engine on run-up is thirty revolutions low due to the weather, the mechanic said.

As Lindbergh himself explains the situation:

Plane ready; engine ready; earth-inductor compass set on course. The long, narrow runway stretches out ahead. Over the telephone wires at its end lies the Atlantic Ocean; and beyond that, mythical as the rainbow's pot of gold, Europe and Paris. This is the moment I've planned for, day and night, all these months past. The decision is mine. No other man can take that responsibility. The mechanics, the engineers, the blue-uniformed police officers standing there behind the wing, everyone has done his part. Now, it's up to me.

Their eyes are intently on mine. They've seen planes crash before. They know what a wrong decision means. If I shake my head, there'll be no complaint, no criticism; I'll be welcomed back into their midst, back to earth and life; for we are separated by something more than the few yards that lie between us. It seems almost the difference between the future and the past, to be decided by a movement of my head. A shake, and we'll be laughing and joking together, laying new plans, plodding over the wet grass toward hot coffee and a warm breakfast—all men of the earth. A nod, and we'll be separated—perhaps forever.[1]

The Flight

7:52 A.M. Takeoff from Roosevelt Field, Long Island, New York. Mud, rain, and fog complicate the departure. Lindbergh clears telephone wires at the end of the runway by only 20 feet.

8:52 A.M. Over Rhode Island, 100 miles from Roosevelt Field, 3500 miles to go. Altitude 600 feet; Airspeed 102 miles per hour; Ceiling 2000 feet; Visibility 5 miles; True course 51 degrees; Compass course 63 degrees.

9:52 A.M. Between Boston and Cape Cod. Altitude 150 feet; Ceiling 4000 feet; Visibility unlimited; Airspeed 107 miles per hour; True course 56 degrees; Compass course 70 degrees.

10:52 A.M. Over water. Burning 16 gallons of gasoline per hour. Altitude 50 feet; Ceiling unlimited; Airspeed 104 miles per hour; True course 57 degrees; Compass course 73 degrees.

11:52 A.M. Approaching Nova Scotia. Altitude 200 feet; Airspeed 103 miles per hour; True course 58 degrees; Compass course 78 degrees. He is six miles southeast of course.

12:52 P.M. Over Nova Scotia. Wind is 30 miles per hour from the West forcing a crab correction of 15 degrees. Altitude 700 feet; Airspeed 102 miles per hour; True course 60 degrees; Compass course 82 degrees. Storm clouds are forming.

1:52 P.M. Beginning the seventh hour, over Nova Scotia. 3000 miles to go. Altitude 900 feet; Ceiling 1500 broken; Airspeed 101 miles per hour; True course 61 degrees; Compass course 84 degrees.

2:52 P.M. Still over Nova Scotia. Altitude 600 feet; Airspeed 96 miles per hour; True course 64 degrees; Compass course 89 degrees. Storm recedes to the North. Lindbergh sees fog, his most dreaded condition, directly ahead.

3:52 P.M. Leaving Cape Breton Island for a 200 miles stretch of water to Newfoundland. Altitude 500 feet; Airspeed 94 miles per hour; True course 64 degrees; Compass Course 91 degrees. Lindbergh is fighting the urge to sleep. Sleep is winning.

4:52 P.M. Over ice fields in the Atlantic. Altitude 150 feet; Airspeed 95 miles per hour; True course 73 degrees; Compass course 102 degrees. Lindbergh has trouble holding course, causing repeated corrections.

5:52 P.M. Placentia Bay, along the southeastern coast of Newfoundland. Altitude 300 feet; Airspeed 92 miles per hour; True course 70 degrees; Compass course 100 degrees.

6:52 P.M. Sunset over Newfoundland. Altitude 700 feet; Airspeed 98 miles per hour; True course 68 degrees; Compass course 99 degrees. Lindbergh has covered 1100 miles in 11 hours, exactly. Never before has an airplane overflown Newfoundland without landing. Lindbergh leaves the continent of North America.

7:52 P.M. Over an iceberg laden Atlantic. Altitude 800 feet; Airspeed 90 miles per hour; True course 65 degrees; Compass course 97 degrees. Fog below and 5 miles visibility above. Lindbergh begins a climb to 7500 feet to stay out of clouds. He figures he has a strong tailwind.

8:52 P.M.   Nighttime over the Atlantic. Altitude 9300 feet; Airspeed 90 miles per hour; True course 66 degrees; Compass course 99 degrees. During the next hour Lindbergh will be forced into towering clouds where he will begin to pick up ice at 10500 feet. He sets a limit of 15000 feet as his maximum altitude to escape clouds. He considers descending into warmer air.

9:52 P.M.   Clear of clouds in haze, cloud formations farther away. Altitude 10500 feet; Airspeed 87 miles per hour; True course 66 degrees; Compass course 99 degrees. The moon begins to rise.

10:52 P.M.   Altitude 10200 feet; Airspeed 86 miles per hour; True course 69 degrees; Compass course 99 degrees. Now 1500 miles from New York, 2100 miles to go. Lindbergh is losing the battle to stay awake. He is still angling on a northward course on the great circle route. Soon the course will turn southward. Lindbergh starts confusing stars overhead with the lights of non-existent ships at sea.

11:52 P.M.   Altitude 10000 feet; Airspeed 90 miles per hour; True course 70 degrees; Compass course 103 degrees. Clear above clouds.

12:52 A.M.   Closer now to Europe than America. Altitude 9600 feet; Airspeed 88 miles per hour; True course 72 degrees; Compass course 106 degrees. High thin overcast. Lindbergh only wants sleep, nothing else. Yet he realizes

that sleep means death and failure. He must be intermittently sleeping: He makes repeated course corrections in excess of 10 degrees in both directions.

1:52 A.M.   1800 miles to Paris. Altitude 9000; Airspeed 87 miles per hour; Lindbergh fails to record his true course or his compass course. Lindbergh begins to wonder what difference a few degrees can make. Figuring out his new heading is beyond his resolve and his ability. Suddenly, he realizes that it is daylight again.

2:52 A.M.   Beginning the 20th hour. Altitude 8800 feet; Airspeed 89 miles per hour; Ceiling: flying between cloud layers. True course and compass course not recorded. The altimeter has not been reset since Newfoundland, by flying close to the water. That was 8 hours ago. He descends to near sea level and determines that he has a quartering tailwind there. But he encounters fog and begins a climb to 1500 feet. He frequently loses control of the airplane as he fights sleep, but recovers each time.

During the   Lindbergh misses the 3:52 A.M. log entry. He reasons that it's not worth the effort anyway. He is so tired that he cannot both control the airplane and make entries in the log. He has energy enough only to fly the airplane and keep track of fuel management.

21st hour.   The Spirit of St. Louis has 5 fuel tanks: a nose tank, a fuselage tank, a left wing tank, a center wing tank, and a right wing tank. He switches tanks hourly.

4:52 A.M.   Still on instruments. He wonders what happened to the forecast high-pressure area that was supposed to be over the North Atlantic. His log entries are confined to fuel management. Over and over again he falls asleep with his eyes open, knowing all the time this is what's happening, but unable to prevent it. (p. 387) He finds himself just above the mountainous ocean waves, flying in salt spray form the wave tops. He climbs.

6:05 A.M.   The 23rd hour. No entries again. What difference does it make, he wonders. No entries in the log for over 3 hours. Lindbergh flies above, below and between layers of clouds.

The 24th

hour.

Lindbergh decides to abandon any further effort to keep his log. He figures that he is 2300 miles from New York, 1300 miles from Paris, and maybe 700 miles from Ireland. But he is beginning to realize that he can no longer accurately deal with figures.

Endnote

1. The Spirit of St. Louis, p. 182.

APPENDIX 6

Women in Early Aviation

Women had been involved in aviation, in one way or another, since Elisabeth Thible of Lyons, France, went aloft in a hot air balloon in 1784. By 1834, some twenty-two women had piloted their own balloons on the continent of Europe. In 1886, Mary H. Myers set an altitude record of over 20,000 feet (without oxygen) in a balloon above the fields of rural Pennsylvania, and in 1903, Cuban born Aida de Acosta became the first woman to pilot a powered machine in flight in a dirigible over Paris, France.

The first woman to earn a pilot's certificate anywhere in the world was Raymonde de Laroche, a French adventuress who also raced early motorcars. Granted a license by the Federation Aeronautique Internacionale (F.A.I.) on March 8, 1910, she was seriously injured four months later when she crashed during an air race competing against the likes of Louis Bleriot. Both legs were broken, as was one arm, and she sustained head and internal injuries. Two years later she was again back to racing the primitive airplanes of the day. She was killed in an airplane crash in 1919 in which she was riding as a passenger.

Helene Dutrieu was licensed shortly after. She flew nonstop over the 28 mile stretch from Ostend to Brugges, in Belgium, only five months after her first flight. She entered an air race in Florence, Italy, in May 1911 and, as the only woman in the field, triumphed over her 15 male competitors to win the Italian King's Cup. She was also known for her avant-garde ways: she flew airplanes without wearing a corset.

The first American woman to make a solo flight was Blanche Stuart Scott on September 6, 1910, although without official observers to confirm, she would not receive official acknowledgment. She had previously gained some measure of notoriety by driving an Overland motorcar from San Francisco to New York in 1910 as a publicity stunt for the Willys-Overland Company, the automobile manufacturer. Driving through the country was so simple and uncomplicated, she showed, even a woman could do it. At the time, Glenn Curtiss had founded an exhibition-flying troupe that performed around the country. Miss Scott was taught to fly at Hammondsport, N.Y. by Glenn Curtiss himself, and she became a daring and successful member of the troupe, making up to $5,000 a week at a time when the average weekly salary for men was $300 and for women was $144.[1]

Official recognition for the first woman to solo an airplane in the United States was given to Bessica Raiche, who had earned a doctor of medicine degree at Tufts Medical School in 1903. Along with her husband, a New York City attorney, they built their own biplane in the living room of their Mineola, N.Y. summer home. When it was ready, they removed the front wall of the house and rolled it out into the street. Mineola Field was a center for early aviation activity and it was there in 1907 that they first tested their machine. Their airplanes went through several iterations, but by 1910 they had completed a Curtiss-type pusher biplane that was propelled by a 40 horsepower engine. Lateral control was achieved by a sort of wing flap connected to a harness worn by the pilot, which operated the wing flaps when the pilot leaned one way or the other. First trials on September 15, 1910, resulted in a crash with Bessica at the controls, but by September 26, repairs had been made and she completed the first official solo of the aircraft by an American woman. The Aeronautical Society of New York presented her with a medal in commemoration of the event with the words "the nation's first intentional solo by a woman."

Although the husband and wife airplane construction team built additional aircraft, and sold them, they each in time returned to their professions of medicine and law, apparently content with their adventure.

Harriett Quimby is easily the most acknowledged of the early women aviators. (See Figure App 5-1.) She was a newspaper and periodical reporter in the early 1900s, living first in San Francisco and then in New York City. She was the first American woman to earn her license (number 37) from the F.A.I. on August 2, 1911. She gained international recognition as the first woman to fly the English Channel when she crossed from Dover to Hardelot, France, 25 miles south of Calais, in a borrowed Bleriot monoplane on April 16, 1912. Her brief but illustrious flying career came to an end on July 1, 1912, when she fell from her new Bleriot monoplane over Boston Harbor before 5,000 spectators. Seatbelts were not worn in those days.

Source: Library of Congress.

FIGURE APP 6-1 Harriet Quimby was the first American woman to earn her license from F.A.I. on August 2, 1911.

It is not generally appreciated that early women aviators taught men to fly. A German, Melli Beese, started a flying school in 1912 in Berlin, and the Englishwoman Hilda Hewlett taught World War I British pilots in fighter aircraft. In the United States, Marjorie Stinson instructed Canadian airmen slated for service in Britain, having taught over 100 before she had reached the age of 22. Marjorie Stinson was the youngest licensed female pilot in the United States at age 20, and her sister, Katherine, was the fourth woman in this country to be licensed by F.A.I. Katherine also became the first woman to fly the U.S. Mail (in Montana), and became known as one of the most daring aerobatic, or stunt pilots as they were then known, in the country. She made a flying tour of Japan and China in 1916, performing aerobatic maneuvers previously unseen in those countries, for crowds that numbered in excess of 25,000 people. In the process she became an icon for the women of those countries, whose prevailing customs were even more restrictive for women than those in the West.

Victor Carlstrom set the American non-stop distance record on November 2, 1916 by flying 452 miles on a course between Chicago and New York. Less than three weeks later, Ruth Law, who had earned her license in 1912, broke that record over the same course by flying 590 miles from Chicago to Hornell, New York. It should be remembered that this was the route over the Allegheny Mountains that would claim the lives of many airmail pilots in the years to come. Upon reaching New York City the next day, she was acclaimed in newspapers the country over, and was feted in a series of banquets attended by President Woodrow Wilson, Admiral Robert E. Peary, the first man to set foot at the North Pole (April 6, 1909), and Captain Roald Amundsen, first to the South Pole (December 14, 1911).

During the 1920s, women continued to enter the field of aviation, and to continue to expand the limits of their participation. Adrienne Bolland, a Frenchwoman who was licensed in 1920, set an aerobatic record by performing 212 consecutive loops that year. She then had her airplane shipped to Argentina and flew it from Mendoza to Chile, becoming the first woman to cross the Andes by airplane on April 1, 1921.

Facing both gender and race barriers to her aspirations, Bessie Coleman became the first black female pilot licensed by F.A.I. on June 15, 1921. She was taught to fly at Ecole d'Aviation des Freres in Le Crotoy, France, and was the only woman in her 62-person class. Bessie Coleman had arrived in France by way of Atlanta, Texas, her birthplace, and from Chicago, where she had lived after leaving Texas. Her two older brothers had been in the U.S. Army in France during World War I, and had returned with stories of life there, and especially about women aviators. Bessie was befriended by the publisher of *The Chicago Defender,* Robert Abbott, who assisted her in her aspirations to travel to France for flying lessons. On her return to the United States, he sponsored flying exhibitions, which featured her as "the world's greatest woman flyer." She attained countrywide recognition on her own merit, and became an advocate for equal rights for all people. She was killed when she fell from the open cockpit of her biplane on April 30, 1926 while preparing for an exhibition in Jacksonville, Florida.

Sophie Mary Pierce (later Lady Mary Heath), was an Irishwoman who emigrated to England and became known for her athletic prowess as a member of the Great Britain Athletics Olympic Team in the early 1920s. She wrote *Athletics for Women and Girls: How to Be an Athlete and Why* in 1925, which followed her presentations to the International Olympic Committee that same year. She shared the world record for the women's high jump and became British javelin champion. In 1926 she was granted a commercial airplane license by the International Commission for Air Navigation after successfully contesting the Commission's ban on awarding commercial licenses to women. She held several altitude records for light planes. In 1927–28, less than a year after Lindbergh's solo flight over the Atlantic, she made the first solo flight from Capetown, South Africa to Cairo in an Avro Avian monoplane, and then extended that with a flight on to London. She then began a tour of England and the United States, being received by President and Mrs. Coolidge in 1928. The Jacksonville Journal recorded her visit to that Florida city on January 4, 1929:

She made the wings fast in flying position, climbing around the plane like a great cat . . . She was clad in a colorful cretonne smock and wore high, soft leather boots . . . She spun the propeller and started the engine herself while a score of men and boys stood open-mouthed in a semi-circle.

These were some of the women who preceded Amelia Earhart.

Endnote

1. <Camps, Enriqueta, Universitat Pompeu Fabra, April 2001, http://www.clarku.edu/faculty/brown/papers/camp1.pdf>.

APPENDIX 7

Calbraith Perry Rodgers

A Wright brothers' airplane (a model B, modified for the flight) would be the first airplane to fly coast-to-coast in the United States in 1911, piloted by a nearly deaf, cigar smoking 32 year old motorcycle racer and yachtsman of independent means. This was Cal Rodgers, great-grandnephew of Captain Oliver Hazard Perry (who defeated a British squadron at the Battle of Lake Erie in the War of 1812), and the great-grandson of Commodore Matthew Calbraith Perry (who was in command of the U.S. Navy contingent that sailed into Tokyo Bay in 1853), the latter being credited with the opening of feudalistic and xenophobic Japan to U.S. and international trade for the first time. Cal Rodgers wanted to follow in his esteemed forefathers' footsteps, but he was denied admission to the United States Naval Academy due to the hearing deficiency that had resulted from an onset of scarlet fever when he was six years old.

It could be said that Cal Rodgers had been at loose ends for most of his adult life. At six feet four inches tall, he had excelled at football in college, but thereafter he seemed to be unable to find his niche. He was never required to work for a salary due to his financial station, and he spent his days after college in "gentlemen's" pursuits and in amateur sports adventures. Cal's cousin, Lt. John Rodgers, was in 1911 a recent graduate of the Naval Academy, and he had been assigned to take flying lessons at the Wright brothers' flying school in Dayton, Ohio (Huffman Prairie) as a part of the fledgling Naval Aviation program. It was there during the first half of 1911, while visiting with his cousin, that Cal Rodgers encountered his first airplane up close.

Cal received ninety minutes of flight instruction from Orville Wright and considered that he was ready for solo flight. Orville disagreed, so Cal just bought one of the Wright's Model Bs and took off on his own. He entered his first aerial competition in July 1911, and in August, he won $11,000 at the International Aviation Meet in Chicago for endurance aloft.

Not quite one year earlier, in October 1910, publisher William Randolph Hearst had offered a prize of $50,000 for any person who could fly coast-to-coast within a period of thirty days from start to finish. In spite of no serious threat to the prize money from anyone else, Rodgers decided that he could win that endurance prize as well. Orville Wright, again, disagreed with the brash Rodgers, believing that the state of the aviation art had not progressed to the point where any flying machine could endure such a trial. Undaunted, Rodgers lined up financial support from the Chicago meat packer J. Ogden Armour, who had just inaugurated a new five cent soft drink called the "Vin Fiz." Armour seized on the idea of a cross-country publicity campaign as being just the right promotion for his new drink and agreed to finance the venture. (See Figure App 6-1.)

The modified Model B was dubbed the "Vin Fiz" and carried the designation "EX," which denoted that it was for exhibition flying. The primary distinguishing characteristic of the Model B was the absence of the forward elevator, or canard, which had been the primary vertical control device on all prior Wright models, including the "A." The Model B was larger than the EX, with a wingspan of 38.5 feet to only 32 feet for the exhibition model. Both craft used twin pusher-type propellers chain driven by the 35 horsepower water-cooled motor, but the EX was built specifically for the stresses of exhibition flying. It carried no instruments, and Rodgers sat in an open chair located on the lower wing structure, completely exposed to the elements.

Armour also agreed to commission a three-car train to accompany the cross-country effort and to carry a contingent of mechanics and support personnel, including the famed Charley Tay-

lor, who had built the Wright internal combustion engine used in the first successful flight of the Flyer at Kitty Hawk. The train, known as the "Vin Fiz Special," was pulled by a steam engine, and consisted of a day coach, a Pullman sleeping car, and a "hangar" car containing tools, spare parts, and a Palmer-Singer automobile with which to fetch Rodgers and return him to the Pullman at the end of each day. Both Cal's mother and his wife, Mabel, went along for moral support, as did a revolving assortment of friends, dignitaries, and newspaper reporters.

The adventure began on September 17, 1911 at the Sheepheads Bay Race Track on Long Island, where he lifted off to begin the first leg of the 4,000-mile odyssey (See Figure App 6-2.). His route would necessarily follow railroad tracks in order to make use of the "Vin Fiz Special" maintenance crew, but also because there were no navigation aids to guide his progress, nor were there any aerial charts, airports, or support facilities of any kind. The "iron compass," the railroad tracks that would still be used to

CAL RODGERS 9/17/11

Source: Library of Congress.

FIGURE APP 7-1 Cal Rodgers just before beginning his cross-country odyssey on Sept. 17, 1911.

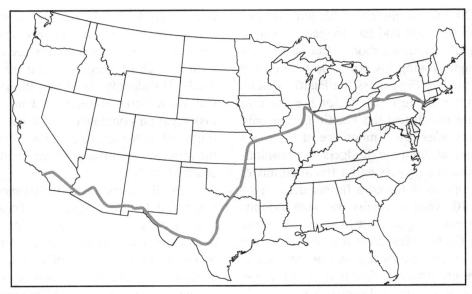

FIGURE APP 7-2 Flight of the "Vin Fiz," 1911.

guide the first airmail pilots later in the decade, ran westerly toward the great city of Chicago, on the far side of the daunting Allegheny Mountains. These same mountains would provide the greatest obstacle to the establishment of successful cross-country airmail in the years to come, but now they lay directly ahead of Rodgers.

Although exact historical sources are scarce, it appears that Rodgers elected to proceed northwest from Sheepheads Bay, to Middletown, New York, for his first leg of 84 miles, which he accomplished easily and, as he said, he "didn't even knock the ashes off my cigar." But this pleasant beginning was not to be a harbinger of good things to come. Although the northwest route would avoid the harshest portions of the vaunted Alleghenies, flat land it was not. The troubles began as he left Middleton when he crashed on takeoff. Difficulties continued as he made his way west toward Elmira, New York, then down into Pennsylvania, and finally on into the flat country of Ohio.

By October 9, 1911, Rodgers had made it only to Chicago. He was just one third of the way across the country and it was becoming obvious that the Hearst time limitation for the prize money could not be met. He reached an accommodation with the Armour organization, nevertheless, to press on, prize or no prize. At Chicago the route turned south, partly because of the established rail lines and cities lying in that direction and partly to prepare for the southern circumvention of the highest portions of the Rocky Mountains. At stops along the way, crowds increased in size and enthusiasm. In Kansas City, the authorities closed the schools to celebrate the remarkable effort.

Enroute, the mechanics were kept busy refurbishing the Vin Fiz after the constant mishaps encountered on takeoff and landings. An accurate tabulation of the number of crashes over the course of the journey is not available to us, but estimates range from sixteen to thirty-nine, depending on the prevailing distinction between a "hard landing" and a "crash." Cal fared little better than the airplane, and he flew in bandages over most of the route and in leg casts over some of it.

By the time he and the Vin Fiz hobbled into Pasadena, California on November 5, 1911, it had been 49 days since he lifted off from the East Coast. A crowd estimated in number from

10,000 to 20,000 was there to greet him. He had made some 69 stops and had logged a total of 82 hours and 4 minutes airborne. But he was not quite through proving his point: he wanted the wheels of the Vin Fiz to kiss the Pacific waters. On November 12 he took off for the 20-mile hop to Long Beach and the Pacific Ocean only to experience after just 8 miles one of his worst crashes of all, at Compton. Rodgers was hospitalized with internal injuries and a fractured ankle, and his recuperation forced a further delay until December 10, when he finally was able to complete his meandering and perilous coast-to-coast expedition. Crowds cheered as Rodgers taxied the weary Vin Fiz into the lapping surf of the Pacific, his ever-present cigar clenched in his teeth. It had been 84 days since he left Sheepheads Bay.

Cal Rodgers had become a celebrity, as his progress had been faithfully heralded by the countries' newspapers during the course of the journey. As King of the Tournament of Roses Parade on New Year's Day 1912, he flew over the gathered marching bands and floats, dropping carnations to those assembled there. He was awarded a medal by the Aero Club of New York later that month, with President of the United States Taft in attendance.

Back in California on April 3, 1912, he was observed to take off from Long Beach, not far from where he had brought his continental odyssey to its tortured end. He proceeded out over the Long Beach pier and was seen flying along with a flock of seagulls when his new Wright Model B suddenly dived into the Pacific Ocean. Calbraith Perry Rodgers did not survive. An investigation concluded that a seagull had been impacted by the airplane and had lodged between the articulating surfaces of the rudder, rendering control hopeless.

Cal Rodgers' accomplishment has been relegated to the status of a footnote in the annals of aviation history, yet it stands as one of the many similar stories of the sacrifices of the gallant pioneers of flight. He was one of those who placed his love of flying and his capacity to endure ahead of his own safety and comfort.

❝ If you are looking for perfect safety, you will do well to sit on a fence and watch the birds; but if you really wish to learn, you must mount a machine and become acquainted with its tricks by actual trial. ❞

—Wilbur Wright, from an address to the Western Society of Engineers in Chicago, 18 September 1901.

APPENDIX 8

Accidents Involving Passenger Fatalities

U.S. Airlines (Part 121) 1982–Present

The NTSB wishes to make clear to all users of the following list of accidents that the information it contains cannot, by itself, be used to compare the safety either of operators or of aircraft types. Airlines that have operated the greatest numbers of flights and flight hours could be expected to have suffered the greatest number of fatal-to-passenger accidents (assuming that such accidents are random events, and not the result of some systematic deficiency). Similarly, the most used aircraft types would tend to be involved in such accidents more than lesser used types. The NTSB also cautions the user to bear in mind when attempting to compare today's airline system to prior years that airline activity (and hence exposure to risk) has risen by almost 100% from the first year depicted to the last.

Date	Location	Operator	Aircraft Type	Passengers Fatal	Passengers Surv
1/13/82	WASHINGTON, DC	AIR FLORIDA	BOEING 737-222	70	4
1/23/82	BOSTON, MA	WORLD AIRWAYS	MCDONNELL DOUGLAS DC-10-30	2	198
7/09/82	NEW ORLEANS, LA	PAN AMERICAN WORLD AIRWAYS	BOEING 727-235	137	0
11/08/82	HONOLULU, HI	PAN AMERICAN WORLD AIRWAYS	BOEING 747-100	1	274
01/09/83	BRAINERD, MN	REPUBLIC AIRLINES	CONVAIR 580-11-A	1	29
10/11/83	PINCKNEYVILLE, IL	AIR ILLINOIS	HAWKER SIDDELEY HS-748-2A	7	0
01/01/85	LA PAZ, BOLIVIA	EASTERN AIR LINES	BOEING 727-225	21	0
01/21/85	RENO, NV	GALAXY AIRLINES	LOCKHEED 188C	64	1
08/02/85	DALLAS/FT WORTH, TX	DELTA AIRLINES	LOCKHEED L-1011-385-1	126	26

Continued

Date	Location	Operator	Aircraft Type	Passengers	
				Fatal	Surv
09/06/85	MILWAUKEE, WI	MIDWEST EXPRESS AIRLINES	DOUGLAS DC-9-14	27	0
12/12/85	GANDER, NEWFOUNDLAND	ARROW AIRWAYS	DOUGLAS DC-8-63	248	0
02/04/86	NEAR ATHENS, GREECE	TRANS WORLD AIRLINES	BOEING 727-231	4	110
02/14/87	DURANGO, MX	PORTS OF CALL	BOEING 707-323B	1	125
08/16/87	ROMULUS, MI	NORTHWEST AIRLINES	MCDONNELL DOUGLAS DC-9-82	148	1
11/15/87	DENVER, CO	CONTINENTAL AIRLINES	MCDONNELL DOUGLAS DC-9-14	25	52
12/07/87	SAN LUIS OBISPO, CA	PACIFIC SOUTHWEST AIRLINES	BRITISH AEROSPACE BAE-146-200	38	0
08/31/88	DALLAS/FT WORTH, TX	DELTA AIRLINES	BOEING 727-232	12	89
12/21/88	LOCKERBIE, SCOTLAND	PAN AMERICAN WORLD AIRWAYS	BOEING 747-121	243	0
02/08/89	SANTAMARIA, AZORES	INDEPENDENT AIR	BOEING 707	137	0
02/24/89	HONOLULU, HI	UNITED AIRLINES	BOEING 747-122	9	328
07/19/89	SIOUX CITY, IA	UNITED AIRLINES	MCDONNELL DOUGLAS DC-10-10	110	175
09/20/89	FLUSHING, NY	USAIR	BOEING 737-400	2	55
12/27/89	MIAMI, FL	EASTERN AIR LINES	BOEING 727-225B	1	46
10/03/90	CAPE CANAVERAL, FL	EASTERN AIR LINES	MCDONNELL DOUGLAS DC-9-31	1	90
12/03/90	ROMULUS, MI	NORTHWEST AIRLINES	MCDONNELL DOUGLAS DC-9-14	7	33
02/01/91	LOS ANGELES, CA	USAIR	BOEING 737-300	20	63
03/03/91	COLORADO SPGS, CO	UNITED AIRLINES	BOEING 737-291	20	0
03/22/92	FLUSHING, NY	USAIR	FOKKER 28-4000	25	22
07/02/94	CHARLOTTE, NC	USAIR	DOUGLAS DC-9-30	37	20
09/08/94	ALIQUIPPA, PA	USAIR	BOEING B-737-300	127	0
10/31/94	ROSELAWN, IN	AMERICAN EAGLE	ATR-72-212	64	0
12/20/95	CALI, COLOMBIA	AMERICAN AIRLINES	BOEING B-757	152	4
05/11/96	MIAMI, FL	VALUJET AIRLINES	MCDONNELL DOUGLAS DC-9	105	0
07/06/96	PENSACOLA, FL	DELTA AIRLINES	MCDONNELL DOUGLAS MD-88	2	140
07/17/96	MORICHES, NY	TRANS WORLD AIRLINES	BOEING 747	212	0
08/02/97	LIMA, PERU	CONTINENTAL AIRLINES	BOEING 757-200	1	141
12/28/97	PACIFIC OCEAN	UNITED AIRLINES	BOEING 747	1	373
06/01/99	LITTLE ROCK, AR	AMERICAN AIRLINES	MCDONNELL DOUGLAS MD-80	10	129
01/31/00	POINT MUGU, CA	ALASKA AIRLINES	MCDONNELL DOUGLAS MD-83	83	0

Date	Location	Operator	Aircraft Type	Passengers	
				Fatal	Surv
09/11/01	NEW YORK CITY, NY	AMERICAN AIRLINES	BOEING 767-200	81	0
09/11/01	NEW YORK CITY, NY	UNITED AIRLINES	BOEING 767-200	56	0
09/11/01	ARLINGTON, VA	AMERICAN AIRLINES	BOEING 757-200	58	0
09/11/01	SHANKSVILLE, PA	UNITED AIRLINES	BOEING 757	37	0
11/12/01	BELLE HARBOR, NY	AMERICAN AIRLINES	AIRBUS INDUSTRIE A300-600	251	0
01/08/03	CHARLOTTE, NC	US AIRWAYS EXPRESS	Beech 1900	19	0
10/19/04	KIRKSVILLE, MO	CORPORATE AIRLINES	British Aerospace Jetstream 32	11	2
12/19/05	MIAMI, FL	CHALKS OCEAN AIRWAYS	Grumman G-73T	18	0
08/27/06	LEXINGTON, KY	COMAIR	Bombardier CRJ-100	47	0

The NTSB wishes to make clear to all users of the preceding list of accidents that the information it contains cannot, by itself, be used to compare the safety either of operators or of aircraft types. Airlines that have operated the greatest numbers of flights and flight hours could be expected to have suffered the greatest number

■ U.S. Commuters (Part 135) 1982–Present

The NTSB wishes to make clear to all users of the following list of accidents that the information it contains cannot, by itself, be used to compare the safety either of operators or of aircraft types. Airlines that have operated the greatest numbers of flights and flight hours could be expected to have suffered the greatest number of fatal-to-passenger accidents (assuming that such accidents are random events, and not the result of some systematic deficiency). Similarly, the most used aircraft types would tend to be involved in such accidents more than lesser used types. The NTSB also cautions the user to bear in mind when attempting to compare today's airline system to prior years that airline activity (and hence exposure to risk) has risen by more than 35% from the first year depicted to the last.

Date	Location	Operator	Aircraft Type	Passengers	
				Fatal	Surv
02/21/1982	PROVIDENCE, RI	PILGRIM AIRLINES	DEHAVILLAND DHC-6	1	9
12/09/1982	NEAR KLAWOCK, AK	TYEE AIRLINES, INC.	DEHAVILLAND DHC-2	7	0
08/17/1983	PEACH SPRINGS, AZ	LAS VEGAS AIRLINES	PIPER PA-31-350	9	0
03/05/1984	CUMBERLAND, MD	CUMBERLAND AIRLINES	PIPER PA-31	2	0
07/21/1984	TAU, MANUA	ISL SOUTH PACIFIC ISLAND	DEHAVILLAND DCH-6-300	1	10
08/02/1984	VIEQUES, PR	VIEQUES AIR LINK, INC. BRITTEN	NORMAN BN-2A ISLANDER	8	0
08/24/1984	SAN LUIS OBISPO, CA	WINGS WEST AIRLINES, INC.	BEECH C-99	13	0
09/07/1984	NAPLES, FL	PROVINCETOWNBOSTON AIRLINES	CESSNA 402C	1	4
12/06/1984	JACKSONVILLE, FL	PROVINCETOWNBOSTON AIRLINES	EMBRAER BANDEIRANTE EMB-110P1	11	0

Continued

Date	Location	Operator	Aircraft Type	Passengers	
				Fatal	Surv
12/17/1984	BAINBRIDGE, NY	SUSQUEHANNA AIRLINES, INC.	PIPER PA-23-250	2	0
02/04/1985	SOLDOTNA, AK	NORTH PACIFIC AIRLINES	BEECH 65-A80	7	0
02/06/1985	ALTUS, OK	ALTUS AIRLINE, INC.	CESSNA 402B	1	0
04/26/1985	NEW YORK, NY	NEW YORK HELICOPTERS	AEROSPATIALE SA360C DAUPHIN	1	5
08/25/1985	AUBURN, ME	BAR HARBOR AIRLINES	BEECH 99	6	0
09/23/1985	GROTTOES, VA	HENSON AIRLINES	BEECH B99	12	0
11/01/1985	BETHEL, AK	HERMENS AIR, INC.	CESSNA 208	1	2
03/13/1986	ALPENA, MI	SIMMONS AIRLINES	EMBRAER EMB-110P1	2	5
10/28/1986	ST. CROIX, VI	VIRGIN ISLAND SEAPLANE SHUTTLE	GRUMMAN G-73	1	12
01/15/198-7	KEARNS, UT	SKY WEST AIRLINES INC. (SKY WEST AIRLINES/ WESTERN EXPR)	SWEARINGEN SA-226TC	6	0
03/04/1987	ROMULUS, MI	FISHER BROTHERS AVIATION INC. (NORTHWEST AIRLINK)	CASA C-212-CC	7	9
04/01/1987	ANCHORAGE, AK	WILBUR'S FLIGHT OPERATIONS (WILBUR'S INC.)	CESSNA 402	1	0
11/23/1987	HOMER, AK	RYAN AIR SERVICE, INC.	BEECH 1900C	16	3
12/23/1987	KENAI, AK	SOUTH CENTRAL AIR, INC.	PIPER PA-31-350	5	2
12/23/1987	MAUNALOA, HI	PANORAMA AIR TOURS (PANORAMA AIR TOURS)	PIPER PA-31-350	7	0
01/19/1988	BAYFIELD, CO	TRANS COLORADO AIRLINES (TRANS COLORADO)	FAIRCHILD SA-227-AC	7	8
02/19/1988	CARY, NC	AVAIR, INC. (AMERICAN EAGLE)	FAIRCHILD SA-227-AC	10	0
04/19/1989	PELICAN, AK	CHANNEL FLYING SERVICE	DEHAVILLAND DHC-2	1	0
07/30/1989	HAINES, AK	SKAGWAY AIR SERVICE	PIPER PA-32-301	2	2
10/28/1989	HALAWA, MOLOKAI, HI	ALOHA ISLANDAIR	DE HAVILLAND DHC-6-300	18	0
12/26/1989	PASCO, WA	NPA/UNITED EXPRESS (UNITED EXPRESS)	BRITISH AEROSPACE BAE-3101	4	0
09/03/1990	KALTAG, AK	FRONTIER FLYING SERVICE	PIPER PA-31-325	3	6
02/01/1991	LOS ANGELES, CA	SKYWEST AIRLINES, INC.	FAIRCHILD SA-227-AC	10	0
04/05/1991	BRUNSWICK, GA	ATLANTIC SOUTHEAST AIRLINES	EMBRAER EMB-120RT	20	0
07/10/1991	BIRMINGHAM, AL	L'EXPRESS AIRLINES, INC.	BEECH C99	12	1
08/20/1991	KETCHIKAN, AK	TEMSCO HELICOPTERS, INC. (TEMSCO AIRLINES)	PILATUS BRITTEN-NORMAN BN-2A-26 ISLANDER	3	0
09/11/1991	EAGLE LAKE, TX	CONTINENTAL EXPRESS	EMBRAER 120	11	0

5555

Date	Location	Operator	Aircraft Type	Passengers Fatal	Surv
12/10/1991	TEMPLE BAR, AZ	LAS VEGAS AIRLINES, INC.	PIPER PA-31-350	4	0
01/03/1992	GABRIELS, NY	COMMUTAIR (USAIR EXPRESS)	BEECH 1900C	1	1
01/23/1992	CLEWISTON, FL	AIR SUNSHINE INC.	CESSNA 402C	1	0
06/07/1992	MAYAGUEZ, PR	EXECUTIVE AIR CHARTER, INC. (AMERICAN EAGLE)	CASA 212	3	0
06/08/1992	ANNISTON, AL	GP EXPRESS AIRLINES, INC.	BEECH C99	2	2
10/27/1992	SAIPAN, MP	PACIFIC ISLAND AVIATION, INC.	CESSNA 310R	2	0
10/31/1992	GRAND JUNCTION, CO	ALPINE AVIATION (ALPINE AIR)	PIPER PA-42	2	0
11/08/1992	KIANA, AK	BAKER AVIATION INC.	CESSNA 402C	2	0
04/03/1993	NOME, AK	RYAN AIR SERVICE, INC	CESSNA 207	1	0
07/12/1993	LAS VEGAS, NV	AIR NEVADA AIRLINES	CESSNA 402C	2	0
12/01/1993	HIBBING, MN	EXPRESS AIRLINES II, INC. (NORTHWEST AIRLINK)	JETSTREAM BA-3100	16	0
01/07/1994	COLUMBUS, OH	ATLANTIC COAST AIRLINES (UNITED EXPRESS)	JETSTREAM 4101	2	3
12/13/1994	MORRISVILLE, NC	FLAGSHIP AIRLINES (AMERICAN EAGLE)	BAE JETSTREAM 3201	15	5
08/21/1995	CARROLLTON, GA	ATLANTIC SOUTHEAST AIRLINES (DELTA CONNECTOR)	EMBRAER EMB-120RT	7	19
11/19/1996	QUINCY, IL	GREAT LAKES AVIATION (UNITED EXPRESS)	BEECH 1900	10	0
01/09/1997	IDA, MI	COMAIR	EMBRAER 120	26	0
02/08/1997	ST. THOMAS, VI	AIR SUNSHIHE	CESSNA 402C	2	2
04/10/1997	WAINWRIGHT, AK	HAGELAND AVIATION	CESSNA 208B	4	0
06/27/1997	NOME, AK	OLSON AIR SERVICE	CESSNA 207	1	0
11/08/1997	BARROW, AK	HAGELAND AVIATION SERVICES	CESSNA 208B	7	0
09/05/1999	WESTERLY, RI	NEW ENGLAND AIRLINES	PIPER PA-32-260	2	2
12/07/1999	BETHEL, AK	GRANT AVIATION	CESSNA 207	5	0
09/18/2000	NUIQSUT, AK	CAPE SMYTHE AIR SERVICE	PIPER PA-31T3	4	5
10/03/2001	DECATUR ISLAND, WA	WEST ISLE AIR	CESSNA 172N	2	0
10/10/2001	DILLINGHAM, AK	PENINSULA AIRWAYS	CESSNA 208	9	0
07/13/2003	TREASURE CAY, BAHAMAS	AIR SUNSHINE	CESSNA 402C	2	7
12/14/2006	PORT HEIDEN, AK	PENINSULA AIRWAYS	PIPER PA-32-301	1	0

The NTSB wishes to make clear to all users of the preceding list of accidents that the information it contains cannot, by itself, be used to compare the safety either of operators or of aircraft types. Airlines that have operated the greatest numbers of flights and flight hours could be expected to have suffered the greatest number of fatal-to-passenger accidents (assuming that such accidents are random events, and not the result of some systematic deficiency). Similarly, the most used aircraft types would tend to be involved in such accidents more than lesser used types. The NTSB also cautions the user to bear in mind when attempting to compare today's airline system to prior years that airline activity (and hence exposure to risk) has risen by more than 35% from the first year depicted to the last.

updated September 2005

GLOSSARY

Administrative Law Judge (ALJ)—A person appointed pursuant to civil service regulations to hold hearings and make determinations of fact and law. Most commonly in aviation, ALJs conduct trials de novo as first level appeals in FAA certificate actions against airmen.

Aerial Experiment Association—A scientific association formed in 1907 by Alexander Graham Bell and consisting of Bell, Glenn Curtis, J. A. D. McCurdy, F. W. Baldwin, and Lt. Thomas Selfridge. The purpose of the organization was to study aeronautics and to design and build a practical airplane.

Aerodrome—The name given by Samuel P. Langley to the flying machine he designed in 1893. His aerodrome no. 5, a 14 pound model powered by small steam engine, flew for a distance of over one-half mile in 1896. The aerodrome employed "planes" (wings), or flat horizontal surfaces mounted to the fuselage, to achieve lift.

Air Transport Association—Trade association composed of U.S. certificated air carriers.

Airport Improvement Program Funds (AIP)—Funds derived primarily from taxes on passenger tickets and aviation fuels used in non-commercial operations and used to pay for improvements to the nation's airports and air traffic control system.

Airship—A lighter than air, elongated balloon-like vehicle with engines for propulsion and external devices (rudders and elevators) for control.

Airway—A route through navigable airspace defined by aids to navigation designated by the FAA, 10 miles in width, and that extends upward from the beginning of navigable airspace to 27,000 feet altitude.

Airworthiness—Term used to describe the legal or mechanical status of an aircraft with regard to its readiness for flight.

Antarctica—The Earth's southernmost and fifth-largest continent. It has an area of 5,400,000 square miles, of which 108,000 (2 percent) is ice-free. It has the highest average elevation of all the continents, and is the driest, coldest, and most windy. It has very little precipitation and is, therefore, the largest desert in the world. Animals that have adapted to its environment include penguins, various kinds of seals, and several species of birds.

Apogee—In an elliptical orbit path, the point at which a satellite is farthest from the Earth.

Arianespace—The French company (Arianespace SA), founded in 1980, which undertakes the production, operation and marketing of the Ariane 5 rocket launcher. It was the world's first commercial space transportation company.

Assembly Line—An innovation employed in the assembly of early Ford automobiles that required workers to perform essentially the same task or tasks on each automobile in the assembly process as the automobile being assembled slowly proceeded down the assembly line by means of a mechanized conveyor.

Astronautics—A branch of engineering (astronautical engineering) that deals with machines designed to work outside of the Earth's atmosphere. The science of the design, construction, and operation of spacecraft.

Atmosphere, Earth's—The layer of gases surrounding the planet, which are retained by Earth's gravity. It is composed of nitrogen (78 percent), oxygen (20.95 percent), argon (.93 percent), carbon dioxide (.038 percent), and trace amounts of other gases. The atmosphere absorbs ultraviolet radiation and reduces temperature extremes of day and night periods.

Available Seat Mile (ASM)—Statistical measure used to describe one seat flown one mile. An aircraft with 100 seats flown a distance of 100 miles represents 10,000 ASMs.

Axis Powers—An alliance of Germany, Italy, and Japan before and during World War II.

Cabotage—Originally, the term for coastwise shipping within the borders of a single country so as to effect commerce between two or more points within that country. In international civil aviation, it describes the practice reserved to domestic airlines only to serve a second point (airport) within a single country from an initial point (airport). Cabotage has not been granted so far in international civil aviation.

CAM Routes—Contract airmail routes awarded by the U.S. post office department beginning in 1925 to companies and individuals in the private sector, granting to them the exclusive right to carry U.S. mail by air between designated points in the country.

Certificate of Public Convenience and Necessity—A certificate granted by the Department of Transportation upon a finding that an air carrier utilizing aircraft with a seating capacity in excess of 60 seats has met the fitness requirements set out in the federal aviation regulations.

Chapter 11—The section of the United States bankruptcy code (11 U.S.C. 1113, et. seq.) designed to allow a corporation to reorganize its operations under the protection of the bankruptcy court and to secure temporary relief from claims of creditors during the period of reorganization. Invoking the provisions of chapter 11 allows the corporation to continue operations even though it is technically bankrupt (liabilities exceed assets).

Civil Aeronautics Administration—Agency of the United States created by the 1940 amendments to the Civil Aeronautics Act of 1938 and charged with the administration of non-military safety programs, air traffic control, and airway development. It was one of the forerunners of the Federal Aviation Administration.

Civil Aeronautics Board—Independent board formed by the 1940 amendment to the Civil Aeronautics Act of 1938 for the purpose of administering the economic regulation of the airlines. The CAB ceased to exist on December 31, 1984, pursuant to the provisions of the Airline Deregulation Act of 1978.

Civil Reserve Air Fleet (CRAF)—Designation of aircraft of U.S. certificated carriers that may be activated, with crew, for exclusive military use in the national interest in cases of emergency.

Code of Federal Regulations (CFRs)—Codification of federal agency regulations that are promulgated by such agencies pursuant to authority given in statutes passed by the congress of the United States. The CFR is arranged into 50 titles, each dealing with a different subject matter, and it is revised and updated annually.

Code Sharing—Marketing devices used by airlines in advertising, sales and reservations that allow originating airlines designations (two letter code) to be carried through to connecting airlines flight segments, even though such subsequent segments are conducted by an entirely different airline.

Cold War—A period of conflict, tension, and competition between the United States and the Soviet Union between the late 1940s until the early 1990s. The Cold War period was characterized by costly defense spending, a massive arms race in conventional and nuclear weapons, and proxy wars.

Common Law—Law that is a result of contested cases between parties in litigation and which results in opinions handed down by courts. Common law was the "judge-made" law of England that was in use in the colonies prior to the American Revolution, and which was adopted by the newly created states of the new American republic. Common law is to be distinguished from statutory law, or legislation, which is created on the federal level in the Congress of the United States, and on the state level in the various legislatures of the states.

Computer Reservation Systems (CRS)—A development made possible by the advent of real-time computer technology beginning in the 1960s, applied to the complexities of airlines' passenger reservations operations. CRS became a major marketing tool for the airlines during the 1980s, and provided immediate analytical perspectives in airline operations not previously possible, including information that allowed last minute seat pricing changes to optimize passenger load factors. Several airlines own these systems and they are used by travel agents.

Convention—An international agreement among nations governing international civil aviation operations.

Department of Transportation—Cabinet level department of the United States government created by congress in 1966, and which began operations in 1967. The legislation, for the first time, gathered into the DOT all federal agencies and functions having to do with any aspect of transportation. The administration of aviation was placed within a new agency called the Federal Aviation Administration. Upon its creation, the Department of Transportation was the fourth largest department in the federal government.

Depression—A period of economic stress that persists over an extended period, accompanied by poor business conditions and high unemployment.

Deregulation—Term used in referring to the Airline Deregulation Act of 1978, which ended the economic regulation of the airlines by the federal government.

Dirigible—See airship.

Due Process—Constitutional guarantee given to all persons in the United States by the fifth and fourteenth amendments to the U.S. constitution that life or liberty may not be taken or abridged by the federal government or any state government without certain procedural and substantive safeguards being observed. Among these are the right to confront witnesses and to cross examine them, the right to a fair trial before an impartial jury, the right to competent counsel, and the right to just compensation for property taken by the government in the public interest.

Enplanements—Term used to describe the number of passengers boarding a flight.

Essential Air Service—Government subsidized airline service to rural areas of the U.S. made necessary by effects of airline deregulation in 1978.

Export-Import Bank—Governmental agency designed to support transactions between domestic suppliers and foreign consumers by providing financing that is not available in the commercial markets.

FAA/AST—The Office of Commercial Space Transportation in the Federal Aviation Administration that approves all commercial rocket launch operations. This Office regulates launch sites, publishes quarterly launch forecasts, and holds annual conferences with the space launch industry. FAA/AST was created by the Commercial Space Launch Act of 1985.

Federal Register—Published under the authority of Congress five days a week, providing official notice of agency proposed rule making, adoption of rules and regulations, and congressional activities.

Federation Aeronautique Internationale (FAI)—A nongovernmental, nonprofit international organization founded in 1905 whose basic aim is the furthering of aeronautical and astronautical activities worldwide. It has some 100-member countries. FAI establishes rules for the control and certification of world aeronautical and astronautical records.

Four Course Radio Range—The first non-visual navigation system ever developed. It utilized low frequency radio waves to transmit steady morse code signals as a homing device to airplanes along the first airways.

General Agreement on Tariffs and Trade (GATT)—Created in 1947, GATT was a multinational agreement designed to promote and allow unfettered access by all nations to the benefits of world free enterprise by reducing protectionist barriers to free trade. It was replaced in 1995 by the World Trade Organization.

General Maritime Law—The common law of admiralty, or the law of the sea, originating in England and adopted by the United States after the American Revolution.

Geostationary orbit—A geosynchronous orbit in the Earth's equatorial plane, directly above the equator. A GSO has zero degrees of inclination and remains in the equatorial plane at all times. To an observer on Earth, it will appear to remain motionless in the sky. Also called a "Clarke Orbit" due to the first use of the phrase by science fiction writer, Arthur C. Clarke in 1945. Satellites in GSO orbit in the direction of the Earth's rotation at an altitude of approximately 22,240 miles above mean sea level. A GSO orbital period is equal to the Earth's rotational period, known as the sidereal day.

Geosynchronous orbit—An orbit around the Earth with an orbital period identical to the sidereal rotation period, or the period of Earth rotation. A geosynchronous orbit differs from a geostationary orbit in that the former may have an inclination from the equatorial plane, so that it passes above and below the plane of the equator during the Earth day.

Guggenheim Fund—A charitable fund established in 1926 by Daniel Guggenheim for the promotion of aeronautics. The fund paid for the establishment of engineering programs at universities, including aeronautical engineering degree programs at Stanford, MIT, Harvard, and others. Competition sponsored by the fund resulted in the first STOL (short takeoff and landing) ever built. The fund was responsible for many other innovations that greatly contributed to the safety of aviation.

Hub and Spoke—The system of airline operations that concentrates the arrival and departure of multiple scheduled aircraft at one central airport (the hub) at or near the same time to allow passengers (arriving from one of the outlying feeder airports at the end of the spoke) to connect with other arriving flights at the hub (each arriving from a different outlying airport) in order to continue their flight to a different outlying destination airport. The system allows maximum utilization of smaller aircraft by airlines but places a huge strain on air traffic control and airport facilities.

ICBM—Intercontinental ballistic missile, or long-range missile designed for the delivery of nuclear weapons. All five of the nations with permanent seats on the United Nations Security Council have operational ICBM systems. France and the United Kingdom have submarine launch capacity and China, the Russian Federation, and the United States have both submarine and land-based launch capability.

Inclination—The angle between an orbital path and a plane of reference. The most common plane of reference used in artificial earth satellite orbit is the equatorial plane. The angle of inclination is stated in degrees.

Institute of Medicine, The—Chartered in 1970 as a component of the National Academy of Sciences, the IOM is a nonprofit organization specifically created to give advice to the federal government on matters of biomedical science, medicine, and health.

International Air Transport Association (IATA)—Association of international air carriers operating as a trade association with liaison responsibilities to the international civil aviation organization (ICAO). IATA also serves as the clearinghouse for interline accounting, servicing the accounts of 380 airlines.

International Civil Aviation Organization (ICAO)—An organ of the United Nations created in 1947 by the Chicago Convention. It has facilitated the integration of international airline operations since World War II, including the adoption of standards for navigation, communication, and aircraft certification.

Joint Aviation Authorities—Association of European countries formed in 1970 for the purpose of coordinating standards for certification of aircraft, and since 1989 it has been charged with coordinating safety efforts similar to the FAA in the United States. Responsibility for aviation safety within the European union is expected to be taken over on a permanent basis by the European Aviation Safety Agency (EASA).

Labor Union—An organized association of workers, often in a trade, formed to protect and further their rights and interests.

Laissez-Faire Policy—Governmental abstention from interfering in economic or commercial affairs.

Load Factor—The percentage of available seats that are filled with paying passengers. Revenue passenger miles divided by available seat miles.

Low Earth orbit—An orbit around the Earth ranging from an altitude of 124 miles to 1240 miles above the Earth's surface. Most human activity in space has been conducted in LEO orbits.

Major Carrier—An airline with annual revenues of more than $1 billion.

Marshall Plan—A program inaugurated by the United States, and participated in by most of the Western European nations, designed to provide economic assistance to the nations of Western Europe in the aftermath of World War II. It was the single most effective and successful international cooperative plan ever conceived in peacetime, and was responsible for the economic recovery of those war-torn nations after 1945.

Medium Earth orbit—An orbit around the Earth above LEO (at a high of 1240 miles) and geosynchronous orbit (around 22,240 miles). The most common use for satellites in this region is for navigation (GPS satellites orbit at around 12,552 miles). Orbital periods for MEO satellites is from 2 hours to 12 hours.

Minimum Wage—Legislatively mandated hourly wage that, at a minimum, must be paid to all qualifying workers by affected employers.

Monopoly—Control or advantage obtained by one supplier or producer over the commercial market within a given region. The market condition existing when only one economic entity produces a particular product or provides a particular service. The term is now commonly applied also to situations that approach but do not strictly meet this definition.

Monroney Aeronautical Center—Location of FAA aircraft registry and recordation activities, airman records branch, the civil aeromedical institute (CAMI), and training center. It is located in Oklahoma City, OK.

Mutually assured destruction (MAD)—A doctrine of military strategy in which a full-scale use of nuclear weapons by one of two opposing sides would effectively result in the destruction of both. It is an evolutionary defense strategy based on the concept that neither the United States nor its enemies will ever start a nuclear war because the other side will retaliate massively. MAD is a product of the 1950s that has little relevance to the major defense threats of the 21st century.

National Academy of Engineering, The—Founded in 1964, the NAE operates under the same Congressional Act of Incorporation that established the National Academy of Sciences, and performs the same functions for the federal government in engineering matters as does the NAS in scientific matters.

National Academy of Sciences, The—Created by statute and signed into law by Abraham Lincoln on March 3, 1863, the NAS is an honorific society of distinguished scholars engaged in scientific research. It investigates, examines, experiments, and reports upon any subject of science or art whenever called upon to do so by any department of the government.

National Academies, The—Composed of four separate organizations (the National Academy of Sciences, the National Academy of Engineering, the Institute of Medicine, and the National Research Council), this collection of experts serves in a pro bono capacity as a public service to address critical national issues and to give advice to the federal government and the public.

National Advisory Committee for Aeronautics (NACA)—Established by the United States government in 1915 to direct and conduct research and experimentation in aeronautics. NACA was formed because of the perception that the United States had fallen behind the European countries in the emerging field of aeronautics during World War I. NACA was the forerunner of NASA.

National Carrier—An airline with annual revenues of between $100 million and $1 billion.

National Mediation Board—Agency created by the Railway Labor Act (RLA) to mediate major issues arising under the RLA with a view to avoiding strikes, work stoppages, and interruptions of national transportation services.

National Reconnaissance Office, The—The NRO was established in 1960 to develop the nation's satellite reconnaissance systems. It is part of the Department of Defense, and is one of the 16 intelligence agencies in the United States. It designs, builds, and operates the reconnaissance satellites of the U.S. government.

National Research Council, The—A component of the National Academies, the mission of the NRC is to improve government decision making and public policy, increase public education and understanding, and promote the acquisition and dissemination of knowledge in matters involving science, engineering, technology, and health.

National Transportation Safety Board—Created by the Department of Transportation Act of 1966, the NTSB is now an independent federal agency charged with the primary responsibility of investigating transportation accidents, making findings of the "probable cause" of such accidents, and making recommendations for system improvements to assist in preventing future accidents. It is responsible under Part 830 of the Federal Aviation Regulations for receiving notification of aircraft accidents and incidents and for administration of the aviation disaster family assistance act.

Nodal period—The time that elapses between successive passages of a satellite through successive ascending nodes (or descending nodes) of an artificial Earth satellite. An orbital node is one of the two points where the satellite's orbit crosses a plane of reference. The most common plane of reference is the Earth's equatorial plane. Orbits that are contained in the plane of reference are called non-inclined. Orbits that cross the plane of reference are in inclined orbits.

Notice of Propose Rulemaking—The Administrative Procedures Act requires that all agencies in the United States government provide notice to the public of any intent to adopt new rules or regulations, setting for the particulars of the proposed rule and the basis for its adoption.

Part 121 Regulations—FAA safety regulations applicable to commercial operations of aircraft with 10 or more seats.

Part 135 Regulations—FAA safety regulations applicable to commercial operations of aircraft with fewer than 10 seats.

Passenger Facility Charges (PFCs)—A per passenger enplanement fee charged by airports, collected by airlines in addition to the passenger airfare, to be used for financing airport capital improvements.

Patent—The governmental grant of a right, privilege, or authority. A patent granted to an invention recognized by industry or the scientific community as pioneering, unexpected, and unprecedented.

Peenemunde—Situated in the northeast of Germany on the Baltic coast, this area was occupied by the German Reich Air Ministry in 1936 as a research center. Its location permitted rocket test flights over water with monitoring capability for some 200 miles along the coast. Experimentation and development of rocket systems, radar systems, and night-navigation were conducted here.

Perigee—In an elliptical orbit path, the point at which a satellite is closest to the Earth.

Perimeter Rules—Restrictions applied to arriving aircraft at New York LaGuardia and Washington National (now Reagan) that requires arriving nonstop flights to have originated within a certain radius, in miles, from the airport (1,500 miles for LaGuardia and 1,250 miles for National). The purpose of perimeter rules was to encourage the use of JFK airport and Dulles airport, which were then relatively new.

Predatory Practices—Unfair exclusionary airline practices designed to prevent or minimize competition from other airlines, usually competition from new entrant or smaller airlines.

Presidential Emergency Board—A panel of experts appointed by the President of the United States pursuant to the provisions of the Railway Labor Act whose function is to make a last-ditch effort to effect a compromise between labor and management to prevent a work stoppage and consequent disruption of national transportation services.

Recession—Period characterized by a sharp slowdown in economic activity, declining employment, and a decrease in investment and consumer spending.

Reconnaissance satellite—An Earth observation satellite or communication satellite deployed for military or intelligence purposes, also known as a "spy satellite."

Regional Carrier—An airline with annual revenues of less than $100 million whose service generally is limited to a particular geographic region.

Rubicon—A river in northern Italy flowing eastward from the Apennines to the Adriatic Sea. "Crossing the Rubicon" is a popular idiom meaning to go past a point of no return. Julius Caesar crossed the river in 49 B.C. deliberately as an act of war.

Saturn V—A multistage liquid-fuel expendable rocket used in the NASA Apollo and Skylab programs.

Sidereal day—The period of time needed for the Earth to complete one complete rotation around its axis. The sidereal day is about four minutes shorter than the solar day.

Slots—A device initiated by the FAA in 1969 in an attempt to alleviate congestion at four airports in the U.S.—Chicago O'Hare, Washington National (now Reagan), New York JFK, and New York LaGuardia. The procedure grants to participating air carriers a specific time and date for either landing or taking off from one of these airports.

Smithsonian Institution—In 1826, James Smithson, a British scientist, drew up his last will and testament, naming his nephew as beneficiary. Smithson stipulated that, should the nephew die without heirs (as he would in 1835), the estate should go "to the United States of America, to found at Washington, under the name of the Smithsonian Institution, an establishment for the increase and diffusion of knowledge among men."

Solar day—The average period of time needed for the sun to return to its highest point (24 hours).

Statute—A written law enacted by a legislative body.

Tariff—Publication of an air carrier in which notice is provided of fares and rates, and any special rules or conditions upon which the transportation of persons or property is subject.

Trial de Novo—A proceeding that is conducted as an original proceeding to find facts based on the presentation of evidence in the proceeding and to make conclusions of law applicable to the case based on the facts presented.

Van Allen radiation belts—Two layers of radiation outside of the earth's atmosphere extending from 400 to 40,000 miles into space. The belts are named for James A. Van Allen, the American astrophysicist who first predicted the belts. The charged particles of which the belts are composed circulate along the Earth's magnetic lines of force extending from the area above the equator to the North pole, to the South Pole, and circle back to the equator. These particles are believed to originate in periodic solar flares and become trapped by the Earth's magnetic field. They are responsible for the aurora borealis.

Versailles Treaty—The peace treaty that officially ended World War I between the Allied and Associated Powers and Germany. The treaty is generally regarded as punitive against Germany, requiring Germany to accept full responsibility for causing the war, to disarm, to make substantial territorial concessions and to pay reparations. The terms of the treaty caused widespread resentment in Germany, and became the focal point for radical political activity during the 1920s in Germany. The National Socialist Party, led by Adolf Hitler, used its extremely punitive provisions as justification for many of its territorial expansions and its rearmament during the 1930s.

Widebody Aircraft—Aircraft with more than one aisle in the passenger cabin, such as the Boeing 747, 767 and 777, L-1011, DC-10, and Airbus A300 and A310.

William J. Hughes Technical Center—Center for research and development programs conducted by the FAA. It is located near Atlantic City, N.J.

Wing-warping—Innovation by the Wright brothers employed on their gliders, and later on the Flyer, that effected a bending of the outer trailing edges of the upper and lower wing surfaces by means of ropes and pulleys manipulated by the operator that allowed, for the first time, a means to control lateral stability of the machine in flight. The U.S. patent office granted patent no. 821,393 to the Wrights on May 22, 1903.

World Trade Organization (WTO)—Successor to GATT effective in 1995, the WTO governs international trade in all respects. The goal of the WTO is to facilitate the international movement of products, goods, and services for the betterment of signatory countries and their citizens.

Yield—Average revenue per revenue passenger mile expressed in cents per mile.

Yield Management—The process made possible by computers that allows airlines to set and revise prices for a particular flight based on real-time information.

Zeppelin—Large airship originally built by Ferdinand Adolf von Zeppelin in 1900. Zeppelins were used in passenger service and in war, the last of which was the Hindenburg, which burned upon attempting to dock at Lakehurst, N.J., in 1937 after a transatlantic voyage.

BIBLIOGRAPHY

——, *Airlines 101-A Primer for Dummies*, The Airline Monitor, November 1998.

——, *Airlines Treat Patron 'Like Cattle' Feds Say*, Aviation Week and Space Technology, August 7, 2000.

——, *Chronology of Presidential Emergency Boards Under the Railway Labor Act*, Catherwood Library, School of Industrial and Labor Relations, Electronic Archive, Miscellaneous Documents <http://www.ilr.cornell.edu/library/e archive/miscellaneous/?pqge.airlines%2Fairlines>, 2002.

——, *A Chronology of Strikes in the Airline Industry*, Catherwood Library, School of Industrial and Labor Relations, Electronic Archive, Miscellaneous Documents <http://www.ilr.cornell.edu/library/e archive/miscellaneous/?page=airlines%2Fairlines>, 2002.

——, *Federal and State Coordination: Aviation Noise Policy and Regulation*, 46 Administrative Law Review 413–427, 1994.

——, *Hell's Bells*, Smithsonian Magazine, May 2002, pp. 28–29.

Air Transport Association, *Airlines in Crisis—The Perfect Storm*, 2003.

Air Transport Association, *2002 Annual Report*, 2002.

Air Transport Association, *The Airline Handbook*, 2001.

Air Transport Association, *State of the U.S. Airline Industry: A Report on Recent Trends for U.S. Air Carriers*, 2002.

Air Transport Association, *U.S. Air Carrier Industry Review and Outlook*, Talk by David Swierenga, Chief Economist, Air Transport Association, to National Business Economics Issue Council, Las Vegas, Nevada, February 12, 2002.

Air Transport Association, *U.S. Carrier Industry Review and Outlook*, 2002.

The Airline Builders, Time-Life Books, 1981.

Alfred E. Kahn, *Deregulation: Looking Backward and Looking Forward*, 7 Yale J. on Reg. 325, 331 (Summer 1990).

Allied Pilots Association, *The Birth of APA*, http://www.alliedpilots.org/index.asp, 2002.

Ambrose, Stephen, *Nothing Like It in the World: The Men Who Built the Transcontinental Railroad 1863–1869*, Simon and Schuster, New York, 2000.

Bailey, Elizabeth E., *Airline Deregulation: Confronting the Paradoxes*, Regulation, Vol. 15, No. 3, Summer 1992.

Borenstein, Severin, *Hubs and Higher Fares: Dominance and Market Power in the United States Airline Industry*, Rand Journal of Economics, Vol. 20, 1989, pp. 47–92.

Bornstein, Aaron, *Grounded. Frank Lorenzo and the Destruction of Eastern Airlines*, Simon and Schuster, New York, 1990.

Costello, Frank J., *The Lessons of Airline Deregulation*, Zuckert, Scoutt, and Rosenberger, LLP, web site. www.zsrlaw.com.

Cremieux, Pierre-Yves 1996. *The Effect of Deregulation on Employee Earnings: Pilots, Flight Attendants, and Mechanics, 1959–1992*, Industrial and Labor Relations Review, Vol. 49, No. 2 (January) pp. 223–242.

Crouch, Tom D., *The Bishop's Boys: A Life of Wilbur and Orville Wright*, W. W. Norton and Co., New York, 1990.

David, Carl, *The Impact of Deregulation on the Employment and Wages of Airline Mechanics*, Industrial and Labor Relations Review, Vol. 39, No. 4, July 1986.

Dempsey, Paul Stephen, *Airport Monopolization: Barriers to Entry and Impediments to Competition,* Testimony before the United States House of Representatives, Committee on the Judiciary-Hearings on the State of Competition in the Airline Industry, June 14, 2000.

Dempsey, Paul Stephen, *Antitrust Law and Policy in Transportation: Monopoly is the Name of the Game,* 21 Ga. L. Rev. 505 (1987).

Dempsey, Paul Stephen, *Competition in the Air: European Union Regulation of Commercial Aviation,* Journal of Air Law and Commerce, Summer 2001.

Dooley, Frank J., *Déjà vu for Airline Industrial Relations,* Journal of Labor Research, Vol. XV, No. 2, Spring 1994.

Douglas, John W., Aerospace Industries Association of America, Testimony before the Subcommittee on Aviation, Committee on Transportation and Infrastructure, U.S. House of Representatives, July 26, 2001.

Emme, Eugene M., comp., *Aeronautics and Astronautics: An American Chronology of Science and Technology in the Exploration of Space, 1915–1960* (Washington, D.C.: National Aeronautics and Space Administration, 1961) pp. 26–32.

Gandt, Robert, *Skygods,* William Morrow and Company, Inc., New York, 1995.

Gann, Ernest K., *Fate is the Hunter*, Simon and Schuster, Inc., 1961.

General Accounting Office Report, *Airline Competition: DOT's Implementation of Airline Regulatory Deregulation* (GAO/RECD-89-93, June 28, 1989).

General Accounting Office Report, *Airline Deregulation: Barriers to Entry Continue to Limit Competition in Several Key Domestic Markets,* (Letter Report, GAO/ RCED-97-4, October 18, 1996).

General Accounting Office Report, *Changes in Airfares, Service, and Safety Since Airline Deregulation* (GAO/T-RECD-96-126, April 25, 1996).

Groenewege, Adrianus D., *Compendium of International Civil Aviation,* International Aviation Development Corporation, 1996.

Hendricks, Wallace and Feuille, Peter and Szersen, Carol, *Regulation, Deregulation, and Collective Bargaining in Airlines,* Industrial and Labor Relations Review, Vol. 34, No. 1, October 1980.

Heppenheimer, T. A., *Turbulent Skies,* John Wiley and Sons, 1995.

The jetAge, Time-Life Books, 1982.

International Air Transport Association, History of IATA, http://wwwl.iata.org/about/history.htm, 2002.

International Civil Aviation Organization, History of ICAO, http://www icao.int/, 2002.

Kahn, Alfred E., *Change, Challenge, and Competition: A Review of the Airline Commission Report,* Regulation, Vol. 16, No. 3, 1993.

Kahn, Alfred E., Statement before The United States House of Representatives, Committee on the Judiciary, *The State of Competition in the Airline Industry,* June 14, 2000.

Kelly, Fred, *The Wright Brothers: A Biography Authorized by Orville Wright,* Ballentine Books, New York, 1956.

Komans, N. A., *Bonfires to Beacons,* Smithsonian Institution Press: Washington, D.C. 1989.

Leonhardt, David with Michelene Maynard, *Troubled Airlines Face Reality: The Cheap Fares Have a Price,* New York Times, August 18, 2002.

Lindbergh, Charles A., *The Spirit of St. Louis,* Charles Scribner's Sons, New York, 1953.

Lipinski, William O., *An Evaluation of the US.—E.U. Trade Relationship* <http://www.house.gov./lipinski/aviation.htm>, 2002.

Logsdon, John M., *Return to flight: Richard H. Truly and the Recovery from the Challenger Accident,* in Pamela E. Mack, editor, *From Engineering to Big Science: The NACA and NASA Collier Trophy Research Project Winners, NASA SP-4219* (Washington: Government Printing Office, 1998).

Lynn, Matthew, *Birds of Prey,* Four Walls Eight Windows, New York 1977; a revised edition first published by Reed International Books, Ltd., London, 1995.

Miles, Richard B., *Competition in the U.S. Manufacturing Industry,* Testimony before the Aviation Subcommittee, Committee on Transportation and Infrastructure, U.S. House of Representatives, June 26, 2001.

Morrison, Steven A. and Winston, Clifford, *The Evolution of the Airline Industry,* Brookings Institution, Washington, D.C., 1995.

Nannes, John M., Deputy Assistant Attorney General, Antitrust Division, *The Importance of Entry Conditions in Analyzing Airlines Antitrust Issues,* Talk before the Industrial Aviation Club, Washington, D.C., July 20, 1999.

Nature, Volume 472, Issue 7341, April 2011.

Nannes, John M., Deputy Assistant Attorney General, Antitrust Division, *Statement Before the Committee on Transportation and Infrastructure,* United States House of Representative Concerning Antitrust Analysis of Airline Mergers, June 13, 2000.

Nay, Leslie A., *The Determinants of Concession Bargaining in the Airline Industry,* Industrial and Labor Relations Review, Vol. 44, No. 2, June 1991.

Northrup, Herbert R., *The New Employee Relations Climate in Airlines,* Industrial and Labor Relations Review, Vol. 36, No. 2, June 1983.

Northrup, Herbert R., *The Rise and Demise of PATCO,* Industrial and Labor Relations Review, Vol. 37, No. 2, June 1984.

Peterson, Barbara and Glab, Jonas, *Rapid Descent,* Simon and Schuster, New Mexico, 1994.

Petzinger, Thomas, Jr., *Hard Landing,* Three Rivers Press, 1996.

Poole, Robert W., Jr., *More Airline Competition—Yet Another Reason for Airport Privitization,* Reason Public Policy Institute, December 1999.

Poole, Robert W., Jr. and Butler, Viggo, *Airline Deregulation: The Unfinished Revolution,* Reason Public Policy Institute, March 1999.

Robson, John E., *Airline Deregulation—Twenty Years of Success and Counting,* Regulation, Spring 1998, pp. 17–22.

Rowe, Jonathon and Cahn, Edgar, *Time Dollars,* Rodale 1992.

Sampson, Anthony, *Emperors of the Sky: The Politics, Contests, and Cartels of World Airlines,* Random House, 1984.

Servan-Schrieber, Jean-Jacques, *Le Defi Americain,* Penguin Books, Hammondsworth, 1967.

Slater, Rodney, Testimony before the Aviation Subcommittee, Committee on Transportation and Infrastructure, U.S. House of Representatives, February 5, 2000.

Solberg, Carl, *Conquest of the Skies,* Little Brown and Company, 1979.

Sterling, Robert, Eagle: *The Story of American Airlines,* St. Martins Press, 1995.

Sterling, Robert, *Howard Hughes' Airline: An Informal History of TWA,* St. Martin's/Markk, 1983.

Thierer, Adam D., *20th Anniversary of Airline Deregulation: Cause for Celebration, Not Re-regulation,* The Heritage Foundation, April 22, 1998.

Thomas, Steven L., and Officer, Dennis, and Johnson, Nancy Brown, *The Capital Market Response to Wage Negotiations in the Airlines,* Industrial Relations, Vol. 34, No. 2, April 1995.

Thronicroft, Kenneth W., *Airline Deregulation and the Airline Labor Market,* Journal of Labor Research, Vol. X, No. 2, Spring 1989.

Time Magazine, *Hunting the Predators,* Vol. 151, No. 15, April 20, 1998.

U.S. Department of Transportation, Bureau of Transportation Statistics, *Airport Activity Statistics of Certificated Air Carriers,* Summary Tables: Twelve Months Ending December 31, 1999, BTSO 1-03, Washington, D.C. 2001.

U.S. Department of Transportation, Bureau of Transportation Statistics, *Airport Activity Statistics of Certificated Air Carriers,* Summary Tables ending December 31, 1999, BTSO1-03, Washington, D.C. 2001.

U.S. Department of Transportation, FAA/OST Task Force, *Airport Business Practices and Their Impact on Airline Competition,* October 1999.

U.S. Department of Transportation, FAA Strategic Plan, 1998. http://api.hq.faa.gov/spo pubs.htm# ANCHOR98 3, 2002.

U.S. Department of Transportation, *Enforcement Policy Regarding Unfair Exclusionary Conduct in the Air Transportation Industry* (Docket No. ST-98-3713) January 17, 2001.

U.S. Department of Transportation, *International Aviation Developments—Global Deregulation Takes Off (First Report),* December 1999.

U.S. Department of Transportation, *International Aviation Developments, Second Report—Transportation Deregulation—The Alliance Network Effect,* October 2000.

U.S. Department of Transportation, *Statement of Enforcement Policy Regarding Unfair Exclusionary Conduct,* (Docket No. OST 98-3713, Notice 98-16) April 1998.

U.S. Department of Transportation, *Statement of U.S. International Air Transportation Policy,* Federal Register, Vol. 60, No. 85, May 3, 1995.

Venneri, Samuel L., Associate Administrator, Office of Aerospace Technology, NASA, Statement before the Subcommittee of Aviation, Committee on Transportation and Infrastructure, U.S. House of Representatives, July 26, 2001.

Wilson, John R. M., *Turbulence Aloft: The Civil Aeronautics Administration Amid Wars and Rumors of Wars, 1938–1953,* Washington: Government Printing Office, 1979.

Winston, Clifford, *Economic Deregulation: Days of Reckoning for Macroeconomists,* Journal of Economic Literature, Vol. 31, No. 3, September 1993, pp. 1263–1289.

Wright, Nancy Allison, *The Reluctant Pioneer and Air Mail's Origin,* Air Mail Pioneers News, 1998–2001.

Zagorin, Adam, *Hunting the Predators,* Daily Magazine, Vol. 151, No. 15, April 20, 1998.

Cases

Diaz v. Pan American World Airways, Inc., 442 F. 2d 385 (5th Cir. 1972)

Minestere Public v. Lucas Asjes ("Nouvelles Frontieres") (Joined Cases 209-213/84) 36 L.E. 173, Eur. Ct. R. 1425 (1986)

Massachusetts Commonwealth v. Hunt, 45 NAA, 111 (1842)

National Labor Relations v. Bildisco, 465 U.S. 513 (1984).

Nouvellas Frontieres (see *Minestere Public v. Lucas Asjes,* above, for citation).

Pacific Air Transport v. U.S.; Boeing Air Transport v. U.S.; United Airline Transport Corporation v. U.S., 98 Ct. Cl. 649 (1942).

Pan American World Airways Inc v. United States, 371 U.S. 296, 306-308 (1963).

Panama Refining Co. v. Ryan, 298 U.S. 388 (1935).

Parker v. Brown, 317 U.S. 341 (1943).

The National Association of Clean Air Agencies v. E.P.A., 489 F.3d 1221 (D.C. Cir. 2007).

United States v. CAB, 766 F.2d 1107 (7th Cir. 1985).

Western Airlines v. Port Authority of New York and New Jersey, 658 F. Supp. 952 (SDNY 1986); aff'd 817 F.2d 222 (2nd Cir. 1987).

Statutes

Interstate Commerce Act

Feb. 4, 1887, ch 104, 24 Stat. 379, 49 USCS §§ 1–22, 25–27, 153, 153 nt., 301–312, 314–327, 901–923, 1001–1022.

Elkins Act

Elkins Act (Interstate Commerce)

Feb. 19, 1903, ch 708, 32 Stat. 847, 49 USCS §§ 41–43.

Hepburn Act

Hepburn Act (Interstate Commerce)

June 29, 1906, ch 3591, 34 Stat. 595, 49 USCS § 20 (11, 12).

Mann-Elkins Act

June 18, 1910, ch 309, 36 Stat. 539, 49 USCS §§ 1, 4, 6, 10, 13, 15, 16, 20, 50.

Transportation Acts

Feb. 28, 1920, ch 91, 41 Stat. 456, 49 USCS §§ 1–6, 10–18, 19a, 20, 20a, 26, 27, 71–74, 76–80, 137, 141, 142, 316, 1361 nt.

May 8, 1920, ch 172, 41 Stat. 590, 49 USCS § 75.

Aug. 13, 1940, ch 666, 54 Stat. 788, 40 USCS § 316.

Jan. 7, 1941, ch 938, 54 Stat. 1226, 49 USCS § 73.

Oct. 25, 1972, P.L. 92–550, 86 Stat. 1163, 49 USCS § 66.

Nov. 6, 1978, P.L. 95–598, 40 USCS § 316.

Airmail Acts

Feb. 2, 1925, ch 128, 43 Stat. 805 (See 39 USCS § 5401 et seq.).

Feb. 21, 1925, ch 283, 43 Stat. 960.

June 3, 1926, ch 460, 44 Stat. 692.

March 8, 1928, ch 149, 45 Stat. 248.

May 17, 1928, ch 603, 45 Stat. 594.

March 2, 1929, ch 478, 45 Stat. 1450.

April 29, 1930, ch 223, 46 Stat. 259.

March 27, 1934, ch 100, 48 Stat. 508.

June 12, 1934, ch 466, 48 Stat. 933.

June 19, 1934, ch 652, 48 Stat. 1102.

June 26, 1934, ch 762, 48 Stat. 1243.

Aug. 14, 1935, ch 530, 49 Stat. 614.

Aug. 24, 1935, ch 638, 49 Stat. 744.

Aug. 20, 1937, ch 718, 50 Stat. 725.

Jan. 14, 1938, ch 9, 52 Stat. 6.

April 15, 1938, ch 157, 52 Stat. 218.

June 23, 1938, ch 601, 52 Stat. 997.

July 6, 1945, ch 274, 59 Stat. 451.

Aug. 14, 1946, ch 963, 60 Stat. 1062.

June 23, 1948, ch 607, 62 Stat. 576.

June 29, 1948, ch 717, 62 Stat. 1097.

July 3, 1948, ch 830, 62 Stat. 1261.

Aug. 30, 1949, ch 523, 63 Stat. 680.

May 27, 1958, P.L. 85–426, 72 Stat. 138.

Aug. 23, 1958, P.L. 85–726, 72 Stat. 808.

Air Commerce Act of 1926

May 20, 1926, ch 344, 44 Stat. 568 (See 49 USCS §§ 1301, 1472, 1473, 1507–1509).

Aug. 5, 1950, ch 591, 64 Stat. 414 (See 49 USCS §§ 1472, 1473, 1509).

Oct. 11, 1951, ch 495, 65 Stat. 407 (See 49 USCS § 1509).

Aug. 8, 1953, ch 379, 67 Stat. 489 (See 49 USCS § 1508).

Railway Labor Act

May 20, 1926, ch 347, 44 Star. 577 (See 15 USCS §§ 21, 45) 18 USCS § 373; 28 USCS §§ 1291–1294; 45 USCS §§ 151–163, 181188.

June 21, 1934, ch 691, 48 Stat. 1185, 45 USCS §§ 151–158, 160162.

April 10, 1936, ch 166, 49 Stat. 1189, 45 USCS §§ 181–188.

Jan. 10, 1951, ch 1220, 64 Stat. 1238, 45 USCS § 152.

Aug. 31, 1964, P.L. 88–542, 78 Stat. 748, 45 USCS § 154.

June 20, 1966, P.L. 89–456, 80 Stat. 208, 45 USCS § 153.

April 23, 1970, P.L. 91–234, 84 Stat. 199, 45 USCS § 153.

Oct. 15, 1970, P.L. 91–452, 84 Stat. 930, 45 USCS § 157.

Aug. 4, 1988, P.L. 100–380, 102 Stat. 896.

Oct. 19, 1994, P.L. 103–380, 108 Stat. 3512.

Dec. 29, 1995, P.L. 104–88, 45 USCS § 151.

Oct. 9, 1996, P.L. 104–264, 45 USCS § 151.

Norris-La Guardia Act (Labor Disputes)

March 23, 1932, ch 90, 47 Stat. 70, 29 USCS §§ 101–115.

Nov. 8, 1984, P.L. 98–620, 29 USCS § 110.

National Labor Relations Act

July 5, 1935, ch 372, 49 Stat. 449, 29 USCS §§ 151–166.

Motor Carrier Act

Aug. 9, 1935, ch 498, 49 Stat. 543, 15 USCS § 77c; 49 USCS §§ 1–5, 6–13, 15–17, 19–20a, 22, 26, 27, 301–327.

Civil Aeronautics Act of 1938

June 23, 1938, ch 601, 52 Stat. 973 (See 49 USCS §§ 1301–1542).

Federal Airport Act

May 13, 1946, ch 251, 60 Stat. 170, 49 USCS §§ 1101–1119.

Federal Aviation Act of 1958

Aug. 23, 1958, P.L. 85-726, 72 Stat. 731, 14 USCS §§ 81, 82, 90; 15 USCS § 45; 16 USCS § 7a; 31 USCS § 686; 48 USCS §§ 485–485d; 49 USCS §§ 212, 486 nt., 1101, 1102, 1103, 1105, 1108, 1111, 1116, 1151, 1152 and others; 50 USCS § 123; 50 USCS Appx §§ 1622–1622c.

Airport and Airway Development Act of 1970

May 21, 1970, P.L. 91–258, 84 Stat. 219, 49 USCS §§ 1701 et seq., 1701 nt., 1711–1727.

Nov. 27, 1971, P.L. 92–174, 85 Stat. 491, 49 USCS §§ 1711–1715, 1717.

June 18, 1973, P.L. 93–44, 87 Stat. 88, 49 USCS §§ 1711, 1712, 1714, 1716, 1717.

Feb. 18, 1980, P.L. 96–193, 49 USCS §§ 1711 et seq.

April 7, 1986, P.L. 99–272, 49 USCS Appx § 1741.

Oct. 22, 1986, P.L. 99–514, 49 USCS Appx § 1741.

Noise Control Act of 1972

Oct. 27, 1972, P.L. 92–574, 86 Stat. 1234, 42 USCS §§ 49014918; 49 USCS § 1431.

Airport Development Acceleration Act

June 18, 1973, P.L. 93–44, 87 Stat. 88, 49 USCS §§ 1513, 1711, 1712, 1714, 1716, 1717.

Airline Deregulation Act of 1978

Oct. 24, 1978, P.L. 95–504, 49 USCS §§ 1301, 1301 nt., 1302 et seq.

Feb. 15, 1980, P.L. 96–192, 49 USCS § 1341 nt.

Oct. 31, 1994, P.L. 103–429, 49 USCS Appx § 1301 nt.

Motor Carrier Act of 1980

July 1, 1980, P.L. 96–296, 49 USCS § 10101 nt.

Sept. 20, 1982, P.L. 97–261, 49 USCS § 10706 nt.

Jan. 6, 1983, P.L. 97–424, 49 USCS § 10927 nt.

Oct. 30, 1984, P.L. 98–554, 49 USCS § 10927 nt.

Nov. 18, 1988, P.L. 100–690, 49 USCS § 10927 nt.

Nov. 16, 1990, P.L. 101–615, 49 USCS § 10927 nt.

Staggers Rail Act of 1980

Oct. 14, 1980, P.L. 96–448, 49 USCS § 10101.

Dec. 21, 1982, P.L. 97–375, 49 USCS S 1654a.

Airport Improvement Program Temporary Extension Act of 1994

May 26, 1994, P.L. 103–260, 26 USCS § 9502; 49 USCS Appx §§ 1348 nt., 2201 nt., 2204, 2206, 2207, 2212.

Oct. 31, 1994, P.L. 103–429, 49 USCS Appx § 2204.

Airport and Airway Improvement Act of 1982

Sept. 3, 1982, P.L. 97–248, 49 USCS §§ 2201 et seq.

Oct. 2, 1982, P.L. 97–276, 49 USCS § 2207.

Jan. 6, 1983, P.L. 97–424, 49 USCS §§ 2204, 2205, 2206.

Dec. 30, 1987, P.L. 100–223, 49 USCS Appx §§ 2226, 2227.

Aug. 14, 1988, P.L. 100–393, 102 Star. 971.

Nov. 3, 1988, P.L. 100–591, 49 USCS Appx § 2205.

Aug. 4, 1989, P.L. 101–71, 49 USCS Appx § 2212.

May 4, 1990, P.L. 101–281, 49 USCS Appx § 2210.

Nov. 5, 1990, P.L. 101–508, 49 USCS Appx §§ 2201–2207, 2227.

Oct. 31, 1992, P.L. 102–581, 49 USCS Appx §§ 2201–2212, 2226c, 2227.

May 26, 1994, P.L. 103–260, 49 USCS Appx §§ 2204, 2206, 2207, 2212.

Airport Noise and Capacity Act of 1990

Nov. 5, 1990, P.L. 101–508, 49 USCS Appx §§ 2151 nt., 21512158.

Federal Aviation Administration Research, Engineering, and Development Authorization Act of 1994

Aug. 23, 1994, P.L. 103–305, 49 USCS §§ 40101 nt.

Wendell H. Ford Aviation Investment and Reform Act for the 21st Century

April 5, 2000, P.L. 106–181, 114 Star. 61, 49 USCS § 40101 nt.

Sherman Anti-Trust Act (Trusts)

July 2, 1890, ch 647, 26 Stat. 209, 15 USCS §§ 1–7.

July 7, 1955, ch 281, 69 Stat. 282, 15 USCS §§ 1–3.

Oct. 8, 1982, P.L. 97–290, 15 USCS § 6a.

Clayton Act (Anti-Trust Act)

Oct. 15, 1914, ch 323, 38 Stat. 730, 15 USCS §§ 12–27, 44; 29 USCS § 52.

Dec. 29, 1950, ch 1184, 64 Stat. 1125, 15 USCS §§ 18, 21.

July 7, 1955, ch 283, 69 Stat. 282, 15 USCS §§ 15a, 15b, 16.

July 23, 1959, P.L. 86–107, 73 Stat. 243, 15 USCS § 21.

Sept. 12, 1980, P.L. 96–349, 15 USCS §§ 15 et seq.

Dec. 29, 1982, P.L. 97–393, 15 USCS § 15.

Oct. 4, 1984, P.L. 98–443, 98 Stat. 1708, 15 USCS §§ 18, 21.

Aug. 9, 1989, P.L. 101–73, 15 USCS § 18a.

Nov. 16, 1990, P.L. 101–588, 15 USCS §§ 15a, 19, 20.

Dec. 17, 1993, P.L. 103–203, 15 USCS § 19.

Dec. 29, 1995, P.L. 104–88, 15 USCS § 18, § 21, § 26.

Feb. 8, 1996, P.L. 104–104, 15 USCS § 18.

Oct. 27, 1998, P.L. 105–297, 15 USCS § 27a.

Nov. 12, 1999, P.L. 106–102, 15 USCS § 18a.

Posse Comitatus Act

June 18, 1878, 20 Stat. 152, 18 USC 1385

Panama Canal Act

August 24, 1912, P.L. 62-337, 37 Stat. 560, 48 USC Chapter 6

Communication Satellite Act

August 31, 1962, P.L. 87-624, 78 Stat. 241, 47 USC 701

Civil Rights Act, Title VII

July 2, 1964, P.L. 88-352, 42 USC 2000

Age Discrimination Act

December 15, 1967, P.L. 90-202, 81 Stat. 602, 29 USC 621

Railroad Revitalization and Regulatory Reform Act

February 5, 1976, P.L. 94-210, 90 Stat. 31, 45 USC 801

Commercial Space Act

October 30, 1984, P.L. 98-575, 49 USC 2601

Implementing Recommendations of the 9/11 Commission Act

January 9, 2007, P.L. 110-53, 121 Stat. 266, 6 USC 195

Airline Safety and Aviation Administration Extension Act

July 28, 2010, P.L. 111-216, 124 Stat. 2348, 49 USC 106

INDEX

CPSIA information can be obtained
at www.ICGtesting.com
Printed in the USA
LVHW010513061219
639566LV00001B/1

9 781465 270740